WISCONSIN
· BLUE BOOK ·

2017 · 2018

Published biennially by
the Wisconsin Legislative Reference Bureau

To view a pdf of the 2017–2018 *Wisconsin Blue Book*, go to
http://legis.wisconsin.gov/lrb/publications/wisconsin-blue-book

Wisconsin Legislative Reference Bureau
One East Main Street, Suite 200, Madison, WI 53703
http://legis.wisconsin.gov/lrb
©2017 Joint Committee on Legislative Organization, Wisconsin Legislature
All rights reserved. Published 2017.
Printed in the United States of America

ISBN 978-0-9752820-9-0

Sold and distributed by:
Document Sales Unit
Department of Administration
2310 Darwin Road
Madison, WI 53704
608-243-2441, 800-362-7253
DOADocumentSalesInformation@wisconsin.gov

Front cover: Four figural sculptures sit at the base of the Capitol dome in Madison. These figures were created in the 1910s by a group of stonecutters following the designs of sculptor Karl Bitter. Work on the Capitol building, the third built in Madison after fire destroyed the second, was concluded in 1917. A celebration of the Capitol's centennial has been ongoing throughout 2017. WHI IMAGE ID 9570

Back cover: The statuary group Prosperity and Abundance stands above the Northwest Pavilion of the Capitol. Karl Bitter explained that the statues were not meant to be "an assemblage of art objects," but "organic parts of the structure." The groups, which have stood for over 100 years, underwent cleaning and repair during the Capitol restoration project from 1993 to 2001. KATHLEEN SITTER

Scott Walker
Office of the Governor

Fellow Wisconsinites,

We are working and winning for Wisconsin.

Since 2011, we have put in place bold, commonsense, conservative reforms to make our state a better place to live, work, and raise a family. The results are impressive.

More people are working today than ever before in our state's history. Unemployment rates in most counties are the lowest ever. And we are now a Top 10 state for business, up from 41st in 2010, according to Chief Executive Magazine.

Our tax reforms have put billions of dollars back in the hands of the hardworking taxpayers, and Wisconsin is a Top 10 state in reducing the overall tax burden over the previous five years. Our cumulative income tax reductions will save the typical Wisconsin family some $1,500. That's real money.

We also put in place reforms that helped the government be a better steward of taxpayer money. We have reduced waste, fraud, and abuse in state government, and independent studies show our Act 10 reforms have saved schools and local and state government some $5 billion.

Overall, our reforms brought us here to the point where we have a better budget outlook. It's what we call the Reform Dividend, and our priorities fall into three categories: Student Success, Accountable Government, and Rewarding Work. Our budget proposal includes major new investments and conservative reforms in each of these areas.

Wisconsin's future is bright, but we're not done yet. We are working and winning for Wisconsin.

It is my honor to serve as your governor. I hope the *Blue Book* is a useful resource for you to learn more about our state government.

Together, we are moving Wisconsin *Forward*.

Scott Walker

INTRODUCTION

On March 8, 2017, legislative leaders and staff gathered in the Wisconsin Senate Parlor to receive the 2016 Kevin B. Harrington award for Excellence in Democracy Education. The award, presented by the National Conference of State Legislatures, is given to an individual or organization that furthers the understanding of the principles and practices of representative democracy. In presenting the award to the Wisconsin legislature, NCSL highlighted the many civics programs and activities of the Wisconsin legislature, but specifically mentioned one publication that exemplifies the award's values—the *Wisconsin Blue Book*.

The *Blue Book*, published since 1853, may be the oldest publication of the state. It was initially a manual for the Wisconsin State Assembly, a pocket-size volume, under 100 pages, for legislators to have quick access to information about state government. Over the decades, the *Blue Book* evolved in size, scope, and purpose. The *Blue Book's* many iterations were caused by the increased availability of information about state government and by the fact that its audience grew to include all state government and the public. By 2015, the *Blue Book* was almost 1,000 pages, filled with dense statistical information. It was an almanac of Wisconsin government.

The 2017 *Blue Book* marks the next iteration in its evolution. The new *Blue Book* is intended as an introduction to Wisconsin state and local government, but not necessarily as the primary source for this information. We live during a time of unparalleled access to information. More information about state government, and more timely information, can be accessed through the Internet than could ever be assembled in one volume by a team of researchers. The 2017 *Blue Book* recognizes this fact. The new *Blue Book* contains biographies of all legislators, descriptions of executive and judicial branch agencies, and vital statistics on Wisconsin government and elections. But it does not reproduce information that is dated or that can be obtained more easily and accurately elsewhere.

Those who have used the *Blue Book* will appreciate the continuity of the information in the 2017 edition. The topics covered are familiar and much of the statistical information is the same. But there are new discussions about the structure and operation of Wisconsin government, including essays on the legislature and the state budget, public education, and local government. Descriptions of government agencies are shorter than in past editions, but readers are directed to Internet websites that contain a wealth of information. The key statistical tables are retained, but information peripheral to state and local government is not included. The *Blue Book* is a working document, intended as an introduction for the general public and students of politics to learn about Wisconsin.

The *Blue Book* is authored by Legislative Reference Bureau staff. New data was compiled, new tables assembled, new essays written, and material from past *Blue Book*s was reorganized. It was a team undertaking in every way, best exemplified by the researching and writing of the feature article about women in the Wisconsin legislature. In the summer of 2016, LRB staff met with all women legislators, as well as past women legislators, to document their service in the legislature. Interviews were conducted in the capitol building, in legislative district offices, and even in private residences. Much was learned from the interviews and these lessons are captured in the article, "Knocking on the Door: Women in the Wisconsin Legislature." The article documents women legislators' campaigns for office, experiences in the legislature, and their challenges and successes. Every reader will appreciate the vital role that women have played in shaping and leading the modern Wisconsin legislature.

The *Blue Book* is a major undertaking that required LRB staff commitment, time, and leadership. Four employees deserve special recognition: Christopher Siciliano, Lauren Jackson, Nancy Warnecke, and Kira Langoussis Mochal. In addition to performing their other legislative duties, they led the project from start to finish. The information assembled in this volume, the visual design of the material, and the recognition of what is required of a hardbound publication in the Internet Age come from their efforts and vision. We are grateful for their contributions.

Richard A. Champagne, Chief
Wisconsin Legislative Reference Bureau

TABLE OF CONTENTS

3 About Wisconsin

4 Statistics and Reference

1

ELECTED OFFICIALS

Scott Walker, Governor

Republican

Biography: Born Colorado Springs, Colorado, November 2, 1967; married; 2 children. ▪ Graduate Delavan-Darien High School, 1986; attended Marquette University, 1986–90. ▪ Former salesman, IBM Corporation; financial developer, American Red Cross. ▪ Elected to Assembly in June 1993 special election. Reelected 1994–2000. Resigned May 9, 2002. Milwaukee County Executive 2002–10.

Current office: Elected governor 2010. Reelected 2014.

Contact: governor@wisconsin.gov; 608-266-1212; PO Box 7863, Madison, WI 53707-7863.

Rebecca Kleefisch, Lieutenant Governor
Republican

Biography: Born Pontiac, Michigan, August 7, 1975; married; 2 children. ▪ Graduate Anthony Wayne High School (Whitehouse, Ohio), 1993; B.A. in Journalism, University of Wisconsin-Madison, 1997. ▪ Former news reporter; media and marketing consultant. ▪ Member: National Lieutenant Governors Association; National Rifle Association, Aerospace States Association (manufacturing chair), Executive Committee of Republican Lieutenant Governors Association.

Current office: Elected lieutenant governor 2010. Reelected 2014.

Contact: ltgov@wisconsin.gov; 608-266-3516; PO Box 2043, Madison, WI 53701-2043.

Brad D. Schimel, Attorney General
Republican

Biography: Born West Allis, Wisconsin, February 18, 1965; married; 2 children. ▪ Graduate Mukwonago High School, 1983; B.A. Political Science, University of Wisconsin-Waukesha, University of Wisconsin-Milwaukee, 1987; J.D. University of Wisconsin-Madison, 1990. ▪ Attorney. ▪ Former member: Addiction Resource Council (treasurer); Interfaith Senior Programs (president); Potawatomi Boy Scout Council (advisory board); Rotary International; Safe Babies, Healthy Families (president); University of Wisconsin-Waukesha Foundation (vice president); Waukesha Food Pantry (board director). ▪ Waukesha County assistant district attorney (1990–2007); Waukesha County district attorney (2007–15).

Current office: Elected attorney general 2014. Member ex officio: Board of Commissioners of Public Lands.

Contact: 608-266-1221; Room 114 East, State Capitol, PO Box 7857, Madison, WI 53707-7857.

Tony Evers, State Superintendent of Public Instruction
nonpartisan office

Biography: Born Plymouth, Wisconsin, November 5, 1951; married; 3 children, 6 grandchildren. ▪ Graduate Plymouth High School, 1969; B.S. University of Wisconsin-Madison, 1973; M.S. University of Wisconsin-Madison, 1976; Ph.D. University of Wisconsin-Madison, 1986. ▪ Former teacher, technology coordinator, principal, Tomah; superintendent of schools, Oakfield, Verona; CESA 6 administrator, Oshkosh; deputy state superintendent of public instruction. ▪ Member: Council of Chief State School Officers (board of directors member in 2017, president in 2016). ▪ Former member: Wisconsin Association of CESA Administrators; Wisconsin Association of School District Administrators.

Current office: Elected state superintendent 2009. Reelected since 2013. Member ex officio: University of Wisconsin Board of Regents; Wisconsin Technical College System Board.

Contact: dpistatesuperintendent@dpi.wisconsin.gov; 608-266-1771; 125 South Webster Street, PO Box 7841, Madison, WI 53707-7841.

Matt Adamczyk, State Treasurer
Republican

Biography: Born Milwaukee, Wisconsin, June 9, 1978; single. ▪ Graduate Pius XI High School, 1996; B.A. University of Wisconsin-Madison, 2000. ▪ Small business manager. Former educator; legislative aide. ▪ Member: Republican Party of Milwaukee County; National Rifle Association; Americans for Prosperity.

Current office: Elected state treasurer 2014. Member ex officio: Board of Commissioners of Public Lands; Wisconsin Insurance Security Fund.

Contact: 608-266-1714; Room B38 West, State Capitol, Madison, WI 53701.

Douglas J. La Follette, Secretary of State
Democrat

Biography: Single. ▪ B.S. in Chemistry, Marietta College, 1963; M.S. in Chemistry, Stanford University, 1964; Ph.D. in Organic Chemistry, Columbia University, 1967. ▪ Former director of training and development with an energy marketing company; assistant professor, University of Wisconsin-Parkside; public affairs director, Union of Concerned Scientists; owner and operator of a small business; research associate, University of Wisconsin-Madison. ▪ Member: American Solar Energy Society; Audubon Society; Friends of the Earth; Phi Beta Kappa. ▪ Former member: Council of Economic Priorities; American Federation of Teachers; Federation of American Scientists; Lake Michigan Federation; Southeastern Wisconsin Coalition for Clean Air; Clean Wisconsin (formerly Wisconsin Environmental Decade, founder). ▪ Elected to Senate 1972.

Current office: Elected secretary of state 1974 and 1982. Reelected since 1986. Member ex officio: Board of Commissioners of Public Lands.

Contact: doug.lafollette@wisconsin.gov; 608-266-8888 press 3; PO Box 7848, Madison, WI 53707-7848.

▪ ▪ ▪

STATE SUPREME COURT JUSTICES

Shirley S. Abrahamson

Biography: Born New York City, December 17, 1933.
■ Graduate Hunter College High School, 1950; B.A.
New York University, 1953; J.D. Indiana University
Law School, 1956; S.J.D. University of Wisconsin Law
School, 1962; D.L. (honorary): Willamette University,
1978; Ripon College, 1981; Beloit College, 1982; Capital University, 1983; John Marshall Law School, 1984;
Northeastern University, 1985; Indiana University, 1986; Northland College,
1988; Hamline University, 1988; Notre Dame University, 1993; Suffolk University, 1994; DePaul University, 1996; Lawrence University, 1998; Marian College,
1998; Roger Williams University School of Law, 2007. ■ Member: American
Philosophical Society (elected 1998); American Academy of Arts and Sciences
(fellow 1997). ■ Recipient: American Bar Association *John Marshall Award*
2010; National Center for State Courts *Harry L. Carrico Award for Judicial
Innovation* 2009; Wisconsin Counties Association *Friend of County Government Award* 2007; American Judicature Society *Dwight D. Opperman Award*
2004 and *Herbert Harley Award* 1999; American Bar Association Commission
on Women in the Profession *Margaret Brent Women Lawyers of Achievement
Award* 1995; University of Wisconsin-Madison *Distinguished Alumni Award*
1994. Featured in *Great American Judges: An Encyclopedia 2003.*

Current office: Appointed to Supreme Court August 1976 to fill vacancy created
by death of Chief Justice Horace W. Wilkie. Elected to full term 1979. Reelected
1989, 1999, and 2009. Became chief justice August 1, 1996, upon the retirement
of Chief Justice Roland B. Day; served as chief justice until 2015.

Ann Walsh Bradley

Biography: Born Richland Center, Wisconsin, July 5,
1950; married; 4 children. ■ Graduate Richland Center
High School; B.A. Webster College (St. Louis, Missouri); J.D. University of Wisconsin-Madison (Knapp
Scholar), 1976. ■ Former high school teacher, practicing attorney, and Marathon County circuit court
judge. ■ Member: Board of Managerial Trustees, International Association of Women Judges; elected member of the American Law

Institute; state coordinator for iCivics; Wisconsin Bench Bar Committee; University of Wisconsin Law School Board of Visitors; American Bar Association; State Bar of Wisconsin; Federal-State Judicial Council; lecturer for the American Bar Association's Asian Law Initiative, International Judicial Academy, and Institute of International Education. ▪ Former member: Board of Directors, National Association of Women Judges; Board of Directors and vice chair, International Judicial Academy; Board of Directors, International Association of Women Judges; American Judicature Society; National Conference on Uniform State Laws; Wisconsin Judicial College (associate dean and faculty); Wisconsin Rhodes Scholarship Committee (chair); Wisconsin Judicial Council; Wisconsin Equal Justice Task Force; Wisconsin Judicial Conference (executive committee, legislative committee, judicial education committee); Civil Law Committee (executive committee); Task Force on Children and Families; Board of Directors, Wisconsin State Public Defender; Committee on the Administration of Courts. ▪ Recipient: American Judicature Society's *Herbert Harley Award*; *Business and Professional Woman of the Year*; *Business Woman of the Year Athena Award*; *Women in the Law Award*.

Current office: Elected to Supreme Court 1995. Reelected 2005 and 2015.

Patience Drake Roggensack, Chief Justice

Biography: Born Joliet, Illinois, July 7; married; 3 children. ▪ Graduate Lockport Township High School; B.A. Drake University; J.D. University of Wisconsin-Madison Law School (cum laude). ▪ Former practicing attorney. ▪ Participation: Commissioner, Uniform Laws Commission; Fellow, American Bar Foundation; Wisconsin Judicial Council; Supreme Court Rules Procedure Committee; Supreme Court Finance Committee; Committee for Public Trust and Confidence in the Courts; American Bar Association; State Bar Association of Wisconsin; Western District of Wisconsin Bar Association (past president); Dane County Bar Association, served on Personnel Review Board (supreme court delegate); 2005 Judicial Conference (cochair); 2005 Statewide Bench Bar Conference (cochair). ▪ Board service on: YMCA; YWCA; Wisconsin Center for Academically Talented Youth; Olbrich Botanical Society; International Women's Forum (past president); A Fund For Women; Friends of the Arboretum. ▪ Court of Appeals judge, District IV (1996–2003). Served on Judicial Conference (legislative liaison); Publication Committee for the Court of Appeals; State Court/Tribal Court Planning Committee (cochair); Personnel Review Board (appeals court delegate).

Current office: Elected to Supreme Court 2003. Reelected 2013. Elected chief justice May 1, 2015. Reelected 2017.

Annette K. Ziegler

Biography: Born Grand Rapids, Michigan, March 6, 1964; married with children. ▪ Graduate Forest Hills Central High School; B.A. in Business Administration and Psychology, Hope College (Holland, Michigan), 1986; J.D. Marquette University Law School, 1989. ▪ Former practicing attorney (civil litigation), 1989–95. Pro bono special assistant district attorney, Milwaukee County, 1992, 1996. Assistant U.S. attorney, Eastern District of Wisconsin, 1995–97. Washington County Circuit Court judge, 1997–2007. Court of Appeals District II (Judicial Exchange Program 1999). Deputy chief judge, Third Judicial District. Judicial faculty at various seminars. ▪ Chair, Judicial Education Commission. Court liaison, Board of Bar Examiners. Commissioner, Uniform State Laws Commission. ▪ Member: State Bar of Wisconsin; American Bar Association; American Law Institute (elected member); American Bar Foundation (fellow); International Women's Forum; Washington County Bar Association; Milwaukee County Bar Association; Eastern District of Wisconsin Bar Association; Wisconsin Judicial Council, State Bar of Wisconsin Bench & Bar Committee; Boys & Girls Club of Washington County (trustee board president); Marquette University Law School Advisory Board; Rotary Club West Bend-Noon. ▪ Former member: Governor's Juvenile Justice Commission; Criminal Benchbook Committee; Criminal Jury Instruction Committee; Legal Association for Women; James E. Doyle American Inn of Court.

Current office: Elected to Supreme Court 2007. Reelected 2017.

Michael J. Gableman

Biography: Born West Allis, Wisconsin, September 18, 1966. Raised in Waukesha County. ▪ Graduate New Berlin West High School, 1984; B.A. in History and Education, Ripon College, 1988; J.D. Hamline University Law School, 1993. ▪ Former teacher of American History, Milwaukee Public School System, George Washington High School, 1988–89. Former law clerk, Minnesota District Court and Wisconsin Circuit Court. Former practicing attorney. Deputy corporation counsel, Forest County, 1997–99. Assistant district attorney, Langlade County, 1996–99. Assistant district attorney, Marathon County, 1998–99. District attorney, Ashland County, appointed 1999, elected 2002. Administrative law judge, Department of Workforce Development, 2002. Burnett County Circuit Court judge, appointed 2002, elected 2003. Established inmate community service program, juvenile community service program, drug and alcohol court, restorative justice program (six-year chair) in Burnett County. Former professor of law at Hamline University Law School (criminal procedure and professional responsibility). ▪ Member: State Bar of Wisconsin; Grantsburg Rotary International; Siren Fraternal Order of Moose. ▪ Former member: Ashland County Republican Party (chair); Ashland Knights of Columbus (Grand Knight); Ashland Masons; Milwaukee Teachers Association; Burnett County Drug and Alcohol Court (founding and first presiding judge); Siren Rotary International; Siren Fraternal Order of Moose.

Current office: Elected to Supreme Court 2008.

Rebecca Grassl Bradley

Biography: Born Milwaukee, Wisconsin, August 2, 1971. ▪ Graduate Divine Savior Holy Angels High School; B.S. with honors in Business Administration and Business Economics, Marquette University, 1993; J.D. University of Wisconsin-Madison, 1996. ▪ Former practicing attorney, 1996–2012; Milwaukee County Circuit Court judge, appointed 2012, elected 2013; District I Court of Appeals judge, appointed 2015. ▪ Member: Supreme Court Finance Committee; Supreme Court Legislative Committee; Board of Advisors, Federalist Society, Milwaukee Lawyers Chapter; Board of Governors, St. Thomas More Lawyers Society; Wisconsin State Advisory Committee, U.S. Commission on Civil Rights; Wisconsin Trial Judges Association. ▪ Former member: Wisconsin Juvenile Jury Instructions Committee; Wisconsin Juvenile Benchbook Committee; Milwaukee Trial Judges Association. ▪ In private practice: American Arbitration Association arbitrator; chair, Business Law Section, State Bar of Wisconsin.

Current office: Appointed to Supreme Court October 2015 to fill vacancy created by death of Justice N. Patrick Crooks. Elected to full term 2016.

Daniel Kelly

Biography: Born Santa Barbara, California, 1964; married; 5 children. ▪ Graduate B.S. Political Science and Spanish, Carroll College, 1986; J.D. Regent University Law School (Virginia Beach, Virginia), 1991, where he was editor-in-chief of the Law Review. ▪ Former shareholder in one of Wisconsin's oldest and largest law firms; law clerk for Wisconsin Court of Appeals Judge Ralph Adam Fine (1991–92); law clerk and staff attorney, Office of Special Masters, U.S. Court of Federal Claims (1992–96). ▪ Member: Board of Advisors, Federalist Society, Milwaukee Lawyers Chapter; Wisconsin State Advisory Committee, U.S. Commission on Civil Rights; President's Advisory Council, Carroll University. ▪ Former member: Old World Wisconsin Foundation (board member); Milwaukee Forum.

Current office: Appointed to Supreme Court July 2016 to fill vacancy created by resignation of Justice David T. Prosser.

▪ ▪ ▪

Tammy Baldwin, U.S. Senator

Democrat

Biography: Born Madison, Wisconsin, February 11, 1962. Voting address: Madison, Wisconsin. ▪ Graduate Madison West High School; A.B. in Mathematics and Government, Smith College (Massachusetts), 1984; J.D. University of Wisconsin-Madison, 1989. ▪ Former practicing attorney, 1989–92. ▪ Madison City Council, 1986; Dane County Board, 1986–94. ▪ State legislative service: Elected to Assembly, 78th District, 1992–96 (served until January 4, 1999).

Congress: Elected to U.S. House of Representatives 1998. Reelected 2000–10. Elected to U.S. Senate 2012. Committee assignments, 115th Congress: **Appropriations** and its subcommittees on Agriculture, Rural Development, Food and Drug Administration, and Related Agencies; Department of Defense; Department of Homeland Security; Departments of Labor, Health and Human Services and Education and Related Agencies; and Military Construction and Veterans Affairs and Related Agencies. **Commerce, Science and Transportation** and its subcommittees on Aviation Operations, Safety, and Security; Communications, Technology, Innovation and the Internet; Oceans, Atmosphere, Fisheries, and Coast Guard; Space, Science and Competitiveness; and Surface Transportation and Merchant Marine Infrastructure, Safety and Security. **Health, Education, Labor and Pension** and its subcommittees on Employment and Workplace Safety; and Primary Health and Retirement Security.

Contact: Washington—202-224-5653; 709 Hart Senate Office Building, Washington, D.C. 20510. Eau Claire—715-832-8424; 402 Graham Street, Suite 206, Eau Claire, WI 54701. Green Bay—920-498-2668; 1039 West Mason Street, Suite 119, Green Bay, WI 54303. La Crosse—608-796-0045; 205 5th Avenue South, Room 216, La Crosse, WI 54601. Madison—608-264-5338; 30 West Mifflin Street, Suite 700, Madison, WI 53703. Milwaukee—414-297-4451; 633 West Wisconsin Avenue, Suite 1920, Milwaukee, WI 53203. Wausau—715-261-2611; 2100 Stewart Avenue, Suite 250B, Wausau, WI 54401.

Website: www.baldwin.senate.gov

Ron Johnson, U.S. Senator

Republican

Biography: Born Mankato, Minnesota, April 8, 1955; 3 children. Voting address: Oshkosh, Wisconsin. ▪ Graduate Edina High School, 1973; B.S.B. University of Minnesota, 1977. ▪ Former CEO, plastics manufacturing company. ▪ Former member: Partners in Education Council, Oshkosh Chamber of Commerce (business cochair); Oshkosh Opera House Foundation (treasurer); Lourdes Foundation (board president); Diocese of Green Bay Finance Council; Oshkosh Chamber of Commerce Board of Directors (chair-elect); Oshkosh Area Community Foundation Investment Council.

Congress: Elected to U.S. Senate 2010. Reelected 2016. Committee assignments, 115th Congress: **Homeland Security and Governmental Affairs** (chair), its Permanent Subcommittee on Investigations, and its subcommittees on Federal Spending Oversight and Emergency Management; and Regulatory Affairs and Federal Management. **Budget. Commerce, Science and Transportation** and its subcommittees on Communications, Technology, Innovation and the Internet; Oceans, Atmosphere, Fisheries and Coast Guard; and Surface Transportation and Merchant Marine Infrastructure, Safety and Security. **Foreign Relations** and its subcommittees on Europe and Regional Security Cooperation (chair); Near East, South Asia, Central Asia and Counterterrorism; and Western Hemisphere, Transnational Crime, Civilian Security, Democracy, Human Rights and Global Women's Issues.

Contact: Washington—202-224-5323; 328 Hart Senate Office Building, Washington, D.C. 20510. Milwaukee—414-276-7282; 517 East Wisconsin Avenue, Suite 408, Milwaukee, WI 53202. Oshkosh—920-230-7250; 219 Washington Avenue, Suite 100, Oshkosh, WI 54901.

Website: www.ronjohnson.senate.gov

Paul Ryan, U.S. Representative

Republican, 1st Congressional District

Biography: Born Janesville, Wisconsin, 1970; married; 3 children. Voting address: Janesville, Wisconsin. ▪ Graduate Janesville Craig High School; B.A. in Economics and Political Science, Miami University of Ohio, 1992. ▪ Former aide to U.S. Senator Robert Kasten and employed at family construction business. ▪ Member: Janesville Bowmen, Inc.; St. John Vianney's Parish.

Congress: Elected to U.S. House of Representatives 1998. Reelected since 2000. Speaker of the House of Representatives since October 29, 2015.

Contact: Washington—202-225-3031; 888-909-7926 (toll free); 1233 Longworth House Office Building, Washington, D.C. 20515. Janesville—608-752-4050; 20 South Main Street, Suite 10, Janesville, WI 53545. Kenosha—262-654-1901; 5031 7th Avenue, Kenosha, WI 53140. Racine—262-637-0510; 216 6th Street, Racine, WI 53403.

Website: http://paulryan.house.gov

Mark Pocan, U.S. Representative

Democrat, 2nd Congressional District

Biography: Born Kenosha, Wisconsin, August 14, 1964; married. Voting address: Town of Vermont, Wisconsin. ▪ Graduate Mary D. Bradford High School (Kenosha); B.A. University of Wisconsin-Madison, 1986. ▪ Small businessperson. ▪ State legislative service: Elected to Assembly, 78th District, 1998–2010 (served until January 3, 2013).

Congress: Elected to U.S. House of Representatives 2012. Reelected since 2014. Committee assignments, 115th Congress: **Appropriations** and its subcommittees on Labor, Health and Human Services, Education, and Related Agencies; and on Agriculture, Rural Development, Food and Drug Administration and Related Agencies.

Contact: Washington—202-225-2906; 1421 Longworth House Office Building, Washington, D.C. 20515. Beloit—608-365-8001; 100 State Street, 3rd floor, Beloit, WI 53511. Madison—608-258-9800; 10 East Doty Street, Suite 405, Madison, WI 53703.

Website: http://pocan.house.gov

Ron Kind, U.S. Representative

Democrat, 3rd Congressional District

Biography: Born La Crosse, Wisconsin, March 16, 1963; married; 2 children. Voting address: La Crosse, Wisconsin. ▪ Graduate Logan High School; B.A. Harvard University, 1985; M.A. London School of Economics (England); J.D. University of Minnesota Law School, 1990. ▪ Attorney. Former La Crosse County assistant district attorney and State of Wisconsin special prosecutor. ▪ Member: U.S. Supreme Court Bar; State Bar of Wisconsin and La Crosse County Bar Association; Association of State Prosecutors; Democratic Party; Wisconsin Harvard Club (board of directors); Boys and Girls Club of La Crosse (board of directors); Coulee Council on Alcohol and Other Drug Abuse (board of directors); Moose Club; Optimist Club.

Congress: Elected to U.S. House of Representatives 1996. Reelected since 1998. Committee assignments, 115th Congress: **Ways and Means** and its subcommittees on Health; and Trade.

Contact: Washington—202-225-5506; 1502 Longworth House Office Building, Washington, D.C. 20515-4906. Eau Claire—715-831-9214; 131 S. Barstow Street, Suite 301, Eau Claire, WI 54701. La Crosse—608-782-2558; 205 5th Avenue South, Suite 400, La Crosse, WI 54601.

Website: https://kind.house.gov

Gwendolynne S. Moore, U.S. Representative

Democrat, 4th Congressional District

Biography: Born Racine, Wisconsin, April 18, 1951; 3 children. Voting address: Milwaukee, Wisconsin. ▪ Graduate North Division High School (Milwaukee); B.A. in Political Science, Marquette University, 1978; certification in Credit Union Management, Milwaukee Area Technical College, 1983. ▪ Former housing officer with Wisconsin Housing and Economic Development Authority; development specialist with Milwaukee City Development; program and planning analyst with Wisconsin Departments of Employment Relations and Health and Social Services. ▪ Member: National

Black Caucus of State Legislators; National Conference of State Legislatures—Host Committee, Milwaukee 1995; National Black Caucus of State Legislators—Host Committee (chair) 1997; Wisconsin Legislative Black and Hispanic Caucus (chair since 1997). ▪ State legislative service: Elected to Assembly 1988 and 1990; elected to Senate 1992, 1996, and 2000. Senate President Pro Tempore 1997, 1995 (effective 7/15/96).

Congress: Elected to U.S. House of Representatives 2004. Reelected since 2006. Committee assignments, 115th Congress: **Financial Services** and its subcommittees on Financial Institutions and Consumer Credit; on Monetary Policy and Trade (ranking minority member); and on Oversight and Investigations.

Contact: Washington—202-225-4572; 2252 Rayburn House Office Building, Washington, D.C. 20515. Milwaukee—414-297-1140; 316 North Milwaukee Street, Suite 406, Milwaukee, WI 53202-5818.

Website: https://gwenmoore.house.gov

F. James Sensenbrenner, Jr., U.S. Representative
Republican, 5th Congressional District

Biography: Born Chicago, Illinois, June 14, 1943; married; 2 children, 1 grandchild. Voting address: Menomonee Falls, Wisconsin. ▪ Graduate Milwaukee Country Day School, 1961; A.B. Stanford University, 1965; J.D. University of Wisconsin-Madison Law School, 1968. ▪ Attorney. Former assistant to State Senate Majority Leader Jerris Leonard and to U.S. Congressman Arthur Younger. ▪ Member: State Bar of Wisconsin; Riveredge Nature Center; American Philatelic Society; Waukesha County Republican Party. ▪ Former member: Whitefish Bay Jaycees; Shorewood Men's Club. ▪ Recipient: Government of Japan *Order of the Rising Sun, Gold and Silver Star*; European Parliament *Schuman Medal*. ▪ State legislative service: Elected to Assembly 1968–74. Elected to Senate in April 1975 special election. Reelected in 1976. Assistant minority leader 1977.

Congress: Elected to U.S. House of Representatives 1978. Reelected since 1980. Committee assignments, 115th Congress: **Foreign Affairs** and its subcommittees on Africa, Global Health, Global Human Rights and International Organizations; and on Europe, Eurasia and Emerging Threats. **Judiciary** and its subcommittees on Crime, Terrorism, Homeland Security and Investigations; and on Immigration and Border Security (chair).

Contact: Washington—202-225-5101; 2449 Rayburn House Office Building, Washington, D.C. 20515-4905. District—262-784-1111; 800-242-1119 (toll free) 120 Bishops Way, Room 154, Brookfield, WI 53005-6294.

Website: http://sensenbrenner.house.gov

Glenn Grothman, U.S. Representative
Republican, 6th Congressional District

Biography: Born Milwaukee, Wisconsin, July 3, 1955. Voting address: Glenbeulah, Wisconsin. ▪ Graduate Homestead High School (Mequon); B.B.A.; J.D. University of Wisconsin-Madison. ▪ Former practicing attorney. ▪ Member: Kiwanis-West Bend Early Risers; Loyal Order of the Moose-West Bend; Kettle Moraine Symphony (board member); ABATE of Wisconsin; Rotary Club of Fond du Lac. ▪ Recipient: The Association of Mature American Citizens *Friend of AMAC*; International Food Distributors Association *Thomas Jefferson Award* 2016; American Conservative Union *Award for Conservative Achievement* 2015; FreedomWorks *Freedom Fighter Award* 2016; Asian American Hotel Owners Association 2015; U.S. Chamber of Commerce *Spirit of Enterprise Award* 2014; National Retail Federation *Hero on Main Street* 2016, 2015; WMC *Exemplar Award* for work on manufacturing tax credit 2012; Wisconsin Farm Bureau's *Friend of Farm Bureau Award* 2016; NFIB *Guardian of Small Business Award* 2016. ▪ State legislative service: Elected to Assembly in December 1993 special election. Reelected 1994–2002. Elected to Senate 2004. Reelected 2008–12. Assistant Majority Leader 2013, 2011; Assistant Minority Leader 2009; Minority Caucus Chair 2007; Majority Caucus Vice Chair 2003, 2001, 1999.

Congress: Elected to U.S. House of Representatives since 2014. Committee assignments, 115th Congress: **Education and the Workforce** and its subcommittees on Higher Education and Workforce Development; and on Workforce Protections. **Oversight and Government Reform** and its subcommittees on Health Care, Benefits, and Administrative Rules; and on Intergovernmental Affairs. **Budget.**

Contact: Washington—202-225-2476; 1217 Longworth House Office Building,

Washington, D.C. 20515. District—920-907-0624; 24 West Pioneer Road, Fond du Lac, WI 54935.

Website: https://grothman.house.gov

Sean P. Duffy, U.S. Representative
Republican, 7th Congressional District

Biography: Born October 3, 1971; married; 7 children. Voting address: Weston, Wisconsin. ▪ Graduate Hayward High School; B.A. in Business Marketing, St. Mary's (Winona, Minnesota), 1994; J.D. William Mitchell College of Law, 1999. ▪ Attorney. Former special prosecutor and district attorney, Ashland County.

Congress: Elected to U.S. House of Representatives 2010. Reelected since 2012. Committee assignments, 115th Congress: **Financial Services** and its subcommittee on Capital Markets, Securities and Investments.

Contact: Washington—202-225-3365; 2330 Rayburn House Office Building, Washington, D.C. 20515. Hayward—715-392-3984; 15954 Rivers Edge Drive, Suite 206, Hayward, WI 54843. Hudson—715-808-8160; 502 2nd Street, Suite 202, Hudson, WI 54016. Wausau—715-298-9344; 208 Grand Avenue, Wausau, WI 54403.

Website: https://duffy.house.gov

Mike Gallagher, U.S. Representative
Republican, 8th Congressional District

Biography: Born Green Bay, Wisconsin, March 3, 1984. Voting address: Green Bay, Wisconsin. ▪ A.B. Princeton University; Master's in Security Studies, Georgetown University; Ph.D. in International Relations, Georgetown University. Iraq War Veteran, intelligence officer, served in U.S. Marine Corps 2006–13. ▪ Former staffer, U.S. Senate Foreign Relations Committee; senior global market strategist at a fuel management services company.

Congress: Elected to U.S. House of Representatives 2016. Committee assignments, 115th Congress: **Armed Forces. Homeland Security** and its subcommittees on Counterterrorism and Intelligence; and on Cybersecurity and Infrastructure Protection.

Contact: Washington—202-225-5665; 1007 Longworth House Office Building, Washington, D.C. 20515. Appleton—920-380-0061; 333 West College Avenue, Appleton, WI 54911.

Website: https://gallagher.house.gov

■ ■ ■

U.S. Congressional Districts

DOUGLAS
BAYFIELD
IRON
ASHLAND
VILAS
BURNETT WASHBURN SAWYER
FLORENCE
PRICE ONEIDA
FOREST
POLK BARRON RUSK
7
MARINETTE
TAYLOR LINCOLN LANGLADE
ST. CROIX CHIPPEWA
DUNN MENOMINEE OCONTO
PIERCE MARATHON
EAU CLAIRE CLARK SHAWANO **8** DOOR
PEPIN
BUFFALO KEWAUNEE
WOOD PORTAGE WAUPACA OUTAGAMIE BROWN
TREM-
PEALEAU JACKSON
3 MANITOWOC
LA CROSSE MONROE ADAMS WAUSHARA WINNEBAGO CALUMET
JUNEAU MARQUETTE **6**
VERNON GREEN
LAKE FOND DU LAC SHEBOYGAN
COLUMBIA
CRAWFORD RICHLAND SAUK DODGE WASH- OZAUKEE
INGTON
5
2 DANE WAUKESHA **4**
IOWA JEFFERSON
GRANT MILWAUKEE
LAFAYETTE GREEN ROCK WALWORTH **1** RACINE
KENOSHA

STATE LEGISLATURE

2017 State Senate Officers

President Roth

President Pro Tempore
Marklein

Majority Leader
Fitzgerald

Assistant Majority
Leader Vukmir

Minority Leader
Shilling

Assistant Minority
Leader Bewley

Chief Clerk Renk

Sergeant at Arms Blazel

2017 State Assembly Officers

Speaker Vos

Speaker Pro Tempore
August

Majority Leader
Steineke

Assistant Majority
Leader Brooks

Minority Leader Barca

Assistant Minority
Leader Hesselbein

Chief Clerk Fuller

Sergeant at Arms
Tonnon Byers

Senate District 1
Assembly Districts 1, 2, 3

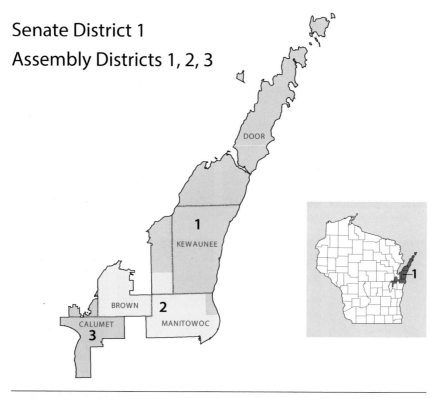

Frank Lasee, Senate District 1
Republican

Biography: Born Oceanside, California, December 11, 1961; married; 7 children. Voting address: Town of Ledgeview, Wisconsin. ▪ B.A. University of Wisconsin-Green Bay, 1986. ▪ Full-time legislator. Former manufacturing computer hardware and software salesman, business long-distance salesman. Former real estate salesman. ▪ Former member: Optimists; Rotary; Telecommunications Specialists of Wisconsin. ▪ Town of Ledgeview chair, 1993–97.

Legislature: Elected to Assembly 1994–2006. Elected to Senate since 2010. Leadership positions: Majority Caucus Chair 2013. Committee assignments, 2017: Insurance, Housing and Trade (chair); Natural Resources and Energy (vice chair); Labor and Regulatory Reform.

Contact: Sen.Lasee@legis.wisconsin.gov; 608-266-3512; Room 316 South, State Capitol, PO Box 7882, Madison, WI 53707-7882.

Joel C. Kitchens, Assembly District 1

Republican

Biography: Born Washington, D.C., September 20, 1957; married; 3 children. Voting address: Sturgeon Bay, Wisconsin. ▪ Graduate Ballard High School, Louisville, Kentucky, 1975; B.S. Ohio State University, 1979; D.V.M. Ohio State University, 1983. ▪ Large animal veterinarian. ▪ Member: Sturgeon Bay Moravian Church; Wisconsin Veterinary Medical Association; American Veterinary Medical Association. ▪ Sturgeon Bay Board of Education, 2000–14.

Legislature: Elected to Assembly since 2014. Committee assignments, 2017: Children and Families (chair); Education (vice chair); Agriculture; Environment and Forestry; Financial Institutions; Tourism.

Contact: Rep.Kitchens@legis.wisconsin.gov; 608-266-5350; 888-482-0001 (toll free); 920-743-7990 (district); Room 10 West, State Capitol, PO Box 8952, Madison, WI 53708.

André Jacque, Assembly District 2

Republican

Biography: Born Beaver Dam, Wisconsin, October 13, 1980; married; 5 children. Voting address: De Pere, Wisconsin. ▪ Graduate Green Bay Southwest 1999; B.S. University of Wisconsin-Madison, 2003; graduate certificate from University of Wisconsin-Madison La Follette Institute of Public Affairs. ▪ Full-time legislator. Former communications director, transit planning coordinator, grant-writing consultant. ▪ Member: Wisconsin Council on Domestic Abuse; Wisconsin Small Business Environmental Council; Green Bay Area Crimestoppers (board member); Golden House Domestic Abuse Shelter Community Leadership Council; Brown County Taxpayers Association; Knights of Columbus; Civil Air Patrol. ▪ Former member: Brown County Teen Leadership (board member); Brown County United Way (marketing and communications committee); Higher Educational Aids Board, 2001–03. ▪ Recipient: Wisconsin Coalition Against Domestic Violence *Legislative Champion Award*; Wisconsin Counties Association *Outstanding Legislator Award*; Pro-Life Wisconsin *Legislator of the Year*; NFIB *Guardian of Small Business*

Award; Wisconsin Family Council *William Wilberforce Freedom Award*; Brown County Crime Prevention Foundation *Crimefighter Award*; Manitowoc County Substance Abuse Prevention Coalition *IMPACT Recognition*; Wisconsin Coalition of Virtual School Families *Shining Star of Education Reform*; Dairy Business Association *Legislative Excellence Award*; Phillips Foundation *Distinguished Young Conservative Leader of the Year*; Green Bay Area Chamber of Commerce *Legislator of the Year*; Mothers Against Drunk Driving (MADD) *Legislator of the Year*; Wisconsin Towns Association *Friend of Towns*; Wisconsin Professional Police Association *Law Enforcement Honor Roll*; U.S. Chamber of Commerce Institute for Legal Reform *State Legislative Achievement Award*.

Legislature: Elected to Assembly since 2010. Committee assignments, 2017: Criminal Justice and Public Safety; Health; Judiciary; Regulatory Licensing Reform; State Affairs; Ways and Means; Joint Committee on Information Policy and Technology.

Contact: Rep.Jacque@legis.wisconsin.gov; 608-266-9870; 888-534-0002 (toll free); 920-819-8066 (district); Room 212 North, State Capitol, PO Box 8952, Madison, WI 53708.

Ron Tusler, Assembly District 3
Republican

Biography: Born Appleton, Wisconsin, March 21, 1984; married (Devon), parents (Bill and Beverly), sister (Liz Tusler Meyer), brother-in-law (Anthony Meyer). Voting address: Harrison, Wisconsin. ▪ Graduate Neenah High School, 2002; Degree in Urban Education, History, Honors from University of Wisconsin-Milwaukee, 2007; Juris Doctor from Marquette University Law School, 2010. ▪ Small business owner, law practice. Attorney. Former student attorney, Winnebago County District Attorney's Office. Former student teacher, Milwaukee Public Schools. ▪ Member: Appleton Area Jaycees (chair; president; treasurer); Heart of the Valley Chamber of Commerce; Republican Party of Outagamie County (chair; vice chair; communications director). ▪ Former Member: St. Thomas More Society (vice president); Native American Law Society (treasurer); Boy Scouts of America-Gathering Waters District (membership chair; executive officer).

Legislature: Elected to Assembly 2016. Committee assignments, 2017: Education; Environment and Forestry; Natural Resources and Sporting Heritage;

Insurance; Judiciary. Additional appointments, 2017: Commission on Uniform State Laws.

Contact: Rep.Tusler@legis.wisconsin.gov; 608-266-5831; 888-534-0003 (toll free); 920-749-0400 (district); Room 22 West, State Capitol, PO Box 8953, Madison, WI 53708.

Senate District 2
Assembly Districts 4, 5, 6

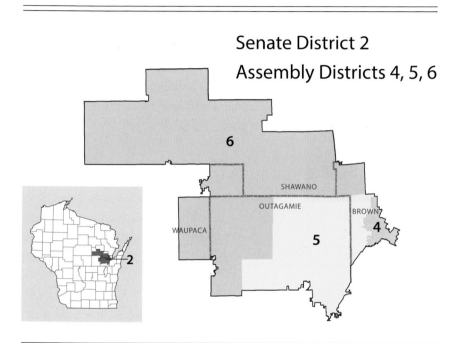

Robert L. Cowles, Senate District 2
Republican

Biography: Born Green Bay, Wisconsin, July 31, 1950. Voting address: Green Bay, Wisconsin. ■ B.S. University of Wisconsin-Green Bay, 1975; graduate work University of Wisconsin-Green Bay. ■ Current small business owner and legislator. Former director of an alternative energy division for a communications construction company. ■ Member: Allouez Kiwanis; Salvation Army Volunteer; National Caucus of Environmental Legislators (board member).

Legislature: Elected to Assembly 1982–86 (resigned 4/21/87). Elected to Senate in April 1987 special election. Reelected since 1988. Committee assignments,

2017: Natural Resources and Energy (chair); Joint Legislative Audit Committee (cochair); Transportation and Veterans Affairs; Joint Committee on Information Policy and Technology.

Contact: Sen.Cowles@legis.wisconsin.gov; 608-266-0484; 800-334-1465 (toll free); 608-267-0304 (fax); 920-448-5092 (district); 920-448-5093 (district fax); Room 118 South, State Capitol, PO Box 7882, Madison, WI 53707-7882.

David Steffen, Assembly District 4
Republican

Biography: Born October 12, 1971; married; 1 child. Voting address: Howard, Wisconsin. ▪ Graduate Ashwaubenon High School, 1990; B.A. in Political Science, University of Wisconsin-Madison, 1995. ▪ Small business owner since 2009. ▪ Former and current memberships: Howard Small Business Partnership (founder); Howard Go Green Save Green Initiative (founder, chair); Ashwaubenon Business Association (president); Prevent Blindness—Northeastern Wisconsin (president); Team Lambeau (executive director); Green Bay Area Chamber of Commerce State and Federal Issues Committee (chair). ▪ Village of Howard Board of Trustees, 2007–15; Brown County Board of Supervisors, 2012–15.

Legislature: Elected to Assembly since 2014. Committee assignments, 2017: Energy and Utilities (vice chair); Insurance; Local Government; Urban Revitalization; Ways and Means.

Contact: Rep.Steffen@legis.wisconsin.gov; 608-266-5840; 888-534-0004 (toll free); Room 21 North, State Capitol, PO Box 8953, Madison, WI 53708.

Jim Steineke, Assembly District 5
Republican

Biography: Born Milwaukee, Wisconsin, November 23, 1970; married; 3 children. Voting address: Kaukauna, Wisconsin. ▪ Graduate Wauwatosa West High School, 1989; attended University of Wisconsin-Milwaukee and University of Wisconsin-Oshkosh. ▪ Realtor, salesman. ▪ Member: Realtors Association of Northeast Wisconsin; Wisconsin Realtors

Association. ▪ Town of Vandenbroek supervisor, 2005–07; town chair, 2007–11. Outagamie County supervisor, 2006–11.

Legislature: Elected to Assembly since 2010. Leadership positions: Majority Leader 2017, 2015; Assistant Majority Leader 2013. Committee assignments, 2017: Rules (chair); Assembly Organization (vice chair); Employment Relations (vice chair); Joint Committee on Employment Relations; Joint Committee on Legislative Organization; Joint Legislative Council.

Contact: Rep.Steineke@legis.wisconsin.gov; 608-266-2401; 888-534-0005 (toll free); Room 115 West, State Capitol, PO Box 8953, Madison, WI 53708.

Gary Tauchen, Assembly District 6
Republican

Biography: Born Rice Lake, Wisconsin, November 23, 1953; single. Voting address: Bonduel, Wisconsin. ▪ Graduate Bonduel High School, 1971; attended University of Wisconsin-Madison, 1971–72; B.S. in Animal Science, University of Wisconsin-River Falls, 1976. ▪ Dairy farmer. ▪ Member: Wisconsin Farm Bureau; Badger AgVest, LLC (director); Professional Dairy Producers of Wisconsin (former director); Dairy Business Association; Wisconsin Livestock Identification Consortium (former director, former chair); Brown, Shawano, Outagamie, Waupaca County Republican Party; Shawano Area Chamber of Commerce; Shawano County Dairy Promotions (former director); Cooperative Resources International (former vice chair); AgSource Cooperative Services (former chair); National Dairy Herd Improvement Association (former director); University of Wisconsin Center for Dairy Profitability (former chair); Shawano Rotary.

Legislature: Elected to Assembly since 2006. Leadership positions: Minority Caucus Sergeant at Arms 2009. Committee assignments, 2017: Small Business Development (chair); State Affairs (vice chair); Agriculture; Energy and Utilities; Family Law; Tourism.

Contact: Rep.Tauchen@legis.wisconsin.gov; 608-266-3097; 888-529-0006 (toll free); 715-758-6181 (district); Room 13 West, State Capitol, PO Box 8953, Madison, WI 53708.

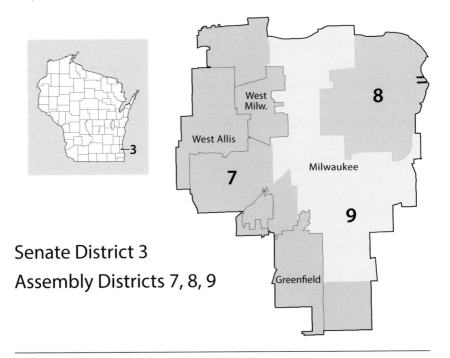

Senate District 3
Assembly Districts 7, 8, 9

Tim Carpenter, Senate District 3
Democrat

Biography: Born Milwaukee, Wisconsin. Voting address: Milwaukee, Wisconsin. ▪ Graduate Pulaski High School; B.A. University of Wisconsin-Milwaukee; M.A. University of Wisconsin-Madison La Follette Institute. ▪ Full-time legislator. ▪ Member: Sierra Club; Jackson Park Neighborhood Association; Story Hill Neighborhood Association; Milwaukee VA Soldiers Home Advisory Council; Milwaukee LGBT Community Center; Wisconsin Humane Society. ▪ Recipient: Wisconsin Professional Police Association *Law Enforcement Honor Roll*, 2014; Mothers Against Drunk Driving *Legislator of the Year*, 2015; Wisconsin Public Health Association's *Champion of Public Health*, 2008; Coalition of Wisconsin Aging Groups *Russ Feingold Award for Service to Seniors*, 2007; Shepherd Express *Best State Legislator*, 2008; Wisconsin League of Conservation Voters *Conservation Champion*, 2014, 2008; Shepherd Express *Legislator of the Year*, 2003; Wisconsin Professional Fire Fighters *Legislator of the Year*, 2002; Environmental Decade *Clean 16 Awards*.

Legislature: Elected to Assembly 1984–2000. Elected to Senate since 2002.

Leadership positions: President Pro Tempore 2011 (effective 7/17/12), 2007; Speaker Pro Tempore 1993. Committee assignments, 2017: Government Operations, Technology and Consumer Protection; Transportation and Veterans Affairs; Joint Committee on Information Policy and Technology; Joint Survey Committee on Tax Exemptions. Additional appointments, 2017: Wisconsin Economic Development Corporation Board; Transportation Projects Commission; State Fair Park Board; Council on Domestic Abuse.

Contact: Sen.Carpenter@legis.wisconsin.gov; 608-266-8535; 800-249-8173 (toll free); 608-282-3543 (fax); Room 109 South, State Capitol, PO Box 7882, Madison, WI 53707-7882.

Daniel Riemer, Assembly District 7

Democrat

Biography: Born Milwaukee, Wisconsin, December 10, 1986; single. Voting address: Milwaukee, Wisconsin. ▪ Graduate Rufus King High School (Milwaukee), 2005; B.A. University of Chicago, 2009; J.D. University of Wisconsin Law School, 2013. ▪ Full-time legislator. ▪ Member: Wisconsin State Bar Association; World Economic Forum: Global Shapers, Milwaukee Hub; Eisenhower Fellows.

Legislature: Elected to Assembly since 2012. Committee assignments, 2017: Public Benefit Reform; Veterans and Military Affairs; Ways and Means; Workforce Development; Joint Review Committee on Criminal Penalties.

Contact: Rep.Riemer@legis.wisconsin.gov; 608-266-1733; 888-529-0007 (toll free); Room 122 North, State Capitol, PO Box 8953, Madison, WI 53708.

JoCasta Zamarripa, Assembly District 8

Democrat

Biography: Born Milwaukee, Wisconsin, March 8, 1976. Voting address: Milwaukee, Wisconsin. ▪ Graduate St. Joan Antida High School (Milwaukee), 1994; BFA University of Wisconsin-Milwaukee, 2005. ▪ Full-time legislator. Former nonprofit professional.

Legislature: Elected to Assembly since 2010. Leadership positions: Minority Caucus Vice Chair 2015,

2013. Committee assignments, 2017: Campaigns and Elections; Criminal Justice and Public Safety; Health; Small Business Development; State Affairs.

Contact: Rep.Zamarripa@legis.wisconsin.gov; legis.wisconsin.gov/assembly/zamarripa; 608-267-7669; 888-534-0008 (toll free); Room 112 North, State Capitol, PO Box 8953, Madison, WI 53708.

Josh Zepnick, Assembly District 9
Democrat

Biography: Born Milwaukee, Wisconsin, March 21, 1968; married. Voting address: Milwaukee, Wisconsin. ▪ Graduate Rufus King High School (Milwaukee); B.A. University of Wisconsin-Madison, 1990; M.A. University of Minnesota, 1998. ▪ Full-time legislator. Former project consultant, Milwaukee Jobs Initiative, Milwaukee Community Service Corps, and Urban Economic Development Association of Wisconsin; research associate, Center for Democracy and Citizenship; aide to State Senator Bob Jauch and Congressman David R. Obey. ▪ Member: Jackson Park Neighborhood Association; Jackson Park Business Association; South Side Business Club. ▪ Former member: UFCW Local 1444.

Legislature: Elected to Assembly since 2002. Committee assignments, 2017: Energy and Utilities; Family Law; Federalism and Interstate Relations; Financial Institutions; Mental Health.

Contact: Rep.Zepnick@legis.wisconsin.gov; 608-266-1707; 888-534-0009 (toll free); Room 7 North, State Capitol, PO Box 8953, Madison, WI 53708.

Senate District 4
Assembly Districts 10, 11, 12

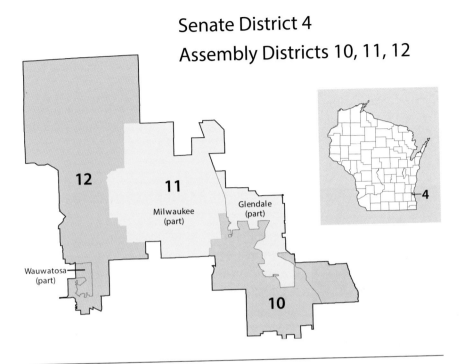

Lena C. Taylor, Senate District 4

Democrat

Biography: Born Milwaukee, Wisconsin, July 25, 1966; 1 child. Voting address: Milwaukee, Wisconsin. ▪ Graduate Rufus King High School (Milwaukee), 1984; B.A. in English, University of Wisconsin-Milwaukee, 1990; J.D. Southern Illinois University-Carbondale, 1993. ▪ Attorney. ▪ Member: State Superintendent's Equity in the Every Student Succeeds Act Stakeholder Council; Alpha Kappa Alpha (Wisconsin State Connection Coordinator); National Organization of Black Elected Legislative Women (ambassador); Boy Scouts Three Harbors Council (advisory board); NAACP; Milwaukee Community Justice Council (vice president); Teen Pregnancy Prevention Oversight Committee; Integrated Reentry Employment Strategies Executive Committee; NCSL Women's Legislative Network Board; Medical College of Wisconsin Cancer Center Community Advisory Board; Democratic Party of Wisconsin (former first vice chair). ▪ Milwaukee Metropolitan Sewerage District Commissioner, 2010–14.

Legislature: Elected to Assembly in April 2003 special election. Elected to Senate since 2004. Committee assignments, 2017: Joint Committee on Finance; Judiciary and Public Safety; Agriculture, Small Business and Tourism; Joint Legislative Council; Joint Review Committee on Criminal Penalties; Law Revision Committee.

Contact: Sen.Taylor@legis.wisconsin.gov; Facebook: Senator Lena Taylor; Twitter: @sentaylor; 608-266-5810; 414-342-7176 (district); Room 5 South, State Capitol, PO Box 7882, Madison, WI 53707-7882.

David Bowen, Assembly District 10
Democrat

Biography: Born Milwaukee, Wisconsin, January 28, 1987; married. Voting address: Milwaukee, Wisconsin. ▪ Graduate Bradley Technology High School, 2005; Scholar of Education Policy and Community Studies at the University of Wisconsin-Milwaukee. ▪ Member: Milwaukee County Juvenile Detention Alternative Initiative Advisory Committee; Beyond the Bell Milwaukee (steering committee); Black Youth Project 100; African American Breastfeeding Network (advisory board); Democratic Party of Wisconsin (vice chair); State Innovation Exchange; Democratic Party of Wisconsin (advisory board); Association of State Democratic Chairs. ▪ Former member: American Legacy Foundation Activism Fellow. ▪ Recipient: Public Allies *Alumni of the Year 2013 Change Maker Award*; Community Action Program *Executive Champion Against Poverty*; Young Elected Officials Network *Leader of the Year—Public Service Leadership Award*; Amani Neighborhood Award; Northwest Side CDC *Unsung Hero Award* 2014; Safe and Sound Borchert Field C.A.R.E.S. *Certificate for Outstanding Community Building Advocate*. ▪ Milwaukee County Board of Supervisors, 2012–14.

Legislature: Elected to Assembly since 2014. Committee Assignments, 2017: Children and Families; Corrections; Education; Financial Institutions; Labor; Urban Revitalization; Legislative Council Study Committee on School Data.

Contact: Rep.Bowen@legis.wisconsin.gov; 608-266-7671; 888-534-0010 (toll free); Room 3 North, State Capitol, PO Box 8952, Madison, WI 53708.

Jason M. Fields, Assembly District 11
Democrat

Biography: Born Milwaukee, Wisconsin, January 29, 1974; single. Voting address: Glendale, Wisconsin. ▪ Graduate Milwaukee Lutheran High School, 1992; B.S. in Business Management, Cardinal Stritch University, 2014. ▪ CEO of investment firm; certified financial education instructor (CFEI). Former stockbroker; investment banker; business owner. ▪ Member: Prince Hall Masons; Alpha Phi Alpha Fraternity, Inc.; Independent Order of Odd Fellows; Elks Lodge of Milwaukee #46; International Society of Business Leaders.

Legislature: Elected to Assembly 2004–2010. Reelected 2016. Committee assignments, 2017: Urban Revitalization (vice chair); Agriculture; Financial Institutions; Jobs and the Economy.

Contact: Rep.Fields@legis.wisconsin.gov; 608-266-3756; 888-534-0011 (toll free); 414-810-7196 (district); Room 412 North, State Capitol, PO Box 8952, Madison, WI 53708.

Frederick P. Kessler, Assembly District 12
Democrat

Biography: Born Milwaukee, Wisconsin, January 11, 1940; married; 2 children. Voting address: Milwaukee, Wisconsin. ▪ Graduate Milwaukee Lutheran High School and Capitol Page School, 1957; B.A. University of Wisconsin-Madison, 1962; L.L.B. University of Wisconsin, 1966. ▪ Labor arbitrator. ▪ Member: Goethe House (vice president, former president); Milwaukee Chapter ACLU (board member, former president); World Affairs Council of Milwaukee (board member); Wisconsin Bar Association; Labor/Employment Relations Association (advisory committee member); Democratic Party; DANK (German-American National Congress), Milwaukee chapter (former vice president); Milwaukee Donauschwaben; Amnesty International Group 107 (former chair); Milwaukee Turners; NAACP; Fair Elections Project (initiator and convener of the group that filed Whitford v. Gill in federal court). ▪ Former member: City of Milwaukee Harbor Commission. ▪ Recipient: Wisconsin ACLU *Eunice Edgar Lifetime Service Award*, 2008; State Bar of Wisconsin *Scales of Justice Award*, 2010; German Immersion Foundation *Lifetime Achievement Award*, 2013. ▪ Presidential Elector for President Barack Obama, 2012. County court judge (Milwaukee County), 1972–78; Circuit court judge (Milwaukee County), 1978–81, 1986–88. On January 11, 1961, his 21st birthday, he became the youngest person, up to that time, ever to serve in the legislature.

Legislature: Elected to Assembly 1960, 1964–70, and since 2004. Committee assignments, 2017: Agriculture; Campaigns and Elections; Constitution and Ethics; Criminal Justice and Public Safety; Insurance.

Contact: Rep.Kessler@legis.wisconsin.gov; 608-266-5813; 888-534-0012 (toll free); 414-535-0266 (district); Room 111 North, State Capitol, PO Box 8952, Madison, WI 53708.

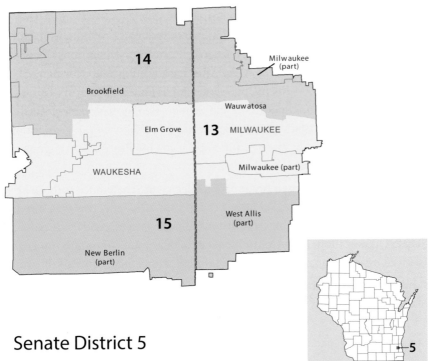

Senate District 5
Assembly Districts 13, 14, 15

Leah Vukmir, Senate District 5
Republican

Biography: Born Milwaukee, Wisconsin, April 26, 1958; 2 children. Voting address: Brookfield, Wisconsin. ▪ Graduate Brookfield East High School, 1976; B.S. in Nursing, Marquette University, 1980; M.S. in Nursing, University of Wisconsin-Madison, 1983. ▪ Registered nurse with 37 years of experience including more than 20 years as a certified pediatric nurse practitioner; research fellow, Wisconsin Policy Research Institute; past president and cofounder of Parents Raising Educational Standards in Schools (PRESS). Nationally recognized authority and speaker on educational issues and educational standards. ▪ Member: Republican Party of Waukesha County; Republican Party of Milwaukee County; American Legislative

Exchange Council (Center to Protect Free Speech chair, 2016 national chair); GOPAC (advisory board member). ▪ Former member: Standards and Assessments Subcommittee of Governor Thompson's Task Force on Education and Learning; English/Language Arts Task Force of Governor Thompson's Council on Model Academic Standards; West Allis Speedskating Club (former ASU Speedskating referee). ▪ Recipient: Center for Education Reform's *Unsung Hero Award* 1998; Brookfield East High School *Alumni Achievement Award* 2002; American Legislative Exchange Council *Legislator of the Year* 2009; *Right Women Iron Lady Award* 2014; Americans for Prosperity-Wisconsin *Champion of Free Speech Award* 2015–16.

Legislature: Elected to Assembly 2002–08. Elected to Senate since 2010. Leadership positions: Assistant Majority Leader 2017, 2015 (effective 9/26/2015). Committee assignments, 2017: Health and Human Services (chair); Education; Senate Organization; Joint Committee on Finance; Joint Committee on Legislative Organization. Additional appointments, 2017: State Fair Park Board.

Contact: Sen.Vukmir@legis.wisconsin.gov; 608-266-2512; Room 415 South, State Capitol, PO Box 7882, Madison, WI 53707-7882.

Rob Hutton, Assembly District 13
Republican

Biography: Born Milwaukee, Wisconsin, April 7, 1967; married; 4 children. Voting address: Brookfield, Wisconsin. ▪ Graduate Brookfield East High School, 1985; B.A. in History, University of Wisconsin-Whitewater, 1990. ▪ 20 years executive experience in trucking industry. ▪ Waukesha County supervisor, 2005–12.

Legislature: Elected to Assembly since 2012. Committee assignments, 2017: Government Accountability and Oversight (chair), Corrections (vice chair); Federalism and Interstate Relations; Regulatory Licensing Reform; Small Business Development.

Contact: Rep.Hutton@legis.wisconsin.gov; 608-267-9836; 888-534-0013 (toll free); 414-380-9665 (district); Room 220 North, State Capitol, PO Box 8952, Madison, WI 53708.

Dale Kooyenga, Assembly District 14

Republican

Biography: Born Oak Lawn, Illinois, February 12, 1979; married; 4 children. Voting address: Brookfield, Wisconsin. ▪ Graduate Chicago Christian High School, 1997; A.A. Moraine Valley Community College, 2000; B.A. Lakeland College, 2000; M.B.A. Marquette University, 2007. ▪ Certified public accountant. Member U.S. Army Reserve, 2005–present. Iraq War veteran. ▪ Member: American Legion; American Institute of Certified Public Accountants; Wisconsin Institute of Certified Public Accountants, LISC.

Legislature: Elected to Assembly since 2010. Committee assignments, 2017: Joint Committee on Finance (vice chair).

Contact: Rep.Kooyenga@legis.wisconsin.gov; 608-266-9180; 888-534-0014 (toll free); Room 324 East, State Capitol, PO Box 8952, Madison, WI 53708.

Joe Sanfelippo, Assembly District 15

Republican

Biography: Born Milwaukee, Wisconsin, February 26, 1964; married; 3 children. Voting address: New Berlin, Wisconsin. ▪ Graduate Thomas More High School, 1982; attended Marquette University, 1982–84. ▪ Small businessman; currently operates a small Christmas tree farm. Owned and operated a landscaping business for 20 years. ▪ Member: St. John the Evangelist Parish, Greenfield. ▪ Milwaukee County Board of Supervisors, 2008–12.

Legislature: Elected to Assembly since 2012. Committee assignments, 2017: Health (chair); Campaigns and Elections (vice chair); Financial Institutions; Mental Health; Transportation; Urban Revitalization.

Contact: Rep.Sanfelippo@legis.wisconsin.gov; 608-266-0620; 888-534-0015 (toll free); Room 306 North, State Capitol, PO Box 8953, Madison, WI 53708.

Senate District 6
Assembly Districts 16, 17, 18

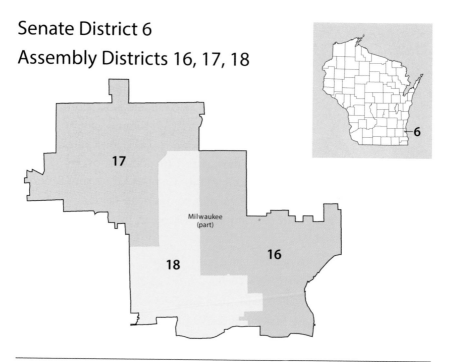

LaTonya Johnson, Senate District 6
Democrat

Biography: Born Somerville, Tennessee, June 22, 1972; 1 child. Voting address: Milwaukee, Wisconsin. ▪ Graduate Bay View High School, 1990; B.S. in Criminal Justice, Tennessee State University, 1997; attended University of Wisconsin-Milwaukee, 1990–92. ▪ Full-time legislator. Former family child care provider/owner, 2002–12; insurance agent, 2000–02; financial employment planner, 1997–2000. ▪ Member: AFSCME Wisconsin Child Care Providers Together Local 502 (former president); AFSCME District Council 48 (former vice president); African American Chamber of Commerce; Emerge Wisconsin, Class of 2012; CBTU-Coalition of Black Trade Unionists; Milwaukee Democratic Legislative Caucus (former chair), Wisconsin Women in Government (board member).

Legislature: Elected to Assembly 2012 and 2014. Elected to Senate 2016. Committee assignments, 2017: Economic Development, Commerce and Local Government; Education; Health and Human Services; Public Benefits, Licensing and State-Federal Relations. Additional appointments, 2017: Wisconsin Center District Board;

Child Abuse and Neglect Prevention Board; Milwaukee Child Welfare Partnership Council; Metropolitan Milwaukee Sewerage District Commission.

Contact: Sen.Johnson@legis.wisconsin.gov; 608-266-2500; 877-474-2000 (toll free); 414-313-1241 (district); Room 22 South, State Capitol, PO Box 7882, Madison, WI 53707-7882.

Leon D. Young, Assembly District 16
Democrat

Biography: Born Los Angeles, California, July 4, 1967; single. Voting address: Milwaukee, Wisconsin. ▪ Graduate Rufus King High School; attended University of Wisconsin-Milwaukee. ▪ Full-time legislator. Former police aide and police officer. ▪ Member: Democratic Party; Harambee Ombudsman Project; Milwaukee Police Association; League of Martin; House of Peace (Love Committee); NAACP; Urban League; Social Development Commission Minority Male Forum on Corrections; National Black Caucus of State Legislators' Task Force on African American Males; 100 Black Men; Milwaukee Metropolitan Fair Housing; Boy Scouts of America (Urban Emphasis Committee); Martin Luther King Community Center (Revitalization Committee).

Legislature: Elected to Assembly since 1992. Committee assignments, 2017: Financial Institutions; Housing and Real Estate; Insurance; Joint Survey Committee on Tax Exemptions.

Contact: Rep.Young@legis.wisconsin.gov; 608-266-3786; 888-534-0016 (toll free); 414-374-7414 (district); Room 11 North, State Capitol, PO Box 8953, Madison, WI 53708.

David Crowley, Assembly District 17
Democrat

Biography: Born Milwaukee, Wisconsin, May 14, 1986; married; 2 children. Voting address: Milwaukee, Wisconsin. ▪ Graduate Bay View High School; attended University of Wisconsin-Milwaukee. ▪ Former executive assistant/ policy director to Senator Nikiya Harris Dodd, Wisconsin Legislature; legislative assistant to Milwaukee County Supervisor

Nikiya Harris; field organizer for the Democratic Party of Wisconsin; African American statewide organizer for Feingold Senate Committee. ▪ Member: ACLU-Milwaukee Chapter Board (chair 2014–16); YMCA of Greater Milwaukee; Americorps/Public Allies Alumni; Prince Hall F&A Mason, Asher Lodge #7; Urban League of Young Professionals; Community Brainstorming Conference; NAACP.

Legislature: Elected to Assembly 2016. Committee assignments, 2017: Criminal Justice and Public Safety; Jobs and the Economy; Small Business Development; Transportation; Workforce Development.

Contact: Rep.Crowley@legis.wisconsin.gov; 608-266-5580; 888-534-0017 (toll free); Room 5 North, State Capitol, PO Box 8952, Madison, WI 53708.

Evan Goyke, Assembly District 18
Democrat

Biography: Born Neenah, Wisconsin, November 24, 1982; married. Voting address: Milwaukee, Wisconsin. ▪ Graduate Edgewood High School (Madison), 2001; B.A. in Political Science, St. John's University (Minnesota), 2005; J.D. Marquette University Law School, 2009. ▪ Attorney. Former state public defender. ▪ Member: St. Michael's/St. Rose of Lima Catholic Church; American Federation of Teachers Local 4822; ACLU; NAACP; State Bar of Wisconsin; Milwaukee Young Lawyers Association (former board member); Historic Concordia Neighborhood Association; Eagle Scout, Boy Scouts of America; Progressive Community Health Center (board member); Milwaukee Democratic Delegation (former chair).

Legislature: Elected to Assembly since 2012. Committee assignments, 2017: Corrections; Criminal Justice and Public Safety; Family Law; Housing and Real Estate; Veterans and Military Affairs. Additional appointments, 2017: Wisconsin Housing and Economic Development Authority Board; Evidence-Based Decision Making Subcommittee of the Criminal Justice Coordinating Council.

Contact: Rep.Goyke@legis.wisconsin.gov; 608-266-0645; 888-534-0018 (toll free); Room 322 West, State Capitol, PO Box 8952, Madison, WI 53708.

Senate District 7
Assembly Districts 19, 20, 21

Chris Larson, Senate District 7

Democrat

Biography: Born Milwaukee County, Wisconsin, November 12, 1980; married; 2 children. Voting address: Milwaukee, Wisconsin. ▪ Graduate Thomas More High School, 1999; degree in Finance, University of Wisconsin-Milwaukee, 2007. ▪ Full-time legislator. Former business manager. ▪ Member: American Civil Liberties Union; UW-Milwaukee Alumni Association; League of Conservation Voters; Bay View Neighborhood Association; Planned Parenthood Advocates of Wisconsin; Sierra Club; Humboldt Park Friends; South Side Business Club of Milwaukee; Bay View Historical Society; Arbor Day Foundation; Tri-Wisconsin; Badgerland Striders; Bay View Lions Club; Lake Park Friends; MPTV Friends. ▪ Former member: Airport Area Economic Development Group; Young Elected Officials; Coalition to Save the Hoan Bridge (cofounder); WISPIRG (campus intern). ▪ Milwaukee County Board of Supervisors, 2008–10.

Legislature: Elected to Senate since 2010. Leadership positions: Minority Leader 2013. Committee assignments, 2017: Agriculture, Small Business and Tourism;

Education; Insurance, Housing and Trade; Joint Committee for Review of Administrative Rules.

Contact: Sen.Larson@legis.wisconsin.gov; 608-266-7505; 800-361-5487 (toll free); Room 20 South, State Capitol, PO Box 7882, Madison, WI 53707-7882.

Jonathan Brostoff, Assembly District 19
Democrat

Biography: Born September 25, 1983; married. Voting address: Milwaukee, Wisconsin. ▪ B.A. in Political Science, University of Wisconsin-Milwaukee, 2011. ▪ Full-time legislator. Former district director for Senator Larson; backup shift supervisor—Pathfinders; program director, SDC Family Support Center; public ally, Americorps; volunteer, Street Beat, Big Brothers, Big Sisters, Casa Maria. ▪ Member: Democratic Party of Milwaukee County (board member); Bay View Neighborhood Association; Historic Water Tower Neighborhood Association; Planned Parenthood; Urban Ecology Center; America's Black Holocaust Museum (board member). ▪ Former member: ACLU-Wisconsin (board member); Tikkun Ha-Ir (board member).

Legislature: Elected to Assembly since 2014. Committee assignments, 2017: Aging and Long-Term Care; Government Accountability and Oversight; Mental Health; Natural Resources and Sporting Heritage; Regulatory Licensing Reform.

Contact: Rep.Brostoff@legis.wisconsin.gov; 608-266-0650; 888-534-0019 (toll free); Room 420 North, State Capitol, PO Box 8952, Madison, WI 53708.

Christine Sinicki, Assembly District 20
Democrat

Biography: Born Milwaukee, Wisconsin, March 28, 1960; married; 2 children. Voting address: Milwaukee, Wisconsin. ▪ Graduate Bay View High School. Bowhay Institute Fellow, La Follette School, University of Wisconsin-Madison, 2001; Flemming Fellow, Center for Policy Alternatives, 2003. ▪ Former small business manager. ▪ Member: Delegate—U.S. President Electoral College, 2000; American Council of Young Political Leaders, Delegate to Israel and Palestine, 2001; Milwaukee Committee on Domestic

Violence and Sexual Assault; Wisconsin Civil Air Patrol, Major; Milwaukee City Council Parents and Teachers Association; Bay View Historical Society; Bay View Neighborhood Association; State Assembly Milwaukee Caucus (chair 2005, 2003). ▪ Former member: State Minimum Wage Council (governor's appointee), 2005; Assembly Democratic Task Force on Working Families (chair), 2003. ▪ Recipient: Wisconsin Environmental Decade *Clean 16* 2000; Wisconsin Ob/Gyn Physicians' *Legislator of the Year* 2000; Wisconsin Coalition Against Domestic Violence *DV Diva* 2003; Wisconsin Department of Veterans Affairs *Certificates of Commendation* 2006, 2005; Wisconsin League of Conservation Voters *Conservation Champion* 2016, 2014, 2011, 2009, 2007; Wisconsin Women's Alliance *Legislation Award* 2009–10; Professional Firefighters of Wisconsin *Legislator of the Year* 2010; Wisconsin Grocers Association *Friend of Grocers* 2010; Cudahy Veterans' *Service Award* 2010; AMVETS *State Legislative Advocacy Award* 2011. ▪ Milwaukee School Board, 1991–98.

Legislature: Elected to Assembly since 1998. Leadership positions: Minority Caucus Sergeant at Arms 2017; Minority Caucus Secretary 2001. Committee assignments, 2017: Consumer Protection; Labor; State Affairs; Urban Revitalization; Veterans and Military Affairs.

Contact: Rep.Sinicki@legis.wisconsin.gov; 608-266-8588; 888-534-0020 (toll free); 414-481-7667 (district); Room 114 North, State Capitol, PO Box 8953, Madison, WI 53708.

Jessie Rodriguez, Assembly District 21
Republican

Biography: Born Puerto el Triunfo, El Salvador, July 5, 1977; married. Voting address: Oak Creek, Wisconsin. ▪ Graduate Alexander Hamilton High School (Milwaukee), 1996; B.A. Marquette University, 2002. ▪ Full-time legislator. Former analyst for a supermarket company; outreach coordinator for Hispanics for School Choice.

Legislature: Elected to Assembly in November 2013 special election. Reelected since 2014. Leadership positions: Majority Caucus Secretary 2017, 2015. Committee assignments, 2017: Family Law (chair); Education; Energy and Utilities.

Contact: Rep.Rodriguez@legis.wisconsin.gov; 608-266-0610; 888-534-0021 (toll free); Room 204 North, State Capitol, PO Box 8953, Madison, WI 53708.

Senate District 8
Assembly Districts 22, 23, 24

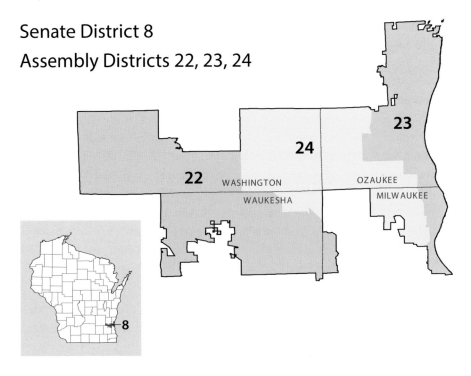

Alberta Darling, Senate District 8
Republican

Biography: Born Hammond, Indiana, April 28; widowed; 2 children, 3 grandchildren. Voting address: River Hills, Wisconsin. ▪ Graduate University of Wisconsin-Madison; postgraduate work University of Wisconsin-Milwaukee. ▪ Former teacher and marketing director. ▪ Member: North Shore Rotary; College Savings Program Board (EdVest); Junior League of Milwaukee (former president); Wisconsin Children's Caucus (cofounder); Milwaukee Child Welfare Partnership Council; NCSL Budgets and Revenue standing committee (vice chair); Fostering Futures Policy Advisory Council; NCSL Task Force on State and Local Taxation. ▪ Former member: Next Door Foundation; Public Policy Forum; Wisconsin Strategic Planning Council for Economic Development; Greater Milwaukee Committee; Goals for Greater Milwaukee 2000 Project (executive committee); United Way Board (chair, allocations committee); Tempo Professional Women's Organization; Future Milwaukee (president); Milwaukee Forum; Children's

Service Society of Wisconsin (board of directors); American Red Cross of Wisconsin (executive committee, board of directors); League of Women Voters; Today's Girls/Tomorrow's Women, Boys & Girls Club (founder); NCSL Education Committee (chair); YMCA (board member). ▪ Recipient: *Shining Star of Education Reform*; Hispanic Chamber of Commerce *Government Advocates Award*; Greater Milwaukee Committee *Leadership Award*; Leukemia and Lymphoma Society *Legislative Leadership Award*; Wisconsin Manufacturers and Commerce *Working for Wisconsin*; American Conservative Union Foundation *Defender of Liberty Award*; *Friend of Grocers*; Coalition of Wisconsin Aging Groups *Tommy G. Thompson Award for Service*; RightWisconsin *Iron Lady Award*, *Margaret Thatcher Award*; *Wisconsin Charter Champion Award*; National MS Hall of Fame Inductee; American Cancer Society *Legislative Champion*; Fair Air Coalition *Friend of Education*; Metropolitan Milwaukee Association of Commerce *Champion of Commerce*; Wisconsin Head Start Directors Association *Award of Excellence*; National Association of Community Leadership *Leadership Award*; United Way *Gwen Jackson Leadership Award*; St. Francis Children's Center *Children Service Award.*

Legislature: Elected to Assembly in May 1990 special election. Reelected November 1990. Elected to Senate since 1992. Committee assignments, 2017: Joint Committee on Finance (cochair); Education (vice chair); Economic Development, Commerce and Local Government; Joint Committee on Employment Relations; Joint Legislative Audit Committee; Joint Legislative Council. Additional appointments, 2017: Wisconsin Housing and Economic Development Authority Board.

Contact: Sen.Darling@legis.wisconsin.gov; 608-266-5830; Room 317 East, State Capitol, PO Box 7882, Madison, WI 53707-7882.

Janel Brandtjen, Assembly District 22
Republican

Biography: Born Milwaukee, Wisconsin, March 27; married; 2 children. Voting address: Menomonee Falls, Wisconsin. ▪ Graduate Marshall High School; B.B.A. in Finance and Marketing, University of Wisconsin-Milwaukee, 1988. ▪ Business owner. ▪ Member: Republican Party of Waukesha, Washington, and Milwaukee Counties; Republican Women of Waukesha, Washington, and Milwaukee Counties; National Rifle Association (lifetime member); Menomonee Falls Optimist Club; Immanuel Lutheran Church. ▪ Recipient: Wisconsin Pro-Life *Legislator of the Year* 2016; Wisconsin Family Action *Friends of Family, Life and Liberty* 2016; Associated Builders & Contractors *Building Wisconsin Award* 2016; MMAC *Champion of Commerce* 2015–16; WDA Dental Academy Award 2015. ▪ Waukesha County supervisor, 2008–16.

Legislature: Elected to Assembly since 2014. Committee assignments, 2017: Government Accountability and Oversight (vice chair); Corrections; Public Benefit Reform; Science and Technology; Urban Revitalization; Workforce Development; Joint Committee on Information Policy and Technology.

Contact: Rep.Brandtjen@legis.wisconsin.gov; 608-267-2367; 888-534-0022 (toll free); Room 221 North, State Capitol, PO Box 8952, Madison, WI 53708.

Jim Ott, Assembly District 23
Republican

Biography: Born Milwaukee, Wisconsin, June 5, 1947; married; 2 sons, 1 grandchild. Voting address: Mequon, Wisconsin. ▪ Graduate Milwaukee Washington High School, 1965; B.S. University of Wisconsin-Milwaukee, 1970; M.S. University of Wisconsin-Milwaukee, 1975; J.D. Marquette University, 2000. ▪ Full-time legislator. Former broadcast meteorologist and instructor at University of Wisconsin-Parkside. Served in U.S. Army, 1970–73; Vietnam veteran. ▪ Member: State Bar of Wisconsin; American Meteorological Society; Mequon/Thiensville Noon Rotary; Mequon/Thiensville Chamber of Commerce; American Legion; Ozaukee County Republican Party; North Shore Branch Milwaukee County Republican Party; Lumen Christi Catholic Church (past parish council president). ▪ Recipient: National Weather Service *Public Service Award* 2006; Archbishops Vatican II *Service Award* 1999; Vietnam Campaign Medal and Meritorious Unit Citation; Emerging Political Leaders Program; BILLD Leadership Fellow; MADD *Legislator of the Year* 2016, 2015, 2013; Wisconsin Chiefs of Police Association *True Friend of the Law Enforcement Community* 2016; Trout Unlimited recognition 2015; MMAC *Champion of Commerce* 2016, 2015.

Legislature: Elected to Assembly since 2006. Committee assignments, 2017: Judiciary (chair); Criminal Justice and Public Safety; Veterans and Military Affairs; Joint Committee for Review of Administrative Rules; Law Revision

Committee (cochair). Additional appointments, 2017: Judicial Council; Miller Park District Board of Directors (appointed by governor).

Contact: Rep.OttJ@legis.wisconsin.gov; 608-266-0486; 888-534-0023 (toll free); Room 317 North, State Capitol, PO Box 8953, Madison, WI 53708-8953.

Dan Knodl, Assembly District 24
Republican

Biography: Born Milwaukee, Wisconsin, December 14, 1958; 4 children. Voting address: Germantown, Wisconsin. ▪ Graduate Menomonee Falls East High School, 1977; attended University of Wisconsin-Madison. ▪ Resort owner. ▪ Member: Washington County Convention and Visitors Bureau; Ozaukee/Washington Land Trust; Pike Lake Sportsmans Club. ▪ Pike Lake Protection District 2000–present (secretary). Washington County Board, 2006–08.

Legislature: Elected to Assembly since 2008. Leadership positions: Majority Caucus Chair 2017; Assistant Majority Leader 2015, 2011. Committee assignments, 2017: Joint Committee on Information Policy and Technology (cochair); Assembly Organization; Labor; Rules; State Affairs.

Contact: Rep.Knodl@legis.wisconsin.gov; 608-266-3796; 888-529-0024 (toll free); Room 218 North, State Capitol, PO Box 8952, Madison, WI 53708.

Senate District 9
Assembly Districts 25, 26, 27

Devin LeMahieu, Senate District 9
Republican

Biography: Born Sheboygan, Wisconsin, August 8, 1972; single. Voting address: Oostburg, Wisconsin. ▪ Graduate Sheboygan County Christian High School, 1991; B.A. in Business Administration and Political Science, Dordt College (Sioux Center, Iowa), 1995. ▪ Publisher/owner, Lakeshore Weekly. ▪ Member: Oostburg Kiwanis Club (former president); Oostburg Chamber of Commerce; Sheboygan County Chamber of Commerce; Oostburg Civic Pride Committee; Bethel OPC (deacon); NRA (life member). ▪ Recipient: Wisconsin Wildlife Association *State Conservation Legislator of the Year* 2015; League of Wisconsin Municipalities *Strong Municipal Supporter* 2016; Cemetery and Cremation Association *Legislator of the Year* 2016; Wisconsin Counties Association *Outstanding Legislator Award* 2016; Wisconsin Academy of Family Physicians *Friend of Family Medicine* 2016; ABC-Wisconsin *Building Wisconsin Award* 2016; Wisconsin Grocers Association *Friend of Grocers* 2016; Wisconsin Builders Association *Friend of Housing* 2016; Wisconsin Manufacturers and Commerce *Working for Wisconsin*

2016; Metropolitan Milwaukee Association of Commerce *Champion of Commerce* 2016; Wisconsin Coalition for International Adoption *Friend of International Adoption* 2016. ▪ Sheboygan County Board supervisor, 2006–15, Human Resources Committee, 2006–15 (chair, 2010–14), Finance Committee, 2012–15, Executive Committee, 2010–12.

Legislature: Elected to Senate 2014. Committee assignments, 2017: Elections and Utilities (chair); Revenue, Financial Institutions and Rural Issues (vice chair); Health and Human Services; Joint Committee for Review of Administrative Rules; Law Revision Committee. Additional appointments, 2017: State Council on Alcohol and Other Drug Abuse; Wisconsin Aerospace Authority.

Contact: Sen.LeMahieu@legis.wisconsin.gov; SenatorDevin.com; Facebook: Senator Devin LeMahieu; Twitter: @senatordevin; 608-266-2056; 888-295-8750 (toll free); Room 323 South, State Capitol, PO Box 7882, Madison, WI 53707-7882.

Paul Tittl, Assembly District 25
Republican

Biography: Born Delavan, Wisconsin, November 23, 1961; married; 2 children, 3 grandchildren. Voting address: Manitowoc, Wisconsin. ▪ Graduate Lincoln High (Manitowoc), 1980. ▪ Owner, vacuum and sewing center. ▪ Member: National Rifle Association; Eagles Manitowoc; Manitowoc County Home Builders Association. ▪ Former member: Economic Development Corporation; Wastewater Treatment Facility Board; Manitowoc Crime Prevention Committee; Community Development Authority; Safety Traffic and Parking Commission; Wisconsin Utility Tax Association, 2009–13; WCA Taxation and Finance Steering Committee, 2010–13; WCA Judicial and Public Safety Steering Committee, 2010–13. ▪ Manitowoc City Council, 2004–08 (president 2006–07); Manitowoc County Board of Supervisors, 2006–13 (chair 2010–12).

Legislature: Elected to Assembly since 2012. Committee assignments, 2017: Mental Health (chair); Consumer Protection (vice chair); Jobs and the Economy; Natural Resources and Sporting Heritage; Veterans and Military Affairs.

Contact: Rep.Tittl@legis.wisconsin.gov; 608-266-0315; 888-529-0025 (toll free); 920-682-6203 (district, home); Room 219 North, State Capitol, PO Box 8953, Madison, WI 53708.

Terry Katsma, Assembly District 26
Republican

Biography: Born Sheboygan, Wisconsin, April 23, 1958; married; 3 children, 5 grandchildren. Voting address: Oostburg, Wisconsin. ▪ Graduate Sheboygan County Christian High School, 1976; B.A. in Business Administration, Dordt College (Sioux Center, Iowa), 1980; M.B.A. Marquette University, 1985. ▪ Full-time legislator. Former community bank president and CEO. ▪ Member: Oostburg State Bank Board of Directors (former president and CEO); Oostburg Chamber of Commerce (former president-elect); Oostburg Kiwanis Club (former president); Oostburg Christian Reformed Church (former elder and deacon); Random Lake Area Chamber of Commerce; Republican Party of Sheboygan County; NRA; Sheboygan County Chamber of Commerce; Workbound, Inc. (former president); YMCA of Sheboygan County Board of Managers. ▪ Former member: Trinity Christian College Board of Trustees (Palos Heights, Illinois-treasurer); Dordt College Board of Trustees (vice chair); Sheboygan County Christian High School (board president); Oostburg Christian School Board (secretary); Oostburg Community Education Foundation.

Legislature: Elected to Assembly since 2014. Committee assignments, 2017: Financial Institutions (chair); Ways and Means (vice chair); Federalism and Interstate Relations; Housing and Real Estate; Insurance; Workforce Development. Additional appointments, 2017: Building Commission.

Contact: Rep.Katsma@legis.wisconsin.gov; 608-266-0656; 888-529-0026 (toll free); Room 208 North, State Capitol, PO Box 8952, Madison, WI 53708.

Tyler Vorpagel, Assembly District 27
Republican

Biography: Born Plymouth, Wisconsin, March 24, 1985; married; one child. Voting address: Plymouth, Wisconsin. ▪ Graduate Plymouth High School, 2003; B.A. in Political Science, B.S. in Public Administration, University of Wisconsin-Green Bay, 2007. Completed 2016 Emerging Leader Program at University of Virginia Darden School of Business. ▪ Full-time legislator. Former district director, Congressman Tom

Petri. ▪ Member: Sheboygan County Youth Apprenticeship Grant Advisory Committee; Sheboygan Elks #299; National Association of Parliamentarians; Republican Party of Sheboygan County (former member executive committee); 6th District Republican Party (former vice chair); former Republican Party of Wisconsin Executive Committee. ▪ Former member: Plymouth Rotary; Exchange Club (president).

Legislature: Elected to Assembly since 2014. Committee assignments, 2017: Federalism and Interstate Relations (chair); Public Benefit Reform (vice chair); Children and Families; State Affairs; Transportation.

Contact: Rep.Vorpagel@legis.wisconsin.gov; 608-266-8530; 888-529-0027 (toll free); Room 127 West, State Capitol, PO Box 8953, Madison, WI 53708.

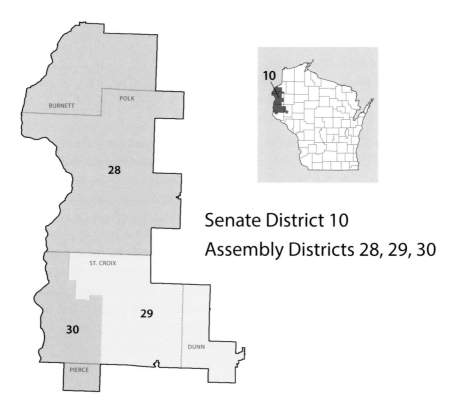

Senate District 10
Assembly Districts 28, 29, 30

Sheila E. Harsdorf, Senate District 10
Republican

Biography: Born St. Paul, Minnesota, July 25, 1956; 1 son. Voting address: River Falls, Wisconsin. ▪ Graduate River Falls High School; B.S. in Animal Science, University of Minnesota, 1978; Wisconsin Rural Leadership Program, graduate of first class, 1986. ▪ Member: Pierce County Republican Party; Pierce County Farm Bureau (former director and treasurer); Luther Memorial Church. ▪ Former member: Wisconsin State FFA Sponsors Board (chair); Wisconsin Conservation Corps Board (secretary); Kinnickinnic River Land Trust Board; Pierce County Dairy Promotion Committee (past chair); Wisconsin State ASCS Committee; Advisory Council on Small Business, Agriculture and Labor for Federal Reserve Bank of Minneapolis.

Legislature: Elected to Assembly 1988–96. Elected to Senate since 2000. Leadership positions: Majority Caucus Chair 2017, 2015; Majority Caucus Vice Chair

2013, 2011; Minority Caucus Vice Chair 2009; Majority Caucus Sergeant at Arms 2005. Committee assignments, 2017: Universities and Technical Colleges (chair); Joint Committee on Information Policy and Technology (cochair); Public Benefits, Licensing and State-Federal relations (vice chair); Agriculture, Small Business and Tourism; Joint Committee on Finance. Additional appointments, 2017: Midwestern Higher Education Compact.

Contact: Sen.Harsdorf@legis.wisconsin.gov; 608-266-7745; 800-862-1092 (toll free); 608-282-3550 (fax); Room 122 South, PO Box 7882, Madison, WI 53707-7882.

Adam Jarchow, Assembly District 28
Republican

Biography: Born St. Paul, Minnesota, November 10, 1978; married; 2 children. Voting address: Balsam Lake, Wisconsin. ▪ Graduate Clear Lake High School, 1997; B.S. in Finance, University of South Florida, 2001; J.D. University of Florida, 2004. ▪ Attorney. ▪ Member: Polk County Economic Development Corporation (secretary); National Rifle Association; Polk County Sportsmen's Club; Wisconsin Bear Hunters' Association; Apple River Fire Department.

Legislature: Elected to Assembly since 2014. Committee assignments, 2017: Financial Institutions (vice chair); Joint Review Committee on Criminal Penalties (cochair); Constitution and Ethics; Energy and Utilities; Tourism.

Contact: Rep.Jarchow@legis.wisconsin.gov; 608-267-2365; 888-529-0028 (toll free); Room 19 North, State Capitol, PO Box 8952, Madison, WI 53708.

Rob Stafsholt, Assembly District 29
Republican

Biography: Born St. Croix County, Wisconsin; single; 1 child. Voting address: New Richmond, Wisconsin. ▪ Graduate New Richmond Public Schools; attended University of Wisconsin-Eau Claire, University of Wisconsin-River Falls. ▪ Small business owner of residential rental and real estate investment company. Farmer. Former co-owner of a salad and food dressings manufacturing and sales company; mortgage loan originator. ▪ Member: Farm Bureau; National Rifle Association (life member); New Richmond Chamber of Commerce; Sportsmen's Alliance; SCI. ▪ Former Member: Erin Prairie Township Planning Commission; Wisconsin Bear Hunters' Association (board of directors); Wisconsin Association of Mortgage Brokers; NWTF.

Legislature: Elected to Assembly 2016. Committee assignments, 2017: Colleges and Universities; Financial Institutions; Insurance; Natural Resources and Sporting Heritage.

Contact: Rep.Stafsholt@legis.wisconsin.gov; 608-266-7683; 888-529-0029 (toll free); Room 17 North, State Capitol, PO Box 8953, Madison, WI 53708.

Shannon Zimmerman, Assembly District 30
Republican

Biography: Born Madison, Wisconsin, March 15, 1972; married; 2 children. Voting address: River Falls, Wisconsin. ▪ Attended Augusta High School; Chippewa Valley Technical College; UW-Milwaukee. ▪ Founder and CEO, language translation company. Small business owner. Coached youth football for 7 years. ▪ Member: UW-River Falls Foundation Board; UW-River Falls Chancellor's Advisory Committee; Rotary. ▪ Former member: Board of Wisconsin Department of Workforce Development.

Legislature: Elected to Assembly 2016. Committee assignments, 2017: Colleges and Universities; Education; Jobs and the Economy; Tourism.

Contact: Rep.Zimmerman@legis.wisconsin.gov; 608-266-1526; 888-529-0030 (toll free); Room 18 North, State Capitol, PO Box 8953, Madison, WI 53708.

Senate District 11
Assembly Districts 31, 32, 33

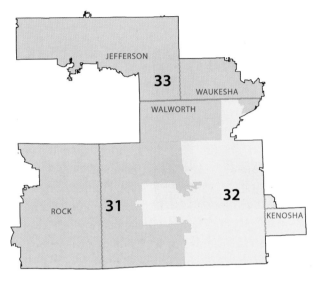

Stephen L. Nass, Senate District 11
Republican

Biography: Born Whitewater, Wisconsin, October 7, 1952. Voting address: Whitewater, Wisconsin. ▪ Graduate Whitewater High School; B.S. University of Wisconsin-Whitewater, 1978; M.S. Ed. in School Business Management, University of Wisconsin-Whitewater, 1990. ▪ Owner, rental property business. Former payroll benefits analyst and information analyst/negotiator. Member of Wisconsin Air National Guard (retired, CMSgt, 33 years of service), served in Middle East in Operations Desert Shield and Desert Storm. ▪ Member: American Legion; Veterans of Foreign Wars; Mukwonago Business Breakfast Club. ▪ Former member: University of Wisconsin-Whitewater Board of Visitors, 1979–89. ▪ Whitewater City Council, 1977–81.

Legislature: Elected to Assembly 1990–2012. Elected to Senate 2014. Committee assignments, 2017: Joint Committee for Review of Administrative Rules (cochair); Labor and Regulatory Reform (chair); Universities and Technical Colleges (vice chair); Education.

Contact: Sen.Nass@legis.wisconsin.gov; 608-266-2635; 800-578-1457 (toll free); 262-495-3424 (district); Room 10 South, State Capitol, PO Box 7882, Madison, WI 53707-7882.

Amy Loudenbeck, Assembly District 31
Republican

Biography: Born Midland, Michigan, September 29, 1969; married. Voting address: Clinton, Wisconsin. ▪ Graduate Hinsdale Central High School (Hinsdale, Illinois), 1987; B.A. in Political Science, International Relations, University of Wisconsin-Madison, 1991; studied abroad in Kingston, Jamaica. ▪ Former chamber of commerce executive, compliance manager, environmental/engineering services project manager. ▪ Member: Wisconsin Family Impact Seminar (advisory board member); Wisconsin DNR Green Tier Advisory Board. ▪ Former member: Town of Linn Fire Department. ▪ Town of Clinton supervisor, 2010–12.

Legislature: Elected to Assembly since 2010. Committee assignments, 2017: Joint Committee on Finance. Additional appointments, 2017: State Capitol and Executive Residence Board (vice chair); Educational Communications Board.

Contact: Rep.Loudenbeck@legis.wisconsin.gov; 608-266-9967; 888-529-0031 (toll free); Room 304 East, State Capitol, PO Box 8952, Madison, WI 53708.

Tyler August, Assembly District 32
Republican

Biography: Born Wisconsin, January 26, 1983; single. Voting address: Lake Geneva, Wisconsin. ▪ Graduate Big Foot High School, 2001; attended University of Wisconsin-Eau Claire and University of Wisconsin-Madison; completed 2012 Emerging Leader Program at University of Virginia Darden School of Business. ▪ Full-time legislator. Former chief of staff to Representative Thomas Lothian. ▪ Member: Republican Party of Wisconsin (former board member); Republican Party of First Congressional

District (former chair); Republican Party of Walworth County (former chair, vice chair); National Rifle Association. ▪ Recipient: American Conservative Union *Defender of Liberty* 2012; GOPAC *Emerging Leader* 2012.

Legislature: Elected to Assembly since 2010. Leadership positions: Speaker Pro Tempore 2017, 2015. Committee assignments, 2017: Joint Survey Committee on Tax Exemptions (cochair); Assembly Organization; Government Accountability and Oversight; Insurance; Rules; Joint Legislative Council.

Contact: Rep.August@legis.wisconsin.gov; 608-266-1190; Room 119 West, State Capitol, PO Box 8952, Madison, WI 53708.

Cody J. Horlacher, Assembly District 33
Republican

Biography: Born Burlington, Wisconsin, April 10, 1987; married. Voting address: Mukwonago, Wisconsin. ▪ Graduate East Troy High School, 2006; B.A. in Marketing, University of Wisconsin-Whitewater, 2010; J.D. Marquette University Law School, 2014. ▪ Attorney. Former special prosecutor, Walworth County; former assistant district attorney, Walworth County. ▪ Member: Carroll University President's Advisory Council; Wisconsin State Bar; Old World Wisconsin Foundation (board of trustees). ▪ Former member: Walworth County Republican Party (secretary, vice chair, chair); Federalist Society.

Legislature: Elected to Assembly since 2014. Committee assignments, 2017: Regulatory Licensing Reform (chair); Judiciary (vice chair); Agriculture; Campaigns and Elections; Criminal Justice and Public Safety. Additional appointments, 2017: Wisconsin Historical Society Board of Curators.

Contact: Rep.Horlacher@legis.wisconsin.gov; 608-266-5715; 888-529-0033 (toll free); Room 214 North, State Capitol, PO Box 8952, Madison, WI 53708.

Senate District 12
Assembly Districts 34, 35, 36

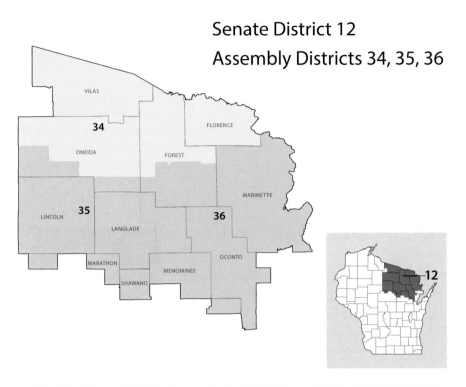

Tom Tiffany, Senate District 12
Republican

Biography: Born Wabasha, Minnesota, December 30, 1957; married; 3 children. Voting address: Town of Little Rice, Wisconsin. ▪ Graduate Elmwood High School, 1976; B.S. in Agricultural Economics, University of Wisconsin-River Falls, 1980. ▪ Dam tender, Wisconsin Valley Improvement Company. ▪ Member: National Rifle Association; Ruffed Grouse Society. ▪ Town of Little Rice supervisor, 2009–13.

Legislature: Elected to Assembly 2010. Elected to Senate since 2012. Committee assignments, 2017: Sporting Heritage, Mining, and Forestry (chair); Agriculture, Small Business, and Tourism (vice chair); Revenue, Financial Institutions, and Rural Issues; Joint Committee on Finance; Joint Survey Committee on Tax Exemptions.

Contact: Sen.Tiffany@legis.wisconsin.gov; 608-266-2509; Room 409 South, State Capitol, PO Box 7882, Madison, WI 53707-7882.

Rob Swearingen, Assembly District 34
Republican

Biography: Born Oneida County, Wisconsin, July 23, 1963; married; 2 children. Voting address: Rhinelander, Wisconsin. ▪ Graduate Rhinelander High School, 1981. ▪ Restaurant owner/operator. ▪ Member: Tavern League of Wisconsin (former president, zone vice president, district director); American Beverage Licensees (former member, board of directors); Oneida County Tavern League (former president, vice president); Rhinelander Chamber of Commerce; Oneida County Republican Party.

Legislature: Elected to Assembly since 2012. Committee assignments, 2017: State Affairs (chair); Tourism (vice chair); Environment and Forestry; Small Business Development; Joint Survey Committee on Tax Exemptions. Additional appointments, 2017: Building Commission (chair of Higher Education Subcommittee).

Contact: Rep.Swearingen@legis.wisconsin.gov; 608-266-7141; 888-534-0034 (toll free); 715-369-5493 (district); Room 123 West, State Capitol, PO Box 8953, Madison, WI 53708.

Mary J. (Czaja) Felzkowski, Assembly District 35
Republican

Biography: Born Tomahawk, Wisconsin, September 25, 1963; married, 5 children. Voting address: Irma, Wisconsin. ▪ Graduate Tomahawk High School, 1981; B.S. in Finance and Economics, University of Wisconsin-River Falls, 1986. ▪ Insurance agency owner. ▪ Member: Tomahawk Main Street, Inc. (former president); Tomahawk Regional Chamber of Commerce; Tomahawk Child Care (former president); National Alliance for Insurance Education  and Research (board member); NRA (lifetime member); Professional Insurance Agents of Wisconsin (former board member, secretary, treasurer, vice president, president, national director).

Legislature: Elected to Assembly since 2012. Committee assignments, 2017: Joint Committee on Finance.

Contact: Rep.Felzkowski@legis.wisconsin.gov; 608-266-7694; 888-534-0035 (toll free); Room 306 East, State Capitol, PO Box 8952, Madison, WI 53708; PO Box 321, Tomahawk, WI 54487 (district).

Jeffrey L. Mursau, Assembly District 36
Republican

Biography: Born Oconto Falls, Wisconsin, June 12, 1954; married; 4 sons, 11 grandchildren. Voting address: Crivitz, Wisconsin. ▪ Graduate Coleman High School, 1972; attended University of Wisconsin-Oshkosh. ▪ Small business owner; electrical contractor. ▪ Member: Crivitz Ski Cats waterski team (advisor, former president); Crivitz Lions Club; Crivitz, Wisconsin-Crivitz, Germany Sister City Organization (former director); Wings Over Wisconsin; St. Mary's Catholic Church; Fourth Degree Knights of Columbus; Friends of Governor Thompson State Park; Master Loggers Certifying Board. ▪ Recipient: Crivitz Business Association Citizen of the Year 1994. ▪ Crivitz Village President, 1991–2004.

Legislature: Elected to Assembly since 2004. Committee assignments, 2017: Environment and Forestry (chair); Agriculture; Education; Natural Resources and Sporting Heritage; Tourism.

Contact: 608-266-3780; 888-534-0036 (toll free); Room 113 West, State Capitol, PO Box 8953, Madison, WI 53708.

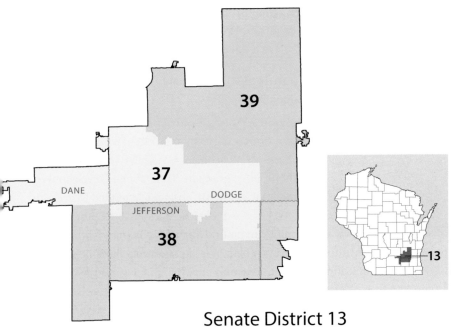

Senate District 13
Assembly Districts 37, 38, 39

Scott L. Fitzgerald, Senate District 13

Republican

Biography: Born Chicago, Illinois, November 16, 1963; married; 3 children. Voting address: Juneau, Wisconsin. ▪ Graduate Hustisford High School, 1981; B.S. in Journalism, University of Wisconsin-Oshkosh, 1985; U.S. Army Armor Officer Basic Course, 1985; U.S. Army Command and General Staff College. ▪ Former associate newspaper publisher; U.S. Army Reserve Lieutenant Colonel (retired). ▪ Member: Dodge County Republican Party (chair, 1992–94); Juneau Lions Club; Reserve Officers Association; Knights of Columbus.

Legislature: Elected to Senate since 1994. Leadership positions: Majority Leader 2017, 2015, 2013, 2011 (through 7/24/12); Minority Leader 2011 (effective 7/24/12), 2009, 2007; Majority Leader 9/17/04 to 11/10/04. Committee assignments, 2017: Senate Organization (chair); Joint Committee on Employment Relations; Joint Committee on Legislative Organization; Joint Legislative Council.

Contact: Sen.Fitzgerald@legis.wisconsin.gov; 608-266-5660; Room 211 South, State Capitol, PO Box 7882, Madison, WI 53707-7882.

John Jagler, Assembly District 37
Republican

Biography: Born Louisville, Kentucky, November 4, 1969; married; 3 children. Voting address: Watertown, Wisconsin. ▪ Graduate Oak Creek High School, 1987; graduate Trans-American School of Broadcasting (Madison), 1989; attended University of Wisconsin-Parkside, 1987–88. ▪ Realtor; owner, family-run natural dog treat company; owner, communications consulting company. Former radio morning show host, news anchor; communications director, Assembly Speaker Jeff Fitzgerald. ▪ Member: Down Syndrome Association of Wisconsin; Honorable Order of Kentucky Colonels; Watertown Elks Club. ▪ Former member: Radio TV News Directors Association; Milwaukee Press Club.

Legislature: Elected to Assembly since 2012. Committee assignments, 2017: Housing and Real Estate (chair); Mental Health (vice chair); Constitution and Ethics; Education; Insurance; Rules; State Affairs.

Contact: Rep.Jagler@legis.wisconsin.gov; 608-266-9650; 888-534-0037 (toll free); Room 316 North, State Capitol, PO Box 8952, Madison, WI 53708.

Joel Kleefisch, Assembly District 38
Republican

Biography: Born Waukesha, Wisconsin, June 8, 1971; married; 2 children. Voting address: Oconomowoc, Wisconsin. ▪ Graduate Waukesha North High School, 1989; B.A. Pepperdine University, 1993. ▪ Former investigative television news reporter for WISN-TV; legislative policy advisor and constituent director. ▪ Member: Watertown Elks Club;

Watertown Moose Club; Ducks Unlimited; National Wild Turkey Federation; National Rifle Association; Wings Over Wisconsin; Lakewatch Volunteer Organization (founder).

Legislature: Elected to Assembly since 2004. Leadership positions: Minority

Caucus Vice Chair 2009. Committee assignments, 2017: Natural Resources and Sporting Heritage (chair); Corrections; Family Law; State Affairs.

Contact: Rep.Kleefisch@legis.wisconsin.gov; 608-266-8551; 888-534-0038 (toll free); Room 216 North, State Capitol, PO Box 8952, Madison, WI 53708.

Mark L. Born, Assembly District 39

Republican

Biography: Born Beaver Dam, Wisconsin, April 14, 1976; married; 1 child. Voting address: Beaver Dam, Wisconsin. ▪ Graduate Beaver Dam High School, 1994; B.A. in Political Science and History, Gustavus Adolphus College (St. Peter, Minnesota), 1998. ▪ Full-time legislator. Former corrections supervisor, Dodge County Sheriff's Department. ▪ Member: Downtown Beaver Dam, Inc.; Friends of Horicon Marsh; Beaver Dam Area Arts Association; Dodge County Historical Society (vice president); Leadership Beaver Dam Steering Committee; Beaver Dam Lake Improvement Association (former vice president); Republican Party of Dodge County (former chair); Beaver Dam Elks Lodge 1540; St. John's Lutheran Church, Beaver Dam. ▪ Beaver Dam Fire and Police Commission, 2003–05; Beaver Dam City Council, 2005–09.

Legislature: Elected to Assembly since 2012. Committee assignments, 2017: Rules; Joint Committee on Finance. Additional appointments, 2017: State Capitol and Executive Residence Board; University of Wisconsin Hospitals and Clinics Authority Board.

Contact: Rep.Born@legis.wisconsin.gov; 608-266-2540; 888-534-0039 (toll free); Room 320 East, State Capitol, PO Box 8952, Madison, WI 53708.

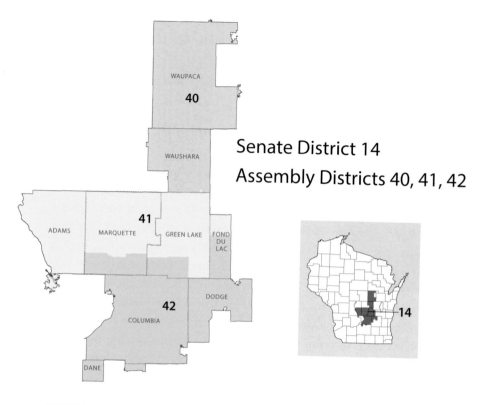

Senate District 14
Assembly Districts 40, 41, 42

Luther S. Olsen, Senate District 14
Republican

Biography: Born Berlin, Wisconsin, February 26, 1951; married. Voting address: Ripon, Wisconsin. ▪ Graduate Berlin High School, 1969; B.S. University of Wisconsin-Madison, 1973; Wisconsin Rural Leadership Program Group IV, 1990–92. ▪ Partner in farm supply dealerships. ▪ Member: NCSL Education Committee (cochair, 2012–14). ▪ Former member: Waushara County Fair Board (director); Family Health/La Clinica director, 1995–99. ▪ Berlin Area School Board, 1976–97 (president 1986–95).

Legislature: Elected to Assembly 1994–2002. Elected to Senate since 2004. Committee assignments, 2017: Education (chair); Joint Committee on Finance (vice chair); Insurance, Housing and Trade (vice chair); Natural Resources and Energy. Additional appointments, 2017: Education Commission of the States, Educational Communications Board, State Capitol and Executive Residence

Board, University of Wisconsin Hospitals and Clinics Authority Board, Women's Council.

Contact: Sen.Olsen@legis.wisconsin.gov; 608-266-0751; 800-991-5541 (toll free); Room 313 South, State Capitol, PO Box 7882, Madison, WI 53707-7882.

Kevin David Petersen, Assembly District 40
Republican

Biography: Born Waupaca, Wisconsin, December 14, 1964; married; 2 children. Voting address: Waupaca, Wisconsin. ▪ Graduate Waupaca High School, 1983; B.S.M.E. University of New Mexico, 1989. ▪ Co-owner of family-run electronics corporation. Served in U.S. Navy sub service, 1983–94; Persian Gulf War veteran; U.S. Naval Reserve member, 1994–2008. ▪ Member: Waupaca County Republican Party; Waushara County Republican Party; VFW Post 1037 (life member); AMVETS Post 1887 (life member); American Legion Post 161; Manawa Chamber of Commerce; Waupaca Area Chamber of Commerce; New London Area Chamber of Commerce; National Rifle Association. ▪ Town of Dayton supervisor, 2001–07.

Legislature: Elected to Assembly since 2006. Committee assignments, 2017: Insurance (chair); Science and Technology (vice chair); Energy and Utilities; Financial Institutions; Public Benefit Reform; Ways and Means.

Contact: Rep.Petersen@legis.wisconsin.gov; 608-266-3794; 888-947-0040 (toll free); Room 105 West, State Capitol, PO Box 8953, Madison, WI 53708.

Joan Ballweg, Assembly District 41
Republican

Biography: Born Milwaukee, Wisconsin, March 16, 1952; married; 3 children, 2 grandchildren. Voting address: Markesan, Wisconsin. ▪ Graduate Nathan Hale High School, West Allis, Wisconsin, 1970; attended University of Wisconsin-Waukesha; B.A. in Elementary Education, University of Wisconsin-Stevens Point, 1974. ▪ Co-owner of farm equipment business. Former first grade teacher. ▪ Member: Markesan Chamber of

Commerce (former treasurer); Waupun Chamber of Commerce; Green Lake County Farm Bureau; Waupun Memorial Hospital (board of directors, former chair); Agnesian HealthCare Enterprises LLC management committee (former secretary); volunteer, Markesan District Schools; Markesan PTA (former president); Markesan AFS Chapter (hosting coordinator, president, former host family, liaison). ▪ Former member: FEMA V Regional Advisory Council. ▪ Recipient: Markesan District Education Association *Friend of Education Award* 1990. ▪ Markesan City Council, 1987–91; mayor of Markesan, 1991–97.

Legislature: Elected to Assembly since 2004. Leadership positions: Majority Caucus Chair 2013, 2011. Committee assignments, 2017: Joint Committee for Review of Administrative Rules (cochair); Regulatory Licensing Reform (vice chair); Children and Families; Colleges and Universities; Mental Health; Rules; Tourism; Joint Legislative Council.

Contact: Rep.Ballweg@legis.wisconsin.gov; 608-266-8077; 888-534-0041 (toll free); 920-398-3708 (district); Room 210 North, State Capitol, PO Box 8952, Madison, WI 53708.

Keith Ripp, Assembly District 42
Republican

Biography: Born Madison, Wisconsin, November 13, 1961; married; 3 children. Voting address: Lodi, Wisconsin. ▪ Graduate Lodi High School, 1980; University of Wisconsin-Madison, Farm and Industry Short Course, 1981. ▪ Farmer and small business owner. ▪ Member: Wisconsin Soybean Marketing Board (former president, vice president); Badger Agvest LLC (former president and cofounder); Wisconsin Corn Growers Association (former president, vice president); Wisconsin Farm Bureau; Lodi FFA Alumni (former president, cofounder); Columbia and Dane County Republican Party; Yellow Thunder Snowmobile Club; Ducks Unlimited. ▪ Town of Dane supervisor, 2006–08.

Legislature: Elected to Assembly since 2008. Committee assignments, 2017: Transportation (chair); Local Government (vice chair); Agriculture; Natural Resources and Sporting Heritage; Workforce Development.

Contact: Rep.Ripp@legis.wisconsin.gov; 608-266-3404; 888-534-0042 (toll free); Room 223 North, State Capitol, PO Box 8953, Madison, WI 53708.

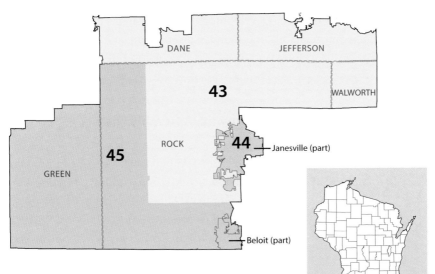

Senate District 15
Assembly Districts 43, 44, 45

Janis Ringhand, Senate District 15

Democrat

Biography: Born Madison, Wisconsin, February 13, 1950; married; 2 children, 5 grandchildren, 1 great-grandchild. Voting address: Evansville, Wisconsin. ▪ Graduate Evansville High School, 1968; Associate Degree Madison Area Technical College, 1985. ▪ Full-time legislator. Former accountant for small businesses, executive director of nonprofit.
▪ Member: Rock County Literacy Connection; Evansville Chamber of Commerce; VFW Auxiliary Post 6905 (former president); Evansville Energy Independence Team. ▪ Former member: Stoughton Hospital Board (chair); Creekside Place, Inc. (board of directors); Evansville Community Partnership (secretary). ▪ Evansville City Council, 1998–2002, 2008–10. Mayor of Evansville, 2002–06.

Legislature: Elected to Assembly 2010–12. Elected to Senate 2014. Leadership positions: Minority Caucus Vice Chair 2017; Minority Caucus Secretary 2013. Committee assignments, 2017: Economic Development, Commerce and Local Government; Labor and Regulatory Reform; Revenue, Financial Institutions and Rural Issues; Workforce Development, Military Affairs and Senior Issues. Additional appointments, 2017: Building Commission.

Contact: Sen.Ringhand@legis.wisconsin.gov; 608-266-2253; 608-882-5879 (district); Room 3 South, State Capitol, PO Box 7882, Madison, WI 53707-7882.

Don Vruwink, Assembly District 43
Democrat

Biography: Born Auburndale, Wisconsin, June 12, 1952; married; 1 child. Voting address: Milton, Wisconsin. ▪ Graduate Auburndale High School, 1970; B.A. in Broad Field Social Studies, Political Science and Coaching Minor, University of Wisconsin-Stevens Point, 1975; M.A. in History, University of Wisconsin-Whitewater, 1986. ▪ Full-time legislator. Retired teacher, Milton School District. Former Parks and Recreation Director, City of Milton. Former Milton High School basketball, football and softball coach. ▪ Member: Farm Bureau; League of Conservation Voters. ▪ Channel 3000 *Top Notch Teacher*, 2011; Milton Athletic Hall of Fame, 2011; Wisconsin Fastpitch Coaches Hall of Fame, 2014; Milton Chamber of Commerce *Lifetime Achievement Award*, 2014. ▪ Milton City Council 2011–15 (president 2014–15); Milton School Board 2016–present.

Legislature: Elected to Assembly 2016. Committee assignments, 2017: Agriculture; Colleges and Universities; Education; Rural Development and Mining; Tourism.

Contact: Rep.Vruwink@legis.wisconsin.gov; 608-266-3790; 888-534-0043 (toll free); Room 5 North, State Capitol, PO Box 8953, Madison, WI 53708.

Debra Kolste, Assembly District 44
Democrat

Biography: Born O'Neill, Nebraska, June 20, 1953; married; 3 children. Voting address: Janesville, Wisconsin. ▪ Graduate Kimball County High School (Kimball, Nebraska), 1971; B.S. in Medical Technology, University of Nebraska, 1975. ▪ Full-time legislator. Former medical technologist. ▪ Member: League of Women Voters; Friends of Rotary Gardens; Janesville Performing Arts Center (board member). ▪ Former member:

Mercy Health Systems Volunteers (president); Rock Futbol Soccer League (founding board member); PTO Board; PTA Board; YMCA of Northern Rock County Board of Directors. ▪ Janesville School Board, 2000–09.

Legislature: Elected to Assembly since 2012. Committee assignments, 2017: Aging and Long-Term Care; Health; Public Benefit Reform; Rules; Science and Technology; Small Business Development; Transportation; Legislative Council Study Committee on Volunteer Firefighter and Emergency Medical Technician Shortages.

Contact: Rep.Kolste@legis.wisconsin.gov; 608-266-7503; 888-947-0044 (toll free); Room 8 North, State Capitol, PO Box 8952, Madison, WI 53708.

Mark Spreitzer, Assembly District 45

Democrat

Biography: Born Evanston, Illinois, December 16, 1986; single. Voting address: Beloit, Wisconsin. ▪ Graduate Northside College Preparatory High School (Chicago, Illinois), 2005; B.A. in Political Science, Beloit College, 2009. ▪ Full-time legislator. Former assistant director of alumni and parent relations and annual support, Beloit College. ▪ Member: United Church of Beloit (deacons board and governing council); Welty Environmental Center (board president); Young Democrats of Wisconsin (2nd CD chair); New Leaders Council (advisory board); Wisconsin League of Conservation Voters; Fair Wisconsin; Democratic Party of Rock County; Wisconsin Farmers Union; Young Elected Officials Network; Greater Beloit Chamber of Commerce Rising Professionals; National Caucus of Environmental Legislators; Great Lakes Legislative Caucus. ▪ Former member: Community Action, Inc. of Rock and Walworth Counties (board member); City of Beloit Appointment Review Committee (chair). ▪ Recipient: WFU *Friend of the Family Farmer* 2017; Fair Wisconsin *Community Advocate of the Year* 2014. ▪ Beloit City Council, 2011–15 (president, 2014–15).

Legislature: Elected to Assembly since 2014. Leadership positions: Minority Caucus Chair 2017. Committee assignments, 2017: Agriculture; Assembly Organization; Local Government; Natural Resources and Sporting Heritage; Rules; Rural Development and Mining; Workforce Development.

Contact: Rep.Spreitzer@legis.wisconsin.gov; 608-266-1192; 888-534-0045 (toll free); Room 113 North, State Capitol, PO Box 8953, Madison, WI 53708.

Senate District 16
Assembly Districts 46, 47, 48

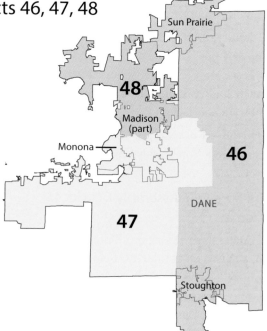

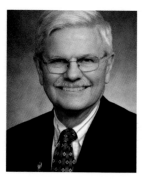

Mark Miller, Senate District 16
Democrat

Biography: Born Boston, Massachusetts, February 1, 1943. Voting address: Monona, Wisconsin. ▪ Graduate Middleton High School; B.S. University of Wisconsin-Madison; Bowhay Institute for Legislative Leadership Development (BILLD), 1999; Flemming Fellows Leadership Institute, 2002. ▪ Former military pilot; Wisconsin Air National Guard, 1966–95 (retired Lieutenant Colonel); former real estate property manager. ▪ Dane County Board of Health, 1998–2004; Board of Health for Madison and Dane County, 2004–07. Dane County Board of Supervisors, 1996–2000.

Legislature: Elected to Assembly 1998–2002. Elected to Senate since 2004. Leadership positions: Minority Caucus Chair 2017; Minority Leader 2011 (through 7/17/12); Majority Leader 2011 (effective 7/17/12); Majority Caucus Chair 2007. Committee assignments, 2017: Agriculture, Small Business and Tourism; Elections and Utilities; Natural Resources and Energy; Joint

Legislative Audit Committee; Joint Legislative Council. Additional appointments, 2017: Midwest Interstate Passenger Rail Commission.

Contact: Sen.Miller@legis.wisconsin.gov; 608-266-9170; 608-221-2701 (district); Room 19 South, State Capitol, PO Box 7882, Madison, WI 53707-7882.

Gary Alan Hebl, Assembly District 46
Democrat

Biography: Born Madison, Wisconsin, May 15, 1951; married; 3 children, 2 grandsons. Voting address: Sun Prairie, Wisconsin. ▪ Graduate Sun Prairie High School, 1969; B.A. in Political Science, University of Wisconsin-Madison, 1973; Gonzaga University Law School, 1976; Bowhay Institute, 2008. ▪ Attorney and owner of a title insurance company. Sacred Hearts eighth grade basketball coach, 1980–99. ▪ Member: Wisconsin League of Conservation Voters; Dane County Bar Association; Wisconsin Bar Association; Sun Prairie Optimist Club (former president); Sun Prairie Chamber of Commerce (former president); U.W. Flying Club (former board chair); AOPA; EAA Young Eagles Program; Knights of Columbus (fourth degree member); Sun Prairie Cable Access Board; YMCA (former president); Sun Prairie Public Library Board (former president); Sacred Heart Parish Council (former trustee); Sun Prairie Quarterback Club (former president). ▪ Recipient: State Bar of Wisconsin *Scales of Justice Award* 2009–10; Wisconsin Dietetic Association *Nutrition Champion Award* 2010; Pharmacy Society of Wisconsin *Legislator of the Year* 2010, 2009; Sun Prairie Star poll *Best Attorney in Sun Prairie* 2008–16; *James J. Reininger Award* for lifetime achievement 2008; Wisconsin Association of PEG Channels *Friend of Access Award* 2010, 2007; Wisconsin League of Conservation Voters *Conservation Champion* 2013–14, 2011–12, 2009–10, 2005–06; Sun Prairie Exchange Club *Book of Golden Deeds Award* 2003; Chamber of Commerce *Judith Krivsky Business Person of the Year Award* 2002; Sun Prairie Business and Education Partnership *Outstanding Small Business of the Year* 2001; Sun Prairie High School Wall of Success 2015.

Legislature: Elected to Assembly since 2004. Committee assignments, 2017: Colleges and Universities; Education; Environment and Forestry; Judiciary; Joint Committee for Review of Administrative Rules.

Contact: Rep.Hebl@legis.wisconsin.gov; 608-266-7678; Room 120 North, State Capitol, PO Box 8952, Madison, WI 53708.

Jimmy Anderson, Assembly District 47
Democrat

Biography: Born El Paso, Texas, August 26, 1986; raised in Patterson, California; married. Voting address: Fitchburg, Wisconsin. ▪ Graduate Patterson High School, 2004; B.A. summa cum laude California State University, Monterey Bay, 2008; J.D. University of Wisconsin Law School, 2012. ▪ Nonprofit director. ▪ Member: Wisconsin State Bar Association.

Legislature: Elected to Assembly 2016. Committee assignments, 2017: Colleges and Universities; Environment and Forestry; Federalism and Interstate Relations; Regulatory Licensing Reform; Science and Technology; Joint Committee for Review of Administrative Rules.

Contact: Rep.Anderson@legis.wisconsin.gov; 608-266-8570; 888-302-0047 (toll free); Room 9 North, State Capitol, PO Box 8952, Madison, WI 53708.

Melissa Sargent, Assembly District 48
Democrat

Biography: Born Madison, Wisconsin, March 28, 1969; married; 4 sons. Voting address: Madison, Wisconsin. ▪ Graduate Madison East High School, 1987; B.A. University of Wisconsin-Madison, 1991. Graduate Bowhay Institute for Legislative Leadership Development; Emerging Leaders Program, University of Virginia, 2014; Toll Fellowship, 2015.

▪ Small business owner. ▪ Member: Women in Government (state director); WiLL/WAND (state director); Emerge Wisconsin (board of directors); Dane County Democratic Party; Democratic Party; Make Room for Youth; Friends of Cherokee Marsh. ▪ Former member: Midwest Shiba Inu Dog Rescue (president); Gompers PTO (president). ▪ Recipient: National Federation of Women Legislators *Woman of Excellence*; WiLL *Pacesetter Award*; Arc Dane County *Elected Official of the Year* 2014; Citizen Action *Activist Achievement Award* 2014; *Eleanor Roosevelt Award* nominee 2013; Wisconsin League of Conservation Voters *Conservation Champion* 2016, 2014. ▪ Dane County Board of Supervisors, 2010–14.

Legislature: Elected to Assembly since 2012. Committee assignments, 2017: Energy and Utilities; Mental Health; Small Business Development; Joint Committee on Information Policy and Technology; Joint Legislative Audit Committee.

Contact: Rep.Sargent@legis.wisconsin.gov; 608-266-0960; Room 321 West, State Capitol, PO Box 8953, Madison, WI 53708.

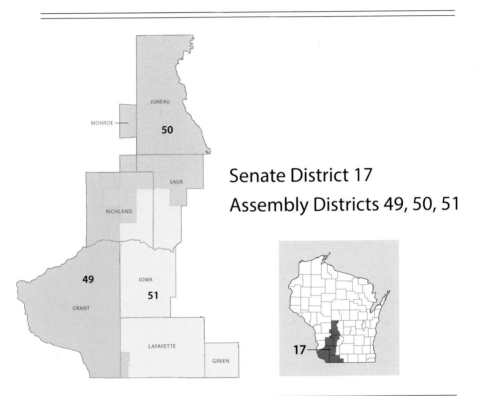

Senate District 17

Assembly Districts 49, 50, 51

Howard Marklein, Senate District 17
Republican

Biography: Born Madison, Wisconsin, October 3, 1954; married; 2 children, 3 stepchildren, 4 grandchildren. Voting address: Spring Green, Wisconsin. ▪ Graduate River Valley High School (Spring Green), 1972; B.B.A. University of Wisconsin-Whitewater, 1976. ▪ Certified public accountant; certified fraud examiner. ▪ Member: St. John's Catholic Church,

Spring Green (finance committee member); Taliesin Preservation Inc. Board of Trustees (treasurer); National Rifle Association (member). ▪ Former member: University of Wisconsin-Whitewater National Alumni Association (president); University of Wisconsin-Whitewater Foundation (board of directors president); Fort Health Care Board of Directors (chair, treasurer); Fort Atkinson Rotary Club (president); Fort Atkinson Chamber of Commerce (president); Whitewater Chamber of Commerce (president); Dodgeville Chamber of Commerce (vice president). ▪ Recipient: WMC *Working for Wisconsin Award* 2016, 2014, 2012; MMAC *Champion of Commerce Award* 2016, 2014, 2012; Wisconsin Pork Association *Distinguished Service Award* 2013; Wisconsin Newspaper Association *Badger Award* 2013; Wisconsin Aquaculture Association *Legislator of the Year* 2013; Dairy Business Association *Legislative Excellence Award* 2016, 2012; Wisconsin Auto Collision Technicians Association *Legislator of the Year* 2016; Wisconsin Towns Association *Friend of Towns* 2016; Associated General Contractors *Legislator of the Year* 2016; Wisconsin Counties Association *Outstanding Legislator* 2016; Wisconsin Builders Association *Friend of Housing* 2016, 2015; Wisconsin Association of Local Health Departments and Boards & Wisconsin Public Health Association *Friend of Public Health* 2016.

Legislature: Elected to Assembly 2010, 2012. Elected to Senate 2014. Leadership positions: President Pro Tempore 2017. Committee assignments, 2017: Revenue, Financial Institutions and Rural Issues (chair); Transportation and Veterans Affairs (vice chair); Workforce Development, Military Affairs and Senior Issues; Joint Committee on Finance; Joint Legislative Council. Additional appointments, 2017: Transportation Projects Commission; Mississippi River Parkway Commission.

Contact: Sen.Marklein@legis.wisconsin.gov; 608-266-0703; 608-588-5632 (district); Room 8 South, State Capitol, PO Box 7882, Madison, WI 53707-7882.

Travis Tranel, Assembly District 49
Republican

Biography: Born Dubuque, Iowa, September 12, 1985; married; 5 children. Voting address: Cuba City, Wisconsin. ▪ Graduate Wahlert Catholic High School (Dubuque, Iowa), 2004; B.A. Loras College (Dubuque, Iowa), 2007. ▪ Dairy farmer, small business owner. ▪ Member: St. Joseph Sinsinawa Parish Council, 2010–12 (president, 2011–12); Wisconsin

Farm Bureau; Knights of Columbus; National Rifle Association; Ducks Unlimited; Platteville Regional Chamber of Commerce; Grant County Republican Party. ▪ Recipient: DBA *Legislative Excellence Award* 2016, 2014, 2012; WMC *Working for Wisconsin Award* 2016, 2014, 2012; MMAC *Champion of Commerce Award* 2014, 2012; WAFP *Friends of Family Medicine* 2014; WATA *Ambassador Award* 2015.

Legislature: Elected to Assembly since 2010. Committee assignments, 2017: Tourism (chair); Colleges and Universities (vice chair); Agriculture; Energy and Utilities; Insurance; Small Business Development. Additional appointments, 2017: Governor's Council on Tourism.

Contact: Rep.Tranel@legis.wisconsin.gov; 608-266-1170; 888-872-0049 (toll free); Room 302 North, State Capitol, PO Box 8953, Madison, WI 53708.

Ed Brooks, Assembly District 50
Republican

Biography: Born Baraboo, Wisconsin, July 1, 1942; married; 3 children, 5 grandchildren. Voting address: Reedsburg, Wisconsin. ▪ Graduate Webb High School (Reedsburg), 1960; B.S. in Agricultural Economics, University of Wisconsin-Madison, 1965. ▪ Farmer. Former county supervisor for USDA-FmHA; loan officer for PCA Madison; chair for 18 years of a Wisconsin-based, multi-state, dairy product cooperative. Served in U.S. Army Reserve, 1965–71. ▪ Member: Wisconsin Federation of Co-ops (former chair); Wisconsin Farm Bureau; American Legion Post 350. ▪ Former member: CALS BOV; Endeavor 4-H Club (leader); St. John Lutheran Church (past president church council). ▪ Recipient: Dairy Business Association *Legislative Excellence Award* 2016, 2014; American Conservative Union *Defender of Liberty* 2013–14; Wisconsin Electric Cooperative's *Enlightened Legislator of the Year Award* 2014; Wisconsin Academy of Family Physicians *Friend of Family Medicine* 2013–14; Wisconsin Counties Association *Outstanding Legislator Award* 2013–14; *Friend of Cooperatives* 2012; Associated Builders and Contractors *Building Wisconsin Award* 2016, 2014; Wisconsin Town Association *Friend of Wisconsin Towns* 2014, 2011; WMC *Working for Wisconsin Award* 2015–16, 2013–14, 2011–12; *Friend of Education* 1998; *Friend of Extension*; Wisconsin Grocers Association *Friend of Grocers* 2014. ▪ Town of Reedsburg supervisor, 1979–85; town chair, 1985–present.

Legislature: Elected to Assembly since 2008. Committee assignments, 2017: Local Government (chair); Jobs and the Economy (vice chair); Agriculture; Corrections; Rural Development and Mining; Transportation; Workforce Development.

Contact: Rep.Brooks@legis.wisconsin.gov; 608-266-8531; 877-947-0050 (toll free); Room 20 North, State Capitol, PO Box 8952, Madison, WI 53708.

Todd Novak, Assembly District 51
Republican

Biography: Born Dodgeville, Wisconsin, April 23, 1965; 2 children. Voting address: Dodgeville, Wisconsin. ▪ Graduate Iowa-Grant High School, 1983; attended Southwest Technical College, 1983–85. ▪ Former government/associate newspaper editor, 1990–2014. ▪ Member: Wisconsin League of Municipalities; NRA; Wisconsin Farm Bureau. ▪ Former member: Iowa County Humane Society (founding member, treasurer); Wisconsin Newspaper Association; National Newspaper Association. ▪ Recipient: Gathering Waters *Policymaker of the Year*; WISCAP *William Steiger Human Services Award*; MMAC *Champion of Commerce*; WMC *Working for Wisconsin Award*; WNA *Legislative Service Award*; WCA *Outstanding Legislator Award*; WPHCA *Friend of Community Health Centers*; WAFP *Friend of Family Medicine Award*; LWM *Municipal Champion Award*. ▪ Southwest Regional Planning Commission, 2012–present. Mayor of Dodgeville, 2012–present.

Legislature: Elected to Assembly since 2014. Committee assignments, 2017: Joint Survey Committee on Retirement Systems (cochair); Agriculture (vice chair); Criminal Justice and Public Safety; Local Government; Mental Health; Rural Development and Mining; Ways and Means.

Contact: Rep.Novak@legis.wisconsin.gov; 608-266-7502; 888-534-0051 (toll free); 608-574-0100 (district); Room 312 North, State Capitol, PO Box 8953, Madison, WI 53708.

Senate District 18
Assembly Districts 52, 53, 54

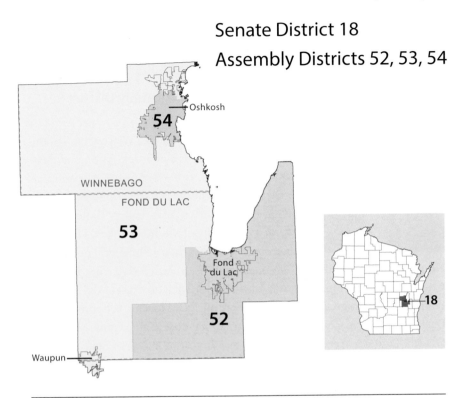

Dan Feyen, Senate District 18

Republican

Biography: Born New Holstein, Wisconsin; married; 2 children. Voting address: Fond du Lac, Wisconsin. ▪ Graduate New Holstein High School, 1986; Diploma in Printing, Fox Valley Technical College, 1988. ▪ Print and bindery coordinator. ▪ Member: Knights of Columbus; Elks Club; Fond du Lac County Republican Party (chair); 6th District Republican Party (chair). ▪ Former member: Jaycees Fond du Lac County (past president); Fond du Lac Advisory Parks Board.

Legislature: Elected to Senate 2016. Committee assignments, 2017: Economic Development, Commerce and Local Government (chair); Financial Services, Constitution and Federalism; Universities and Technical Colleges; Workforce Development, Military Affairs and Senior Issues (vice chair); Joint Survey Committee on Tax Exemptions (cochair). Additional appointments, 2017: Wisconsin Economic Development Corporation Board.

Contact: Sen.Feyen@legis.wisconsin.gov; 608-266-5300; Room 306 South, State Capitol, PO Box 7882, Madison, WI 53707-7882.

Jeremy Thiesfeldt, Assembly District 52
Republican

Biography: Born Fond du Lac, Wisconsin, November 22, 1966; married; 4 children. Voting address: Fond du Lac, Wisconsin. ▪ Graduate Kettle Moraine Lutheran High School (Jackson), 1985; B.S. in Elementary Education, Martin Luther College, 1989; attended University of Minnesota, 1992. ▪ Full-time legislator. Former teacher. ▪ Member: Fond du Lac Noon Rotary; Fond du Lac County Republican Party; Redeemer Lutheran Church, Thrivent Financial; National Rifle Association; Fond du Lac Association of Commerce; Leadership Fond du Lac Alumni; Wisconsin Farm Bureau; Wisconsin Civil Air Patrol. ▪ Former member: Camp Croix; Minnesota District Lutheran Teachers' Conference; Wisconsin Lutheran State Teachers' Conference; Wisconsin Area Lutheran Educators' Conference. ▪ Fond du Lac City Council, 2005–10.

Legislature: Elected to Assembly since 2010. Committee assignments, 2017: Education (chair); Constitution and Ethics (vice chair); Family Law; Judiciary; Transportation.

Contact: Rep.Thiesfeldt@legis.wisconsin.gov; 608-266-3156; 888-529-0052 (toll free); 920-933-2086 (district); Room 16 West, State Capitol, PO Box 8953, Madison, WI 53708.

Michael Schraa, Assembly District 53
Republican

Biography: Born Fort Carson, Colorado, April 17, 1961; married; 3 children. Voting address: Oshkosh, Wisconsin. ▪ Graduate Oshkosh North High School, 1979; attended University of Wisconsin-Oshkosh, 1980–82. ▪ Restaurant owner. Former stock broker/investment advisor. ▪ Member: Winnebago County Republican Party (executive board); Fond du Lac County Republican Party; Oshkosh Chamber of Commerce; Calvary Son Rise

Church (Oshkosh); Wisconsin Independent Business; NRA; Winnebago County Farm Bureau; Fond du Lac County Farm Bureau. ▪ Former member: Southwest Rotary; NFIB; Oshkosh Jaycees; Big Brothers/Big Sisters; Exchange Club.

Legislature: Elected to Assembly since 2012. Committee assignments, 2017: Corrections (chair); Federalism and Interstate Relations (vice chair); Campaigns and Elections; Labor; Public Benefit Reform.

Contact: Rep.Schraa@legis.wisconsin.gov; 608-267-7990; 888-534-0053 (toll free); Room 107 West, State Capitol, PO Box 8953, Madison, WI 53708.

Gordon Hintz, Assembly District 54
Democrat

Biography: Born Oshkosh, Wisconsin, November 29, 1973; married; 1 daughter. Voting address: Oshkosh, Wisconsin. ▪ Graduate Oshkosh North High School, 1992; B.A. Hamline University (St. Paul, Minnesota), 1996; M.P.A. University of Wisconsin-Madison, 2001. ▪ Municipal consultant. Former legislative staff assistant, U.S. Representative Jay Johnson, U.S. Senator Herb Kohl; former management and budget analyst, City of Long Beach, California; former instructor, Political Science Department, University of Wisconsin-Oshkosh. ▪ Member: Oshkosh Rotary Club; First Congregational Church; Oshkosh Public Museum; Winnebagoland Housing Coalition; Winnebago County Safe Streets Committee; Winnebago County Democratic Party; Oshkosh Food Co-op.

Legislature: Elected to Assembly since 2006. Committee assignments, 2017: Joint Committee on Finance; Government Accountability and Oversight; Joint Legislative Council.

Contact: Rep.Hintz@legis.wisconsin.gov; www.gordonhintz.com; Facebook: Gordon Hintz; Twitter: @GordonHintz; 608-266-2254; 888-534-0054 (toll free); 920-232-0805 (district); Room 109 North, State Capitol, PO Box 8952, Madison, WI 53708.

Senate District 19
Assembly Districts 55, 56, 57

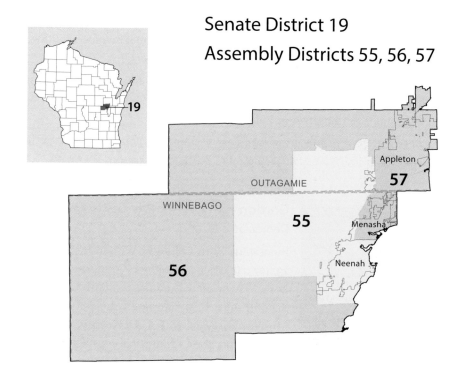

Roger Roth, Senate District 19
Republican

Biography: Born Appleton, Wisconsin, February 5, 1978; married; 3 children. Voting address: Appleton, Wisconsin. ▪ Graduate St. Mary Central High School (Menasha), 1996; B.S. in History, University of Wisconsin-Oshkosh, 2001. ▪ Self-employed home builder. 2d Lt. in the Wisconsin Air National Guard; Iraq War veteran. ▪ Member: American Legion; AMVETS; Veterans of Foreign Wars.

Legislature: Elected to Assembly 2006–08. Elected to Senate 2014. Leadership positions: President of the Senate 2017. Committee assignments, 2017: Joint Committee on Employment Relations (cochair); Joint Committee on Legislative Organization (cochair); Joint Legislative Council (cochair); Senate Organization; Joint Committee on Information Policy and Technology.

Contact: Sen.Roth@legis.wisconsin.gov; 608-266-0718; 800-579-8717 (toll free); Room 220 South, State Capitol, PO Box 7882, Madison, WI 53707-7882.

Mike Rohrkaste, Assembly District 55
Republican

Biography: Born Dayton, Ohio, September 24, 1958; married; 2 children. Voting address: Neenah, Wisconsin. ▪ Graduate Chaminade-Julienne High School (Dayton, Ohio), 1976; B.S. Michigan State University, 1980; Masters in Labor and Industrial Relations, Michigan State University, 1982. ▪ Full-time legislator. Former chief human resources officer, vice president of human resources; over 30 years business/human resources experience. ▪ Member: YMCA of Fox Cities (board member); Samaritans Counseling Center Fox Valley (board member); Neenah Club; Fox Cities Morning Rotary; Calvary Bible Church. ▪ Former member: Fox Valley Christian Academy (board member).

Legislature: Elected to Assembly since 2014. Committee assignments, 2017: Joint Committee on Finance.

Contact: Rep.Rohrkaste@legis.wisconsin.gov; 608-266-5719; 888-534-0055 (toll free); 920-284-9507 (district); Room 321 East, State Capitol, PO Box 8953, Madison, WI 53708.

Dave Murphy, Assembly District 56
Republican

Biography: Born Appleton, Wisconsin, November 26, 1954; married; 2 children. Voting address: Greenville, Wisconsin. ▪ Graduate Hortonville High School, 1972; University of Wisconsin-Fox Valley, 1972–74; Wisconsin School of Real Estate, 1975. ▪ Full-time legislator. Former owner, fitness center and agri-business; real estate broker. ▪ Member: Greenville Lions Club; Zion Lutheran Church Council. ▪ Former member: Paper Valley Soccer Club (vice president).

Legislature: Elected to Assembly since 2012. Committee assignments, 2017: Colleges and Universities (chair); Campaigns and Elections; Financial Institutions; Health; Housing and Real Estate; Workforce Development.

Contact: Rep.Murphy@legis.wisconsin.gov; 608-266-7500; 888-534-0056 (toll free); 920-574-2075 (district); Room 318 North, State Capitol, PO Box 8953, Madison, WI 53708.

Amanda Stuck, Assembly District 57
Democrat

Biography: Born Appleton, Wisconsin, December 16, 1982; married; 2 children. Voting address: Appleton, Wisconsin. ▪ Graduate Appleton North High School, 2001; B.A. in Political Science, University of Wisconsin-Oshkosh, 2007; Master of Public Administration degree, University of Wisconsin-Oshkosh, 2012. ▪ Full-time legislator. Former housing specialist, Appleton Housing Authority; legislative aide, Congressman Steve Kagan; rural mail carrier.

Legislature: Elected to Assembly since 2014. Committee assignments, 2017: Energy and Utilities; Housing and Real Estate; Jobs and the Economy; Natural Resources and Sporting Heritage.

Contact: Rep.Stuck@legis.wisconsin.gov; 608-266-3070; 888-534-0057 (toll free); Room 4 West, State Capitol, PO Box 8953, Madison, WI 53708.

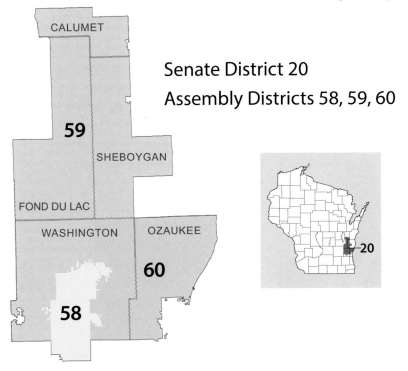

Senate District 20
Assembly Districts 58, 59, 60

Duey Stroebel, Senate District 20

Republican

Biography: Born Cedarburg, Wisconsin, September 1, 1959; married; 8 children. Voting address: Town of Cedarburg, Wisconsin. ▪ Graduate Cedarburg High School, 1978; B.B.A. University of Wisconsin-Madison, 1984; M.S. University of Wisconsin-Madison, 1987. ▪ Real estate. ▪ Member: Ozaukee Board of Realtors; Cedarburg Chamber of Commerce; Greater Cedarburg Foundation (former president); Concordia University President's Council; Farm Bureau; ABATE of Wisconsin; West Bend Chamber of Commerce; Saukville Chamber of Commerce. ▪ Former member: City of Cedarburg Downtown Ad Hoc Committee; Ozaukee Bank and Cornerstone Bank (board of directors). ▪ Town of Cedarburg Parks Commission, 2001–04; Town of Cedarburg Planning Commission, 2003–05; Cedarburg School Board, 2007–12.

Legislature: Elected to Assembly in May 2011 special election. Reelected 2012. Elected to Senate in April 2015 special election. Reelected 2016. Committee assignments, 2017: Government Operations, Technology and Consumer

Protection (chair); Financial Services, Constitution and Federalism (vice chair); Judiciary and Public Safety; Joint Committee for Review of Administrative Rules. **Contact:** Sen.Stroebel@legis.wisconsin.gov; SenatorStroebel.com; Twitter: @SenStroebel; Facebook: Senator Duey Stroebel; 608-266-7513; 800-662-1227 (toll free); 262-822-1520 (district); Room 18 South, State Capitol, PO Box 7882, Madison, WI 53707-7882.

Bob Gannon, Assembly District 58
Republican

Biography: Born Mequon, Wisconsin, January 6, 1959; married; 2 children. Voting address: Slinger, Wisconsin. ▪ Graduate West Bend East High School, 1977; attended various colleges and vocational courses. ▪ Owner, independent insurance agency, hotel and investment property. ▪ Member: West Bend Sunrise Rotary (former president); West Bend Economic Development (former vice president); Still Waters United Methodist; Independent Insurance Agents of Wisconsin; Professional Insurance Agents of Wisconsin; Life Member NRA; West Bend Chamber of Commerce (former president). ▪ Former member: Family Promise of Washington County (president); West Bend Jaycees (president); Washington County Youth Hockey Association (president).

Legislature: Elected to Assembly since 2014. Committee assignments, 2017: Urban Revitalization (chair); Children and Families (vice chair); Corrections; Insurance; State Affairs.

Contact: Rep.Gannon@legis.wisconsin.gov; 608-264-8486; 888-534-0058 (toll free); Room 12 West, State Capitol, PO Box 8952, Madison, WI 53708.

Jesse Kremer, Assembly District 59
Republican

Biography: Born Moline, Illinois, February 28, 1977; married; 3 children. Voting address: Kewaskum, Wisconsin. ▪ Graduate Kettle Moraine Lutheran High School, 1995; A.S. Fox Valley Technical College, 1997; Certificate, Firefighter and Police Recruit Academy, Waukesha County Technical College, 1999; Certificate, EMT-Basic, Milwaukee Area

Technical College, 1999. ▪ Pilot, small business owner, firefighter/ EMT. Former emergency services dispatcher, flight instructor, airline captain, charter pilot. Served in Army National Guard and U.S. Army Reserve 2002–10; Iraq War veteran. ▪ Member: Kewaskum Volunteer Fire Department; American Legion Fohl-Martin Post 483.

Legislature: Elected to Assembly since 2014. Committee assignments, 2017: Criminal Justice and Public Safety (vice chair); Aging and Long-Term Care; Colleges and Universities; Constitution and Ethics; Corrections; Health; Public Benefit Reform.

Contact: Rep.Kremer@legis.wisconsin.gov; www.RepKremer.com; 608-266-9175; 888-534-0059 (toll free); Room 17 West, State Capitol, PO Box 8952, Madison, WI 53708.

Robert Brooks, Assembly District 60
Republican

Biography: Born Rockford, Illinois, July 13, 1965; married; 2 children. Voting address: Saukville, Wisconsin. ▪ Graduate Orfordville Parkview High School, 1983; attended University of Wisconsin-La Crosse, 1983–86. ▪ Real estate broker since 1990, restaurant/tavern owner. ▪ Former member: Stars and Stripes Honor Flight (board of directors); Wisconsin County Mutual (board of directors); Wisconsin Board of Realtors; Ozaukee County Tavern League (board of directors). ▪ Former commissioner, Southeastern Wisconsin Regional Planning Commission. Ozaukee County Board, 2000–14.

Legislature: Elected to Assembly since 2014. Leadership positions: Assistant Majority Leader 2017. Committee assignments, 2017: Joint Legislative Council (cochair); Assembly Organization; Housing and Real Estate; Rules; Rural Development and Mining; Joint Committee on Legislative Organization.

Contact: Rep.Rob.Brooks@legis.wisconsin.gov; 608-267-2369; 888-534-0060 (toll free); 262-268-7880 (district); Room 309 North, State Capitol, PO Box 8952, Madison, WI 53708.

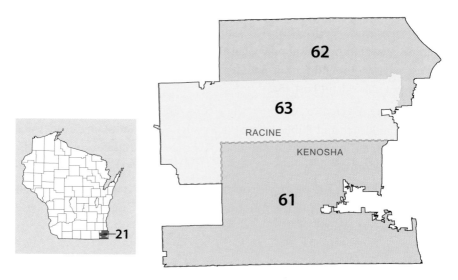

Senate District 21
Assembly Districts 61, 62, 63

Van H. Wanggaard, Senate District 21
Republican

Biography: Born Ft. Leavenworth, Kansas, April 1952; married; 2 children, 2 grandchildren. Voting address: Racine, Wisconsin. ▪ Graduate Racine Lutheran High School, 1970; Racine Police Academy; Wisconsin State Patrol Academy Accident Investigation; Northwestern University Traffic Institute-Reconstruction; U.S. Coast Guard National SAR School; attended John F. Kennedy University, California; University of Wisconsin-Extension; University of Wisconsin-Parkside; Green Bay Technical College; Milwaukee Area Technical College; Fox Valley Technical College. ▪ Full-time legislator. Retired traffic investigator, Racine Police Department; adjunct instructor, Gateway Technical College and Northwestern Traffic Institute; police liaison and security, Racine Unified School District. ▪ Member: National Rifle Association (life member); Racine County Line Rifle Club (board of directors); Racine Police Credit Union (former president, vice president). ▪ Former member: Racine Zoological Society (board of directors); Racine Jaycees; Racine Police Explorers (advisor); Traffic Accident Consultants, Inc. (board of directors); Association of SWAT Personnel; Racine Innovative Youth Service (board); Hostage Negotiation Team, RAPD; Racine Junior Deputy Sheriffs Association; Racine Alateen (advisor); National Association for Search and Rescue (PSAR chair). ▪ Racine Police and Fire Commission, 2003–13 (chair, vice chair, secretary). Racine County Board, 2002–11.

Legislature: Elected to Senate 2010. Reelected 2014. Leadership positions: Majority Caucus Vice Chair 2017, 2015. Committee assignments, 2017: Judiciary and Public Safety (chair); Labor and Regulatory Reform (vice chair); Joint Review Committee on Criminal Penalties (cochair); Law Revision Committee (cochair); Elections and Utilities; Joint Legislative Council.

Contact: Sen.Wanggaard@legis.wisconsin.gov; 608-266-1832; 866-615-7510 (toll free); Room 319 South, State Capitol, PO Box 7882, Madison, WI 53707-7882.

Samantha Kerkman, Assembly District 61
Republican

Biography: Born Burlington, Wisconsin, March 6, 1974; 2 children. Voting address: Town of Salem, Wisconsin. ▪ Graduate Wilmot High School; B.A. University of Wisconsin-Whitewater, 1996. ▪ Member: Kenosha Area Business Alliance; Twin Lakes Chamber and Area Business Association; Twin Lakes American Legion Auxiliary Post 544; VFW  Auxiliary, Bloomfield Center Post 5830; St. Alphonsus Catholic Church. ▪ Former member: Burlington Area Chamber of Commerce; Powers Lake Sportsmen Club.

Legislature: Elected to Assembly since 2000. Leadership positions: Majority Caucus Sergeant at Arms 2017, 2015, 2013, 2011. Committee assignments, 2017: Joint Legislative Audit Committee (cochair); Children and Families; Federalism and Interstate Relations; Judiciary; Ways and Means.

Contact: Rep.Kerkman@legis.wisconsin.gov; www.legis.state.wi.us/assembly/kerkman/Pages/default.aspx; 608-266-2530; 888-529-0061 (toll free); 262-279-1037 (district); Room 315 North, State Capitol, PO Box 8952, Madison, WI 53708; PO Box 156, Powers Lake, WI 53159 (district).

Thomas Weatherston, Assembly District 62
Republican

Biography: Born Buffalo, New York, February 15, 1950; 1 child. Voting address: Racine, Wisconsin. ▪ Graduate Williamsville Central High School, 1968; A.A.S. in Construction Management, Erie Community College, 1975; B.S. in Industrial Engineering, State University College of New York at Buffalo, 1977. ▪ Full-time legislator. Former director of facilities management at Modine Manufacturing Company; adjunct instructor at Gateway Technical College. Vietnam veteran, served in U.S. Air Force, 1968–72. ▪ Member: Vietnam Veterans of America Chapter 767; Veterans of Foreign Wars Post 10301. ▪ Former member: Kiwanis; Racine Area Veterans, Inc. (president); St. Catherine High School (board member); Salvation Army (advisory board). ▪ Caledonia Utility District Commission, 2011–13. Caledonia village trustee, 2010–13.

Legislature: Elected to Assembly since 2012. Committee assignments, 2017: Aging and Long Term Care (chair); Workforce Development (vice chair); Energy and Utilities; Financial Institutions; Transportation; Urban Revitalization; Veterans and Military Affairs.

Contact: Rep.Weatherston@legis.wisconsin.gov; 608-266-0731; 888-534-0062 (toll free); Room 307 North, State Capitol, PO Box 8953, Madison, WI 53708.

Robin J. Vos, Assembly District 63
Republican

Biography: Born Burlington, Wisconsin, July 5, 1968. Voting address: Burlington, Wisconsin. ▪ Graduate Burlington High School, 1986; University of Wisconsin-Whitewater, 1991. ▪ Owner of several small businesses. Former congressional district director; former legislative assistant. ▪ Member: Rotary Club (past president); Racine/Kenosha Farm Bureau; Knights of Columbus; Racine County Republican Party; Racine Area Manufacturers and Commerce; Union Grove Chamber of Commerce; Burlington Chamber of Commerce. ▪ University of Wisconsin Board of Regents, 1989–91. Racine County Board, 1994–2004 (former chair of Finance and Personnel committees).

Legislature: Elected to Assembly since 2004. Leadership positions: Speaker of the Assembly 2017, 2015, 2013; Cochair, Joint Committee on Finance, 2011.

Contact: Rep.Vos@legis.wisconsin.gov; SpeakerVos.com; 608-266-9171; 888-534-0063 (toll free); 608-282-3663 (fax); 262-514-2597 (district); Room 217 West, State Capitol, PO Box 8953, Madison, WI 53708.

Senate District 22
Assembly Districts 64, 65, 66

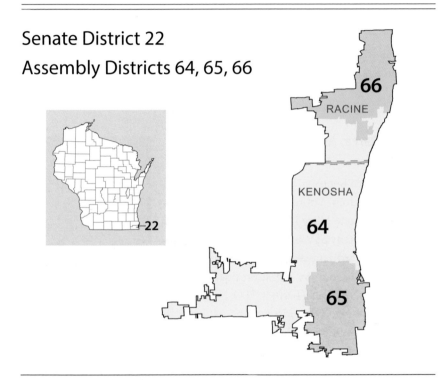

Robert W. Wirch, Senate District 22
Democrat

Biography: Born Kenosha, Wisconsin, November 16, 1943; married; 2 children. Voting address: Somers, Wisconsin. ▪ Graduate Mary D. Bradford High School; B.A. University of Wisconsin-Parkside, 1970. ▪ Full-time legislator. Former factory worker and liaison to JTPA programs. Served in Army Reserve, 1965–71. ▪ Member: Danish Brotherhood; Kenosha Sport Fishing and Conservation Association; Democratic Party of Wisconsin. ▪ Former member: Kenosha Boys and Girls Club (board of directors). ▪

Kenosha County supervisor, 1986–94 (served on Health and Human Services Committee, Welfare Board, and Developmental Disabilities Board).

Legislature: Elected to Assembly 1992. Reelected 1994. Elected to Senate since 1996. Leadership positions: Minority Caucus Chair 2003. Committee assignments, 2017: Government Operations, Technology and Consumer Protection; Labor and Regulatory Reform; Sporting Heritage, Mining and Forestry; Joint Committee for Review of Administrative Rules.

Contact: Sen.Wirch@legis.wisconsin.gov; 608-267-8979; 262-694-7379 (district); 888-769-4724 (office hotline); Room 127 South, State Capitol, PO Box 7882, Madison, WI 53707-7882.

Peter W. Barca, Assembly District 64
Democrat

Biography: Born Kenosha, Wisconsin, August 7, 1955; married; 2 children. Voting address: Kenosha, Wisconsin. ▪ Graduate Mary D. Bradford High School, 1973; B.S. University of Wisconsin-Milwaukee, 1977; attended Harvard University; M.A. University of Wisconsin-Madison, 1983. ▪ Past president, Aurora Association International; Former CEO, Northpointe Resources; National Ombudsman and Midwest Regional Administrator, U.S. Small Business Administration. ▪ Member: Foundation Board of Directors, University of Wisconsin-Parkside; International Society for ISCTR (cofounder, secretary/treasurer); WISITALIA (past president). ▪ Former member: Committee to Found the Boys and Girls Club of Kenosha (chair); Lake County Partnership on Economic Development (executive committee) and Economic Development Committee on Small Business (chair); Small Business Forum of DNC (national cochair); Kenosha Family and Aging Services (board member); Kenosha Incubator Association (chair); Partnership for a Stronger Economy (chair).

Legislature: Elected to Assembly 1984–92 (resigned 6/8/93 upon election to U.S. Congress). Reelected since 2008. Leadership positions: Minority Leader 2017, 2015, 2013, 2011; Majority Caucus Chair 2009, 1993, 1991. Committee assignments, 2017: Assembly Organization; Rules; Joint Committee on Employment Relations; Joint Committee on Information Policy and Technology; Joint Committee on Legislative Organization; Joint Legislative Council. Additional appointments, 2017: Wisconsin Economic Development Corporation Board.

Contact: Rep.Barca@legis.wisconsin.gov; 608-266-5504; 888-534-0064 (toll free); Room 201 West, State Capitol, PO Box 8952, Madison, WI 53708.

Tod Ohnstad, Assembly District 65
Democrat

Biography: Born Eau Claire, Wisconsin, May 21, 1952; married. Voting address: Kenosha, Wisconsin. ▪ Graduate Altoona Public High School, 1970; attended University of Wisconsin-Parkside. ▪ Former member: UAW Local 72 (chair of trustees, shop committeeman, bargaining committee, executive board). ▪ City of Kenosha alderman, 2008–14.

Legislature: Elected to Assembly since 2012. Committee assignments, 2017: Jobs and the Economy; Labor; State Affairs; Tourism; Ways and Means; Workforce Development.

Contact: Rep.Ohnstad@legis.wisconsin.gov; 608-266-0455; 888-534-0065 (toll free); 262-764-1950 (district); Room 128 North, State Capitol, PO Box 8953, Madison, WI 53708.

Cory Mason, Assembly District 66
Democrat

Biography: Born Racine, Wisconsin, January 25, 1973; married; 2 daughters, 1 son. Voting address: Racine, Wisconsin. ▪ Graduate Case High School (Racine); B.A. in Philosophy, University of Wisconsin-Madison. ▪ Full-time legislator. ▪ Member: Great Lakes Legislative Caucus (chair); National Caucus of Environmental Legislators; River Alliance of Wisconsin (former board member); University of Wisconsin Center for Tobacco Research and Intervention (former board member). ▪ Former member: Wisconsin Coastal Management Board; Redevelopment Authority of Racine, 2005–11 (commissioner).

Legislature: Elected to Assembly since 2006. Committee assignments, 2017: Environment and Forestry; Labor; Tourism; Joint Legislative Council; Joint Survey Committee on Retirement Systems.

Contact: Rep.Mason@legis.wisconsin.gov; 608-266-0634; 888-534-0066 (toll free); Room 6 North, State Capitol, PO Box 8953, Madison, WI 53708.

Senate District 23
Assembly Districts 67, 68, 69

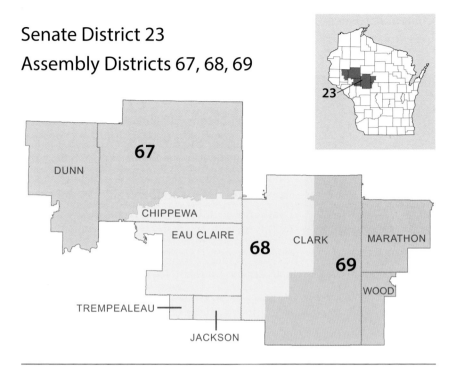

Terry Moulton, Senate District 23

Republican

Biography: Born Whitefish, Montana, July 19, 1946; married; 2 children, 8 grandchildren. Voting address: Chippewa Falls, Wisconsin. ▪ Graduate Chippewa Falls High School, 1964; attended University of Wisconsin-Eau Claire. ▪ Owner of archery and tackle shop and fishing tackle manufacturer. Former hospital accountant and business manager. ▪ Member: Chippewa Falls and Eau Claire Chambers of Commerce; Archery Range and Retailers Organization; Muskies, Inc.; Chippewa Bowhunters; Chippewa Rod and Gun; Eau Claire Archers; Eau Claire Rod and Gun Club.

Legislature: Elected to Assembly 2004, 2006. Elected to Senate since 2010. Committee assignments, 2017: Agriculture, Small Business, and Tourism (chair); Health and Human Services (vice chair); Sporting Heritage, Mining and Forestry; Joint Legislative Council. Additional appointments, 2017: Building Commission; Council on Tourism; Evidence-Based Decision Making Subcommittee of the Criminal Justice Coordinating Council.

Contact: Sen.Moulton@legis.wisconsin.gov; 608-266-7511; 888-437-9436 (toll free); Room 310 South, State Capitol, PO Box 7882, Madison, WI 53707-7882.

Robert Summerfield, Assembly District 67

Republican

Biography: Born Eau Claire, Wisconsin, February 24, 1980; raised Bloomer, Wisconsin; married; 3 children. Voting address: Bloomer, Wisconsin. ▪ Graduate Bloomer High School, 1998; B.S. in Business Administration, University of Wisconsin-Stout, 2002. ▪ Small business owner; supper club manager. ▪ Member: Bloomer Chamber of Commerce; Bloomer Rod & Gun; Tavern League of Wisconsin; Chippewa County Tavern League; NRA; Good Shepherd Lutheran Church (Bloomer, Wisconsin).

Legislature: Elected to Assembly 2016. Committee assignments, 2017: Colleges and Universities; Small Business Development; State Affairs; Tourism; Veterans and Military Affairs.

Contact: Rep.Summerfield@legis.wisconsin.gov; 608-266-1194; 888-534-0067 (toll free); 715-568-1796 (district); Room 7 West, State Capitol, PO Box 8953, Madison, WI 53708.

Kathy Bernier, Assembly District 68

Republican

Biography: Born Eau Claire, Wisconsin, April 29, 1956; 3 children, 6 grandchildren. Voting address: Lake Hallie, Wisconsin. ▪ Graduate Chippewa Falls Senior High School, 1974; B.A. University of Wisconsin-Eau Claire, 1998; Certificate in Public Management Essentials, University of Wisconsin-Green Bay, 2005. ▪ Member: American Legislative Exchange Council; Assembly of State Legislatures; Chippewa Falls Chamber of Commerce; Eau Claire Area Chamber of Commerce; Lake Hallie Optimists Club; National Foundation for Women Legislators (board of directors); Wisconsin County Clerks Association (lifetime member); National Conference of State Legislatures, Elections and Redistricting Committee. ▪ Former member: Wisconsin Women in Government; Wisconsin County Constitutional Officers;

Chippewa County Humane Association; Kiwanis Noon Club. ▪ Chippewa County clerk, 1999–2011; Village of Lake Hallie trustee, 2007–11 and 2015–16. **Legislature:** Elected to Assembly since 2010. Committee assignments, 2017: Campaigns and Elections (chair); Health (vice chair); Aging and Long-Term Care; Criminal Justice and Public Safety; Tourism; Ways and Means.

Contact: Rep.Bernier@legis.wisconsin.gov; 608-266-9172; 888-534-0068 (toll free); 715-720-0326 (district); Room 314 North, State Capitol, PO Box 8952, Madison, WI 53708.

Bob Kulp, Assembly District 69
Republican

Biography: Born Elkhart, Indiana, March 21, 1966; married; 7 children, 7 grandchildren. Voting address: Stratford, Wisconsin. ▪ Roofing and insulation contractor. ▪ Member: National Roofing Contractors Association (board member); Construction Specifications Institute-Wausau Chapter (past president); Small Business Administration Regulatory Fairness Board (former board member); Wausau Area Builders Association (former member, governmental committee); Noon Rotary Club of Marshfield.

Legislature: Elected to Assembly in November 2013 special election. Reelected since 2014. Committee assignments, 2017: Labor (chair); Rural Development and Mining (vice chair); Jobs and the Economy; State Affairs; Transportation; Workforce Development.

Contact: Rep.Kulp@legis.wisconsin.gov; 608-267-0280; 888-534-0069 (toll free); Room 15 West, State Capitol, PO Box 8952, Madison, WI 53708.

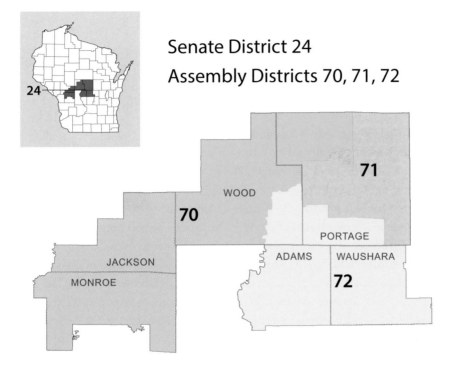

Senate District 24
Assembly Districts 70, 71, 72

Patrick Testin, Senate District 24
Republican

Biography: Born Madison, Wisconsin, June 9, 1988; married. Voting address: Stevens Point, Wisconsin. ▪ Graduate Marinette High School, 2006; B.S. in Political Science, University of Wisconsin-Stevens Point, 2011. ▪ Former sales professional for Wisconsin-based wine distributor. ▪ Member: Stevens Point Elk Lodge 641; Ignite Leadership Network of Portage County.

Legislature: Elected to Senate 2016. Committee assignments, 2017: Workforce Development, Military Affairs and Senior Issues (chair); Judiciary and Public Safety (vice chair); Sporting Heritage, Mining and Forestry (vice chair); Joint Survey Committee on Retirement Systems (cochair); Agriculture, Small Business and Tourism; Economic Development, Commerce and Local Government.

Contact: Sen.Testin@legis.wisconsin.gov; 608-266-3123; Room 131 South, State Capitol, PO Box 7882, Madison, WI 53707-7882.

Nancy Lynn VanderMeer, Assembly District 70
Republican

Biography: Born Evergreen Park, Illinois, December 15, 1958; married. Voting address: Tomah, Wisconsin. ▪ Graduate Evergreen Park Community High School, 1976; B.S. in Psychology, University of Wisconsin-La Crosse, 1988. ▪ Automobile dealer, small business owner, family dairy farmer. ▪ Member: Jackson County Local Emergency Planning Commission; Farm Bureau; Gloria Dei Lutheran Church (former council president); Tomah Chamber of Commerce (former board of directors member); Tomah Memorial Hospital Board (former officer); American Business Women's Association (former member, president); NRA; American Legion Auxiliary; board of directors of the nonprofit Handishop Industries. ▪ Recipient: Sparta Area School District *Certificate of Recognition* 2015; WCSEA *Legislative Award* 2016; Wisconsin Academy of Family Physicians 2016 *Friend of Family Medicine*; Dairy Business Association *Legislative Excellence Award* 2016; Wisconsin Library Association *Wisconsin Library Champion* 2016.

Legislature: Elected to Assembly since 2014. Committee assignments, 2017: Rural Development and Mining (chair); Veterans and Military Affairs (vice chair); Agriculture; Consumer Protection; Mental Health; Science and Technology; Small Business Development.

Contact: Rep.VanderMeer@legis.wisconsin.gov; 608-266-8366; 888-534-0070 (toll free); Room 11 West, State Capitol, PO Box 8953, Madison, WI 53708.

Katrina Shankland, Assembly District 71
Democrat

Biography: Born Wausau, Wisconsin, August 4, 1987; single. Voting address: Stevens Point, Wisconsin. ▪ Graduate Wittenberg-Birnamwood High School, 2005; B.A. in Political Science, University of Wisconsin-Madison, 2009; attended Marquette University, 2005–06, University of Wisconsin-Marathon County, 2004–05 ▪ Full-time legislator. Former nonprofit professional. ▪ Member: Early Years Collaborative Advocacy and Awareness Steering Committee; Wisconsin Legislative Children's Caucus; Wisconsin Legislative Sportsmen's Caucus; National Caucus of Environmental

Legislators; Young Elected Officials Network; Council of State Governments Henry Toll Fellow, 2013; Midwest Renewable Energy Association; Clean Wisconsin; Portage County Business Council; Central Rivers Farmshed; Portage County Democratic Party.

Legislature: Elected to Assembly since 2012. Leadership positions: Assistant Minority Leader 2015. Committee assignments, 2017: Joint Committee on Finance; Rural Development and Mining. Additional appointments, 2017: Governor's Council on Workforce Investment; Wisconsin Environmental Education Board.

Contact: Rep.Shankland@legis.wisconsin.gov; 608-267-9649; 888-534-0071 (toll free); Room 304 West, State Capitol, PO Box 8953, Madison, WI 53708.

Scott S. Krug, Assembly District 72
Republican

Biography: Born Wisconsin Rapids, Wisconsin, September 16, 1975; married; 6 children. Voting address: Rome, Wisconsin. ▪ Graduate Lincoln High School, 1993; attended University of Wisconsin-Stevens Point; A.D. Mid-State Technical College, 1999; B.A.S. in Psychology, University of Wisconsin-Green Bay, 2008. ▪ Employment and training specialist. Former Wood County drug court coordinator, jail discharge planner; Juneau County sheriff's deputy. ▪ Member: Heart of Wisconsin Chamber of Commerce; Wisconsin Rapids Rotary. ▪ Recipient: Wisconsin Industrial Energy Group *Legislator of the Year Award* 2014; Dairy Business Association *Legislative Excellence Award* 2014, 2012; Wisconsin Paper Council *Legislator of the Year* 2014; Child Support Enforcement Association *Legislator of the Year* 2014; League of Conservation Voters *Honor Roll* 2014; Wisconsin Troopers Association *Legislator of the Year* 2014; Wisconsin Counties Association *Outstanding Legislator* 2014; WMC *Working for Wisconsin Award* 2016, 2014, 2012; Third Congressional District *State Legislator of the Year* 2012.

Legislature: Elected to Assembly since 2010. Committee assignments, 2017: Public Benefit Reform (chair); Environment and Forestry (vice chair); Children and Families; Colleges and Universities; Criminal Justice and Public Safety; Family Law; Government Accountability and Oversight.

Contact: Rep.Krug@legis.wisconsin.gov; 608-266-0215; 888-529-0072 (toll free); Room 207 North, State Capitol, PO Box 8952, Madison, WI 53708.

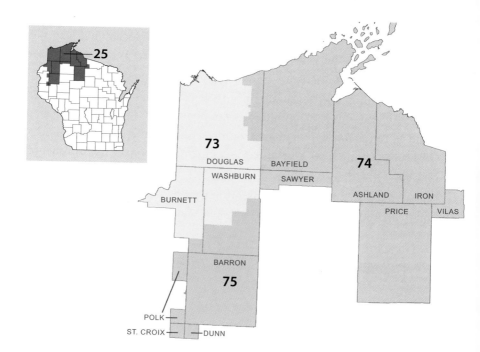

Senate District 25
Assembly Districts 73, 74, 75

Janet Bewley, Senate District 25
Democrat

Biography: Born Painesville, Ohio, November 10, 1951; married; 5 children, 4 grandchildren. Voting address: Mason, Wisconsin. ▪ Graduate James Ford Rhodes High School (Cleveland, Ohio), 1969; B.A. Case Western Reserve University, 1973; M. Ed. University of Maine, 1977. ▪ Full-time legislator. Former Community Relations Officer, Wisconsin Housing and Economic Development Authority; former Dean of Students, Northland College; former executive director, Mary H. Rice Foundation. ▪ One of the original cast members at Lake Superior Big Top Chautauqua and current member of the Rittenhouse Chamber Singers. ▪ Ashland City Council, 2007–09.

Legislature: Elected to Assembly 2010–12. Elected to Senate 2014. Leadership positions: Assistant Minority Leader 2017. Committee assignments, 2017: Economic Development, Commerce and Local Government; Education; Insurance, Housing and Trade; Senate Organization; Universities and Technical Colleges; Joint Committee on Legislative Organization. Additional appointments, 2017: State Council on Alcohol and Other Drug Abuse; Council on Tourism; Wisconsin Housing and Economic Development Authority Board; Wisconsin Council on Forestry; Governor's Task Force on Opioid Abuse.

Contact: Sen.Bewley@legis.wisconsin.gov; 608-266-3510; 800-469-6562 (toll free); 715-746-4100 (district); Room 126 South, State Capitol, PO Box 7882, Madison, WI 53707-7882.

Nick Milroy, Assembly District 73

Democrat

Biography: Born Duluth, Minnesota, April 15, 1974; married; 3 children. Voting address: South Range, Wisconsin. ▪ Graduate Superior Senior High School, 1992; B.S. University of Wisconsin-Superior, 1998; attended University of Wisconsin-Eau Claire, 1999–2000. ▪ Full-time legislator. Former fisheries biologist. Served in U.S. Navy, 1992–94, U.S. Naval Reserve, 1994–2000; deployed to Persian Gulf during Operation Southern Watch. ▪ Member: Executive Board of the Great Lakes Caucus of the Council of State Governments; Wisconsin Chapter of the Congressional Sportsmen's Foundation (cochair); National Conference of Environmental Legislators; Douglas County Democratic Party (former secretary). ▪ Former member: Lake Superior Binational Forum; St. Louis River Watershed TMDL Partnership (board of directors); American Fisheries Society; Duluth-Superior Metropolitan Interstate Council (policy board member); Head of the Lakes Fair (board of directors). ▪ Superior City Council, 2005–09.

Legislature: Elected to Assembly since 2008. Committee assignments, 2017: Environment and Forestry; Natural Resources and Sporting Heritage; Rural Development and Mining; Veterans and Military Affairs. Additional appointments, 2017: Wisconsin Council on Forestry; Wisconsin Sporting Heritage Council.

Contact: Rep.Milroy@legis.wisconsin.gov; 608-266-0640; 888-534-0073 (toll free); 715-392-8690 (district); Room 126 North, State Capitol, PO Box 8953, Madison, WI 53708.

Beth Meyers, Assembly District 74
Democrat

Biography: Born Ashland, Wisconsin, May 29, 1959; married; 2 children. Voting address: Bayfield, Wisconsin. ▪ Graduate Bayfield High School, 1977; B.S. Northland College (Ashland, Wisconsin), 1989. ▪ Full-time legislator. Former executive director, CORE Community Resources. Former board member Apostle Islands Area Community Fund. ▪ Bayfield County Board of Supervisors, 2010–15 (Executive Committee; Personnel Committee; Library Board chair; County Tribal Relations Committee vice chair; Northern Wisconsin Community Action Program Committee vice chair; Health Department Committee chair).

Legislature: Elected to Assembly since 2014. Leadership positions: Minority Caucus Secretary 2017, 2015. Committee assignments, 2017: Aging and Long-Term Care; Energy and Utilities; Financial Institutions; Transportation; Special Committee on State-Tribal Relations.

Contact: Rep.Meyers@legis.wisconsin.gov; 608-266-7690; 888-534-0074 (toll free); Room 409 North, State Capitol, PO Box 8953, Madison, WI 53708.

Romaine Robert Quinn, Assembly District 75
Republican

Biography: Born Rice Lake, Wisconsin, July 30, 1990. Voting address: Chetek, Wisconsin. ▪ Graduate Rice Lake High School, 2009; interdisciplinary B.A. in Political Science with emphasis on Public Leadership, University of Wisconsin-Green Bay, 2014; attended University of Wisconsin-Barron County and University of Wisconsin-Eau Claire. ▪ Full-time legislator. Former Coca-Cola salesman. ▪ Rice Lake City Council, 2009–10; mayor of Rice Lake, 2010–12.

Legislature: Elected to Assembly since 2014. Leadership positions: Majority Caucus Vice Chair 2017. Committee assignments, 2017: Science and Technology (chair); Natural Resources and Sporting Heritage (vice chair); Colleges and Universities; Education; Labor; Regulatory Licensing Reform; Rural Development and Mining.

Contact: Rep.Quinn@legis.wisconsin.gov; 608-266-2519; 888-534-0075 (toll free); Room 323 North, State Capitol, PO Box 8953, Madison, WI 53708.

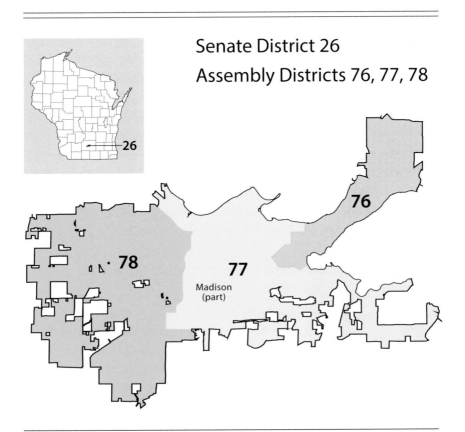

Senate District 26
Assembly Districts 76, 77, 78

76

78

77

Madison
(part)

Fred Risser, Senate District 26
Democrat

Biography: Born Madison, Wisconsin, May 5, 1927; married; 3 children. Voting address: Madison, Wisconsin. ▪ Attended Carleton College (Minnesota), University of Wisconsin-Madison; B.A. University of Oregon, 1950; LL.B. University of Oregon, 1952. ▪ Attorney. World War II veteran; Navy. ▪ Member: State Bar of Wisconsin and Oregon and Dane

County Bar Associations; NCSL (past member National Executive Committee); CSG (past member National Executive Committee, Midwestern Conference chair 1993, 1982). ▪ Presidential Elector 2012, 2008, 1964.

Legislature: Elected to Assembly 1956–60. Elected to Senate in 1962 special election. Reelected since 1964. Longest serving legislator in Wisconsin history and longest serving state legislator in U.S. history. Leadership positions: President of the Senate 2011 (effective 7/17/12), 2009, 2007, 2001, 1999, 1997 (effective 1/15/97 to 4/20/98), 1995 (effective 7/9/96), also 1979 to 4/20/93; Comajority Leader 2001 (effective 10/22/02); Assistant Minority Leader 1995 (effective 1/5/95 to 7/12/96), 1993 (effective 4/20/93), also 1965; Senate President Pro Tempore 1977, 1975; Minority Leader 1967–73. Committee assignments, 2017: Elections and Utilities; Financial Services, Constitution and Federalism; Judiciary and Public Safety; Joint Legislative Council; Law Revision Committee. Additional appointments, 2017: Educational Communications Board; State Historical Society Board of Curators; State Capitol and Executive Residence Board; Commission on Uniform State Laws.

Contact: Sen.Risser@legis.wisconsin.gov; 608-266-1627; Room 130 South, State Capitol, PO Box 7882, Madison, WI 53707-7882.

Chris Taylor, Assembly District 76
Democrat

Biography: Born January 13, 1968, Los Angeles, California; married; 2 children. Voting address: Madison, Wisconsin. ▪ Graduate Birmingham High School (Van Nuys, California), 1986; B.A. University of Pennsylvania, 1990; J.D. University of Wisconsin Law School, 1995. ▪ Full-time legislator. Former public policy director, Planned Parenthood of Wisconsin and practicing attorney. ▪ Member: State Bar of Wisconsin; Wisconsin League of Conservation Voters; Planned Parenthood Advocates of Wisconsin; Planned Parenthood Federation; Sierra Club; Democratic Party of Wisconsin. ▪ Former member: Public Interest Law Board (legislative subcommittee chair).

Legislature: Elected to Assembly in August 2011 special election. Reelected since 2012. Committee assignments, 2017: Campaigns and Elections; Children and Families; Health; Judiciary; Ways and Means.

Contact: Rep.Taylor@legis.wisconsin.gov; 608-266-5342; Room 306 West, State Capitol, PO Box 8953, Madison, WI 53708.

Terese Berceau, Assembly District 77

Democrat

Biography: Born Green Bay, Wisconsin, August 23, 1950. Voting address: Madison, Wisconsin. ▪ B.S. University of Wisconsin-Madison, 1973; graduate studies in Urban and Regional Planning, University of Wisconsin-Madison. ▪ Staff, University of Wisconsin-Madison Robert M. La Follette School; staff, Wisconsin Counties Association; real estate sales; substitute teacher. ▪ Member: Democratic Party of Wisconsin; Planned Parenthood Advocates of Wisconsin; ACLU. ▪ Former member: Monona Terrace Community and Convention Center Board; Greater Madison Convention and Visitors Bureau Board; Governor's Council on Domestic Abuse. ▪ Recipient: Wisconsin Coalition Against Domestic Violence *Legislative Champion Award* 2010; Wisconsin Women's Network *Stateswoman of the Year* 2006; Wisconsin League of Conservation Voters Award 2002–10; Wisconsin Council of the Blind *Legislator of the Year* 2005; Wisconsin Coalition Against Sexual Assault *Voices of Courage Award* 2005; Wisconsin Alliance of Cities *Urban Families Recognition* 2004; Domestic Abuse Intervention Services *Certificate of Recognition* 2004; Wisconsin Coalition Against Domestic Violence *DV Diva Award* 2003; Domestic Abuse Intervention Service *Public Service Award* 2002; National Alliance for the Mentally Ill-Dane County *Community Action Citizen Award* 2003. ▪ City of Madison Community Development Authority (chair 1989–92); Dane County Board of Supervisors, 1992–2000.

Legislature: Elected to Assembly since 1998. Committee assignments, 2017: Colleges and Universities; Constitution and Ethics; Consumer Protection; Insurance; Local Government; Joint Legislative Audit Committee.

Contact: Rep.Berceau@legis.wisconsin.gov; www.terese.org; 608-266-3784; Room 104 North, State Capitol, PO Box 8952, Madison, WI 53708.

Lisa Subeck, Assembly District 78

Democrat

Biography: Born Chicago, Illinois, June 17, 1971; single. Voting address: Madison, Wisconsin. ▪ Graduate Rich Central High School, 1989; B.A. University of Wisconsin-Madison, 1993. ▪ Full-time legislator. Former early childhood education/Head Start program manager; technical college instructor; nonprofit executive director. ▪ Former member: American Federation of Teachers. ▪ City of Madison Common Council, 2011–15.

Legislature: Elected to Assembly since 2014. Committee assignments, 2017: Children and Families; Family Law; Health; Local Government; Public Benefit Reform.

Contact: Rep.Subeck@legis.wisconsin.gov; 608-266-7521; 888-534-0078 (toll free); Room 418 North, State Capitol, PO Box 8953, Madison, WI 53708.

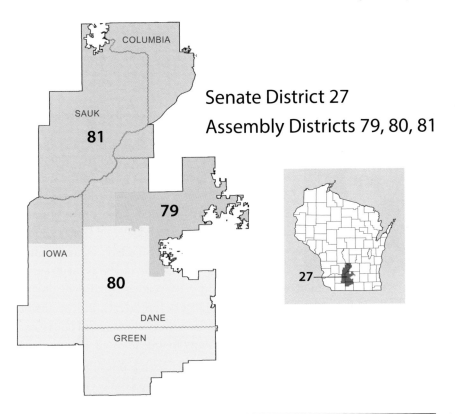

Senate District 27
Assembly Districts 79, 80, 81

Jon B. Erpenbach, Senate District 27
Democrat

Biography: Born Middleton, Wisconsin, January 28, 1961; married; 2 children. Voting address: Middleton, Wisconsin. ▪ Graduate Middleton High School; attended University of Wisconsin-Oshkosh, 1979–81. ▪ Former communications director, legislative aide, radio personality, short order cook, meat packer, truck driver, and City of Middleton recreation instructor.

Legislature: Elected to Senate since 1998. Leadership positions: Minority Leader 2003. Committee assignments, 2017: Health and Human Services; Sporting Heritage, Mining and Forestry; Workforce Development, Military Affairs and Senior Issues; Joint Committee on Finance; Joint Survey Committee on Retirement Systems; Legislative Study Committee on the Preservation of Burial Sites.

Contact: Sen.Erpenbach@legis.wisconsin.gov; 608-266-6670; 888-549-0027 (district, toll free); Room 7 South, State Capitol, PO Box 7882, Madison, WI 53707-7882.

Dianne Hesselbein, Assembly District 79
Democrat

Biography: Born Madison, Wisconsin, March 10, 1971; married; 3 children. Voting address: Middleton, Wisconsin. ▪ Graduate La Follette High School (Madison), 1989; B.S. University of Wisconsin-Oshkosh, 1993; M.A. Edgewood College, 1996. ▪ Full-time legislator. ▪ Member: Dane County Democratic Party; Friends of Pheasant Branch; Clean Wisconsin; Middleton Action Team; VFW Ladies Auxiliary Council. ▪ Former member: Parent Teacher Organization (president); Boy Scouts of America (cubmaster); Girl Scouts troop leader. ▪ Middleton-Cross Plains Area School District Board, 2005–08. Dane County Board, 2008–14.

Legislature: Elected to Assembly since 2012. Leadership positions: Assistant Minority Leader 2017. Committee assignments, 2017: Assembly Organization; Natural Resources and Sporting Heritage; Rules; State Affairs; Veterans and Military Affairs; Joint Committee on Legislative Organization; Joint Legislative Council.

Contact: Rep.Hesselbein@legis.wisconsin.gov; 608-266-5340; Room 119 North, State Capitol, PO Box 8952, Madison, WI 53708.

Sondy Pope, Assembly District 80
Democrat

Biography: Born Madison, Wisconsin, April 27, 1950; married. Voting address: Mount Horeb, Wisconsin. ▪ Graduate River Valley High School; attended Madison Area Technical College and Edgewood College. ▪ Former Associate Director of the Foundation for Madison's Public Schools. ▪ Member: National Caucus of Environmental Legislators; Honorary Life Member, Wisconsin Congress of Parents and Teachers; Midwestern Higher Education Compact Commission; Fellow, Bowhay Institute, La Follette School,

University of Wisconsin-Madison; Fellow, Flemming Institute, Center for Policy Alternatives; Oakhill Correctional Institute Advisory Board; WiLL/WAND National Women's Leadership; State Innovation Exchange; Agrace HospiceCare Patient and Family Partnership Council; Agrace HospiceCare Ethics Committee.

Legislature: Elected to Assembly since 2002. Committee assignments, 2017: Consumer Protection; Corrections; Education; Government Accountability and Oversight; Rules; Legislative Council Study Committee on Student Data. Additional appointments, 2017: Read to Lead Development Council; State Superintendent's Equity in ESSA Stakeholders Council.

Contact: Rep.Pope@legis.wisconsin.gov; 608-266-3520; 888-534-0080 (toll free); Room 118 North, State Capitol, PO Box 8953, Madison, WI 53708.

Dave Considine, Assembly District 81
Democrat

Biography: Born Janesville, Wisconsin, March 29, 1952; married; 5 children. Voting address: Baraboo, Wisconsin. ▪ Graduate Mukwonago Union High School, 1970; B.S. in Education, University of Wisconsin-Whitewater, 1974; certificate in EBD, University of Wisconsin-Madison, 1990; M.A. in Education, Viterbo University, 2005; certificates—instructor certificate, autism spectrum, and enhanced verbal skills, Crisis Prevention Institute (Milwaukee), 2008, 2010, 2013. ▪ Full-time legislator. Former dairy goat farmer, special education teacher. ▪ Member: Columbia County Democratic Party; Pheasants Forever; Ducks Unlimited. ▪ Former member: Baraboo Education Association (president); American Dairy Goat Association (judge); Wisconsin Dairy Goat Association (president); Crisis Prevention Institute (instructor).

Legislature: Elected to Assembly since 2014. Committee assignments, 2017: Agriculture; Corrections; Education; Mental Health; Tourism.

Contact: 608-266-7746; 888-534-0081 (toll free); Room 303 West, State Capitol, PO Box 8952, Madison, WI 53708.

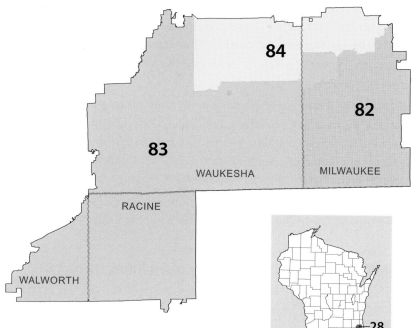

Senate District 28
Assembly Districts 82, 83, 84

David Craig, Senate District 28
Republican

Biography: Born Waukesha, Wisconsin, March 16, 1979; married; 6 children. Voting address: Big Bend, Wisconsin. ▪ Graduate Wisconsin Lutheran High School, 1997; attended University of Wisconsin-Waukesha; B.A. University of Wisconsin-Milwaukee, 2002. ▪ Realtor. Former aide to Congressman Paul Ryan. ▪ Village of Big Bend trustee, 2008–10.

Legislature: Elected to Assembly in May 2011 special election. Reelected 2012, 2014. Elected to Senate 2016. Committee assignments, 2017: Financial Services, Constitution and Federalism (chair); Government Operations, Technology and Consumer Protection (vice chair); Insurance, Housing and Trade; Public Benefits, Licensing and State-Federal Relations; Joint Survey Committee on Retirement Systems.

Contact: Sen.Craig@legis.wisconsin.gov; 608-266-5400; Room 104 South, State Capitol, PO Box 7882, Madison, WI 53707-7882.

Ken Skowronski, Assembly District 82
Republican

Biography: Born Milwaukee, Wisconsin, May 31, 1938; widowed; 2 children. Voting address: Franklin, Wisconsin. ▪ Graduate Boys Tech High School, 1958; journeyman carpenter, MATC (Milwaukee), 1961; NARI certified remodeler. ▪ General contractor; radio host, monthly talk show; 4-H construction skills instructor; seminar speaker, Wisconsin Burglar and Fire Alarm Association and WPR. Wisconsin Air National Guard, 1956–62. ▪ Member: Milwaukee/NARI Foundation (trustee, former president); Franklin Noon Lions Club (trustee, former president); Polish Heritage Alliance (board member); Knights of Columbus (former deputy grand knight); National Rifle Association (endowment life member); Ducks Unlimited (life member); Rocky Mountain Elk Foundation (life member); South Suburban Chamber of Commerce (former board member); Milwaukee/NARI Chapter (former president); NARI National Foundation/NRF (former president). ▪ Former member: Franklin Lions Club (president); NKBA Wisconsin/Upper Michigan Chapter (treasurer); City of Franklin Plan Commission; City of Franklin Economic Development Commission (chair); City of Franklin Community Development Authority; City of Franklin 50th Anniversary Committee (chair). ▪ Recipient: City of Franklin *Distinguished Service Award* 1983; Lions International *Melvin Jones Fellowship Award* 1995; Remodeling Magazine *Big 50 Industry Impact Award* 1992; National Brand Names Foundation *First Place Remodelers Award* 1972; Milwaukee/NARI Chapter *Hank Fenderbosh Award* 1995, *Harold Hammerman Award* (nominee) 1994–95, *Lifetime Achievement Award* 2002, 1997. ▪ Alderman, City of Franklin 2005–14.

Legislature: Elected to Assembly in December 2013 special election. Reelected since 2014. Committee assignments, 2017: Veterans and Military Affairs (chair); Consumer Protection; Health; Local Government; Natural Resources and Sporting Heritage; Small Business Development; Transportation.

Contact: Rep.Skowronski@legis.wisconsin.gov; 608-266-8590; 888-534-0082 (toll free); 414-425-2034 (district); Room 209 North, State Capitol, PO Box 8953, Madison, WI 53708.

Chuck Wichgers, Assembly District 83
Republican

Biography: Born Milwaukee, Wisconsin, July 4, 1965; married to wife Michelle (Hocking) Wichgers from Big Bend, Wisconsin; 8 children. Voting address: Muskego, Wisconsin. ▪ Graduate Muskego High School, 1983; Waukesha County Technical College, 1984–85. ▪ Medical sales offering conservative options for pain management. Coach for softball, basketball, football. Volunteer, along with wife and children, assisting nursing home residents to get to weekly religious services. Education curriculum watchdog. Former occupations in sales and marketing, and in entrepreneurship and management. ▪ Member: Various pro-life groups across Wisconsin; church committees and organizations. ▪ Former Member: Muskego Hoops Booster Club (cofounder); Moose Club; Preserve Muskego (president); Janesville Road Reconstruction Advisory Committee. ▪ City of Muskego alderman, 1999–2002; Waukesha County supervisor, 1999–2002.

Legislature: Elected to Assembly 2016. Committee assignments, 2017: Constitution and Ethics; Education; Environment and Forestry; Government Accountability and Oversight; Health; Jobs and the Economy.

Contact: Rep.Wichgers@legis.wisconsin.gov; 608-266-3363; 888-534-0083 (toll free); 414-507-3140 (district); Room 121 West, State Capitol, PO Box 8953, Madison, WI 53708.

Michael Kuglitsch, Assembly District 84
Republican

Biography: Born Milwaukee, Wisconsin, February 3, 1960; married; 4 children. Voting address: New Berlin, Wisconsin. ▪ Graduate New Berlin West High School, 1978; B.A. in Business, University of Wisconsin-Whitewater, 1983. ▪ Business consultant. ▪ Former member: Wisconsin Restaurant Association (president); Wisconsin Bowling Centers Association (president); New Berlin Chamber of Commerce (president).

Legislature: Elected to Assembly since 2010. Committee assignments, 2017: Energy and Utilities (chair); Labor (vice chair); Government Accountability and Oversight; Rules; Rural Development and Mining; Joint Survey Committee on Retirement Systems.

Contact: Rep.Kuglitsch@legis.wisconsin.gov; 608-267-5158; 888-534-0084 (toll free); Room 129 West, State Capitol, PO Box 8952, Madison, WI 53708.

Senate District 29
Assembly Districts 85, 86, 87

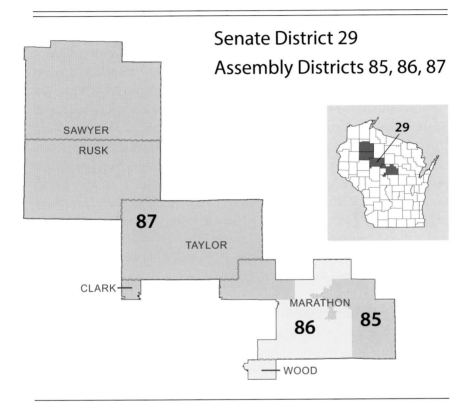

Jerry Petrowski, Senate District 29
Republican

Biography: Born Wausau, Wisconsin, June 16, 1950; married; 4 children, 3 grandchildren. Voting address: Marathon, Wisconsin. ▪ Graduate Newman High School (Wausau); attended University of Wisconsin-Marathon County and Northcentral Technical College. ▪ Former ginseng, dairy, and beef farmer. Served in Army Reserve, 1968–74. ▪ Member: Seventh Congressional District, Marathon, Wood, Taylor, Rusk, Sawyer, Price, Lincoln, Portage, and Shawano County Republican Parties;

Farm Bureau; National Rifle Association; Friends of Rib Mountain; Wausau Elks; Marathon Lions. ▪ Former member: Wisconsin Rifle and Pistol Association; International Brotherhood of Electrical Workers Local #1791; Childcare Connection Board; Department of Transportation Law Enforcement Advisory Council; Marathon County Hunger Coalition. ▪ Recipient: American Heart Association *Legislator of the Year Award* 2016, 2014; End Domestic Abuse Wisconsin *Legislative Leader Award* 2014; Wisconsin VFW *Legislator of the Year Award* 2014; Wisconsin American Legion *Legislator of the Year Award* 2014; Wisconsin Vietnam Veterans *Legislator of the Year Award* 2002; Wisconsin Department of Veterans Affairs *Certificate of Commendation* 2005; Wisconsin Towns Association *Friend of Wisconsin Towns Award* 2016, 2014, 2011; Wisconsin Counties Association *Outstanding Legislator Award* 2014; Wisconsin Urban and Rural Transit Association *Legislative Statesman of the Year* 2014; Wisconsin Professional Police Association *Legislator of the Year Award* 2014; Wisconsin Troopers Association *Legislator of the Year Award* 2014, 2003; Center for Driver's License Recovery and Employability *Legislative Champion Award* 2014; State Bar of Wisconsin *Scales of Justice Award* 2014; Wisconsin Dental Association *Champion Award* 2013 & *Award of Honor (Mission of Mercy)* 2011; Wisconsin Academy of Family Physicians *Friend of Family Medicine Award* 2016, 2014; American Academy of Pediatrics *Childhood Legislative Advocate of the Year* 2005; Wisconsin Council on Physical Disabilities *Appreciation Award* 2014; Wisconsin Public Health Association *Friend of Public Health* 2016; Wisconsin Electric Cooperatives Association *Enlightened Legislator of the Year Award* 2013; Wisconsin Farm Bureau *Friend of Agriculture Award* 2006, 2004; Wisconsin Dairy Business Association Award 2014, 2012, 2010, 2008; Wisconsin Grocers Association *Friend of the Grocers Award* 2016, 2014, 2012, 2008, 2006; Wisconsin Pork Association *Distinguished Public Service Award* 2016; WMC *Working for Wisconsin Award* 2016, 2014, 2012, 2002, 2000; MMAC *Champion of Commerce Award* 2016, 2014; Wisconsin Builders Association *Friend of Housing Award* 2016, 2013, 2006; Associated Builders and Contractors of Wisconsin *Building Wisconsin Award* 2014; State Farm Insurance *Golden Car Seat Award* 2007; Chiropractic Society of Wisconsin *Legislator of the Year Award* 2014; Allied Health Chiropractic Centers *Commitment and Dedication to the Chiropractic Profession Award* 2004; 3M *Award of Appreciation* 2001; Wisconsin Paper Council *Champion of Paper Award* 2007; Wisconsin Technical College System *Legislator of the Year* 2016; Wisconsin Technical College District Boards Association *Legislator of the Year* 2016; UWSP Paper Science

Foundation *Friends of the Foundation Award* 2005; The American Conservative Union *Defender of Liberty Award* 2013; Wisconsin Ginseng Board *Assistance to the Wisconsin Ginseng Industry Award* 2005; Wisconsin Bear Hunters Association *Hero Award* 2014, 2012.

Legislature: Elected to Assembly 1998–2010. Elected to Senate in June 2012 special election. Reelected 2014. Leadership positions: Majority Caucus Sergeant at Arms 2003–07. Committee assignments, 2017: Transportation and Veterans Affairs (chair); Economic Development, Commerce and Local Government (vice chair); Agriculture, Small Business, and Tourism; Joint Legislative Council. Additional appointments, 2017: Building Commission; Transportation Projects Commission; Council on Highway Safety.

Contact: Sen.Petrowski@legis.wisconsin.gov; 608-266-2502; Room 123 South, State Capitol, PO Box 7882, Madison, WI 53707-7882.

Patrick Snyder, Assembly District 85
Republican

Biography: Born Boone, Iowa, October 10, 1956; married to Shawn for 36 years; 2 children, Amy (spouse Chris) Heitman and Dan (spouse Becky) Snyder. Voting address: Schofield, Wisconsin. ▪ Graduate Oelwein Community High School (Iowa), 1974; Degree in Communications, University of Iowa, 1974–78. ▪ Former congressional staffer for Congressman Sean Duffy (2.5 years); Radio host for WSAU (12 years). ▪ Member: Wausau Noon Rotary; ELKS Club; United Way's Hunger Coalition and Housing and Homelessness Committee; Marathon County Health Department's Alcohol and Other Drugs (AODA) Committee; Marathon County Department of Social Services' Administrative Review Panel. ▪ Former member: St. Therese Parish Council. ▪ Former alder for the City of Schofield.

Legislature: Elected to Assembly 2016. Committee assignments, 2017: Aging and Long-Term Care; Campaigns and Elections; Children and Families; Jobs and the Economy; Mental Health; Urban Revitalization; Workforce Development.

Contact: Rep.Snyder@legis.wisconsin.gov; 608-266-0654; 888-534-0085 (toll free); 715-359-4981 (district); Room 9 West, State Capitol, PO Box 8953, Madison, WI 53708.

John Spiros, Assembly District 86
Republican

Biography: Born Akron, Ohio, July 28, 1961; married; 5 children (1 son-in-law), 3 grandchildren. Voting address: Marshfield, Wisconsin. ▪ Graduate Marietta High School (Marietta, Ohio), 1979; A.A.S. in Criminal Justice, MTCC (Omaha, Nebraska), 1985. ▪ Vice president, safety and claims management for a transport company. Served in U.S. Air Force, 1979–85. ▪ Member: Trucking Industry Defense Association (board president 2015–17; executive committee 2013–17); Wisconsin Farm Bureau; Marshfield Elks Club. ▪ Former member: Marshfield Rotary Club. ▪ City of Marshfield alderman, 2005–13.

Legislature: Elected to Assembly since 2012. Committee assignments, 2017: Criminal Justice and Public Safety (chair); Transportation (vice chair); Labor; Mental Health; Joint Legislative Council.

Contact: Rep.Spiros@legis.wisconsin.gov; 608-266-1182; 888-534-0086 (toll free); Room 15 North, State Capitol, PO Box 8953, Madison, WI 53708.

James W. Edming, Assembly District 87
Republican

Biography: Born Ladysmith, Wisconsin, November 22, 1945; married; 3 sons, 2 granddaughters, 1 great granddaughter. Voting address: Glen Flora, Wisconsin. ▪ Graduate Flambeau High School (Tony), 1964; Teacher's Certificate Taylor County Teacher's College, 1967; attended University of Wisconsin-Superior, University of Wisconsin-Eau Claire, University of Wisconsin-Menomonie, University of Wisconsin-Barron County. ▪ Convenience store owner, metal stamping company owner, farmer. Former frozen pizza manufacturer. ▪ Member: 3rd degree Master Mason; 32nd degree Scottish Rite; Shriner; NRA (gun instructor); Model T Ford Club. Rusk County Hospital Board, 1980–82, 2010–present. ▪ Rusk County Board of Supervisors, 1976–87.

Legislature: Elected to Assembly since 2014. Committee assignments, 2017: Small Business Development (vice chair); Agriculture; Environment and Forestry; Health; Natural Resources and Sporting Heritage; Veterans and Military Affairs.

Contact: Rep.Edming@legis.wisconsin.gov; 608-266-7506; 888-534-0087 (toll free); 715-475-9292 (district); Room 109 West, State Capitol, PO Box 8952, Madison, WI 53708.

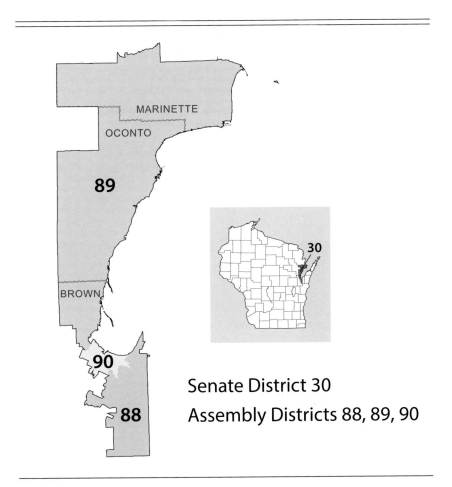

Senate District 30
Assembly Districts 88, 89, 90

Dave Hansen, Senate District 30
Democrat

Biography: Born Green Bay, Wisconsin, December 18, 1947; married; 3 children, 11 grandchildren. Voting address: Green Bay, Wisconsin. ▪ Graduate Green Bay West High School; B.S. University of Wisconsin-Green Bay, 1971. ▪ Full-time legislator. Former teacher. Former truck driver for Green Bay Department of Public Works. Former Teamster's

Union steward. ▪ Former member: Brown County Human Services Board (chair); N.E.W. Zoo Advisory Board; Brown County Education and Recreation Committee (chair); Great Lakes Compact Commission. ▪ Brown County Board supervisor, 1996–2002.

Legislature: Elected to Senate since 2000. Leadership positions: Assistant Minority Leader 2015, 2013, 2011, 2005, 2003; Majority Leader 2009 (effective 12/15/10); Assistant Majority Leader 2011 (effective 7/24/12), 2009, 2007. Committee assignments, 2017: Natural Resources and Energy; Transportation and Veterans Affairs; Universities and Technical Colleges. Additional appointments, 2017: Transportation Projects Commission.

Contact: Sen.Hansen@legis.wisconsin.gov; 608-266-5670; 866-221-9395 (toll free); 920-391-2000 (district); Room 106 South, State Capitol, PO Box 7882, Madison, WI 53707-7882.

John J. Macco, Assembly District 88
Republican

Biography: Born Green Bay, Wisconsin, September 23, 1958; married; 2 children; 4 grandchildren. Voting address: De Pere, Wisconsin. ▪ Graduate Green Bay Southwest High School, 1976; attended NWTC and University of Wisconsin-Green Bay. ▪ Founder of regional financial planning group. Founder of regional retail franchise. Business consultant. ▪ Member: National Rifle Association; Experimental Aircraft Association. ▪ Former board member: American Cancer Society of Wood County; Old Main Street Marshfield; Old Main Street De Pere; Old Main Street Green Bay; U.S. Ski Patrol; Aircraft Owners and Pilots Association. Former Deacon and Church Elder at Central Church, Green Bay.

Legislature: Elected to Assembly since 2014. Committee assignments, 2017: Ways and Means (chair); Joint Legislative Audit Committee (co-vice chair); Aging and Long-Term Care; Consumer Protection; Jobs and the Economy; Regulatory Licensing Reform; Transportation.

Contact: Rep.Macco@legis.wisconsin.gov; 608-266-0485; 888-534-0088 (toll free); Room 308 North, State Capitol, PO Box 8953, Madison, WI 53708.

John Nygren, Assembly District 89
Republican

Biography: Born Marinette, Wisconsin, February 27, 1964; married; 3 children. Voting address: Marinette, Wisconsin. ▪ Graduate Marinette High School, 1982; attended University of Wisconsin-Marinette. ▪ Insurance and financial representative. Former restaurant owner and operator. ▪ Member: Jaycees (lifetime member, former chapter, state, U.S. president); Marinette Elks Club; Marinette Moose Lodge; Marinette Kiwanis (former president); Marinette County Republican Party (former chair). ▪ City of Marinette Recreation and Planning Board, 2003–06.

Legislature: Elected to Assembly since 2006. Committee assignments, 2017: Joint Committee on Finance (cochair); Joint Committee on Employment Relations; Joint Legislative Audit Committee; Joint Legislative Council.

Contact: Rep.Nygren@legis.wisconsin.gov; 608-266-2343; 888-534-0089 (toll free); Room 309 East, State Capitol, PO Box 8953, Madison, WI 53708.

Eric Genrich, Assembly District 90
Democrat

Biography: Born Green Bay, Wisconsin, 1979; married; 2 children. Voting address: Green Bay, Wisconsin. ▪ Graduate Notre Dame Academy, 1998; B.A. University of Wisconsin-Madison, 2002; MLIS University of Wisconsin-Milwaukee, 2010. ▪ Full-time legislator. Former librarian and legislative aide. ▪ Member: Emerging Leaders Society of the Brown County United Way; Brown County Historical Society; Democratic Party of Brown County; AFSCME Local 1901B; Current Young Professionals Network; Green Bay Economic Development Authority; Wisconsin Public Utility Institute (board of directors); Council of State Governments Midwest Legislative Conference Education Committee (vice chair) and Executive Committee.

Legislature: Elected to Assembly since 2012. Committee assignments, 2017:

Education; Energy and Utilities; Insurance; Regulatory Licensing Reform; Science and Technology.

Contact: Rep.Genrich@legis.wisconsin.gov; 608-266-0616; 888-534-0090 (toll free); 920-593-8528 (district); Room 320 West, State Capitol, PO Box 8952, Madison, WI 53708.

Senate District 31
Assembly Districts 91, 92, 93

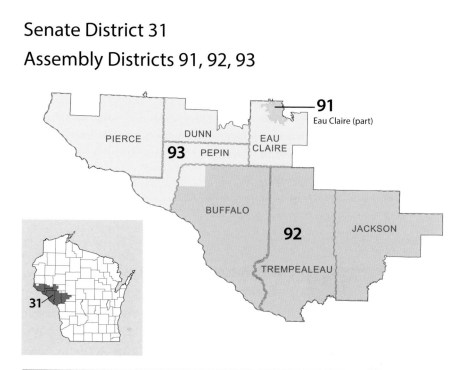

Kathleen Vinehout, Senate District 31
Democrat

Biography: Born June 16, 1958; married; 1 child. Voting address: Alma, Wisconsin. ▪ B.S. with honors in Education, Southern Illinois University, 1980; M.P.H. St. Louis University, 1982; Ph.D. St. Louis University, 1987; A.D. in Agriculture. ▪ Organic farmer. Former dairy farmer, university professor, health care manager. ▪ Member: Wisconsin Farmers Union; Wisconsin Farm Bureau Federation (former board member, Buffalo County); Alma Chamber of Commerce; Democratic Party of Buffalo County (former chair);

Andrew Blackfoot American Legion Auxiliary Post 129. ▪ Former member: Buffalo County Agricultural Fair Association (board member); American Federation of Teachers (treasurer, Local 4100). ▪ Recipient: Sierra Club *Environmental Champion* 2014; Wisconsin Public Health Association *Friend of Public Health* 2014; Wisconsin Farmers Union *Friend of Farmers Union Award* 2013; Wisconsin Congress of Parents and Teachers *Joan Dykstra Friends of Children Award* 2012; Wisconsin Aquaculture Association *Friend of Wisconsin Aquaculture* 2011; La Crosse Area Development Council *Triangle of Achievement*; AFSCME Council 40 *Protector of Quality Services Award* 2010; School Administrators Alliance *Legislator of the Year* 2010; Wisconsin Academy of Family Physicians *Friend of Family Medicine*; Wisconsin Grocers Association *Friend of Grocers* 2010; Wisconsin Crop Production Association *Outstanding Service to Agriculture Award*; Wisconsin Association of County Homes *Outstanding Legislative Service Award* 2010; Wisconsin Troopers Association *Legislator of the Year* 2010; Wisconsin League of Conservation Voters *Conservation Champion* 2014, 2010, 2008; Wisconsin Association of PEG Channels *Friend of Access* 2008; Wisconsin Association of FFA *Honorary State FFA Degree* 2008; Pharmacy Society of Wisconsin *Legislator of the Year* 2008; Wisconsin Federation of Cooperatives *Friend of Cooperatives* 2008. ▪ Mississippi River Regional Planning Commission, 2004–11.

Legislature: Elected to Senate since 2006. Leadership positions: Minority Caucus Vice Chair 2015, 2013, 2011; Majority Caucus Vice Chair 2009. Committee assignments, 2017: Agriculture, Small Business and Tourism; Financial Services, Constitution and Federalism; Public Benefits, Licensing and State-Federal Relations; Revenue, Financial Institutions and Rural Issues; Joint Committee on Information Policy and Technology; Joint Legislative Audit Committee.

Contact: Sen.Vinehout@legis.wisconsin.gov; 608-266-8546; 877-763-6636 (toll free); Room 108 South, State Capitol, PO Box 7882, Madison, WI 53707-7882.

Dana Wachs, Assembly District 91
Democrat

Biography: Born Eau Claire, Wisconsin, August 25, 1957; married; 3 children. Voting address: Eau Claire, Wisconsin. ▪ Graduate Memorial High School (Eau Claire), 1975; attended University of Wisconsin-Eau Claire 1975–76; B.S. Marquette University, 1981; J.D. Valparaiso University, 1985. ▪ Attorney (Martindale-Hubbell AV Rated; National Trial Lawyers

Top 100). ▪ Member: American Bar Association; Wisconsin State Bar; Eau Claire County Bar Association; Wisconsin Association of Justice; Chippewa Valley Astronomical Association; Wisconsin Farmers Union; Muskies, Inc. ▪ Eau Claire City Council, 2009–12 (Eau Claire City-County Board of Health, Eau Claire Transit Commission, Eau Claire Affirmative Action Committee, Eau Claire Parks and Waterways Committee, L.E. Phillips Memorial Library Board, Eau Claire Economic Policy Advisory Committee).

Legislature: Elected to Assembly since 2012. Committee assignments, 2017: Colleges and Universities; Constitution and Ethics; Judiciary; Transportation. Additional appointments, 2017: Building Commission.

Contact: Rep.Wachs@legis.wisconsin.gov; 608-266-7461; 888-534-0091 (toll free); Room 107 North, State Capitol, PO Box 8953, Madison, WI 53708.

Treig E. Pronschinske, Assembly District 92
Republican

Biography: Born Eau Claire, Wisconsin, July 7, 1978; married; 1 child. Voting address: Mondovi, Wisconsin. ▪ Graduate Memorial High School, 1996; degree in Construction Management, Chippewa Valley Technical College, 1997. ▪ Small business owner; general construction contractor. ▪ Member: Mondovi Fire Department (volunteer firefighter); Mondovi Ambulance Commission; Gilmanton Community Club; Junior Achievement volunteer. ▪ Former  member: Mondovi Youth Baseball Association (president); Big Brothers, Big Sisters. ▪ Mayor of Mondovi, 2014–present.

Legislature: Elected to Assembly 2016. Committee assignments, 2017: Children and Families; Environment and Forestry; Housing and Real Estate; Rural Development and Mining.

Contact: Rep.Pronschinske@legis.wisconsin.gov; 608-266-7015; 888-534-0092 (toll free); Room 18 West, State Capitol, PO Box 8953, Madison, WI 53708.

Warren Petryk, Assembly District 93
Republican

Biography: Born Eau Claire, Wisconsin, January 24, 1955; single. Voting address: Eleva, Wisconsin. ▪ Eagle Scout, November 1969; Badger Boys State 1972; Graduate and Valedictorian, Boyceville High School, 1973; attended University of Wisconsin-Stout; earned B.A. with highest honors University of Wisconsin-Eau Claire, 1978. ▪ Worked 15 years in community relations for United Cerebral Palsy of West Central Wisconsin; cofounder of musical entertainment group "The Memories" (started 1972). ▪ Member: Eau Claire, Menomonie, Ellsworth, and Prescott Chambers of Commerce; National Rifle Association; Eau Galle-Rush River, Ellsworth, Durand, Rock Falls, and Arkansaw Sportsmen's Clubs; Wisconsin Farm Bureau; Cleghorn Lions Club; Chippewa Valley Council of Boy Scouts of America (board of directors). ▪ Recipient: Wisconsin Veterans of Foreign Wars *Legislator of the Year* 2013; Wisconsin AMVETS *Veteran's Advocate of the Year* 2014; Wisconsin Electrical Cooperatives Association *Most Enlightened Legislator* 2016; Wisconsin School Nutritionists Association *Legislator of the Year* 2016; Wisconsin Manufacturers and Commerce *Working for Wisconsin Award* (every term); *Dairy Business Association Award* (every term).

Legislature: Elected to Assembly since 2010. Committee assignments, 2017: Workforce Development (chair); Aging and Long-Term Care (vice chair); Colleges and Universities; Energy and Utilities; Financial Institutions; Insurance; Veterans and Military Affairs; Legislative Council Study Committee on Rural Broadband. Additional appointments, 2017: Governor's Council on Workforce Investment (since 2012).

Contact: Rep.Petryk@legis.wisconsin.gov; 608-266-0660; 888-534-0093 (toll free); Room 103 West, State Capitol, PO Box 8953, Madison, WI 53708.

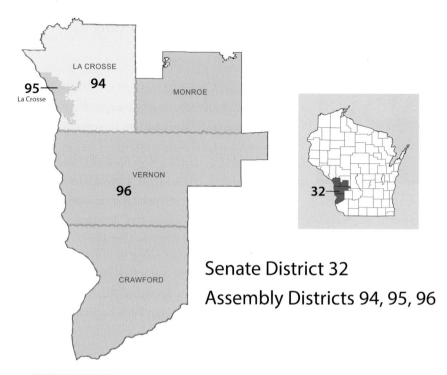

Senate District 32
Assembly Districts 94, 95, 96

Jennifer Shilling, Senate District 32
Democrat

Biography: Born Oshkosh, Wisconsin, July 4; married; 2 children. Voting address: La Crosse, Wisconsin. ▪ Graduate Buffalo Grove High School (Illinois); B.A. in Political Science and Public Administration, University of Wisconsin-La Crosse, 1992. ▪ Former congressional aide and legislative aide. ▪ Member: University of Wisconsin-La Crosse Alumni Association (former president); La Crosse County League of Women Voters; La Crosse County Democratic Party (former chair); University of Wisconsin-La Crosse Chancellor's Community Council; Viterbo University Board of Advisors; La Crosse Area Chamber of Commerce; La Crosse County Local Emergency Planning Committee; La Crosse Area Habitat for Humanity Women Build; Vernon Women's Alliance; Viroqua Chamber Main Street; Riverfront La Crosse Community Advisory Board. ▪ La Crosse County Board, 1990–92.

Legislature: Elected to Assembly 2000–10. Elected to Senate in August 2011 special election. Reelected since 2012. Leadership positions: Minority Leader

2017, 2015; Minority Caucus Sergeant at Arms 2005. Committee assignments, 2017: Senate Organization; Joint Committee on Employment Relations; Joint Committee on Legislative Organization; Joint Legislative Council. Additional appointments, 2017: Disability Board.

Contact: Sen.Shilling@legis.wisconsin.gov; 608-266-5490; 800-385-3385 (toll free); Room 206 South, State Capitol, PO Box 7882, Madison, WI 53707-7882.

Steve Doyle, Assembly District 94
Democrat

Biography: Born La Crosse, Wisconsin, May 21, 1958; married; 2 children. Voting address: Onalaska, Wisconsin. ▪ Graduate Aquinas High School, 1976; B.A. University of Wisconsin-La Crosse, 1980; J.D. University of Wisconsin Law School, 1986. ▪ Attorney. Former instructor, University of Wisconsin-La Crosse. ▪ Former member: Family Resource Center (board member); Family and Children's Center (board member); Coulee Region Humane Society (board member, president). ▪ La Crosse County Board, 1986–present (chair, 2002–11).

Legislature: Elected to Assembly in May 2011 special election. Reelected since 2012. Leadership positions: Minority Caucus Vice Chair 2017. Committee assignments, 2017: Federalism and Interstate Relations; Financial Institutions; Insurance; Rules; State Affairs; Ways and Means.

Contact: Rep.Doyle@legis.wisconsin.gov; 608-266-0631; 888-534-0094 (toll free); 608-783-1204 (district); 608-784-7299 (district); Room 124 North, State Capitol, PO Box 8952, Madison, WI 53708.

Jill Billings, Assembly District 95
Democrat

Biography: Born Rochester, Minnesota, January 19, 1962; 2 children. Voting address: La Crosse, Wisconsin. ▪ Graduate Stewartville High School, 1980; B.A. Augsburg College, Minneapolis, Minnesota, 1989. Council of State Governments: BILLD Fellow, 2012, Toll Fellow, 2014. ▪ Full-time legislator. Former teacher of English and Citizenship to Hmong adults.

■ Member: Wisconsin Legislative Children's Caucus (cochair); Wisconsin Family Impact Seminar Advisors Committee; Viterbo University Board of Advisors; University of Wisconsin-La Crosse Chancellor's Community Council; La Crosse County League of Women Voters; La Crosse Area Chamber of Commerce; La Crosse Health Families Advisory Committee; Preservation Alliance of La Crosse. ■ La Crosse County Board, 2004–12.

Legislature: Elected to the Assembly in November 2011 special election. Reelected since 2012. Committee assignments, 2017: Children and Families; Colleges and Universities; Small Business Development; Tourism; Transportation; Workforce Development; Legislative Council Study Committee on Reducing Recidivism and Removing Impediments to Ex-Offender Employment. Additional appointments, 2017: Child Abuse and Neglect Prevention Board; State Council on Alcohol and Other Drug Abuse; Governor's Task Force on Opioid Abuse; Mississippi River Parkway Commission.

Contact: Rep.Billings@legis.wisconsin.gov; 608-266-5780; 888-534-0095 (toll free); Room 307 West, State Capitol, PO Box 8952, Madison, WI 53708.

Lee Nerison, Assembly District 96
Republican

Biography: Born La Crosse, Wisconsin, July 31, 1952; married; 3 children, 5 grandchildren. Voting address: Westby, Wisconsin. ■ Graduate Viroqua High School, 1970; University of Wisconsin-Madison Farm and Industry Short Course, 1971. ■ Farmer. Former dairy farmer. ■ Member: Coon Valley Lions. ■ Former member: Vernon Co-op Oil and Gas (board member, secretary); Viroqua FFA Alumni (reporter); Westby FFA Alumni; Church Council (vice president, treasurer). ■ Vernon County Board, 1998–2006 (chair 2002–06).

Legislature: Elected to Assembly since 2004. Committee assignments, 2017: Agriculture (chair); Consumer Protection; Natural Resources and Sporting Heritage; Veterans and Military Affairs.

Contact: Rep.Nerison@legis.wisconsin.gov; 608-266-3534; 888-534-0096 (toll free); 608-634-4562 (district); Room 310 North, State Capitol, PO Box 8953, Madison, WI 53708.

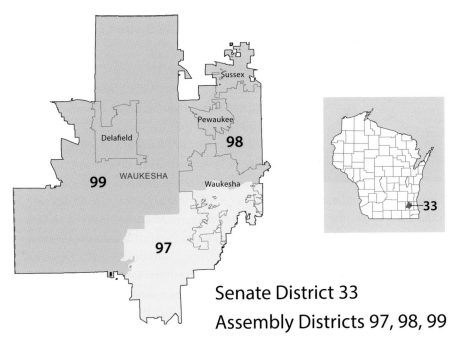

Senate District 33
Assembly Districts 97, 98, 99

Chris Kapenga, Senate District 33

Republican

Biography: Born Zeeland, Michigan, February 19, 1972; married; 2 children. Voting address: Delafield, Wisconsin. ▪ Graduate Holland Christian (Holland, Michigan), 1990; B.S. in Accountancy, Calvin College (Grand Rapids, Michigan), 1994. ▪ Business owner. Certified public accountant. ▪ Member: Assembly of State Legislatures (copresident); NFIB; Elmbrook Church Financial Counseling (director). ▪ Former member: WSCA School Board (vice chair, treasurer, secretary); WICPA; MMAC; Institute of Management Accountants (board member).

Legislature: Elected to Assembly 2010–14. Elected to Senate in July 2015 special election. Committee assignments, 2017: Public Benefits, Licensing and State-Federal Relations (chair); Elections and Utilities (vice chair); Government Operations, Technology and Consumer Protection; Joint Legislative Audit Committee.

Contact: Sen.Kapenga@legis.wisconsin.gov; 608-266-9174; 800-863-8883 (toll free); Room 15 South, State Capitol, PO Box 7882, Madison, WI 53707-7882.

Scott Allen, Assembly District 97
Republican

Biography: Born Racine, Wisconsin, December 18, 1965; married; 2 children. Voting address: Waukesha, Wisconsin. ▪ Graduate Kettle Moraine High School, 1984; attended University of Wisconsin-Oshkosh, University of Wisconsin-Waukesha; B.A. University of Wisconsin-Milwaukee, 1989; Master of Public Administration and Master of Planning, University of Southern California, 1992. ▪ Sales and leadership coach. Former sales director, home builder, and risk management analyst. Served in U.S. Army Reserve, 1984–90. ▪ Member: Republican Party of Waukesha County; Spring Creek Church. ▪ Former member: Greater Milwaukee Association of Realtors (former board member); Wisconsin Realtors Association; National Association of Realtors; Waukesha Civic Theatre (president). ▪ Waukesha County Community Development Block Grant Board, 2010–14. Alderman, City of Waukesha, 1998–2001.

Legislature: Elected to Assembly since 2014. Committee assignments, 2017: Constitution and Ethics (chair); Housing and Real Estate (vice chair); Financial Institutions; Science and Technology; Small Business Development; Veterans and Military Affairs; Workforce Development. Additional appointments, 2017: Wisconsin Housing and Economic Development Authority Board.

Contact: Rep.Allen@legis.wisconsin.gov; 608-266-8580; 888-534-0097 (toll free); Room 8 West, State Capitol, PO Box 8952, Madison, WI 53708.

Adam Neylon, Assembly District 98
Republican

Biography: Born Elgin, Illinois, December 30, 1984; married; 1 child. Voting address: Pewaukee, Wisconsin. ▪ Graduate H.D. Jacobs High School, 2003; B.A. Carroll University, 2008. ▪ Small business owner. Former legislative staffer for U.S. Representative Jim Sensenbrenner and Republican leadership in the Wisconsin Assembly. Council of State Governments 2014 Bowhay Institute for Legislative Leadership Development (BILLD) Fellow. ▪ Member: 100th Anniversary Capitol Commemorative Commission; President's Advisory Council at Carroll University; Republican Party of Waukesha

County (former youth chair); National Rifle Association. ■ Recipient: American Conservative Union *Conservative Achievement Award* 2015–16, 2013–14; Milwaukee Metropolitan Association of Commerce *Champion of Commerce Award* 2015–16, 2013–14; Wisconsin Dairy Business Association *Legislative Excellence Award* 2015; Wisconsin Manufacturers and Commerce Working for Wisconsin Award 2015–16, 2013–14; Wisconsin Family Action *Friend of Family, Life & Liberty Award* 2015–16.

Legislature: Elected to Assembly in April 2013 special election. Reelected since 2014. Committee assignments, 2017: Jobs and the Economy (chair); Energy and Utilities; Science and Technology; Joint Committee for Review of Administrative Rules. Additional appointments, 2017: Small Business Regulatory Review Board (cochair).

Contact: Rep.Neylon@legis.wisconsin.gov; 608-266-5120; 888-534-0098 (toll free); Room 125 West, State Capitol, PO Box 8953, Madison, WI 53708.

Cindi S. Duchow, Assembly District 99
Republican

Biography: Born Waukesha, Wisconsin; married; 2 children. Voting address: Pewaukee, Wisconsin. ■ Graduate Catholic Memorial High School, 1977; B.S. University of Wisconsin-Madison, 1981. ■ Former manager and fashion specialist for national retailers. ■ Member: St. Anthony's Church; Republican Party of Waukesha County, Leadership Circle; Volunteer Service Club of Pewaukee Lake (former president); Pewaukee Yacht Club. ■ Former member: Waukesha Youth Hockey Association board. ■ Town of Delafield supervisor, 2013–16.

Legislature: Elected to Assembly in September 2015 special election. Reelected in 2016. Committee assignments, 2017: Consumer Protection (chair); Family Law (vice chair); Insurance (vice chair); Education; Local Government; Small Business Development.

Contact: Rep.Duchow@legis.wisconsin.gov; 608-266-3007; 888-534-0099 (toll free); Room 304 North, State Capitol, PO Box 8952, Madison, WI 53708.

Chief Clerks and Sergeants at Arms

Jeffrey Renk, Senate Chief Clerk

Biography: Born Wauwatosa, Wisconsin, January 31, 1960; married; 1 child. Voting address: Fitchburg, Wisconsin. ▪ Graduate Wauwatosa West High School, 1978; attended University of Wisconsin-Milwaukee, 1978–80; B.A. in Political Science, University of Wisconsin-Madison, 1984. ▪ Former Senate Assistant Chief Clerk, 2004–12; computer programmer, Legislative Technology Services Bureau, 1998–2004; Assembly chief clerk staff, 1988–98; Assembly messenger, 1983–88. Member: American Society of Legislative Clerks and Secretaries. Former member: National Association of Legislative Information Technology.

Current office: Elected Senate Chief Clerk 2013. Reelected since 2015.

Contact: 608-266-2517; Room B20 Southeast, State Capitol, PO Box 7882, Madison, WI 53707-7882.

Edward (Ted) A. Blazel, Senate Sergeant at Arms

Biography: Born Quincy, Illinois, June 14, 1972; married; 2 children. Voting address: Madison, Wisconsin. ▪ Graduate Quincy Senior High School, 1990; B.A. St. Norbert College (De Pere), 1994; M.A. Marquette University, 1998. ▪ Member: National Legislative Service and Security Association; Madison Area Youth Soccer Association (board member).

Current office: Elected Senate Sergeant at Arms 2003. Reelected since 2005.

Contact: 608-266-1801; Room B35 South, State Capitol, PO Box 7882, Madison, WI 53707-7882.

Patrick E. Fuller, Assembly Chief Clerk

Biography: Born Toledo, Ohio, February 24, 1954; married; 1 child. Voting address: Ridgeway, Wisconsin. ▪ Graduate St. Francis de Sales High School (Toledo), 1972; B.E. University of Toledo, 1980; M.B.A. Touro University International (Los Alamitos, CA), 2001. ▪ Former director, Wisconsin Troops to Teachers Program, Wisconsin Department of Veterans Affairs, 1998–2000. Vietnam Era and Operation Desert Storm veteran. Served in U.S. Marine Corps, 1972–86; U.S. Army, 1986–97. Member: NRA; Second Marine Division Association; Veterans of Foreign Wars; Disabled Veterans of America; American Legion; Force Recon Association; 75th Ranger Regiment Association.

Current office: Elected Assembly Chief Clerk 2003. Reelected since 2005.

Contact: Patrick.Fuller@legis.wisconsin.gov; 608-266-1501; Suite 401, Risser Justice Center, 17 West Main Street, Madison, WI 53703.

Anne Tonnon Byers, Assembly Sergeant at Arms

Biography: Born Green Bay, Wisconsin, December 14, 1968; married; 2 children. Voting address: McFarland, Wisconsin. ▪ Graduate Green Bay East High School, 1987; attended University of Wisconsin-Green Bay; B.S. University of Wisconsin-Madison, 1991; University of Wisconsin Certified Public Management Program, 2001. ▪ Former Assembly Assistant Sergeant at Arms, 1998–2010; office manager for Assembly Sergeant, 1993–98. Member: Boy Scout Troop 53.

Current office: Elected Assembly Sergeant at Arms 2011. Reelected since 2013.

Contact: Anne.TonnonByers@legis.wisconsin.gov; 608-266-1503; Room 411 West, State Capitol, PO Box 8952, Madison, WI 53708-8952.

▪ ▪ ▪

2

UNITS OF STATE GOVERNMENT

THE LEGISLATURE

Officers of the Senate

President: Roger Roth
President pro tempore: Howard Marklein

Majority leader: Scott L. Fitzgerald
Assistant majority leader: Leah Vukmir
Majority caucus chair: Sheila E. Harsdorf
Majority caucus vice chair: Van Wanggaard

Minority leader: Jennifer Shilling
Assistant minority leader: Janet Bewley
Minority caucus chair: Mark Miller
Minority caucus vice chair: Janis Ringhand

Chief clerk: Jeffrey Renk
Location: B20 South East, State Capitol
Contact: 608-266-2517; PO Box 7882, Madison, WI 53707-7882

Sergeant at arms: Edward A. Blazel
Location: B35 South, State Capitol
Contact: 608-266-1801; PO Box 7882, Madison, WI 53707-7882

Officers of the Assembly

Speaker: Robin J. Vos
Speaker pro tempore: Tyler August

Majority leader: Jim Steineke
Assistant majority leader: Robert Brooks
Majority caucus chair: Dan Knodl
Majority caucus vice chair: Romaine Quinn
Majority caucus secretary: Jessie Rodriguez
Majority caucus sergeant at arms: Samantha Kerkman

Minority leader: Peter W. Barca
Assistant minority leader: Dianne Hesselbein
Minority caucus chair: Mark Spreitzer
Minority caucus vice chair: Steve Doyle

Minority caucus secretary: Beth Meyers
Minority caucus sergeant at arms: Christine Sinicki

Chief clerk: Patrick E. Fuller
Location: 17 West Main Street (on the Capitol Square), Suite 401
Contact: 608-266-1501; PO Box 8952, Madison, WI 53708-8952

Sergeant at arms: Anne Tonnon Byers
Location: 411 West, State Capitol
Contact: 608-266-1503; PO Box 8952, Madison, WI 53708-8952

Legislative hotline: 608-266-9960; 800-362-9472
Website: http://legis.wisconsin.gov
Number of employees: 188 (senate, includes the 33 senators); 330 (assembly, includes the 99 representatives)
Total budget 2015–17: $152,372,200 (includes the legislative service agencies)

Overview

Wisconsin's legislature makes the laws of the state. The legislature also controls the state's purse strings: no money can be paid out of the treasury unless the legislature enacts a law that specifically appropriates it. At the same time, the legislature is required to raise revenues sufficient to pay for the state's expenditures, and it is required to audit the state's accounts. The legislature can remove any elective office holder in state government, including the governor, from office for wrongdoing. It can also remove a judge or supreme court justice from office for any reason that in its judgment warrants it. The legislature can override the governor's veto of legislation. Finally, the legislature has charge of the two avenues by which the Wisconsin Constitution can be amended. The legislature can propose amendments for the people to vote on; and it can set in motion the process for calling a constitutional convention.

The legislature has two houses: the senate and the assembly. The senate is composed of 33 senators, each elected for a four-year term from a different senate district. The assembly is composed of 99 representatives, each elected for a two-year term from a different assembly district. Each senate district comprises the combined territory of three assembly districts. Elections are held in November of each even-numbered year. The terms of 17 senate seats expire in alternate even-numbered years from the terms of the other 16. If a midterm vacancy occurs in the office of senator or representative, it is filled through a special election called by the governor.

On January 3, 2017, senators from even-numbered districts were sworn in for the new legislative session by Supreme Court Justice Daniel Kelly *(left)*. Senators serve four-year terms, and elections alternate every two years between even-numbered and odd-numbered districts.

A new legislature is sworn into office in January of each odd-numbered year, and it meets in continuous session for the full biennium until its successor is convened. The 2017 Legislature is the 103rd Wisconsin Legislature. It convened on January 3, 2017, and will continue until January 7, 2019.

Apparatus for conducting business

Rules. The Wisconsin Constitution prescribes a number of specific procedural requirements for the legislature (for example, that each house must keep and publish a journal of its proceedings; and that a roll-call vote, rather than a voice vote, must be taken in certain circumstances). For the most part, however, the legislature determines for itself the manner in which it conducts its business. Each house of the legislature has adopted rules that codify its own practices, and the two houses have adopted joint rules that deal with relations between the houses and administrative proceedings common to both. Either house can change its own rules by passing a resolution, and the two houses can change the joint rules by passing a joint resolution.

Officers. Each house elects from among its members a presiding officer and an officer to stand in for the presiding officer as needed. The presiding officer or stand-in chairs the house's meetings and authenticates the house's acts, orders, and proceedings. In the senate, these officers are the president and president pro tempore; in the assembly, they are the speaker and speaker pro tempore.

Each house also elects two individuals who are not legislators to serve as the house's chief clerk and sergeant at arms. The chief clerk is the clerk for the house's meetings. The chief clerk also manages the house's paperwork, records, and general operations. The sergeant at arms maintains order in and about the house's meeting chamber and supervises the house's messengers.

Within each house, the members from each political party organize as a caucus and elect officers to coordinate their activity. Caucus officers include the majority leader and assistant majority leader and the minority leader and assistant minority leader.

The senate majority leader and the assembly speaker play major and roughly parallel roles in guiding the activities of their houses, as a result of special responsibilities that the rules in their houses assign to their offices.

Former Senator Mary Lazich *(left)*, who served as senate president in 2015 and retired in 2017, passes on the gavel of office to new Senate President Roger Roth of Appleton during Inauguration Day ceremonies.

JAY SALVO, LEGISLATIVE PHOTOGRAPHER

Senate Minority Leader Jennifer Shilling *(left)* and Senate Majority Leader Scott Fitzgerald *(right)* steer their respective caucuses. Leaders coordinate with caucus members on policy positions and work to prioritize which legislation will be the focus of each session.

These responsibilities include appointing the members of committees, serving on the committee that determines what business will be scheduled for the house's meetings, and serving on the committee that makes staffing and budget decisions for the house's operations.

Committees. The legislature does much of its work in committees. Legislative committees study proposed legislation to determine whether it should be given further consideration by the houses. They review the performance and expenditures of state agencies. And they conduct inquiries to inform the public and the legislature about important issues facing the state.

Each committee is assigned a general area of responsibility or a particular matter to look into and, within the scope of its assignment, can hold hearings to gather information and executive sessions (deliberative meetings) to decide what recommendations and reports it will make. (Some committees can do more than make recommendations and reports. For example, the Joint Committee on Finance can approve requests from state agencies for supplemental funding.) With rare exceptions, all committee proceedings are open to the public.

(BOTH PHOTOS) JAY SALVO, LEGISLATIVE PHOTOGRAPHER

Committee work is where much of the work of developing policy and evaluating legislative proposals is done. *(top)* Representatives Sondy Pope, Evan Goyke, and Dave Considine *(left to right)* listen to testimony in the Assembly Committee on Corrections. *(above)* The Assembly Committee on Children and Families hears testimony from staff of the Department of Children and Families on child abuse and neglect reports in 2016.

Each house has its own committees, and the two houses together have joint committees. Usually, every member of the legislature serves on at least one committee. Each house committee includes members from the two major political parties, but more of the members are from the majority party. On a joint committee, which includes members from both houses, more of the members from each house are from the majority party in that house. For some members on some committees, membership is automatic and based on another office that they hold (ex officio membership), but otherwise committee members are appointed. The senate majority leader and the assembly speaker make the appointments in their respective houses but honor the nominations of the minority leader for the minority party appointments. They also designate the committee chairs and the joint committee cochairs, except when those positions are held ex officio.

The standing committees in each house operate through the legislature's entire biennial session. They are created under the rules of the house and consist exclusively of legislators from the house. Most of the standing committees have responsibility for one or more specific subject areas—e.g., "transportation" or "health." However, the Committee on Senate Organization has organizational responsibilities: it schedules, and determines the agendas for, the senate's meetings; and it decides matters pertaining to the senate's personnel, expenditures, and general operations. In the assembly, these organizational responsibilities fall, respectively, to the Assembly Committee on Rules and the Committee on Assembly Organization.

In addition to the standing committees in the houses, there are several joint standing committees, which likewise operate through the entire biennial session. These committees are created in the statutes rather than under the legislature's rules. Three of these committees include nonlegislators in addition to the legislators from both houses. The responsibilities of the joint committees are described on pages 153–172.

Special committees can also be appointed in either house or by the two houses jointly. Committees of this type are created to study a problem or conduct an investigation and report their findings to the house or the legislature. Special committees cease to exist when they have completed their assignments.

Meetings. Early in the biennial session, the legislature adopts a joint resolution to establish its session schedule. The session schedule specifies the floorperiods for the session. A floorperiod is a day or span of days that is reserved for meetings of the full houses. Committees can meet on any day. When a house meets during a floorperiod, it meets in regular session.

The legislature can also call itself into extraordinary session for any day or span of days. The call requires a majority vote of the members of the committee on organization in each house, or the adoption of a joint resolution in both houses, or a joint petition signed by a majority of the members of each house. In addition, the call must specify what business can be considered during the session. An extraordinary session can have the effect of extending

JAY SALVO, LEGISLATIVE PHOTOGRAPHER

The Assembly Speaker leads the majority party in that house and largely determines the course of its legislative business. Speaker Robin Vos *(left)* has led the assembly since 2013. Here he confers with assembly leadership from both parties during the special session focusing on opioid abuse.

a floorperiod so that it begins earlier or ends later than originally scheduled. In such cases, the terms "extended session" and "extended floorperiod" are sometimes used. An extraordinary session can also overlap a floorperiod, and a house can meet in extraordinary session and in regular session at different times during the same day.

The governor can call the legislature into special session at any time. When the legislature convenes in special session, it can act only upon the matters specified in the governor's call. Special sessions can occur during floorperiods and during extraordinary sessions, and a house can meet in special session and in regular or extraordinary session at different times during the same day.

Notices and records. Each house issues a calendar for each of its meetings. The calendar lists the business that will be taken up at the meeting.

The legislature publishes on the Internet a schedule of committee activities that indicates the time, place, and business scheduled for each committee meeting.

Each house keeps a record of its actions known as the daily journal.

The legislature issues the *Bulletin of the Proceedings of the Wisconsin Legislature* periodically during the biennial session. Each issue contains a cumulative record of actions taken on bills, resolutions, and joint resolutions;

Senate President Pro Tempore Howard Marklein *(right)* oversees the floor sessions when the senate president is unavailable. Senate Chief Clerk Jeff Renk *(left)* keeps track of legislative business for the body.

information on administrative rule changes; and a listing of statutes affected by acts.

Employees. Each house employs staff for its members and staff to take care of general administrative matters. In addition, the legislature maintains five service agencies to provide it with legal advice; bill drafting services; budgetary, economic, and fiscal analysis; public policy analysis; research and information services; committee staffing; auditing services; and information technology advice and services.

How a bill becomes a law

A bill is a formal document that proposes to make a new law or change an existing law. For a bill to become a law, two things must happen: 1) The bill must be enacted—that is, it must be passed in identical form by both houses of the legislature and either agreed to by the governor or passed again by both houses over the governor's veto; and 2) The enacted bill must be published.

First reading. A bill takes the first step toward becoming a law when a member of the legislature introduces it in the member's house. This is done by filing the bill with the chief clerk. The chief clerk then assigns the bill its

(BOTH PHOTOS) JAY SALVO, LEGISLATIVE PHOTOGRAPHER

Senate Assistant Majority Leader Leah Vukmir *(left)* and Senate Assistant Minority Leader Janet Bewley *(right)* help guide their parties on policy issues. In 2017, five women and five men were serving in leadership positions in the senate.

bill number (e.g., Assembly Bill 15), and the presiding officer refers the bill to a standing committee or joint standing committee.

A bill must be given three readings, on three different days, before the house can pass it. Each reading is followed by a different stage in the house's deliberation process. Introduction and referral to committee are considered a bill's first reading and are followed by committee review.

Committee review. When a bill is referred to a committee, it remains in the committee until the committee reports it out to the house or the house acts to withdraw it. The committee chair (or cochairs if a joint committee) determines whether the committee will meet to consider a bill and, if so, whether it will hold a hearing or an executive session or both. In the senate, though not in the assembly, a bill that has not received a public hearing cannot be placed on the calendar for a meeting of the full house. And in both houses, a committee cannot report a bill out to the house unless it holds an executive session.

A committee holds a hearing on a bill to gather information, either from the public at large or from specifically invited persons. A committee holds an executive session on a bill to decide what recommendation it will make to the house. The committee can recommend passage of the bill as originally introduced, passage of the bill with amendments, passage of a substitute amendment, or rejection of the bill. Unless it recommends rejection, the committee reports the bill, together with its recommendation, out to the house. In limited circumstances (such as a tie vote), a committee can report a bill without a recommendation.

If a bill is reported out by a committee, or if it is withdrawn from a committee by the house, it is generally sent to the house's scheduling committee—the Committee on Senate Organization or the Assembly Committee on Rules—so that it can be scheduled for consideration at a meeting of the house. (Sometimes, however, a bill is referred to another committee for that committee to review. In such cases, the bill remains in that other committee, just as it did in the previous committee, until it is reported out or withdrawn.)

Scheduling. A bill that reaches the scheduling committee cannot advance further unless the scheduling committee schedules it for a meeting of the house or the house acts to withdraw it. The scheduling committee is not required to schedule the bill for a meeting of the house. If the house withdraws a bill from the scheduling committee, the bill is automatically scheduled for a future meeting of the house. (In the senate, it is placed on the calendar for the senate's

For the last four sessions, Assembly Minority Leader Peter Barca of Kenosha has had the task of making sure the minority party in the 99-member body is heard.

GREG ANDERSON, LEGISLATIVE PHOTOGRAPHER

next succeeding meeting; in the assembly, on the calendar for the assembly's second succeeding meeting.) If a bill is scheduled for a meeting of the house, it can be given its second reading at that meeting.

Second reading. A bill's second reading is a formal announcement that the chief clerk makes at the time when the bill is about to be considered. Following this announcement, the house debates and votes on amendments and substitute amendments to the bill (any that the standing committee recommended and any that are offered by members). This stage ends if the house votes affirmatively to engross the bill. Such a vote means that the house has decided on the final form that the bill will take and is ready to consider passage of the bill in that final form. However, the house cannot proceed to consider passage until the bill has been given its third reading—and this cannot be done until a different day. The house can suspend this restriction by a unanimous voice vote or a two-thirds roll call vote. If the house does not suspend the restriction, the bill is automatically scheduled for a future meeting of the house. (In the senate, it is placed on the calendar for the senate's next succeeding meeting; in the assembly, on the calendar for the assembly's second succeeding meeting.)

Third reading. A bill's third reading, like its second, is a formal announcement that the chief clerk makes at the time when the bill is about to be considered. Following this announcement, the house debates the question whether the bill, in the final form that the house had decided on previously, should be passed. Members can speak for and against passage only; no further amendments can be offered. When all members finish speaking, they vote. If the bill is passed, it is ready to be messaged to the other house. Messaging occurs automatically following a reconsideration period specified in the rules of the house, unless, within that period, the house chooses to reconsider its action in passing the bill. (In the senate, the reconsideration period extends through the senate's next meeting; in the assembly, through the seventh order of business at the assembly's next meeting. Generally, only a member who voted for passage can make a motion for reconsideration.) Alternatively, the house can suspend its rules to message the bill immediately, by a unanimous voice vote or a two-thirds roll call vote.

Action in the second house. When the bill is received in the other house, it goes through substantially the same process as in the first house. If the second house ultimately passes the bill, which it can do with or without additional amendments, it messages the bill back to the house of origin.

Subsequent action in the houses. If the second house adopted additional amendments, the house of origin must determine whether it agrees to those amendments. If the house of origin rejects or amends the amendments, it can message the bill back to the second house. The houses can message the bill back and forth repeatedly until it has been passed in identical form by both. Alternatively, the houses can create a conference committee, consisting of members from each house, to develop a compromise version. If the conference committee proposes a compromise version, the houses can vote on it but cannot adopt amendments. The compromise version is considered in

Committee attendance makes up a large part of the legislative workload. *(below)* Senator Alberta Darling *(left)* and Senator Jerry Petrowski enjoy a lighter moment during a January committee meeting. *(bottom)* At a meeting of the Assembly Committee on Criminal Justice and Public Safety, Chief Deputy Ed Janke of the Oconto County Sheriff's Office, Representative David Steffen of Green Bay, and Deputy Adam Day *(left to right)* speak in favor of a bill that would expand the definition of "hate crime" to include law enforcement officers.

Groups of legislators will often hold a press conference at the capitol to announce legislative initiatives for specific issues. Assembly Majority Leader Jim Steineke was joined by Representative Treig Pronschinske and Representative Jessie Rodriguez *(left to right)* to announce their work on a package of bills to address homelessness in Wisconsin.

the second house first; if it passes in the second house, it is messaged to the house of origin.

Action by the governor. If a bill is passed in identical form by both houses, it is sent to the governor. The governor has six days (excluding Sundays) in which to take action on a bill after receiving it. If the governor takes no action, the bill is enacted on the seventh day. If the governor signs the bill, the bill is enacted on the day it is signed. If the governor vetoes the bill, it goes back to the house of origin. If the governor signs the bill but vetoes part of it—which is permitted in the case of appropriation bills—the signed part is enacted on the day it is signed and the vetoed part goes back to the house of origin.

Publication and effective date. A bill or part of a bill that has been enacted

Seeing their bill signed by the governor is a high point of many legislators' careers. Freshman Representative Rob Summerfield *(far right)* shepherded Assembly Bill 194 through the legislative process and saw it enacted by Governor Walker on May 24, 2017, as Act 7. Senator Terry Moulton, next to Summerfield, was the main co-sponsor of the bill.

is called an act. An act becomes a law when it is published in the manner prescribed by the legislature. The legislature has provided for each act to be published on the Internet no later than the day after its date of enactment. An act goes into effect on the second day after its date of enactment, unless the act specifies that it goes into effect on a different date.

Veto override. A bill or part of a bill that the governor has vetoed can become a law if the legislature passes it again over the governor's veto. The procedure is different than when the bill was passed the first time. The only question considered is passage, and this question can be taken up immediately; the three-readings process is not repeated and amendments cannot be offered. In addition, passage requires a two-thirds vote in each house, rather than a simple majority vote. Any action on a veto begins in the house of origin. If a vote is taken in the house of origin and two-thirds of the members present and voting agree to pass the vetoed bill or vetoed part of a bill, the bill or part is messaged to the other house. If a vote is taken in the second house and two-thirds of the members present and voting agree to pass the bill or part, the bill or part is enacted on the day the vote is taken. The enacted bill or part is then published and becomes a law in the same way as other acts. If either house does not take a vote or fails to muster a two-thirds vote, the bill or part advances no further, and the governor's veto stands.

JAY SALVO, LEGISLATIVE PHOTOGRAPHER

Senator David Craig, chair of the Committee on Financial Services, Constitution and Federalism, asks questions during a joint hearing on proposals related to calling a national constitutional convention in order to add an amendment requiring a balanced budget.

Senate standing committees

Administrative Rules Nass, *chair*; LeMahieu, *vice chair*; Stroebel; Larson, *ranking minority member*; Wirch

Agriculture, Small Business and Tourism Moulton, *chair*; Tiffany, *vice chair*; Harsdorf, Petrowski, Testin; Taylor, *ranking minority member*; Miller, Larson, Vinehout

Economic Development, Commerce and Local Government Feyen, *chair*; Petrowski, *vice chair*; Darling, Testin; Ringhand, *ranking minority member*; Bewley, Johnson

Education Olsen, *chair*; Darling, *vice chair*; Nass, Vukmir; Larson, *ranking minority member*; Bewley, Johnson

Elections and Utilities LeMahieu, *chair*; Kapenga, *vice chair*; Wanggaard; Miller, *ranking minority member*; Risser

Finance Darling, *chair*; Olsen, *vice chair*; Harsdorf, Marklein, Tiffany, Vukmir; Taylor, *ranking minority member*; Erpenbach

Financial Services, Constitution and Federalism Craig, *chair*; Stroebel, *vice chair*; Feyen; Vinehout, *ranking minority member*; Risser

Government Operations, Technology and Consumer Protection Stroebel, *chair*; Craig, *vice chair*; Kapenga; Wirch, *ranking minority member*; Carpenter

Health and Human Services Vukmir, *chair*; Moulton, *vice chair*; LeMahieu; Erpenbach, *ranking minority member*; Johnson

Insurance, Housing and Trade Lasee, *chair*; Olsen, *vice chair*; Craig; Bewley, *ranking minority member*; Larson

Judiciary and Public Safety Wanggaard, *chair*; Testin, *vice chair*; Stroebel; Risser, *ranking minority member*; Taylor

Labor and Regulatory Reform Nass, *chair*; Wanggaard, *vice chair*; Lasee; Wirch, *ranking minority member*; Ringhand

Natural Resources and Energy Cowles, *chair*; Lasee, *vice chair*; Olsen; Miller, *ranking minority member*; Hansen

Public Benefits, Licensing and State-Federal Relations Kapenga, *chair*; Harsdorf, *vice chair*; Craig; Johnson, *ranking minority member*; Vinehout

Revenue, Financial Institutions and Rural Issues Marklein, *chair*; LeMahieu, *vice chair*; Tiffany; Ringhand, *ranking minority member*; Vinehout

Senate Organization Fitzgerald, *chair*; Roth, *vice chair*; Vukmir; Shilling, *ranking minority member*; Bewley

Sporting Heritage, Mining and Forestry Tiffany, *chair*; Testin, *vice chair*; Moulton; Wirch, *ranking minority member*; Erpenbach

Transportation and Veterans Affairs Petrowski, *chair*; Marklein, *vice chair*; Cowles; Carpenter, *ranking minority member*; Hansen

Universities and Technical Colleges Harsdorf, *chair*; Nass, *vice chair*; Feyen; Hansen, *ranking minority member*; Bewley

Workforce Development, Military Affairs and Senior Issues Testin, *chair*; Feyen, *vice chair*; Marklein; Ringhand, *ranking minority member*; Erpenbach

Assembly standing committees

Administrative Rules Ballweg, *chair*; Neylon, Ott; Hebl, *ranking minority member*; Anderson

Aging and Long-Term Care Weatherston, *chair*; Petryk, *vice chair*; Bernier, Snyder, Macco, Kremer; Meyers, *ranking minority member*; Kolste, Brostoff

Agriculture Nerison, *chair*; Novak, *vice chair*; Tauchen, Ripp, Tranel, E. Brooks, Kitchens, VanderMeer, Mursau, Edming, Horlacher; Considine, *ranking minority member*; Kessler, Spreitzer, Fields, Vruwink

Assembly Organization Vos, *chair*; Steineke, *vice chair*; R. Brooks, August, Knodl; Barca, *ranking minority member*; Hesselbein, Spreitzer

Audit Kerkman, *chair*; Macco, *vice chair*; Nygren; Sargent, *ranking minority member*; Berceau

Campaigns and Elections Bernier, *chair*; Sanfelippo, *vice chair*; Snyder, Horlacher, Schraa, Murphy; Kessler, *ranking minority member*; Zamarripa, Taylor

Children and Families Kitchens, *chair*; Gannon, *vice chair*; Snyder, Vorpagel, Kerkman, Ballweg, Pronschinske, Krug; Taylor, *ranking minority member*; Billings, Subeck, Bowen

Colleges and Universities Murphy, *chair*; Tranel, *vice chair*; Zimmerman, Quinn, Summerfield, Petryk, Ballweg, Krug, Stafsholt, Kremer; Berceau, *ranking minority member*; Wachs, Billings, Hebl, Vruwink, Anderson

Constitution and Ethics Allen, *chair*; Thiesfeldt, *vice chair*; Jagler, Kremer, Wichgers, Jarchow; Kessler, *ranking minority member*; Berceau, Wachs

Consumer Protection Duchow, *chair*; Tittl, *vice chair*; Skowronski, Nerison, Macco, VanderMeer; Berceau, *ranking minority member*; Sinicki, Pope

Corrections Schraa, *chair*; Hutton, *vice chair*; Brandtjen, E. Brooks, Kremer, Kleefisch, Gannon; Bowen, *ranking minority member*; Pope, Goyke, Considine

Criminal Justice and Public Safety Spiros, *chair*; Kremer, *vice chair*; Bernier, Ott, Jacque, Horlacher, Novak, Krug; Goyke, *ranking minority member*; Kessler, Zamarripa, Crowley

Education Thiesfeldt, *chair*; Kitchens, *vice chair*; Jagler, Zimmerman,

Senator Chris Kapenga, Representative Kathy Bernier, and Representative Daniel Knodl *(left to right)* testify at a joint public hearing in March 2017.

Rodriguez, Tusler, Mursau, Quinn, Duchow, Wichgers; Pope, *ranking minority member*; Genrich, Considine, Hebl, Bowen, Vruwink

Employment Relations Vos, *chair*; Steineke, *vice chair*; Nygren; Barca, *ranking minority member*

Energy and Utilities Kuglitsch, *chair*; Steffen, *vice chair*; Rodriguez, Weatherston, Petersen, Tauchen, Tranel, Jarchow, Petryk, Neylon; Zepnick, *ranking minority member*; Sargent, Genrich, Stuck, Meyers

Environment and Forestry Mursau, *chair*; Krug, *vice chair*; Pronschinske, Kitchens, Swearingen, Edming, Wichgers, Tusler; Mason, *ranking minority member*; Hebl, Milroy, Anderson

Family Law Rodriguez, *chair*; Duchow, *vice chair*; Thiesfeldt, Tauchen, Krug, Kleefisch; Goyke, *ranking minority member*; Subeck, Zepnick

Federalism and Interstate Relations Vorpagel, *chair*; Schraa, *vice chair*; Kerkman, Hutton, Katsma; Zepnick, *ranking minority member*; Anderson

Finance Nygren, *chair*; Kooyenga, *vice chair*; Loudenbeck, Felzkowski, Born, Rohrkaste; Hintz, *ranking minority member*; Shankland

Financial Institutions Katsma, *chair*; Jarchow, *vice chair*; Allen, Sanfelippo, Stafsholt, Petryk, Weatherston, Murphy, Petersen, Kitchens; Doyle, *ranking minority member*; Young, Zepnick, Bowen, Meyers, Fields

Government Accountability and Oversight Hutton, *chair*; Brandtjen, *vice*

Addressing the floor for the first time is an important moment in every legislator's tenure. Representative Jimmy Anderson of Fitchburg made his first address in May 2017 and was greeted with applause from members of both parties.

chair; Krug, Wichgers, Kuglitsch, August; Pope, *ranking minority member*; Hintz, Brostoff

Health Sanfelippo, *chair*; Bernier, *vice chair*; Edming, Skowronski, Kremer, Wichgers, Murphy, Jacque; Kolste, *ranking minority member*; Zamarripa, Subeck, Taylor

Housing and Real Estate Jagler, *chair*; Allen, *vice chair*; Katsma, R. Brooks, Murphy, Pronschinske; Stuck, *ranking minority member*; Young, Goyke

Insurance Petersen, *chair*; Duchow, *vice chair*; Gannon, Steffen, Jagler,

Petryk, Tusler, Tranel, Katsma, August, Stafsholt; Genrich, *ranking minority member*; Young, Berceau, Doyle, Kessler

Jobs and the Economy Neylon, *chair*; E. Brooks, *vice chair*; Zimmerman, Kulp, Tittl, Macco, Snyder, Wichgers; Ohnstad, *ranking minority member*; Stuck, Fields, Crowley

Judiciary Ott, *chair*; Horlacher, *vice chair*; Thiesfeldt, Jacque, Tusler, Kerkman; Wachs, *ranking minority member*; Hebl, Taylor

Labor Kulp, *chair*; Kuglitsch, *vice chair*; Spiros, Knodl, Schraa, Quinn; Sinicki, *ranking minority member*; Bowen, Ohnstad

Local Government E. Brooks, *chair*; Ripp, *vice chair*; Novak, Duchow, Steffen, Skowronski; Subeck, *ranking minority member*; Berceau, Spreitzer

Mental Health Tittl, *chair*; Jagler, *vice chair*; Ballweg, Novak, Sanfelippo, Snyder, VanderMeer, Spiros; Considine, *ranking minority member*; Sargent, Brostoff, Zepnick

Natural Resources and Sporting Heritage Kleefisch, *chair*; Quinn, *vice chair*; Tittl, Edming, Nerison, Mursau, Skowronski, Ripp, Tusler, Stafsholt; Milroy, *ranking minority member*; Hesselbein, Spreitzer, Stuck, Brostoff

Public Benefit Reform Krug, *chair*; Vorpagel, *vice chair*; Brandtjen, Schraa, Kremer, Petersen; Subeck, *ranking minority member*; Kolste, Riemer

Regulatory Licensing Reform Horlacher, *chair*; Ballweg, *vice chair*; Hutton, Jacque, Macco, Quinn; Brostoff, *ranking minority member*; Genrich, Anderson

Rules Steineke, *chair*; Vos, August, R. Brooks, Knodl, Ballweg, Kuglitsch, Jagler, Born; Barca, *ranking minority member*; Hesselbein, Spreitzer, Doyle, Pope, Kolste

Rural Development and Mining VanderMeer, *chair*; Kulp, *vice chair*; Novak, R. Brooks, Quinn, E. Brooks, Kuglitsch, Pronschinske; Spreitzer, *ranking minority member*; Milroy, Shankland, Vruwink

Science and Technology Quinn, *chair*; Petersen, *vice chair*; Brandtjen, Allen, Neylon, VanderMeer; Genrich, *ranking minority member*; Kolste, Anderson

Small Business Development Tauchen, *chair*; Edming, *vice chair*; Tranel, Hutton, Allen, Swearingen, Summerfield, Duchow, VanderMeer,

Skowronski; Sargent, *ranking minority member*; Zamarripa, Billings, Kolste, Crowley

State Affairs Swearingen, *chair*; Tauchen, *vice chair*; Jagler, Jacque, Knodl, Kleefisch, Gannon, Summerfield, Kulp, Vorpagel; Zamarripa, *ranking minority member*; Sinicki, Ohnstad, Hesselbein, Doyle

Tourism Tranel, *chair*; Swearingen, *vice chair*; Jarchow, Ballweg, Tauchen, Summerfield, Kitchens, Bernier, Mursau, Zimmerman; Billings, *ranking minority member*; Ohnstad, Mason, Considine, Vruwink

Transportation Ripp, *chair*; Spiros, *vice chair*; Thiesfeldt, Weatherston, Kulp, Sanfelippo, Vorpagel, E. Brooks, Skowronski, Macco; Wachs, *ranking minority member*; Kolste, Meyers, Billings, Crowley

Urban Revitalization Gannon, *chair*; Fields, *vice chair*; Steffen, Snyder, Weatherston, Sanfelippo, Brandtjen; Sinicki, Bowen

Veterans and Military Affairs Skowronski, *chair*; VanderMeer, *vice chair*; Petryk, Allen, Edming, Nerison, Summerfield, Ott, Tittl, Weatherston; Hesselbein, *ranking minority member*; Milroy, Sinicki, Goyke, Riemer

Assembly Assistant Majority Leader Robert Brooks answers questions and clarifies information for committee members on a proposal he has co-sponsored.

JAY SALVO, LEGISLATIVE PHOTOGRAPHER

Ways and Means Macco, *chair*; Katsma, *vice chair*; Kerkman, Novak, Steffen, Jacque, Bernier, Petersen; Taylor, *ranking minority member*; Riemer, Ohnstad, Doyle

Workforce Development Petryk, *chair*; Weatherston, *vice chair*; Murphy, Ripp, Allen, Katsma, Kulp, E. Brooks, Brandtjen, Snyder; Billings, *ranking minority member*; Spreitzer, Riemer, Ohnstad, Crowley

Joint legislative committees and commissions

Joint committees and commissions are created by statute and include members from both houses. Three joint committees include members who are not legislators. Commissions include gubernatorial appointees and, in two cases, the governor.

Joint Committee for Review of Administrative Rules

Senators: Nass, *cochair*; LeMahieu, Stroebel; Larson, *ranking minority member*; Wirch

Representatives: Ballweg, *cochair*; Neylon, Ott; Hebl, *ranking minority member*; Anderson

Senator Nass: Sen.Nass@legis.wisconsin.gov; 608-266-2635; Room 10 South, State Capitol, PO Box 7882, Madison, WI 53707-7882

Representative Ballweg: Rep.Ballweg@legis.wisconsin.gov; 608-266-8077; Room 210 North, State Capitol, PO Box 8952, Madison, WI 53708-8952

The Joint Committee for Review of Administrative Rules must review proposed rules and may object to the promulgation of rules as part of the legislative oversight of the rule-making process. It also may suspend rules that have been promulgated; suspend or extend the effective period of emergency rules; and order an agency to put policies in rule form.

Following standing committee review, a proposed rule must be referred to the joint committee. The joint committee must meet to review proposed rules that receive standing committee objections, and may meet to review any rule received without objection. The joint committee generally has 30 days to review the rule, but that period may be extended in certain cases. The joint committee may concur or nonconcur in the standing committee's action or may on its own accord object to a proposed rule or portion of a rule. If it objects or concurs in a standing committee's objection, it must introduce bills concurrently in both houses to prevent promulgation of the rule. If either bill is enacted, the agency may not adopt the rule unless specifically authorized to do so by a subsequent legislative enactment. The joint committee may also request that an agency modify a proposed rule.

The joint committee may suspend a rule that was previously promulgated after holding a public hearing. Within 30 days following the suspension, the joint committee must introduce bills concurrently in both houses to repeal the suspended rule. If either bill is enacted, the rule is repealed and the agency may not promulgate it again unless authorized by a subsequent legislative action. If both bills fail to pass, the rule remains in effect and may not be suspended again.

The joint committee receives notice of any action in a circuit court for declaratory judgments about the validity of a rule and may intervene in the action with the consent of the Joint Committee on Legislative Organization.

The joint committee is composed of five senators and five representatives, and the membership from each house must include representatives of both the majority and minority parties.

State of Wisconsin Building Commission

Governor: Scott Walker, *chair*
Senators: Moulton, *vice chair*; Petrowski; Ringhand
Representatives: Swearingen, Katsma; Wachs
Other members: Bob Brandherm (citizen member appointed by governor)
Nonvoting advisory members from Department of Administration: John Klenke (administrator, Division of Facilities Development), *commission secretary*; Kevin Trinastic, R. J. Binau, David Erdman, Jillian Quarne

Contact: 608-266-1855; 101 East Wilson Street, 7th Floor, Madison, WI 53703; PO Box 7866, Madison, WI 53707-7866

The State of Wisconsin Building Commission coordinates the state building program, which includes the construction of new buildings; the remodeling, renovation, and maintenance of existing facilities; and the acquisition of lands and capital equipment. The commission determines the projects to be incorporated into the building program and biennially makes recommendations concerning the building program to the legislature, including the amount to be appropriated in the biennial budget. The budget for the state building program for 2015–17 was $848,728,000. The commission oversees all state construction, except highway development. In addition, the commission may authorize expenditures from the State Building Trust Fund for construction, remodeling, maintenance, and planning of future development. The commission has supervision over all matters relating to the contracting of state debt.

A group of assembly Democrats held a press conference in March 2017 to announce that they would introduce legislation to prohibit the state from investing in companies that contract to build a border wall between the United States and Mexico. Representative JoCasta Zamarripa, Representative David Bowen, and Representative Lisa Subeck *(left to right)* present their case to the media.

All transactions for the sale of instruments that result in a state debt liability must be approved by official resolution of the commission.

The eight-member commission includes three senators and three representatives. Both the majority and minority parties in each house must be represented, and one legislator from each house must also be a member of the State Supported Programs Study and Advisory Committee. The governor serves as chair. One citizen member serves at the pleasure of the governor. The Department of Administration provides staffing for the commission, and several department employees serve as nonvoting, advisory members.

Joint Review Committee on Criminal Penalties

Senators: Wanggaard, *cochair*; Taylor
Representatives: Jarchow, *cochair*; Riemer
Other members: Brad D. Schimel (attorney general); Jon E. Litscher (secretary of corrections); Kelli S. Thompson (state public defender); James T. Bayorgeon, David G. Deininger (reserve judges appointed by supreme court); Bradley Gehring, Maury Straub (public members appointed by governor)

Senator Wanggaard: Sen.Wanggaard@legis.wisconsin.gov; 608-266-1832; Room 319 South, State Capitol, PO Box 7882, Madison, WI 53707-7882
Representative Jarchow: Rep.Jarchow@legis.wisconsin.gov; 608-267-2365; Room 19 North, State Capitol, PO Box 8952, Madison, WI 53708-8952

The Joint Review Committee on Criminal Penalties reviews any bill that creates a new crime or revises a penalty for an existing crime when requested to do so by the chair of a standing committee in the house of origin to which the bill was referred. The presiding officer in the house of origin may also request a report from the joint committee if the bill is not referred to a standing committee.

Reports of the joint committee on bills submitted for its review concern the costs or savings to public agencies; the consistency of proposed penalties with existing penalties; whether alternative language is needed to conform the proposed penalties to existing penalties; and whether any acts prohibited by the bill are already prohibited under existing law.

Once a report is requested for a bill, a standing committee may not vote on the bill and the house of origin may not pass the bill before the joint committee submits its report or before the 30th day after the request is made, whichever is earlier.

The joint committee includes one majority and one minority party member from each house of the legislature; the members from the majority party serve as cochairs. The attorney general, secretary of corrections, and state public defender serve ex officio. The supreme court appoints one reserve judge residing somewhere within judicial administrative districts 1 to 5 and another from

Floor sessions can be as much about strategy as they are about policy. Speaker Pro Tempore Tyler August *(right)* and Majority Caucus Secretary Jessie Rodriguez confer during a break in action.

districts 6 to 10. The governor appoints two public members—an individual with law enforcement experience and an elected county official.

Joint Committee on Employment Relations

Senators: Roth (senate president), *cochair*; Fitzgerald (majority leader), Darling (cochair, Joint Committee on Finance); Shilling (minority leader)

Representatives: Vos (assembly speaker), *cochair*; Steineke (majority leader), Nygren (cochair, Joint Committee on Finance); Barca (minority leader)

Contact: Legislative Council Staff, 608-266-1304; 1 East Main Street, Suite 401, Madison, WI 53703-3382

The Joint Committee on Employment Relations approves all changes to the collective bargaining agreements that cover state employees represented by unions, and the compensation plans for nonrepresented state employees. These plans and agreements include pay adjustments; fringe benefits; performance awards; pay equity adjustments; and other items related to wages, hours, and conditions of employment. The committee also approves the assignment of certain unclassified positions to the executive salary group ranges.

The Division of Personnel Management in the Department of Administration submits the compensation plans for nonrepresented employees to the committee. One plan covers all nonrepresented classified employees and certain officials outside the classified service, including legislators, justices of the supreme court, court of appeals judges, circuit court judges, constitutional officers, district attorneys, heads of executive agencies, division administrators, and others designated by law. The faculty and academic staff of the University of Wisconsin System are covered by a separate compensation plan, which is based on recommendations made by the University of Wisconsin Board of Regents.

After public hearings on the nonrepresented employee plans, the committee may modify the plans, but the committee's modifications may be disapproved by the governor. The committee may set aside the governor's disapproval by a vote of six committee members.

In the case of unionized employees, the Division of Personnel Management or, for University of Wisconsin bargaining units, the Board of Regents or the University of Wisconsin-Madison, submits tentative agreements negotiated between it and certified labor organizations to the committee. If the committee disapproves an agreement, it is returned to the bargaining parties for renegotiation.

When the committee approves an agreement for unionized employees, it introduces those portions requiring legislative approval in bill form and recommends passage without change. If the legislature fails to pass the bill, the agreement is returned to the bargaining parties for renegotiation.

The committee is composed of eight members: the presiding officers of each house; the majority and minority leaders of each house; and the cochairs of the Joint Committee on Finance. It is assisted in its work by the Legislative Council Staff and the Legislative Fiscal Bureau.

Joint Committee on Finance

Senators: Darling, *cochair*; Olsen, *vice chair*; Harsdorf, Marklein, Tiffany, Vukmir; Taylor, *ranking minority member*; Erpenbach
Representatives: Nygren, *cochair*; Kooyenga, *vice chair*; Loudenbeck, Felzkowski, Born, Rohrkaste; Hintz, *ranking minority member*; Shankland

Senator Darling: Sen.Darling@legis.wisconsin.gov; 608-266-5830; Room 317 East, State Capitol, PO Box 7882, Madison, WI 53707-7882
Representative Nygren: Rep.Nygren@legis.wisconsin.gov; 608-266-2343; Room 309 East, State Capitol, PO Box 8953, Madison, WI 53708-8953

The Joint Committee on Finance examines legislation that deals with state income and spending. The committee also gives final approval to a wide variety of state payments and assessments. Any bill introduced in the legislature that appropriates money, provides for revenue, or relates to taxation must be referred to the committee.

The committee introduces the biennial budget as recommended by the governor. After holding a series of public hearings and executive sessions, it submits its own version of the budget as a substitute amendment to the governor's budget bill for consideration by the legislature.

At regularly scheduled quarterly meetings, the committee considers agency requests to adjust their budgets. It may approve a request for emergency funds if it finds that the legislature has authorized the activities for which the appropriation is sought. It may also transfer funds between existing appropriations and change the number of positions authorized to an agency in the budget process.

When required, the committee introduces legislation to pay claims against the state, resolve shortages in funds, and restore capital reserve funds of the Wisconsin Housing and Economic Development Authority to the required level. As an emergency measure, it may reduce certain state agency appropriations when there is a decrease in state revenues.

The committee is composed of the eight senators on the Senate Finance Committee and the eight representatives on the Assembly Finance Commit-

(top) The assembly conducts business in a chamber that is over 100 years old yet makes use of advanced tools and technology to administer its operations. *(above)* The grand settings are open to the public and allow present and future voters of Wisconsin, such as this group of students, to visit the corridors of power and learn how their government functions.

(BOTH PHOTOS) GREG ANDERSON, LEGISLATIVE PHOTOGRAPHER

tee. It includes members of the majority and minority party in each house. The cochairs are appointed in the same manner as are the chairs of standing committees in their respective houses.

Joint Committee on Information Policy and Technology

Senators: Harsdorf, *cochair*; Cowles, Roth; Carpenter, *ranking minority member*; Vinehout

Representatives: Knodl, *cochair*; Jacque, Brandtjen; Barca, *ranking minority member*; Sargent

Senator Harsdorf: Sen.Harsdorf@legis.wisconsin.gov; 608-266-7745; Room 122 South, State Capitol, PO Box 7882, Madison, WI 53707-7882
Representative Knodl: Rep.Knodl@legis.wisconsin.gov; 608-266-3796; Room 218 North, State Capitol, PO Box 8952, Madison, WI 53708-8952

The Joint Committee on Information Policy and Technology reviews information management practices and technology systems of state and local units of government to ensure economic and efficient service, maintain data security and integrity, and protect the privacy of individuals who are subjects of the databases. It studies the effects of proposals by the state to expand existing information technology or implement new technologies. With the concurrence of the Joint Committee on Finance, it may direct the Department of Administration to report on any information technology system project that could cost $1 million or more in the current or succeeding biennium. The committee may direct the Department of Administration to prepare reports or conduct studies and may make recommendations to the governor, the legislature, state agencies, or local governments based on this information. The University of Wisconsin Board of Regents is required to submit a report to the committee semiannually, detailing each information technology project in the University of Wisconsin System costing more than $1 million or deemed "high-risk" by the board. The committee may make recommendations on the identified projects to the governor and the legislature. The committee is composed of three majority and two minority party members from each house of the legislature.

Joint Legislative Audit Committee

Senators: Cowles, *cochair*; Darling (cochair, Joint Committee on Finance), Kapenga; Vinehout, *ranking minority member*; Miller
Representatives: Kerkman, *cochair*; Macco, Nygren (cochair, Joint Committee on Finance); Sargent, *ranking minority member*; Berceau

The senate and assembly parlors can function as retreats for quiet work or private conversation among legislators. Senator Chris Larson of Milwaukee takes a moment to work on his laptop in 2015.

Senator Cowles: Sen.Cowles@legis.wisconsin.gov; 608-266-0484; Room 118 South, State Capitol, PO Box 7882, Madison, WI 53707-7882
Representative Kerkman: Rep.Kerkman@legis.wisconsin.gov; 608-266-2530; Room 315 North, State Capitol, PO Box 8952, Madison, WI 53708-8952

The Joint Legislative Audit Committee advises the Legislative Audit Bureau, subject to general supervision of the Joint Committee on Legislative Organization. The committee is composed of the cochairs of the Joint Committee on Finance, plus two majority and two minority party members from each house of the legislature. The committee evaluates candidates for the office of state auditor and makes recommendations to the Joint Committee on Legislative Organization, which selects the auditor.

The committee may direct the state auditor to undertake specific audits and review requests for special audits from individual legislators or standing committees, but no legislator or standing committee may interfere with the auditor in the conduct of an audit.

The committee reviews each report of the Legislative Audit Bureau and then confers with the state auditor, other legislative committees, and the audited agencies on the report's findings. It may propose corrective action and direct that follow-up reports be submitted to it.

The annual State of the State address brings both houses together in the assembly chamber *(top)*, where the governor *(above)* greets legislators and lays out his agenda for the new year.

The committee may hold hearings on audit reports, request the Joint Committee on Legislative Organization to investigate any matter within the scope of the audit, and request investigation of any matter relative to the fiscal and performance responsibilities of a state agency. If an audit report cites financial deficiencies, the head of the agency must report to the Joint Legislative Audit

Committee on remedial actions taken. Should the agency head fail to report, the committee may refer the matter to the Joint Committee on Legislative Organization and the appropriate standing committees.

When the committee determines that legislative action is needed, it may refer the necessary information to the legislature or a standing committee. It can also request information from a committee on action taken or seek advice of a standing committee on program portions of an audit. The committee may introduce legislation to address issues covered in audit reports.

Joint Legislative Council

Senators: Roth (senate president), *cochair*; Darling (cochair, Joint Committee on Finance), Fitzgerald (majority leader), Marklein (president pro tempore), Moulton, Petrowski, Wanggaard; Shilling (minority leader), *ranking minority member*; Taylor (ranking minority member, Joint Committee on Finance), Risser, Miller

Representatives: R. Brooks (designated by assembly speaker), *cochair*; Vos (assembly speaker), Steineke (majority leader), August (speaker pro tempore), Nygren (cochair, Joint Committee on Finance), Ballweg, Spiros; Barca (minority leader), *ranking minority member*; Hintz (ranking minority member, Joint Committee on Finance), Mason, Hesselbein

Legislative Council Staff: Terry C. Anderson, *director*; Jessica Karls-Ruplinger, *deputy director*; Scott Grosz, *rules clearinghouse director*; Margit Kelley, *rules clearinghouse assistant director*

Contact: leg.council@legis.wisconsin.gov; 608-266-1304; 1 East Main Street, Suite 401, Madison, WI 53703-3382

Website: http://lc.legis.wisconsin.gov

Publications: *General Report of the Joint Legislative Council to the Legislature*; *State Agency Staff Members with Responsibilities Related to the Legislature*; *Wisconsin Legislator Briefing Book*; *Directory of Joint Legislative Council Committees*; *Comparative Retirement Study*; *A Citizen's Guide to Participation in the Wisconsin State Legislature*; rules clearinghouse reports; staff briefs; information memoranda on substantive issues considered by council committees; staff memoranda; amendment and act memoranda.

Number of employees: 34.17

Total budget 2015–17: $7,897,200

The Joint Legislative Council creates special committees made up of legislators and members of the public to study various problems of state and local government. Study topics are selected from requests presented to the council by law, joint resolution, and individual legislators. After research, expert testimony, and public hearings, the study committees draft proposals and submit them to the council, which must approve those drafts it wants introduced in the legislature as council bills.

The council is assisted in its work by the Legislative Council Staff. The staff provides legal and research assistance to all of the legislature's substantive standing committees and joint statutory committees (except the Joint Committee on Finance) and assists individual legislators on request. The staff operates the rules clearinghouse to review proposed administrative rules and assists standing committees in their oversight of rulemaking. The staff also assists the legislature in identifying and responding to issues relating to the Wisconsin Retirement System.

By law, the Legislative Council Staff must be strictly nonpartisan and must observe the confidential nature of the research and drafting requests it receives. The law requires that state agencies and local governmental units cooperate fully with the council staff in its carrying out of its statutory duties. The Joint Committee on Legislative Organization appoints the director of the Legislative Council Staff from outside the classified service. The director appoints the other staff members from outside the classified service.

The council consists of 22 legislators. The majority of them serve ex officio, and the remainder are appointed in the same manner as members of standing committees. The president of the senate and the speaker of the assembly serve as cochairs, but each may designate another member to serve as cochair and each may decline to serve on the council. The council operates two permanent statutory committees and various special committees appointed to study selected subjects.

PERMANENT COMMITTEES OF THE COUNCIL

Special Committee on State-Tribal Relations Representative Mursau, *chair*; Senator Vinehout, *vice chair*; Senators Carpenter, Lazich; Representatives Edming, Meyers; Dee Ann Allen (Lac du Flambeau Band of Lake Superior Chippewa Indians), Bryan Bainbridge (Red Cliff Band of Lake Superior Chippewa Indians), Russell Barber (Lac Courte Oreilles Tribal Governing Board), Gary Besaw (Menominee Indian Tribe of Wisconsin), Wilfrid Cleveland (Ho-Chunk Nation), Michael Decorah (St. Croix Chippewa Indians of Wisconsin), Harold Frank (Forest County Potawatomi

Community), Shannon Holsey (Stockbridge-Munsee Community), Chris McGeshick (Sokaogon Chippewa Community), Lisa Summers (Oneida Nation)

State-Tribal Relations Technical Advisory Committee Tom Bellavia (Department of Justice), Kelly Jackson (Department of Transportation), David O'Connor (Department of Public Instruction), Michele Allness (Department of Natural Resources), Andrew Evenson (Department of Workforce Development), Thomas Ourada (Department of Revenue), Gail Nahwahquaw (Department of Health Services), Stephanie Lozano (Department of Children and Families)

The Special Committee on State-Tribal Relations is appointed by the Joint Legislative Council each biennium to study issues related to American Indians and the Indian tribes and bands in this state and develop specific recommendations and legislative proposals relating to such issues. Legislative membership includes not fewer than six nor more than 12 members with at least one member of the majority and the minority party from each house. The council appoints no fewer than six and no more than 11 members from names submitted by federally recognized Wisconsin Indian tribes or bands

Another occasion for a joint meeting of the senate and the assembly is the annual State of the Tribes address. During his 2016 address, speaker Mic Isham of the Lac Courte Oreilles recognized Wilfrid Cleveland (*standing*), President of the Ho-Chunk Nation; Brooks Boyd of the Forest County Potawatomi Community; and Melinda Danforth of the Oneida Nation (*left to right*).

GREG ANDERSON, LEGISLATIVE PHOTOGRAPHER

With only 33 members in the senate and four-year terms, senators have a chance to form working relationships that reach across the aisle. Senator Mark Miller *(left)* and Senator Alberta Darling have worked together for more than ten years.

JAY SALVO, LEGISLATIVE PHOTOGRAPHER

or the Great Lakes Inter-Tribal Council. The council may not appoint more than one member recommended by any one tribe or band or the Great Lakes Inter-Tribal Council.

The Technical Advisory Committee, consisting of representatives of eight major executive agencies, assists the Special Committee on State-Tribal Relations.

Law Revision Committee Senators Wanggaard, *cochair*, LeMahieu, Risser, Taylor; Representatives Ott, *cochair*, August, Riemer, Wachs

The Law Revision Committee is appointed each biennium by the Joint Legislative Council. The membership of the committee is not specified, but it must include majority and minority party representation from each house. The committee reviews minor, remedial changes to the statutes as proposed by state agencies and reviews opinions of the attorney general and court decisions declaring a Wisconsin statute unconstitutional, ambiguous, or otherwise in need of revision. It considers proposals by the Legislative Reference Bureau to correct statutory language and session laws that conflict or need revision, and it may submit recommendations for major law revision projects to the Joint Legislative Council. It also serves as the repository for interstate compacts and agreements and makes recommendations to the legislature regarding revision of such agreements.

SPECIAL COMMITTEES OF THE COUNCIL REPORTING IN 2017

Legislative Council Study Committee on Access to Civil Legal Services
Representative Horlacher, *chair*; Senator Stroebel, *vice chair*; Senator Wirch; Representatives Ballweg, Stuck, Subeck; Erin Boyd, Rick Esenberg, James Gramling, Kimberly Haas, Gregg Moore, David Pifer, David Prosser, Michael Rust, Amy Wochos, Glenn Yamahiro

The study committee is directed to review the funding and delivery of legal services for the indigent in civil cases. The committee shall review the need for legal services by indigent civil litigants, identify additional non-GPR sources of revenue to provide civil legal services for the indigent, and review current operations.

Legislative Council Study Committee on Publication of Government Documents and Legal Notices
Representative Spiros, *chair*; Senator Miller, *vice chair*; Representatives Genrich, Jacque; Matt Blessing, Caroline Burmaster, Tim Lyke, Heather Rogge, Michael Schlaak, Mark Stodder, Maribeth Witzel-Behl

The study committee is directed to update and recodify Wis. Stats. Chapters 35 and 985, relating to the publication and distribution of government documents and legal notices respectively, to reflect technological advances and remove obsolete provisions. The committee shall also study whether, and in what circumstances, current law regarding the publication and distribution of government documents and legal notices, including qualifications for official newspapers, should be modified to allow for information to be made available only electronically or through nontraditional media outlets. The committee shall recommend legislation regarding any such modifications.

Legislative Council Study Committee on Reducing Recidivism and Removing Impediments to Ex-Offender Employment
Senator Darling, *chair*; Representative Hutton, *vice chair*; Senator Taylor; Representatives Billings, Goyke, Nygren; Edward Bailey, David Borowski, Earl Buford, Jerome Dillard, Sadique Isahaku, Eric Johnson, Mary Prosser, Amy Schabel, Lisa Stark, Kelli Thompson

The study committee is directed to review effective strategies and best practices for reducing recidivism. The committee shall consider evidence-based strategies to decrease recidivism that have achieved success in Wisconsin or in other states for possible expansion or implementation, investigate systems of earned-time credits for possible implementation as part of a recidivism reduction program, and explore existing impediments to reacclimating to society, including: continuity of medication, impediments to occupational licensure and professional credentials, and other collateral consequences of conviction.

Legislative Council Study Committee on Rural Broadband Senator Marklein, *chair*; Representative Petryk, *vice chair*; Representatives Meyers, Spreitzer; Scott Behn, Ronald Brisbois, Jim Costello, Philip Hejtmanek, Mike Hill, Michelle Olson, Jean Pauk, Ben Rivard, Kelly Shipley

The study committee is directed to review the Wisconsin Broadband Expansion Grant Program and the extent to which it has encouraged construction of broadband infrastructure in areas of the state with few broadband service providers. The committee shall discuss the criteria used to evaluate applications and award grants, consider alternatives for determining eligibility and prioritizing proposed projects, consider alternative methods for encouraging construction of broadband infrastructure, and identify options to recommend.

Legislative Council Study Committee on School Data Representative Thiesfeldt, *chair*; Senator LeMahieu, *vice chair*; Senator Larson; Representatives Bowen, Murphy, Pope; Kevin Bruggink, Sally Flaschberger, Wendy Greenfield, Nicole Hafele, Kelly Hoyland, John Humphries, Kim Kaukl, Margaret Murphy, Ann Steenwyk

The study committee is directed to review all student data gathered by the Department of Public Instruction (DPI) and the data security measures that protect student privacy. The committee will study whether the data is required by federal law, state statute, or administrative rule and the purposes for which the data is utilized, and consider developing legislation to limit the types of student data collected by DPI and to improve the security of that data.

Legislative Council Study Committee on the Preservation of Burial Sites Representative Loudenbeck, *chair*; Representative R. Brooks, *vice chair*; Senator Erpenbach; Representative Considine; Conrad Goodkind, William Green, David Grignon, Kira Kaufmann, Justin Oeth, E. Glen Porter, Bill Quackenbush, Robert Shea, Chad Wuebben

The study committee is directed to review section 157.70, Wisconsin Statutes, to determine whether the statute adequately balances the interests of scientists, landowners, developers, and others with an interest in a burial site, including those with a kinship interest and those with a general cultural, tribal, or re-

Assistant Minority Leader Dianne Hesselbein makes a point during the debate about Assembly Bill 109, relating to towns withdrawing from county zoning ordinances. Hesselbein was able to give her personal perspective, as she formerly served on the Dane County Board.

ligious affiliation with the burial site. The committee shall consider whether modifications to these procedures are necessary to protect all interests related to any human burial site encountered during archaeological excavation, metallic or nonmetallic mining, construction, agricultural activities, environmental impact assessments, or other ground-disturbing activities, without causing avoidable or undue delay or hardship to any person who has an interest in using the land on which the burial site is located.

Legislative Council Study Committee on Volunteer Firefighter and Emergency Medical Technician Shortages Senator Nass, *chair*; Representative Kremer, *vice chair*; Senator Bewley; Representative Kolste; John Eich, J. Timothy Hillebrand, Gregory Michalek, Jodie Olson, Jeff Rickaby, David Seager Jr., Dana Sechler, James Small, Jody Stoker, Jay Tousey, Gene Wright

The study committee is directed to examine issues related to the shortage of volunteer firefighters and emergency medical technicians (EMTs) in the state, particularly in rural areas, and propose measures to address the shortage. Specifically, the committee shall study: the magnitude of volunteer shortages, the areas of the state most affected, and the potential impact of shortages on public health and safety and economic development; whether current training and continuing education requirements contribute to the shortage; relationships between full-time and volunteer emergency response departments and the impact that the shortage of volunteers has on non-volunteer departments in neighboring communities; and whether the creation of organizations, particularly in rural areas, may help address the shortage. The committee shall develop legislative options to meet the needs of full-time and volunteer fire departments, including proposals designed to increase the recruitment and retention of volunteer firefighters throughout the state.

Joint Committee on Legislative Organization

Senators: Roth (senate president), *cochair*; Fitzgerald (majority leader), Vukmir (assistant majority leader); Shilling (minority leader), Bewley (assistant minority leader)

Representatives: Vos (assembly speaker), *cochair*; Steineke (majority leader), R. Brooks (assistant majority leader); Barca (minority leader), Hesselbein (assistant minority leader)

Contact: Legislative Council Staff, 608-266-1304; 1 East Main Street, Suite 401, Madison, WI 53703-3382

The Joint Committee on Legislative Organization is the policy-making body for the Legislative Audit Bureau, the Legislative Fiscal Bureau, the Legislative Reference Bureau, and the Legislative Technology Services Bureau. In this capacity, it assigns tasks to each bureau, approves bureau budgets, and sets the salary of bureau heads. The committee selects the four bureau heads, but it acts on the recommendation of the Joint Legislative Audit Committee when appointing the state auditor. The committee also selects the director of the Legislative Council Staff.

The committee may inquire into misconduct by members and employees of the legislature. It oversees a variety of operations, including the work schedule for the legislative session, computer use, space allocation for legislative offices and legislative service agencies, parking on the State Capitol Park grounds, and sale and distribution of legislative documents. The committee recommends which newspaper should serve as the official state newspaper for publication of state legal notices. It advises the Elections Commission on its operations and, upon recommendation of the Joint Legislative Audit Committee, may investigate any problems the Legislative Audit Bureau finds during its audits. The committee may employ outside consultants to study ways to improve legislative staff services and organization.

The ten-member committee consists of the presiding officers and party leadership of both houses. The committee has established a Subcommittee on Legislative Services to advise it on matters pertaining to the legislative institution, including the review of computer technology purchases. The Legislative Council Staff provides staff assistance to the committee.

Joint Survey Committee on Retirement Systems

Senators: Testin, *cochair*; Craig; Erpenbach
Representatives: Novak, *cochair*; Kuglitsch; Mason
Other members: Charlotte Gibson (assistant attorney general appointed by attorney general), Robert J. Conlin (secretary of employee trust funds), Ted Nickel (insurance commissioner), Tim Pederson (public member appointed by governor)

Contact: Legislative Council Staff, 608-266-1304; 1 East Main Street, Suite 401, Madison, WI 53703-3382

The Joint Survey Committee on Retirement Systems makes recommendations on legislation that affects retirement and pension plans for public officers and employees, and its recommendations must be attached as an appendix to each retirement bill. Neither house of the legislature may consider such a bill until the committee submits a written report that describes the proposal's purpose, probable costs, actuarial effect, and desirability as a matter of public policy.

The ten-member committee includes two majority party members and one minority party member from each house of the legislature. An experienced actuary from the Office of the Commissioner of Insurance may be designated to serve in the commissioner's place on the committee. The public member cannot be a participant in any public retirement system in the state and is expected to "represent the interests of the taxpayers." Appointed members serve four-year terms unless they lose the status upon which the appointment was based. The committee is assisted by the Legislative Council Staff in the performance of its duties, but may contract for actuarial assistance outside the classified service.

Joint Legislative State Supported Programs Study and Advisory Committee (Appointments had not yet been made as of June 1, 2017.)

Members of the Joint Legislative State Supported Programs Study and Advisory Committee visit and inspect the State Capitol and all institutions and office buildings owned or leased by the state. They are granted free and full access to all parts of the buildings, the surrounding grounds, and all persons associated with the buildings. The committee may also examine any institution, program, or organization that receives direct or indirect state financial support.

The committee consists of five senators and six representatives. Members appointed from each house must represent the two major political parties, and one legislator from each house must also be a member of the State of Wisconsin Building Commission. Assistance to the committee is provided by the Legislative Council Staff.

Joint Survey Committee on Tax Exemptions

Senators: Feyen, *cochair*; Tiffany; Carpenter
Representatives: August, *cochair*; Swearingen; Young
Other members: Richard G. Chandler (secretary of revenue), Paul Connell (Department of Justice representative appointed by attorney general), Kimberly Shaul (public member appointed by governor)

Contact: Legislative Council Staff, 608-266-1304; 1 East Main Street, Suite 401, Madison, WI 53703-3382

The Joint Survey Committee on Tax Exemptions considers all legislation related to the exemption of persons or property from state or local taxes. It is assisted by the Legislative Council Staff.

Any legislative proposal that provides a tax exemption must be referred to the committee immediately upon introduction. Neither house of the legislature may consider the proposal until the committee has issued its report, attached as an appendix to the bill, describing the proposal's legality, desirability as public policy, and fiscal effect. In the course of its review, the committee is authorized to conduct investigations, hold hearings, and subpoena witnesses. For an executive budget bill that provides a tax exemption, the committee must prepare its report within 60 days.

The committee includes two majority party members and one minority party member from each house of the legislature. The public member must be familiar with the tax problems of local government. Members' terms expire on January 15 of odd-numbered years.

Transportation Projects Commission

Governor: Scott Walker, *chair*
Senators: Cowles, Marklein, Petrowski; Carpenter, Hansen

JAY SALVO, LEGISLATIVE PHOTOGRAPHER

Ann O'Leary of Evansville, the 69th person to hold the title of Alice in Dairyland, addresses the assembly from the rostrum. Alice in Dairyland travels the state as Wisconsin's agricultural ambassador. Behind her is Representative Mark Spreitzer, whose district includes the Evansville area.

Representatives: Ripp, Spiros, 1 vacancy; Spreitzer, 1 vacancy
Other members: Jean Jacobson, Barbara Fleisner LaMue, Michael Ryan (citizen members appointed by governor)
Nonvoting members: Dave Ross (secretary of transportation)
Commission secretary: Kris Sommers

Contact: 608-266-3341; Hill Farms State Transportation Building, Room 901, 4802 Sheboygan Avenue, Madison, WI 53705; PO Box 7913, Madison, WI 53707-7913

The Transportation Projects Commission includes three majority party and two minority party members from each house of the legislature. The commission reviews Department of Transportation recommendations for major highway projects. The department must report its recommendations to the commission by September 15 of each even-numbered year, and the commission, in turn, reports its recommendations to the governor or governor-elect, the legislature, and the Joint Committee on Finance before December 15 of each even-numbered year. The department must also provide the commission with a status report on major transportation projects every six months. The commission also approves the preparation of environmental impact or assessment statements for potential major highway projects.

Commission on Uniform State Laws

Members: Joanne Huelsman (former state senator), *chair*; Aaron Gary (designated by Legislative Reference Bureau chief), *secretary*; Senator Risser; Representatives Tusler, Riemer; Margit Kelley (designated by director, Legislative Council Staff); John Macy, Justice Annette Kingsland Ziegler (public members appointed by governor)

Contact: 608-261-6926; 1 East Main Street, Suite 200, Madison, WI 53701-2037

The Commission on Uniform State Laws examines subjects on which interstate uniformity is desirable, cooperates with the national Uniform Law Commission, and advises the legislature on uniform laws and model laws.

The commission consists of four current or former legislators, two public members, and two members representing legislative service agencies.

Legislative service agencies

Legislative Audit Bureau

State auditor: Joe Chrisman
Special assistant to the state auditor: Anne Sappenfield
Deputy state auditor for program evaluation: Paul Stuiber
Audit directors: Sherry Haakenson, Carolyn Stittleburg, Dean Swenson, Kendra Eppler

Contact: AskLAB@legis.wisconsin.gov; 608-266-2818; 877-FRAUD-17 (fraud, waste, and mismanagement hotline); 22 East Mifflin Street, Suite 500, Madison, WI 53703-2512
Website: http://legis.wisconsin.gov/lab
Publications: Audit reports of individual state agencies and programs; biennial reports.
Number of employees: 86.80
Total budget 2015–17: $16,641,400

The Legislative Audit Bureau is responsible for conducting financial and program audits to assist the legislature in its oversight function. The bureau performs financial audits to determine whether agencies have conducted and reported their financial transactions legally and properly. It undertakes program audits to analyze whether agencies have managed their programs efficiently and effectively and have carried out the policies prescribed by law.

The bureau's authority extends to executive, legislative, and judicial agencies; authorities created by the legislature; special districts; and certain service providers that receive state funds. The bureau may audit any county, city, village, town, or school district at the request of the Joint Legislative Audit Committee.

The bureau provides an annual audit opinion on the state's comprehensive financial statements by the Department of Administration and prepares audits and reports on the financial transactions and records of state agencies at the state auditor's discretion or at the direction of the Joint Legislative Audit Committee. The bureau maintains a toll-free number to receive reports of fraud, waste, and mismanagement in state government.

Typically, the bureau's program audits are conducted at the request of the

Two of the younger members of the assembly include Representative Tyler Vorpagel *(left)*, age 32, who is serving in his second session, and Representative Daniel Riemer, age 30, who is serving in his third session.

JAY SALVO, LEGISLATIVE PHOTOGRAPHER

New legislators find they can turn to their colleagues for guidance in navigating the legislative environment. Representative Cindi Duchow *(right)*, who is beginning her first full term, consults with Representative Mary Felzkowski.

Joint Legislative Audit Committee, initiated by the state auditor, or required by legislation. The reports are reviewed by the Joint Legislative Audit Committee, which may hold hearings on them and may introduce legislation in response to audit recommendations.

The director of the bureau is the state auditor, who is appointed by the Joint Committee on Legislative Organization upon the recommendation of the Joint Legislative Audit Committee. Both the state auditor and the bureau's staff are appointed from outside the classified service and are strictly nonpartisan.

STATUTORY ADVISORY COUNCIL

Municipal Best Practices Reviews Advisory Council Steve O'Malley, Adam Payne (representing the Wisconsin Counties Association); Mark Rohloff (representing the League of Wisconsin Municipalities); Richard Nawrocki (representing the Wisconsin Towns Association) (All are appointed by the state auditor.)

The Municipal Best Practices Reviews Advisory Council advises the state auditor on the selection of county and municipal service delivery practices to be reviewed by the state auditor. The state auditor conducts periodic reviews of procedures and practices used by local governments in the delivery of governmental services; identifies variations in costs and effectiveness of such services between counties and municipalities; and recommends practices to save money or provide more effective service delivery. Council members are chosen from candidates submitted by the organizations represented.

Legislative Council Staff

Director: Terry C. Anderson
Deputy director: Jessica Karls-Ruplinger
Rules clearinghouse director: Scott Grosz
Rules clearinghouse assistant director: Margit Kelley

Contact: 1 East Main Street, Suite 401, Madison, WI 53703-3382; 608-266-1304; leg.council@legis.wisconsin.gov
Website: http://lc.legis.wisconsin.gov

See the entry for the Joint Legislative Council, beginning on page 163.

Legislative Fiscal Bureau

Director: Robert Wm. Lang
Assistant director: David Loppnow
Program supervisors: Jere Bauer, Paul Ferguson, Charles Morgan, Rob Reinhardt, Al Runde
Supervising analysts: Kendra Bonderud, Jon Dyck
Administrative assistant: Becky Hannah
Supervising program assistant: Sandy Swain

Contact: fiscal.bureau@legis.wisconsin.gov; 608-266-3847; 1 East Main Street, Suite 301, Madison, WI 53703
Website: http://legis.wisconsin.gov/lfb
Publications: Biennial budget and budget adjustment summaries: summaries of state agency budget requests; cumulative and comparative summaries of the governor's proposals, Joint Committee on Finance provisions and legislative amendments, and separate summaries of legislative amendments when necessary; summary of governor's partial vetoes. Informational reports on various state programs, budget issue papers, and revenue estimates. (Reports and papers available on the Internet or upon request.)
Number of employees: 35.00
Total budget 2015–17: $7,995,400

The Legislative Fiscal Bureau develops fiscal information for the legislature, and its services must be impartial and nonpartisan. One of the bureau's principal duties is to staff the Joint Committee on Finance and assist its members. As part of this responsibility, the bureau studies the state budget and its long-range implications, reviews state revenues and expenditures, suggests alternatives to the committee and the legislature, and prepares a report detailing earmarks in the budget bill. In addition, the bureau provides information on all other bills before the committee and analyzes agency requests for new positions and appropriation supplements outside of the budget process.

The bureau provides fiscal information to any legislative committee or legislator upon request. On its own initiative, or at legislative direction, the bureau may conduct studies of any financial issue affecting the state. To aid the bureau in performing its duties, the director or designated employees are granted access to all state departments and to any records maintained by the agencies relating to their expenditures, revenues, operations, and structure.

The Joint Committee on Legislative Organization is the policy-making body for the Legislative Fiscal Bureau, and it selects the bureau's director. The director is assisted by program supervisors responsible for broadly defined subject areas of government budgeting and fiscal operations. The director and all bureau staff are chosen outside the classified service.

Legislative Reference Bureau

Chief: Richard A. Champagne
Deputy chief: Cathlene M. Hanaman
Legal services manager: Joe Kreye
Information services manager: Stefanie Rose
Administrative services manager: Wendy L. Jackson

Contact: 608-266-3561 (legal); 608-266-0341 (reference); 1 East Main Street, Suite 200, Madison, WI 53703; PO Box 2037, Madison, WI 53701-2037
Website: http://legis.wisconsin.gov/lrb
Publications: Wisconsin Statutes; Laws of Wisconsin; Wisconsin Administrative Code and Register; *Wisconsin Blue Book*; informational, legal, and research reports.
Number of employees: 60.00
Total budget 2015–17: $12,383,800

The Legislative Reference Bureau provides nonpartisan, confidential bill drafting and other legal services to the Wisconsin Legislature. The bureau employs a staff of attorneys and editors who serve the legislature and its members and who draft and prepare all legislation, including the executive budget bill, for introduction in the legislature. Bureau attorneys also draft legislation at the request of state agencies. The bureau publishes all laws enacted during each biennial legislative session and incorporates the laws into the Wisconsin Statutes. The bureau prints the Wisconsin Statutes every two years and updates continuously the Wisconsin Statutes on the Wisconsin Legislature's Internet site. The bureau publishes and updates the Wisconsin Administrative Code and the Wisconsin Administrative Register on the Internet site.

The Legislative Reference Bureau also employs research analysts and librarians who provide information and research services to the legislature and the public. The bureau publishes the *Wisconsin Blue Book* and informational, legal, and research reports. The bureau responds to inquiries from legislators, legislative staff, and the public on current law and pending legislation and the operations of the legislature and state government. The bureau operates a legislative library that contains an extensive collection of materials pertaining to Wisconsin government and politics. The bureau compiles and publishes the Assembly Rules, Senate Rules, and Joint Rules. The bureau maintains for public inspection the drafting records of all legislation introduced in the Wisconsin Legislature, beginning with the 1927 session.

The Joint Committee on Legislative Organization is the policy-making body for the Legislative Reference Bureau, and it selects the bureau chief. The chief employs all bureau staff. The chief and the bureau staff serve outside the classified service.

The state capitol is celebrating its centennial in 2017 with several events, including this kick-off in the rotunda in January. The current capitol was completed in 1917 after nearly ten years of planning and construction. More information can be found at https://capitol100th.wisconsin.gov.

JAY SALVO, LEGISLATIVE PHOTOGRAPHER

Legislative Technology Services Bureau

Director: Jeff Ylvisaker
Business manager: Erin Esser
Enterprise operations manager: Matt Harned
Geographic information systems manager: Tony Van Der Wielen
Software development manager: Doug DeMuth
Technical support manager: Nate Rohan

Contact: 608-264-8582; 17 West Main Street, Suite 200, Madison, WI 53703
Website: http://legis.wisconsin.gov/ltsb
Number of employees: 43.00
Total budget 2015–17: $8,545,200

The Legislative Technology Services Bureau provides confidential, nonpartisan information technology services and support to the Wisconsin Legislature. The bureau creates, maintains, and enhances specialized software used for bill drafting, floor session activity, and committee activity, managing constituent interactions, producing the Wisconsin Statutes and the Wisconsin Administrative Code, and publishing the *Wisconsin Blue Book*. It supports the publication of legislative documents including bills and amendments, house journals, daily calendars, and the *Bulletin of the Proceedings*. The bureau also maintains network infrastructure, data center operations, electronic communications, desktops, laptops, printers, and other technology devices. It keeps an inventory of computer hardware and software assets and manages technology replacement schedules. It supports the redistricting project following each decennial U.S. Census and provides mapping services throughout the decade. The bureau also supports the legislature during floor sessions, delivers audio and video services, manages the technology for the Wisconsin Legislature's websites, and offers training services for legislators and staff in the use of information technology.

The bureau's director is appointed by the Joint Committee on Legislative Organization and has overall management responsibilities for the bureau. The director appoints bureau staff; both the director and the staff serve outside the classified service.

Office of the Governor

Governor: Scott Walker
Chief of staff: Rich Zipperer
Location: 115 East, State Capitol, Madison
Contact: govgeneral@wisconsin.gov; 608-266-1212; PO Box 7863, Madison, WI 53707-7863
Website: https://walker.wi.gov
Number of employees: 37.25
Total budget 2015–17: $7,953,000

The governor is the state's chief executive. Voters elect the governor and lieutenant governor on a joint ballot to a four-year term. Most of the individuals, commissions, and boards that head the major executive branch agencies are appointed by, and serve at the pleasure of, the governor, although many of these appointments require senate confirmation. The governor reviews all bills passed by the legislature and can veto an entire bill and, in the case of an appropriation bill, can veto parts of a bill. A two-thirds vote of the members present in each house of the legislature is required to override the governor's veto. In addition, the governor can call the legislature into special session to deal with specific legislation.

If a vacancy occurs in the state senate or assembly, state law directs the governor to call a special election. Vacancies in elective county offices and judicial positions can be filled by gubernatorial appointment for the unexpired terms or until a successor is elected. The governor may dismiss sheriffs, district attorneys, coroners, and registers of deeds for cause.

Finally, the governor serves as commander in chief of the Wisconsin National Guard when it is called into state service during emergencies, such as natural disasters and civil disturbances.

Subordinate statutory boards, councils, and committees

STATE COUNCIL ON ALCOHOL AND OTHER DRUG ABUSE

The State Council on Alcohol and Other Drug Abuse coordinates and reviews the efforts of state agencies to control and prevent alcohol and drug abuse. It evaluates program effectiveness, recommends improved programming, educates people about the dangers of drug abuse, and allocates responsibility for

DEPARTMENT OF WORKFORCE DEVELOPMENT

Governor Walker visits Beloit High School to meet with students participating in the Department of Workforce Development's Youth Apprenticeship Program.

various alcohol and drug abuse programs among state agencies. The council also reviews and provides an opinion to the legislature on proposed legislation that relates to alcohol and other drug abuse policies, programs, or services.

COUNCIL ON MILITARY AND STATE RELATIONS

The Council on Military and State Relations assists the governor by working with the state's military installations, commands and communities, state agencies, and economic development professionals to develop and implement strategies designed to enhance those installations. It advises and assists the governor on issues related to the location of military installations and assists and cooperates with state agencies to determine how those agencies can better serve military communities and families. It also assists the efforts of military families and their support groups regarding quality-of-life issues for service members and their families.

COUNCIL ON VETERANS EMPLOYMENT

The Council on Veterans Employment advises and assists the governor and state agencies with the recruitment and employment of veterans so as to increase veteran employment in state government.

Independent entities attached for administrative purposes

DISABILITY BOARD

Members: Scott Walker (governor), Patience Roggensack (chief justice of the supreme court), Senator Roth (senate president), Senator Shilling (senate minority leader), Representative Vos (assembly speaker), Representative Barca (assembly minority leader), Robert Golden (dean, UW Medical School)

The Disability Board is authorized to determine when a temporary vacancy exists in the office of the governor, lieutenant governor, secretary of state, treasurer, state superintendent of public instruction, or attorney general because the incumbent is incapacitated due to illness or injury.

Nongovernmental entities with gubernatorial appointments

WISCONSIN HUMANITIES COUNCIL

Executive director: Dena Wortzel
Contact: contact@wisconsinhumanities.org; 608-262-0706; 3801 Regent Street, Madison, WI 53705
Website: www.wisconsinhumanities.org

The Wisconsin Humanities Council is an independent affiliate of the National Endowment for the Humanities. It is supported by state, federal, and private funding. Its mission is to create and support programs that use history, culture, and discussion to strengthen community life in Wisconsin. The governor appoints six members to the council. Other members are elected by the council.

THE MEDICAL COLLEGE OF WISCONSIN, INC.

President and CEO: John Raymond, Sr.
Contact: 414-955-8296; 8701 Watertown Plank Road, Milwaukee, WI 53226
Website: www.mcw.edu
State appropriation 2015–17: $20,399,700

The Medical College of Wisconsin, Inc., is a private nonprofit institution located in Milwaukee that operates a school of medicine, school of pharmacy, and graduate school of biomedical sciences. The college receives state funds for education, training, and research; for its family medicine residency program; and for cancer research. The college is required to fulfill certain reporting requirements concerning its finances, student body, and programs. The governor appoints two members to the board of trustees with the advice and consent of the senate.

Governor's special committees

The committees listed below were created or continued by Governor Scott Walker by executive order to conduct studies and provide advice. Members serve at the governor's pleasure. These committees submit final reports to the governor or governor-elect prior to the beginning of a new gubernatorial term and, unless continued by executive order, expire on the fourth Monday of January of the year in which a new gubernatorial term begins.

COUNCIL ON AUTISM

Aligned to: Department of Health Services; 1 West Wilson Street, Madison, WI 53703
Contact: Andrea Jacobson; AndreaL.Jacobson@dhs.wisconsin.gov; 608-261-5998
Website: https://autismcouncil.wisconsin.gov

Created by Governor Jim Doyle in 2005 and continued by Governor Walker, the Council on Autism advises the Department of Health Services on strategies for implementing statewide supports and services for children with autism. A majority of its members are parents of children with autism or autism spectrum disorders.

BICYCLE COORDINATING COUNCIL

Aligned to: Department of Transportation; 4802 Sheboygan Avenue, PO Box 7913, Madison, WI 53707-7913
Contact: Jill Mrotek Glenzinski; jill.mrotekglenzinski@dot.wi.gov; 608-267-7757

Created by Governor Tommy G. Thompson in 1991 and continued most recently by Governor Walker, the Bicycle Coordinating Council's concerns include encouraging the use of the bicycle as an alternative means of transportation, promoting bicycle safety and education, promoting bicycling as a recreational and tourist activity, and disseminating information about state and federal funding for bicycle programs.

WISCONSIN COASTAL MANAGEMENT COUNCIL

Aligned to: Department of Administration; 101 East Wilson Street, PO Box 8944, Madison, WI 53708-8944
Contact: Michael Friis; michael.friis@wisconsin.gov; coastal@wisconsin.gov; 608-267-7982
Website: www.doa.state.wi.us/divisions/intergovernmental-relations/Wisconsin-Coastal-Management

The Wisconsin Coastal Management Council was created by acting Governor Martin J. Schreiber in 1977 to comply with provisions of the federal Coastal Zone Management Act of 1972 and to implement Wisconsin's Coastal Management Program. It was continued most recently by Governor Walker. The council advises the governor with respect to Wisconsin's coastal management efforts.

CRIMINAL JUSTICE COORDINATING COUNCIL

Aligned to: Department of Justice; 608-266-1221; PO Box 7857, Madison, WI 53707-7857

Website: https://cjcc.doj.wi.gov

Created by Governor Walker in 2012, the Criminal Justice Coordinating Council is tasked with assisting the governor in directing, collaborating with, and coordinating the services of state, local, and private actors in the criminal justice system to increase public safety and the system's efficiency and effectiveness. Members of the council represent various aspects of the state's criminal justice system.

GOVERNOR'S COMMITTEE FOR PEOPLE WITH DISABILITIES

Aligned to: Department of Health Services; 1 West Wilson Street, Room 551, Madison, WI 53703

Contact: Dan Johnson; dan.johnson@wisconsin.gov; 608-267-9582

Website: https://gcpd.wisconsin.gov/

The Governor's Committee for People with Disabilities, in its present form, was established in 1976 by Governor Patrick J. Lucey and has since been continued by each succeeding governor. The committee's functions include advising the governor on a broad range of issues affecting people with disabilities, including involvement in the workforce, reviewing legislation affecting people with disabilities, and promoting public awareness of the needs and abilities of people with disabilities.

EARLY CHILDHOOD ADVISORY COUNCIL

Aligned to: Department of Children and Families; 201 East Washington Avenue, 2nd Floor, PO Box 8916 Madison, WI 53708-8916

Contact: Amanda Reeve; Amanda.Reeve@wisconsin.gov; 608-422-6079

Website: https://dcf.wisconsin.gov/ecac

Governor Jim Doyle created the Early Childhood Advisory Council in 2008 in accordance with federal law, and Governor Walker has continued it. The council advises the governor on the development of a comprehensive statewide early childhood system by, among other things, conducting needs assessments, developing recommendations for increasing participation of children in early childhood services, assessing the capacity of higher education to support the development of early childhood professionals, and making recommendations for the improvement of early learning standards.

EARLY INTERVENTION INTERAGENCY COORDINATING COUNCIL

Aligned to: Department of Health Services; 1 West Wilson Street, Madison, WI 53703
Contact: Terri Enters; Terri.Enters@wisconsin.gov; 608-267-3270
Website: https://b3icc.wisconsin.gov

First established by Governor Tommy G. Thompson in 1987, re-established by Governor Thompson in 1998, and continued most recently by Governor Walker, the Early Intervention Interagency Coordinating Council was created pursuant to federal law. The council assists the Department of Health Services in the development and administration of early intervention services, referred to as the "Birth to Three Program," for infants and toddlers with developmental delays and their families. The council's members include parents of children with disabilities.

GOVERNOR'S COUNCIL ON FINANCIAL LITERACY

Aligned to: Department of Financial Institutions, Office of Financial Literacy; PO Box 8861, Madison, WI 53708-8861
Contact: David Mancl; david.mancl@dfi.wisconsin.gov; 608-267-1713
Website: www.wdfi.org/ymm/govcouncilfinlit

Created by Governor Jim Doyle in 2005 and continued by Governor Walker, the Governor's Council on Financial Literacy works with state agencies, private entities, and nonprofit associations to improve financial literacy among Wisconsin citizens. The council also promotes the financial literacy awareness and education campaign called Money Smart Week.

HISTORICAL RECORDS ADVISORY BOARD

Aligned to: State Historical Society of Wisconsin; 816 State Street, Madison, WI 53706
Contact: Matthew Blessing; matthew.blessing@wisconsinhistory.org; 608-264-6480
Website: www.wisconsinhistory.org/Content.
aspx?dsNav=N:4294963828-4294963805&dsRecordDetails=R:CS3558

Continued most recently by Governor Walker, the Historical Records Advisory Board enables the state to participate in a grant program of the National Historical Publications and Records Commission. The board also promotes the availability and use of historic records as a key to understanding American culture.

HOMELAND SECURITY COUNCIL

Contact: 608-242-3075; 2400 Wright Street, PO Box 14587, Madison, WI 53708-0587

Website: http://homelandsecurity.wi.gov

Created by Governor Jim Doyle in 2003 and continued by Governor Walker, the Homeland Security Council advises the governor and coordinates the efforts of state and local officials concerning the prevention of and response to potential threats to the homeland security of Wisconsin.

INDEPENDENT LIVING COUNCIL OF WISCONSIN

Executive director: Mike Bachhuber

Contact: director@ilcw.org; 608-256-9257; 866-656-4010 (toll free); 3810 Milwaukee Street, Madison, WI 53714

Website: www.wis-il.net/council

Governor Tommy G. Thompson created the Independent Living Council of Wisconsin in 1994. Governor Jim Doyle established the council as a nonprofit entity in 2004, and Governor Walker has continued it. In coordination with the Division of Vocational Rehabilitation in the Department of Workforce Development, the council maintains the state's plan for independent living services for people with disabilities. The majority of the council's members are persons with disabilities. At least one member must be a director of a center for independent living, and at least one member must represent Native American vocational rehabilitation programs.

GOVERNOR'S INFORMATION TECHNOLOGY EXECUTIVE STEERING COMMITTEE

Aligned to: Department of Administration; 101 East Wilson Street, PO Box 7864, Madison, WI 53707

Contact: Vicky Halverson; vicky.halverson@wisconsin.gov

Governor Walker created the Governor's Information Technology Executive Steering Committee in 2013. It is responsible for the effective and efficient application of information technology assets across state agencies.

GOVERNOR'S JUDICIAL SELECTION ADVISORY COMMITTEE

Aligned to: Office of the Governor; Room 115 East, State Capitol, PO Box 7863, Madison, WI 53707-7863

Contact: Katie Ignatowski; katie.ignatowski@wisconsin.gov; 608-266-1212

Governor Walker created the Governor's Judicial Selection Advisory Committee in 2011. The committee recommends candidates to the governor to fill judicial vacancies in the state courts.

GOVERNOR'S JUVENILE JUSTICE COMMISSION

Aligned to: Department of Justice; PO Box 7857, Madison, WI 53707-7857
Contact: Nina Emerson; emersonnj@doj.state.wi.us; 608-261-6626

Governor Tommy G. Thompson created the Juvenile Justice Advisory Group in 1989. In 1991, he recreated it as the Governor's Juvenile Justice Commission, which was continued most recently by Governor Walker. The commission distributes federal grant moneys for the improvement of the juvenile justice system in the state. It also advises the governor and the legislature concerning juvenile justice issues.

GOVERNOR'S TASK FORCE ON OPIOID ABUSE

Aligned to: Department of Health Services; 1 West Wilson Street, Room 551, Madison, WI 53703

Created by Governor Scott Walker in 2016, the Governor's Task Force on Opioid Abuse advises the governor regarding opioid abuse in the state. The task force gathers and reviews data; analyzes actions taken in Wisconsin, as well as actions taken in other states and by the National Governors Association Compact to Fight Opioid Addiction; and makes policy recommendations.

GOVERNOR'S COUNCIL ON PHYSICAL FITNESS AND HEALTH

Aligned to: Office of the Governor; 608-267-1212; Room 115 East, State Capitol, PO Box 7863, Madison, WI 53707-7863
Website: www.fitness-health.wisconsin.gov/index.asp?locid=132

Governor Anthony Earl established the Governor's Council on Physical Fitness and Health in 1983, and Governor Walker recreated it in 2012. The council develops policy recommendations to improve the status of and educate the public concerning children's health, physical fitness, and nutrition. The council also encourages obesity prevention for all state residents.

STATE REHABILITATION COUNCIL

Aligned to: Department of Workforce Development, Division of Vocational Rehabilitation; 608-261-0076; 201 East Washington Avenue, PO Box 7852, Madison, WI 53707-7852
Website: http://dwd.wisconsin.gov/dvr/wrc

Created by Governor Tommy G. Thompson in 1999 and continued most recently by Governor Walker, the State Rehabilitation Council advises the Department of Workforce Development on a statewide vocational rehabilitation plan for disabled individuals required by federal law.

WISCONSIN TECHNOLOGY COMMITTEE

Aligned to: Wisconsin Technology Council; 455 Science Drive, Suite 240, Madison, WI 53711
Contact: Tom Still; 608-442-7557; 888-443-5285 (toll free)
Website: http://wisconsintechnologycouncil.com

Created by Governor Walker in 2011, the Wisconsin Technology Committee consists of the members of the Wisconsin Technology Council, a nonprofit corporation that was created by state legislation but later removed from the statutes. The committee provides a means by which the council can coordinate with state government. The council assists the state in promoting the creation, development, and retention of science- and technology-based businesses.

TELECOMMUNICATIONS RELAY SERVICE COUNCIL

Aligned to: Department of Administration, Division of Enterprise Technology; 101 East Wilson Street, 8th Floor, PO Box 7844, Madison, WI 53707-7844
Contact: Jack R. Cassell; jack.cassell@wisconsin.gov; 608-234-4781

Created by Governor Tommy G. Thompson in 1990 and continued most recently by Governor Walker, the Telecommunications Relay Service Council advises the state concerning telecommunications relay service, including with respect to rates and availability. The members include one speech-impaired person, one hearing-impaired person, one speech-impaired and hearing-impaired person, and one person not having a speech or hearing impairment.

GOVERNOR'S COUNCIL ON WORKFORCE INVESTMENT

Aligned to: Department of Workforce Development; 201 E. Washington Avenue, Madison, WI 53703; PO Box 7972, Madison, WI 53707-7972; 608-266-5336
Website: www.wi-cwi.org

Governor Tommy G. Thompson created the Governor's Council on Workforce Investment in 1999. Governor Scott Walker reconstituted the council in 2015 as a result of changes to federal law. The council is charged with carrying out certain duties and functions established under federal law governing state workforce development boards, including recommending strategies that align workforce development resources to support economic development, promoting programs to increase the number of skilled workers in the workforce and provide resources to job seekers, and recommending strategies that align workforce development resources to support economic development.

Office of the Lieutenant Governor

Lieutenant governor: Rebecca Kleefisch
Chief of staff: Daniel Suhr
Location: 19 East, State Capitol, Madison
Contact: ltgov@wisconsin.gov; 608-266-3516; PO Box 2043, Madison, WI 53702-2043
Website: www.ltgov.wisconsin.gov
Number of employees: 4.00
Total budget 2015–17: $574,200

The lieutenant governor is the state's second-ranking executive officer, a position comparable to that of the vice president of the United States. If the incumbent governor dies, resigns, or is removed from office, the lieutenant governor becomes governor for the balance of the unexpired term. The lieutenant governor serves as acting governor while the governor is unable to perform the duties of the office due to impeachment, incapacitation, or absence from the state. If there is a vacancy in the office of lieutenant governor, the governor must nominate a successor to serve, upon confirmation by both the senate and assembly, for the remainder of the unexpired term.

The governor may designate the lieutenant governor to represent the governor's office on any statutory board, commission, or committee on which the governor is entitled to membership, on any nonstatutory committee established by the governor, and on any intergovernmental body created to maintain relationships with federal, state, and local governments or regional agencies. The governor may ask the lieutenant governor to coordinate certain state services and programs the governor is directed by law to coordinate.

Voters elect the governor and lieutenant governor on a joint ballot to four-year terms. Candidates are nominated independently in the partisan August primary, but voters cast a combined ballot for the two offices in the November election.

Department of Administration

Department secretary: Scott Neitzel
Deputy secretary: Cate Zeuske
Location: State Administration Building; 101 East Wilson Street, Madison
Contact: 608-266-1741; PO Box 7864, Madison, WI 53707-7864
Website: www.doa.wi.gov
Number of employees: 926.73
Total budget 2015–17: $2,257,947,600

The Department of Administration is administered by a secretary who is appointed by the governor with the advice and consent of the senate.

The department provides a wide range of services to other state agencies, including personnel management, payroll, accounting systems, and legal services. The department administers the state civil service system. The department administers the state's information system, procurement policies and contracts, fleet transportation, and risk management. It oversees the state's buildings and leased office space, as well as statewide facilities project planning and analysis. The department oversees the Capitol Police. It administers a federal and state funded low-income household energy assistance program and offers program assistance and funds to address homelessness and support affordable housing, public infrastructure, and economic development opportunities. It provides fiscal and policy analysis to the governor for development of executive budget proposals. It regulates racing, charitable gaming, and Indian gaming. The department advises the Building Commission and the governor on the issuance of state debt. It administers finances for the clean water revolving loan fund program. It manages the state's Section 529 College Savings programs and the local government investment pool. Finally, the department provides a variety of services to the public and state, local, and tribal governments.

Subordinate statutory boards, councils, and committees

COUNCIL ON AFFIRMATIVE ACTION

Contact: 101 E. Wilson Street, 4th Floor, Madison, WI 53703

The Council on Affirmative Action advises the administrator of the Division of Personnel Management in the department, evaluates affirmative action programs throughout the classified service, seeks compliance with state and federal regulations, and recommends improvements in the state's affirmative action efforts.

CERTIFICATION STANDARDS REVIEW COUNCIL

The Certification Standards Review Council reviews the Department of Natural Resources laboratory certification and registration program and makes recommendations on programs for testing water, wastewater, waste material, soil, and hazardous substances.

COUNCIL ON SMALL BUSINESS, VETERAN-OWNED BUSINESS AND MINORITY BUSINESS OPPORTUNITIES

The Council on Small Business, Veteran-Owned Business and Minority Business Opportunities advises the department on how to increase the participation of small businesses, veteran-owned businesses, and minority businesses in state purchasing.

STATE EMPLOYEES SUGGESTION BOARD

Website: http://suggest.wi.gov

The State Employees Suggestion Board administers an awards program to encourage unusual and meritorious suggestions and accomplishments by state employees that promote economy and efficiency in government functions.

Independent entities attached for administrative purposes

BOARD ON AGING AND LONG-TERM CARE

Members: Eva Arnold, Barbara Bechtel, Michael Brooks, Tanya L. Meyer, Valerie Palarski, James Surprise, Dale Taylor
Executive director: Heather A. Bruemmer
Contact: boaltc@wisconsin.gov; 608-246-7013; 1402 Pankratz Street, Suite 111, Madison, WI 53704
Website: http://longtermcare.wi.gov
Number of employees: 40.50
Total budget 2015–17: $6,071,600

The Board on Aging and Long-Term Care reports to the governor and the legislature on matters relating to long-term care for the aged and disabled. The board monitors the development and implementation of federal, state, and local laws and regulations related to long-term care facilities and investigates complaints from persons receiving long-term care. The board operates the Medigap Helpline, which provides information on insurance designed to supplement Medicare.

OFFICE OF BUSINESS DEVELOPMENT

Director: Nancy Mistele

Deputy director: Joe Knilans

Contact: 608-267-7873; PO Box 7864, Madison, WI 53707

The Office of Business Development provides administrative support to the Small Business Regulatory Review Board.

CLAIMS BOARD

Chair: Corey Finkelmeyer

Secretary: Christopher Green

Contact: patricia.reardon@wisconsin.gov; 608-264-9595; PO Box 7864, Madison, WI 53707-7864

Website: www.claimsboard.wi.gov

Number of employees: 0.00

Total budget 2015–17: $50,000

The Claims Board investigates and makes recommendations on all money claims against the state for $10 or more. The findings and recommendations are reported to the legislature, and no claim may be considered by the legislature until the board has made its recommendation.

COLLEGE SAVINGS PROGRAM BOARD

Administrator: James DiUlio

Contact: 608-264-7899; PO Box 7864, Madison, WI 53707-7871

Website: http://529.wi.gov

The College Savings Program Board administers the Edvest, Tomorrow's Scholar, and Tuition Units plans, which provide for investment accounts with certain tax advantages that are held in a trust fund to cover higher education expenses.

DEPOSITORY SELECTION BOARD

Members: Matt Adamczyk (state treasurer), Scott Neitzel (secretary of administration), Richard G. Chandler (secretary of revenue)

The Depository Selection Board establishes procedures to be used by state agencies to select depositories for public funds and to contract for depository services.

ELECTRONIC RECORDING COUNCIL

Chair: Sharon Hoffman

The Electronic Recording Council adopts standards regarding the electronic recording of real estate documents to be promulgated by rule by the department.

DIVISION OF HEARINGS AND APPEALS

Administrator: Brian Hayes
Contact: dhamail@wisconsin.gov; 608-266-7709; 5005 University Avenue, Suite 201, Madison, WI 53705-5400
Website: www.doa.wi.gov/divisions/Hearings-and-Appeals
Number of employees: 83.15
Total budget 2015–17: $17,241,400

The Division of Hearings and Appeals decides contested proceedings for the Department of Natural Resources, cases arising under the Department of Justice's Crime Victim Compensation Program, and appeals related to actions of the Departments of Health Services, Children and Families, Safety and Professional Services, and Agriculture, Trade and Consumer Protection. It hears appeals from the Department of Transportation, including those related to motor vehicle dealer licenses, highway signs, motor carrier regulation, and disputes arising between motor vehicle dealers and manufacturers. The division conducts hearings for the Department of Corrections on probation, parole, and extended supervision revocation and juvenile aftercare supervision. It handles contested cases for the Department of Public Instruction, the Department of Employee Trust Funds, and the Low-Income Home Energy Assistance Program of the Department of Administration. Other agencies may contract with the division for hearing services.

INCORPORATION REVIEW BOARD

Chair: Dawn Vick
Location: 101 East Wilson Street, 9th Floor, Madison
Contact: wimunicipalboundaryreview@wi.gov; 608-264-6102; PO Box 1645, Madison, WI 53701
Website: http://doa.wi.gov/municipalboundaryreview

The Incorporation Review Board reviews petitions for incorporating territory as a city or village to determine whether the petition meets certain statutory standards and is in the public interest.

INTEROPERABILITY COUNCIL

Chair: Matthew Joski

The Interoperability Council develops strategies and makes recommendations on how to achieve and operate a statewide public safety interoperable communication system.

LABOR AND INDUSTRY REVIEW COMMISSION

Chair: Laurie McCallum
Location: Public Broadcasting Building, 3319 West Beltline Highway, Madison
Contact: lirc@wisconsin.gov; 608-266-9850; PO Box 8126, Madison, WI 53708-8126
Website: http://lirc.wisconsin.gov
Number of employees: 26.50
Total budget 2015–17: $6,354,200

The Labor and Industry Review Commission reviews the decisions of the Department of Workforce Development related to unemployment insurance, worker's compensation, fair employment, and public accommodations. The commission also hears appeals about discrimination in postsecondary education involving a person's physical condition or developmental disability.

NATIONAL AND COMMUNITY SERVICE BOARD

Chair: Lisa Delmore
Executive director: Jeanne M. Duffy
Contact: 608-261-6716; 1 West Wilson Street, Room B274, Madison, WI 53703
Website: www.servewisconsin.wi.gov
Number of employees: 5.00
Total budget 2015–17: $8,483,300

The National and Community Service Board prepares a plan for providing national service programs (which must ensure outreach to organizations serving underrepresented populations) and provides a system to recruit and place participants in national service programs. The board receives and distributes funds from governmental and private sources and acts as an intermediary between the Corporation for National and Community Service and local agencies.

BOARD FOR PEOPLE WITH DEVELOPMENTAL DISABILITIES

Chair: Patrick Young
Contact: bpddhelp@wi-bpdd.org; 608-266-7826; 888-332-1677 (toll free); 608-266-6660 (TTY); 101 East Wilson Street, Room 219, Madison, WI 53703-2796
Website: http://wi-bpdd.org
Number of employees: 7.75
Total budget 2015–17: $2,800,100

The Board for People with Developmental Disabilities advises the department, other state agencies, the legislature, and the governor on matters related to developmental disabilities.

PUBLIC RECORDS BOARD

Chair: Matthew Blessing
Executive secretary: Linda Barth; lindas1.barth@wisconsin.gov
Contact: 608-267-7693; 101 East Wilson Street, Madison, WI 53703
Website: http://publicrecordsboard.wi.gov

The Public Records Board is responsible for the preservation of important state records, the cost-effective management of records by state agencies, and the orderly disposition of state records that have become obsolete. State agencies must have written approval from the board to dispose of records they generate or receive.

SMALL BUSINESS REGULATORY REVIEW BOARD

Members: Senator Testin, Representative Neylon, Steve Davis, Erich Korth, Pravin Raikar, Melissa Remis, Jim Ring, Connie Smith, Guy Wood

The Small Business Regulatory Review Board reviews state agency rules and guidelines, proposed rules, and emergency rules to determine whether they place an unnecessary burden on small businesses.

STATE CAPITOL AND EXECUTIVE RESIDENCE BOARD

Chair: Senator Risser

The State Capitol and Executive Residence Board directs the maintenance of the property, furnishings, and furniture of the capitol and executive residence. The board must approve all renovations, repairs, installation of fixtures, decorative items, and furnishings for the grounds and buildings of the capitol and executive residence.

STATE USE BOARD

Chair: Jean Zweifel
Contact: Bureau of Procurement, Division of Enterprise Operations; 608-266-5462; PO Box 7867, Madison, WI 53707-7867
Number of employees: 1.50
Total budget 2015–17: $264,700

The State Use Board oversees state purchases of goods and services from charitable organizations or nonprofit institutions that employ individuals with severe disabilities for at least 75 percent of the direct labor used in providing the goods or services.

TAX APPEALS COMMISSION

Members: Lorna Hemp Boll, David D. Wilmoth, David L. Coon
Legal assistant: Nancy Batz; nancy.batz@wisconsin.gov; 608-266-9754
Contact: 608-266-1391; 5005 University Avenue, Suite 110, Madison, WI 53705
Number of employees: 5.00
Total budget 2015–17: $1,128,800

The Tax Appeals Commission hears and decides appeals of assessments and determinations made by the Department of Revenue involving state-imposed taxes and state tax assessments of manufacturing property. The commission also adjudicates disputes between taxpayers and the Department of Transportation regarding certain motor vehicle taxes and fees. In addition, the commission has jurisdiction over cases involving the reasonableness of municipally imposed fees. The commission's decisions may be appealed to circuit court.

DIVISION OF TRUST LANDS AND INVESTMENTS

Executive secretary: Jonathan B. Barry
Deputy secretary: Tom German
Location: 101 East Wilson Street, 2nd Floor, Madison
Contact: bcplinfo@wisconsin.gov; 608-266-1370; PO Box 8943, Madison, WI 53708-8943
Website: http://bcpl.wisconsin.gov

The Division of Trust Lands and Investments assists the Board of Commissioners of Public Lands in its work and is under the direction and supervision of that board. The division is headed by an executive secretary who is appointed by the board. See the entry for the Board of Commissioners of Public Lands, beginning on page 232.

WASTE FACILITY SITING BOARD

Members: (all seats currently vacant)
Acting executive director: Brian Hayes
Contact: dhamail@wisconsin.gov; 608-266-7709; 5005 University Avenue, Suite 201, Madison, WI 53705-5400
Website: www.doa.wi.gov/Divisions/Hearing-and-Appeals/Waste-Facility-Siting-Board

Number of employees: 0.00
Total budget 2015–17: $91,000

The Waste Facility Siting Board supervises a mandated negotiation-arbitration procedure between applicants for new or expanded solid or hazardous waste facility licenses and local committees composed of representatives from the municipalities affected by proposed facilities. It is authorized to make final awards in arbitration hearings and can enforce legal deadlines and other obligations of applicants and local committees during the process.

WOMEN'S COUNCIL

Chair: Mary Jo Baas
Executive director: Christine Lidbury
Contact: womenscouncil@wisconsin.gov; 608-266-2219; 101 East Wilson Street, 9th Floor, Madison, WI 53702
Website: http://womenscouncil.wi.gov
Number of employees: 1.00
Total budget 2015–17: $287,600

The Women's Council identifies barriers that prevent women in Wisconsin from participating fully and equally in all aspects of life. The council advises state agencies about how current and emerging state policies, laws, and rules have an impact on women; recommends changes to the public and private sectors and initiates legislation to further women's economic and social equality and improve this state's tax base and economy; and disseminates information on the status of women.

Department of Agriculture, Trade and Consumer Protection

Board of Agriculture, Trade and Consumer Protection: Miranda Leis, *chair*
Department secretary: Ben Brancel
Deputy secretary: Jeff Lyon
Location: 2811 Agriculture Drive, Madison
Contact: 608-224-5012; PO Box 8911, Madison, WI 53708-8911
Website: https://datcp.wi.gov
Number of employees: 644.79
Total budget 2015–17: $191,655,000

The Department of Agriculture, Trade and Consumer Protection is directed and supervised by the Board of Agriculture, Trade and Consumer Protection

(*top*) An entomologist with the Department of Agriculture, Trade and Consumer Protection checks a trap for agricultural pests as part of the department's growing season survey that helps farmers with pest control. (*above*) An inspector for the Division of Food and Recreational Safety tests water samples to be sure a water park is safe.

and is administered by a secretary. The members of the board and the secretary are appointed by the governor with the advice and consent of the senate.

The department regulates agriculture, trade, and commercial activity in Wisconsin for the protection of the state's citizens. It enforces the state's primary consumer protection laws, including those relating to deceptive advertising, unfair business practices, and consumer product safety. The department oversees enforcement of Wisconsin's animal health and disease control laws and conducts a variety of programs to conserve and protect the state's vital land, water, and plant resources. The department licenses and inspects food-related businesses to ensure the safety of food produced or sold in Wisconsin. The department administers financial security programs to protect agricultural producers, facilitates the marketing of Wisconsin agricultural products in interstate and international markets, and promotes agricultural development.

Subordinate statutory boards, councils, and committees

AGRICULTURAL EDUCATION AND WORKFORCE DEVELOPMENT COUNCIL

Website: www.wiaglink.org

The Agricultural Education and Workforce Development Council recommends policies and other changes to improve agricultural education across educational systems and to support employment in industries related to agriculture, food, and natural resources. It also advises state agencies on matters relating to integrating agricultural education and workforce development systems.

AGRICULTURAL PRODUCER SECURITY COUNCIL

The Agricultural Producer Security Council advises the department on the administration and enforcement of the agricultural producer security program, which reimburses grain, milk, and vegetable producers and grain warehouse keepers if a purchaser defaults on payment.

FARM TO SCHOOL COUNCIL

Contact: 608-224-5046

The Farm to School Council advises the department regarding the promotion and administration of farm to school programs and reports to the legislature on the needs of those programs.

FERTILIZER RESEARCH COUNCIL

Website: https://frc.soils.wisc.edu

The Fertilizer Research Council reviews and recommends projects involving research on soil management, soil fertility, and plant nutrition as well as research on surface and groundwater problems related to fertilizer use. The department secretary grants final approval for project funding. These research projects are granted to the University of Wisconsin System and are financed through funds generated from the sale of fertilizer and soil or plant additives in Wisconsin.

Independent entities attached for administrative purposes

BIOENERGY COUNCIL

Chair: Jamie Derr

Contact: 608-224-5041

The Bioenergy Council advises the department regarding voluntary best management practices for sustainable biomass and biofuels production.

LAND AND WATER CONSERVATION BOARD

Chair: Mark E. Cupp

Contact: 608-224-4630

The Land and Water Conservation Board advises the secretary and department regarding soil and water conservation and animal waste management. It reviews and makes recommendations to the department on county land and water resource plans and funding allocations to county land conservation committees. The board also advises the University of Wisconsin System about needed research and education programs related to soil and water conservation and assists the Department of Natural Resources with issues related to runoff from agriculture and other rural sources of pollution.

LIVESTOCK FACILITY SITING REVIEW BOARD

Members: Lee Engelbrecht, Bob Selk, Ray Diederich, Bob Topel, Scott Sand, Jerome Gaska, 1 vacancy

Contact: SitingBoard@wisconsin.gov

The Livestock Facility Siting Review Board may review certain decisions made by political subdivisions relating to the siting or expansion of livestock facilities such as feedlots. An aggrieved person may challenge the decision of a city, village, town, or county government approving or disapproving the siting or expansion of a livestock facility by requesting that the board review the decision. If the board determines that a challenge is valid, it must reverse the decision of the governmental body. The decision of the board is binding on the governmental body, but either party may appeal the board's decision in circuit court.

VETERINARY EXAMINING BOARD

Chair: Philip C. Johnson

Contact: 608-224-4353

The Veterinary Examining Board determines the education and experience required for obtaining veterinary licenses and veterinary technician certifications and develops and evaluates examinations for obtaining these licenses and certifications. The board also establishes and enforces standards of professional conduct for veterinarians and veterinary technicians.

Department of Children and Families

Department secretary: Eloise Anderson
Deputy secretary: Ron Hunt
Location: 201 East Washington Avenue, 2nd Floor, Madison
Contact: dcfweb@wisconsin.gov; 608-422-7000; PO Box 8916, Madison, WI 53708-8916
Website: https://dcf.wisconsin.gov
Number of employees: 797.01
Total budget 2015–17: $2,497,486,500

The Department of Children and Families is administered by a secretary who is appointed by the governor with the advice and consent of the senate.

The department provides or oversees county provision of various services to assist children and families, including services for children in need of protection or services, adoption and foster care services, the licensing of facilities that provide out-of-home care for children, background investigations of child caregivers, child abuse and neglect investigations, and community-based juvenile justice services. The department administers the Wisconsin Works (W-2) public assistance program, including the Wisconsin Shares child care subsidy program, the YoungStar child care quality improvement program, the child support enforcement and paternity establishment program, and programs related to the federal Temporary Assistance to Needy Families (TANF) income support program. The department also works to ensure that families have access to high quality and affordable early childhood care and education and administers the licensing and regulation of child care centers.

Subordinate statutory boards, councils, and committees

READ TO LEAD DEVELOPMENT COUNCIL

The Read to Lead Development Council makes recommendations to the secretary of children and families and the state superintendent of public instruction regarding recipients of literacy and early childhood development grants. It annually submits a report on its operation to the appropriate standing committees of the legislature.

COUNCIL ON DOMESTIC ABUSE

The Council on Domestic Abuse reviews applications for domestic abuse services grants, advises the department and the legislature on matters of domestic abuse policy, and, in conjunction with the Judicial Conference, develops forms for filing petitions for domestic abuse restraining orders and injunctions.

RATE REGULATION ADVISORY COMMITTEE

The Rate Regulation Advisory Committee advises the department regarding rates for child welfare agencies, residential care centers, and group homes.

Independent entities attached for administrative purposes

CHILD ABUSE AND NEGLECT PREVENTION BOARD

Chair: Teri Zywicki
Executive director: Michelle Jensen Goodwin
Contact: PreventionBoard@wisconsin.gov; 608-266-6871; 110 East Main Street, Suite 810, Madison, WI 53703-3316
Website: https://preventionboard.wi.gov
Number of employees: 6.00
Total budget 2015–17: $6,082,400

The Child Abuse and Neglect Prevention Board administers the Children's Trust Fund, which was created to develop and fund strategies that prevent child maltreatment in Wisconsin. In addition, the board recommends to the governor, the legislature, and state agencies changes needed in state programs, statutes, policies, budgets, and rules to reduce child abuse and neglect and improve coordination among state agencies.

MILWAUKEE CHILD WELFARE PARTNERSHIP COUNCIL

Chair: Mark Mertens
Contact: Deanna Alexander; 414-343-5759; 635 North 26th Street, Milwaukee, WI 53233

The Milwaukee Child Welfare Partnership Council makes recommendations to the department and the legislature regarding policies and plans to improve the child welfare system in Milwaukee County.

Department of Corrections

Department secretary: Jon E. Litscher
Deputy secretary: Cathy Jess

Location: 3099 East Washington Avenue, Madison
Contact: 608-240-5000; PO Box 7925, Madison, WI 53707-7925
Website: www.doc.wi.gov
Number of employees: 10,101.32
Total budget 2015–17: $2,440,157,400

The Department of Corrections is administered by a secretary who is appointed by the governor with the advice and consent of the senate. The department administers Wisconsin's state prisons, community corrections programs, and juvenile corrections programs. It supervises the custody and discipline of all inmates and operates programs to rehabilitate offenders and reintegrate them into society. It also supervises offenders on probation, parole, and extended supervision; monitors compliance with deferred prosecution programs; and may make recommendations for pardons or commutations of sentence when requested by the governor. The department maintains the sex offender registry and monitors sex offenders and sexually violent persons who are subject to GPS tracking.

Subordinate statutory boards, councils, and committees

CORRECTIONS SYSTEM FORMULARY BOARD

The Corrections System Formulary Board establishes written guidelines, to be applied uniformly throughout the state's correctional institutions, for making therapeutic alternate drug selections for prisoners.

Independent entities attached for administrative purposes

INTERSTATE ADULT OFFENDER SUPERVISION BOARD

Members: Michael Bohren, Robert Berry, Jay Laufenberg, 2 vacancies

The Interstate Adult Offender Supervision Board appoints the Wisconsin representative to the Interstate Commission for Adult Offender Supervision. The board advises and exercises oversight and advocacy concerning the state's participation in the Interstate Compact for Adult Offender Supervision and on the operation of the compact within this state.

COUNCIL ON OFFENDER REENTRY

Chair: Silvia Jackson

The Council on Offender Reentry coordinates reentry initiatives across the state, including by promoting collaboration in the provision of transition services and training opportunities, identifying funding sources, and developing methods of information sharing.

PAROLE COMMISSION

Chair: Daniel Gabler

Contact: 608-240-7280; 2418 Cross Roads Dr., Suite 1000, PO Box 7960, Madison, WI 53718

The Parole Commission conducts regularly scheduled interviews to consider the parole of eligible inmates and is responsible for notifying victims and law enforcement about parole decisions.

PRISON INDUSTRIES BOARD

Members: James Jackson, Bill G. Smith, Tracey Isensee, Jon Litscher, James Langdon, 4 vacancies

The Prison Industries Board develops a plan for the manufacture and marketing of prison industry products and the provision of prison industry services and research and development activities.

STATE BOARD FOR INTERSTATE JUVENILE SUPERVISION

Members: Shelley Hagan, T. Christopher Dee, Tanya Nelson, 2 vacancies

The State Board for Interstate Juvenile Supervision advises and exercises oversight and advocacy concerning the state's participation in the Interstate Compact for Juveniles and on the operation of the compact within this state.

Educational Communications Board

Chair: Rolf Wegenke
Executive director: Gene Purcell
Contact: 608-264-9600; 3319 West Beltline Highway, Madison, WI 53713
Website: www.ecb.org
Number of employees: 55.18
Total budget 2015–17: $38,418,100

The Educational Communications Board oversees the statewide public broadcasting system. It plans, constructs, operates, and maintains the infrastructure necessary for the state's public radio and television networks and oversees operation of the Emergency Alert System, the Amber Alert System, National Weather Service transmitters, a telecommunication operations center, and other transmitters and satellite facilities. The board operates the statewide Wisconsin Public Radio and Wisconsin Public Television services in partnership with the University of Wisconsin-Extension.

Elections Commission

Commissioners: Mark L. Thomsen, *chair*; Beverly Gill, Julie M. Glancey, Ann S. Jacobs, Jodi Jensen, Steve King
Administrator: Michael Haas
Location: 212 East Washington Avenue, 3rd Floor, Madison
Contact: elections@wi.gov; 608-266-8005; 866-VOTE-WIS (toll-free voter help line); PO Box 7984, Madison, WI 53707-7984
Website: http://elections.wi.gov
Number of employees: 31.75
Total budget 2015–17: (not applicable, the commission was not in existence for the full biennium)

The Elections Commission consists of six members and can include additional members in certain circumstances. The majority and minority leaders of the senate and assembly each appoint one member. The governor appoints two members who were formerly county or municipal clerks, selecting one each from lists prepared by the legislative leadership of the two major political parties. If another political party qualified for a separate ballot and received at least 10 percent of the vote in the most recent gubernatorial election, the governor must appoint an additional member selected from a list prepared by that party. The governor's appointments must be confirmed by a majority of the members of the senate, but can serve on the commission prior to confirmation. The commission appoints an administrator to direct and supervise the commission's staff. This appointment must be confirmed by the senate, but the commission can select a person to serve as interim administrator while the confirmation is pending. The administrator serves as the chief election officer of the state.

The commission is responsible for ensuring compliance with state election laws and with the federal Help America Vote Act of 2002, which established certain requirements regarding the conduct of federal elections in the state. In this capacity, the commission trains and certifies all municipal clerks and chief election inspectors in the state to promote uniform election procedures. In addition, the commission is responsible for the design and maintenance of the statewide voter registration system. Every municipality in the state must use this system to administer federal, state, and local elections.

Department of Employee Trust Funds

Employee Trust Funds Board: Wayne Koessl, *chair*
Department secretary: Robert Conlin

Deputy secretary: John Voelker
Location: 801 West Badger Road, Madison
Contact: 608-266-3285; 877-533-5020 (toll free); PO Box 7931, Madison, WI 53707-7931
Website: http://etf.wi.gov
Number of employees: 267.20
Total budget 2015–17: $89,722,100

The Department of Employee Trust Funds is directed and supervised by the Employee Trust Funds Board. The board consists of 13 members, one of whom is the governor (or a designee). The department is administered by a secretary who is appointed by the board.

The department administers various benefit programs available to state and local public employees, including the Wisconsin Retirement System, health and life insurance programs for active and retired employees of the state and participating local governments, a deferred compensation program, and employee-funded reimbursement account plans. The department serves all state employees and teachers and most municipal employees, with the notable exceptions of employees of the City of Milwaukee and Milwaukee County.

The board sets policy for the department; appoints the department secretary; approves tables used for computing benefits, contribution rates, and actuarial assumptions; authorizes all annuities except for disability; approves or rejects the department's administrative rules; and generally oversees benefit programs administered by the department, except the group insurance and deferred compensation programs.

Subordinate statutory boards, councils, and committees

DEFERRED COMPENSATION BOARD

Website: http://etf.wi.gov/boards/board_dc.htm

The Deferred Compensation Board oversees deferred compensation plans offered to state and local employees and contracts with deferred compensation plan providers.

GROUP INSURANCE BOARD

Website: http://etf.wi.gov/boards/board_gib.htm

The Group Insurance Board oversees the group health, life, income continuation, and other insurance programs offered to state employees, covered local employees, and retirees.

TEACHERS RETIREMENT BOARD

Website: http://etf.wi.gov/boards/board_tr.htm

The Teachers Retirement Board advises the Employee Trust Funds Board about retirement matters related to teachers, recommends and approves or rejects administrative rules, authorizes payment of disability annuities for teachers, and hears appeals of staff determinations regarding disability annuities for teacher participants.

WISCONSIN RETIREMENT BOARD

Website: http://etf.wi.gov/boards/board_wr.htm

The Wisconsin Retirement Board advises the Employee Trust Funds Board about retirement matters related to state and local general and protective employees and performs the same functions for these employees as the Teachers Retirement Board does for teachers.

Ethics Commission

Commissioners: James "Mac" Davis, David R. Halbrooks, Katie McCallum, Pat Strachota, Timothy Van Akkeren, Jeralyn Wendelberger

Administrator: Brian M. Bell

Location: 212 East Washington Avenue, Third Floor, Madison

Contact: ethics@wi.gov (general and code of ethics questions); ethicsCFIS@wi.gov (campaign finance); lobbying@wi.gov (lobbying); 608-266-8123; PO Box 7984, Madison, WI 53707-7984

Website: https://ethics.wi.gov; https://cfis.wi.gov (Campaign Finance Information System); https://lobbying.wi.gov (Eye On Lobbying)

Number of employees: 8.00

Total budget 2015–17: (not applicable, the commission was not in existence for the full biennium)

The Ethics Commission consists of six members and can include additional members in certain circumstances. The majority and minority leaders of the senate and assembly each appoint one member. The governor appoints two members who were formerly elected judges, selecting one each from lists prepared by the legislative leadership of the two major political parties. If another political party qualified for a separate ballot and received at least 10 percent of the vote in the most recent gubernatorial election, the governor must appoint an additional member selected from a list prepared by that party. The governor's appointments must be confirmed by a majority of the members of the senate, but can serve on the commission prior to confirmation. The commission appoints an administrator to direct and supervise the commission's staff. This appointment must be confirmed by the senate, but the commission can select a person to serve as interim administrator while the confirmation is pending.

The commission administers Wisconsin's campaign finance laws, lobbying laws, and ethics laws. The commission is the campaign finance filing officer for political organizations that are required to file campaign finance reports with the state, and provides forms, training materials, and assistance to local campaign filing officers (municipal, county, and school district clerks). Lobbyists must obtain a license from the commission; and organizations that employ a lobbyist must register and file reports with the commission detailing the time and money they spend on lobbying. State officials, candidates, and nominees must annually file with the commission statements detailing their economic interests.

Department of Financial Institutions

Department secretary: Jay Risch
Deputy secretary: Jim Podewils
Location: 201 West Washington Avenue, Suite 500, Madison
Contact: 608-261-9555; PO Box 8861, Madison, WI 53708-8861
Website: www.wdfi.org
Number of employees: 139.54
Total budget 2015–17: $37,165,700

The Department of Financial Institutions is administered by a secretary who is appointed by the governor with the advice and consent of the senate. The department regulates state-chartered banks, savings banks, and savings and loan associations. The department also registers securities and securities industry members and regulates securities offerings, securities industry operations, corporate takeovers, and franchise offerings. It examines and files organizational documents and annual reports for corporations, limited liability companies, and other business entities. It also licenses and regulates the mortgage banking industry and other financial service providers, including payday lenders, high-interest consumer lenders, collection agencies, check cashing services, check sellers, credit counseling and debt settlement services, and automobile sales finance companies. The department administers the Uniform Commercial Code filing system and the Wisconsin Consumer Act. It also issues notary public commissions and registers trademarks, trade names, and brands. It registers and regulates charitable organizations, persons involved with solicitations on behalf of charitable organizations, and professional employer organizations. It also issues video service franchises to cable television operators.

Subordinate statutory boards, councils, and committees

BANKING REVIEW BOARD

The Banking Review Board advises the Division of Banking in the department on matters related to banks and banking and reviews the division's administrative actions.

SAVINGS INSTITUTIONS REVIEW BOARD

The Savings Institutions Review Board advises the Division of Banking in the department on matters related to savings banks and savings and loan associations and reviews the division's administrative actions.

Independent entities attached for administrative purposes

OFFICE OF CREDIT UNIONS

Director: Kim Santos
Credit Union Review Board: Colleen Woggon, Lisa M. Greco, Danny Wollin, Christopher P. Butler, Sherri O. Stumpf
Location: 201 West Washington Avenue, Suite 500, Madison
Contact: 608-261-9543; PO Box 14137, Madison, WI 53708-0137
Website: www.wdfi.org/fi/cu

The Office of Credit Unions regulates state-chartered credit unions. The Credit Union Review Board advises the Office of Credit Unions on matters relating to credit unions and reviews the office's administrative actions.

Department of Health Services

Department secretary: Linda Seemeyer
Deputy secretary: Tom Engels
Location: Wilson Street State Human Services Building, 1 West Wilson Street, Madison
Contact: 608-266-9622; 1 West Wilson Street, PO Box 7850, Madison, WI 53707-7850
Website: www.dhs.wisconsin.gov

Number of employees: 6,112.33
Total budget 2015–17: $22,924,602,400

The Department of Health Services is administered by a secretary who is appointed by the governor with the advice and consent of the senate.

The Department of Health Services administers a wide range of services to clients in the community and at state institutions; regulates certain care providers, including emergency medical technicians; oversees vital records, including birth, death, marriage, and divorce certificates; and supervises and consults with local public and voluntary agencies. The department promotes and protects public health in Wisconsin through various services and regulations addressing environmental and occupational health, family and community health, chronic and communicable disease prevention and control, and programs relating to maternal and child health. The department provides access to health care for low-income persons, the elderly, and people with disabilities and administers the Medical Assistance (Medicaid), BadgerCare Plus, SeniorCare, chronic disease aids, general relief, and FoodShare programs. Additionally, the department administers programs that provide long-term support for the elderly and people with disabilities, including Family Care, IRIS, Aging and Disability Resource Centers, Community Relocation Initiative, Community Integration Initiative, Pathways to Independence, and the Community Options Program. The department licenses and regulates programs and facilities that provide health, long-term

Wisconsin residents receiving FoodShare benefits have access to the FoodShare Employment and Training program to help them learn job skills.

DEPARTMENT OF HEALTH SERVICES

Participants in the IRIS Medicaid waiver program are able to enjoy and be part of their communities while also having their long-term care needs met.

care, and mental health and substance abuse services, including assisted living facilities, nursing homes, home health agencies, and facilities serving people with developmental disabilities, including three state-operated centers for persons with developmental disabilities. The department administers programs to meet mental health and substance abuse prevention, diagnosis, early intervention, and treatment needs in community and institutional settings, including two state-owned, inpatient mental health institutes, Mendota Mental Health Institute and Winnebago Mental Health Institute. Mendota Mental Health Institute houses a secure treatment unit to meet the mental health needs of male adolescents from the Department of Corrections' juvenile institutions. The department also operates the Wisconsin Resource Center as a medium security facility for mentally ill prison inmates whose treatment needs cannot be met by the Department of Corrections and provides treatment at the Sand Ridge Secure Treatment Center for individuals civilly committed under the sexually violent persons law.

Subordinate statutory boards, councils, and committees

COUNCIL ON BIRTH DEFECT PREVENTION AND SURVEILLANCE

Contact: Peggy Helm-Quest; Peggy.HelmQuest@wisconsin.gov; 608-267-2945

Website: https://cbdps.wisconsin.gov

The Council on Birth Defect Prevention and Surveillance makes recommendations to the department regarding the administration of the Wisconsin Birth Defects Registry, which documents diagnoses and counts the number of birth defects for children up to age two. The council advises what birth defects are to be reported; the content, format, and procedures for reporting; and the contents of the aggregated reports.

COUNCIL ON BLINDNESS

The Council on Blindness makes recommendations to the department and other state agencies on services, activities, programs, investigations, and research that affect persons who are blind or visually impaired.

COUNCIL FOR THE DEAF AND HARD OF HEARING

Website: https://dhhcouncil.wisconsin.gov

The Council for the Deaf and Hard of Hearing advises the department on the provision of effective services to deaf, hard-of-hearing, late-deafened, and deaf-blind people.

MEDICAID PHARMACY PRIOR AUTHORIZATION ADVISORY COMMITTEE

The Medicaid Pharmacy Prior Authorization Advisory Committee advises the department on issues related to prior authorization decisions concerning prescription drugs on behalf of Medical Assistance recipients.

COUNCIL ON MENTAL HEALTH

Website: https://mhc.wisconsin.gov

The Council on Mental Health advises the department, governor, and legislature on mental health programs; provides recommendations on the expenditure of federal mental health block grants; reviews the department's plans for mental health services; and serves as an advocate for the mentally ill.

PUBLIC HEALTH COUNCIL

The Public Health Council advises the department, the governor, the legislature, and the public on progress made in the implementation of the department's ten-year public health plan and coordination of responses to public health emergencies.

TRAUMA ADVISORY COUNCIL

The Trauma Advisory Council advises the department on developing and implementing a statewide trauma care system.

Advisory entities authorized under s. 15.04 (1) (c)

NEWBORN SCREENING ADVISORY GROUP: UMBRELLA COMMITTEE

The Newborn Screening Advisory Umbrella Committee advises the department regarding a statutorily required program that generally requires that newborn infants receive blood or other diagnostic tests for congenital and metabolic disorders.

Independent entities attached for administrative purposes

EMERGENCY MEDICAL SERVICES BOARD

Chair: Jerry Biggart
Contact: 608-266-1568; PO Box 2659, Madison, WI 53701-2659

The Emergency Medical Services Board appoints an advisory committee of physicians to advise the department on the selection of the state medical director for emergency medical services and to review that person's performance. The board also advises the director on medical issues; reviews emergency medical service statutes and rules concerning the transportation of patients; and recommends changes to the department and the Department of Transportation.

COUNCIL ON PHYSICAL DISABILITIES

Chair: Ben Barrett
Coordinator: Dan Johnson
Contact: dan.johnson@wisconsin.gov; 608-267-9582; TTY/TDD/Relay: WI Relay 711; 1 West Wilson Street, Room 551, Madison, WI 53703
Website: https://cpd.wisconsin.gov

The Council on Physical Disabilities develops and modifies the state plan for services to persons with physical disabilities. The council advises the secretary of health services, recommends legislation, encourages public understanding of the needs of persons with physical disabilities, and promotes programs to prevent physical disability.

Higher Educational Aids Board

Members: Margaret Farrow, Stephen Willett, Kathleen Sahlhoff, Robert Welch, Jeff Cichon, Michelle Thompson, Jacob Lubenow, Nathaniel Helm-Quest, Steve Midthun, Jennifer Kammerud, Benjamin Zellmer
Nonvoting member: 1 vacancy

Executive secretary: John Reinemann
Location: 131 West Wilson Street, Suite 902, Madison
Contact: HEABmail@wi.gov; 608-267-2206; PO Box 7885, Madison, WI 53707-7885
Website: http://heab.wi.gov
Number of employees: 10.00
Total budget 2015–17: $284,475,800

The Higher Educational Aids Board consists of the superintendent of public instruction and ten members appointed by the governor without senate confirmation. The board has added one nonvoting member to represent tribal institutions of higher education. The governor appoints the board's executive secretary. The board is responsible for the management and oversight of the state's student financial aid system for Wisconsin residents attending institutions of higher education. The board also enters into interstate agreements and performs student loan collection services.

Independent entities attached for administrative purposes

DISTANCE LEARNING AUTHORIZATION BOARD

Members: Morna Foy, Ray Cross, Rolf Wegenke, David Dies, Barb Lundberg
Contact: John Reinemann; john.reinemann@wi.gov; 608-267-2206
Website: http://heab.wi.gov/DLAB

The Distance Learning Authorization Board may, on behalf of the state and subject to review by the Joint Committee on Finance, enter into the State Authorization Reciprocity Agreement administered under the Midwestern Higher Education Compact or any other interstate reciprocity agreement related to state authorization and oversight of postsecondary institutions that offer distance education beyond the borders of the states in which they are located. The board administers and enforces any agreement entered into and reviews, authorizes, and monitors eligible postsecondary institutions.

State Historical Society of Wisconsin

Board of Curators: Dave Anderson, Angela Bartell, John Decker, Lane Earns, Ramona Gonzalez, Conrad Goodkind, Norbert Hill, Jr., Representative Horlacher, Gregory Huber, Joanne Huelsman, George Jacobs, Jr., Carol McChesney Johnson, Representative Kessler, James Klauser, Patty Loew, Thomas Maxwell, Susan McLeod, Lowell Peterson, Jerry Phillips, Senator

Risser, Brian Rude, Walter Rugland, Phillip Schauer, Michael Schmudlach, Sam Scinta, Thomas Shriner, Jr., Robert Smith, John Thompson, Chia Youyee Vang, Senator Wanggaard, Keene Winters, Michael Youngman, Aharon Zorea

Director: Ellsworth H. Brown

Location: 816 State Street, Madison (archives and library); 30 North Carroll Street, Madison (museum)

Contact: 608-264-6400 (general); 608-264-6535 (library and archives); 608-264-6555 (museum); 816 State Street, Madison, WI 53706

Website: www.wisconsinhistory.org

Number of employees: 129.04

Total budget 2015–17: $45,744,100

The State Historical Society of Wisconsin, also known as the Wisconsin Historical Society, is both a state agency and a membership organization. The society's Board of Curators includes eight statutory appointments and up to 30 members who are elected according to the society's constitution and bylaws. Three board members are appointed by the governor with the advice and consent of the senate. The board selects the society's director, who serves as administrative head and as secretary to the board.

The mission of the society is to help connect people to the past. The society has a statutory duty to collect and preserve historical and cultural resources

Villa Louis in Prairie du Chien is one of several historic sites operated by the State Historical Society of Wisconsin. The estate was established by the Dousman family in the 1840s and rebuilt in the 1870s in the Italian Villa style.

related to Wisconsin and to make them available to the public. To meet these objectives, the society maintains a major history research collection in Madison and in 13 area research centers. The society also operates the Wisconsin Historical Museum in Madison, ten other museums and historic sites throughout the state, an office at the Northern Great Lakes Visitor Center, a field services office in Eau Claire, and statewide school services programs. The society owns the Circus World Museum, which is operated by the Circus World Museum Foundation. The society provides public history programming such as National History Day and collaborates with other agencies such as Wisconsin Public Television to deliver history programming to the public. The society provides technical services and advice to nearly 400 affiliated local historical societies throughout the state. The society conducts, publishes, and disseminates research on Wisconsin and U.S. history and serves as the state's historic preservation office, which facilitates the preservation of historic structures and archaeological sites and administers the state and national registers of historic places. The society is also responsible for implementation of the state's Burial Sites Preservation Law.

Independent entities attached for administrative purposes

BURIAL SITES PRESERVATION BOARD

Members: Ellsworth H. Brown, Kathryn C. Egan-Bruhy, Jennifer Haas, Cynthia Stiles, David J. Grignon, Corina Williams, Melinda Young
Nonvoting members: John H. Broihahn, Jim Draeger
Contact: Kim Cook; kim.cook@wisconsinhistory.org; 608-264-6493; 816 State Street, Madison, WI 53706

The Burial Sites Preservation Board assists in the administration of the state's burial sites laws. The board's duties include determining which Indian tribes in Wisconsin have an interest in catalogued burial sites, approving applicants for a registry of persons interested in those sites, reviewing decisions on permit applications to disturb those sites, and reviewing decisions regarding the disposition of human remains and burial objects removed from catalogued and uncatalogued burial sites.

HISTORIC PRESERVATION REVIEW BOARD

Members: Bruce T. Block, Carlen Hatala, Carol McChesney Johnson, Dan J. Joyce, Kubet Luchterhand, David V. Mollenhoff, Neil Prendergast, Sissel Schroeder, Valentine J. Schute, Jr., Daniel J. Stephans, Paul Wolter, Melinda Young, Donna Zimmerman, 2 vacancies

Contact: Peggy Veregin; peggy.veregin@wisconsinhistory.org; 608-264-6501; 816 State Street, Madison, WI 53706

The Historic Preservation Review Board approves nominations to the Wisconsin State Register of Historic Places and the National Register of Historic Places upon recommendation of the state historic preservation officer. The board approves the distribution of federal grants-in-aid for preservation, advises the State Historical Society, and requests comments from planning departments of affected cities, villages, towns, counties, local landmark commissions, and local historical societies regarding properties being considered for nomination to the state and national registers.

Office of the Commissioner of Insurance

Commissioner: Ted Nickel
Deputy commissioner: J.P. Wieske
Location: 125 South Webster Street, Madison
Contact: 608-266-3585; 800-236-8517 (toll free); PO Box 7873, Madison, WI 53707-7873
Website: https://oci.wi.gov
Number of employees: 151.50
Total budget 2015–17: $220,747,300

The Office of the Commissioner of Insurance is administered by the commissioner of insurance, who is appointed by the governor with the advice and consent of the senate. The office supervises the insurance industry in Wisconsin. The office is responsible for examining insurance industry financial practices and market conduct, licensing insurance agents, reviewing policy forms for compliance with state insurance statutes and regulations, investigating consumer complaints, and providing consumer information.

The office administers three segregated insurance funds: the State Life Insurance Fund, the Local Government Property Insurance Fund, and the Injured Patients and Families Compensation Fund. The State Life Insurance Fund offers up to $10,000 of low-cost life insurance protection to any Wisconsin resident who meets prescribed risk standards. The Local Government Property Insurance Fund provides coverage for local governments against fire loss, as well as optional coverage for certain property damage they may incur. The Injured Patients and Families Compensation Fund provides medical malpractice coverage for qualified health care providers on claims in excess of a provider's underlying coverage. The office also oversees the Health Care Liability Insurance Plan, which provides liability coverage for hospitals, physicians, and other health care providers in Wisconsin.

Subordinate statutory boards, councils, and committees

BOARD OF DIRECTORS OF THE INSURANCE SECURITY FUND

The Board of Directors of the Insurance Security Fund administers a fund that protects certain insurance policyholders and claimants from excessive delay and loss in the event of insurer liquidation. The fund consists of accounts for life insurance, allocated annuities, disability insurance (includes health), HMO insurers, other insurance (includes property and casualty), and fund administration. The fund supports continuation of coverage under many life, annuity, and health policies. It is financed by assessments paid by most insurers in this state. The board's advice and recommendations to the commissioner are not subject to the state's open records law.

BOARD OF GOVERNORS OF THE INJURED PATIENTS AND FAMILIES COMPENSATION FUND/ WISCONSIN HEALTH CARE LIABILITY INSURANCE PLAN

The Board of Governors of the Injured Patients and Families Compensation Fund/ Wisconsin Health Care Liability Insurance Plan oversees the health care liability plans for licensed physicians and certified registered nurse anesthetists, medical partnerships and corporations, cooperative sickness care associations, ambulatory surgery centers, hospitals, some nursing homes, and certain other health care providers. The board also supervises the Injured Patients and Families Compensation Fund, which pays medical malpractice claims in excess of a provider's underlying coverage.

INJURED PATIENTS AND FAMILIES COMPENSATION FUND PEER REVIEW COUNCIL

The Injured Patients and Families Compensation Fund Peer Review Council reviews, within one year of the first payment on a claim, each claim for damages arising out of medical care provided by a health care provider or provider's employee, if the claim is paid by any of the following: the Injured Patients and Families Compensation Fund, a mandatory health care risk-sharing plan, a private health care liability insurer, or a self-insurer. The council can recommend adjustments in fees paid to the Injured Patients and Families Compensation Fund and the Wisconsin Health Care Liability Insurance Plan or premiums paid to private insurers, if requested by the insurer.

State of Wisconsin Investment Board

Chair: David Stein
Executive director: Michael Williamson
Location: 121 East Wilson Street, Madison
Contact: 608-266-2381; PO Box 7842, Madison, WI 53707-7842
Website: www.swib.state.wi.us
Number of employees: 166.35
Total budget 2015–17: $93,707,200

The State of Wisconsin Investment Board consists of the secretary of administration or his or her designee and eight other members, six of whom are appointed by the governor with the advice and consent of the senate. The board appoints the executive director.

The board is responsible for investing the assets of the Wisconsin Retirement System and the State Investment Fund. The board's investments are managed by its own professional staff and by outside money managers. As of December 31, 2015, the board managed about $100 billion in assets. The largest portion of the assets managed by the board, about 93 percent, is the trust funds of the Wisconsin Retirement System. For purposes of investment, the retirement system's assets are divided into two funds: the core fund, which is a broadly diversified portfolio that includes stocks, bonds, and other assets, and the variable fund, which is an all-stock fund. About 6 percent of the assets under management by the board are in the State Investment Fund, which is the state's cash management fund, and which is also available to local units of government through the Local Government Pooled-Investment Fund, a separate fund within the State Investment Fund. The board also manages the assets of the following trust funds, which together account for about 1 percent of the board's total assets under management: the Local Government Property Insurance Fund, the State Life Insurance Fund, the State Historical Society of Wisconsin Endowment Trust Fund, the Injured Patients and Families Compensation Fund, and the Tuition Trust Fund.

Department of Justice

Attorney general: Brad D. Schimel
Deputy attorney general: Paul W. Connell
Location: 114 East, State Capitol (attorney general's office); 17 West Main Street, Madison (Department of Justice)

Contact: 608-266-1221; PO Box 7857, Madison, WI 53707-7857
Website: www.doj.state.wi.us
Number of employees: 689.74
Total budget 2015–17: $255,426,600

The Department of Justice is headed by the attorney general, a constitutional officer who is elected on a partisan ballot to a four-year term. The department provides legal advice and representation, investigates criminal activity, and provides various law enforcement services for the state. The department appears for the state and prosecutes or defends all civil and criminal actions and proceedings in the court of appeals or the supreme court in which the state is interested or a party. The department prosecutes or defends all civil cases sent or remanded to any circuit court in which the state is a party. The department also represents the state in criminal cases on appeal in federal court.

Subordinate statutory boards, councils, and committees

CRIME VICTIMS COUNCIL

The Crime Victims Council provides advice and recommendations to the attorney general on the rights of crime victims, improving the criminal justice response to victims, and other issues affecting crime victims.

Mobile Crime Scene Response Units assist law enforcement at major crime scenes and bring the evidence back to crime labs in Madison, Milwaukee, and Wausau.

DEPARTMENT OF JUSTICE

Independent entities attached for administrative purposes

CRIME VICTIMS RIGHTS BOARD

Members: Timothy Gruenke, Paul Susienka, Trisha Anderson, Charles S. McGee, Rebecca Rapp

The Crime Victims Rights Board has the authority to review complaints filed by a victim of a crime that allege that a public official, public employee, or public agency violated the victim's rights. The board may issue a private or public reprimand for a violation, seek appropriate equitable relief on behalf of a victim, or bring a civil action to assess a forfeiture for an intentional violation. The board may issue a report or recommendation concerning the rights of crime victims and the provision of services to crime victims.

LAW ENFORCEMENT STANDARDS BOARD

Chair: Christopher Domagalski
Contact: Tony Barthuly, Training and Standards Bureau director; barthulyja@doj.state.wi.us; 608-266-9606; 17 W. Main St., PO Box 7070, Madison, WI 53707-7070
Curriculum Advisory Committee: Todd Thomas, Jerry Staniszewski, Richard Oliva, Ron Tischer, Greg Leck, Michael Hartert, Sam Wollin, Ron Cramer, Nate Dreckman, Mark Podoll, Joe Fath, Mike Lukas, Paul Matl, Sara Gossfeld-Benzing.

The Law Enforcement Standards Board sets minimum education and training standards for law enforcement and tribal law enforcement officers. The board certifies persons who meet professional standards as qualified to be law enforcement, tribal law enforcement, jail, or juvenile detention officers. The board consults with other government agencies regarding the development of training schools and courses, conducts research to improve law enforcement and performance, and evaluates governmental units for compliance with board standards.

The Curriculum Advisory Committee advises the Law Enforcement Standards Board on the establishment of curriculum requirements for training of law enforcement, tribal law enforcement, and jail and secure detention officers.

Department of Military Affairs

Commander in chief: Scott Walker (governor)
Adjutant general: Major General Donald P. Dunbar
Deputy adjutant general for army: Brig. Gen. Mark E. Anderson

Deputy adjutant general for air: Brig. Gen. Gary L. Ebben
Administrator, Division of Emergency Management: Brian M. Satula
Location: 2400 Wright Street, Madison
Contact: 608-242-3000 (general); 800-943-0003 (24-hour hotline for emergencies and hazardous materials spills); PO Box 8111, Madison, WI 53708-8111
Website: http://dma.wi.gov (Department of Military Affairs and Wisconsin National Guard); http://emergencymanagement.wi.gov (Division of Emergency Management)
Number of state employees: 457.10
Total state budget 2015–17: $211,534,700
Total federal budget: approximately $260 million annually

The governor is the commander in chief of the state's military forces, which are organized as the Wisconsin National Guard within the Department of Military Affairs. The department is directed by an adjutant general who is appointed by the governor without senate advice and consent. The department also includes the Division of Emergency Management, which is headed by an administrator who is appointed by the governor with the advice and consent of the senate.

The Wisconsin National Guard is maintained by both the federal and the state governments. (When it is called up in an active federal duty status, the president of the United States, rather than the governor, becomes its commander in chief.) The federal mission of the National Guard is to provide trained units to the U.S. Army and U.S. Air Force in time of war or national emergency. Its state mission is to assist civil authorities, protect life and property, and preserve peace, order, and public safety in times of natural or human-caused emergencies. The federal government provides arms and ammunition, equipment and uniforms, major outdoor training facilities, pay for military and support personnel, and training and supervision. The state provides personnel; conducts training as required under the National Defense Act; and shares the cost of constructing, maintaining, and operating armories and other military facilities.

The Division of Emergency Management coordinates the development and implementation of the state emergency operations plan; provides assistance to local jurisdictions in the development of their programs and plans; administers private and federal disaster and emergency relief funds; administers the Wisconsin Disaster Fund; and maintains the state's 24-hour duty officer reporting and response system. The division also conducts training programs in emergency planning for businesses and state and local officials, as well as educational programs for the general public. It also prepares for off-site radiological emergencies at nuclear power plants and provides assistance for various emergencies such as prison disturbances and natural disasters.

Department of Natural Resources

Natural Resources Board: Terry Hilgenberg, *chair*
Department secretary: Cathy L. Stepp
Deputy secretary: Kurt Thiede
Location: State Natural Resources Building (GEF 2), 101 South Webster Street, Madison
Contact: 888-936-7463 (TTY access via relay 711); PO Box 7921, Madison, WI 53707-7921
Website: http://dnr.wi.gov
Number of employees: 2,549.10
Total budget 2015–17: $1,109,384,300

The Department of Natural Resources is directed and supervised by the Natural Resources Board and is administered by a secretary. The members of the board and the secretary are appointed by the governor with the advice and consent of the senate.

The department is responsible for implementing state and federal laws that protect and enhance Wisconsin's natural resources, including its air, land, water, forests, wildlife, fish, and plants. It coordinates the many state-administered programs that protect the environment and provides a full range of outdoor recreational opportunities for Wisconsin residents and visitors.

Subordinate statutory boards, councils, and committees

DRY CLEANER ENVIRONMENTAL RESPONSE COUNCIL

The Dry Cleaner Environmental Response Council advises the department on matters related to the Dry Cleaner Environmental Response Program, which is administered by the department and which provides awards to dry cleaning establishments for assistance in the investigation and cleanup of environmental contamination.

COUNCIL ON FORESTRY

The Council on Forestry advises the governor, legislature, department, and other state agencies on topics relating to forestry in Wisconsin, including protection from fire, insects, and disease; sustainable forestry; reforestation and forestry genetics; management and protection of urban forests; increasing the public's knowledge and awareness of forestry issues; forestry research; economic development and marketing of forestry products; legislation affecting forestry; and staff and funding needs for forestry programs.

METALLIC MINING COUNCIL

The Metallic Mining Council advises the department on matters relating to the reclamation of mined land and the disposal of metallic mine-related waste. The council is currently inactive.

NATURAL AREAS PRESERVATION COUNCIL

The Natural Areas Preservation Council advises the department on matters pertaining to the protection of natural areas that contain native biotic communities and habitats for rare species. It also makes recommendations about gifts or purchases for the state natural areas system.

NONMOTORIZED RECREATION AND TRANSPORTATION TRAILS COUNCIL

The Nonmotorized Recreation and Transportation Trails Council carries out studies and advises the governor, the legislature, the department, and the Department of Transportation on matters related to nonmotorized recreation and transportation trails.

The Department of Natural Resources releases thousands of game farm pheasants to public hunting lands every year. The release below was aided by students at Richland Center High School.

DEPARTMENT OF NATURAL RESOURCES

OFF-HIGHWAY MOTORCYCLE COUNCIL

The Off-Highway Motorcycle Council makes recommendations to the department on matters relating to off-highway motorcycle corridors and routes and the operation of off-highway motorcycles.

OFF-ROAD VEHICLE COUNCIL

The Off-Road Vehicle Council advises the department, the Department of Transportation, the governor, and the legislature on all matters relating to all-terrain vehicle trails and routes.

SMALL BUSINESS ENVIRONMENTAL COUNCIL

The Small Business Environmental Council advises the department on the effectiveness of assistance programs to small businesses that enable the businesses to comply with the federal Clean Air Act. It also advises on the fairness and effectiveness of air pollution rules promulgated by the department and the U.S. Environmental Protection Agency regarding their impact on small businesses.

SNOWMOBILE RECREATIONAL COUNCIL

The Snowmobile Recreational Council carries out studies and makes recommendations to the governor, the legislature, the department, and the Department of Transportation regarding all matters affecting snowmobiling.

SPORTING HERITAGE COUNCIL

The Sporting Heritage Council advises the governor, the legislature, and the Natural Resources Board about issues relating to hunting, trapping, fishing, and other types of outdoor recreation activities.

STATE TRAILS COUNCIL

The State Trails Council advises the department about the planning, acquisition, development, and management of state trails.

Advisory entities authorized under s. 15.04 (1) (c)

FIRE DEPARTMENT ADVISORY COUNCIL

The Fire Department Advisory Council was chartered in 1994 as an official advisory council to the state forester. The purpose of the council is to strengthen partnerships between the department and the rural fire service in Wisconsin. The council advises and assists the state forester on operational issues related to the department's forest fire management program to provide for an effective rural community fire protection program. In addition, the council provides fundamental guidance on the Forest Fire Protection Grant administration.

URBAN FORESTRY COUNCIL

The Urban Forestry Council advises the state forester and the department on the best ways to preserve, protect, expand, and improve Wisconsin's urban and community forest resources. The council gives awards to outstanding individuals, organizations, and communities that further urban forestry in Wisconsin.

Independent entities attached for administrative purposes

GROUNDWATER COORDINATING COUNCIL

Chair: Patrick Stevens

The Groundwater Coordinating Council advises state agencies on the coordination of nonregulatory programs related to groundwater management. Member agencies exchange information regarding groundwater monitoring, budgets for groundwater programs, data management, public information efforts, laboratory analyses, research, and state appropriations for research.

INVASIVE SPECIES COUNCIL

Chair: Paul Schumacher

The Invasive Species Council conducts studies related to controlling invasive species and makes recommendations to the department regarding a system for classifying invasive species under the department's statewide invasive species control program and regarding procedures for awarding grants to public and private agencies engaged in projects to control invasive species.

LAKE MICHIGAN COMMERCIAL FISHING BOARD

Members: Charles W. Henriksen, Richard R. Johnson, Michael LeClair, Mark Maricque, Dean Swaer, Neil A. Schwarz, Dan Pawlitzke

The Lake Michigan Commercial Fishing Board reviews applications for transfers of commercial fishing licenses between individuals, establishes criteria for allotting catch quotas to individual licensees, assigns catch quotas when the department establishes special harvest limits, and assists the department in establishing criteria for identifying inactive license holders.

LAKE SUPERIOR COMMERCIAL FISHING BOARD

Members: Maurine Halvorson, Craig Hoopman, Jeff Bodin, 2 vacancies

The Lake Superior Commercial Fishing Board reviews applications for transfers of commercial fishing licenses between individuals, establishes criteria for allotting catch quotas to individual licensees, assigns catch quotas when

DEPARTMENT OF NATURAL RESOURCES

Putting on kids fishing clinics is one of the many ways the Department of Natural Resources works with local organizations to build an appreciation for the state's natural resources.

the department establishes special harvest limits, and assists the department in establishing criteria for identifying inactive license holders.

LOWER WISCONSIN STATE RIVERWAY BOARD

Chair: Frederick Madison

The Lower Wisconsin State Riverway Board is responsible for protecting and preserving the scenic beauty and natural character of the riverway. The board reviews permit applications for buildings, walkways and stairways, timber harvests, nonmetallic mining, utility facilities, public access sites, bridges, and other structures in the riverway and issues permits for activities that meet established standards.

COUNCIL ON RECYCLING

Chair: James Birmingham

The Council on Recycling promotes implementation of the state's solid waste reduction, recovery, and recycling programs; helps public agencies coordinate programs and exchange information; advises state agencies about creating administrative rules and establishing priorities for market development; and advises the department and the University of Wisconsin System about education and research related to solid waste recycling. The council also promotes a regional and interstate marketing system for recycled materials and reports to the legislature about market development and research to encourage recycling. The council advises the department about statewide public information activities and advises the governor and the legislature.

WISCONSIN WATERWAYS COMMISSION

Chair: James F. Rooney

The Wisconsin Waterways Commission may conduct studies to determine the need for recreational boating facilities; approve financial aid to local governments for development of recreational boating projects, including the acquisition of weed harvesters; and recommend administrative rules for the recreational facilities boating program.

Affiliated entity

CONSERVATION CONGRESS

The Conservation Congress is a publicly elected citizen advisory group, and its district leadership council advises the Natural Resources Board on all matters under the board's jurisdiction.

Office of the State Public Defender

Public Defender Board: Daniel M. Berkos, *chair*
State public defender: Kelli Thompson
Deputy state public defender: Michael Tobin
Location: 17 South Fairchild Street, Suite 500, Madison
Contact: 608-266-0087; PO Box 7923, Madison, WI 53707-7923
Website: www.wispd.org
Number of employees: 614.85
Total budget 2015–17: $172,893,000

The Office of the State Public Defender provides legal representation to indigent persons and to persons otherwise entitled to such representation. The state public defender, who must be a member of the state bar, serves at the pleasure of the Public Defender Board. Board members are appointed by the governor with the advice and consent of the senate.

Attorneys are assigned by the state public defender to persons charged with a crime sentencible by imprisonment and in other cases, such as cases involving paternity determinations, termination of parental rights, emergency detentions, involuntary commitments, modification of bifurcated sentences, and certain appeals.

Department of Public Instruction

State superintendent of public instruction: Tony Evers
Deputy state superintendent: Mike Thompson
Location: State Education Building (GEF 3), 125 South Webster Street, Madison
Contact: 608-266-3390; 800-441-4563 (toll free); 608-267-2427 (TDD); PO Box 7841, Madison, WI 53707-7841
Website: www.dpi.wi.gov
Number of employees: 634.05
Total budget 2015–17: $13,298,178,000

The Department of Public Instruction is headed by the state superintendent of public instruction, a constitutional officer who is elected on the nonpartisan spring ballot for a term of four years. The department provides guidance and technical assistance to support public elementary and secondary education in Wisconsin. The department also administers the Milwaukee, Racine, and Statewide Parental Choice Programs; the Special Needs Scholarship Program;

the open enrollment program; and a number of educational and other services for children and their families.

The department offers a broad range of programs and professional services to local school administrators and staff. It also reviews and approves educator preparation programs and licenses teachers, pupil services personnel, administrators, and library professionals. The department distributes state and federal aids to supplement local tax revenue, improve curriculum and school operations, ensure education for children with disabilities, offer professional guidance and counseling, and develop school and public library resources. The department also administers the Wisconsin Educational Services Program for the Deaf and Hard of Hearing and the Wisconsin Center for the Blind and Visually Impaired.

Finally, the department provides assistance for the development and improvement of public and school libraries. The department fosters interlibrary cooperation and resource sharing and promotes information and instructional technology in schools and libraries. The department also acts as a state-level clearinghouse for interlibrary loan requests; administers BadgerLink (https://badgerlink.dpi.wi.gov), the statewide full-text database project that allows access to thousands of magazines, newsletters, newspapers, pamphlets, and historical documents; and, in collaboration with other Wisconsin library organizations, manages BadgerLearn, the statewide portal that provides continuing education resources for library professionals.

Subordinate statutory boards, councils, and committees

ADVISORY COUNCIL ON ALCOHOL AND OTHER DRUG ABUSE PROGRAMS

Contact: Brenda Jennings; brenda.jennings@dpi.wi.gov

The Council on Alcohol and Other Drug Abuse Programs advises the state superintendent about programs to prevent or reduce alcohol, tobacco, and other drug abuse by minors.

BLIND AND VISUAL IMPAIRMENT EDUCATION COUNCIL

The Blind and Visual Impairment Education Council provides advice on educational and library services to blind and visually impaired people and provides advice on the services of the Wisconsin Center for the Blind and Visually Impaired.

DEAF AND HARD-OF-HEARING EDUCATION COUNCIL

Contact: Marla Walsh; marla.walsh@wsd.12k.wi.us

The Deaf and Hard-of-Hearing Education Council advises the state superintendent on issues related to pupils who are hearing impaired and informs the state superintendent on services, programs, and research that could benefit those pupils.

COUNCIL ON LIBRARY AND NETWORK DEVELOPMENT

Contact: Roslyn Wise; roslyn.wise@dpi.wi.gov

The Council on Library and Network Development advises the state superintendent and the administrator of the Division for Libraries and Technology to ensure that all state citizens have access to library and information services.

PROFESSIONAL STANDARDS COUNCIL FOR TEACHERS

The Professional Standards Council for Teachers advises the state superintendent regarding licensing and evaluating teachers; evaluation and approval of teacher education programs; the status of teaching in Wisconsin; school board practices to develop effective teaching; peer mentoring; evaluation systems; and alternative dismissal procedures.

SCHOOL DISTRICT BOUNDARY APPEAL BOARD

Contact: Janice Zmrazek; janice.zmrazek@dpi.wi.gov

Panels consisting of three or seven members of the School District Boundary Appeal Board hear appeals related to school district creation and dissolution, annexation, and boundary disputes.

COUNCIL ON SPECIAL EDUCATION

Contact: Anna Moffit; anna@wifamilyties.org; 608-446-3290

The Council on Special Education advises the state superintendent on matters related to meeting the needs and improving the education of children with disabilities.

Board of Commissioners of Public Lands

Members: Douglas J. La Follette (secretary of state), Matt Adamczyk (state treasurer), Brad D. Schimel (attorney general)

Division of Trust Lands and Investments: Jonathan B. Barry, *executive secretary*; Tom German, *deputy secretary*; Richard Sneider, *chief investment officer*

Location: 101 East Wilson Street, 2nd Floor, Madison

Contact: bcplinfo@wisconsin.gov; 608-266-1370; PO Box 8943, Madison, WI 53708-8943

Website: http://bcpl.wisconsin.gov
Number of employees: 9.50
Total budget 2015–17: $3,267,800

The Board of Commissioners of Public Lands is a body established in the Wisconsin Constitution. The board is composed of the secretary of state, state treasurer, and attorney general. The board manages the state's remaining trust lands, manages trust funds primarily for the benefit of public education, and maintains the state's original 19th-century land survey and land sales records. The board is assisted in its work by the Division of Trust Lands and Investments, an entity attached to the Department of Administration for administrative purposes.

The board holds title to nearly 76,000 acres of school trust lands. These lands are managed for timber production, natural area preservation, and public use. The board manages four trust funds, totaling over $1 billion in assets. The largest of these is the Common School Fund. The principal of this fund continues to grow through the collection of fees, fines, and forfeitures that accrue to the state. The board invests the moneys of this fund in state and municipal bonds. It also loans moneys from this fund directly to Wisconsin municipalities and school districts through the State Trust Fund Loan Program. These loans are used for economic development, school repairs and improvements, local infrastructure and utilities, and capital equipment and vehicles. The net earnings of the Common School Fund are distributed annually by the Department of Public Instruction to all of Wisconsin's public school districts and provide the sole source of state aid for public school library media and resources. The other trust funds are used to support the University of Wisconsin and the state's general fund.

Public Service Commission

Members: Ellen Nowak, *chair*; Lon Roberts, Mike Huebsch
Executive assistant to the chair: William Jordahl
Location: 610 North Whitney Way, 3rd Floor, Madison
Contact: pscrecordsmail@wisconsin.gov (general); PSCPublicRecordsRe
quest@Wisconsin.gov (public records requests); 608-266-5481; 888-816-3831
(toll free); 608-266-2001 (consumer complaints); 800-225-7729 (consumer
complaints, toll free); PO Box 7854, Madison, WI 53707-7854
Website: http://psc.wi.gov
Number of employees: 143.00
Total budget 2015–17: $53,240,700

The Public Service Commission consists of three commissioners appointed by the governor with the advice and consent of the senate for six-year terms. The governor appoints one of the commissioners as chair for a two-year term. A commissioner may not have a financial interest in a railroad, public utility, or water carrier; may not be a candidate for public office; and is subject to certain restrictions regarding political activity.

The commission is responsible for regulating Wisconsin's public utilities and ensuring that utility services are provided to customers safely, reliably, and at prices reasonable to both ratepayers and utility owners. The commission also regulates the rates and services of electric, natural gas distribution, water, and municipal combined water and sewer utilities. The commission's responsibilities include determining levels for adequate and safe service; overseeing compliance with renewable energy and energy conservation and efficiency requirements; approving public utility bond sales and stock offerings; and approving mergers, consolidations, and ownership changes regarding public utilities. The commission also considers applications for major construction projects, such as power plants, transmission lines, and wind farms. In addition to ensuring public utility compliance with statutes, administrative codes, and record-keeping requirements, commission staff investigates and mediates consumer complaints.

The commission has limited jurisdiction over landline telecommunications providers and services. The commission certifies various types of telecommunications providers; manages the Universal Service Fund; handles some wholesale disputes between telecommunications providers, including interconnection agreement filings and disputes; and administers telephone numbering resources. In general, the commission has no jurisdiction over electric cooperatives, liquefied petroleum gas, fuel oil, wireless telephone, or cable television. Also, although the commission has no jurisdiction over Internet service, it does provide oversight for statewide broadband mapping and planning and makes grants for constructing broadband infrastructure in underserved areas.

Subordinate statutory boards, councils, and committees

UNIVERSAL SERVICE FUND COUNCIL

Contact: Jeff Richter, Universal Service Fund director; jeff.richter@wiscon sin.gov; 608-267-9624; PO Box 7854, Madison, WI 53707-7854

The Universal Service Fund Council advises the commission on the administration of the Universal Service Fund, which assists low-income customers, customers in areas where telecommunications service costs are relatively high, and customers with disabilities in obtaining affordable access to basic telecommunications services. The Universal Service Fund director acts as the liaison between the Public Service Commission and the council.

WIND SITING COUNCIL

The Wind Siting Council advises the commission on the promulgation of rules relating to restrictions that a political subdivision may impose on the installation of a wind energy system, including setback requirements that provide reasonable protection from any health effects. The council also surveys the peer-reviewed scientific research regarding the health impacts of wind energy systems and studies state and national regulatory developments regarding the siting of wind energy systems.

Independent entities attached for administrative purposes

OFFICE OF THE COMMISSIONER OF RAILROADS

Commissioner of railroads: Yash Wadhwa
Location: 610 North Whitney Way, Suite 110, Madison
Contact: 608-266-0276; PO Box 7854, Madison, WI 53707-7854
Website: http://ocr.wi.gov
Number of employees: 6.00
Total budget 2015–17: $1,183,700

The governor appoints the commissioner of railroads with the advice and consent of the senate for a six-year term. The commissioner may not have a financial interest in railroads or water carriers and may not serve on or under any committee of a political party. The Office of the Commissioner of Railroads enforces regulations related to railway safety and determines the safety of highway crossings, including the adequacy of railroad warning devices. The office also has authority over the rates and services of intrastate water carriers.

Department of Revenue

Department secretary: Richard G. Chandler
Deputy secretary: Eileen O'Neill
Location: 2135 Rimrock Road, Madison
Contact: 608-266-2486 (individuals); 608-266-2776 (businesses); PO Box 8933, Madison, WI 53708-8933
Website: www.revenue.wi.gov
Number of employees: 1,202.28
Total budget 2015–17: $418,882,900

The Department of Revenue is administered by a secretary who is appointed by the governor with the advice and consent of the senate. The department administers all major state tax laws except the insurance premiums tax and enforces the state's alcohol beverage and tobacco laws. It estimates state revenues, forecasts state economic activity, helps formulate tax policy, and administers the Wisconsin Lottery. The department also determines the equalized value of taxable property and assesses manufacturing and telecommunications company property for property tax purposes. It administers local financial assistance programs and assists local governments in their property assessments and financial management. The department also oversees Wisconsin's Unclaimed Property program to match taxpayers with unclaimed financial assets.

Subordinate statutory boards, councils, and committees

STATE BOARD OF ASSESSORS

The State Board of Assessors investigates objections to the amount, valuation, or taxability of real or personal manufacturing property, as well as objections to the penalties issued for late filing or nonfiling of required manufacturing property report forms.

FARMLAND ADVISORY COUNCIL

The Farmland Advisory Council advises the department on implementing use-value assessment of agricultural land and reducing expansion of urban sprawl. It reports annually to the legislature on the usefulness of use-value assessment as a way to preserve farmland and reduce the conversion of farmland to other uses. The council also recommends changes to the shared revenue formula to compensate local governments adversely affected by use-value assessment.

Independent entities attached for administrative purposes

INVESTMENT AND LOCAL IMPACT FUND BOARD

Chair: Richard Chandler

The Investment and Local Impact Fund Board administers the Investment and Local Impact Fund, created to help municipalities alleviate costs associated with social, educational, environmental, and economic impacts of metalliferous mineral mining. The board certifies to the Department of Administration the amount of the payments to be distributed to municipalities from the fund. It also provides funding to local governments throughout the development of a mining project.

Department of Safety and Professional Services

Department secretary: Laura Gutiérrez
Deputy secretary: Eric Esser
Location: 1400 East Washington Avenue, Madison
Contact: 608-266-2112; PO Box 8935, Madison, WI 53708-8935
Website: http://dsps.wi.gov
Number of employees: 247.14
Total budget 2015–17: $102,535,200

The Department of Safety and Professional Services is administered by a secretary who is appointed by the governor with the advice and consent of the senate.

The department administers and enforces laws to ensure safe and sanitary conditions in public and private buildings, including by reviewing plans and performing inspections of commercial buildings and certain of their components and systems.

The department is also responsible for ensuring the safe and competent practice of various licensed occupations and businesses in Wisconsin. The department provides direct regulation or licensing of certain occupations and businesses. In addition, numerous boards are attached to the department that are responsible for regulating other occupations and businesses. In general, these boards determine the education and experience required for credentialing, develop and evaluate examinations, and establish standards for professional conduct. The department or the relevant board may reprimand a credential holder in a field that it regulates; limit, suspend, or revoke the credential of a practitioner who violates laws or rules; and, in some cases, impose forfeitures. The department provides administrative services to the boards and policy assistance in such areas as evaluating and establishing new professional licensing programs, creating routine procedures for legal proceedings, and adjusting policies in response to public needs. The department also investigates and prosecutes complaints against credential holders and assists with drafting administrative rules.

Subordinate statutory boards, councils, and committees

AUTOMATIC FIRE SPRINKLER SYSTEM CONTRACTORS AND JOURNEYMEN COUNCIL

Contact: Brittany Lewin, *executive director*; brittany.lewin@wisconsin.gov; 608-261-5406

The Automatic Fire Sprinkler System Contractors and Journeymen Council advises the department on rules for credentials required for installing and maintaining automatic fire sprinkler systems.

COMMERCIAL BUILDING CODE COUNCIL

Contact: Brittany Lewin, *executive director*; brittany.lewin@wisconsin.gov; 608-261-5406

The Commercial Building Code Council advises the department on rules relating to public buildings and buildings that are places of employment. The council also reviews and makes recommendations pertaining to the department's rules for constructing, altering, adding to, repairing, and maintaining those types of buildings.

CONTRACTOR CERTIFICATION COUNCIL

Contact: Brittany Lewin, *executive director*; brittany.lewin@wisconsin.gov; 608-261-5406

The Contractor Certification Council makes recommendations to the department regarding rules for continuing education and examination requirements for building contractors for one-family and two-family dwellings and for certifying financial responsibility of those contractors.

CONTROLLED SUBSTANCES BOARD

Contact: Chad Zadrazil, *managing director*; Chad.Zadrazil@wisconsin.gov; 608-266-0011

The Controlled Substances Board classifies controlled substances into schedules that regulate the prescription, use, and possession of controlled substances. The board also approves special use permits for controlled substances.

CONVEYANCE SAFETY CODE COUNCIL

Contact: Brittany Lewin, *executive director*; brittany.lewin@wisconsin.gov; 608-261-5406

The Conveyance Safety Code Council makes recommendations to the department pertaining to safety standards for elevators, escalators, and similar conveyances.

MANUFACTURED HOUSING CODE COUNCIL

Contact: Brittany Lewin, *executive director*; brittany.lewin@wisconsin.gov; 608-261-5406

The Manufactured Housing Code Council makes recommendations to the department pertaining to standards for the construction, installation, and sale of manufactured homes.

PLUMBERS COUNCIL

Contact: Brittany Lewin, *executive director*; brittany.lewin@wisconsin.gov; 608-261-5406

The Plumbers Council advises the department on rules for credentials required for plumbing.

SIGN LANGUAGE INTERPRETER COUNCIL

Contact: Dan Williams, *executive director*; Dan1.Williams@wisconsin.gov; 608-267-7223

The Sign Language Interpreter Council advises the department on rules for the practice of sign language interpreters and grants temporary and permanent exemptions from a department-issued license for sign language interpreters.

UNIFORM DWELLING CODE COUNCIL

Contact: Brittany Lewin, *executive director*; brittany.lewin@wisconsin.gov; 608-261-5406

The Uniform Dwelling Code Council reviews and makes recommendations for department rules pertaining to the construction and inspection of one-family and two-family dwellings.

Independent entities attached for administrative purposes

Except for the Building Inspector Review Board, these are the occupation and business regulating boards described in the write-up of the department given above. (In each case, the occupations or businesses regulated are indicated by the entity's name.)

ACCOUNTING EXAMINING BOARD

Chair: John S. Scheid
Contact: Brittany Lewin, *executive director*; brittany.lewin@wisconsin.gov; 608-261-5406

EXAMINING BOARD OF ARCHITECTS, LANDSCAPE ARCHITECTS, PROFESSIONAL ENGINEERS, DESIGNERS AND PROFESSIONAL LAND SURVEYORS

Chair: Rosheen Styczinski
Architect section chair: (vacant)
Designer section chair: (vacant)

Engineer section chair: Mark E. Mayer
Landscape architect section chair: Rosheen M. Styczinski
Land surveyor section chair: Bruce D. Bowden
Contact: Brittany Lewin, *executive director*; brittany.lewin@wisconsin.gov;
608-261-5406

ATHLETIC TRAINERS AFFILIATED CREDENTIALING BOARD (affiliated to Medical Examining Board)

Chair: Ryan A. Berry
Contact: Thomas Ryan, *executive director*; Thomas.Ryan@wisconsin.gov;
608-261-2378

AUCTIONEER BOARD

Chair: Jerry L. Thiel
Contact: Dan Williams, *executive director*; Dan1.Williams@wisconsin.gov;
608-267-7223

BUILDING INSPECTOR REVIEW BOARD

Members: Donald A. Esposito, David R. Huebsch, Gary Roehrig, James S. Micech, Benjamin E. Noffke
Contact: Brittany Lewin, *executive director*; brittany.lewin@wisconsin.gov;
608-261-5406

The Building Inspector Review Board reviews allegations of misconduct made against building inspectors. The board may revoke a building inspector's certification if it finds an allegation to be valid. The board may also modify or reverse a building inspector's decision that the board determines is erroneous.

CEMETERY BOARD

Members: Francis J. Groh, Patricia A. Grathen, Bernard G. Schroedl, Kathleen M. Cantu, John M. Reinemann, 1 vacancy
Contact: Dan Williams, *executive director*; Dan1.Williams@wisconsin.gov;
608-267-7223

CHIROPRACTIC EXAMINING BOARD

Chair: Patricia A. Schumacher
Contact: Thomas Ryan, *executive director*; Thomas.Ryan@wisconsin.gov;
608-261-2378

COSMETOLOGY EXAMINING BOARD

Chair: Vicky L. McNally

Contact: Brittany Lewin, *executive director*; brittany.lewin@wisconsin.gov; 608-261-5406

DENTISTRY EXAMINING BOARD

Chair: Mark T. Braden
Contact: Brittany Lewin, *executive director*; brittany.lewin@wisconsin.gov; 608-261-5406

DIETITIANS AFFILIATED CREDENTIALING BOARD (affiliated to Medical Examining Board)

Chair: Scott M. Krueger
Contact: Thomas Ryan, *executive director*; Thomas.Ryan@wisconsin.gov; 608-261-2378

FUNERAL DIRECTORS EXAMINING BOARD

Members: Eric Lengell, Marla E. Michaelis, D. Bruce Carlson, Marc A. Eernisse, Aziz K. Al-Sager, 1 vacancy
Contact: Dan Williams, *executive director*; Dan1.Williams@wisconsin.gov; 608-267-7223

EXAMINING BOARD OF PROFESSIONAL GEOLOGISTS, HYDROLOGISTS AND SOIL SCIENTISTS

Chair: William N. Mode
Geologist section chair: William N. Mode
Hydrologist section chair: Randall J. Hunt
Soil scientist section: (all seats currently vacant)
Contact: Dan Williams, *executive director*; Dan1.Williams@wisconsin.gov; 608-267-7223

HEARING AND SPEECH EXAMINING BOARD

Chair: Thomas W. Sather
Contact: Thomas Ryan, *executive director*; Thomas.Ryan@wisconsin.gov; 608-261-2378

MARRIAGE AND FAMILY THERAPY, PROFESSIONAL COUNSELING AND SOCIAL WORK EXAMINING BOARD

Chair: Gregory E. Winkler
Marriage and family therapist section chair: Alice Hanson-Drew
Professional counselor section chair: Allison L. Gordon
Social worker section chair: Gregory E. Winkler

Contact: Dan Williams, *executive director*; Dan1.Williams@wisconsin.gov; 608-267-7223

MASSAGE THERAPY AND BODYWORK THERAPY AFFILIATED CREDENTIALING BOARD (affiliated to Medical Examining Board)

Chair: Elizabeth C. Krizenesky

Contact: Thomas Ryan, *executive director*; Thomas.Ryan@wisconsin.gov; 608-261-2378

MEDICAL EXAMINING BOARD

Chair: Kenneth B. Simons

Contact: Thomas Ryan, *executive director*; Thomas.Ryan@wisconsin.gov; 608-261-2378

Advisory councils assisting the board: Council on Anesthesiologists Assistants, Michael L. Bottcher, *chair*; Perfusionists Examining Council, Shawn E. Mergen, *chair*; Council on Physician Assistants, Jeremiah L. Barrett, *chair*; Respiratory Care Practitioners Examining Council, William D. Rosandick, *chair*

BOARD OF NURSING

Chair: Sheryl A. Krause

Contact: Dan Williams, *executive director*; Dan1.Williams@wisconsin.gov; 608-267-7223

NURSING HOME ADMINISTRATOR EXAMINING BOARD

Chair: Timothy J. Conroy

Contact: Thomas Ryan, *executive director*; Thomas.Ryan@wisconsin.gov; 608-261-2378

OCCUPATIONAL THERAPISTS AFFILIATED CREDENTIALING BOARD (affiliated to Medical Examining Board)

Chair: Brian B. Holmquist

Contact: Thomas Ryan, *executive director*; Thomas.Ryan@wisconsin.gov; 608-261-2378

OPTOMETRY EXAMINING BOARD

Chair: Ann Meier Carli

Contact: Thomas Ryan, *executive director*; Thomas.Ryan@wisconsin.gov; 608-261-2378

PHARMACY EXAMINING BOARD

Chair: Thaddeus J. Schumacher

Contact: Dan Williams, *executive director*; Dan1.Williams@wisconsin.gov; 608-267-7223

PHYSICAL THERAPY EXAMINING BOARD

Chair: Shari L. Berry
Contact: Thomas Ryan, *executive director*; Thomas.Ryan@wisconsin.gov; 608-261-2378

PODIATRY AFFILIATED CREDENTIALING BOARD (affiliated to Medical Examining Board)

Chair: William W. Weis
Contact: Thomas Ryan, *executive director*; Thomas.Ryan@wisconsin.gov; 608-261-2378

PSYCHOLOGY EXAMINING BOARD

Chair: Daniel A. Schroeder
Contact: Dan Williams, *executive director*; Dan1.Williams@wisconsin.gov; 608-267-7223

RADIOGRAPHY EXAMINING BOARD

Chair: Donald A. Borst
Contact: Thomas Ryan, *executive director*; Thomas.Ryan@wisconsin.gov; 608-261-2378

REAL ESTATE APPRAISERS BOARD

Chair: Lawrence R. Nicholson
Contact: Thomas Ryan, *executive director*; Thomas.Ryan@wisconsin.gov; 608-261-2378

REAL ESTATE EXAMINING BOARD

Chair: Randal F. Savaglio
Contact: Brittany Lewin, *executive director*; brittany.lewin@wisconsin.gov; 608-261-5406
Advisory councils assisting the board: Council on Real Estate Curriculum and Examinations, Kitty M. Jedwabny, *chair*

Office of the Secretary of State

Secretary of state: Douglas La Follette
Location: B41 West, State Capitol, Madison

Contact: statesec@wisconsin.gov; 608-266-8888; PO Box 7848, Madison, WI 53707-7848
Website: www.sos.state.wi.us
Number of employees: 2.00
Total budget 2015–17: $536,800

The secretary of state is a constitutional officer elected for a four-year term by partisan ballot in the November general election. The secretary of state maintains the official acts of the legislature and governor and keeps the Great Seal of the State of Wisconsin, affixing it to all official acts of the governor. Along with the attorney general and the state treasurer, the secretary of state serves on the Board of Commissioners of Public Lands. The secretary of state may also be called upon to act as governor under certain circumstances, for example, if the sitting governor dies or resigns and there is a vacancy in the Office of Lieutenant Governor.

Office of the State Treasurer

State treasurer: Matt Adamczyk
Location: Room B41 West, State Capitol, Madison
Contact: 608-266-1714; Room B41 West, State Capitol, Madison, WI 53701
Website: www.statetreasury.wisconsin.gov
Number of employees: 1.00
Total budget 2015–17: $346,600

The state treasurer is a constitutional officer elected for a four-year term by partisan ballot in the November general election. The state treasurer signs certain checks and financial instruments and helps to promote the state's unclaimed property program. Along with the attorney general and secretary of state, the state treasurer serves on the Board of Commissioners of Public Lands.

Technical College System

Technical College System Board: John Schwantes, *president*
System president and state director: Morna K. Foy
Location: 4622 University Avenue, Madison
Contact: 608-266-1207; PO Box 7874, Madison, WI 53707-7874
Website: www.wtcsystem.edu
Number of employees: 55.00
Total budget 2015–17: $1,114,153,500

The Technical College System Board is the coordinating and oversight agency for the Technical College System. The governor, with the advice and consent of the senate, appoints ten of the board's 13 members, nine to serve six-year terms and a technical college student to serve a two-year term. The remaining members are the state superintendent of public instruction, the secretary of workforce development, and the president of the Board of Regents of the University of Wisconsin System (but each of these officers may designate another individual to serve in his or her place).

The board establishes statewide policies for the educational programs and services provided by the state's 16 technical college districts. (The districts, in turn, are responsible for the direct operation of the technical colleges, including setting academic and grading standards and hiring instructional staff for their programs.) The board defines, approves, evaluates, and reviews educational programs; provides guidance to the technical college districts in developing financial policies and standards; distributes state and federal aid; sets student fees; sets standards for and approves building projects; oversees district budgets and enrollments; coordinates state and federal grant programs and student financial aid; and supports services for students.

The board also coordinates with the University of Wisconsin System on

Chef John Johnson, a culinary arts instructor at Madison College, provides guidance to students preparing for an event at the college.

TECHNICAL COLLEGE SYSTEM

programming and college transfer courses and with other state agencies on vocational and technical education programs and apprentice training.

Independent entities attached for administrative purposes

EDUCATIONAL APPROVAL BOARD

Chair: Don Madelung
Executive secretary: David C. Dies
Contact: 608-266-1996; 431 Charmany Drive, Suite 102, Madison, WI 53719
Website: http://eab.state.wi.us
Number of employees: 6.50
Total budget 2015–17: $1,423,600

The Educational Approval Board is responsible for regulating and evaluating private, for-profit postsecondary schools; out-of-state, nonprofit colleges and universities offering distance education to Wisconsin residents; and in-state, nonprofit institutions incorporated after 1991. The board currently oversees 217 schools serving approximately 30,000 students annually.

Department of Tourism

Department secretary: Stephanie Klett
Deputy secretary: Sarah Klavas
Location: 201 West Washington Avenue, 2nd Floor, Madison
Contact: 608-266-2161; 800-432-8747; PO Box 8690, Madison, WI 53708-8690
Website: www.travelwisconsin.com (information for tourists); http://industry.travelwisconsin.com (information for the tourism industry)
Number of employees: 31.00
Total budget 2015–17: $31,863,200

The Department of Tourism is administered by a secretary who is appointed by the governor with the advice and consent of the senate. The department promotes travel to Wisconsin's scenic, historic, artistic, educational, and recreational sites. Travel sectors targeted by the department include leisure, meetings and conventions, sports, group tours, and international. Through planning, research, and assistance it provides guidance to the tourism and recreation industry to aid in the development of facilities. It also assists cooperative projects between profit and nonprofit tourism ventures and encourages local tourism development.

DEPARTMENT OF TOURISM

Every September, the Chequamegon Fat Tire Festival brings cycling enthusiasts of all ages to northern Wisconsin from around the world.

Subordinate statutory boards, councils, and committees

ARTS BOARD

Executive director: George Tzougros
Contact: artsboard@wisconsin.gov; 608-266-0190; PO Box 8690, Madison, WI 53708-8690
Website: https://artsboard.wisconsin.gov
Number of employees: 4.00
Total budget 2015–17: $3,155,400

The Arts Board studies and assists artistic and cultural activities in the state, assists communities in developing their own arts programs, and plans and implements financial support programs for individuals and organizations engaged in the arts, including apprenticeships, artists-in-education programs, challenge grants, community activities, fellowships, opportunity grants, program assistance and support, and programs for presenters. The board also provides matching grants to local arts agencies and municipalities through the Wisconsin Regranting Program.

COUNCIL ON TOURISM

The Council on Tourism advises the secretary about tourism, including by encouraging Wisconsin-based companies to promote the state in their advertisements and by formulating a statewide marketing plan.

Independent entities attached for administrative purposes

KICKAPOO RESERVE MANAGEMENT BOARD

Chair: Ronald M. Johnson
Executive director: Marcy West
Contact: kickapoo.reserve@krm.state.wi.us; 608-625-2960; S3661 State Highway 131, La Farge, WI 54639
Website: http://kvr.state.wi.us
Number of employees: 0.00
Total budget 2015–17: $0

The Kickapoo Reserve Management Board manages the approximately 8,600 acre Kickapoo Valley Reserve through a joint management agreement with the Ho-Chunk Nation. The Kickapoo Valley Reserve exists to preserve and enhance the area's environmental, scenic, and cultural features and provides facilities

Several ferries connect tourists from Bayfield, at the tip of northern Wisconsin, to Madeline Island; there, they can visit historic sites or take in the scenery of the Apostle Islands.

for the use and enjoyment of visitors. Subject to the approval of the governor, the board may purchase land for inclusion in the reserve and trade land in the reserve under certain conditions. The board also may lease land for purposes consistent with the management of the reserve or for agricultural purposes.

STATE FAIR PARK BOARD

Chair: John Yingling
Chief executive officer: Kathleen O'Leary
Contact: wsfp@wistatefair.com; 414-266-7000; 414-266-7100 (ticket office); 800-884-FAIR (events information); 640 South 84th Street, West Allis, WI 53214
Website: www.wistatefair.com
Number of employees: 48.00
Total budget 2015–17: $48,003,900

The State Fair Park Board manages the State Fair Park, including the development of new facilities. The board provides a permanent location for the annual Wisconsin State Fair and for major sports events, agricultural and industrial expositions, and other programs of civic interest.

Department of Transportation

Department secretary: Dave Ross
Deputy secretary: Bob Seitz
Location: Hill Farms State Transportation Building, 4802 Sheboygan Avenue, Madison
Contact: 608-266-3581; PO Box 7910, Madison, WI 53707-7910
Website: www.wisconsindot.gov
Number of employees: 3,494.54
Total budget 2015–17: $5,689,553,100

The Department of Transportation is administered by a secretary who is appointed by the governor with the advice and consent of the senate.

The department is responsible for the planning, promotion, and protection of all transportation systems in the state. Its major responsibilities involve highways, motor vehicles, motor carriers, traffic law enforcement, railroads, waterways, mass transit, and aeronautics. The department issues vehicle titles and registrations and individual identification cards and examines and licenses drivers. The department works with several federal agencies in the administration of federal transportation aids. It also cooperates with departments at the

The Wisconsin State Patrol, part of the Department of Transportation, not only enforces traffic laws but conducts public outreach on traffic safety to young drivers.

state level in travel promotion, consumer protection, environmental analysis, and transportation services for elderly and handicapped persons.

Subordinate statutory boards, councils, and committees

COUNCIL ON HIGHWAY SAFETY

The Council on Highway Safety advises the department secretary about highway safety matters.

RUSTIC ROADS BOARD

The Rustic Roads Board oversees the application and selection process of locally nominated county highways and local roads for inclusion in the Rustic Roads network. The Rustic Roads program is a partnership between local officials and state government to showcase some of Wisconsin's most picturesque and lightly traveled roadways for the leisurely enjoyment of hikers, bikers, and motorists.

COUNCIL ON UNIFORMITY OF TRAFFIC CITATIONS AND COMPLAINTS

The Council on Uniformity of Traffic Citations and Complaints recommends forms used for traffic violations.

University of Wisconsin System

Board of Regents: Regina Millner, John Behling, Tony Evers, José Delgado, Margaret Farrow, Michael M. Grebe, Eve Hall, Tim Higgins, Janice Mueller, Drew Petersen, Tracey Klein, S. Mark Tyler, Bryan Steil, Gerald Whitburn, Lisa Erickson, 3 vacancies

Executive director and corporate secretary: Jane Radue

System Administration: Raymond W. Cross, *president*
Contact: 608-262-2321; 1720 Van Hise Hall, 1220 Linden Drive, Madison, WI 53706
Website: www.wisconsin.edu
Number of employees: 34,655.26
Total budget 2015–17: $11,758,980,000

UW-MADISON

Chancellor: Rebecca Blank
Contact: 608-262-1234; 161 Bascom Hall, 500 Lincoln Drive, Madison, WI 53706
Website: www.wisc.edu

UW-MILWAUKEE

Chancellor: Mark Mone
Contact: 414-229-1122; PO Box 413, Milwaukee, WI 53201
Website: www.uwm.edu

UW-EAU CLAIRE

Chancellor: James C. Schmidt
Contact: 715-836-4636; 105 Garfield Avenue, PO Box 4004, Eau Claire, WI 54702-4004
Website: www.uwec.edu

UW-GREEN BAY

Chancellor: Gary L. Miller
Contact: 920-465-2000; 2420 Nicolet Drive, Green Bay, WI 54311-7001
Website: www.uwgb.edu

UW-LA CROSSE

Chancellor: Joe Gow
Contact: 608-785-8000; 1725 State Street, La Crosse, WI 54601-9959
Website: www.uwlax.edu

UW-OSHKOSH

Chancellor: Andrew J. Leavitt
Contact: 920-424-1234; 220 Dempsey Hall, 800 Algoma Boulevard, Oshkosh, WI 54901
Website: www.uwosh.edu

UW-PARKSIDE

Chancellor: Deborah L. Ford
Contact: 262-595-2345; PO Box 2000, Kenosha, WI 53141-2000
Website: www.uwp.edu

UW-PLATTEVILLE

Chancellor: Dennis J. Shields
Contact: 608-342-1491; 2508 Ullsvik Hall, 1 University Plaza, Platteville, WI 53818
Website: www.uwplatt.edu

UW-RIVER FALLS

Chancellor: Dean Van Galen
Contact: 715-425-3911; 116 North Hall, 410 South Third Street, River Falls, WI 54022
Website: www.uwrf.edu

UW-STEVENS POINT

Chancellor: Bernie L. Patterson
Contact: 715-346-0123; Room 213 Old Main, 2100 Main Street, Stevens Point, WI 54481
Website: www.uwsp.edu

UW-STOUT

Chancellor: Bob Meyer
Contact: 715-232-1122; PO Box 790, Menomonie, WI 54751
Website: www.uwstout.edu

UW-SUPERIOR

Chancellor: Renée Wachter
Contact: 715-394-8101; Belknap and Catlin Avenue, PO Box 2000, Superior, WI 54880
Website: www.uwsuper.edu

(*top*) UW-Milwaukee is connecting students with careers in the growing water industry through a program called "See Yourself Succeeding in STEM," which places students from area technical colleges in internships at water-related businesses. Research in the lab at UW-Milwaukee's School of Freshwater Sciences is part of the Water SYS-STEM internship. (*above*) A UW-Stout professor works with a student in a video compositing class.

UW-WHITEWATER

Chancellor: Beverly A. Kopper

Contact: 262-472-1234; 800 West Main Street, Whitewater, WI 53190-1790

Website: www.uww.edu

UW COLLEGES AND UW-EXTENSION

Chancellor: Cathy Sandeen

Contact: 608-262-3786; 432 North Lake Street, Madison, WI 53706

Website: www.uwc.edu (UW Colleges); www.uwex.edu (UW-Extension)

The University of Wisconsin System is governed by an 18-member Board of Regents, which consists of 14 citizen members, two student members, the president of the Technical College System Board or his or her designee, and the state superintendent of public instruction. The citizen and student members are appointed by the governor subject to senate confirmation. The Board of Regents appoints the president of the UW System, who has executive responsibility for system operation and management. The Board of Regents also appoints the chancellors for each four-year university and one chancellor who administers both UW Colleges and UW-Extension.

The prime responsibilities of the UW System are teaching, public service, and research. The system provides postsecondary academic education for about 180,000 students, including approximately 156,000 undergraduates. The system consists of 13 four-year universities, 13 two-year colleges, and extension programs known as UW-Extension. Two of the four-year universities (UW-Madison and UW-Milwaukee) offer bachelor's, master's, doctoral, and professional degrees. The remaining four-year universities (UW-Eau Claire, UW-Green Bay, UW-La Crosse, UW-Oshkosh, UW-Parkside, UW-Platteville, UW-River Falls, UW-Stevens Point, UW-Stout, UW-Superior, and UW-Whitewater) offer associate, bachelor's, master's, and clinical/professional doctoral degree programs. The two-year colleges comprise an institution known as UW Colleges, which offers Associate of Arts and Science and Bachelor of Applied Arts and Sciences degrees at college campuses and through UW Colleges Online. UW-Extension provides statewide access to system resources and research in partnership with all system campuses, counties, three tribal nations, and other public and private organizations.

Programs required by statute

OFFICE OF THE STATE CARTOGRAPHER

State cartographer: Howard Veregin

Contact: 608-262-3065; 384 Science Hall, 550 North Park Street, Madison, WI 53706-1491
Website: www.sco.wisc.edu

GEOLOGICAL AND NATURAL HISTORY SURVEY

Director and state geologist: Ken Bradbury
Contact: 608-262-1705; 3817 Mineral Point Road, Madison, WI 53705-5100
Website: http://wgnhs.uwex.edu

UW CENTER FOR AGRICULTURAL SAFETY AND HEALTH

Interim director: Cheryl Skjolaas
Contact: 608-265-0568; 201 Agricultural Engineering Building, 460 Henry Mall, Madison, WI 53706
Website: http://fyi.uwex.edu/agsafety

WISCONSIN CENTER FOR ENVIRONMENTAL EDUCATION

Director: Laurie Gharis
Contact: 715-346-4973; 800 Reserve Street, Stevens Point, WI 54481
Website: www.uwsp.edu/cnr-ap/wcee

AREA HEALTH EDUCATION CENTER

Director: Nancy Sugden
Contact: 608-263-4927; 4251 Health Sciences Learning Center, 750 Highland Avenue, Madison, WI 53705
Website: www.ahec.wisc.edu

WISCONSIN STATE HERBARIUM

Director: Kenneth Cameron
Contact: 608-262-2792; Birge Hall, 460 Lincoln Drive, Madison, WI 53706
Website: http://herbarium.wisc.edu

PSYCHIATRIC HEALTH EMOTIONS RESEARCH INSTITUTE

Director: Ned Kalin
Contact: 608-263-6079; 6001 Research Park Boulevard, Madison, WI 53719

ROBERT M. LA FOLLETTE SCHOOL OF PUBLIC AFFAIRS

Director: Donald Moynihan
Contact: 608-262-3581; 1225 Observatory Drive, Madison, WI 53706
Website: www.lafollette.wisc.edu

STATE SOILS AND PLANT ANALYSIS LABORATORY
Director: Robert Florence
Contact: 715-387-2523; 2611 Yellowstone Drive, Marshfield, WI 54449
Website: https://uwlab.soils.wisc.edu

INSTITUTE FOR URBAN EDUCATION
Director: Tracey Nix
Contact: 414-229-6507; Enderis Hall, UW-Milwaukee, 2400 East Hartford Avenue, Room 568, Milwaukee, WI 53211
Website: http://uwm.edu/education/community/partnerships/institute-urban-edu

JAMES A. GRAASKAMP CENTER FOR REAL ESTATE
Executive director: Michael Brennan
Contact: 608-263-4392; Grainger Hall, 975 University Avenue, Madison, WI 53706
Website: http://bus.wisc.edu/centers/james-a-graaskamp-center-for-real-estate

SCHOOL OF VETERINARY MEDICINE
Dean: Mark D. Markel
Contact: 608-263-6716; 2015 Linden Drive West, Madison, WI 53706-1102
Website: www.vetmed.wisc.edu

Subordinate statutory boards, councils, and committees

RURAL HEALTH DEVELOPMENT COUNCIL
Contact: 608-261-1883; 800-385-0005 (toll free); Wisconsin Office of Rural Health, UW School of Medicine and Public Health, 310 N. Midvale Boulevard, Suite 301, Madison, WI 53705

The Rural Health Development Council consists of 17 members appointed by the governor, with the advice and consent of the senate, for five-year terms and the secretary of health services or his or her designee. The council advises the Board of Regents on matters related to loan assistance programs for physicians, dentists, and other health care providers.

Independent entities attached for administrative purposes

LABORATORY OF HYGIENE BOARD
Members: James Morrison, James Wenzler, Barry Irmen, Jeffery Kindrai, Robert Corliss, Richard Moss, Karen McKeown, Mark Aquino, Michelle Wachter, 2 vacancies

Nonvoting member and laboratory director: Charles D. Brokopp
Contact: 608-890-0288 (Administrative Office); 608-262-6386 and
800-862-1013 (Clinical Laboratories); 608-224-6202 and 800-442-4618
(Environmental Health Laboratory); 608-224-6210 and 800-446-
0403 (Occupational Health Laboratory); 608-224-4302 and 800-462-
5261 (Proficiency Testing); 465 Henry Mall, Madison, WI 53706-1501
(Clinical Laboratories); 2601 Agriculture Drive, Madison, WI 53718-6780
(Environmental and Occupational Health Laboratories, Forensic Toxicology,
Safety and Health Consultation, and Proficiency Testing)
Website: www.slh.wisc.edu
Number of employees: 309.75
Total budget 2015–17: $69,055,600

The Laboratory of Hygiene Board oversees the Laboratory of Hygiene, which provides laboratory services for state agencies and local health departments in the areas of water quality, air quality, public health, and contagious diseases. The laboratory performs tests and consults with physicians, health officers, local agencies, private citizens, and resource management officials to prevent and control diseases and environmental hazards. As part of the UW-Madison, the laboratory provides facilities for teaching and research in the fields of public health and environmental protection.

VETERINARY DIAGNOSTIC LABORATORY BOARD

Members: Sandra C. Madland, Ben Brancel, Charles Czuprynski, Mark
Markel, Sherry Shaw, Alissa Grenawalt, James Meronek, Casey Davis, Ray
Pawlisch
Nonvoting member and laboratory director: Philip Bochsler
Contact: 608-262-5432; 800-608-8387 (toll free); 445 Easterday Lane,
Madison, WI 53706
Website: www.wvdl.wisc.edu
Number of employees: 94.50
Total budget 2015–17: $22,861,400

The Veterinary Diagnostic Laboratory Board oversees the Veterinary Diagnostic Laboratory, which provides animal health testing and diagnostic services on a statewide basis for all types of animals.

Department of Veterans Affairs

Department secretary: Daniel J. Zimmerman
Deputy secretary: Tom Rhatican

Board of Veterans Affairs: Larry Kutschma, *chair*
Location: 201 West Washington Avenue, Madison
Contact: 608-266-1311; 1-800-WIS-VETS (toll free); PO Box 7843, Madison, WI 53707-7843
Website: www.wisvets.com
Number of employees: 1,294.20
Total budget 2015–17: $283,746,000

The Department of Veterans Affairs is administered by a secretary who must be a veteran and is appointed by the governor with the advice and consent of the senate. The department includes the Board of Veterans Affairs, consisting of nine members who must be veterans and are appointed by the governor with the advice and consent of the senate. The board advises the secretary on the promulgation of administrative rules necessary to carry out the powers and duties of the department.

The department administers an array of grants, benefits, programs, and services to eligible veterans, their families, and organizations that serve veterans. It operates the Wisconsin veterans homes at Chippewa Falls, King, and Union Grove, which provide short-term rehabilitation and long-term skilled nursing care to eligible veterans (and, to the extent of their resources, to the

The University of Wisconsin Band greets veterans during its annual Salute to Veterans Tailgate event during football season. The event brings student athletes together with active and former military personnel in the state.

DEPARTMENT OF VETERANS AFFAIRS

spouses and parents of veterans). The department also operates the Southern Wisconsin Veterans Memorial Cemetery at Union Grove, the Northern Wisconsin Veterans Memorial Cemetery near Spooner, and the Central Wisconsin Veterans Memorial Cemetery at King. Finally, the department operates the Wisconsin Veterans Museum in Madison.

Subordinate statutory boards, councils, and committees

COUNCIL ON VETERANS PROGRAMS

The Council on Veterans Programs studies and presents policy alternatives and recommendations to the Board of Veterans Affairs.

Department of Workforce Development

Department secretary: Ray Allen
Deputy secretary: Georgia Maxwell
Location: 201 East Washington Avenue, Madison
Contact: 608-266-3131; PO Box 7946, Madison, WI 53707-7946
Website: www.dwd.wisconsin.gov
Number of employees: 1,620.55
Total budget 2015–17: $722,646,600

The Department of Workforce Development is administered by a secretary who is appointed by the governor with the advice and consent of the senate.

The department operates the state's job center network (https://jobcenter ofwisconsin.com); manages the Fast Forward worker training grant program; operates adult and youth apprenticeship programs; collects, analyzes, and distributes labor market information; monitors migrant workers services; provides vocational rehabilitation services to help people with disabilities achieve their employment goals; and offers comprehensive employment and training programs and services to youth and adults, including veterans with service-connected disabilities. The department also oversees the unemployment insurance and worker's compensation programs. Finally, the department enforces wage and hour laws; prevailing wage laws; leave and benefits laws; child labor laws; civil rights laws; plant closing laws; and laws regulating migrant labor contractors and camps.

Subordinate statutory boards, councils, and committees

WISCONSIN APPRENTICESHIP COUNCIL

Contact: 608-266-3332; PO Box 7972, Madison, WI 53707-7972

DEPARTMENT OF WORKFORCE DEVELOPMENT

Department of Workforce Development Secretary Ray Allen joins Milwaukee Public School leaders at Bradley Tech High School to learn more about expanded Career and Technical Education opportunities available to students.

The Wisconsin Apprenticeship Council advises the department on matters pertaining to Wisconsin's apprenticeship system.

COUNCIL ON MIGRANT LABOR

Contact: 608-266-0002; PO Box 7972, Madison, WI 53707-7972

The Council on Migrant Labor advises the department and other state officials about matters affecting migrant workers.

SELF-INSURERS COUNCIL

Contact: 608-266-6841; PO Box 7901, Madison, WI 53707-7901

The Self-Insurers Council assists the department in administering the self-insurance program, under which an employer can be permitted to cover its worker's compensation costs directly rather than by purchasing insurance. The council ensures that those employers applying for self-insurance are financially viable and monitors the financial status of employers in the self-insurance pool.

COUNCIL ON UNEMPLOYMENT INSURANCE

Contact: 608-266-1639; PO Box 8942, Madison, WI 53708-8942

The Council on Unemployment Insurance advises the legislature and the department about unemployment insurance matters.

COUNCIL ON WORKER'S COMPENSATION

Contact: 608-266-6841; PO Box 7901, Madison, WI 53707-7901

The Council on Worker's Compensation advises the legislature and the department about worker's compensation matters.

HEALTH CARE PROVIDER ADVISORY COMMITTEE

Contact: 608-266-6841; PO Box 7901, Madison, WI 53707-7901

The Health Care Provider Advisory Committee advises the department and the Council on Worker's Compensation on the standards that the department uses when it determines whether treatment provided to an injured employee was necessary treatment that is compensable by worker's compensation insurance.

Independent entities attached for administrative purposes

EMPLOYMENT RELATIONS COMMISSION

Chair: James R. Scott
Chief legal counsel: Peter G. Davis
Location: 4868 High Crossing Boulevard, Madison
Contact: werc@werc.state.wi.us; 608-243-2424; PO Box 7870, Madison, WI 53707-7870
Website: http://werc.wi.gov
Number of employees: 9.01
Total budget 2015–17: $3,071,700

The Employment Relations Commission promotes collective bargaining and peaceful labor relations in the private and public sectors. The commission determines various types of labor relations cases and issues decisions arising from state employee civil service appeals. The commission also provides mediation and grievance arbitration services as well as training and assistance to parties interested in labor-management cooperation and a consensus approach to resolving labor relations issues.

Authorities

Wisconsin Aerospace Authority

Board of directors chair: Thomas Crabb

The Wisconsin Aerospace Authority is directed to promote and develop the state's space-related industry and coordinate these activities with governmental entities, the aerospace industry, businesses, educational organizations, and the Wisconsin Space Grant Consortium. The authority's other duties include securing adequate funding for spaceport facilities and services, sponsoring events to attract space-related businesses to Wisconsin, advertising the use of spaceports to the public, and establishing a safety program.

The authority is a public corporation whose board consists of the director of the consortium, six appointees of the governor, one senator appointed by the president of the senate, and one assembly representative appointed by the speaker of the assembly. Other than the director of the consortium, board members must be Wisconsin residents with experience in the commercial space industry, education, finance, or some other significant experience related to the functions of the authority.

Wisconsin Economic Development Corporation

Board of directors chair: Lisa Mauer
Chief executive officer: Mark Hogan
Chief operating officer: Tricia Braun
Location: 201 West Washington Avenue, Madison
Contact: 855-469-4249; PO Box 1687, Madison, WI 53701
Website: http://inwisconsin.com
Total state appropriation 2015–17: $65,001,400

The Wisconsin Economic Development Corporation is a public corporation that develops, implements, and administers programs to provide business support and expertise and financial assistance to companies that are investing and creating jobs in Wisconsin and to promote new business start-ups and business expansion and growth in the state. The authority was established in 2011 and assumed many of the functions previously performed by the former Department of Commerce. WEDC is governed by a 14-member board that includes six appointees of the governor and four appointees of legislative leaders of both parties from both houses. WEDC may issue bonds and incur other debt to achieve its public purposes. WEDC's bonds and other debt do not create a debt of the state.

Fox River Navigational System Authority

Board of directors chair: S. Timothy Rose
Chief executive officer: Robert J. Stark
Contact: 920-759-9833; 1008 Augustine Street, Kaukauna, WI 54130-1608
Website: www.foxlocks.org

The Fox River Navigational System Authority is a public corporation that is responsible for the rehabilitation, repair, and management of the navigation system on or near the Fox River, and it may enter into contracts with third parties to operate the system. The authority may charge fees for services provided to watercraft owners and users of navigational facilities, enter into contracts with nonprofit organizations to raise funds, and contract debt, but it may not issue bonds. Annually, the authority must submit an audited financial statement to the Department of Administration. The authority is governed by a nine-member board of directors that includes six appointees of the governor, two each from Brown, Outagamie, and Winnebago Counties.

Wisconsin Health and Educational Facilities Authority

Board of directors chair: James Dietsche
Executive director: Dennis P. Reilly
Contact: info@whefa.com; 262-792-0466; 18000 West Sarah Lane, Suite 300, Brookfield, WI 53045-5841
Website: www.whefa.com

The Wisconsin Health and Educational Facilities Authority is a public corporation governed by a seven-member board, whose members are appointed by the governor with the advice and consent of the senate. No more than four of the members may be of the same political party. The governor appoints the chair.

WHEFA issues bonds on behalf of private nonprofit facilities to help them finance their capital costs. The authority has no taxing power. WHEFA's bonds are not a debt, liability, or obligation of the State of Wisconsin or any of its subdivisions. The authority may issue bonds to finance any qualifying capital project, including new construction, remodeling, and renovation; expansion of current facilities; and purchase of new equipment or furnishings. WHEFA may also issue bonds to refinance outstanding debt.

Wisconsin Housing and Economic Development Authority

Board of directors chair: Ivan Gamboa
Executive director: Wyman B. Winston
Contact: info@wheda.com; 608-266-7884 or 800-334-6873 (Madison); 414-227-4039 or 800-628-4833 (Milwaukee); PO Box 1728, Madison, WI 53701-1728; 201 West Washington Avenue, Suite 700, Madison, WI 53703; 611 West National Avenue, Suite 110, Milwaukee, WI 53204 (Milwaukee office)
Website: www.wheda.com

The Wisconsin Housing and Economic Development Authority is a public corporation governed by a 12-member board that includes six appointees of the governor and four legislators representing both parties and both houses. WHEDA administers numerous loan programs and other programs and projects that provide housing and related assistance to Wisconsin residents, including single and multifamily housing for individuals and families of low and moderate income, and that promote and support home ownership. WHEDA also finances loan guarantees and administers other programs to support business and agricultural development in the state. WHEDA issues bonds to support its operations, which, however, do not create a debt of the state.

Lower Fox River Remediation Authority (inactive)

The Lower Fox River Remediation Authority is a public corporation that is authorized to issue assessment bonds for eligible waterway improvement costs, which generally include environmental investigation and remediation of the Fox River extending from Lake Winnebago to the mouth of the river in Lake Michigan, and including any portion of Green Bay in Lake Michigan that contains sediments discharged from the river. The state is not liable for the authority's bonds, and the bonds are not a debt of the state. The authority is governed by a seven-member board, appointed by the governor with the advice and consent of the senate, and no more than four members may be from the same political party.

University of Wisconsin Hospitals and Clinics Authority

Board of directors chair: Robert Golden
Chief executive officer: Alan Kaplan
Contact: 608-263-6400 or 800-323-8942; 600 Highland Avenue, Madison, WI 53792
Website: www.uwhealth.org

The University of Wisconsin Hospitals and Clinics Authority is a public corporation governed by a 16-member board of directors that includes the cochairs of the Joint Committee on Finance and six appointees of the governor. The authority operates the UW Hospital and Clinics, including the American Family Children's Hospital, and related clinics and health care facilities. Through the UW Hospital and Clinics and its other programs, the authority delivers health care, including care for the indigent; provides an environment for instruction of physicians, nurses, and other health-related disciplines; sponsors and supports health care research; and assists health care programs and personnel throughout the state.

The authority is self-financing. It derives much of its income from charges for clinical and hospital services. The authority also may issue bonds to support its operations, which, however, do not create a debt of the state, and may seek financing from the Wisconsin Health and Educational Facilities Authority.

Nonprofit corporations

Bradley Center Sports and Entertainment Corporation

Board of directors chair: Ted D. Kellner
Contact: 414-227-0400; 1001 North 4th Street, Milwaukee, WI 53203
Website: www.bmoharrisbradleycenter.com

The Bradley Center Sports and Entertainment Corporation is a public non-profit corporation, created as an instrumentality of the state to receive the donation of the Bradley Center, a sports and entertainment facility located in Milwaukee County, from the Bradley Center Corporation. The corporation's board of directors is made up of nine members appointed by the governor, none of whom may be an elected public official. Its responsibility is to own and operate the center for the economic and recreational benefit of the residents of Wisconsin. The Bradley Center is the home of the Milwaukee Bucks basketball team and the Marquette University men's basketball team. Other events held at the facility include family entertainment shows and concerts. The corporation and the Wisconsin Center District must enter into transfer agreements under which the corporation must transfer to the district, upon the completion of new sports and entertainment arena facilities that will be home to the Milwaukee Bucks, the Bradley Center and land under its control. Following the transfer, the Bradley Center is to be demolished, although its parking structure may continue to exist and operate.

Wisconsin Artistic Endowment Foundation (inactive)

The legislature created the Wisconsin Artistic Endowment Foundation as a public nonprofit corporation for the purpose of supporting the arts, distributing funds, and facilitating the conversion of donated property into cash to support the arts. It is currently inactive. The foundation may not be dissolved except by an enactment of the legislature.

Regional planning commissions

Regional planning commissions advise cities, villages, towns, and counties on the planning and delivery of public services to the residents of a defined region, and they prepare and adopt master plans for the physical development of the region they serve.

The commissions may conduct research studies; make and adopt plans for the physical, social, and economic development of the region; provide advisory services to local governmental units and other public and private agencies; and coordinate local programs that relate to their objectives. The functions of commissions are solely advisory to the political subdivisions comprising the region.

Currently, there are nine regional planning commissions serving all but five of the state's 72 counties. Their boundaries are based on factors including common topographical and geographical features; the extent of urban development; the existence of special or acute agricultural, forestry, or other rural problems; and the existence of physical, social, and economic problems of a regional character.

Regional planning commissions have developed and assisted with projects in areas including rail and air transportation, waste disposal and recycling, highways, air and water quality, farmland preservation and zoning, land conservation and reclamation, outdoor recreation, parking and lakefront studies, and land records modernization.

Membership of regional planning commissions varies according to conditions defined by statute. The commissions are funded through state and federal planning grants, contracts with local governments for special planning services, and a statutorily authorized levy of up to 0.003 percent of equalized real estate value charged to each local governmental unit.

Wisconsin's regional planning commissions have established the Association of Wisconsin Regional Planning Commissions. The association's purposes include assisting the study of common problems and serving as an information clearinghouse.

Bay-Lake Regional Planning Commission

Counties in region: Brown, Door, Florence, Kewaunee, Manitowoc, Marinette, Oconto, Sheboygan
Chair: Mike Hotz
Executive director: Cindy J. Wojtczak

Contact: 920-448-2820; 425 South Adams Street, Suite 201, Green Bay, WI 54301
Website: www.baylakerpc.org

Capital Area Regional Planning Commission

Counties in region: Dane
Chair: Larry Palm
Deputy director: Steve Steinhoff
Contact: info@capitalarearpc.org; 608-266-4137; City-County Building, 210 Martin Luther King Jr. Boulevard, Room 362, Madison, WI 53703
Website: www.capitalarearpc.org

East Central Wisconsin Regional Planning Commission

Counties in region: Calumet, Fond du Lac, Green Lake (not participating), Marquette (not participating), Menominee, Outagamie, Shawano, Waupaca, Waushara, Winnebago
Chair: Jerry Erdmann
Executive director: Eric W. Fowle
Contact: 920-751-4770; 400 Ahnaip Street, Suite 100, Menasha, WI 54952-3100
Website: www.ecwrpc.org

Mississippi River Regional Planning Commission

Counties in region: Buffalo, Crawford, Jackson, La Crosse, Monroe, Pepin, Pierce, Trempealeau, Vernon
Chair: James Kuhn
Executive director: Gregory D. Flogstad
Contact: plan@mrrpc.com; 608-785-9396; 1707 Main Street, Suite 435, La Crosse, WI 54601
Website: www.mrrpc.com

North Central Wisconsin Regional Planning Commission

Counties in region: Adams, Forest, Juneau, Langlade, Lincoln, Marathon, Oneida, Portage (not participating), Vilas, Wood
Chair: Paul Millan
Executive director: Dennis L. Lawrence
Contact: info@ncwrpc.org; 715-849-5510; 210 McClellan Street, Suite 210, Wausau, WI 54403
Website: www.ncwrpc.org

Northwest Regional Planning Commission

Counties in region: Ashland, Bayfield, Burnett, Douglas, Iron, Price, Rusk, Sawyer, Taylor, Washburn

Participating tribal nations: Bad River, Lac Courte Oreilles, Lac du Flambeau, Red Cliff, St. Croix

Chair: Douglas Finn

Executive director: Sheldon Johnson

Contact: info@nwrpc.com; 715-635-2197; 1400 South River Street, Spooner, WI 54801

Website: www.nwrpc.com

Southeastern Wisconsin Regional Planning Commission

Counties in region: Kenosha, Milwaukee, Ozaukee, Racine, Walworth, Washington, Waukesha

Regional planning commission areas

Chair: Charles L. Colman
Executive director: Michael G. Hahn
Contact: sewrpc@sewrpc.org; 262-547-6721; W239 N1812 Rockwood Drive,
PO Box 1607, Waukesha, WI 53187-1607
Website: www.sewrpc.org

Southwestern Wisconsin Regional Planning Commission

Counties in region: Grant, Green, Iowa, Lafayette, Richland
Chair: Jeanetta Kirkpatrick
Executive director: Troy Maggied
Contact: info@swwrpc.org; 608-342-1636; 20 South Court Street, PO Box
262, Platteville, WI 53818
Website: www.swwrpc.org

West Central Wisconsin Regional Planning Commission

Counties in region: Barron, Chippewa, Clark, Dunn, Eau Claire, Polk,
St. Croix
Chair: Jess Miller
Executive director: Lynn Nelson
Contact: wcwrpc@wcwrpc.org; 715-836-2918; 800 Wisconsin Street,
Building D2, Room 401, Mail Box 9, Eau Claire, WI 54703
Website: www.wcwrpc.org

Other regional entities

Madison Cultural Arts District Board (inactive)

Arts districts are local governmental units that may acquire, construct, operate,
and manage cultural arts facilities. A local district may issue revenue bonds,
invest funds, set standards for the use of facilities, and establish and collect fees
for usage. The Madison Cultural Arts District Board's activities are suspended
until requested otherwise.

Professional Football Stadium District

Board of directors chair: Ann Patteson
Executive director: Pat Webb
Contact: 920-965-6997; 1229 Lombardi Avenue, At Lambeau Field, Green
Bay, WI 54304

The Professional Football Stadium District is an owner and landlord of Lambeau Field, the designated home of the Green Bay Packers football team. It is a local governmental unit that may acquire, construct, equip, maintain, improve, operate, and manage football stadium facilities or hire others to do the same. Maintenance and operation of the stadium is governed by provisions of the Lambeau Field Lease Agreement by and among the district; Green Bay Packers, Inc.; and the City of Green Bay. The district board consists of seven members who are appointed by local elected officials.

Southeast Wisconsin Professional Baseball Park District

Governing board chair: Don Smiley
Executive director: Michael R. Duckett
Contact: contact@millerparkdistrict.com; 414-902-4040; Miller Park, One Brewers Way, Milwaukee, WI 53214
Website: www.millerparkdistrict.com

The Southeast Wisconsin Professional Baseball Park District is the majority owner of Miller Park, the home of the Milwaukee Brewers Baseball Club. It is a local governmental unit that may acquire, construct, maintain, improve, operate, and manage baseball park facilities, which include parking lots, garages, restaurants, parks, concession facilities, entertainment facilities, and other related structures. The district is also authorized to issue bonds for certain purposes related to baseball park facilities. To pay off the bonds, the district may impose a sales tax and a use tax. A city or county within the district's jurisdiction may make loans or grants to the district, expend funds to subsidize the district, borrow money for baseball park facilities, or grant property to the state dedicated for use by a professional baseball park.

The district includes Milwaukee, Ozaukee, Racine, Washington, and Waukesha counties. The district's governing board consists of 13 members appointed by the governor and elected officials from within its jurisdiction. The governor appoints the chair of the governing board.

Wisconsin Center District

Board of directors chair: Scott Neitzel
President and CEO: Russ Staerkel
Contact: 414-908-6000; 400 West Wisconsin Avenue, Milwaukee, WI 53203
Website: www.wcd.org

The Wisconsin Center District is a local governmental unit that may acquire, construct, and operate an exposition center and related facilities; enter into contracts and grant concessions; mortgage district property and issue bonds; and invest funds as the district board considers appropriate. The Wisconsin Center District operates the University of Wisconsin-Milwaukee Panther Arena, the Milwaukee Theatre, and the Wisconsin Center. It will also assist in the development and construction of sports and entertainment facilities, including a new arena for the Milwaukee Bucks. Following the completion of the sports and entertainment facilities, the Wisconsin Center District will oversee the demolition of the Bradley Center.

The district is funded by operating revenue and special sales taxes on hotel rooms, restaurant food and beverages, and car rentals within its taxing jurisdiction. The district board has 17 members, including legislative leaders, local government finance officials, and members who are appointed by the governor, Milwaukee County executive, city of Milwaukee mayor, and city of Milwaukee common council president.

Interstate compacts

Wisconsin has entered with other states into various interstate compacts, under which the compacting states agree to coordinate their activities related to a particular matter according to uniform guidelines or procedures. Some of these compacts include provisions creating an interstate entity made up of representatives from the compacting states, while others do not.

Interstate entities created by interstate compacts

EDUCATION COMMISSION OF THE STATES

Wisconsin delegation: Scott Walker (governor), *chair*
Contact: 303-299-3600; 700 Broadway, Suite 810, Denver, CO 80203
Website: www.ecs.org

The Education Commission of the States was established to foster national cooperation among executive, legislative, educational, and lay leaders of the various states concerning education policy and the improvement of state and local education systems. The seven-member Wisconsin delegation includes the governor and the state superintendent of public instruction.

GREAT LAKES COMMISSION

Wisconsin delegation: Patrick Stevens, *chair*
Executive director: Tim A. Eder

Contact: 734-971-9135; 2805 South Industrial Highway, Suite 100, Ann Arbor, MI 48104-6791
Website: www.glc.org

The Great Lakes Commission was established under the Great Lakes Basin Compact to promote the orderly, integrated, and comprehensive development, use, and conservation of the water and related natural resources of the Great Lakes basin and St. Lawrence River. Its members include the eight Great Lakes states of Illinois, Indiana, Michigan, Minnesota, New York, Ohio, Pennsylvania, and Wisconsin with associate member status for the Canadian provinces of Ontario and Québec. A three-member delegation, appointed by the governor, represents Wisconsin on the commission. The commission develops and recommends the adoption of policy positions by its members and offers advice on issues such as clean energy, climate change, habitat and coastal management, control of aquatic invasive species, water quality, and water resources.

GREAT LAKES PROTECTION FUND

Wisconsin representatives to the board of directors: Richard Meeusen, Kevin L. Shafer
Executive director: Russell Van Herik
Contact: 847-425-8150; 1560 Sherman Avenue, Suite 1370, Evanston, IL 60201
Website: www.glpf.org

The Great Lakes Protection Fund is a private nonprofit corporation, the members of which are the governors of Illinois, Michigan, Minnesota, New York, Ohio, Pennsylvania, and Wisconsin. The purpose of the corporation is to finance projects for the protection and cleanup of the Great Lakes. The corporation is managed by a board of directors composed of two representatives from each member state. The governor appoints the two representatives from this state.

GREAT LAKES–ST. LAWRENCE RIVER BASIN WATER RESOURCES COUNCIL

Wisconsin members: Scott Walker (governor); Cathy Stepp (secretary of natural resources), *governor's designated alternate*
Executive director: David Naftzger
Contact: cglg@cglg.org; 312-407-0177; 20 North Wacker Drive, Suite 2700, Chicago, IL 60606
Website: www.glslcompactcouncil.org

The Great Lakes-St. Lawrence River Basin Water Resources Council is charged with aiding, promoting, and coordinating the activities and programs of the Great Lakes states concerning water resources management in the Great Lakes-St. Lawrence River basin. The council may promulgate and enforce rules and regulations as may be necessary for the implementation and enforcement of the Great Lakes-St. Lawrence River Basin Water Resources Compact. The legally binding compact governs withdrawals, consumptive uses, conservation and efficient use, and diversions of basin water resources, and the council may initiate legal actions to compel compliance with the compact. In addition, the council must review and approve proposals from certain parties for the withdrawal, diversion, or consumptive use of water from the basin that is subject to the compact.

Under the compact, the governors from the states of Illinois, Indiana, Michigan, Minnesota, New York, Ohio, Pennsylvania, and Wisconsin jointly pursue intergovernmental cooperation and consultation to protect, conserve, restore, improve, and effectively manage the waters and water dependent natural resources of the basin. The governor serves as Wisconsin's representative on the council.

GREAT LAKES-ST. LAWRENCE RIVER WATER RESOURCES REGIONAL BODY

Wisconsin members: Scott Walker (governor); Cathy Stepp (secretary of natural resources), *governor's designated alternate*
Secretary: David Naftzger
Contact: cglg@cglg.org; 312-407-0177; 20 North Wacker Drive, Suite 2700, Chicago, IL 60606
Website: www.glslregionalbody.org

The Great Lakes-St. Lawrence River Water Resources Regional Body is an entity charged with aiding and promoting the coordination of the activities and programs of the Great Lakes states and provinces concerned with water resources management in the Great Lakes and St. Lawrence River basin. The regional body may develop procedures for implementation of the Great Lakes-St. Lawrence River Basin Sustainable Water Resources Agreement, which is a good-faith agreement between Great Lakes states and provinces that governs withdrawals, consumptive uses, conservation and efficient use, and diversions of basin water resources. The regional body must review and approve proposals from certain parties for the withdrawal, diversion, or consumptive use of water from the basin that is subject to the agreement.

The members of the regional body are the governors from the states of

Illinois, Indiana, Michigan, Minnesota, New York, Ohio, Pennsylvania, and Wisconsin, and the premiers of Ontario and Québec. The governor serves as Wisconsin's representative on the regional body. The members of the body jointly pursue intergovernmental cooperation and consultation to protect, conserve, restore, improve, and manage the waters and water dependent natural resources of the basin.

INTERSTATE COMMISSION FOR JUVENILES

Wisconsin member: Shelley Hagan (compact administrator, Office of Juvenile Offender Review, Division of Juvenile Corrections, Department of Corrections)
Contact: icjadmin@juvenilecompact.org; 859-721-1061; 836 Euclid Avenue, Suite 322, Lexington, KY 40502
Website: www.juvenilecompact.org

The Interstate Commission for Juveniles was established under the Interstate Compact for Juveniles. The compact is designed to coordinate the supervision of juveniles on probation and parole who move across state lines and assists states in returning youth who run away, escape, or abscond across state lines. The commission has the authority to promulgate rules that have the force of law and enforce compliance with the compact.

INTERSTATE INSURANCE PRODUCT REGULATION COMMISSION

Wisconsin member: Ted Nickel (commissioner of insurance)
Contact: 202-471-3962; 444 North Capitol Street NW, Hall of the States, Suite 700, Washington, DC 20001-1509
Website: www.insurancecompact.org

The Interstate Insurance Product Regulation Commission was established under the Interstate Insurance Product Regulation Compact. The compact's purposes are to promote and protect the interest of consumers of, and establish uniform standards for, annuity, life, disability income, and long-term care insurance products; establish a central clearinghouse for the review of those insurance products and related matters such as advertising; and improve the coordination of regulatory resources and expertise among the various insurance agencies of the member states.

INTERSTATE WILDLIFE VIOLATOR COMPACT BOARD OF ADMINISTRATORS

Wisconsin member: Jennifer McDonough (compact administrator, Department of Natural Resources)

Contact: Wisconsin Department of Natural Resources; 608-267-0859; PO Box 7921, Madison, WI 53707-7921

The Interstate Wildlife Violator Compact is intended to promote compliance with laws and rules relating to the management of wildlife resources in the member states. The compact establishes a process for handling a wildlife resources law violation by a nonresident in a member state as if the violator were a resident of that state. The compact also requires each member state to recognize the revocation or suspension of an individual's wildlife resources privileges in another member state. The compact board of administrators resolves all matters relating to the operation of the compact.

LOWER ST. CROIX MANAGEMENT COMMISSION

Wisconsin member: Dan Baumann (designated by secretary of natural resources)
Contact: Department of Natural Resources, West Central Region; 715-839-3722; 1300 West Clairemont Avenue, Eau Claire, WI 54701

The Lower St. Croix Management Commission was created to provide a forum for discussion of problems and programs associated with the Lower St. Croix National Scenic Riverway. It coordinates planning, development, protection, and management of the riverway among Wisconsin, Minnesota, and the U.S. government.

MIDWEST INTERSTATE LOW-LEVEL RADIOACTIVE WASTE COMMISSION

Wisconsin member: Stanley York
Contact: mwllrwc@midwestcompact.org; 608-267-4793; PO Box 2659, Madison, WI 53701-2659
Website: www.midwestcompact.org

The Midwest Interstate Low-Level Radioactive Waste Commission administers the Midwest Interstate Low-Level Radioactive Waste Compact. The compact is an agreement between the states of Indiana, Iowa, Minnesota, Missouri, Ohio, and Wisconsin that provides for the cooperative and safe disposal of commercial low-level radioactive waste.

MIDWEST INTERSTATE PASSENGER RAIL COMMISSION

Wisconsin members: Scott Walker (governor); Representative E. Brooks; Senator Miller; 1 vacancy (private sector representative appointed by governor)

Contact: 630-925-1922; 701 East 22nd Street, Suite 110, Lombard, IL 60148
Website: www.miprc.org

The Midwest Interstate Passenger Rail Commission brings together state leaders from the members of the Midwest Interstate Passenger Rail Compact to advocate for passenger rail improvements. The commission also works to educate government officials and the public with respect to the advantages of passenger rail. The current members of the compact are Illinois, Indiana, Kansas, Michigan, Minnesota, Missouri, Nebraska, North Dakota, and Wisconsin.

MIDWESTERN HIGHER EDUCATION COMMISSION

Wisconsin members: Representative Ballweg; Margaret Farrow; Senator Harsdorf; Donald G. Madelung; Rolf Wegenke; Morna K. Foy (alternate); Jessica Tormey (alternate)
Contact: 612-677-2777; 105 Fifth Avenue South, Suite 450, Minneapolis, Minnesota 55401
Website: www.mhec.org

The Midwestern Higher Education Commission was organized to further higher educational opportunities for residents of states participating in the Midwestern Higher Education Compact. The commission may enter into agreements with states, universities, and colleges to provide student programs and services. The commission also studies the compact's effects on higher education.

MILITARY INTERSTATE CHILDREN'S COMPACT COMMISSION

Wisconsin commissioner: Shelley Joan Weiss
State Council on the Interstate Compact on Educational Opportunity for Military Children: Tony Evers (state superintendent of public instruction); John Hendricks (Sparta school district superintendent); Lt. Col. John Blaha (Wisconsin National Guard); Ryan Nilsestuen (Department of Public Instruction); Gregg Curtis (Department of Public Instruction); Senator Testin; Shelley Joan Weiss (nonvoting member); Becky Walley (military school liaison, nonvoting member)
Contact: mic3info@csg.org; 859-244-8000; 1776 Avenue of The States, Lexington, KY 40511
Website: www.mic3.net

The Military Interstate Children's Compact Commission oversees implementation of the Interstate Compact on Educational Opportunity for Military Children. The compact is intended to facilitate the education of children of military families and remove barriers to educational success due to frequent moves and parent deployment.

The commission is composed of one commissioner from each of the compacting states. In each compacting state, a council or other body in state government administers the compact within that state. In Wisconsin, the compact is administered by the State Council on the Interstate Compact on Educational Opportunity for Military Children.

MISSISSIPPI RIVER PARKWAY COMMISSION

Wisconsin commission: Sherry Quamme, *chair*
Contact: mrpc@pilchbarnet.com; 866-763-8310; National Office, 701 East Washington Avenue, #202, Madison, WI 53703
Website: http://mrpcmembers.com

The Mississippi River Parkway Commission coordinates development and preservation of Wisconsin's portion of the Great River Road corridor along the Mississippi River. It assists and advises state and local agencies about maintaining and enhancing the scenic, historic, economic, and recreational assets within the corridor and cooperates with similar commissions in other Mississippi River states and the province of Ontario. The 16-member Wisconsin commission includes 12 voting members, including four legislative members who represent the two major political parties in each house, and four nonvoting ex officio members, the secretaries of tourism, natural resources, and transportation, and the director of the historical society. The commission selects its own chair who is Wisconsin's sole voting representative at national meetings of the Mississippi River Parkway Commission.

UPPER MISSISSIPPI RIVER BASIN ASSOCIATION

Wisconsin representative: Dan Baumann (appointed by governor)
Executive director: Dave Hokanson
Contact: 651-224-2880; 415 Hamm Building, 408 St. Peter Street, St. Paul, MN 55102
Website: www.umrba.org

The Upper Mississippi River Basin Association is a nonprofit regional organization created by Illinois, Iowa, Minnesota, Missouri, and Wisconsin to facilitate cooperative action regarding the basin's water and related land resources. The association consists of one voting member from each state and sponsors studies of river-related issues, cooperative planning for use of the region's resources, and an information exchange. The organization also enables the member states to develop regional positions on resource issues and to advocate for the basin states' collective interests before the U.S. Congress and federal agencies. The association is involved with programs related to commercial navigation, ecosystem restoration, water quality, aquatic nuisance species, hazardous spills, flood risk management, water supply, and other water resource issues. Six federal agencies with major water resources responsibilities serve as advisory members: the Environmental Protection Agency, the U.S. Army Corps of Engineers, and the U.S. departments of Agriculture, Homeland Security, the Interior, and Transportation.

Interstate compacts without interstate entities

INTERSTATE COMPACT ON ADOPTION AND MEDICAL ASSISTANCE

Requires each member state to cooperate with other states to ensure that children with special needs who were adopted in or from another member state receive medical and other benefits. The Department of Children and Families administers the compact in Wisconsin.

INTERSTATE COMPACT FOR ADULT OFFENDER SUPERVISION

Creates cooperative procedures for individuals placed on parole, probation, or extended supervision in one state to be supervised in another state if certain conditions are met. The Department of Corrections administers the compact in Wisconsin.

INTERSTATE CORRECTIONS COMPACT

Authorizes Wisconsin to contract with member states for the confinement of Wisconsin inmates in those states and to receive inmates from member states. The Department of Corrections administers the compact in Wisconsin.

INTERSTATE AGREEMENT ON DETAINERS

Allows a member state to obtain temporary custody of an individual incarcerated in another member state to conduct a trial on outstanding charges.

EMERGENCY MANAGEMENT ASSISTANCE COMPACT

Authorizes member states to provide mutual assistance to other states in an emergency or disaster declared by the governor of the affected state. Under the compact, member states cooperate in emergency-related training and formulate plans for interstate cooperation in responding to a disaster. The Division of Emergency Management in the Department of Military Affairs administers the compact in Wisconsin.

INTERSTATE MEDICAL LICENSURE COMPACT

Provides an expedited process for physicians to become licensed to practice medicine in multiple states. The Medical Examining Board administers the compact in Wisconsin.

INTERSTATE COMPACT ON MENTAL HEALTH

Facilitates treatment of patients with mental illness and mental disabilities by the cooperative action of the member states, to the benefit of the patients, their families, and society.

NURSE LICENSURE COMPACT

Authorizes a nurse licensed in a member state to practice nursing in any other member state without obtaining a license in that state. The Department of Safety and Professional Services administers the compact in Wisconsin.

INTERSTATE COMPACT ON THE PLACEMENT OF CHILDREN

Provides a uniform legal and administrative framework governing the interstate placement of abused, neglected, or dependent children, the interstate placement of children through independent or private adoption, and the interstate placement of any child into residential treatment facilities. The Department of Children and Families administers the compact in Wisconsin.

INTERSTATE AGREEMENT ON QUALIFICATION OF EDUCATIONAL PERSONNEL

Authorizes a state education official designated by each member state to contract with other member states to recognize the credentials of educators from those member states and facilitate the employment of qualified educational personnel.

Wisconsin Supreme Court

Justices: Patience Drake Roggensack, *chief justice*; Shirley S. Abrahamson, Ann Walsh Bradley, Annette K. Ziegler, Michael J. Gableman, Rebecca Grassl Bradley, Daniel Kelly
Clerk of the supreme court: Diane Fremgen
Supreme court commissioners: Nancy Kopp, Mark Neuser, Julie Rich, David Runke

Location: Room 16 East, State Capitol, Madison (supreme court); 110 East Main Street, Madison (clerk)
Contact: 608-266-1298 (supreme court); 608-266-1880 (clerk); 608-266-7442 (commissioners); PO Box 1688, Madison, WI 53701-1688
Website: https://wicourts.gov
Number of employees: 38.50
Total budget 2015–17: $10,579,300

The Wisconsin Supreme Court is the highest court in Wisconsin's court system. It is the final authority on matters pertaining to the Wisconsin Constitution and the highest tribunal for all actions begun in the state court system, except those involving federal constitutional issues appealable to the U.S. Supreme Court. In addition, it has supervisory and administrative authority over all courts in the state. In this capacity, it establishes procedural rules and codes of conduct for the courts and for the practice of law, and it regulates and disciplines attorneys, judges, and justices.

The supreme court consists of seven justices elected for ten-year terms. They are chosen in statewide elections on the nonpartisan April ballot and take office on the following August 1. The Wisconsin Constitution provides that only one justice can be elected in any single year. In the event of a vacancy, the governor may appoint a person to serve until an election can be held to fill the seat.

The justices elect one of themselves to be the chief justice for a term of two years. The chief justice serves as administrative head of the court system. Any four justices constitute a quorum for conducting court business.

The court decides which cases it will hear. Decisions of a lower court are not appealable to the supreme court as a matter of right.

The supreme court exercises its appellate jurisdiction to review a decision of a lower court if three or more justices approve a petition for review or if the court decides on its own motion to review a matter that has been appealed to the court of appeals. It exercises its original jurisdiction as the first court to hear a case if four or more justices approve a petition requesting it to do so.

The majority of cases advance from the circuit court to the court of appeals before reaching the supreme court, but the supreme court can bypass the court of appeals, either on its own motion or at the request of the parties; in addition, the court of appeals may certify a case to the supreme court, asking the high court to take the case directly from the circuit court.

The supreme court does not take testimony. Instead, it decides cases on the basis of written briefs and oral argument. It is required by statute to deliver its decisions in writing, and it may publish them as it deems appropriate.

Wisconsin Court of Appeals

Chief judge: Lisa S. Neubauer
Clerk of the court of appeals: Diane Fremgen

Location: 110 East Main Street, Suite 215, Madison (clerk)
Contact: 608-266-1880; PO Box 1688, Madison, WI 53701-1688
Website: https://wicourts.gov/courts/appeals/index.htm
Number of employees: 75.50
Total budget 2015–17: $21,384,200

DISTRICT I

Kitty K. Brennan, *presiding judge*; Joan F. Kessler, William W. Brash III, Timothy G. Dugan
Contact: 414-227-4680; 330 East Kilbourn Avenue, Suite 1020, Milwaukee, WI 53202-316

DISTRICT II

Paul F. Reilly, *presiding judge*; Lisa S. Neubauer, Mark D. Gundrum, Brian K. Hagedorn
Contact: 262-521-5230; 2727 North Grandview Boulevard, Suite 300, Waukesha, WI 53188-1672

DISTRICT III

Lisa K. Stark, *presiding judge*; Thomas M. Hruz, Mark A. Seidl
Contact: 715-848-1421; 2100 Stewart Avenue, Suite 310, Wausau, WI 54401-1700

DISTRICT IV

JoAnne F. Kloppenburg, *presiding judge*; Paul Lundsten, Gary E. Sherman, Brian W. Blanchard, Michael R. Fitzpatrick

Contact: 608-266-9250; 10 East Doty Street, Suite 700, Madison, WI 53703-3397

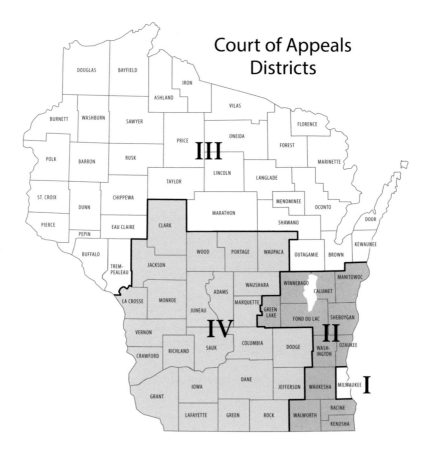

The Wisconsin Court of Appeals consists of 16 judges serving in four districts. The Wisconsin Supreme Court appoints one of these judges to be the chief judge and to serve as administrative head of the court of appeals for a three-year term. The clerk of the supreme court serves as the clerk for the court of appeals.

Court of appeals judges are elected for six-year terms in the nonpartisan April election and begin their terms of office on the following August 1. They must reside in the district from which they are elected. Only one court of

Wisconsin Supreme Court Chief Justice Patience Drake Roggensack discusses the Judiciary with newly elected legislators in the Supreme Court Hearing Room as Justice Rebecca Grassl Bradley looks on. The visit was part of a broader new legislator orientation program conducted by the Wisconsin Legislative Council on December 6, 2016.

appeals judge may be elected in a district in any one year. In the event of a vacancy, the governor may appoint a person to serve until an election can be held to fill the seat.

The court of appeals has both appellate and supervisory jurisdiction, as well as original jurisdiction to issue prerogative writs. The final judgments and orders of a circuit court may be appealed to the court of appeals as a matter of right. Other judgments or orders may be appealed upon leave of the appellate court.

The court usually sits as a three-judge panel to dispose of cases on their merits. However, a single judge may decide certain categories of cases, including juvenile cases; small claims; municipal ordinance and traffic violations; and mental health and misdemeanor cases. No testimony is taken in the appellate court. The court relies on the trial court record and written briefs in deciding a case, and it prescreens all cases to determine whether oral argument is needed. Both oral argument and "briefs only" cases are placed on a regularly issued calendar. The court gives criminal cases preference on the calendar when it is possible to do so without undue delay of civil cases.

Decisions of the appellate court are delivered in writing, and the court's publication committee determines which decisions will be published. With certain exceptions, only published opinions have precedential value and may be cited as controlling law in Wisconsin. Unpublished opinions that are authored by a judge and issued after July 1, 2009, may be cited for their persuasive value.

Circuit Court

Website: https://wicourts.gov/courts/circuit/index.htm
Number of state-funded employees: 527.00
Total budget 2015–17: $195,406,000

DISTRICT 1

Maxine White, *chief judge*; Holly Szablewski, *administrator*
Contact: 414-278-5113; Milwaukee County Courthouse, 901 North 9th Street, Room 609, Milwaukee, WI 53233-1425

DISTRICT 2

Jason Rossell, *chief judge*; Louis Moore, *administrator*
Contact: 262-636-3133; Racine County Courthouse, 730 Wisconsin Avenue, Racine, WI 53403-1274

DISTRICT 3

Jennifer Dorow, *chief judge*; Michael Neimon, *administrator*
Contact: 262-548-7209; Waukesha County Courthouse, 515 West Moreland Boulevard, Room 359, Waukesha, WI 53188-2428

DISTRICT 4

Barbara Hart Key, *chief judge*; Jon Bellows, *administrator*
Contact: 920-424-0028; 415 Jackson Street, Room 510, PO Box 2808, Oshkosh, WI 54903-2808

DISTRICT 5

James P. Daley, *chief judge*; Theresa Owens, *administrator*
Contact: 608-267-8820; Dane County Courthouse, 215 South Hamilton Street, Madison, WI 53703-3290

DISTRICT 6

Gregory Potter, *chief judge*; Ron Ledford, *administrator*
Contact: 715-345-5295; 3317 Business Park Drive, Suite A, Stevens Point, WI 54481-8834

DISTRICT 7

Robert VanDeHey, *chief judge*; Patrick Brummond, *administrator*
Contact: 608-785-9546; La Crosse County Law Enforcement Center, 333 Vine Street, Room 3504, La Crosse, WI 54601-3296

DISTRICT 8

James Morrison, *chief judge*; Thomas Schappa, *administrator*
Contact: 920-448-4281; 414 East Walnut Street, Suite 100, Green Bay, WI 54301-5020

DISTRICT 9

Gregory Huber, *chief judge*; Susan Byrnes, *administrator*
Contact: 715-842-3872; 2100 Stewart Avenue, Suite 310, Wausau, WI 54401

DISTRICT 10

Scott Needham, *chief judge*; Donald Harper, *administrator*
Contact: 715-245-4105; St. Croix Government Center, 1101 Carmichael Road, Suite 1260, Hudson, WI 54016-7708

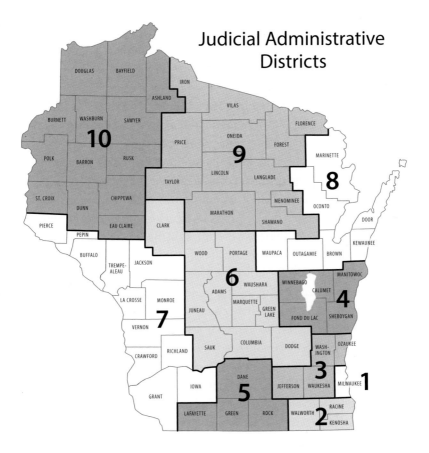

Judicial Administrative Districts

The circuit court is the trial court of general jurisdiction in Wisconsin. It has original jurisdiction in both civil and criminal matters unless exclusive jurisdiction is given to another court. It also reviews state agency decisions and hears appeals from municipal courts. Jury trials are conducted only in circuit courts.

The circuit court consists of numerous judges serving in 69 circuits. Each circuit consists of the territory of a single county, except for three two-county circuits (Buffalo-Pepin, Florence-Forest, and Menominee-Shawano). Because of the varying size of their caseloads, some circuits have a single judge, while others have multiple judges. Each judge in a circuit holds court separately—circuit judges do not sit as a panel to hear cases—and each judgeship is called a branch of the circuit. Forty circuits had multiple branches as of August 1, 2016, and there were a total of 249 circuit branches in the state.

Circuit judges are elected for six-year terms on a nonpartisan basis in the April election and take office the following August 1. The governor may fill circuit court vacancies by appointment, and the appointees serve until a successor is elected. The state pays the salaries of circuit judges and court reporters. It also covers some of the expenses for interpreters, guardians ad litem, judicial assistants, court-appointed witnesses, and jury per diems. Counties bear the remaining expenses for operating the circuit courts.

The circuit court is divided into ten administrative districts, each supervised by a chief judge appointed by the supreme court from the district's circuit judges. A judge usually cannot serve more than three successive two-year terms as chief judge. The chief judge has authority to assign judges, manage caseflow, supervise personnel, and conduct financial planning.

The chief judge in each district appoints a district court administrator from a list of candidates supplied by the director of state courts. The administrator manages the nonjudicial business of the district at the direction of the chief judge.

Circuit court commissioners are appointed by the circuit court to assist the court, and they must be attorneys licensed to practice law in Wisconsin. They may be authorized by the court to conduct various civil, criminal, family, small claims, juvenile, and probate court proceedings. Their duties include issuing summonses, arrest warrants, or search warrants; conducting initial appearances; setting bail; conducting preliminary examinations and arraignments; imposing monetary penalties in certain traffic cases; conducting certain family, juvenile, and small claims court proceedings; hearing petitions for mental commitments; and conducting uncontested probate proceedings. On their own authority, court commissioners may perform marriages, administer oaths, take depositions, and issue subpoenas and certain writs.

The statutes require the circuit court for Milwaukee County to have full-time family, small claims, and probate court commissioners. In all other counties, the circuit court is required to have a family court commissioner.

Municipal Court

Website: https://wicourts.gov/courts/municipal/index.htm

The legislature has authorized cities, villages, and towns to establish municipal courts to exercise jurisdiction over municipal ordinance violations that have monetary penalties. In addition, municipal courts have authority to rule on the constitutionality of municipal ordinances.

Municipal courts can have multiple branches (judges who hold court separately), and two or more municipalities can form a joint court. As of February 2017, there were 232 municipal courts with 235 municipal judges; and there were 70 joint courts, serving a total of 249 municipalities. The cities of Milwaukee and Madison have the state's only full-time municipal courts.

Upon convicting a defendant, the municipal court may order payment of a forfeiture plus costs and surcharges, or, if the defendant agrees, it may require community service in lieu of a forfeiture. In general, municipal courts may also order restitution up to $10,000. In traffic cases, a municipal court may

Supreme Court Justice Daniel Kelly addresses guests before administering the oath of office to newly elected Wisconsin state senators during a swearing-in ceremony held in the Senate Chambers on January 3, 2017.

TOM SHEEHAN, WISCONSIN SUPREME COURT

suspend or revoke a driver's license. Municipal courts have the authority to handle first offense Operating While Under the Influence cases.

If a defendant fails to pay a forfeiture or make restitution, the municipal court may suspend the driver's license or commit the defendant to jail. Municipal court decisions may be appealed to the circuit court for the county where the offense occurred.

Municipal judges are elected at the nonpartisan April election and take office on May 1. The term of office is four years, unless the municipality has adopted a charter ordinance designating a two-year term. The governing body determines the judge's salary. There is no state requirement that the office be filled by an attorney, but a municipality may enact such a qualification by ordinance. If a municipal judge is ill, disqualified, or unavailable, the chief judge of the circuit court administrative district containing the municipality may transfer the case to another municipal judge.

Auxiliary entities

Office of the Director of State Courts

Director of state courts: Randy Koschnick
Deputy director for court operations: Sara Ward-Cassady
Deputy director for management services: Brian Lamprech

Location: Room 16 East, State Capitol, Madison (director); 110 East Main Street, Madison (staff)
Contact: 608-266-6828 (director); PO Box 1688, Madison, WI 53701-1688 (director); 110 East Main Street, Madison, WI 53703 (staff)
Website: https://wicourts.gov
Number of employees: 147.75
Total budget 2015–17: $40,766,600

The director of state courts is appointed by the supreme court and is the chief nonjudicial officer of the Wisconsin court system. The director is responsible for the management of the court system and advises the supreme court, particularly on matters relating to improvements to the court system. The director supervises most state-level court personnel; develops the court system's budget; and directs the courts' work on legislation, public information, and information systems. This office also controls expenditures; allocates space and equipment; supervises judicial education, interdistrict assignment of active and reserve judges, and planning and research; and administers the medical malpractice mediation system.

State Bar of Wisconsin

Board of Governors, officer members: Francis W. Deisinger, *president*; Paul G. Swanson, *president-elect*; Ralph M. Cagle, *past president*; Mary Lynne Donohue, *secretary*; John E. Danner, *treasurer*; Amy E. Wochos, *chair of the board*

Board of Governors, district elected members: Eric L. Andrews, Karen M. Bauer, Howard J. Bichler, John A. Birsdall, Daniel J. Blinka, Truscenialyn Brooks, Bruce J. Brovold, Douglas S. Buck, Andrew J. Chevrez, Milton L. Childs, Kathleen Chung, Michael J. Cohen, Byron B. Conway, Daniel P. Fay, Martin P. Gagne, Adam Y. Gerol, Jeff Goldman, Anthony J. Gray, Kimberly K. Haines, Steven C. Harvey, Gregg M. Herman, Christopher B. Hughes, Jill M. Kastner, Timothy T. Kay, Deanne M. Koll, Peggy A. Lautenschlager, Amanda J. Ley, Kelly J. Mattingly, Kelly Mould, Randall L. Nash, John R. Orton, Christopher E. Rogers, Charles "Chuck" Stertz, Jeffrey R. Wisnicky, Nicholas C. Zales

Board of Governors, other members: Ryan A. Blay (young lawyers division); Robert G. Barrington (government lawyers division); James J. Casey, Jr., Debra E. Kuper, H. Charles Stahmer, Viet-Hanh Nguyen Winchell, David M. Werwie (nonresident lawyers division); Mark G. Petri (senior lawyers division); James Marshall, Christine Procknow, James Wenzler (nonlawyer members); Makda Fessahaye, Benjamin E. Reyes, Starlyn R. Tourtillott, Amesia Xiong (nonvoting minority bar liaisons)

Executive director: Larry J. Martin

Location: 5302 Eastpark Boulevard, Madison
Contact: service@wisbar.org; 608-257-3838 (general); 800-362-9082 (lawyer referral and information service); PO Box 7158, Madison, WI 53707-7158
Website: www.wisbar.org

The State Bar of Wisconsin is a mandatory professional association of all attorneys who hold a Wisconsin law license. The State Bar works to raise professional standards, improve the administration of justice and the delivery of legal services, and provide continuing legal education to lawyers. The State Bar conducts legal research in substantive law, practice, and procedure and develops related reports and recommendations. It also maintains the roll of attorneys, collects mandatory assessments imposed by the supreme court for supreme court boards and to fund civil legal services for the poor, and performs other administrative services for the judicial system.

Attorneys may be admitted to the State Bar by the full Wisconsin Supreme

Court or by a single justice. The governance and structure of the State Bar are established by the supreme court.

State Law Library

State law librarian: Julie Tessmer
Deputy law librarian: Amy Crowder

Location: 120 Martin Luther King, Jr. Blvd., 2nd Floor, Madison
Contact: wsll.ref@wicourts.gov (reference); 800-322-9755 (toll free); 608-266-1600 (circulation); 608-267-9696 (reference); PO Box 7881, Madison, WI 53707-7881
Website: http://wilawlibrary.gov

The State Law Library is a public library open to all citizens of Wisconsin. The library supports the information needs of the justices, judges, and staff of the Wisconsin court system. The library is administered by the supreme court, which appoints the state law librarian and determines the rules governing library access. The library acts as a consultant and resource for circuit court libraries throughout the state. Milwaukee County and Dane County contract with the State Law Library for management and operation of their courthouse libraries (the Milwaukee County Law Library and the Dane County Law Library).

The library's collection features session laws, statutory codes, case reporters, administrative rules, and legal indexes of the U.S. government, all 50 states, and U.S. territories. It also includes legal and bar periodicals and legal treatises and encyclopedias relevant to all major areas of law. As a federal depository library, it selects federal documents to complement the legal collection. The collection circulates to judges and court staff, attorneys, legislators, and government personnel. The library offers reference, legal research guidance, and document delivery services, as well as training in the use of legal research tools, databases, and websites.

Lawyer Regulation System

Office of Lawyer Regulation: Keith L. Sellen, *director*
Preliminary Review Committee: Frank Lo Coco, *chair*
Special Preliminary Review Panel: Robert A. Mathers, *chair*
Board of Administrative Oversight: Charles Dykman, *chair*

Contact: 608-267-7274; 877-315-6941 (toll free); 110 East Main Street, Suite 315, Madison, WI 53703-3383

Doug Middleton, a state Department of Corrections employee, installs a new sign at the Wisconsin State Law Library in Madison. The facility, located within the Risser Justice Center, was named in honor of former legislator and retired Wisconsin Supreme Court Justice David T. Prosser Jr. on October 19, 2016.

Number of employees: 27.50
Total budget 2015–17: $6,093,500

The Lawyer Regulation System assists the supreme court in supervising the practice of law and protecting the public from professional misconduct by persons practicing law in Wisconsin. The system includes several entities.

The Office of Lawyer Regulation receives and evaluates all complaints, inquiries, and grievances related to attorney misconduct or medical incapacity. The office is headed by a director who is appointed by the supreme court. The office must investigate any grievance that appears to support an allegation of possible attorney misconduct or incapacity, and the attorney in question must cooperate with the investigation. After investigation, the director decides whether the matter should be forwarded to the Preliminary Review Committee, be dismissed, or be diverted for alternative action. The director may also obtain the attorney's consent to a private or public reprimand.

If the director does forward a matter to the Preliminary Review Committee and a panel of that committee determines there is cause to proceed, the director may seek disciplinary action, ranging from private reprimand to filing a formal complaint with the supreme court that requests public reprimand, license suspension or revocation, monetary payment, or imposing conditions on the continued practice of law. An attorney may be offered alternatives to formal disciplinary action, including mediation, fee arbitration, law office management assistance, evaluation and treatment for alcohol and other substance abuse, psychological evaluation and treatment, monitoring of the attorney's practice or trust account procedures, continuing legal education, ethics school, or the multistate professional responsibility examination.

Formal disciplinary actions for attorney misconduct are filed by the director with the supreme court, which appoints an attorney or reserve judge to be the referee for each such action. Referees conduct hearings on complaints of attorney misconduct, petitions alleging attorney medical incapacity, and petitions for reinstatement. They make findings, conclusions, and recommendations and submit them to the supreme court for review and appropriate action. Only the supreme court has the authority to suspend or revoke a lawyer's license to practice law in Wisconsin.

If the director receives an allegation of misconduct or incapacity pertaining to an attorney who works in or is retained to assist the Lawyer Regulation System, the director must refer the matter to a special investigator of the Special Investigative Panel. This panel is composed of attorneys who are appointed by the supreme court and who are not currently working in or retained by the Lawyer Regulation System. The special investigator commences an investigation if there is enough information to support the allegation, but otherwise may close the matter. After an investigation, the special investigator can dismiss the matter or submit an investigative report to the Special Preliminary Review Panel. If this panel determines, after receiving an investigative report from a special investigator, that there is cause to proceed, the special investigator can proceed to file a complaint with the supreme court and prosecute the matter personally or may assign that responsibility to counsel retained by the director for such purposes.

The Board of Administrative Oversight monitors and assesses the performance of the Lawyer Regulation System and reports its findings to the supreme court. The board reviews with the supreme court the operation of the Lawyer Regulation System, proposes for consideration by the supreme court substantive and procedural rules related to the regulation of lawyers, and proposes to the supreme court the annual budget for the Office of Lawyer Regulation, after consulting with the director of that office.

Board of Bar Examiners

Chair: Steven M. Barkan
Director: Jacquelynn B. Rothstein

Contact: bbe@wicourts.gov; 110 East Main Street, Suite 715, PO Box 2748, Madison, WI 53701-2748
Website: https://wicourts.gov/courts/offices/bbe.htm
Number of employees: 8.00
Total budget 2015–17: $1,536,000

The Board of Bar Examiners administers all bar admissions; it writes and grades the bar examination, reviews motions for admission on proof of practice, and conducts character and fitness investigations of all candidates for admission to the bar, including diploma privilege graduates. The board also administers the Wisconsin mandatory continuing legal education requirement for attorneys.

Judicial Commission

Members: Mark Barrette, Eileen Burnett, William E. Cullinan, Frank J. Daily, Brian K. Hagedorn, Kendall M. Kelley, Steve C. Miller, Joseph L. Olson, Robert H. Papke
Executive director: Jeremiah C. Van Hecke

Contact: judcmm@wicourts.gov; 608-266-7637; 110 East Main Street, Suite 700, Madison, WI 53703-3328
Website: https://wicourts.gov/judcom
Number of employees: 2.00
Total budget 2015–17: $603,200

The Judicial Commission conducts investigations regarding allegations of misconduct by or permanent disability of a justice, judge, or court commissioner.

The commission's investigations are confidential. If the commission finds probable cause that a justice, judge, or court commissioner has engaged in misconduct or has a disability that substantially impairs his or her judicial performance, the commission must file a formal complaint of misconduct or a petition regarding disability with the supreme court.

The commission then prosecutes a proceeding against the judge before a three-judge panel or, if the commission so requested when it filed the complaint or petition, before a jury. The panel of judges, or a single judge to preside over a jury proceeding, is selected by the chief judge of the court of appeals. When the proceeding has concluded, the supreme court reviews the findings of fact, conclusions of law, and recommended disposition and determines the appropriate discipline in cases of misconduct or appropriate action in cases of permanent disability.

Judicial Conduct Advisory Committee

Members: D. Todd Ehlers, James Daley, Joan Kessler, William Domina, Daniel P. Koval, Victor Manion, Anton Jamieson, Dan Conley, Randy Morrissette II

Contact: 608-266-6828; PO Box 1688, Madison, WI 53701-1688
Website: https://wicourts.gov/courts/committees/judicialconduct.htm

The Judicial Conduct Advisory Committee gives formal advisory opinions and informal advice regarding whether actions judges are contemplating comply with the Code of Judicial Conduct. It also makes recommendations to the supreme court about amending of the Code of Judicial Conduct or the rules governing the committee.

Judicial Conference

Website: https://wicourts.gov/courts/committees/judicialconf.htm

The Judicial Conference is composed of all supreme court justices, court of appeals judges, circuit court judges, and reserve judges; three municipal court judges designated by the Wisconsin Municipal Judges Association; three judicial representatives of tribal courts designated by the Wisconsin Tribal Judges Association; one circuit court commissioner designated by the Family Court Commissioner Association; and one circuit court commissioner designated by the Judicial Court Commissioner Association.

The Judicial Conference meets at least once a year to recommend improvements in administration of the justice system, conduct educational programs for its members, adopt the revised uniform traffic deposit and misdemeanor bail schedules, and adopt forms necessary for the administration of certain court proceedings.

The Judicial Conference may create study committees to examine particular topics. These study committees must report their findings and recommendations to the next annual meeting of the Judicial Conference. Study committees usually work for one year, unless extended by the Judicial Conference.

Judicial Council

Members: Annette Kingsland Ziegler (justice designated by supreme court); Brian W. Blanchard (judge designated by court of appeals); Randy Koschnick (director of state courts); Michael R. Fitzpatrick, Eugene A. Gasiorkiewicz, Robert P. Van De Hey, Jeffrey A. Wagner (circuit court judges designated by Judicial Conference); Senator Wanggaard (chairperson, senate judicial committee); Representative J. Ott (chairperson, assembly judicial committee); R. Duane Harlow (designated by attorney general); Sarah Walkenhorst Barber (designated by Legislative Reference Bureau chief); Steven Wright (faculty member designated by UW Law School dean); Thomas L. Shriner, Jr. (faculty member designated by Marquette University Law School dean); Devon M. Lee (designated by state public defender); Chuck M. Stertz (State Bar member, designated by president-elect); Thomas W. Bertz, William Gleisner, Sherry D. Coley (State Bar members selected by State Bar); Christian Gossett (district attorney appointed by governor); Dennis Myers, Benjamin J. Pliskie (public members appointed by governor)

Contact: 608-261-8290; 110 East Main Street, Suite 822, Madison, WI 53703
Number of employees: 1.00
Total budget 2015–17: $222,500

The Judicial Council is authorized to advise the supreme court, the governor, and the legislature on any matter affecting the administration of justice in Wisconsin, and it may recommend changes in the jurisdiction, organization, operation, or business methods of the courts that would result in a more effective and cost-efficient court system. The council studies the rules of pleading, practice, and procedure and advises the supreme court about changes that will simplify procedure and promote efficiency.

Judicial Education Committee

Members: Annette Ziegler (designated by supreme court chief justice); Thomas R. Hruz (designated by appeals court chief judge); Randy Koschnick (director of state courts); Steven G. Bauer, Ellen K. Berz, Ellen R. Brostrom, Jennifer R. Dorrow, Thomas J. Gritton, Mark J. McGinnis, Jason A. Rossell, Robert R. Russell (circuit court judges appointed by supreme court); John C. Moore, Alice A. Rudebusch (circuit court commissioners appointed by supreme court); Jini M. Jasti (designated by UW Law School dean); Thomas Hammer (designated by Marquette University Law School dean), Lisa K. Stark (dean, Wisconsin Judicial College)

Contact: JED@wicourts.gov; 608-266-7807; Office of Judicial Education, 110 East Main Street, Room 200, Madison, WI 53703
Website: https://wicourts.gov/courts/committees/judicialed.htm

The Judicial Education Committee approves educational programs for the purpose of continuing education requirements mandated for the judiciary by the supreme court. All supreme court justices and commissioners, appeals court judges and staff attorneys, and circuit court judges and commissioners must earn 60 credit hours of continuing education every six years in approved educational programs. Different credit-hour requirements apply to reserve judges and municipal court judges. The committee monitors compliance with the continuing education requirements and refers instances of noncompliance to the supreme court. The committee is assisted in its work by the Office of Judicial Education in the Office of the Director of State Courts, which also plans and conducts educational seminars for judges and tracks credits earned by judges.

Planning and Policy Advisory Committee

Chair: Patience Drake Roggensack (chief justice of the supreme court)

Contact: 608-266-3121; 110 East Main Street, Room 410, Madison, WI 53703
Website: https://wicourts.gov/courts/committees/ppac.htm

The Planning and Policy Advisory Committee advises the Wisconsin Supreme Court and the director of state courts on planning and policy and assists in a continuing evaluation of the administrative structure of the court system. It participates in the budget process of the Wisconsin judiciary and appoints a subcommittee to confer with the supreme court and the director of state courts in the court's review of the budget. The committee meets at least quarterly, and the supreme court meets with the committee annually. The director of state courts participates in committee deliberations, with full floor and advocacy privileges, but is not a member of the committee and does not have a vote.

3

ABOUT WISCONSIN

KNOCKING
on the DOOR

Women in the Wisconsin Legislature

The Wisconsin Legislature represents all of the people of Wisconsin. Legislators hail from all walks of life and socioeconomic backgrounds and come to the legislature with different life experiences and political outlooks. Members of the legislature represent small towns and villages, major urban centers, university and college towns, thriving suburban communities, and sparsely populated rural areas. They work in business, agriculture, law, education, health care, and many other trades and professions. In their personal and family lives, they resemble other Wisconsin citizens: legislators are husbands and wives, brothers and sisters, and parents and children. The strength and vitality of the Wisconsin Legislature comes from the commonalities between its members and the diverse body of people they represent.

This article introduces the women who serve in the Wisconsin Legislature and discusses their experiences. The article is about representation, about standing for the people of Wisconsin, as seen from the perspectives of women legislators. An article on women legislators is timely and important. In recent years, women have assumed major leadership roles in the legislature. Women are now a vital part of the leadership team in each political party in each house. During the 2015 legislative session, women served as senate president, assistant senate majority leader, senate minority leader, and assistant assembly minority leader; women also served as co-chairs of the Joint Committee on Finance, the Joint Audit Committee, and the Joint Committee for Review of Administrative Rules. These are power positions in Wisconsin government. During the 2015 legislative session, there were 11 senators and 23 representatives who

We would like to thank all of the following women who served in the Wisconsin Legislature for sharing their insights and experiences in public life:

SENATORS IN THE 2015 SESSION

Janet Bewley (D-25)

Alberta Darling (R-8)

Nikiya Harris Dodd (D-6)

Sheila Harsdorf (R-10)

Julie Lassa (D-24)

Mary Lazich (R-28)

Janis Ringhand (D-15)

Jennifer Shilling (D-32)

Lena Taylor (D-4)

Kathleen Vinehout (D-31)

Leah Vukmir (R-5)

REPRESENTATIVES IN THE 2015 SESSION

Joan Ballweg (R-41)

Terese Berceau (D-77)

Kathy Bernier (R-68)

Jill Billings (D-95)

Janel Brandtjen (R-22)

Cindi Duchow (R-99)

Mary Felzkowski (R-35)

Dianne Hesselbein (D-79)

LaTonya Johnson (D-17)

Samantha Kerkman (R-61)

Debra Kolste (D-44)

Amy Loudenbeck (R-31)

Beth Meyers (D-74)

Sondy Pope (D-80)

Jessie Rodriguez (R-21)

Melissa Sargent (D-48)

Katrina Shankland (D-71)

Christine Sinicki (D-20)

Amanda Stuck (D-57)

Lisa Subeck (D-78)

Chris Taylor (D-76)

Nancy VanderMeer (R-70)

JoCasta Zamarripa (D-8)

FORMER MEMBERS OF THE LEGISLATURE

Alice Clausing (senator 1993 through 1999 sessions, D)

Barbara Lorman (senator 1979 through 1993 sessions, R)

Mary Panzer (senate majority leader 2003 to 2004, senator 1993 through 2003 sessions, representative 1979 through 1993 sessions, R)

Judith Biros Robson (senate majority leader 2007, senator 1999 through 2009 sessions, representative 1987 through 1997 sessions, D)

Carol Roessler (senator 1987 through 2007 sessions, representative 1983 through 1987 sessions, R)

Peggy Rosenzweig (senator 1993 through 2001 sessions, representative 1983 through 1993 sessions, R)

Patricia Strachota (assembly majority leader 2014, representative 2005 through 2013 sessions, R)

Barbara Ulichny (senator 1985 through 1991 sessions, representative 1979 through 1983 sessions, D)

Mary Williams (representative 2003 through 2013 sessions, R)

(BOTH PHOTOS) JAY SALVO, LEGISLATIVE PHOTOGRAPHER

The 2015 legislative session included 11 women senators and 23 women representatives. *(top)* Senators Leah Vukmir and Alberta Darling *(seated)* confer on the floor. *(above)* Members of the assembly JoCasta Zamarripa, Terese Berceau, and Melissa Sargent *(left to right)* attend a press conference.

were women. This is down from a peak of 37 women legislators in the 1989 and 2003 legislative sessions. But numbers, although an easy way to gauge women's progress, provide only a partial picture.

Every senator and representative has a story, a narrative about his or her origins, childhood, and family. This article captures some of these stories. A theme that will run throughout the narratives is the importance of parents,

Alice Clausing

MORE TO ACCOMPLISH

For former Senator Alice Clausing, her political drive came from the desire to protect and restore the environment, after moving to Menomonie, Wisconsin, and seeing the poor state of Lake Menomin. She recalls her inauguration:

"When I was elected [in 1992], I was working on that 'Clean the Green' bill. And it was ten days after I was elected [that] the rule took the effect of law. So I got there, and I accomplished, really, my main purpose for going there. And then, when I got there, I'm standing up there taking my oath of office, and they said that I was the tenth woman since 1848 to become a Wisconsin State Senator. And at first, I thought, 'Holy baby, I really accomplished something.' And then I thought, 'You know, there's so much more to accomplish.'"

siblings, friends, and local communities on the career choices of women legislators.

Every person who enters the political arena must first make the heady decision to seek political office. This article documents the different routes that women took before they made the decision to run for the legislature. Many were leaders in their chosen professions or trades, many were active in volunteer and community organizations, and many were accomplished leaders in college or the workplace. Some women decided on their own to seek political office, while others were actively recruited.

Life on the campaign trail is a challenge, with long hours and many demands on a candidate's family. Campaign organizations must be assembled, and candidates must canvass the entire district, knock on constituents' doors, fundraise, and appear in public as often as possible. In addition, public policy positions must be staked out and carefully articulated. These are time-consuming but necessary tasks. This article looks at the campaign experiences of women legislators to see what role, if any, gender played in the campaigns. Among the many questions this article addresses are: Did the media treat women candidates differently or have different expectations for women candidates? How was the candidacy of a woman for legislative office viewed in her community? What lessons were learned on the campaign trail?

There are many possible career routes in the legislature. Some members become experts in a certain public policy area, while others pursue membership on key legislative committees that directly serve their districts' immediate interests. Some play an active role in their political party caucus and pursue a leadership position early in their careers, while others bide their time before seeking a leadership position. Some legislators become active and prominent drafters of legislation, even across many different subject matters, while other legislators play less visible roles in building consensus and forging compromise around legislation drafted by others. None of these paths is exclusive and the usual legislative career path is an amalgam of different roles. This article charts the routes that women legislators took once in office and identifies what obstacles, if any, they confronted in their legislative careers. Many issues will be discussed, such as: Did women legislators have mentors to guide them? Were women encouraged to pursue one path over another? How did partisanship affect their legislative choices?

An important feature of this article is that the legislative careers of women are examined and discussed during different periods. The article therefore focuses not just on women legislators in the 2015 legislature, but also on women who previously served in the legislature. The political atmosphere in the 1990s or early 2000s, after all, may have been very different from that of today and could have contributed to different experiences. For example, partisanship may matter more now than it once did, though this is by no means certain.

Former Senator Peggy Rosenzweig hit the campaign trail frequently during her time in office, which spanned from the early 1980s to the 2000s. Although technology has changed many things related to political campaigns, personal appearances and interactions remain a vital element.

If partisanship matters more, it may be that gender matters less, as voters increasingly base their voting decisions on political party allegiance and less on the gender or ethnicity of the person seeking office. This article looks at these issues and concludes with the reflections of these women as they look back at their legislative experiences, assess their legislative successes, and offer advice to a new generation of women who may wish to pursue political careers in the Wisconsin Legislature.

The title of this article, "Knocking on the Door," is taken from a core experience that every candidate faces on the campaign trail: knocking on the doors of constituents and presenting oneself to the voters. It is a rite of passage for every candidate and demands the most from them, as voters relate their concerns, worries, and problems to candidates. Representative Jessie Rodriguez captured this concisely when she said "the first door you knock on is the hardest." This idea of knocking on the door applied well, we thought, to the experience of women during the last century as they knocked on the doors of the capitol in their quest to gain admittance to the ranks of Wisconsin legislators. More than 5,500 people have served in the Wisconsin Legislature, but only 133 of those have been women. The first women—Mildred Barber, Hellen Brooks, and Helen Thompson—took office as representatives to the assembly in 1925 and the first woman—Kathryn Morrison—was elected to the senate for the 1975 legislative session. Women have been knocking on the door for almost 100 years and, as this article documents, they have gained admittance.

Backgrounds of women legislators

The women of the 2015 legislature hold an extensive breadth of life experience and bring this experience to bear when representing their communities. Their backgrounds vary by geography, age, religious affiliation, race, ethnicity, political experience, education, and employment. The ages of the 34 women who were part of the 2015 legislature ranged from 29 years to 72 years, with the median age being 53.5 years. Of the 23 women in the assembly, five were freshman legislators elected in 2014. (One woman was elected in a special election in 2015.) Of the 11 women in the 2015 senate, two were newly elected in 2014. (Senators in even and odd districts are elected in alternating elections.) In the senate, two women identified themselves as African American. In the assembly, one woman identified herself as African American and two women identified themselves as Latina or Hispanic. Fourteen women identified themselves in the 2015–2016 *Blue Book* as full-time legislators, and seven identified themselves as business owners or participating in small business. The women

WHI IMAGE ID 50361

WHI IMAGE ID 131057

WHI IMAGE ID 65405

Of the more than 5,500 people who have served in the Wisconsin Legislature, only 133 have been women. *(top left)* The 1865 Assembly typifies the legislative profile until 1925, when Mildred Barber, Helen Thompson, and Hellen Brooks *(above, left to right)* were the first women elected to serve in the assembly. It wasn't until 1975 that a woman, Kathryn Morrison *(top right)*, was elected to the senate.

of the 2015 legislature have backgrounds as insurance agents, farmers, teachers, and community leaders, as well as a host of other career experiences. Some are from large families; some are only children. Some stayed close to their roots; others made their way to Wisconsin from other states. Some legislators grew up with an interest in politics; others found their way to politics later in life.

Several women legislators represent their hometown. Senate Assistant Majority Leader Leah Vukmir is from Brookfield originally; after she raised her family in Wauwatosa, she then returned to live in Brookfield. Representative

TRADITIONAL GENDER ROLES

Terese Berceau

For women growing up in the 1950s and 1960s, traditional gender roles sometimes had a large impact on how they were raised. Representative Terese Berceau, who grew up in Green Bay, watched her mother break the constraints of those traditional roles:

"My dad worked a lot. I would call him low white collar. He worked for a pickle factory in Green Bay—[the] Green Bay Pickle Company. We always had pickles in the house, and we didn't necessarily want to eat them. But my mother did not go to work until my last sister entered grade school. She found a job—I think her first job was filing for an insurance company or a doctor's office. Apparently, either she didn't discuss it with my dad or my dad did not take her seriously, because he was very upset. [He came] from a very traditional point of view that he was supposed to be the breadwinner, and he was so upset that when she got her first check, she decided that she would go out and buy him a new television, because that was one of the things he did with his free time. So she went out and bought a television, and he would not watch it; he would not use it. So he had a real hard time with that. I don't know if he ever got over that. And then she topped it off [the time] I called her and she said, in a whisper, 'I bought a house.' And I said, 'Why are you whispering?' 'I didn't tell your dad.' Anyway, she saw a house that she liked. It was a modest home, but it was something that she liked, in a better neighborhood, etc. And she didn't tell my dad. I asked her why, and she said, 'Because he has a toothache and he's in a bad mood.' He, I am told, cried when she told him because it was such an assault on his view of what the man is in charge of."

Amanda Stuck was raised in Appleton and now represents that area in the assembly. Representative Melissa Sargent grew up in Madison and now raises her family in the city while she serves in the assembly. Representative Dianne Hesselbein, who became Assembly Assistant Minority Leader in 2017, is from Madison; though she lived for a time in Texas during her childhood, she now represents a large area of Dane County outside of Madison. Senator Lena Taylor was born and raised in Milwaukee and currently lives on the block on which she grew up. Representative JoCasta Zamarripa grew up in Milwaukee but spoke

Representative JoCasta Zamarripa, who was born and raised in Milwaukee, grew up inspired by women like her grandmother, a migrant farmer who brought her family to Wisconsin, and her aunt, who was politically and socially active in her community.

proudly of her large family network and the unique path her family followed, coming to Wisconsin with roots in Texas and Mexico: "I always credit my grandmother, she was a migrant farmer . . . and she would come up and work in the farm fields picking vegetables. So that's how she discovered Wisconsin, and she decided—she felt like there were a lot of job opportunities here. She felt that there were a lot better economic opportunities for herself and her family."

Other legislators were transplants to their districts. Representative Rodriguez, who represents South Milwaukee, was born in El Salvador and grew up in Salem, Massachusetts. Some, like former Senator Barbara Lorman, are first-generation Americans. Senator Alberta Darling spent her childhood in a Lithuanian community in Cicero, Illinois; she was the only child who spoke English in her grade at school. Former Senator Peggy Rosenzweig lived all over the United States before settling in Wisconsin. She was born in Detroit, then moved with her father during World War II to military posts in Texas and Tennessee. She attended the Julliard School in New York for dance, and after she married, she lived with her husband in Denver, Colorado. After her husband's medical residency, they moved back to the Midwest and settled in Milwaukee. Senator LaTonya Johnson grew up in Tennessee and came to Wisconsin when she was 12 years old. She described her rural Tennessee childhood before arriving in Milwaukee:

> I originally grew up in a small town called LaGrange, Tennessee. It's really, really tiny. I think it has a population of 150 people. And I was raised by my grandmother. My mom gave birth to me when she was 15, so by the time I was probably old enough to remember, my mom had already moved away. And so I grew up in this little three-room shack. And it was a shack—we had no indoor plumbing, so we walked to the well to collect all of our water to bring in to the house. I didn't live in a house with indoor plumbing until I moved to Milwaukee.

JAY SALVO, LEGISLATIVE PHOTOGRAPHER

Senator LaTonya Johnson, who now represents Milwaukee, grew up in a "little three-room shack" in a tiny town in Tennessee, arriving in Wisconsin when she was 12 years old. Later, running a day care for low-income children sparked her interest in running for statewide office.

Most of the legislators grew up in the working class or came, as former Senate President Mary Lazich recounted, from "small humble beginnings." Some said that their families accepted government assistance. Senator Kathleen Vinehout, whose parents met while serving in the military, noted that at times her family received food stamps. Representative Beth Meyers, who was born and raised in northern Wisconsin, worked seasonal jobs on Madeline Island

and said that at the end of the season, people in the area often had to go on unemployment or welfare in order to meet their needs.

The women legislators also had a variety of educational backgrounds. In the 2015 legislature, 19 women had earned bachelor's degrees, 8 had earned master's degrees, 2 had earned law degrees, and one had earned a Ph.D. Several women, including Representatives Jill Billings and Joan Ballweg, were the first in their families to attend college. Senator Janet Bewley, who became Senate Assistant Minority Leader in 2017, was the first person in her family to go to college, and she then went on to graduate school. She was born in Cleveland, Ohio, and lived at home while attending college, then moved to Ashland for

Kathleen Vinehout

A DIFFERENT PATH TO COLLEGE

Senator Kathleen Vinehout recalled:

"There were years when my father only made four thousand dollars a year; of course, this was back in the sixties, but still, four thousand dollars a year. I was the oldest of five children. It wasn't easy at all. So I kind of learned how to get by. I got my first job when I was 14: I became a nurse's assistant, making $2.30 an hour, helping to take care of old people in a nursing home. I very much wanted to go to college, but my parents—especially my dad—didn't want me to. My father felt that a college education was wasted on a woman, that her only role was to get married and have children. When it came time for me to actually apply to go to college, he wouldn't sign my financial aid papers. Of course my family is very poor, so that was a huge blow to me, because I knew I could get in. I really, really, really wanted to go to college.

I became an independent student. I left home the day I turned 18, I continued to work as a nurse's aide, and [I] went to local community college—technical college. I went there for two years. At the time, to be an independent student you had to be away from your parents' home for [a certain] period of time. After that period of time was over, I was able to apply on my own, on my own income. I was accepted at the college that was [the] farthest away from my family home that was still a public university: Southern Illinois University. I went there and became an education major, but I was very, very, very motivated to further my education."

her first job in 1977 and made her home there, becoming the dean of students at Northland College.

Many of the women completed their education later in life. Former Senator Rosenzweig, for example, finished her degree at UW-Milwaukee after having five sons. Representative Kathy Bernier had no plans for higher education when she went through high school in Chippewa Falls: "We were low income, so little did I know—and no one talked to me in high school about it either because I

Representative Joan Ballweg (*left*) was one of the first people in her family to go to college. She is shown here at her high school graduation in 1970, accompanied by her proud aunt, Lis.

was sort of an average student—about higher education. I know that's changed now. So, higher education wasn't an option that I was aware of." However, at age 37, she decided to go to college and earned her bachelor's degree.

Wisconsin has more than 14 million acres of farmland, and many women legislators were raised in rural areas. Former Senator Julie Lassa grew up in

Janet Bewley

A DIFFERENT PATH TO COLLEGE

Senator Janet Bewley remembered:

"I always knew I wanted to go [to college], and I don't know why. Because my dad sat us down and said, 'I'll put the boys through school, but not the girls.' He worked hard, and he truly believed that he was doing the right thing—that the boys needed to grow up and raise a family, and the girls didn't; they would get married, and so we didn't have to have a college education. 'So yeah, go ahead Janet, and if you want to go to college, fine, you know, we won't stop you, but I'm not going to pay [for] you. I'm not going to give you any money for it.' And I [had] no language to say, 'That's wrong,' because that was the way it was done."

Senator Janet Bewley *(center)* was told by her father that he would not pay for her to go to college, but he would pay for her brothers' educations. Bewley attended college and graduate school anyway and eventually became the dean of students at Northland College in northern Wisconsin.

northern Portage County on a dairy farm. She said that she was not able to get involved in too many extracurricular activities until college, as her family had just one car, and they typically made only one trip into Stevens Point per week to run errands. Representative Mary Felzkowski grew up working on her family's Christmas tree farm in Tomahawk, Wisconsin. She helped with the business, which included retail lots not only in Wisconsin, but also in Anchorage and Fairbanks, Alaska. Her father also owned an insurance agency, which she now owns and runs while also serving her hometown area in the assembly. Senator Sheila Harsdorf was raised on a dairy farm in Lake Elmo, Minnesota, and later moved the farm to Beldenville, Wisconsin. She farmed for several years before deciding to follow in her brother's footsteps and run for a seat in the state legislature. Representative Debra Kolste spent her childhood in a small town in western Nebraska. She attended the University of Nebraska and trained as a medical technician. After she married, she moved with her husband, a physician, to a small town in Kansas, where they built their own clinic. They then moved to Janesville to raise their three children in a more urban setting. Representative Bernier was bussed to kindergarten in Chippewa Falls because her rural hometown, Lake Hallie, did not have a kindergarten. She then attended elementary school in a three-room school house, where she had two teachers for four grades of school. Representative Sondy Pope had a similar rural school experience growing up in Iowa County, Wisconsin, on a small family farm. She recalled, "I attended a one-room country school for four years, where anywhere from seven to nine children filled the eight grades. Pumped water, put it in the red wing crock in the morning. Went to the bathroom down on the flat in one of the two buildings. Same school my dad went to."

Other legislators grew up in more urban settings. Former Senator Nikiya Harris Dodd and Representative Christine Sinicki grew up in Milwaukee and came to represent their hometown area in the legislature. Representative Amy Loudenbeck lived in suburban Detroit and suburban Chicago, then attended UW-Madison and decided to stay and make Wisconsin home. She settled with her husband in the Clinton area. Senator Vinehout was born in New York, raised in the Chicago suburbs, and moved to Wisconsin as an adult to become a full-time farmer. Representative Chris Taylor was born in Los Angeles, came to UW-Madison for law school, and remained after graduating. Former Senate Majority Leader Judith Biros Robson was raised in Cleveland, Ohio, and initially attended Ohio State University. However, she came to UW-Madison after having a federal traineeship pulled by the faculty at Ohio State because she was pregnant. She completed her education as a geriatric nurse practitioner at UW-Madison and settled in Wisconsin, where she served almost 23 years in the assembly and the senate.

Many women legislators had politicians in their immediate family. Representative Samantha Kerkman grew up interested in politics, as her father has

Former Senate Majority Leader Judith Biros Robson spent her childhood in Cleveland and came to Wisconsin to finish her college degree. Her grandmother immigrated to the United States from the remote village of Ovčie in Slovakia. Robson is shown here in Slovakia with the headstones of her great-grandparents.

Representative Samantha Kerkman's father was a supervisor for the Town of Randall and got her involved in politics at an early age. She is pictured here with her father, Mark Starzyk *(left)*, visiting the capitol building office of Senator Joseph Andrea *(right)* in the early 1990s.

served on the town board since she was born and took her to political events during her childhood. Senate Minority Leader Jennifer Shilling moved around with her family as her father pursued an interest in public service; he worked for Governor Martin Schreiber and for Secretary of State Vel Phillips. Senator Shilling's grandfathers were also public servants: one was a circuit court judge in northern Wisconsin, and the other was a city council member and mayor.

While some legislators were raised in political families and others, like Representative Kerkman, studied political science, others took a less direct route to legislative service. Legislators have had a variety of careers, including medicine, education, agriculture, and small business. Senator Harsdorf was a farmer before entering politics. When talking about her first election, she said, "I was at a dinner and somebody said, 'Well, what's your background?' And I said, 'I have a degree in animal science.' And they said, 'Oh. Not political science?' [*laughter*] And I said no. And they said, 'Well, you must have minored in poli-sci.' And I said no. And it's important for people to recognize that you can learn the governmental process, but it's very beneficial to bring with you those experiences that you've learned either through having your own business or working for someone else." Representative Ballweg noted that her family's John Deere farm equipment business is one of the larger businesses in

Representative Joan Ballweg's family runs a large farm equipment business in Markesan, which led to her involvement in local politics, then state politics. She is shown here with her husband, Tom, at the business they have run together for over 40 years.

the Markesan community, leading to the family's involvement in the local chamber of commerce and, eventually, politics.

The decision to seek office

The legislators described a variety of influences that led to the decision to run for public office. Many were inspired by example at a young age. Some found that inspiration in a public figure; others had a passion for politics ignited by their own family. And many women legislators described how, later in life, their education, their business experience, or a particular cause or public policy close to their hearts motivated them to run.

One of those who found inspiration in public figures, Representative Stuck, described "[falling] in love with politics and policy" after seeing Bill Clinton speak during his first presidential campaign. Former Senate Majority Leader Robson was "enthralled" with John F. Kennedy and "heeded his challenge to be active for your country, be passionate about your country, be passionate about public service, and really make a difference, just don't complain, and be positive." Some were inspired by more local public figures. Representative Meyers recalled her former supervisor, Rose Gurnoe, who was the tribal chairwoman of the Red Cliff Tribe. It was inspirational, she said, "to know that a woman could be the leader of a tribal nation."

For some, public service was a value instilled by family at an early age. Former Senator Lorman's family was instrumental in her passion for public service: "My family, my dad, loved politics. I was only 15 when he died. But I remember him having these big discussions. He loved Franklin Roosevelt and my mom liked public service. I am a first-generation American. My parents were foreign born, and my mom would say over and over and over, 'You need to give back. You just need to do something because we should be grateful for living here.' So she was always volunteering." Former Senate Majority Leader Mary Panzer grew up with a father who was heavily involved in local and state government in addition to farming and conducting business in insurance,

CHANGES SEEN THROUGH GENERATIONS

Mary Panzer

Former Senate Majority Leader Mary Panzer talked about accompanying her father, Senator Frank Panzer, to work in the 1950s and 1960s, and how the lack of women in the legislature did not match her experience on the family's farm:

"My aunt and my mom were very, very involved in the business, making decisions, and managing and running things, including finances . . . so I found it very odd. I remember asking my dad, 'Why aren't there more women here?' And he said, 'Well, there's no reason why there can't be, and if you want to do that someday, you should do that when you're old enough.'"

Senator Panzer not only became a legislator, but a leader in state politics. She remembers her mother's reaction:

"She loved the fact that her daughter could do things. Like when my dad was in the legislature, the Madison Club was sort of the male bastion, and a woman had to walk in the side door. And it was also a sleeping club. So my mother said to my father, 'When I get to walk in the front door, you get to lay your head on a pillow. Otherwise, no. We're not raising our family, our kids that way. We're not setting those kinds of examples.' So when I got sworn in, she loved to go to the Madison Club, because she could walk in the front door on her daughter's membership."

Former Senate Majority Leader Mary Panzer was joined by her mother, Verna *(left)*, and her daughter, Melissa *(right)*, at her senate swearing-in ceremony in 1993. Like her father, Frank, she became a leader in the state senate.

banking, and accounting. She explained, "While he was running [the farm] with the rest of the family, he also was one of those old-school type of government folks. He was town board chairman, he was county board chairman, and he was president pro tem of the senate . . . I think that really created the impetus to run for office because I saw him do it. He didn't just talk about doing it, you saw how he did it."

Representative Zamarripa also grew up with a politically active family. Her aunt, who helped raise her, was "very involved in the community and politics." She continued:

Christine Sinicki

FINDING OUT SHE WAS RUNNING FOR THE LEGISLATURE

Women often must be encouraged by others or asked multiple times to run for public office. Representative Christine Sinicki was encouraged by her predecessor in the legislature in a very particular way.

"I spent eight years on the Milwaukee School Board, and then my predecessor [Representative Rosemary Potter] [decided] to retire from the legislature. And it's kind of a funny story, the way this all came about. At that time, I really had no intention of running for higher office. I really enjoyed what I was doing on the school board and [with] education. So I called her, and I said, 'So, Rosemary, you got somebody in mind to run?' 'Yeah, don't worry about it,' she said, 'We got somebody, don't worry about it.' A week later, I called her again, 'So, who's running?' 'Don't worry about it. We've got somebody in mind, we've just got to pin her down.' I said, 'Okay, well, it's a woman—is she pro-choice, pro-public education?' 'You're going to love her.' Okay. So a week later, she called me; she said, 'Let's have coffee.' So I said, 'Okay, fine.' [I met] her for coffee and said, 'Who's running?' And she looked at me and [said], 'You are.' And I said, 'Um, no, I'm not.' Then I thought about it for about a week and talked to my family—my husband and kids and my mom and my sisters. And my mom, at first, [said], 'Oh no, no, you can't do this, we need you on the school board.' But I decided that with all that—that was right at the beginning of the voucher program, and there was so much debate around that—I knew the education debate was going to really be at the state level, so I decided I should jump in."

[My aunt] kind of forced me to volunteer as a child, go with her to meetings and then volunteer on campaigns and the like. So as a young adult it became a force of habit for me. And she ran for office. I want to say, historically, she was probably one of the first Hispanic women to ever run for elected office in Wisconsin. She ran for a few different positions: alder, state representative—the same seat that I now hold—and I think maybe school board as well, but never successfully, unfortunately. But I saw that growing up, and so I always credit her for being a big influence in my career decisions.

Sometimes the influence of family came later; Representative Sargent explained how she was inspired to run for office after she became a mother:

I had actually just turned 40 years old and found out I was pregnant, and the world did not know that. I was thinking that I'm very busy doing all these other things. I'm happy with all my dreams. I'm a mom in my city. I'm doing things that I really care about. And I realized as my kids were feeling really frustrated that they needed to do . . . community service, and I was talking to them about stepping up and maybe doing something they thought would be good for the community as opposed to what I was asking them to do, and taking some initiative, and that they were going to reap the benefits by [doing community service]. I actually had one of those moments where all the blood rushed out of my face. And I [told myself], "Shoot I'm kind of acting like my elementary school children by telling people I'm not going to run for office because I'm already doing so much too." It just felt like a real parallel.

The knowledge that women legislators gained in their careers before entering office strongly affected their legislative service. Representative Rodriguez worked with Hispanic communities, including immigrant families and non-native English speakers.

I went to work for a nonprofit called Hispanics for School Choice. And that's where I kind of put a little bit of my experience as an immigrant and seeing my parents struggle to good use. I could relate to the families that the organization was involved [with]. The organization's focus was helping parents learn about the educational choices that were available in the city of Milwaukee. . . . I got to meet a lot of parents that I felt like were like my parents, who were lost, who didn't know how to navigate the system, where to go for assistance, what's available here in the United States if your child is falling behind, if they need other services.

Representative Jessie Rodriguez was born in El Salvador and used her experience to help other Hispanic families learn about the local school system.

Senator Johnson's decision to run for office was motivated by her experience as a small business owner, which raised her awareness of community issues:

I decided that I [had] an interest in running for office once I started doing day care. I started seeing some of the struggles that my day care parents were going through, and how sometimes we have systems in place to protect or help our low-income families that just really don't work, either because they're underfunded or underutilized, or the families just don't have the education or the resources to actually get to where those programs are. . . . I found out that Tamara Grigsby was going to retire from the state legislature, and I was really scared. I was scared about what would happen to our low-income and working families if there wasn't a voice there.

Senator Johnson went on to win the late Representative Grigsby's seat, making advocacy for low-income families her legislative focus.

Like Senator Johnson, Senator Taylor became interested in political change at the start of her career, when her experience as a public defender exposed her to what she felt were flaws in the criminal justice system:

After becoming a lawyer and becoming a public defender, I saw the system was completely jacked up, to say it in really basic terms. Policies that were in place. The system that the public defender and the prosecutor had to deal with. There was just a need for some change, [especially] from a policy perspective. . . . And so the more that I learned about the state of our justice system, it screamed that I needed to go and try to help change policy. I did not want to be the state that leads [the nation in the] incarceration of African American men.

Nearly all of the women we spoke to had to be asked—often multiple times—to run for office. Senator Taylor admitted, "If I could be honest, I ran because I was asked." Senator Taylor is not alone in being encouraged by others before deciding for herself to pursue public office. Though she was actively involved in her community for many years via the Dairy Herd Improvement Association in Buffalo County, Senator Vinehout never considered running for public office until she was asked:

> I was down here [in Madison] for some kind of hearing, and I was kind of recruited by the [Democrats] to come to a press conference they were having about health care. So I told my story and Lena Taylor came up to me, she's a brand new senator, and she said, "Oh my God, girl, you would make a fabulous senator, have you ever thought about running for the senate?" And [I said], "Oh, honey, that's way too much work. I can't possibly do that." As if farming full time wasn't way too much work. It took a couple years to

Senator Lena Taylor became interested in politics during her career as a public defender. Like many women, she had to be asked to run for office; Senator Taylor has, in turn, encouraged and asked other women, such as Senator Kathleen Vinehout, to run for statewide office.

JAY SALVO, LEGISLATIVE PHOTOGRAPHER

dawn on me that this was a possibility. I never ever dreamed that I would be involved in politics, it's totally not my dream at all.

Several years after her conversation with Senator Taylor, and only after more encouragement from people in her community, Senator Vinehout decided to run for office. Senator Bewley described how she decided to run for office: "My kids are grown and living in Ashland, and somebody asked me to run for city council, and I said no. I didn't see it. It's like, why? No. I don't run for office, other people run for office. Then it was like somebody had to ask me three times and then, boom. Why am I saying no? Oh yeah. It's like the bumper sticker, you know, 'Start seeing motorcycles.' We

Though Senator Kathleen Vinehout was asked by others, including Senator Lena Taylor, to run for office, it took her years afterward to believe that a career in politics was a possibility for her.

don't know what we don't see until somebody says, 'Hey, snap out of it. Look. Run for office.' And then you go, 'Oh, oh me, yeah, okay.'"

For many of the women, local government was a critical stepping stone to serving at the state level. About 56 percent of the women in the 2015 Wisconsin Legislature served in a local elected position before winning a seat in the legislature. All agreed that it was a valuable experience. Representative Janel Brandtjen served on her county board for several years before learning that her state representative was retiring and that he wanted to endorse her for his seat. She said, "At that point, you have to say to yourself, this is a tremendous opportunity to not just serve my community, but to serve [as a] legacy for my kids, and then also to impact your direct community. And why wouldn't you take that opportunity? Wouldn't you kick yourself for not saying, 'Hey, I gave it a try to go out and make a difference in [my] community'?"

The campaign experience

Many women had little campaign experience before running for office, and their first campaign often proved the most difficult, introducing them to the rigors and rewards of campaigning. Former Senate President Lazich explained, "In the first campaign, you learn everything the hard way. You start walking,

MEETING THE PUBLIC

Door-to-door campaigning is a vital activity for legislative candidates, letting them meet constituents and learn firsthand about issues in the community. But almost anything can happen out on the campaign trail, as former Representative Mary Williams can attest:

Mary Williams

"There were some very interesting things along the way. I did meet a naked felon. I knocked on a door and this guy opened [it]. He was a nice-looking young man, but he only showed his head . . . kind of peeking out. I told him who I was, and I said, 'I'm running for the state assembly.' And he said, 'Huh?' I said, 'In Madison, the state assembly.' 'Okay.' I said, 'I want to talk to you a little bit, and I hope I can have your vote.' He said, 'I can't vote.' I said, 'You can't?' He opens the door a little more, and I saw he didn't have a shirt on. And okay, it's hot out; it's fall, and it's hot. And he said, 'I can't vote. I'm a felon.' I said, 'Oh my goodness, you are?' 'Yeah.' And well, he opens the door, and there you go. I said, 'Well, it's been nice speaking with you.' I was going to say 'seeing you,' and I thought I'd better not say [that].

But then you have dogs. I always carry dog biscuits with me. I had a Rottweiler come after me. He broke the chain, and he came to a screeching halt right by me. I was between the house and the car. And I looked up, and I said, 'You're going to have to help me, because he's going to kill me.' And honestly, this is the strangest thing, it was like he was frozen. I looked at him, and he just looked at me, and I moved, and he kept looking straight ahead until I got up on the steps. And the lady came running out, 'Oh my God, my dog broke loose.' And I said, 'I already met him.'"

and it's raining, and you don't have your umbrella. You step in a puddle and you're soaking wet. And all of these dumb things [happen]." Representative Rodriguez said that "the first door that you knock on is the hardest. I think the first few doors you knock [on] are the hardest, because you don't know what to expect, what kind of questions people are going to have for you. I didn't know how to prepare for that." Many women still needed the income from their day jobs and had to campaign around their work schedules. Senator Harsdorf recalled, "During that first campaign I was milking cows, doing chores, and farming from first thing in the morning until noon. Then, in the afternoon,

I would go out and campaign until dark." Walking neighborhoods to meet constituents took its toll. Former Representative Mary Williams estimated that she lost 25 pounds during her first campaign; she wore out a brand new pair of tennis shoes and put "just thousands and thousands of miles" on her car.

This door-to-door campaigning, though exhausting, was the activity that the women credited the most for a successful campaign. Whether they were running for school board or state senator, women legislators consistently emphasized how much winning their elections depended upon making personal connections with constituents. This held especially true for legislators' first campaigns, which were frequently for municipal offices such as alderperson or mayor. Through face-to-face discussions, women could tell voters their policy platforms and listen to the voters' concerns. Former Senate President Lazich credited her first win to knocking on "every single door. . . . I listened to their story. And all of that information, you put in your backpack and go home and do your homework."

Even if they knocked on every door, women legislators commonly encountered failure before success. Former Senate Majority Leader Mary Panzer ran for the assembly in 1974 at the age of 21 and lost by only 81 votes. Losing a first campaign, and sometimes many subsequent campaigns, provided many of the women an opportunity to learn from their mistakes and mount a successful

Politicians seeking election to statewide office can cover thousands of miles on foot and by car while on the campaign trail. Door-to-door campaigning, appearances at parades, pancake breakfasts, meet-and-greets, and other local events keep the candidates on the go. Despite pounding the pavement, former Senator Mary Panzer lost her first election, but she continued to learn and work to gain the trust of her constituents.

future run. Representative Lisa Subeck explained that the first time she ran, "I went into it thinking that I was going to print some things on my computer, hand them out to my neighbors, and get elected. I think it was very eye-opening to me that in Madison, you have to raise a lot of money to be able to send a lot of mailings and be able to print literature, and you need to knock on thousands of doors. To me, that was all so brand new." She concluded, "What that [first run] really did for me was open my eyes to how it all works and get me [to] that point where I was ready, next time, to run a strong campaign."

Many women legislators found it challenging to master effective fundraising. Former Representative Williams said that fundraising "was the hardest thing for me to ever do. To sit down and call people and say, 'Can you send me a $500 check or a $100 check?'—that was the most difficult thing for me." Senator Johnson found that "it's exceptionally expensive to run a campaign, and the issues that I've fought hardest on, that are nearest and dearest to my heart, the individuals that I fight for, they don't have money to donate to a campaign." And while she acknowledged that fundraising is crucial to running a campaign, she said, "You have to find a way to make sure that you're raising the type of funds that are true to your values."

Many of the women's early campaigns were small and inexpensive, but expenses tended to amplify over time or when seeking higher office. Senator Janis Ringhand recalled her first campaign for city council: "You really didn't raise any money, you just didn't have to. I think if you spent less than $200, you didn't even have to do a financial report at the local level, so it was really low key. I put an ad in the local paper, had a couple of coffees—local restaurants, sort of meet-and-greets." Former Senate Majority Leader Robson recalled that during her first campaign, "if I got a $25 donation I thought I died and went to heaven; I thought it was just fantastic." She said the budget for her first campaign for the assembly was around $1,000. But by the time of her final campaign, "I think at the end, we were spending nearly

Representative Lisa Subeck says that her first campaign for local office in Madison was "eye-opening" but ultimately led her to be ready to run a strong campaign the next time.

GREG ANDERSON, LEGISLATIVE PHOTOGRAPHER

fifty, sixty, seventy thousand dollars. We were up on the radio; we were putting up big glossy fliers; I was on cable TV. It was really almost entirely different from the first campaign, which was small, personal, doing doors."

Some women who served as volunteers or support staff for other candidates' campaigns started their own first campaigns with more knowledge of the issues and the election process. "But it's different being the candidate," Representative Billings remarked. "It's a little more lonely, even though you are surrounded by people. You're the person who's running for office at the door, asking for money. And you don't want to disappoint everyone and lose. That's what makes you wake up at three in the morning." And whether or not they were successful, these first campaigns helped the legislators gain confidence, expertise, and contacts that were useful in subsequent campaigns. Representative Ballweg found that "there are a lot of the faithful standards that I can always go to now when it comes to putting up campaign signs and supporting me with fundraisers or going out and getting nomination papers, so there is a good core group that I can go back to on a regular basis. I think that's the biggest advantage that an incumbent has. You just keep building on what you've done in years past."

This type of support system proved crucial to winning campaigns. It was acknowledged by all legislators that although there is only one candidate, running for public office is a group effort. Senator Harsdorf said, "I learned very quickly, you don't win a campaign alone. It takes a lot of people willing to invest their time and resources to be successful." At the local level, this support group was often composed of the friends and family of the candidate, and they were often other women. Former Senator Rosenzweig said that the women in her community "worked themselves to the bone" on her campaigns. She told us that she formed lasting emotional bonds with these supporters, even if their political viewpoints later diverged. Former Senate Majority Leader Robson deployed a group of fellow nurses that she dubbed her "white shoe army."

Once the women became candidates for statewide office, political party resources were usually available in addition to local group support. Many Democratic legislators received training from Emerge Wisconsin, part of a nationwide Democratic Party initiative focused on encouraging women to run for elected office. Many Republican women legislators mentioned attending candidate schools sponsored by the Republican Party and receiving assistance from the Republican Assembly Campaign Committee. These training programs helped the candidates master skills like public speaking, effective door-to-door campaigning, and fundraising.

Time in office

The prevailing opinion of women legislators is that the legislative environment has dramatically changed for the better. With exceptions, younger legislators described more equal treatment than those who served in past decades, and long-serving women legislators seemed to find that their gender mattered less as they gained seniority. However, most of the women did describe instances in which they were treated differently than their male colleagues.

In past decades, there were few women legislators. Former Senator Lorman recalled that when she took office in 1979, she was the first woman in the Senate Republican Caucus. When she walked into the room, "These guys were sitting around the conference table with their feet up, smoking cigars." She stood in the doorway, she said, and "didn't know what to do. They just sort of looked up, and Rod Johnston . . . he was a very nice guy, [and] he said, 'You must be our newest member. Come on in. Grab a chair.' That was my welcome." The capitol building at the time reflected the rarity of women legislators. Former Senate Majority Leader Robson recalled that when she was elected to the primarily male assembly in 1987, women "really didn't have a bathroom next to the assembly chambers, we had a converted janitor closet. Which was not befitting of all the marble and the gold and the red velvet and all the rest of that stuff." She interpreted this lack of facilities as being "because women weren't supposed to be there, or weren't ever going to be there." She explained that while it "seems like a trite example . . . it does sort of cement [or] underline the culture of 'It was a man's world.' So being in politics was really considered to be a man's business."

As more women became legislators, attitudes changed. Over the years, women gained seniority and status. Representative Pope explained how the length of her incumbency has affected her interactions with her colleagues:

> Here's the truth of it. At 66, gender stops being much of an issue for people my age. I think it's more of an issue for the younger women. And that may sound silly. But maybe it's the fact that I've been here for 14 years . . . you just garner a little more respect from people who are new, just because you've been here a lot longer than they have. But the sexism, I don't think that applies so much to people like me. We've let our personalities out of the bag, and they know that we don't take off—that if we have a strong opinion, you're going to hear it.

Senator Vinehout has seen firsthand how attitudes toward women in leadership have changed during her tenure. When she took office in 2007, there

USING HUMOR

Jill Billings

Many women legislators, like Representative Jill Billings, use humor to address attitudes about women:

"When I was running for office, a reporter wrote a story about a debate that we did. It talked about me walking in; it was a male, who was a Republican, running against me, a female who was a Democrat. And she talked [about] me walking in with a bright blue jacket and dark pants—didn't mention what he wore at all, but mentioned what I wore. Sometimes you deal with that just by pointing it out. I said, 'Would you ever ask the representative in the next district, my male companion, would you ever comment on what he was wearing?' And humor helps, because I kind of chuckle when I say it. If I can point things out with humor, that helps people accept it. I can give you an example. When you step into the shoes of the representative, it's no longer as much about you, it's about who you represent and the office you hold. I'm a pretty comfortable, relaxed person, but in the building, I don't correct people when they call me Representative Billings. I don't say, 'No, call me Jill,' I accept that. And there is staff that is told, 'You will refer to people as "Representative."' So, I was riding up in the elevator with some people from the [chief] clerk's office—young people. The doors opened, and a lobbyist that I knew from before I became a representative looked at me and said 'Good morning, Gorgeous!' And you heard an 'Uhhhhh' in the elevator. And I pointed to him and said, 'That's Representative Gorgeous to you.' Now, that has not caught on. It's Representative Billings [*laughter*]. I had some people in my home district that called me Representative Gorgeous after I told that story. (Later on, [the lobbyist] said, 'Yeah, I'm sorry about that.') I think you can point things out with humor and help change behavior [for the] better, or often in a way that works."

were three other women in her caucus, including the senate majority leader. But by the end of October that year, the entire senate leadership was men. "What kinds of things happened? There were several older gentlemen who are no longer with us in the senate, who were very outspoken. They dominated the conversation; they cut off the women senators; they demeaned them; and they incessantly told sexist jokes in the caucus." However, after more women joined the caucus and attained leadership positions, the internal dynamics of the caucus changed. Vinehout observed, "The answer to changing it is simple: you have to get more women in office."

Women who began their legislative tenures more recently have served with more women and generally described different relationships with the men with whom they work. "I certainly feel that I've been treated the same as any male colleague," said Representative Ballweg. Representative Nancy VanderMeer believes she has been treated equally, but contends that women legislators still need to have "that enthusiasm and that momentum to continue to represent ourselves . . . create that awareness, let people know we're here." But many of the women still described witnessing or experiencing different treatment based on gender. Sometimes it was fairly explicit, and even noticed by men in the room: Representative Taylor recalled when a male coworker sitting next to her at a committee meeting pointed out behavior that he thought was biased.

JAY SALVO, LEGISLATIVE PHOTOGRAPHER

Representative Chris Taylor once had a male colleague point out biased behavior to her in a committee meeting. She didn't recognize it at first, saying "I think you get used to it . . . You just keep going."

"It was very interesting—it took my male colleague to say to me, 'You know, there's a lot of sexism going on here.' . . . I think you get used to it and you just don't respond to it. You just keep going." Representative Subeck told of her experience when one of her colleagues introduced her to another legislator: "He turned to him and said, 'Have you met Lisa Subeck yet?' Zach, who's my staff, was standing next to me, and this legislator looks at me and then looks over at him and says, 'Oh, do you work for him?' And I said, 'No, this is my legislative aide, Zach.' The look on Zach's face was priceless, too. And the guy actually goes, 'Oh, so you work for her,' like this was some mystery. So, when people say, 'Do you get treated differently?' Yes."

The women's experience with gender bias was not always glaring. "I think there are biases, but they're subtle," explained Representative Billings. "I think that's what's happened as women are in positions of power or leadership. I think we still see sexism and sexism in our society as a whole. It's just often

Former Senator Nikiya Harris Dodd, shown here at a committee meeting in 2015, says she was sometimes made to feel that she wasn't smart enough to be in office because she was a woman.

not as blatant." Former Senator Harris Dodd explained that she was made to feel that, as a woman, she wasn't smart enough, and people "minimized what [her] value was to the process." Representative Sargent told of being in meetings during which women were "talked over in a way that men aren't talked over."

Senator Taylor remembered saying something, then having one of her male colleagues offer the same suggestion: "And then [another] male colleague said it after that, and it sounded brilliant the third time. But the first time, they didn't understand what the heck I was talking about." Representative Stuck, who is 34 years old, said, "Being a younger woman, I've not felt a whole lot of discrimination in the workplace. I always feel like I've been paid pretty fairly, treated pretty fairly. But I would say, this is an interesting experience, to definitely walk in and sort of be dismissed sometimes when you're the only woman, or maybe one of two women, in a room full of men, on a committee, or on the floor where you're in a smaller group where . . . the men sort of just talk around you instead of including you."

Women legislators' interactions with some members of the public often revealed biases different from those sometimes displayed in interactions with their colleagues. Representative Sinicki explained that in her experience, "There is a great deal of respect by other legislators for everybody. I think whether you're

JAY SALVO, LEGISLATIVE PHOTOGRAPHER

Representative Amanda Stuck has experienced a more equal working environment in today's legislature. "I always feel like I've been paid pretty fairly, treated pretty fairly," she said.

a man or a woman, you ran for the seat; you got the votes that were needed; you worked for the seat and I think they do treat you with lots of respect in that way." However, she has also had members of the public arrive at her office to talk to "him." She described it as "just kind of odd at first. People were saying, 'Well, is he here?' I'm like, 'I'm here. Do you want to talk to me?'"

Many women legislators experienced a situation in which a member of the public approached them expecting the legislator to be a man rather than a woman. Former Senate Majority Leader Robson observed, "If I were chairing a meeting, and I was sitting there, and I had a male clerk next to me, people that would come in from the public would assume that the male clerk was the leader or was the chair of the committee." While Robson said that assumption was disconcerting, she commented that others at the meeting often intervened on her behalf: "Usually the staff is so good, they'll say, 'This is Chairman Robson,' and then [the person making the assumption would] be real embarrassed."

Assembly Assistant Minority Leader Katrina Shankland, who is 29 years old, is frequently asked, "Are you just staff?" She responds, "First of all, staff is extremely valuable, so please never say "just." And secondly, I'm the legislator.' They'll [ask], 'Whose office are you with?' And I'll say my name. '[You] work for her?' And [I say], 'No, I am her.' So you wonder how many decades it's going to take before people accept that . . . I feel like there's a learning curve for people who just are not used to young women holding leadership positions." Representative Stuck recounted similar experiences when lobbyists and members of the public look at and talk to her male staffer during meetings, "even though I'm the representative. I often feel like, well, he's my staff person, [but] I make the decisions, so you should be talking to me and asking me questions."

Serving as a woman in office

Some women legislators do not think they need to do their job differently from men. When asked if she felt such a need, Representative Hesselbein replied, "No. I never felt that way." Representative Felzkowski attributed her

Samantha
Kerkman

WHEN HOME AND WORK LIFE COLLIDE

For some women in the legislature, particularly young mothers, a balance between home life and work life is challenging. Representative Samantha Kerkman recalled the times she faced this dilemma:

"I just remember one of the boys was really sick one night, and it was cold out; [he was] probably three months old. Representative [John] Ainsworth and [I] were in the back, and this was when session nights ran really late all the time, consistently. We were here until one, two o'clock in the morning. I was in the back with the baby; I had the visor up and the baby was sleeping. And Representative Ainsworth pulled it down. I remember jumping up off the couch and [saying] 'If you wake this child up!'

Plus, then, I parked across the street, and I remember [someone said], 'Oh, you can park over in GEF 1 building. It's probably better for you.' But then hauling everything back every night was—which you just do, because you love the kids, and I would not change my job. [People said], 'You didn't take any time off?' I said, 'No.' I missed one week of session. There were a lot of helping hands around, too; they would help if the baby was crying on the floor. I think about that today. There were a couple times when the baby was crying really late at night. I pulled him into the side office over there, and I just couldn't get him to calm down. And do I bring him out onto the floor

Representative Samantha Kerkman with her sons, Ian and Evan, in 2016. Since infancy, both of her sons have made appearances with Kerkman on the assembly floor.

and make it louder to try to get off the floor with him? And you think at that moment, 'Oh my gosh, the world is—everybody is—paying attention.' But everyone has been in those shoes."

success in office to her "strong personality" and didn't think that she had to work harder than her male colleagues. Representative Kerkman characterized her approach as "working smarter," which includes having patience with the pace of the legislative process and continuing to work with her colleagues.

Other women legislators, however, believed that they had to compensate for work opportunities that were missed when family took priority. This challenge was greater for those who had to travel long distances to attend committee hearings and legislative sessions. When Senator Taylor joined the legislature, she was a single parent with a young child at home. She had support from her family, but she still had to find the balance between her official duties and her family obligations: "I was commuting, unlike most people who would stay [in Madison], and I would say that it probably was draining on my relationships in the legislature. I probably could have more relationships. Even though I've accomplished a lot, I probably could've accomplished even more if I could've stayed and [done] lunch, coffee, dinner, [and] drinks with my colleagues. But instead, I'm on the road driving back [to Milwaukee]." Representative Ballweg added: "I think one of the things that is different in what I've done is because I'm traveling back and forth every night. I'm not here to go out to eat and have those after-hours conversations that sometimes aid in building those relationships. And because my family was a little bit younger, and I'm only an hour away, I wanted to get home every night as much as possible. So, from that standpoint, it's a little bit of a different dynamic." Former Senator Lorman explained that her situation was challenging because she was widowed, and she always wanted her child to come first: "I think that's different for men because, if there's a spouse, you can call your spouse and say, 'Could you go pick him up or go to the meeting?' Things like that. And I didn't have a spouse then, I was widowed. And so [my son] came first. That made a difference. So I didn't go out for dinner with the guys. I mean, most people don't go home at five. They go out to dinner; they go to the bar; they've got apartments. I didn't have that, so I never got really very close to anybody."

Many other women legislators believed that they had to work harder than their male colleagues because they saw their work as somehow representative of all women in office. Former Assembly Majority Leader Pat Strachota described her efforts: "I didn't let my gender have an impact . . . If I perceived that somebody would—felt that my gender had an impact, I would rise. I would work harder to show them that it wasn't—it had no impact. I think that's the pressure." Some women described feeling like they had something to prove, regardless of whether that feeling was warranted. Representative Meyers said,

"Yes. Women definitely work hard. And it's maybe self-inflicted sometimes. Maybe we do the best job, but we're always trying to do a little bit better because we think someone is behind us going, 'Oh yeah, she's a woman.' I think that is on all of our minds. Maybe I shouldn't speak for women in general, but it is on my mind. You walk into a room, and you're the only woman in the room. Yeah, you better pull your weight and somebody else's, too."

Some women did not believe that they had to work harder but that they needed to adopt a different, more collaborative approach to get results. In looking back on her legislative service, former Senator Robson recalled, "If I'm asked about what the difference is between men leaders and women leaders, I would say . . . that women legislators tend to be more consensus building, that they try to be more inclusive, that they try to build on the issue, not necessarily on the person. They give up their ego, so to speak, and they want the issue to win . . . so that means that, I think, you can get a lot more done. I did that when I was the leader." Representative VanderMeer explained that, when she authored a bill about which she felt very strongly, "instead of just putting out my co-sponsorship on an email, I went to visit as many of my legislators here in the building that I could. A lot like doing doors. It's that face-to-face and sharing that enthusiasm that I can't really put on a piece of paper." Senator Ringhand added, "I think women are just, in general, a little more diplomatic about how they approach some of the issues."

Representative Brandtjen echoed this belief, saying that "as a female legislator . . . you're probably a little more comfortable working together as a team to find that success. And I think women are more team-directed, or team-angled, and working towards making that happen." Representative Ballweg agreed, explaining that she sees that "women are more—in many cases—[interested] in working at consensus building, sometimes, than the gentlemen . . . you know, making personal contacts, phone calls to members, visiting their offices, communication, and trying to explain what the proposal is, things like that." Former Senator Lassa explained:

> I think women are much more willing to sit down and come up with a solution that works for people. Whereas I think sometimes men can get dug in on an issue and not—compromise has become a dirty word in government. But I think in all of our relationships, whether you're married or you're involved with a significant other or you're just part of a family, no one gets their way all the time. You don't. And that doesn't happen at work either. But I think women are much more willing to sit down and see where they

can find some common ground and come up with a solution that works for people, and sometimes men are more reticent to do that.

Particular perspectives

Women legislators generally agreed that they brought a different perspective to the legislature by virtue of their life experiences. "I think everyone brings a unique voice; I think everyone has a story to tell," said Representative Hesselbein. Representative Pope noted, "I think it is important that people understand women bring a different perspective to law-making that men may or may not have." Many women expressed that a plurality of views is what gives representation its depth. Senator Bewley explained, "I think that we bring to our roles whatever parts of ourselves we use as a frame of reference. And I can't help but know that my lens is a female lens. I'm a woman; I have a woman's eyes; and so I'm looking through a woman's eyes. But I try to acknowledge that as long as everybody is aware of the fact that they all have different lenses, and we respect each other's points of view, that we end up with the right vision—total vision—we're okay."

Representative Bernier agreed, saying that "a woman's perspective is going to be a little bit different than a man's. And I think the balance is good. No

Representative Kathy Bernier of Lake Hallie visits one of the grade schools in her district. She believes that every aspect of life, including government, benefits from having both male and female perspectives.

matter what aspect of life—whether it's the legislature or a business or an industry or whatever, whatever realm that you live in or work in—to have male and female perspectives is important." Representative Meyers echoed, "I can't bring the exact perspective [a man] would bring to a conversation, and I think we need to make sure that we have both sides to the conversation."

The women did not all agree that gender was significant in shaping their perspective. As Senator Vukmir said, "I've never really subscribed to the notion that being a woman in politics is different than being a man." However, those who did think that gender was significant explained why. For example, Representative Meyers expressed the belief that women have "a compassion—as mothers, as wives, as women—that we can bring to a situation that a man just can't, and vice versa." Representative Taylor found that being a mother affected the types of issues on which she focuses, saying, "The issue of gun violence has become one of the top things for me because I'm worried about my kids. So I bring that perspective, I think, that a mother brings. I'm a mom first, and so that is always my first inclination as to how to improve the lives of children and how to keep them safe. So, as a mother and working parent, I think I have a perspective that a lot of people don't have."

To Senator Jennifer Shilling of La Crosse, a woman's perspective is essential when the legislature discusses issues such as reproductive health.

JAY SALVO, LEGISLATIVE PHOTOGRAPHER

Other women believed that, when the legislature debated certain issues, a woman's perspective was essential to finding the best solution. Senator Shilling noted that, when it comes to an issue like women's reproductive health, "there is one gender that knows a little bit more personally than the other one." She explained that when the legislature considers those issues, it's important for women to be part of the conversation: "[U.S. Senator] Tammy Baldwin always says, if you're not in the room, they talk about you. If you're in the room, they talk to you. We all bring different experiences that shape us." She added, "I think we are a richer legislature when we have people from all walks of life that run and serve."

The women legislators generally

concurred that their perspectives were shaped by more than their gender; many other influences and experiences make up their identities. As the first and only Republican representative who is Hispanic, Representative Rodriguez noted, "I bring a unique perspective [because] I come from an immigrant background, so poverty, knowledge of the community, knowledge of cultural values and ideas. And so [my colleagues] look upon me to be that voice for them, to help them understand and garner information." She observed, "The funny thing is that when I was elected, I wasn't running as a 'Hispanic' Republican, and that wasn't my focus. When I ran, I wanted to represent my community, [which] is predominantly white." Experiences in office changed her mind: "Although I didn't expect that I needed to be that voice, I feel like I have to now, because I'm there." Former Senator Lorman, when asked if she, as a woman, had a perspective that the legislature otherwise would have lacked, answered, "Probably to some extent, and maybe influenced by the fact that I came from an immigrant background. Maybe because I'm Jewish. Maybe because I was widowed; I had more responsibility for family-raising than some people. I can't say that it was just being a woman." Senator Johnson, who identifies as African American, said that in addition to her gender, "to a large degree, I actually think my color helps me here at the capitol . . . I think I'm able to bring perspectives to the table that other people may not be able to see. It has helped a lot with some of the legislation that I've been able to pass."

Representative Sargent spoke about growing up in a family that did not have a lot of money and learning how to grocery shop with food stamps as a young girl. She explained, "I think that makes me unique. I don't know that there's a lot of people in this building that have had that experience. And I think it's really important that our legislature is made up of different perspectives and different realities." Senator Taylor described her unique lens:

> I know I bring something different to the table. It means something to be a child whose parents divorced. I can speak to that in a way [that] somebody who has walked in those [shoes] can speak. I can speak about being a single parent and the challenges that exist. I know what it is to be an entrepreneur and have a startup. I know what it is to hire people and have to fire people. It's not easy to do those things. I understand the story of the mother who is raising a black boy in America, let alone in Milwaukee in the state of Wisconsin.

She added, "When I am the only person of color to walk in a room, my mere presence brings something different."

All of the women agreed that the legislature is a better and more effective body when more perspectives and experiences are represented. Representative Billings captured this sentiment, noting, "I'm a believer of having a lot of different voices at the table. And I think you're better representatives, you're a better governing body, if you have those varied voices at the table."

Particular concerns

One problem commonly experienced by many women legislators was the attention paid to their clothing and appearance. "I think women just are held to a higher standard," said Representative Shankland. Some found the lack of consensus on what constitutes women's business wear to be problematic. "Men have a pretty basic uniform," said Representative Billings. Representative Ballweg agreed, noting that "when we put in a more formal dress code here at the legislature, it was easy to say that gentlemen need to wear a coat and a tie to be recognized on the floor, but it was impossible to come up with a definition of what professional dress is for ladies."

Representative Billings added that women "kind of have to find a female version of the male suit." The rules, it seems, are endless: "Your hemline has to be so low. You can't show cleavage. The type of jewelry you wear cannot be

The Republican women of the 2015 legislature. Many women legislators described the difficulty of establishing a professional dress code for themselves, knowing that they may be judged more harshly than their male colleagues for their choice of wardrobe.

JAY SALVO, LEGISLATIVE PHOTOGRAPHER

Mary Lazich

COMMUNICATING WITH CONSTITUENTS

Until the mid-1990s, constituents and candidates for office had three ways to communicate with each other: phone call, letter writing, or personal visit. Since the introduction of email and social media, the pace of communication has become much faster and larger in volume, as former Senate President Mary Lazich relates:

"When I first ran, it was all about the doors. Doors, doors, doors. And I still think it is today. But when I ran, it was still the dinosaur age of communications. Email didn't exist back then. We were letter writing. When I came in, in 1993, we wrote letters, and letters were the main form of communication. We had 800 numbers, so some people called us. Cell phones were first coming on. I had this big, huge bag phone that you had in your car. You didn't carry cell phones around. But it was very, very different then. So the letters came in, and then people had to sit down at home and write a letter, and put a stamp on it, and address it. So you didn't get as much communication. These letters came in each day, and staff would help you, and you'd do research, and you would write back to people. It was U.S. Mail back and forth. But when email came . . . [and] people became more savvy . . . [The Joint] Finance Committee, my gosh, we got 500 emails a day. There's just no way to keep up with that. Just no way. And then with TV, everything's very instantaneous. It's just immensely different. It's so different. And the campaigns, then, are immensely different because of the communications, too."

too flashy. You shouldn't wear sleeveless outfits. You shouldn't wear open-toed shoes." She did, however, explain why some of these limitations make sense: "If what you want as a representative of a district is for people to hear your words, you want them to hear your message. And if you're wearing low cleavage or a short, short skirt, or a wild pattern or crazy jewelry, are they listening to your message or are they saying, 'That jewelry is interesting?' You want them to hear your words, so you want them to focus on that and not what you're wearing."

A second problem mentioned by women legislators is the harassment some have faced online. Many women noted that social media has been an effective way for them to communicate with the public and their constituents: "It's an important part of any campaign, or even from the official office, in terms of just getting your message out and letting people know what you're doing," said Representative Stuck. However, social media also opened a new avenue for a type of negative, and often anonymous, comment that is directed primarily at women. Some women legislators, like Representative Pope, address negative online comments by simply avoiding social media altogether or delegating to their staff the tasks of updating their Facebook pages and monitoring their online presence. Others contend that the best way to handle the problem is to ignore it. "You have to be prepared that some people are incredibly amazing to you, and other people are going to tell you everything you don't need to know about yourself," said Representative Brandtjen. She advised: "Grow your alligator skin, and get comfortable in your skin, and be willing to step forward, head high, and be that voice for your community."

Public focus on women's appearance and the online harassment experienced by some women legislators are closely tied. Senator Shilling said that she sometimes receives negative comments about her appearance on social media. She explained, "I've never seen them say that against my male colleagues. . . . People will take these pot shots at women legislators and our looks and our appearance and things like that." Representative Billings related the following experience: "I did a press release the day I co-chaired my first committee meeting, and I had a picture on my Facebook page. And one of my media people called me and commented on the clothes that I wore." "Being a public official means that you're in the public eye and that you're a target of negative comments—gender, sexist comments," said Representative Shankland. However, she explained that it's important not to be silenced by bad online behavior: "It's so easy to get mad at these stupid comments from people who call you terrible words for believing in voting rights or whatever simple thing that you're advocating for at the time, like tax fairness. These comments come out at the weirdest times, and I just started calling them out and saying, 'This is what happens when women are in office.'"

Mentorship

Mentoring in the legislature can echo through many legislative careers. The current woman legislator who was named most frequently as a mentor was Representative Ballweg. For example, Representative Cindi Duchow said that Representative Ballweg was the first person to welcome her to the Assembly, and Representative Bernier referred to her as "the best mentor in the whole wide world." Representative Ballweg, in turn, talked about the importance of the formal mentoring program in the assembly:

JAY SALVO, LEGISLATIVE PHOTOGRAPHER

Representative Joan Ballweg *(left)*, shown with fellow representative Cindi Duchow, has been named by many of her fellow legislators as a mentor to them. Mentorship in the legislature can span many sessions and impart procedural and historical knowledge, as well as provide an important social aspect for many members.

We had a good system of formalized mentors in our caucus, and that was someone who would kind of help you out, tell you how things worked . . . They would sit you on the [assembly] floor next to that person. And in my particular case, it was Jean Hundertmark, who actually was in the district next to mine, so it was [a] very similar type of constituency, and she was coming from a very similar place in that we had kids about the same age and things like that, although she'd been in the legislature for

MILKSHAKE MENTOR

Senator Alberta Darling connected with her first mentor over an invitation to have a milkshake: "I was really lucky that I met Mary Panzer my first day in the legislature. She asked me if I wanted a milkshake. I thought that was very undignified. [*laughter*] You could eat things on the floor in the assembly, and I thought, 'I've worked

Alberta Darling

this hard to have someone ask me if I want a milkshake?' But we became fast friends, and she was a terrific mentor, because she was very reasonable, very bright, very committed to service, and came from a family of individuals very committed to public service. She was a great mentor."

several terms at that point. She was someone that I could talk to and not feel foolish [asking] about what's happening with floor procedure and those kinds of things. Our caucus has tried to keep that going, and I've served as mentor for someone most every term, a couple of gentlemen and a couple of ladies also—tried to do the same thing that Jean did for me.

As for less formal mentoring, Representative Ballweg said, "Informally, I think people, just like in any other organization, seek out folks that they think would have similar interests, similar backgrounds."

All of the women who identified specific mentors agreed that a mentor was a valuable asset. Former Senate Majority Leader Robson remembered the mentorship of Representative Jeannette Bell. "She took us under her wing and she kind of showed us the way and the pitfalls, and also helped organize the women going out for lunch and dinner so we could just be friends and relate to each other and feel like you had some comfort with other women." Robson added that when they were on the assembly floor and it felt a little hostile, "Jeannette always had your back." Representative Brandtjen's assigned mentor was Representative André Jacque. Brandtjen said having a mentor help with

FRESHMAN CHAOS

Former Senate President Lazich talked about when she was first elected to the assembly in 1992 in a class of 23 freshmen representatives, 9 of whom were women. Senator Lazich said she was fortunate to have been assigned a good mentor, "But we all wanted to know more about the rules, and how do we get things done? What do we do on the floor? So [Representative and

Mary Lazich

Minority Caucus Chair] Dave Deininger said, 'Okay, let's get together and I'll help you with that.' So we all went in, and we're all bubbling over with questions, and he doesn't really have a plan to teach us. And we walk out of there, and it was just more chaotic." Deininger did leave them with one piece of advice, Lazich said: "Well, I'll tell you what [Assembly Speaker] Tom Loftus told me when I came into the building: 'There ain't no rules and we don't play fair.' That was our induction. So I go back to my office, and I typed that out in great big letters and slapped it on the wall. And I was quickly told to take that down."

Representative Janel Brandtjen, vice chair of the Assembly Committee on Government Accountability and Oversight, confers with her fellow committee member Representative Tyler August, who is also Speaker Pro Tempore.

"making deadlines, making sure you understand how the different departments work, what they can provide and what they can't provide, and where you go for the information they're not providing, so all kinds of different ways to get information and how you can be successful about that" was "really helpful in getting [work] done." Senator Ringhand said that Representative Pope had been her mentor during her campaign, and that Pope was helpful "because she understood some of the same things I was going through, struggling at home sometimes—I just wish I had an extra hour to do this or do that; she understood that." Mentorship was especially helpful in each legislator's freshman session. Former Senator Lassa said that her former boss, Representative Donald Hasenohrl, was her mentor. Because she had worked as Hasenohrl's chief of staff, she felt pretty comfortable in the capitol when she was first elected. Of Hasenohrl, she said, "He was a really good mentor in helping think through some of the policy issues and providing a really good wealth of knowledge. Because there still is that transition. And when you're first elected, there's so much information coming at you that it's really hard to take it all in and not to be overwhelmed."

Women legislators faced varying degrees of difficulty in finding mentors. Some were set up formally with their mentors. Others said that they had no mentor or that they relied on more informal mentorship, learning from the legislators around them. Former Representative Williams said that the importance of having a mentor in the legislature "depends upon the woman." She continued, "If you are the kind of person that can go and get all your own answers and do all your own research and stuff, it's not quite as important."

Former Senator Harris Dodd discussed the mentoring dynamic she observed during her career: "There were some people who did try to take me under their wing, and there were some people that I kind of sought out. And so it was kind of this really interesting dynamic going on, where I just received some mentorship, and others I rejected based on what my experience with that person was." Senator Taylor explained that although she never had anybody say to her, "I'm going to be your mentor," she chose mentors for herself. "Marvin Pratt became a mentor because he was a neighbor. He was my alderman. He was the standard of what I thought service was . . . He could've told you when he met you what your issue was, what your address was. I call him the 'Rain Man of Politics.'"

Senator Johnson said her first mentor was former Representative Sandy Pasch, but that she doesn't have just one mentor. Instead, she said, "I have people that I watch. And, with that, you have to take it with a grain of salt. I have to separate the things that I don't like about them, but really concentrate and try to mimic the things that I do. So I would say that I have a lot of mentors here in the capitol." Many legislators learned from watching a seatmate on the floor. Former Representative Strachota said that back in 2004, she was paired with then-Representative Vukmir. Strachota remembered sitting on the assembly floor with Vukmir—whom she described as "a strong female representative"— and asking lots of questions. Former Senator Carol Roessler said, "My seatmate was Pat Goodrich, and from time to time, I would ask Pat questions. But as far as a mentor was concerned, no [I did not have one]. And that surely would have been helpful. But again, having Pat as my seatmate was fortunate because I could glean some information and thoughts and assistance from her." Other times, the women roomed together when the legislature was in session, which gave them the opportunity to find, as Senator Roessler described it, "a place for exchange and learning."

Senator Bewley said she has had no single mentor:

I am just enchanted by all the people in this building, and so I really count on different people for different things. But no, I do not have one person who sort of ushered me through. I don't want to say [mentoring] is relatively new, but a woman mentoring another woman, that didn't happen. If it happened, it was almost by accident, and you developed a relationship and then years later you realize, 'Oh, she was a mentor to me.' But now it is more common. And so I just see mentoring opportunities in everybody.

So I'll go to this person because I know that's what he knows and that's where he'll help me, or she is really good and very clear and very honest about that, and so I use people that way.

Representative Duchow mentioned she feels comfortable regularly calling and talking with other women legislators and that she can always rely on "the guys down the hall" in the capitol, referring to Representatives Tyler August, Michael Kuglitsch, Rob Swearingen, and Adam Neylon. Representative Shankland shared that "I always like to collect a few opinions of people I respect so that I have a myriad of ideas, and then I go with whatever I feel was right on the issue."

Not all women legislators were mentored by women, and some found mentorship outside their own party. Representative Hesselbein was paired with Representative Nick Milroy because they were both on the Assembly Committee on Veterans and Military Affairs, as well as the Natural Resources and Sporting Heritage committee:

> It was really great that he is a hunter and a fisherman, and I am not, but I love the resources. I love the outdoors. I want to go on walks with my family just as I want a hunter to be able to hunt, so it was nice to be able to get his perspective on that as well. . . . I could call up Nick and say 'There's this veterans' bill that I have.' It wasn't going well and he gave me some ideas. And I took his ideas, and I was able to pass the bill into law. Very helpful.

Representative Dianne Hesselbein has been mentored by Representative Nick Milroy, her colleague and a co-member of two committees with her in 2015. Milroy was helpful in providing a different perspective for Hesselbein's proposals related to natural resources and veterans issues.

GREG ANDERSON, LEGISLATIVE PHOTOGRAPHER

Leah Vukmir

STARTING FROM SCRATCH

Every legislator has a story about her first day in office and getting acclimated to the legislature. Senate Assistant Majority Leader Leah Vukmir, who began her legislative career in the assembly, remembers that on her first day she literally went back to basics.

"I said, 'What in the world did I get myself into?' There is no manual that really prepares you. You can go through an orientation—bless the hearts of those that try to orient us. You really have no clue until you get here. And I'm not afraid to admit, I admitted this before, that I sat down in my office, [which] was very empty and had dusty bookshelves that had nothing on [them], and there was a children's cartoon book that we give out, *How a Bill Becomes a Law*. And I read it. Now, I did have a working knowledge, because I had come up here to the capitol, and I had been testifying and was involved in various pieces of legislation. But it was one of those chuckle moments where I looked at this, and I went, 'Okay, this is what I've got.' The rest was trial by fire, being thrown and thrust into situations, and learning as you go. But I'm a nurse, and we're used to being in unpredictable environments. We're used to having to be flexible. We're used to having days that don't run where everything happens at an exact time. So in many ways, my nursing background really prepared me very well."

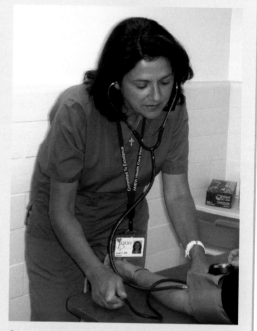

Senator Leah Vukmir has used her background in nursing and teaching to help her navigate the often whirlwind environment of the legislature.

Representative Debra Kolste of Janesville *(left)*, a Democrat, has teamed up with her Republican colleague Representative Amy Loudenbeck *(right)* to improve her proposals and get them through the legislative process.

Representative Kolste, a Democrat, found help across the aisle in Representative Loudenbeck. In talking about the challenges of her first year in the assembly, as a member of the minority party trying to write a bill that might pass, she said, "I did write a bill the first year for the nurse practitioners to be able to prescribe at free health clinics. And I teamed with Amy Loudenbeck, and she actually showed me how to make the bill much better. So I considered her counsel a lot. She was very helpful." Another Democrat, Representative Billings, found assistance in Republican Senator Harsdorf, saying, "When you are in the minority, you have to find a Republican champion, and [Harsdorf] has helped me with legislation in the past two terms."

Representative Felzkowski, when asked whether it is important for new women legislators to be paired with women mentors, replied, "No, I don't think it matters." Her mentor was Representative John Nygren, who had a similar background in the insurance business. Representative Subeck said, "We were asked who our first choices and second choices were and then paired up largely based on that. And my first choices, interestingly, were not women, and I don't know that it's because I didn't want a woman, because certainly some of my not-first choices were women, but I think it was partly products of geography. I wanted somebody in Dane County and somebody who I didn't know."

On the question of whether it is important for women legislators to have women mentors, Representative Rodriguez responded, "Yes, and kind of no." She clarified that for procedural questions, it doesn't matter whether the mentor is a woman or a man. But she added, "Seeing a woman's perspective on issues,

THE BABY BOOMER EXPERIENCE

Barbara Ulichny

Like many women of the Baby Boomer generation, former Senator Barbara Ulichny had her political consciousness raised while attending college and seeing the unrest of the 1968 riots in Chicago. She recalls growing up in a very religious and Republican family, but in the 1970s, she worked for George McGovern's campaign and also ran for Congress. She worked with various groups to change Wisconsin's sexual assault and divorce laws, learning grassroots organizing and becoming familiar with the legislative process. She was elected to the assembly in 1978 and served in the legislature for 14 years. She remembers the many people who helped her become a better legislator:

"My mentor in politics was the late senator and justice Bill Bablitch, because he was our chief author of the sexual assault reform bill in the state senate, and he became my mentor in the process. I also learned a lot from women in the assembly, including Sheehan Donoghue, who was a Republican from Merrill, Wisconsin. I sat next to Midge Miller from Madison; I learned from her to read about and follow the opposition and not only to read about and research the points of view that you agreed with—[to] see what the 'other' side had to say about issues . . . Mary Lou Munts; she and I became friends. And Sharon Metz was my roommate in Madison—Sharon was from Green Bay, Wisconsin. But those were all people who were very impactful for me."

though, is really helpful. I see it a certain way and I talk to other females to see if they see it the same way. Even if we agree on certain things, we disagree on some other things, but they're there as a resource." Senator Ringhand added, "I think it was helpful having a woman mentor because they just understand some of the family side of things, because men wouldn't be as cognizant because they don't address it in the same way." Former Senate President Lazich agreed that women should serve as mentors to other women: "That's something that I'd certainly love to do in my retirement is to mentor young girls, young women, whatever the age, very young children to a women my own age, to be involved and to prepare them for and help them run for elections."

Like former Senate President Lazich, many of the women expressed interest in mentoring the next generation of public servants. Representative Billings remembered encouraging another woman to run for the seat on the county board she had vacated to go to the assembly. The woman responded, "Oh, me? I don't think I know enough about county issues." Representative Billings said, "Neither does anybody else, and I think you can learn them. And I will be here to help you. That's the other thing that helps: if you have women who help mentor, if you feel like you have that support system, then you want to do it."

Representative Bernier said that young women considering going into politics need strong encouragement in the form of mentoring. She explained, "I want to reach out to women in greater Wisconsin to say, if you are city council, if you are county board, if you are school board, or you're a woman serving at the local level, or if you're a woman just interested, you're just a community member interested in running for office, well, I'm here to help you. I'm here to encourage you, and I'm here to tell you how to make that happen. So, we need more mentors out there."

Senator Johnson was unsure whether she had served as an official mentor to anyone but, she added, "I'm always giving my advice, whether it's asked for or not, to some of the younger electeds, and that's because I really want to see them succeed. Especially the individuals from Milwaukee, because I am so proud of Danny Riemer, Mandela Barnes, David Bowen—because these are young men, and for so long in politics, especially in Milwaukee, in order to get to the capitol you needed to be seasoned." Representative Sinicki said, "I do get a lot of our freshmen coming to me, just to ask advice on how to get things done." Her advice was, "What you need to do is just find your niche and run with it."

Senator Shilling, in looking back over her time as Senate Democratic leader, said, "That is one thing I regret, that I didn't do a better job or work with [the National Conference of State Legislatures] or another group for mentoring both in-the-building dynamics and personal life dynamics of how you blend, how you deal with colleagues, how you deal with lobbyists, how you deal with all of these pressures and all the glass balls we're juggling." She concluded, "Mentoring is very important, but it's undervalued."

Across the aisle

Many of the women legislators have worked across the aisle, but said it did not make much difference whether they were working with a man or a woman. Representative Hesselbein said, "There's not a difference for me . . . I think it matters on the issue." Representative Felzkowski agreed: "It's more dictated by the issue." Representative Sargent added, "I think that I work [as] well with women on the other side of the aisle as I [work] with men on the other side of the aisle." Representative Taylor mentioned that "[The] first person who I really worked closely with was [former Republican Representative] Gary Bies... [We] worked on a bill to require that police investigations, when there is an officer-involved death, [are] not led by the department where the officer works... I mean, I just love the guy. I would walk through water, walk through fire for him. I really would. And I don't agree with him on a lot of issues. I mean, we don't agree on a lot of things, but what I saw in Gary Bies was just a . . . very fierce advocate." She went on to mention forming collaborative relationships across the aisle with both men and women, including Representatives Loudenbeck, Kerkman, Jeremy Thiesfeldt, Joel Kleefisch, and Tyler August. Apart from issue-based cooperation, some women acknowledged women legislators' tendency to look out for each other in terms of safety and well-being. Representative Brandtjen said, "We do make sure: 'Do you need a walk to your car?' 'Do you have a room tonight?' 'Do you need a pair of heels? Yours broke.' For, I guess, some of the girl stuff, we do look out for each other more." The legislators also found they could talk about motherhood; former Senator Lassa said, "It's something that you can bond over, on life outside of work. Some of the mutual frustrations in terms of raising children and being a working mom and that type of thing."

Many women noted how tough it has become to maintain genuine friendships with other legislators. Some legislators believed that this was a result of partisanship. Representative Sinicki discussed how socialization has changed in the time that she has been a legislator:

> There is such a partisan feel at this time, in this building, that it's very difficult to form those bonds because what I've seen happen now—you know, when I was first elected, you could debate on the floor all you wanted, you could fight, you could yell, you could debate, but once you walk off that floor, it's over. And that doesn't happen anymore. We don't see a whole lot of socialization anymore. As women, we used to always get together. I had some very good friends on the other side of the aisle many years ago. But we just don't see that anymore. It's sad, but it's true.

Others seconded Representative Sinicki's observation that forming relationships across the aisle has not always been so difficult. A few of the legislators brought up former Lieutenant Governor Barbara Lawton's efforts to form a women's caucus. Former Senator Robson remembered:

> It was very, very informal, the women's caucus. I know that sometimes, if

we felt like we were going to be threatening to the men, we would say that we had a women's caucus. But when we were in the senate, Lieutenant Governor Barb Lawton tried mightily to put together a women's caucus, and she wanted it to be a bipartisan women's caucus. So she organized us for lunch, Republican and Democrat women, and we started meeting for lunch—there would be 25 or more of us that would meet for lunch. We would just talk about everything and nothing, you know, your kids, neighbor stuff, and not necessarily legislation.

Senator Vukmir noted that the events around passage of 2011 Wisconsin Act 10 affected bipartisan relationships:

Clearly, coming in and going to Act 10 with senators leaving, it was a very unprecedented time in our state's history, and you can imagine, then, the chilling effect that it had on relationships. And in the assembly, I had relationships with members on the other side of the aisle and in both houses. When that happened, it was just almost like divorce, so to speak. You know, you just are completely on separate sides of an issue, and it was very polarizing. And it took some time for that chill to go away. I'm happy to say that it has.

While many legislators did not think being a woman provided any significant difference in reaching across the aisle, a few observed that women have a different way of going about getting things done and that this can affect cooperation. Representative Shankland pointed to the federal government shutdown as an example, saying, "I think if anything, all the research that's been done about women in office has shown that they are more cooperative. If you just even look at bills or at Congress shutting down and then reopening because a coalition of women across both parties open[ed] the government, found a deal." She further discussed the ways she thinks that men and women work differently:

I think that—and there's a lot of research that shows this—women can work together in a way that men maybe don't. But I also think it goes the other way. An example: where does a lot of work get done in business? Whether it's insurance or law—on the golf course. How can women be included in that if they can't golf, right? I see that and get frustrated by it because I do think it cuts both ways and it's helpful that women can be allies to each other in the legislature—work across the aisle on key initiatives that support children and families, for example.

Increasing equality

Most of the women wanted to see more women in the legislature and in leadership positions. Representative Shankland observed, "Women being at the table can inform the conversation or change the conversation entirely." Senator Bewley argued that "The leadership should be 51 percent women just because it's simply accurate. When the demographics are accurately represented in leadership, things work better, because everyone is heard. . . . When that representation isn't there, things fall apart." However, while the women legislators wanted to see more women in office, many discouraged the idea of supporting women candidates blindly. Many of the women pointed out that having a diverse legislature encompasses more than just gender equality.

Representative Pope remarked that she wouldn't support a particular candidate just because she is a woman, "because I don't think gender really has that big [of an] influence." Representative VanderMeer added, "I think it's important that we elect the best candidate to represent us, the person that is going to help Wisconsin be the best state in the country. So whoever fulfills that mission should be in the House." Senator Ringhand recalled that she had declined to support some women because she felt they were simply not good candidates, even though people expect her to endorse other women. She reasoned, "It isn't easy; you do get criticized for it, but just because she's a woman doesn't mean she's a good candidate. You really have to pay attention to what the end outcome would be, because I don't want to saddle constituents with a bad choice, and I don't want to support someone I don't have confidence in." Some women legislators wanted the focus to be on their actions, not their gender. Representative Brandtjen told us, "I'm not really comfortable labelling myself as a female legislator. I'm a legislator. All issues are women's issues. All issues have importance."

The majority of women believed that the Wisconsin Legislature benefits from having a variety of opinions and life experiences and that this encompasses much more than just being a woman. Senator Harsdorf shared that "There were some who suggested that I not run again because I had a baby. I've always felt that it's important to not only encourage different [professions to be] represented, but it's also important to allow people at different stages of their life to be able to serve. You don't want to create a legislature where you can't have people with young families able to serve." She also emphasized the need for leadership to be representative of the different geographical parts of the state. Representative Zamarripa described being the only Hispanic member of her caucus: "We've never had a Latino state senator. Those things are

Senator Sheila Harsdorf, shown with Gene Lamere at the 2008 Governor's Fishing Opener, is a farmer, a legislator, and a mother and talks about the need for leadership to come from all types of backgrounds, whether familial, geographical, or professional.

not lost on me, and I feel . . . a sense of isolation, sometimes—not always."

Gains from public service

Many of the women legislators admitted to being reserved before taking office, but found that as the duties of office forced them into the public arena, they grew more comfortable speaking their opinions. A consequence of performing in their new position was a boost in self-confidence. The more they carried out their public responsibilities and duties of office, the more assertive they became in their advocacy. Representative Zamarripa acknowledged, "I was an introvert—very, very shy growing up. I was not the fourth grader that knew they were going to be president." Former Senator Robson spoke about how bashful she was before taking public office, saying, "I used to be very shy. In fact, in high school I could barely speak. I would turn red, beet red; I would stumble; I would not be able to put a coherent sentence together." Robson told us that after she entered public office, "I learned to be a much better speaker . . . to be a lot more confident. I've noticed that I can make decisions a lot quicker, that I can grasp a situation and figure out what the problem is and come up with some solutions." Robson went on to say, "I think women tend to not realize how many skills they have until the occasion arises or they see the problem, and all [of] the sudden it comes into place." Part of this newfound confidence is rooted in the legislators' knowledge that once in office, they speak on behalf of the people who live in their district, not just themselves. Representative Zamarripa described "[knowing] that the influence I wield is not just to benefit myself but to benefit my community and my district, where I was born and raised, I feel a tremendous amount of pride."

The opportunity to learn was another benefit legislators gained from their time in office. Representative Terese Berceau talked about the many roles a legislator plays, commenting, "You get a chance to be a teacher, a social worker, sometimes a star. You get to perform. If you're intellectually curious, there's a ton of interesting things to learn." One of the things that makes serving in the legislature unique is the diversity of subject areas with which one becomes acquainted, and the legislators told us how their time in office both spurred and sated their intellectual curiosity. As Representative Stuck said, "You learn a lot about so many different issues because there's so many things that come before you that you just don't necessarily deal with in your normal life." Former Senator Rosenzweig talked about how she was able to learn about "a whole wide world of things" and praised the state's legislative service agencies in aiding her education, saying, "[T]he service agencies in this state were just phenomenal—I mean everything from [the Legislative Reference Bureau] to [the Legislative] Council, Fiscal Bureau, and finally even the Audit Bureau were just treasures [from] which I learned so much. So when there was an issue, I really got the full understanding of everything."

Representative Kolste acknowledged how fortunate legislators are in the high quality of information they receive, saying, "I've learned more than I could ever share with anybody else. I think about pharmaceuticals in the waste water. Who else gets to go to a conference with experts and learn about pharmaceuticals in the waste water?" Representative Meyers talked about touring a plastics plant where they use robots to make medical molds and learning about barrels with cluster bombs in them that were dropped in Lake Superior during the Cold War; she asked, "Who knew I would be learning that type of stuff?" Representative Kerkman told us, "I have learned to ask a lot more questions, and that it's okay to ask questions and not be afraid to question why." Representative Felzkowski said, "One of the things that happens . . . when you get involved in public office, especially in the assembly, you are exposed to circumstances and issues and perspectives that you've never seen before. And I just think that that's a blessing."

Much of what these legislators have learned has been a product of their face-to-face interactions with their constituents. Senator Darling said, "Getting to meet a lot of nice people and getting to share with them, [by] being with them, some of their priorities and interests, I think that's been the best part." Representative Taylor expressed a similar sentiment, saying, "The best thing about my job is I get to meet amazing people. Like every day. There are amazing people all over the state, amazing people right in my community, that are

Face-to-face interaction with constituents is vital for any legislator to understand the needs of her community and to create opportunities for that community to thrive. *(top)* Representative Beth Meyers, shown at an event in Marengo, Wisconsin, spoke about the wealth of information she has been able to access by visiting areas around her district and the state. *(above)* By holding listening sessions in her district, Representative Mary Felzkowski has been exposed to new issues and perspectives she might never have encountered otherwise.

working every single day to bring about change, to improve our community, and I get to meet them, and I get to hear about what they're doing." Mastering these discussions highlights a skill that legislators said was a vital component of their job: the ability to listen. Former Representative Williams said, "I think I learned better how to communicate. But I turned into a real listener . . . I really listened when my constituents would have a problem. And constituents had said that. 'Just talk to Mary. She'll listen.'" Former Senate President Lazich said, "I don't believe that we're sent here to be a legislator. I think we're sent here to represent the constituents. And, to truly represent them, you have to listen to them—you have to know what's important to them."

Representative Shankland gained a sense of perspective from listening to the people she represents: "I can think of so many stories where people just started crying—grown men, old men, young women, teenagers—just a lot of stories. So that's been, really, just potent and powerful and incredible." Senator Johnson said, "Usually when people have issues, they always have solutions. And the best solutions aren't going to come from here in the capitol because this is not reality. The best solutions for those situations are going to come from the community, and I think that's the one perspective that I've learned." Representative Sargent said she is drawn into her district so that she "can have those conversations and I hear those voices and hear the stories, and I can bring that back and figure out what is working and what is not working. And that's actually where the legislation that I've passed has come from—conversations with people in my community. And that's exciting and that makes me feel proud."

Many of the women legislators said that they used these constituent interactions to determine what was needed in their districts so that they could use their office to provide assistance. Through public service, they gained the personal gratification one receives from helping others. A large facet of the job is helping constituents navigate the bureaucracy, what former Senator Lassa referred to as "constituent service." She explained, "I think most people think that the main part of the job is coming up with new legislation, but actually what my staff and I spend most of our time focusing on is constituent service—if someone's having an issue with one of the state agencies, or they need some sort of help where we act as their liaison in trying to find out what's happening with the state agency." Former Representative Strachota said, "With my constituents, I didn't realize how, when individuals are having difficulties or having trouble navigating the system, how much you can advocate for them and help them through the system. That was very rewarding to me." Senator Lassa referred to constituent service as the "real victories . . . that make you feel really good about the job you're doing." Senator Ringhand shared the following:

> I think the biggest thing for me is when we're able to help constituents—that's really important. In fact, before you came in today, I had two women come in, and one is a constituent and the other was a member of Gilda's

[Club]. I don't know if you're familiar with [Gilda's Club], but they help cancer victims, and my constituent is a cancer survivor. And she had a problem with her health insurance, and they got dropped, basically, because of a mix up in some payment, and so my staff was able to help her and get it straightened out with her husband's employer—got it all back on track—got their insurance back where it should be. She came in today to thank me and wanted a picture taken because she was so grateful, because the company told them it would take 60 days to straighten it all out; my staff intervened, [and] it was done in six days. So those are the rewarding moments, when things like that happen.

Finally, legislators said that they had gained a profound respect for the democratic process and a lasting appreciation of the complexity of the state and its people. Senator Shilling said, "I think I have gained an appreciation for ordinary people doing extraordinary things. I am inspired when I meet people who just are making a go of it, nothing really extraordinary about them, but they are doing extraordinary things." Representative Billings added, "When you think about it, there are only 99 of us [members of the 2015 assembly] in the state—this is a pretty incredible job." Representative Pope admitted, "This is the most frustrating job I've ever had. The most rewarding job I've ever had. The most interesting job I've ever had. And the job where I've felt like I was actually making a difference for people on a large scale." Representative Bernier said, "I've gained a feeling of satisfaction that I've been a part of something bigger than myself." Representative Brandtjen found that she has gained "an appreciation for the state, the different communities, of the different crops that they bring in, and the different specialties that they have, and the different places where they shine or maybe they have shortcomings—and probably a real appreciation for all the resources and all the jobs and all the people as far as the growth and development. It's just an amazing state." While reminiscing about her time in public office, former Senator Alice Clausing said, "I did have experiences that most people would have never had the opportunity to do. And as the memory fades as to the legislation and that kind of work, my memory still stays with the people and the things that I did for them and by them."

Advice to young women

Former Senator Harris Dodd recommended that "any woman who is considering a career in politics, at whatever level, my advice to them is to do it. Don't let anything hold you back. Don't let anyone tell you what you cannot do. And do it fearlessly." Many admitted, as Representative Rodriguez did, that "It is a difficult job, and it can be very demanding, and it can be high pressure." But none expressed regrets about running for or serving in the legislature. Representative Rodriguez added, "Helping people, constituents, it's awesome. It's awesome to see someone thank you for what you've done for them and it's gratifying . . . it's giving back to your community, [and] if you really like your community and you want to see positive changes in the state, then this is the way to do it. This is the job that can help you get there." Senator Bewley said she tells women who are interested in politics, "You will find a new world with new light and new opportunities and new things to learn that you never knew were there, and you will thrive."

Amy Loudenbeck

INSPIRING BY EXAMPLE

Representative Amy Loudenbeck, whose mother was a chemist, understands how important it is for young women to be inspired by examples of women in leadership or nontraditional roles:

"Dianne Hesselbein and I both hosted a Girl Scouts leadership day here at the capitol a few weeks ago. She asked me to do it; she really wanted it to be bipartisan. It's a busy time, it's all day on a Saturday, but I want to do that because I think it's still really important to expose women to other women that are in positions of leadership or power, because maybe they don't think of it as power in the best of ways. My mom, she wasn't baking cookies for my birthday, but she would come in and do science experiments in the classroom for us. She took me to see Geraldine Ferraro speak when I was younger, not because [she] was a Democrat, but just because she was a woman who was going to be on the ballot for a major political party. So those were the kind of things—you want to make sure people have the opportunity to see a role model that maybe looks like them. I used to teach fire prevention. October is fire prevention [month], and so we used to go around to schools, and we'd get the letters back, 'Thank you for coming to our school.' . . . They just thought it was neat because they had never seen a fire fighter that was a woman. Whereas now you see a little more diversity, more gender representation on TV and things like that."

Representative Amy Loudenbeck *(back row, left)* believes it is important for young women to see examples of women in leadership and makes time, even during her busiest periods, to meet with those young women in her community or at the capitol.

When discussing why fewer women than men pursue public office, several of the legislators suggested that women tend to believe that to be qualified to run, they need to have a wide breadth of knowledge and understanding of many topics. But as many women noted, this is not true; many legislators take advantage of the legislature's opportunities to learn about complex issues after they arrive in office. Representative Felzkowski said, "You can't always know everything about everything. Make sure you surround yourself with really good people. And if you don't know, that's okay. Tell people you don't know, but then you look into it. Don't try to have all the answers up front." Representative Bernier added, "I think women sometimes think, 'Well, you know, I have to know this, and I have to do that and whatever.' Men don't know it either. They're learning as they go. They don't know everything."

Representative Berceau advised, "If you think there's something you want to do, just start doing it and you will learn through doing." Many acknowledged the additional pressure women put on themselves in this regard. As Representative Shankland put it, "I've seen so many capable women, who do an outstanding job fighting for the average citizen of Wisconsin, turn it down because of fear that they weren't qualified enough."

The legislators also emphasized that women should not wait for the "perfect time" to jump into public service, because it might never come. Former Senator Lassa reflected, "For so many women, I think they decide, 'Well, I want to raise my kids, and then there will be time for that.' And I think that regardless, and for men as well, if you have the desire to [serve] and interest, and you want to give back, then maybe don't wait. Because we need people's perspectives regardless of [whether] there's someone who's younger or older and in-between, and that helps us make better policy. And I think that's valuable."

After encouraging women to run for office, many legislators went on to give advice on how to run an effective campaign. Legislators advised women to evaluate their beliefs and guiding principles before running for public office, in order to understand why they want to run. Representative Ballweg advised people to "know where you are, know what your goals are, know what you need to accomplish that." Senator Vukmir added, "Have a strong understanding [of] what your guiding principles are, because you'll be tested and pushed in many directions. And so if you have a firm set of what your principles are and if your people in your district elect you, meaning that they agree with that firm set of principles, then it's your responsibility to act on those." Representative Pope pointed out that candidates "just really need to know themselves and their inner core really well before they venture out to speak for 65,000 people." Senator Johnson concurred: "You have to know what you're running for. And you have to let that be your motivation. If I'm just running because I want to be in politics one day, that's not going to be enough to win a seat. But if I'm running because there's a serious issue that I want to address and I literally believe that the survival of my community and my family depends on it, you're not going to lose that race."

Other legislators offered practical advice on how to run a campaign, naming resources available to women candidates. A few that were cited include Emerge Wisconsin, Wisconsin Women in Government, and EMILY's List. Representative Felzkowski also suggested, "Take all the speech and communication classes you can." In addition to formal organizations, assistance can be found close to home. Representative Stuck suggested, "The best thing is to really find people in the community who are already doing it, other women who are already elected or have been elected in the past and get to know them and learn from them."

Another common piece of advice was that experience in local politics is an advantage when running for state office. Many noted that such experience gave them a good introduction to what running a campaign and being an elected official entailed. Some also pointed out that involvement in one's local community can lead to valuable relationships and resources that are helpful when running a state campaign. Representative Stuck advised:

> Just getting involved in the community so you really understand the issues. I've done everything from volunteering at animal shelters to volunteering in my kids' schools to serving on boards in the community. That really gave me a good sense of what was going on in the community so that when it came time to run I had connections, first of all—I knew people in the community—but I also knew what was going on, what people were worried about, so when I showed up at their door, I knew how to respond. I knew how to talk to people about what was going on because [of] having been involved.

Representative Billings agreed:

Look at local office; starting on [the] school board, county board, city council, is great experience for this job, because you learn about so many issues and you learn about simple things like parliamentary procedure and advocating for people in your district—and your district is smaller. I encourage [women] to run for local office and feel like they can get a taste for knocking on doors and all of that. If they enjoy that, then think about the next step. And also, local office is so important . . . I would say, just be involved in your community. Learn about what's important in your community. Learn about the culture of your community, the history of your community. What kind of people live there? What makes your community run? And then, don't

Representative Jill Billings, shown in 2011 in her home district of La Crosse, encourages young women to run for local office to experience not only campaigning but also the day-to-day procedures of holding office itself.

be afraid to jump in. If that's what you want to do, don't be afraid to jump in. You're as good as anybody else.

Every woman legislator had positive advice for young women thinking about pursuing public office. They encouraged women to not let anything hold them back and to believe in themselves: to believe that they are qualified enough and smart enough, have enough life experience, and have something valuable to offer. Senator Darling stated: "We have one of the best and biggest experiments with humanity in terms of the opportunity that our form of government offers . . . it is a very unique position in the world, and I would encourage people to become a part of that." Representative Hesselbein noted the importance of running even if you lose. She said, "I always tell them to absolutely do it. Win or lose. I've won and I've lost, and it's not easy to lose, but it's so worth doing. And I learned so much about myself in the process, even in that failed election." Former Senator Harris Dodd captured all of these sentiments:

> Don't underestimate the experiences you've already had, your talents, what you bring to the table. And be unapologetic about it, I guess, is really the word. If I'm going to encompass all that: be unapologetic about wanting to be a woman in politics. It is okay, you're supposed to be here. You deserve to be here. In fact, the legislature is better when women are in the room. When we're here serving our community, we're making such a difference that it's a better place to be, for everybody, whether it's acknowledged or not. Own the space, own the room, be who you are going to be. ⯑

Elections in Wisconsin

Purposes and days

Wisconsin holds elections for a variety of purposes and, depending on the purpose, on a variety of days.

FILLING THE STATE'S ELECTIVE OFFICES

To fill its elective offices, Wisconsin holds elections on four regular election days.

The general election. On the Tuesday after the first Monday in November of every even-numbered year, Wisconsin elects individuals to fill its partisan elective offices. The elections held on this day are referred to collectively as the "general election."

The partisan offices in Wisconsin are: U.S. senator, U.S. representative, state senator, state representative, governor, lieutenant governor, attorney general, secretary of state, state treasurer, and the county-level offices of district attorney, county clerk, sheriff, clerk of circuit court, register of deeds, treasurer, coroner (in counties that have one), and surveyor (in counties in which the office is elective).

The voters of the entire state elect Wisconsin's U.S. senators, governor, lieutenant governor, attorney general, secretary of state, and state treasurer. The voters of each congressional, senate, and assembly district elect that district's U.S. representative, state senator, or state representative. The voters of each county elect that county's clerk, sheriff, clerk of circuit court, register of deeds, treasurer, coroner, and surveyor and the district attorney for the prosecutorial unit serving the county. (For the prosecutorial unit that serves Menominee and Shawano counties, the voters of both counties elect the district attorney.)

The terms of office for the partisan offices are not all the same length and do not all expire on the same day or in the same year. Accordingly, only some of the partisan offices will be up for election at any particular general election—those, namely, for which the currently running term of office will expire before the next general election is held.

The ballot at each general election lists the offices that are up for election and, under each office, the candidates for the office who have qualified to be listed. Next to each candidate's name, the ballot lists the name of the political party or the principle that the candidate represents.

An individual who wishes to be listed as a candidate on the ballot must file, no later than the June 1 preceding the general election, 1) a declaration of candidacy indicating the office that the individual seeks and the political party or the principle that he or she proposes to represent and 2) nomination papers signed by a prescribed number of voters residing in the governmental jurisdiction or election district that the office serves. In addition, the individual must win a partisan primary election if he or she proposes to represent one of the "recognized" political parties (see below). By contrast, an individual who does not propose to represent a recognized political party will be listed on the general election ballot without participating in a partisan primary election. Such an individual is called an "independent candidate." (In fact, many independent candidates specifically use the term "Independent" in their declarations of candidacy.)

The candidate who receives the most votes cast for a particular office at the general election fills that office when the currently running term of office expires.

The partisan primary. Prior to the general election, on the second Tuesday in August of every even-numbered year, Wisconsin holds primary elections to select the individuals who will be listed on the general election ballot as the candidates of the "recognized" political parties. The elections held on this day are referred to collectively as the "partisan primary."

A political party qualifies as a recognized political party in one of three situations:

- A candidate of the political party won at least 1 percent of the votes cast in Wisconsin, either for a statewide office at the last general election at which the office of governor was up for election, or for U.S. president at the most recent general election; and the political party was a recognized political party for that election.

- An individual representing the political party as an independent candidate won at least 1 percent of the votes cast in Wisconsin, either for a statewide office at the last general election at which the office of governor was up for election, or for U.S. president at the most recent general election; and the political party requests recognized status no later than the April 1 preceding the partisan primary.

- The political party submits, no later than the April 1 preceding the partisan primary, a petition requesting recognized status signed by at least 10,000 Wisconsin voters, including at least 1,000 from each of at least three congressional districts.

A separate primary ballot is prepared for each recognized political party. Each party's ballot lists all of the offices that will be filled at the general election and, under each office, the individuals, if any, who have filed to be candidates for the office and have proposed, in their declarations of candidacy, to represent the party.

A voter at the partisan primary is given a ballot for each of the recognized political parties but can vote on just one of them. The voter can pick any party's ballot for this purpose—voters in Wisconsin are not asked to declare a party affiliation when registering or voting and are not obliged in any other way to pick a particular party's ballot. However, if a voter votes on the ballots of more than one party, none of the voter's votes will be counted.

The individual who receives the most votes cast for a particular office on the ballots of a particular party is selected thereby as that party's candidate for that office at the general election, and his or her name, together with the party's name, will be listed under the office on the general election ballot.

The partisan primary is the exclusive means by which a recognized political party can select a candidate to be listed on the general election ballot. The party must accept as its candidate the individual selected by the voters who vote its ballots. Moreover, if no individual is listed under a particular office on a party's partisan primary ballot (because no one who filed to be a candidate for the office proposed to represent that party), the party will not have a candidate for that office listed on the general election ballot.

The spring election. On the first Tuesday in April of every year, Wisconsin elects individuals to fill its nonpartisan elective offices. The elections held on this day are referred to collectively as the "spring election."

The nonpartisan offices in Wisconsin are: state superintendent of public instruction; supreme court justice; court of appeals judge; circuit court judge; county executive (in counties that have one); county supervisor; county comptroller (in Milwaukee); every elective town, village, and city office; and school board member.

The voters of the entire state elect Wisconsin's state superintendent of public instruction and supreme court justices. The voters of each court of appeals district elect that district's judges. The voters of each county elect the county's county executive (if any) and county comptroller (in Milwaukee) and the circuit court judges for the circuit that serves the county. (For circuits that serve two counties, the voters of both counties elect the circuit court judges.) The voters of each county supervisory district elect that district's county supervisor. The voters of each town elect that town's officers. Village trustees and city alders can be elected at large by the voters of the entire village or city or from election districts by the voters residing in each election district. All other village and city officers are elected at large by the voters of the entire village or city. School board members can be elected at large by the voters of the entire school district; from election districts by the voters residing in each election district; or from election districts by the voters of the entire school district.

Just as with the partisan offices, the terms of office for the nonpartisan offices are not all the same length and do not all expire on the same day or in the same year. At each spring election, accordingly, only those nonpartisan offices are up for election for which the currently running term of office will expire before the next spring election is held.

The ballot at each spring election lists the offices that are up for election and, under each office, the candidates for the office who have qualified to be listed. Ordinarily, no more than two candidates can be listed. The situation is different, however, when multiple, undifferentiated instances of the same office exist in a particular governmental jurisdiction or election district. In many villages, for example, the trustees who make up the village board are elected at large rather than from election districts, and no distinction is made between the "seat" occupied by one trustee and the "seat" occupied by another. In this situation, the ballot can list up to twice as many candidates for an office as the number of seats to be filled. (The ballot would also include an instruction to vote for no more of those candidates than the number of seats to be filled.)

An individual who wishes to be listed as a candidate on the ballot must file, no later than the first Tuesday in the January preceding the spring election, 1) a declaration of candidacy indicating the office that the individual seeks and 2) nomination papers signed by a prescribed number of voters residing in the governmental jurisdiction or election district that the office serves. In addition, the individual must win a spring primary election (see below) if the total number of individuals who file to be candidates for the office is more than two (or, if applicable, is more than twice the number of seats to be filled). By contrast, if the total number of individuals is less than two (or is less than twice the number of seats to be filled), each individual will be listed on the spring election ballot without participating in a spring primary election.[1]

The candidate who receives the most votes cast for a particular office at the spring election fills that office when the currently running term of office expires. (Or, if multiple seats are to be filled for a particular office, the candidates equal in number to the number of those seats who receive the most votes fill those seats when the currently running term of office expires.)

The spring primary. Prior to the spring election, on the third Tuesday in February of every year, Wisconsin holds primary elections to select, for some of the offices that will be filled at the spring election, the individuals who will be listed as candidates on the spring election ballot. The elections held on this day are referred to collectively as the "spring primary."

The ballot at the spring primary lists only those offices for which more than two individuals (or, if applicable, more individuals than twice the number of seats to be filled) have filed to be candidates and, under each office, the individuals who have filed to be candidates for the office. (The ballot also includes for each office an instruction to vote for not more than two individuals or for not more than twice as many individuals as the number of seats to be filled.)

The two individuals (or the individuals equal in number to twice the number of seats to be filled) who receive the most votes cast for an office at a spring primary election will be listed as the candidates for that office on the spring election ballot.

ELECTING THE U.S. PRESIDENT AND VICE PRESIDENT

As part of the process by which the United States elects its president and vice president, Wisconsin holds two elections, each on one of the regular election days just discussed.

At the general election. On the day of the general election, in presidential election years, Wisconsin elects the slate of presidential electors that will be its delegation to the Electoral College, the nationwide body that actually elects the U.S. president and vice president.

The ballot at the general election does not list slates of would-be presidential electors. Rather, it lists the pairs of candidates who are running together, one for president and one for vice president, and who have qualified to be listed. Each of these candidate pairs has its own slate of would-be presidential electors; and a vote cast for a candidate pair is simultaneously a vote cast for its slate.

A pair of individuals can qualify to be listed on the general election ballot as candidates for U.S. president and vice president in two ways. They can be selected by a recognized political party (see above, page 362) to be its candidates. Each recognized political party selects its candidates at a national convention of party members conducted according to rules that the party determines for itself. The pair of individuals that a recognized political party selects will be listed on the general election ballot if 1) the party's state or national chair certifies to the Elections Commission, no later than the first Tuesday in the September preceding the general election, that the individuals are the party's candidates, and 2) each of the individuals files a declaration of candidacy with the Elections Commission by the same deadline.

Alternatively, a pair of individuals can qualify to be listed as independent candidates. To do this, each of the individuals must file with the Elections Commission, no later than the first Tuesday in the August preceding the general election, a declaration of candidacy indicating the office that he or she seeks and the political party or principle that he or she proposes to represent; and the two individuals jointly must file nomination papers nominating them as a pair and signed by a prescribed number of Wisconsin voters.

The slate of presidential electors for each candidate pair must consist of ten individuals, one from each of Wisconsin's eight congressional districts and two more from anywhere in the state.

A slate can be determined in two ways. For the candidates of the recognized political parties, the slates are determined at a special convention held at the state capitol on the first Tuesday in the October preceding the general election. The convention consists of certain officials holding partisan elective offices in state government—the governor, lieutenant governor, attorney general, secretary of state, state treasurer, and those state senators whose seats are not up for election—together with the individuals who will be listed on the general election ballot as the candidates of the recognized political parties for the offices of state senator and state representative. The convention participants meet separately according to the parties they belong to, and each party designates a slate of presidential electors for its pair of candidates for president and vice president. The state chair of each party then certifies that party's slate to the Election Commission.

By contrast, each pair of independent candidates for U.S. president and vice president designates its own slate of presidential electors in its nomination papers.

The slate of presidential electors of the candidate pair that wins the most votes at Wisconsin's general election becomes Wisconsin's delegation to the Electoral College. On the first Monday after the second Wednesday in the December following the general election, this delegation assembles in the state capitol and casts its votes as members of that body.

At the spring election. On the day of the spring election, in presidential election years, Wisconsin conducts its presidential preference primary.

This primary is advisory, rather than binding. Wisconsin's voters indicate which individual they would like a political party to select as its candidate for U.S. president, but Wisconsin law does not require the party's Wisconsin members to vote for that individual at the party's national convention. Rather, the party conducts its convention according to rules that it determines for itself, and it can select its presidential candidate using any mechanism it chooses.

A political party qualifies to participate in Wisconsin's presidential preference primary only if 1) it was a recognized political party (see above, page 362) at Wisconsin's last general election; 2) it had a candidate for governor at that election, and that candidate won at least 10 percent of the votes cast for that office; and 3) its state chair certifies to the Elections Commission, no later than the second Tuesday in the December preceding the presidential preference primary, that the party will participate.

A separate presidential preference primary ballot is prepared for each participating political party. Each party's ballot lists the individuals who wish to be selected as the party's candidate for president and have qualified to be listed.

An individual can qualify to be listed on a party's presidential preference primary ballot in two ways. The individual can be certified by a special committee that meets in the state capitol on the first Tuesday in the January preceding the presidential preference primary. This committee consists of the state chair, one national committeeman, and one national committeewoman of each participating political party; the speaker and the minority leader of the state assembly; the president and the minority leader of the state senate; and an additional member selected by the rest of the committee to be its chair. The committee identifies, for each of the participating political parties, the individuals who are generally recognized in the national media as the party's candidates for U.S. president and any additional individuals that the committee believes should be listed as candidates on the party's ballot. The committee then certifies these candidates to the Elections Commission.

Alternatively, an individual can submit to the Elections Commission, no later than the last Tuesday in January, a petition requesting to be listed as a candidate on a party's ballot. The petition must be signed by a prescribed number of voters from each of Wisconsin's congressional districts.

A voter at the spring election is given a presidential preference primary ballot for each of the participating political parties but can vote on just one of them. As at the partisan primary, the voter can pick any party's ballot to vote on and is not obliged, based on party affiliation or any other criteria, to pick the ballot of a particular party.

FILLING A MIDTERM VACANCY

A "special election" can be held to fill a midterm vacancy in certain elective offices. This kind of election can be held on one of the four regular election days or on a different day.

A vacancy in the office of U.S. senator, U.S. representative, state senator, or state representative can be filled only by a special election called by the governor. A vacancy in the office of attorney general, state superintendent of public instruction, secretary of state, or state treasurer can be filled either by a special election called by the governor, if the vacancy occurs more than six months before the term of office expires, or by appointment by the governor, regardless when the vacancy occurs. (A vacancy in the office of supreme court justice, court of appeals judge, circuit court judge, district attorney, sheriff, coroner, or register of deeds can be filled only by appointment by the governor.)

In some county and municipal offices, a vacancy can be filled either by a special election or by appointment, at the discretion of the local governing body.

An individual who wishes to be listed as a candidate on a special election ballot must file a declaration of candidacy and nomination papers and must also win a special primary election if one is required. For a partisan office, a special primary must be held for each of the recognized political parties if it is the case for any one of them that two or more individuals have proposed in their declarations of candidacy to represent it. For a nonpartisan office, a special primary must be held if three or more individuals file to be candidates.

RECALLING AN ELECTED OFFICIAL FROM OFFICE

A "recall election" can be held to decide whether an elected official will be recalled from office before his or her term of office expires and, if so, who will serve in his or her place for the remainder of the term. This kind of election can be held on one of the four regular election days or on a different day. However, a recall election cannot be held before an official has served one year of his or her term. In addition, no more than one recall election can be held for the same official during a single term of office.

A recall election is held only if voters of the governmental jurisdiction or election district that elected an official file a petition to recall the official. The petition must be signed by a number of voters equal to at least 25 percent of the vote cast for governor in the jurisdiction or district at the last election for governor. In addition, if the petition seeks the recall of a city, village, town, or school district official, it must assert a reason that is related to the duties of the office.

Other than the official named in the recall petition, an individual who wishes to be listed as a candidate on a recall election ballot must file a declaration of candidacy and nomination papers and might also have to win a recall primary election if one is required. The official named in the recall petition might similarly have to win a recall primary but otherwise will be listed on the recall election ballot automatically (unless he or she resigns).

For a partisan office, a recall primary must be held for each recognized political party for which it is the case that two or more individuals (who might include the official named in the recall petition) seek to be listed as its candidate on the recall election ballot. (If only one individual seeks to be listed as a party's candidate, the individual will be listed as such without a primary being held for that party.)

For a nonpartisan office, a recall primary must be held if three or more individuals (who might include the official named in the recall petition) seek to be listed as candidates on the recall election ballot. In contrast to other nonpartisan primaries, if one individual receives over 50 percent of the votes cast at the recall primary, no further election is held, and that individual fills the office for the remaining term.

APPROVING OR REJECTING A PROPOSAL

A "referendum" can be held in Wisconsin to approve or reject a proposal (rather than to choose an individual to fill an office). This kind of election can be held on one of the four regular election days or on a different day.

A referendum can be binding or nonbinding. In the one case, a proposal is implemented automatically if approved by a majority of the voters voting at the referendum; in the other, the voters' approval or rejection is merely advisory.

At the state level, Wisconsin holds binding referenda on proposals 1) to amend the state constitution; 2) to extend the right to vote; and 3) to permit an act of the legislature to take effect in cases in which the legislature has provided that the act's taking effect is contingent upon voter approval.

A referendum ballot presents the referendum proposal in the form of a yes-or-no question, and the voter votes the ballot by marking "yes" or "no." The question on the ballot summarizes the effect of the proposal. The full text of the proposal along with an explanation of its effect must be posted at the polling place.

Administration

The responsibility for administering elections is distributed across several levels of government.

Elections Commission. The state Elections Commission oversees and facilitates the performance of elections-related functions by officials at lower levels of government. The commission:

- Determines the format that must be used for ballots.
- Certifies all equipment and materials used to record votes at elections.
- Trains and certifies officials at lower levels of government.
- Maintains the electronic statewide voter registration list.

The Elections Commission also performs certain functions related to state and national elections. The commission:

- Determines which candidates for elective offices in state and national government qualify to be listed on the ballot. Such candidates must file with the commission their declarations of candidacy, nomination papers, and other documents that demonstrate that they are qualified.
- Tabulates the votes cast in the state at each election held to fill an office in state or national government or to vote on a state referendum.

County clerk. The county clerk performs certain functions related to county, state, and national elections. (In Wisconsin's most populous county, Milwaukee, a special commission performs these functions instead.) The county clerk:

- Determines which candidates for elective offices in county government qualify to be listed on the ballot. Such candidates must file with the county clerk their declarations of candidacy, nomination papers, and other documents that demonstrate that they are qualified.
- Prepares the ballots for elections held to fill offices in county, state, and national government and to vote on county and state referenda and distributes these ballots to the municipalities (cities, villages, and towns) located within the county.
- Processes voter registrations for county residents who ask to register at the county clerk's office and forwards the information obtained to the municipal clerk of the municipality in which the registrant resides so that the municipal clerk can update the electronic statewide registration list. (In some cases, a county clerk, by agreement with a municipal clerk, acts in place of the municipal clerk as that clerk's agent for the performance of all registration functions, including updating the statewide registration list.)
- Tabulates the votes cast in the county at each election held to fill an office in county, state, or national government or to vote on a county or state referendum.

- Reports to the Elections Commission the votes cast in the county related to a state or national election.

Municipal clerk. The municipal clerk—i.e., the city, village, or town clerk—performs certain functions related to municipal, county, state, and national elections. (In Wisconsin's most populous city, Milwaukee, a special commission performs these functions instead.) The municipal clerk:

- Determines which candidates for elective offices in municipal government qualify to be listed on the ballot. Such candidates must file with the municipal clerk their declarations of candidacy, nomination papers, and other documents to demonstrate that they are qualified.

- Prepares the ballots for elections held to fill offices in municipal government and to vote on municipal referenda.

- Processes voter registrations for residents of the municipality and updates the electronic statewide registration list to reflect the information obtained.

- Provides the ballots for each election to the voters who desire to vote; and receives the ballots back from those voters when they cast them. Only the municipal clerk provides ballots to voters and receives cast ballots back; county clerks and the Elections Commission do not.

- Operates polling places in the municipality on the day of an election. Only the municipal clerk operates polling places; county clerks and the Elections Commission do not.

- Tabulates the votes cast in the municipality at each election held to fill an office in municipal, county, state, or national government or to vote on a municipal, county, or state referendum.

- Reports to the county clerk of each county in which the municipality is located the votes cast in the municipality related to a county, state, or national election.

The municipal clerk also handles most matters related to elections held by school districts that are located in whole or part within the municipality. However, the school district clerk determines which candidates for school district elective offices qualify to be listed on the ballot, and such candidates must file with the school district clerk their declarations of candidacy, nomination papers, and other documents to demonstrate that they are qualified.

Voting

Eligibility. To vote at an election in Wisconsin, an individual must be a U.S. citizen, must be 18 years of age or older, and must reside in the governmental jurisdiction or election district for which the election is held. For example, an individual must reside in a particular county to vote at an election held to elect that county's sheriff; and must reside in a particular supervisory district within the county to vote at an election held to elect that district's member of the county board of supervisors.

To establish residence for voting purposes, an individual must reside at the same address for the ten days[2] preceding the election at which he or she wishes to vote.

An individual who has moved to a new address in Wisconsin during the ten days preceding an election but who had resided at his or her former address for the ten days preceding the move is considered to reside at the former address for that election. He or she can vote at the election only if the former address is located within the governmental jurisdiction or election district for which the election is held.

An individual who has resided in Wisconsin for less than ten days but who is otherwise eligible to vote can vote for U.S. president and vice president only, under a special procedure.

Certain individuals are not eligible to vote at any election:

- An individual who has been convicted of treason, felony, or bribery, unless the individual has been pardoned or has completed his or her sentence (including any parole, probation, or extended supervision) for the crime.
- An individual who has been adjudicated incompetent by a court, unless the court has determined that the individual is competent to exercise the right to vote.

In addition, an individual is not eligible to vote at a particular election if the individual has bet upon the result of the election.

Registration. With limited exceptions, an eligible voter must register to vote before he or she will be allowed to vote. Registration is the means by which an individual demonstrates that he or she is eligible to vote.

To register, an individual must fill out, sign, and submit a registration form and present acceptable proof of residence.

On the registration form, the individual must:

- Provide his or her name and date of birth; current address; previous address; and the number and expiration date of his or her Wisconsin driver's license or identification card, if any, or the last four digits of his or her social security number, if any.
- Indicate whether he or she has been convicted of a felony for which he or she has not been pardoned and, if so, whether he or she is incarcerated or on parole, probation, or extended supervision.

- Indicate whether he or she is currently registered to vote at an address other than the current one.
- Certify that he or she is a U.S. citizen, will be 18 years of age or over on the day of the next election, and will have resided at his or her current address for the ten days preceding that day.

Registrants are not asked to indicate a political party affiliation.

Documents that qualify as proof of residence include:

- A current and valid Wisconsin driver's license or identification card.
- A student identification card accompanied by a fee receipt dated within the preceding nine months.
- A property tax bill for the current or previous year.
- A bank statement.
- A utility bill for a period beginning no earlier than 90 days before the next election.

Through the third Wednesday preceding an election, an eligible voter can register in person at the office of the municipal clerk or county clerk, by mail with the municipal clerk, or via an electronic registration system maintained by the Elections Commission and accessible at the website myvote.wi.gov.[3] After that Wednesday and through the Friday preceding the election, an eligible voter can register only in person at the office of the municipal clerk (or of the county clerk, if acting as the municipal clerk's agent for registration purposes). After that Friday, an eligible voter who still has not registered and who wishes to vote at the election must register on the day of the election at his or her polling place.

The Elections Commission maintains an electronic list of all eligible voters who are registered to vote in Wisconsin. Every municipal clerk (or county clerk acting as the agent of a municipal clerk) who processes a registration for an eligible voter must update the list (via an interface provided by the Elections Commission) to reflect the information obtained. The list updates automatically to reflect registrations submitted via the electronic registration system. The list also updates automatically to reflect information reported by the Department of Corrections about individuals who have been convicted of a felony (and are thus ineligible to vote), including the dates they are expected to complete their sentences.

An individual who has registered once does not need to register again, unless the individual changes his or her name or address. However, an individual's registration can be canceled if the individual has not voted for four years and fails to respond to a mailed postcard that asks whether he or she wishes to continue his or her registration. (The Elections Commission sends out the postcards to such voters every two years.)

Military voters and their families who are residents of Wisconsin but are away from home by reason of active duty are not required to register prior to voting. In addition, an individual who has resided in Wisconsin for less than ten days, but who is otherwise eligible to vote, can vote for U.S. president and vice president without being registered. Similarly, a former Wisconsin resident who has moved to another state and is not eligible to vote in the new state can, if he or she is otherwise eligible to vote, vote a Wisconsin absentee ballot for U.S. president and vice president without being registered, during the 24 months after the move.

Voter registration information is generally open to public inspection. However, voters who are victims of certain crimes, such as domestic abuse, sexual assault, and stalking, can request confidential voter status. If a voter qualifies for this status, the municipal clerk updates the electronic statewide registration list to indicate that the voter's registration must be kept confidential and issues a confidential voter identification card to the voter.

Photo identification. With few exceptions,[4] a registered voter (or an eligible voter exempt from registration) who wishes to vote at an election in Wisconsin must present acceptable proof of identification in order to obtain a ballot. In most cases, photo identification is required. Acceptable forms of photo identification include:

- A Wisconsin driver's license or identification card issued by the Wisconsin Department of Transportation.
- A U.S. passport.
- A Veterans Affairs identification card.
- A photo identification card issued by a Wisconsin accredited university, college, or technical college, if certain conditions are satisfied.

Individuals who have a religious objection to being photographed can obtain and present a Wisconsin identification card issued without a photo. In addition, an individual who has had to surrender his or her driver's license to a law enforcement officer within 60 days of the election can present in place of the driver's license the citation or notice that he or she received. A confidential voter can present his or her confidential voter identification card instead of photo identification.

Voting at a polling place. Polling places are operated by the municipal clerk and are open for voting only on the day of an election. Each address in a municipality is served by a designated polling place, and a voter can vote only at the polling place that serves his or her address. (If a registered voter has moved within Wisconsin during the ten days preceding an election, he or she is considered to reside at his or her former address for that election and can vote only at the polling place that serves the former address.) Each polling place is staffed by poll workers who have been trained by the municipal clerk. Each polling place is supplied with duplicate "poll lists" (which are generated from the electronic statewide registration list) of all eligible voters served by the polling place who had registered before the day of the election. Each polling place is also supplied with ballots that are specific to the elections at which voters served by the polling place are eligible to vote.

When an individual comes to a polling place to vote, a poll worker asks him or her to state his or her name and address and to present proof of identification. (A confidential voter can present his or her confidential voter identification card without stating anything or can state just his or her name and the serial number of the card without presenting anything.) A poll worker confirms that the individual's name and address are listed in the poll list, that the name on the proof of identification is consistent with the name on the poll list, and that any photograph on the proof of identification reasonably resembles the individual.[5] The individual is then required to sign the poll list, unless he or she cannot sign due to a physical disability.

Following these preliminaries, the individual is assigned a voter number. A poll worker writes the voter number on the poll list, gives the individual a slip of paper that has the voter number on it, and directs the individual to take the voter number slip to another poll worker, who gives the individual, in exchange for the voter number slip, a paper ballot or a card that will permit the voter to access an electronic ballot on a voting machine.

The voter takes the ballot or card to a voting booth and marks the paper ballot, or marks an electronic ballot via an interface on a voting machine, to indicate his or her votes. After marking a paper ballot, the voter casts it by depositing it through a slot into a locked ballot box or by feeding it into an optical scanning machine. (An optical scanning machine reads and tabulates electronically the votes marked on a paper ballot and stores the ballot in a locked compartment.) After marking an electronic ballot, the voter verifies a record of his or her votes that the voting machine prints on a paper tape, then casts the ballot by giving a direction via the machine's interface. (The voting machine records the voter's votes in its electronic memory, tabulates them electronically, and advances the paper tape so that the record of the voter's votes is stored within a locked compartment.)

Voting by absentee ballot. A registered voter who is unwilling or unable to vote at his or her polling place on the day of an election can vote by absentee ballot instead.

To obtain an absentee ballot, the voter must submit a written request to the municipal clerk. This can be done in person at the clerk's office or at an alternate site designated by the clerk. It can also be done by mail, email, or fax. The general deadline is the Thursday preceding the election.

An in-person requester must present acceptable proof of identification to the municipal clerk or an individual designated by the clerk before he or she will be issued a ballot. Most other requesters must submit a copy of their proof of identification with their request for a ballot.[6]

To cast an absentee ballot, the voter must mark his or her votes on the ballot and seal the marked ballot in a special envelope that is provided with the ballot. The voter must take these actions in the presence of a witness who is an adult U.S. citizen. The voter must also show the unmarked ballot to the witness prior to marking it and must make sure that no one, including the witness, sees the votes that he or she marks. After the ballot is sealed in the special envelope, the voter and the witness must sign a certification that is printed on the special envelope—the voter to attest that he or she is eligible to vote the ballot, will not cast any other ballot at the election, and followed the required procedures in voting the ballot; and the witness to attest that he or she is an adult U.S. citizen and that the voter followed the required procedures in voting the ballot. If the ballot was requested in person, the voter must return it before leaving the municipal clerk's office or alternate site. In these cases, the municipal clerk or an individual designated by the clerk serves as the witness. If the ballot was requested in another way, the voter must seal the special envelope containing the ballot in a second envelope[7] and either mail it or deliver it in person to the municipal clerk so that it is received by the municipal clerk no later than the day of the election.

Campaign finance regulation

Wisconsin regulates campaign finance—the spending of money on campaigning and the giving of money to others to spend on campaigning—in several ways:

- Only a particular kind of entity, called a "committee," is allowed to use money that it has accepted from others to engage in campaign spending and campaign giving. If the amount of money exceeds a specified threshold, a committee must register and file reports of its financial activity.[8]

- Limits are placed on who can give money to a committee and how much money can be given.
- Limits are also placed on some campaign spending, and some campaign spending is subject to special disclosure requirements.

Three kinds of campaigning are covered by the regulations: express advocacy related to a candidate for elective office in state or local government;[9] campaigning related to a state or local referendum question; and campaigning related to the recall of an elected official in state or local government.[10]

COMMITTEES

A "committee" is a group of two or more individuals that comes together, or an organization that is established, specifically for the purpose of accepting money from others[11] and using the money for campaign spending and campaign giving. An entity that is not formed specifically for that purpose—for example, a business or a social club—cannot accept money from others to use for campaign spending or campaign giving; and neither can an individual acting alone. However, such an entity or individual could set up a committee as a separate entity that would be able to do those things.

Registration. A committee must register with a state or local filing officer before it accepts or disburses money above a specified threshold. Wisconsin's regulations distinguish seven types of committee (described in a moment), and specify a different threshold for each type. When a committee registers, it must identify the type of committee it is. It must also identify a single depository account that it will use to accept and disburse money and an individual who will be in charge of the account.

A "candidate committee" is a committee formed by a candidate to campaign for his or her election. A candidate cannot accept or disburse any money except through his or her candidate committee. In addition, a candidate can have only one candidate committee for any one office that he or she seeks. However, the candidate can be the individual in charge of the candidate committee depository account. (For that matter, the candidate can be the sole member of the candidate committee—an exception to the rule that a committee consists of two or more individuals.) A candidate's candidate committee must register with the appropriate filing officer[12] as soon as the candidate qualifies to be considered a candidate.[13]

A "political party" is a committee that qualifies for a separate partisan primary ballot—i.e., it is a "recognized" political party. (See page 362, above.) Local affiliates of a recognized political party that are authorized to operate under the same name are also considered political parties. A political party must register with the Ethics Commission before it accepts or disburses any money in a calendar year. (An entity that calls itself a political party, but that does not meet the criteria just described, would have to register as a different type of committee.)

A "legislative campaign committee" is a committee that is formed by state senators or state representatives of a particular political party to support candidates for legislative office (by engaging in express advocacy on their behalf and by giving money to their candidate committees). A legislative campaign committee must register with the Ethics Commission before it accepts or disburses any money in a calendar year.

A "political action committee," or "PAC," is a committee, other than a candidate committee, political party, or legislative campaign committee, that 1) is formed to engage in express advocacy; 2) might do this independently or in coordination with a candidate, candidate committee, political party, or legislative campaign committee;[14] 3) might also campaign for and against referenda; and 4) might also give money to other committees. A PAC must register with the Ethics Commission if it accepts or disburses more than $2,500 in a calendar year.

An "independent expenditure committee," or "IEC," is a committee, other than a candidate committee, political party, or legislative campaign committee, that 1) is formed to engage in express advocacy; 2) will do this independently only and not in coordination with a candidate, candidate committee, political party, or legislative campaign committee; 3) might also campaign for and against referenda; and 4) might also give money to other committees, but will not give money to a candidate committee or to a committee that is able to give the money subsequently to a candidate committee. An IEC must register with the Ethics Commission if it accepts or disburses more than $2,500 in a calendar year.

A "referendum committee" is a committee that 1) is formed specifically to campaign for or against a referendum and 2) will not attempt to influence how voters vote with respect to a candidate. A referendum committee must register with the appropriate filing officer[15] if it accepts or disburses more than $10,000 in a calendar year.

A "recall committee" is a committee that is formed specifically to campaign for or against the recall of an elected official, including by appealing to voters to sign or not sign the petition that is required to bring about a recall election. A recall committee must register with the appropriate filing officer[16] if it accepts or disburses more than $2,000 in a calendar year.

Reporting financial activity. Each registered committee must file with its filing officer regular reports of its financial activity. Reports are due every January 15 and July 15. A report is also due on the fourth Tuesday in September of an even-numbered year if a committee accepts or disburses money for campaigning related to a partisan office (or to a referendum that will be held on the day of the partisan primary or general election). Other reports are required in advance of each primary and election with respect to which a committee accepts or disburses money. All of a committee's reports are made public within two days of their filing.

Each report must include, among other things:

- A listing of each gift of money received from an individual, specifying the amount and date of the gift and the name and address of the individual.
- A listing of each gift of money received from a committee, specifying the amount and date of the gift and the name and address of the committee.
- A listing of any other income received from any source, specifying the amount, date, and type of the income and the name and address of the source.
- A listing of each gift of money given to another committee, specifying the amount and date of the gift and the name and address of the committee.
- A listing of each other disbursement of money made to any individual or entity, specifying the amount, date, and purpose of the disbursement and the name and address of the individual or entity.

CAMPAIGN GIVING LIMITS

Campaign giving consists of giving money to a committee (necessarily, since an entity that is not a committee cannot use money given by others for campaigning). Wisconsin's regulations place limits on who can give money to a committee and how much money can be given. The limits apply simultaneously to the giver and the recipient; both are guilty if the latter accepts a gift that violates a limit.

Generally, only individuals and committees are allowed to give money to a committee. However, corporations, labor organizations, cooperative associations, and federally recognized American Indian tribes can also give money in certain cases (but not to a candidate committee and not to a committee that is able to give the money subsequently to a candidate committee).

Giving to a candidate committee. An individual can give up to $20,000 to the candidate committee of a candidate for a statewide office (governor, lieutenant governor, attorney general, superintendent of public instruction, secretary of state, state treasurer, or supreme court justice). Other limits apply to other offices, including $2,000 for state senator and $1,000 for state representative.

A candidate committee can give to another candidate committee up to the same amount as an individual can give. (But the candidate committees of candidates who are running together for governor and lieutenant governor can give unlimited amounts to each other.)

A candidate can give unlimited amounts to his or her own candidate committee.

A political party or legislative campaign committee can give unlimited amounts to a candidate committee.

A PAC can give up to $86,000 to the candidate committee of a candidate for governor. Other limits apply to other offices, including: $26,000 for lieutenant governor; $44,000 for attorney general; $18,000 for superintendent of public instruction, secretary of state, state treasurer, or supreme court justice; $2,000 for state senator; and $1,000 for state representative.

No one else can give money to a candidate committee.

Giving to a political party or to a legislative campaign committee. An individual, candidate committee, political party, or legislative campaign committee can give unlimited amounts to a political party or a legislative campaign committee.

A PAC can give up to $12,000 in a calendar year to a political party or legislative campaign committee.

No one else can give money to a political party or legislative campaign committee, unless the political party or legislative campaign committee has established a segregated fund of money that will not be spent on express advocacy or given to a candidate committee. An individual, candidate committee, political party, or legislative campaign committee can give unlimited amounts to such a fund. A PAC can give up to $12,000 in a calendar year to such a fund (in addition to the other money it can give to the political party or legislative campaign committee). A corporation, labor union, cooperative association, or American Indian tribe can also give up to $12,000 in a calendar year to such a fund (even though none of these entities can otherwise give money to the political party or legislative campaign committee).

Giving to a PAC. An individual, candidate committee, political party, legislative campaign committee, or PAC can give unlimited amounts to a PAC. No one else can give money to a PAC.

Giving to an IEC. An individual, candidate committee, political party, legislative campaign committee, PAC, or IEC can give unlimited amounts to an IEC. A corporation, labor union, cooperative association, or American Indian tribe can also give unlimited amounts to an IEC. No one else can give money to an IEC.

Giving to a referendum committee. Individuals and committees can give unlimited amounts to a referendum committee. A corporation, labor union, cooperative association, or American Indian tribe can also give unlimited amounts to a referendum committee. No one else can give money to a referendum committee.

Giving to a recall committee. Individuals and committees other than IECs or referendum committees can give unlimited amounts to a recall committee. No one else can give money to a recall committee.

CAMPAIGN SPENDING LIMITS

Individuals, committees, and entities that are not committees can generally spend unlimited amounts on their own campaigning. The exception is spending on express advocacy that is done in coordination with a candidate, candidate committee, political party, or legislative campaign committee.[17] (See note 14 for the criteria that define coordination.) Spending of this kind is treated as a gift given to the candidate committee of the candidate who is benefitted by the express advocacy. As such, it is subject to the limits (described above) that apply to giving to a candidate committee.

CAMPAIGN SPENDING SPECIAL DISCLOSURE REQUIREMENTS

Special disclosures are required for some kinds of campaign spending. These are the only disclosures that individuals and entities that are not committees must make about their campaign spending.[18] Committees, by contrast, must also report their campaign spending in the regular reports they file covering all of their financial activity.

Specific reporting of certain communications. An individual or an entity that is not a committee, and similarly a PAC or an IEC, that spends $2,500 or more to make express advocacy communications during the 60 days preceding a primary or election must report that spending to the Ethics Commission within 72 hours after the first $2,500 has been spent and within 72 hours after any additional expenditure. Every report for an additional expenditure must specify the date, amount, recipient, and purpose of the expenditure, as well as the name of and office sought by any candidate who is the subject of the express advocacy. The reports are made public within two days of their filing.

Candidate committees, political parties, and legislative campaign committees are not required to report these expenditures other than in their regular financial activity reports.

Information required in certain communications. An individual, committee, or other entity that spends money to make an express advocacy communication or to make a communication to influence the outcome of a recall effort must include in the communication the phrase, "Paid for by," followed by the name of the individual, committee, or other entity.[19] For individuals and entities that are not committees, this requirement applies only to a communication whose cost exceeds $2,500. ▣

NOTES

1. An alternative mechanism exists by which an individual can qualify to be listed on the spring election ballot. A town or village (but no other type of governmental jurisdiction) can hold a special meeting called a caucus to select the individuals who will be the candidates at the spring election for the town's or village's offices. The caucus must be held on or between the January 2 and the January 21 preceding the spring election. The caucus is open to the public, but only the eligible voters of the town or village can participate. The caucus participants propose one or more individuals to be the candidates for each office and vote, if the total number of proposed candidates for a particular office is more than two (or is more than twice the number of seats to be filled), to determine which ones will in fact be the candidates. An individual who is selected at a caucus to be a candidate for a town or village office must subsequently file a declaration of candidacy in order to be listed on the spring election ballot.

2. Wisconsin changed the required number of days of consecutive residence from ten to 28 in 2011, but a U.S. district court found this change to be unconstitutional in 2016. Wisconsin appealed the court's finding, but as of June 2017 the appeal remained pending.

3. To register via the electronic registration system, an individual must possess a current and valid Wisconsin driver's license or identification card. The system requires the individual to enter his or her name, address, and date of birth together with the number of the driver's license or identification card. If the system confirms that the individual's information matches the records of the state Department of Transportation pertaining to the driver's license or identification card, the system permits the individual to register by 1) filling out and submitting an electronic version of the registration form; 2) "signing" the form by authorizing the use of a copy of the signature that he or she provided when applying for the driver's license or identification card; and 3) using as proof of residence the number of his or her driver's license or identification card.

4. Military voters (members of a uniformed service and their families who are residents of Wisconsin but are away from home by reason of active duty) and overseas voters (former Wisconsin residents who no longer reside in the U.S. but remain U.S. citizens) can obtain and vote a Wisconsin absentee ballot without providing proof of identification. Overseas voters are entitled to vote for offices in national government only (U.S. president, vice president, senator, and representative).

5. If an individual's name and address are not listed in the poll list, the poll worker will determine whether the voter is at the wrong polling place or is at the correct polling place but not registered. In the one case, the poll worker will direct the voter to the correct polling place; in the other, the poll worker will tell the voter where to go so that he or she can register.

If an individual's name and address are listed in the poll list but a poll worker believes that the name on the proof of identification is not consistent with the name on the poll list, or that a photograph on the proof of identification does not reasonably resemble the individual, the poll worker must challenge the individual. The individual must reply to the challenge under oath in order to obtain a ballot. If the poll worker does not withdraw the challenge, the individual must also take an oath that he or she is eligible to vote the ballot, and a poll worker must place a special notation in the poll list and on the ballot before issuing it. The individual's votes will be considered valid unless the election officials responsible for counting the votes decide beyond a reasonable doubt, based on evidence presented, that the individual was not eligible to vote or was not properly registered.

If an individual's name and address are listed in the poll list but the individual is unable or unwilling to present proof of identification, he or she is given an opportunity to cast a provisional ballot, rather than a regular ballot. The voter must sign a certification attesting that he or she is eligible to vote the ballot. The provisional ballot will not be counted unless the voter subsequently presents the proof of identification. The voter can return to the polling place to do this, until 8:00 p.m. when the polls close, or the voter can bring the proof of identification to the municipal clerk's office, until 4:00 p.m. on the Friday following the election.

6. But military and overseas voters are exempt from this requirement. (See note 4.)

7. If the ballot was requested by email or fax, the voter must also include in the second envelope a signed printed copy of the request.

8. Another kind of entity, called a "conduit," is subject to similar requirements. Conduits do not spend money on campaigning themselves, nor do they give money to others to spend on campaigning. Rather, they hold money on behalf of givers and pass it on to a committee at the direction of those givers.

9. Express advocacy is communication that includes words such as "vote for," "elect," "support," "vote against," "defeat," or "oppose"; makes reference to a clearly identified candidate; and unambiguously relates to the election or defeat of that candidate. Communication that refers to a candidate but that does not qualify as express advocacy would not, by itself, subject the communicator to Wisconsin's regulations, even if the communication was intended to influence voters' opinion of the candidate.

10. Not covered by the regulations is campaigning related to a candidate for elective office in national government. (That kind of campaigning is regulated under federal law.) There is no national-level referendum or recall process.

11. This could consist of pooling contributions made by the individuals in the group or the members of the organization.

12. The Ethics Commission, if the candidate is seeking office in state government; or a county, municipal, or school district clerk, if the candidate is seeking office in local government.

13. Based on one of the following criteria: 1) filing nomination papers; 2) being certified as the nominee of a political party or a village or town caucus; 3) accepting or disbursing any money in an effort to win a primary or election; 4) being an incumbent elective office holder.

14. Under Wisconsin law, coordination exists in only two situations: 1) a candidate, candidate committee, political party, or legislative campaign committee communicates directly with an individual or with an entity other than a political party or legislative campaign committee to specifically request that the individual or entity make an expenditure for express advocacy, and the individual or entity explicitly assents before making the expenditure; or 2) a candidate, candidate committee, political party, or legislative campaign committee exercises control over an expenditure made for express advocacy by an individual or by an entity other than a political party or legislative campaign committee or exercises control over the content, timing, location, form, intended audience, number, or frequency of the express advocacy.

15. The Ethics Commission, for a statewide referendum; or a county, municipal, or school district clerk, for a local one.

16. The Ethics Commission, if the petition pertains to an official in state government; or a county, municipal, or school district clerk, if it pertains to an official in local government.

17. Also, some entities that enjoy tax-exempt status under federal law, based on the fact that they have limited themselves to specific activities, would lose that status if they were to spend money on campaigning. In addition, a registered committee cannot spend money on a kind of campaigning that is inconsistent with the type of committee that it has registered as.

18. Campaign giving is a different story. For every gift of money that an individual or entity makes to a committee, the individual or entity must disclose to the committee the information (such as name and address) that the committee needs to complete its financial activity reports; and those reports, in turn, are made public shortly after they are filed.

19. An additional phrase—"Not authorized by any candidate or candidate's agent or committee"—must be included in an express advocacy communication that is made independently, rather than in coordination with a candidate, candidate committee, political party, or legislative campaign committee.

Local government in Wisconsin

Government in Wisconsin includes not only the state government, but also numerous local governments that exist and operate under the authority of the state government. Some local governments are "general purpose districts," which have broad authority to administer a particular locale, while others are "special purpose districts," whose authority is limited to the performance of a specific function.

General purpose districts

Counties and municipalities—towns, villages, and cities—are Wisconsin's general purpose districts. The territory of the state is divided into counties, and it is also divided into towns, villages, and cities. Towns lie entirely within the boundaries of counties, but villages and cities can lie across county boundaries.

Historically, counties were created to be administrative subdivisions of the state. Towns were created within counties to enable sparsely populated areas to provide basic services for themselves, whereas villages and cities were created to enable population centers, wherever they had formed, to govern their local affairs.

Today, counties continue to act as the local arm of state government, and towns continue to be providers of basic services, but all general purpose districts have some authority to make decisions about their local affairs.

General purpose districts determine their own budgets and raise money to pay for their operations by establishing fees, imposing property taxes on real property within their boundaries, and incurring debt.

Counties. Wisconsin has 72 counties. County boundaries are drawn by the legislature and specified in state law. County boundary lines generally run north to south and east to west or follow major physical features (such as rivers).

The governing body of a county is the county board. The county board is composed of supervisors who are elected from election districts within the county for two-year terms at the nonpartisan spring election. Each county decides for itself how many supervisors it will have (subject to a statutory maximum that is based on a county's population), and whether their terms will be concurrent or staggered.

In addition to the county board, counties are required to have a central administrative officer. For this purpose, a county can create the office of county executive or county administrator, or it can designate an individual holding an existing elective or appointive office (other than county supervisor) to serve also as the county's administrative coordinator.

A county executive is elected for a four-year term at the nonpartisan spring election. Eleven counties have a county executive, including Wisconsin's eight most populous counties. The county executive directs all administrative functions; proposes to the county board an annual budget for the county; appoints (subject to approval by the county board) members of boards and commissions and heads of departments; and can veto actions of the county board.

A county administrator is appointed by the county board. Twenty-nine counties have a county administrator. The powers and responsibilities of this office are similar to those of a county executive, but a county administrator has no veto power and can be removed by the county board.

A county administrative coordinator, finally, has only the powers and responsibilities assigned by the county board. These could be as extensive as those of a county administrator but need not be. An individual serving as county administrative coordinator has no veto power, and his or her service in this capacity can be terminated by the county board.

Apart from its supervisors and county executive (if any), the elected officers of a county, including the sheriff, district attorney, clerk, and treasurer, are elected for four-year terms at the partisan general election.

Counties administer state programs in a variety of ways. County district attorneys enforce the state's criminal laws, and county jails incarcerate many violators of those laws; county clerks and registers of deeds maintain state-mandated vital and property records; county clerks oversee elections; and county human services departments administer state family and human service programs. In performing these functions for the state, counties have a limited role in determining policy. Rather, the state sets specific standards that counties must abide by.

At the same time, however, counties have some authority to determine policy on local matters. For example, counties can regulate land use in the county (but not within the territory of a city or village), operate county highway systems, and establish recreational programs and social service programs.

Generally, all counties have the same powers and duties, but the legislature has imposed special requirements on the state's most populous county, Milwaukee. Among other things, that county must utilize a specific budgeting procedure that includes various reports and notices and that limits certain types of expenditures; and it must use a county executive system rather than an appointed central administrative officer.

Towns. Wisconsin has 1,253 towns. Town boundaries can be drawn by a county or a circuit court, according to procedures authorized by the legislature, and also by the legislature directly. Town boundary lines, like those of counties, generally run north to south and east to west or follow major physical features. However, town boundary lines can vary from this pattern when part of a town has been incorporated as, or annexed to, a city or village.

The governing body of a town is the town board. This board is typically composed of three supervisors, but towns that meet certain criteria can opt to have up to five. Supervisors are elected at large for two-year terms at the nonpartisan spring election. In towns that have four or five supervisors, the terms can be staggered. One of the supervisor seats is designated for the town board chair, and the supervisor elected to that seat presides over the board's meetings and acts on behalf of the board in certain matters. Towns do not have a separate elected executive officer, but a town can create the appointive position of town administrator to perform administrative functions. Other town officers include the town clerk, treasurer, surveyor, assessor, and constable. Each town can decide for itself whether these officers will be elected or appointed. If elected, they are elected for two-year terms at the nonpartisan spring election. (Towns are also permitted to combine or abolish some of the offices.)

A distinctive feature of the town form of government is the annual town meeting. The annual meeting is held on the third Tuesday of April (or another date set by the voters at the preceding town meeting). During the meeting all eligible voters of the town are entitled to debate and vote on certain matters, including major issues affecting the town, such as establishing the tax levy and authorizing bonding. Determinations of the town meeting are binding on the town board and cannot be overturned by it.

Towns are required to provide certain basic services, in particular fire protection and the maintenance of local roads, and are allowed to provide other basic services, such as law enforcement and garbage collection. Many towns, particularly less populous and more rural ones, do little more than this. However, towns can also make policy on local matters. In particular, a town can opt to exercise village powers (by approving a resolution at a town meeting), in which case it is permitted to take any of the actions a village can take, except actions relating to the structure of its government. The village powers that towns most often exercise are those related to land use regulation. (Towns are otherwise subject to county land use regulation.)

Cities and villages. Wisconsin has 190 cities and 411 villages. City and village boundaries do not follow any particular pattern and are determined when the residents of territory lying within one or more towns incorporate the territory as a city or village. Incorporation is authorized by state law, and several procedures are provided. Typically, residents who wish to incorporate territory file a petition with the circuit court. If the circuit court determines that the petition is formally sufficient and that requirements pertaining to size, population, and population density have been met, the petition is forwarded to the state's Incorporation Review Board. If that board determines that the incorporation is in the public interest, a referendum on the incorporation is held in the territory that is proposed to be incorporated. If the referendum is approved, the city or village is established.

The governing body of a city is the common council, which is composed of alders and, in cities that have one, a mayor. The alders are elected at the nonpartisan spring election. Each city decides for itself how many alders it will have, whether they will be elected at large or from election districts, what the term of office will be, and whether terms will be staggered or concurrent. The mayor is elected at large at the nonpartisan spring election for a term decided by the city. The mayor presides over meetings of the common council but has no vote, except to break a tie.

Cities use two forms of executive organization. In most cities, the mayor is the chief executive officer. The mayor can veto the council's actions and has a general responsibility to ensure that the laws are obeyed and that city officials and employees carry out their duties. Specific responsibilities, however, vary from city to city. In some cities, for example, the mayor proposes an annual budget for the city, but in others the council develops the budget itself. Similarly, the mayor might have authority to appoint many or few of a city's appointive positions.

In place of a mayor, ten cities have created the position of city manager. A city manager is appointed (and can be removed) by the common council. A city manager can attend, but does not preside or vote at, meetings of the council and cannot veto its actions. The responsibilities of a city manager include proposing an annual budget and appointing department heads, unless the common council defines the position differently.

City officers other than alders and the mayor or city manager can be elected or appointed, as decided by the city. If elected, they are elected at the nonpartisan spring election.

The governing body of a village is the village board, which is composed of trustees and a village president. Trustees are elected at the nonpartisan spring election for staggered terms. Each village decides for itself how many trustees it will have, whether they will be elected at large or from election districts, and what the term of office will be. The village president is elected at large at the nonpartisan spring election, for a term decided by the village. The village president presides over meetings of the village board and votes as a trustee. The president also acts on behalf of the board in certain matters.

Villages do not have a separate elected executive officer, but ten villages have created the position of village manager to perform much the same role as a city manager performs in a city. A village manager is appointed (and can be removed) by the village board.

Village officers other than the trustees, president, and village manager (if any) can be elected or appointed, as decided by the village. If elected, they are elected at the nonpartisan spring election.

Cities and villages, like towns, provide basic services. These include fire protection, road maintenance, and police service. To a greater extent than towns or counties, however, cities and villages have broad authority to make local policy. Some powers are granted expressly in state statutes. Among the most characteristic of these are powers related to land use regulation, including authority to make rules that limit land uses in particular areas and that limit the kinds of structures that can be built or maintained in the city or village and authority to grant exceptions to the rules.

Beyond the authority granted in the statutes, however, cities and villages possess "home rule" powers conferred by the state constitution. The home rule provision states that cities and villages have the authority to "determine their local affairs and government, subject only to this constitution and to such enactments of the legislature of statewide concern as with uniformity shall affect every city or every village." While it is not clear exactly what powers the provision grants to cities and villages or to what extent it prohibits the state from restricting local powers, the provision is typically understood to allow cities and villages to take action on local matters without specific authorization from the state. That is, conversely to the situation with towns or counties, cities and villages can take such action unless otherwise prohibited.

An additional power exercised only by cities and villages is the power of annexation: the power to detach territory from a town and attach it to the city or village. There are several different procedures by which an annexation can take place. Usually, all of the owners of property in the territory to be annexed sign on to a petition for annexation that is filed with the annexing city or village. If the petition meets certain statutory requirements and the governing body of the city or village enacts an ordinance approving the annexation, the territory becomes part of the city or village. In most cases, a town has no power to prohibit an annexation of part of its territory (but it can challenge the legality of an annexation in court).

Although cities and villages ordinarily have the same powers and duties, the legislature has imposed special requirements on "1st class" cities, including specific standards for budgeting, public employment, and police and fire department administration. Milwaukee is Wisconsin's only 1st class city currently.

Special purpose districts

Wisconsin has over 1,100 special purpose districts. The legislature has created some special purpose districts directly, and it has also authorized general purpose districts to create certain types of special purpose districts. Although a special purpose district exists only to perform a special function, the scope of its authority and its impact on the people who reside within its jurisdiction can be great. For example, some school districts have jurisdiction over the education of tens of thousands of children and some metropolitan sewerage districts manage sewage for hundreds of thousands of people. Other special purpose districts, however, such as certain public inland lake protection and rehabilitation districts, have authority over a very small geographic area and directly affect only a very small number of people.

School districts. Wisconsin has 422 school districts, which collectively cover the entire territory of the state. District boundaries can be modified, including by subdividing or consolidating existing districts, so long as no territory of the state is left outside of a district. Boundary modifications are typically initiated by the affected districts and might require ratification by referendum. The governing body of a school district is the school board. School board members are elected at the nonpartisan spring election, usually to staggered three-year terms. The number of members on a school board varies between three and 11, and school board members can be elected at large or from election districts. School districts operate primary and secondary schools and otherwise provide educational services to the children who reside in the district. School districts are authorized to levy property taxes and to incur debt.

Technical college districts. Wisconsin has 16 technical college districts, which collectively cover the entire territory of the state. The number of districts and their boundaries were originally determined by a predecessor of the state Technical College System Board, and that agency has the power to reorganize the districts. Technical college districts are governed by boards of nine members who are appointed for staggered three-year terms. Depending on the district, the appointments are made by a committee composed of the county board chairs of the counties that lie within the district or by a committee composed of the school board presidents of the school districts that lie within the district. For the Milwaukee Area Technical College District, the appointing committee is composed of the Milwaukee county executive and the Milwaukee, Ozaukee, and Washington county board chairs. Technical college districts operate technical colleges that provide postsecondary vocational and occupational training to persons who enroll in their programs. Districts are authorized to charge tuition and other fees, levy property taxes, and incur debt.

Metropolitan sewerage districts. Wisconsin has six metropolitan sewerage districts.

The legislature created the Milwaukee Metropolitan Sewerage District (MMSD) in the Milwaukee area. State law authorizes general purpose districts in the rest of the state to create their own metropolitan sewerage districts.

Sewerage districts plan, design, construct, maintain, and operate sewerage systems for the collection, transmission, disposal, and treatment of both sewage and storm water. An 11-member commission governs the MMSD, and five-member commissions govern other sewerage districts. Commissioners of the MMSD are appointed to staggered three-year terms by officials of the municipalities located in Milwaukee County. Commissioners of other sewerage districts are generally appointed to staggered five-year terms by the county board of the county in which the district is located. Funds for a district's projects and operations are generated from property taxes assessed against property located in the district, from the issuance of bonds, and from user fees that are paid by the individuals and businesses that use the district's services. A large district, like the MMSD, provides services both to people who live within its jurisdiction and to people whose municipalities have contracted with it for its services.

Professional sports team stadium districts. Wisconsin has three professional sports team stadium districts. The Southeast Wisconsin Professional Baseball Park District was created by the legislature in 1995 and was authorized to issue bonds to acquire, construct, own, and operate a baseball park and related facilities. The district built, and is the majority owner of, Miller Park, the home stadium of the Milwaukee Brewers baseball team. To pay off the bonds, and to pay for stadium maintenance, the district is authorized to impose a sales tax within the district's jurisdiction, which consists of the counties of Milwaukee, Ozaukee, Racine, Waukesha, and Washington. The district is governed by a board of 13 members: six appointed by the governor, three for two-year terms and three for four-year terms; two appointed by and serving at the pleasure of the Milwaukee county executive for indefinite terms; and one each appointed by and serving at the pleasure of the Racine county executive, Waukesha county executive, Ozaukee county board chair, Washington county board chair, and Milwaukee mayor.

The Professional Football Stadium District was created by the legislature in 1999 and was authorized to issue bonds to finance the renovation of Lambeau Field, the home stadium of the Green Bay Packers football team. To pay off the bonds, the district was authorized to impose a sales tax within the district's jurisdiction, which consists of Brown County. The sales tax was imposed until September 2015, at which time sufficient money had been collected to repay the bonds and to set aside a required reserve fund. Although its purpose has been carried out, the district continues to exist. The district is governed by a board of seven members who are appointed for concurrent two-year terms by elected local officials, including the mayor of Green Bay and the Brown county executive.

The Wisconsin Center District was created in 1994 by the City of Milwaukee under a state law that permits general purpose districts in the state to create a kind of special purpose district called a local exposition district. The district was authorized to issue bonds to build, own, and operate certain entertainment facilities in Milwaukee. (These facilities are known today as the Milwaukee Theatre, Wisconsin Center, and UW-Milwaukee Panther Arena.) To pay off the bonds, the district is authorized to impose special sales taxes in Milwaukee County on hotel rooms, on food and beverages sold in restaurants and taverns, and on car rentals. Operating revenues of the facilities pay for the district's operations. In 2015, the legislature expanded the district's purpose, altered its governance structure, and authorized it to issue bonds to finance the development and construction of a professional basketball arena for the Milwaukee Bucks basketball team. The state, the City of Milwaukee, and Milwaukee County are required to provide the district the money that the district will need to pay off the bonds. The district is governed by a board of 17 members, including the state assembly speaker and minority leader, the state senate majority leader and minority leader, and appointees of the governor, the Milwaukee mayor, the Milwaukee common council president, and the Milwaukee county executive.

Other special purpose districts. State law permits general purpose districts to create certain types of special purpose districts. These include agricultural drainage districts, sanitary districts, public inland lake protection and rehabilitation districts, sewer utility districts, solid waste management systems, long-term care districts, water utility districts, and mosquito control districts. ▣

Public education in Wisconsin

2016–17 school year

The Wisconsin Constitution requires the legislature to make available to all children in the state a free uniform basic education. (Article X, section 3.) At the same time, the constitution does not prohibit the legislature from creating additional forms of publicly funded education; nor does it require the additional forms, if any, to be available to all children, or to be entirely free, or to provide the same basic education as the legislature must make available to all children. (*Davis v. Grover*, 166 Wis. 2d 501, 539, 480 N.W.2d 460, 474 (1992) and *Jackson v. Benson*, 218 Wis. 2d 835, 895, 578 N.W.2d 602, 628 (1998).) This article describes first the general educational system that the legislature has established to meet its obligation under the constitution; and thereafter each of the currently existing additional forms of publicly funded education that the legislature has also created.

The general system

In Wisconsin, every child resides within a school district and is entitled to a free education at a public school operated by that school district. The education provided at the public school must conform to requirements specified in state law.

Wisconsin is organized into 422 school districts. Each school district is governed by a school board whose members are elected by the residents of the district. For the purpose of operating public schools, school districts can, among other things, own and lease property; employ teachers and other personnel; and contract for the provision of services.

State law sets out general educational goals for children attending public schools and requires school districts to provide educational programs that will enable students to attain those goals. State law requires school districts to specify the knowledge and skills that they intend students in each grade to acquire; to maintain sequential curriculum plans; and to define criteria for promoting students to the fifth grade and the ninth grade and for awarding high school diplomas. It requires school districts to schedule a minimum number of hours of direct student instruction in each grade. And it requires school districts to ensure that every teacher and professional staff member holds a certificate, license, or permit to teach issued by the state's Department of Public Instruction (DPI). Within these parameters, and subject to further requirements, school districts have discretion to determine the specifics of their educational programs and policies.

Additional requirements under both state and federal law apply to the education that school districts provide to children with disabilities. A school district must identify, locate, and evaluate children with disabilities who reside in the district. It must develop an individualized education program (IEP) for each such child that describes the special education and related services that the child needs to make progress appropriate for the child's level of ability. It must offer the child an educational setting in which it will provide the special education and related services described in the IEP. And, as long as the child is enrolled in the district, the district must regularly reevaluate the child, review and revise the IEP, and offer the child an educational setting in which it will implement the IEP. In addition, the school district must make special education and related services available to a child with a disability beginning in the year the child attains the age of three and continuing through the year in which the child attains the age of 21.

For state oversight purposes, school districts are required to report various kinds of information to DPI and to administer certain standardized tests every year in every public school to students in specific grades. In addition, DPI is required to publish an annual report, called the school and school district accountability report, that evaluates the performance of every public school and school district. (The individual evaluations in the report are called school or school district "report cards.")

Funding for school district operations comes primarily from state aid and property taxes levied by each district, but also from federal aid and miscellaneous fees, sales, and interest earnings. The amount of state aid that a school district receives is based on several factors, including the number of pupils enrolled in the district's schools. State law limits the total amount of revenue that a school district can raise each year from the state aid it receives for general purposes, the state aid it receives for computers, and the property taxes it levies. However, a school district can exceed its revenue limit if it obtains voter approval at a referendum.

Additional forms of publicly funded education

OPEN ENROLLMENT PROGRAM

Under the Open Enrollment Program, a child can enroll to attend a public school in a school district other than the one in which the child resides. Open enrollment is available to any child in any grade from five-year-old kindergarten up. It is also open to younger children, but only if a child's school district of residence provides the same type of program as the child wishes to attend in the nonresident school district and the child is eligible to attend the program in the child's school district of residence.

In most cases, a child must apply to participate in the Open Enrollment Program in the school year preceding the school year for which the application is made. The nonresident school district in which the child wishes to enroll cannot deny the application except for certain reasons, such as that the non-resident school district does not have space for additional students; that the nonresident school district does not provide the special education or related services specified in the IEP of an applicant who is a child with a disability; that the child has been habitually truant from the nonresident school district in a prior school year; or that the child has been expelled from any school district in the previous three years because of specific behaviors.

Under special circumstances, a child can apply to participate in the program immediately. Circumstances that qualify for this purpose include that a child is or has recently been homeless; that a child has been the victim of repeated bullying or harassment; or that a child's parent, the child's resident school district, and the nonresident school district all agree that attending school in the nonresident school district is in the best interests of the child. In these cases, the resident school district can deny the application if it determines that the special circumstances asserted in the application are not present. The nonresident school district can deny the application for any of the reasons that would be permitted for an ordinary application.

The nonresident school district must afford an open enrollment student the same educational opportunities and programs as it affords a student who resides in the district. In the case of an open enrollment student who is a child with a disability, the nonresident school district must assume, in place of the resident school district, the duties under state and federal law that apply to the education of such children.

For each open enrollment student, the state transfers to the nonresident school district a set amount from the state aid that is allocated for the student's resident school district. In the 2016–17 school year, the general per student transfer amount was $6,748, and the per student transfer amount for a child with a disability was $12,000. (Prior to the 2016–17 school year, the state did not transfer state aid in the case of a child with a disability. Instead, the resident school district made an individualized tuition payment for the child to the nonresident school district.)

The parent rather than the school district is responsible for providing transportation to and from school for an open enrollment student who is not a child with a disability. (But parents can apply to DPI for financial assistance based on need.)

YOUTH OPTIONS PROGRAM

The Youth Options Program allows a student who is attending a public school in grade 11 or 12 to take college courses at the University of Wisconsin System, the Wisconsin Technical College System, a participating private nonprofit institution of higher education in Wisconsin, or a participating tribal college in Wisconsin. In addition to the college credit that a student receives for such a course, a student can receive high school credit if the school district in which the student is enrolled determines that the course qualifies for high school credit and is not comparable to a course already offered in the school district.

The school district pays for each course that a student takes for high school credit (or for both high school and college credit) under the program, if the student successfully completes the course. The student pays for each course that the student takes for college credit only or that the student does not successfully complete. Parents are responsible for providing transportation to and from courses under the Youth Options Program, unless a course is being taken to implement the IEP of a child with a disability. (But parents can apply to DPI for financial assistance based on need.)

COURSE OPTIONS PROGRAM

The Course Options Program allows a student who is attending a public school in any grade to take up to two courses at one time at a public school in another school district, the University of Wisconsin System, the Wisconsin Technical College System, a nonprofit institution of higher education, a tribal college, a charter school, or a nonprofit organization that has been approved by DPI. The school district in which the student is enrolled may deny a student's course options application if the school district determines that the course does not satisfy a graduation requirement, does not support a student's academic and career plan, or conflicts with a student's IEP if the student is a child with a disability.

The Course Options Program includes concurrent enrollment courses (also known as "dual enrollment" and "dual credit" courses). A concurrent enrollment course is provided by an institution of higher education at a public high school under an agreement between the institution and the school district that operates the high school. The course is taught by a school district teacher who, for the purpose of teaching the course, has been certified as an adjunct faculty member by the institution. A student receives college credit from the institution, as well as high school credit from the school district, for completing the course.

In general, the school district in which a student is enrolled pays for a course that the student takes under the Course Options Program. The amount of the payment is equal to the cost of providing the course to the student, as determined by DPI. The entity that provides the course cannot charge a student or the student's school district any more than the amount determined by DPI, unless the entity is an institution of higher education and the student will receive college credit for the course. Parents are responsible for providing transportation to and from courses under the Course Options Program, unless a course is being taken to implement the IEP of a child with a disability. (But parents can apply to DPI for financial assistance based on need.)

CHARTER SCHOOLS

A charter school is a type of public school that is largely exempt from state education laws that apply to other public schools. A charter school is operated by a person identified in a contract that establishes the school, and is subject to the terms of the contract. The contract describes the school's educational program and governance structure and specifies the facilities and funds that will be available to it. The contract is negotiated between and agreed to by the person who will operate the charter school and an entity that has the power to authorize a charter school. Currently, all school districts and nine other entities, discussed below, have this power. The authorizing entity can revoke a charter school contract if the charter school operator fails to comply with the terms of the contract. The authorizing entity can also revoke the contract if the children attending the charter school fail to make sufficient progress towards attaining the general educational goals set out in state law for children attending public schools.

Charter schools are not exempt from state education laws that pertain to public health and safety. In addition, all professional employees of a charter school who have direct contact with students or involvement with the instructional program must hold a license or permit to teach issued by DPI.

Charter school operators must report the same kinds of information to DPI as school districts and administer the same standardized tests to their students as school districts must administer to students in other public schools.

In addition, DPI must include performance evaluations of charter schools in the annual school and school district accountability report.

As public schools, charter schools are not exempt from federal laws pertaining to regular education, the education of children with disabilities, or civil rights.

School district charter schools. A charter school established by a school district is a public school of that school district, even though the school district does not directly operate the charter school. As a result, a school district charter school is subject to school district policies, except as otherwise negotiated in the charter contract. A child who attends a school district charter school is enrolled in the school district just the same as if the child attended a school that the school district operated directly. The school district receives the same amount of state aid or the same open enrollment transfer payment for the child, and the school district has the same duties if the child is a child with a disability. However, a school district cannot require a child to attend a charter school and must provide other public school attendance arrangements for a child who does not wish to attend a charter school.

A school district can establish a "virtual" charter school, which is a kind of charter school at which all or a portion of the instruction is provided on the Internet. A virtual charter school is considered to be located in the school district that establishes it, even if it has no physical presence there. In contrast to the situation with a bricks-and-mortar school, it is feasible under the Open Enrollment Program for children who reside anywhere in the state to attend a virtual charter school.

A school district that establishes a charter school pays the charter school operator an amount negotiated in the charter contract to operate the charter school.

Independent charter schools. Prior to 2015, four entities other than school districts could authorize charter schools: the City of Milwaukee, the University of Wisconsin-Milwaukee, the University of Wisconsin-Parkside, and the Milwaukee Area Technical College District. Five more entities were granted this power in 2015: the Gateway Technical College District, Waukesha County, the College of Menominee Nation, the Lac Courte Oreilles Ojibwa Community College, and the Office of Educational Opportunity in the University of Wisconsin System.

The power of these entities to authorize charter schools is limited in various ways. For example, the Gateway Technical College District cannot authorize a charter school unless the charter school 1) operates only high school grades, 2) provides a curriculum focused on science, technology, engineering, and mathematics or on occupational education and training, and 3) is located in the Gateway Technical College District. In addition, none of these entities can authorize a virtual charter school.

A charter school established by one of these entities (an independent charter school) is not part of any school district. Accordingly, an independent charter school is not subject to any school district's policies. If a child with a disability attends an independent charter school, the charter school operator is subject to the same federal laws pertaining to the education of such children as a school district would be and must evaluate the child, develop an IEP, offer the child an educational setting in which it will provide the special education and services specified in the IEP, and regularly reevaluate the child and revise the IEP.

The state pays an independent charter school operator a set amount for each student attending the independent charter school. In the 2016–17 school year, the per student amount was $8,188 for most of the independent charter schools. For an independent charter school authorized by the College of Menominee Nation or the Lac Courte Oreilles Ojibwa Community College, however, the per student amount in each school year is set to equal the per student amount in the previous school year of a type of federal aid provided to tribal schools.

PARENTAL CHOICE PROGRAMS

Under a parental choice program (sometimes called a "voucher" program), the state makes a payment to a private school, on behalf of a student's parent, for the student to attend the private school. There are three parental choice programs in Wisconsin: the Milwaukee Parental Choice Program, which has been in existence since 1989; the Racine Parental Choice Program, which was created in the 2011–13 biennial budget act; and the Statewide Parental Choice Program, which was created in the 2013–15 biennial budget act.

Each of these programs is available to children whose family income, at the time that the child first participates, is below a specified level (three times the federal poverty level for the Milwaukee and Racine programs and 1.85 times that level for the statewide program). A child must reside in the city of Milwaukee to participate in the Milwaukee program, in the Racine Unified School District to participate in the Racine program, and anywhere else in the state to participate in the statewide program. Except in certain circumstances, a child cannot participate in the Racine or statewide programs if the child was attending a private school in the previous school year other than as a participant in those programs. In addition, a temporary limit has been imposed on the number of children from each school district who can participate in the statewide program. This limit was 1 percent of a school district's student membership in the 2016–17 school year. The limit increases by one percentage point each school year until the 2025–26 school year and ceases to apply after that.

A private school that wishes to participate in a parental choice program must report to DPI, by the February 1 preceding each school year of participation, the number of spaces it has for choice students and pay an annual fee. Additional requirements apply to a private school that has been in continuous operation in this state for less than 12 consecutive months or provides education to fewer than 40 students divided into two or fewer grades.

A student who wishes to participate in a parental choice program must apply to a participating private school during specific enrollment periods. The private school may reject an applicant only if the spaces it has for choice students are full. If a private school rejects an application, the applicant can transfer his or her application to another participating private school. A private school must generally accept applicants on a random basis, but may give preference to applicants who participated in a parental choice program in the previous school year, siblings of such applicants, and siblings of applicants whom the private school has accepted for the current school year on a random basis.

A participating private school must satisfy all state health and safety laws and codes that are applicable to public schools and federal laws prohibiting discrimination on the basis of race, color, or national origin. It must satisfy at least one of four achievement standards to continue participating in the program. And it may not require a choice student to participate in any religious activity. The private school must also provide a prescribed minimum number of hours of direct student instruction in each grade. Additionally, all of the private school's teachers and administrators must have a bachelor's or higher degree, or a license issued by DPI.

Participating private schools must report the same kinds of information to DPI as school districts must report, but only with respect to the choice students attending them. They must also administer the same standardized tests to their choice students as school districts must administer to public school students. In addition, DPI must include an evaluation of each participating private school's performance with respect to its choice students in the annual school and school district accountability report.

A child with a disability who participates in a parental choice program is not entitled to the special education and related services to which he or she would be entitled under state and federal law if he or she attended a public school.

In the 2016–17 school year, the state paid $7,323 to a participating private school for each choice student attending the school in grades kindergarten to eight and $7,969 for each choice student attending in grades 9 to 12. A private school cannot charge tuition to a choice student unless the student's family income exceeds 220 percent of the federal poverty line. A private school can charge a choice student fees related to certain expenses (such as social and extracurricular activities, musical instruments, meals, and transportation) but cannot take adverse action against a choice student or the student's family if the fees are not paid.

SPECIAL NEEDS SCHOLARSHIP PROGRAM

Under the Special Needs Scholarship Program, the state makes a payment (the scholarship) to a private school, on behalf of the parent of a child with a disability, for the child to attend the private school. The program was created in the 2015–17 biennial budget act, and scholarships were first available for the 2016–17 school year. A study of the program will be conducted by the Legislative Audit Bureau and submitted to the legislature by January 9, 2019.

A child with a disability is eligible for a scholarship under the program if five conditions are met. The child must have been enrolled in a public school for the entire school year immediately preceding the first school year for which the child will receive a scholarship. The child must have applied under the Open Enrollment Program to attend public school in one or more non-resident school districts, and every such application must have been denied. The child must have an IEP or services plan in effect. (A services plan out-lines the services that a school district has agreed to provide to a child with a disability whose parent has enrolled the child in a private school rather than in the school district.) The child's parent or guardian must consent to make the child available for reevaluation upon request of the child's school district of residence. And the private school that the child wishes to attend with the scholarship must be accredited and must have notified DPI of its intent to participate in the program.

A private school that wishes to participate in the program must notify DPI of the number of spaces it has available for children who receive a scholarship under the program. A participating private school must accept applications under the program on a first-come first-served basis, but may give preference to siblings of students who are already attending the private school if it receives more applications than the number of spaces it has available.

A participating private school must implement, for each child that receives a scholarship, either 1) the IEP or services plan that the child's school district of residence developed in its most recent reevaluation of the child, or 2) a modified version of that IEP or services plan agreed to between the private school and the child's parent. The private school must also provide the child with any related services agreed to between the private school and the child's parent that are not included in the child's IEP or services plan.

A participating private school must comply with all health and safety laws that apply to public schools; must provide each child who applies for a scholarship with a profile of the private school's special education program; and must submit to DPI an annual school financial information report.

Unless it is also participating in a parental choice program, a private school participating in the Special Needs Scholarship Program is not required to report to DPI the kinds of information that school districts must report or to administer to any of its students the standardized tests that school districts must administer to public school students, and no performance evaluation of the private school is included in the annual school and school district accountability report.

A child with a disability who attends a private school under the program is not entitled to the special education and related services to which he or she would be entitled under state and federal law if he or she attended a public school.

In the 2016–17 school year, the scholarship amount under the Special Needs Scholarship Program was $12,000. There is no limit on the amount of additional tuition or fees that a private school may charge a child who receives a scholarship under the program. Once awarded, a scholarship continues until the child graduates from high school or until the end of the school term in which the child attains the age of 21, whichever comes first, unless upon reevaluation by the child's school district of residence, it is determined that the child is no longer a child with a disability. In that case, the child can continue to receive a scholarship under the program, but the amount of the scholarship is reduced to the per student amount paid under the parental choice programs. ▣

The legislature and the state budget

The legislature has the power of the purse. In Wisconsin, the state government may not spend a single dollar without the legislature specifically authorizing the expenditure by law. The manner in which the legislature controls the expenditure of state funds is through its appropriation power, which is a power granted to the legislature under the Wisconsin Constitution. In the 1936 case *Finnegan v. Dammann*, the Wisconsin Supreme Court defined an appropriation as "the setting aside from the public revenue of a certain sum of money for a specified object, in such a manner that the executive officers of the government are authorized to use that money, and no more, for that object, and no other."[1] It is the legislature that directs the governor and the executive branch in determining what state moneys are to be spent and the purposes for which they may be spent.

The most consequential exercise of the legislature's appropriation power is the enactment of the state budget. The biennial budget bill is easily the most significant piece of legislation that is enacted during the entire legislative session. This is the case for two reasons. First, the biennial budget bill appropriates almost all dollars that will be expended by state government during the two fiscal years covered by the bill. These dollars consist mostly of state taxes and revenues, program and license fees, and federal moneys allocated to Wisconsin. In 2015 Wisconsin Act 55, the state budget act for the 2015–17 fiscal biennium, the legislature authorized the expenditure of over $72 billion in total state government spending from all revenue sources. The second reason for the significance of the biennial budget bill is that it contains most of the governor's public policy agenda for the entire legislative session. The biennial budget bill is generally considered the one bill that "must pass" in order to sufficiently fund state government operations and programs during the fiscal years covered in the bill. As such, there is a strong incentive for the governor, as well as for legislators, to include in the biennial budget bill the major public policy items supported by the governor and the legislators. Hence legislative action on the biennial budget bill not only establishes the state budget, but also creates the major public policy programs of the governor and the legislature. The state budget process is therefore unequaled in its significance for the operations of state government and for its effects on the lives of the men and women who live and work in Wisconsin.

The state budget process: core principles

There are several core principles to the state budget process in Wisconsin. First, the state budget is a biennial budget, covering two years of state government operations and programs, with each fiscal year beginning on July 1 and ending on June 30. Many states have a "drop-dead" date by which a new state budget must be enacted in order for state government to continue to operate. Wisconsin does not have this. In Wisconsin, if a new state budget is not enacted by June 30 of the odd-numbered year, state government continues to operate and its programs are funded, but only at the prior year's appropriation amounts. The governor and the legislature strive to enact the state budget bill before July 1 of the odd-numbered year, and this deadline is usually met, but there is little short-term fiscal impact if it is not.

Second, Wisconsin uses what is known as program budgeting, in which executive branch state agencies are assigned to different functional areas and generally lump-sum appropriations are made to the agencies to fund the programs. The biennial budget bill therefore lists the overall amounts appropriated for agency operations and programs, but does not contain the level of expenditure detail that one might find in a state that uses a so-called "line-item" budget, in which each agency expenditure is specifically budgeted by line in the bill. This level of detail is not found in the biennial budget bill in Wisconsin; instead, it appears in accompanying budget documents, which are not law but which do capture the intentions of the governor and the legislature in budget deliberations. Consequently, that portion of the biennial bill that sets the expenditure levels of state operations and programs is roughly 200 pages in length, which is about 11 or 12 percent of the total number of pages of recent biennial budget bills.

Third, the Wisconsin Constitution requires that the legislature "provide for an annual tax sufficient to defray the estimated expenses of the state for each year."[2] What this means in practice is that Wisconsin has a balanced-budget requirement, in which state expenditures must equal revenues received by the state. Generally speaking, at each stage of the budget process, in which different versions of the budget are formulated and considered, each version of the budget must be balanced by having proposed state expenditures in any fiscal year be less than or equal to anticipated state revenues. This is a real constraint on state budgeting, one that is not found at the federal level.

Finally, the Wisconsin Constitution grants the governor partial veto power over appropriation bills. This partial veto power allows the governor to reduce amounts appropriated to state agencies for their operations and programs by writing in a lower amount, and allows the governor, with limitations, to delete specific words and digits within newly created statutory text in appropriation bills. The governor can thus police the legislature's budget actions. While this power has been curtailed in recent years by amendments to the constitution, the governor still can reduce all state expenditures, or the expenditures of any specific state agency, with the stroke of a pen, subject only to an override of his or her actions by a two-thirds vote of each house of the legislature—an event that last occurred in 1985.

The state budget process: an overview of executive action

Chapter 97, Laws of 1929,[3] required the governor to prepare the executive budget bill, and since 1931 the governor has prepared for introduction each biennial budget bill. The legislature delegated this task to the governor for understandable reasons: as head of the executive branch, the governor can coordinate the expenditures of executive-branch agencies, as well as assess the expenditure needs of each state agency. In addition, the growth in state government in the twentieth century resulted in a level of public policy and budgetary expertise in the executive branch that is generally not available in the legislative branch, which has a much smaller professional staff. Requiring the governor to produce the budget bill allows the legislature to work from a document that may require modification, because of different legislative public policy or budgetary priorities, but which already contains numerous budgetary matters and details that the legislature need not address. The governor's budget is a solid foundation on which the legislature can build its version of the budget and serves both the governor and the legislature well.

There are just a few steps in the preparation of the governor's budget. In the summer of each even-numbered year, the State Budget Office in the Department of Administration submits budget instructions to executive-branch agencies, establishing the manner of submitting budget requests and informing them of any broad fiscal or policy goals that the governor intends the state agencies to achieve. By September 15, state agencies must submit their budget requests to the State Budget Office for review by that office, the state budget director, and the governor. By November 20, the Department of Administration publishes a compilation and summation of the agency budget requests, as well as estimated revenues to the state for the current and forthcoming fiscal biennia. The State Budget Office oversees the preparation of legislation to achieve the governor's budget and policy recommendations. In this endeavor, the State Budget Office works closely with legal counsel at the Legislative

Reference Bureau—the legislature's bill-drafting agency—to draft the statutory language that will ultimately be incorporated into the governor's budget bill. Throughout the process, the governor is briefed on individual items in the budget bill, and the bill is complete only when the governor has signed off on the items in the bill. The governor is then required to deliver the budget bill to the legislature no later than the last Tuesday in January of each odd-numbered year, but the legislature regularly moves this deadline back into February to allow the governor to make changes in the bill once more accurate revenue estimates for the current and forthcoming fiscal biennia are available in late January. When the budget bill is delivered to the legislature, the governor addresses the legislature on the proposals contained in the bill, which more often than not are the key public policy goals of the governor's administration for the entire legislative session.

The first thing to note about the production of the executive budget bill is the role of the State Budget Office. The State Budget Office is headed by the state budget director and consists of about 25 budget analysts who serve in classified civil service positions. These analysts serve both Republican and Democratic gubernatorial administrations in a strictly nonpartisan and highly professional manner and are able to provide independent review of state agency funding requirements, as well as fashion fiscal and nonfiscal policies to achieve the governor's political and public policy aims. The State Budget Office translates the governor's public policy goals into workable and funded programs.

The second thing to note about the production of the executive budget bill is that the State Budget Office works directly with nonpartisan legal counsel in the Legislative Reference Bureau to prepare statutory text that achieves the governor's policy goals. The Legislative Reference Bureau has about 20 licensed attorneys with subject matter and legal expertise in virtually all policy areas. This is significant. The governor's budget bill is drafted in a professional, nonpartisan manner, so that the legislators need only focus on the public policies in the bill and not worry about the bill's legal quality or effectiveness. In addition, when the legislature takes up the governor's budget bill, the Legislative Reference Bureau attorneys who originally drafted the governor's provisions in the bill will be the ones who draft the legislature's alternatives. In this way, often the very same attorneys are working on the same language in the bill throughout the process. The legislature can thus count on experienced and competent legal counsel to prepare its budget bill in an accurate, high-quality, and nonpartisan manner.

Finally, it is important to note the political uses of the executive budget bill. The budget bill is by far the longest and most complex bill before the legislature during the entire biennial session. In recent years the bill has grown substantially in length. From 1961 to 1986, the 13 executive budget bills averaged 367 pages in length. From 1987 to 2012, in contrast, the 13 executive budget bills averaged 1,521 pages in length. This is more than a fourfold increase in the size of the executive budget bill. The 2015 executive budget bill was over 1,800 pages in length.

The executive budget bill is now a blueprint for the legislature for taking up the governor's goals for public policy change. When the governor steps up to the assembly podium to present the budget address to the legislature, an event that is televised throughout the state and broadcast live on the Internet, in many ways the political season commences in Wisconsin.

The state budget process: the role of the legislature

The Wisconsin Legislature is the policymaking body in this state and has the sole power to appropriate all moneys expended by the state. The biennial budget bill is, therefore, every bit as much of a product of legislative deliberation and action as it is of the governor's actions. The governor sets the agenda for legislative action on the budget, but the legislature examines, modifies or rejects, and altogether re-creates what the governor originally had in the budget bill. In addition, the legislature will devise a few policies of its own, often from whole cloth, or it will refashion the governor's policies so that they are barely recognizable from their original form. Much of what the governor has proposed in the budget bill will survive the legislative process, but the document that emerges from the legislature is very much a product of the legislature.

When the governor presents the budget bill to the legislature, it is by law introduced by the Joint Committee on Finance and is referred to that committee. In 1885, a young congressional scholar by the name of Woodrow Wilson, then a professor at Bryn Mawr College, wrote that "Congress in session is Congress on public exhibition, whilst Congress in its committee rooms is Congress at work."[4] This applies perfectly to the Wisconsin Legislature. It is in its several committee rooms that the Wisconsin Legislature does its work, and no committee more exemplifies that work ethic than the Joint Committee on Finance.

The Joint Committee on Finance consists of eight senators and eight representatives to the assembly. All bills that affect revenues, taxes, or expenditures are referred to that committee and must be reported out of that committee before the legislature may take the bill up for consideration and passage. It is fair to say that this committee is the most powerful standing committee in the legislature and is a training ground for legislative leadership. Legislators work on this committee and they work long hours. Upon introduction of the budget bill, the bill is referred to the Joint Committee on Finance and legislative work on the budget begins.

The Joint Committee on Finance does not work alone, but is staffed by the Legislative Fiscal Bureau, a nonpartisan legislative service agency. The Legislative Fiscal Bureau has about the same number of analysts as the State Budget Office, each of whom has policy and budgetary expertise in specific areas of state government. The analysts perform their work in a professional, nonpartisan manner, serving both the majority and minority parties in the legislature. After the budget bill is introduced, Legislative Fiscal Bureau analysts prepare a lengthy, detailed summary document that contains an analysis of every single item in the bill. The summary is written in plain English, is precise and exhaustive in its presentation of the governor's policies, and is hundreds of pages in length. The Legislative Fiscal Bureau summary is the document that forms the basis on which the legislature and the Joint Committee on Finance begin their work on the budget.

The Joint Committee on Finance will often hold hearings around the state on matters in the governor's budget bill, inviting comment from experts, other elected officials, and ordinary citizens. Beginning in April and continuing into May, the Legislative Fiscal Bureau prepares papers on the items contained in the budget bill, laying out alternatives or even new ways to address the same items in the bill. The Legislative Fiscal Bureau derives its alternatives from its own public policy expertise and from committee member involvement in working out alternatives to the governor's programs. Sometimes working groups will form among members of the committee to consider and propose policy alternatives. In April and May, the Joint Committee on Finance meets to approve items it will include in its version of the budget. These are lengthy, often contentious meetings that run late into the evening or early morning. It is not uncommon to see Joint Committee on Finance members and Legislative Fiscal Bureau analysts leaving the Capitol building in the bright light of early morning.

Once the committee has finished its work, the Legislative Fiscal Bureau oversees the production of a substitute amendment that incorporates the committee's version of the budget to replace the governor's budget bill. In this regard, the Legislative Fiscal Bureau gives drafting instructions to attorneys at the Legislative Reference Bureau, who also work around the clock to prepare the substitute amendment. While the executive branch often has six months or more to prepare the governor's budget bill, the Joint Committee on Finance will do its work in a little more than six to eight weeks. It is a hectic and tiring pace, but the end product is now a legislative one.

The committee's substitute amendment is not always the final and complete version of the legislature's budget bill. Each house of the legislature has the option of further amending the substitute amendment to include items of its own design or to modify or reject items included by the Joint Committee on Finance. Whether this occurs, and the extent to which the substitute amendment will be modified, depends on a number of factors, such as whether the same political party is the majority party in both houses, whether legislators who do not serve on the Joint Committee on Finance believe that their interests and concerns have been addressed in the substitute amendment, and the likelihood of the convening of a conference committee on the bill to resolve differences between the two houses. These calculations are based on substantive factors, in that members will work to include items that benefit them or their constituents, as well as on strategic considerations, in that members will want to fortify their own house's position in conference committee negotiations with the other house.

Once the legislature passes its version of the budget bill, most often before July 1, the bill is presented to the governor for signing. As mentioned earlier, the governor has partial veto power over appropriation bills and will use that power to modify what the legislature has wrought in the bill. The governor can reduce appropriations, as well as modify some statutory text. The extent to which the governor will partially veto the bill also depends on a number of factors, such as the partisan makeup of the legislature, the degree to which the governor agrees with what the legislature has done, and whether the governor has made agreements in negotiations with the legislature over what can and cannot be vetoed. Once the governor has signed the bill into law, the budget-making process is concluded, as the only other possible step is for the legislature to override one or more of the governor's partial vetoes—an action, as mentioned earlier, that has not happened since 1985.

Concluding considerations

The state budget-making process is truly a year-long event, beginning in the summer of each even-numbered year when the State Budget Office sends budget instructions to the state agencies, and concluding the following summer with the enactment of the biennial budget act. The process is characterized both by careful deliberation and by frenzied, all-night sessions and meetings. The budget bill is the work product of the governor, every elected member of the Senate and the Assembly, and numerous professional staff in both the executive and legislative branches. There is never an "easy" budget, as each fiscal biennium presents its own unique budgetary and political challenges. But there is never complete gridlock, as the legislature does complete its work. Sometimes the budget will be late, especially when the two houses are controlled by different political parties, but in the end Wisconsin will have a state budget. ▣

NOTES

1. *Finnegan v. Dammann*, 220 Wis. 143, 148, 264 N.W. 622 (1936).

2. Wisconsin Constitution, article VIII, section 5.

3. This would have been called Act 97 if it took effect today; before 1983, a bill that was enacted into law was called a "chapter" rather than an "act."

4. Woodrow Wilson, *Congressional Government, A Study in American Politics* (1885).

Significant enactments of the 2015 Legislature

Administrative law

Act 391 (AB-582) requires an economic impact analysis of a proposed rule to analyze any limitations that the rule would place on the free use of private property, allows for the substitution of a hearing examiner in a contested case hearing involving a decision of the Department of Natural Resources or the Department of Agriculture, Trade and Consumer Protection, and requires a court to accord no deference to a state agency's interpretation of law when reviewing an agency action or decision that restricts a property owner's free use of the owner's property.

Beverages

Act 279 (AB-808) prohibits issuance of an underage alcohol beverage citation to a victim of sexual assault or certain other crimes, or to a bystander present with the victim, if the victim or bystander cooperates with emergency responders.

Business and consumer law

Act 55 (SB-21) makes changes to the laws relating to the governance of the Wisconsin Economic Development Corporation, including prohibiting WEDC from originating new loans totaling more than $10 million in fiscal year 2015–16 and $5 million in fiscal year 2016–17, and prohibits WEDC from originating any new loan after June 30, 2017.

Act 295 (AB-837) revises the state's partnership law by adopting, with modifications, the most recent version of the Revised Uniform Partnership Act.

Children

Act 55 (SB-21) makes the following changes in the laws relating to children:

1. Transfers from the Department of Corrections to the Department of Children and Families supervision of community-based juvenile delinquency-related services provided by counties.

2. Eliminates aftercare and corrective sanctions supervision for juveniles placed under the supervision of DOC and instead requires DOC to provide community supervision for those juveniles.

3. Requires DCF to pay for or provide treatment and services to children who are the victims of sex trafficking.

4. Authorizes DCF to enter into a pay-for-performance contract with an organization to operate a program to reduce recidivism in the city of Milwaukee.

Act 367 (SB-618) expands what constitutes the crime of child sex trafficking, includes child sex trafficking under the definition of "abuse" in the Children's Code, requires the reporting and investigation of certain suspected child abuse cases involving prostitution or child sex trafficking, and makes changes to the information required to be included in a court order or provided to a care provider when a child is placed outside the home.

Constitutional amendments

Enrolled Joint Resolution 2 (Senate Joint Resolution 2), proposed by the 2015 legislature on second consideration, requires the supreme court to elect a chief justice for a term of two years. Previously, the justice with the longest continuous service was automatically chief justice. The amendment was ratified by the voters on April 7, 2015.

Enrolled Joint Resolution 7 (Assembly Joint Resolution 5), proposed by the 2015 legislature on first consideration, eliminates the Office of the State Treasurer from the constitution. The amendment also replaces the state treasurer with the lieutenant governor on the Board of Commissioners of Public Lands. To become a part of the constitution, the 2017 legislature must concur in the amendment, and the amendment must then be ratified by the voters.

Correctional system

Act 206 (SB-248) eliminates the requirement that a person be detained or in custody for at least 12 hours before being subject to a strip search so that a person who is detained or in custody for any period may be subject to a strip search if the person will be incarcerated with another person.

Crime, criminal procedure, and law enforcement

Act 30 (SB-95) criminalizes falsely claiming military service or military honors in order to receive a tangible benefit.

Act 64 (SB-43) limits the crimes that may be investigated in a John Doe hearing to certain felonies under the criminal code or any crime allegedly committed by a law enforcement officer or certain Department of Corrections employees; limits the application of secrecy orders in John Doe proceedings to only judges, prosecuting attorneys, law enforcement personnel, interpreters, and reporters; and imposes a six-month limit on a John Doe proceeding.

Act 80 (AB-8) makes it a Class I felony to install or use a device to intentionally view under another person's outer clothing, or to view another body part that is not otherwise visible, without that person's consent.

Act 109 (AB-220) establishes mandatory minimum periods of confinement in prison for a person who is prohibited from possessing a firearm because he or she was convicted of committing certain violent felonies but who either possesses a firearm within five years of completing a sentence for a felony or for certain violent misdemeanors or uses a firearm to commit certain violent felonies.

Act 238 (SB-383) provides immunity from civil and criminal liability for a health care provider who performs a body cavity search on a person confined in a jail or prison.

Act 370 (AB-630) prohibits a parent or guardian from capturing, distributing, or exhibiting a nude image of a child if the parent or guardian does such activity for sexual arousal, gratification, humiliation, degradation, or monetary or commercial gain.

Act 371 (SB-455) increases the penalties for fourth or subsequent drunken driving offenses and changes the definition of "injury" used for certain drunken driving offenses.

Education

HIGHER EDUCATION

Act 21 (SB-164) requires technical colleges to charge resident tuition to veterans, and their spouses and children, living in this state, regardless of whether they would otherwise be considered state residents, if certain conditions are met.

Act 55 (SB-21) does the following with respect to the University of Wisconsin System:

1. Reduces funding for general program operations in the 2015–17 biennium by $250 million, provides funding for increased fringe benefits costs, eliminates in fiscal year 2016–17 a separate appropriation for UW System administration, and increases the amount the UW System is required to transfer to the medical assistance trust fund.

2. In the 2015–16 and 2016–17 academic years, prohibits increases in resident

undergraduate tuition above the tuition charged in the 2014–15 academic year, except for student-approved differential tuition at UW-Stevens Point.

3. Eliminates requirements for tenure and probationary appointments.

4. Deletes a provision limiting the Board of Regents in accumulating auxiliary reserve funds from student fees.

5. Requires the Board of Regents to identify accountability measures in specified areas and submit them to the legislature for approval.

6. Requires the Board of Regents to create the Office of Educational Opportunity within the UW System, requires the UW System president to appoint the director of that office, and authorizes the director to authorize independent charter schools in certain school districts.

Act 281 (AB-740) increases funding for Wisconsin grants to technical college students.

Act 284 (AB-744) requires institutions of higher education to annually provide a letter to each student that contains certain information about the student's student loans, the institution's cost of attendance, and the amount of grants the student receives. The institution must also provide students with financial literacy information.

PRIMARY AND SECONDARY EDUCATION

Act 53 (SB-32) ends the SAGE Program and creates an achievement gap reduction program under which an eligible school board may enter into a contract with the Department of Public Instruction to receive funding in exchange for implementing strategies to improve the achievement of low-income pupils, such as reducing class size or providing one-on-one tutoring to pupils struggling with reading or mathematics.

Act 55 (SB-21) affects primary and secondary education as follows:

1. Makes changes to parental choice programs, including eliminating the statewide cap on the statewide PCP and increasing the cap on the number of pupils residing in a school district who may participate in the statewide PCP from 1 percent to 10 percent over a ten-year period. Beginning in the 2026–27 school year, there is no participation limit in the statewide PCP.

2. Authorizes the director of the Office of Educational Opportunity in the UW System to authorize independent charter schools in certain school districts. These independent charter schools are treated the same as independent "2r" charter schools.

3. Creates the Special Needs Scholarship Program, under which DPI

makes a payment to a private school on behalf of the parent of a child with a disability.

4. Creates Opportunity Schools and Partnership Programs for certain eligible school districts, including Milwaukee Public Schools.

5. Makes the following changes to the open enrollment program:

a. Eliminates the ability of a resident school district to reject an application for open enrollment because of an undue financial burden.

b. Beginning in the 2016–17 school year, replaces tuition payments for special needs pupils with a $12,000 per pupil transfer amount.

6. Authorizes a school board to allow high school pupils to earn credit by demonstrating proficiency in a subject area or by creating a learning portfolio in a subject area.

7. Requires the MPS school board to prepare an inventory of all school buildings in the school district; to identify the use of those buildings, including whether the building is surplus, underutilized, or vacant; and to provide for the purchase of such eligible school buildings to education operators, including private schools, and other entities.

8. Closes the Special Transfer Program, commonly known as the Chapter 220 Program, to a pupil unless the pupil participated in the program in the 2015–16 school year. Under the program, the state provides aid to school districts to support their voluntary efforts to reduce racial imbalance through inter-district and intra-district pupil transfers.

9. Prohibits the state superintendent from giving any effect to or adopting, or requiring a school board to give any effect to or adopt, any academic standard developed by the Common Core State Standards Initiative.

10. Allows a school board, operator of an independent charter school, or private school participating in a parental choice program to administer alternative, nationally recognized, norm-referenced assessments to pupils in lieu of those adopted by the state superintendent once certain conditions have been satisfied.

Elections

Act 37 (SB-121) makes election law changes, including requiring a write-in candidate to file a registration statement in order for write-in votes for that candidate to be counted; providing that a municipal board of canvassers need not reconvene if the municipal clerk certifies that he or she has received no provisional or absentee ballots between the time of the board's initial canvass and 4 p.m. on the Friday after the election; and providing that a school board referendum held in conjunction with a state, county, municipal, or judicial election must take place at the same polling place and during the same hours as the municipal election.

Act 117 (AB-387) doubles the contribution limits applicable to candidates for state or local office; allows corporations, cooperatives, labor organizations, and American Indian Tribes to make contributions to independent expenditure committees and referendum committees and to segregated funds established by political parties and legislative campaign committees; requires the reporting of expenditures for express advocacy coordinated with a candidate; and makes other changes to the campaign finance laws.

Act 118 (AB-388) eliminates the Government Accountability Board and replaces it with the Elections Commission, which administers and supervises elections, and the Ethics Commission, which administers and supervises ethics, campaign financing, and lobbying regulation.

Act 261 (SB-295) allows an individual with a current state driver's license or identification card to register online to vote; allows an individual to use a veterans identification card as a voter ID; allows occupants of residential care facilities to use intake documents as proof of residence for voter registration; and makes other changes related to elections administration.

Employment

Act 1 (SB-44) is known as the Right-to-Work Act. The act prohibits a person from requiring, as a condition of employment, an individual to refrain or resign from membership in a labor organization, to become or remain a member of a labor organization, or to pay dues or other charges to a labor organization. A person who violates this prohibition is guilty of a Class A misdemeanor.

Act 55 (SB-21) does the following relating to the unemployment insurance law:

1. Requires the Department of Workforce Development to set up a process for requiring certain claimants for UI benefits to take a drug test.

2. Allows an employer to submit to DWD the results of a drug test that was conducted on an individual as a condition of an offer of employment, the results of which may be used to disqualify the individual from receiving UI benefits.

3. Increases administrative penalties for claimants who commit acts of concealment in obtaining unemployment insurance benefits, from 15 percent to 40 percent of the benefits fraudulently obtained.

Act 55 also makes changes to the prevailing wage law, which requires an employee performing certain work on a project of public works to be paid the prevailing wage for the employee's trade or occupation. The changes include the following:

1. Exempting projects undertaken by local governments from the prevailing wage law.

2. Providing for the use of federally determined prevailing wage laws in lieu of rates ascertained by DWD.

3. Restricting the remedies available for a violation of the prevailing wage law.

Act 180 (AB-724) makes the following changes relating to worker's compensation:

1. Reduces the statute of limitations for a traumatic injury from 12 years to 6 years after the date of the injury or the date that worker's compensation was last paid.

2. Eliminates disability and death benefits for an injured employee who violates an employer's drug or alcohol policy if the violation caused the injury.

Act 345 (SB-517) requires certain employers to allow an employee who has been employed for at least one year to take up to six weeks of leave from his or her employment in a given year to serve as a bone marrow or organ donor.

Act 386 (AB-441) creates the Wisconsin Veterans Employment Initiative, which is a program to increase the number of veterans holding positions in state government.

Environment

Act 43 (SB-15) generally prohibits the manufacture or acceptance for sale of a personal care product containing microbeads, which are small, nonbiodegradable plastic particles.

Act 55 (SB-21) makes the following changes to the laws relating to the environment:

1. Sunsets eligibility for reimbursement under the petroleum environmental cleanup fund award program.

2. Reduces bonding authority for the clean water fund by $236,300,000 and increases bonding authority for the safe drinking water loan program by $5,400,000.

Health and social services

Act 55 (SB-21) makes changes related to the laws governing Medical Assistance, including the following:

1. Requires the Department of Health Services to seek waivers of federal Medicaid law to expand Family Care statewide and to make changes to Family Care and IRIS, including providing primary and acute care services as well as long-term care services.

2. Eliminates a three-month ineligibility period for BadgerCare Plus benefits for individuals whose access to other health insurance has ended.

Act 55 also makes the following changes to the Wisconsin Works (W-2) program:

1. Modifies the behaviors that constitute refusal to participate in a W-2 employment position, which results in the participant's ineligibility to participate in the W-2 program for three months.

2. Allows the Department of Children and Families, under the Transform Milwaukee Jobs Program, to pay an employer a wage subsidy that is less than minimum wage while still requiring the employer to pay a participant at least minimum wage.

3. Reduces the lifetime limit on receiving benefits under certain W-2 programs from 60 months to 48 months and allows a W-2 agency to extend this time limit if it determines that the individual is experiencing hardship or that the individual's family includes an individual who has been battered or subjected to extreme cruelty.

Act 55 also changes the laws relating to public assistance, other than W-2, including requiring DHS to screen and, if indicated, test and treat participants in the FoodShare employment and training program who are able-bodied adults for use of a controlled substance without a valid prescription for the controlled substance.

Act 56 (SB-179) prohibits any person from performing or inducing an abortion when the probable postfertilization age of the unborn child is 20 or more weeks unless the pregnant woman is undergoing a medical emergency. When the unborn child is 20 or more weeks probable postfertilization age and the pregnant woman is undergoing a medical emergency, the act generally requires the pregnancy to be terminated in the manner that provides the best opportunity for the unborn child to survive. The act further requires the facility in which an induced abortion is performed to report certain information to DHS and requires that, before an abortion is performed or induced, the woman be informed of the probable postfertilization age of the unborn child, the numerical odds of survival for an unborn child of that age, and the availability of perinatal hospice.

Act 151 (AB-310) requires DHS to apply for federal Title X grants and to distribute the funds received to public entities, including state, county, and local health departments and health clinics, and the Well-Woman Program for family planning and related preventive health services. DHS may distribute any remaining funds to certain nonpublic entities that provide comprehensive primary and preventive care.

Act 263 (AB-659) establishes certain requirements on DHS regulation of opioid treatment systems and narcotic treatment services for opiate addiction relating to the duration of certification, contracts for counseling services, length of narcotic treatment service, and geographic proximity requirements.

Act 265 (AB-366) requires a pain clinic to have a certificate from DHS in order to operate. The act also establishes requirements for pain clinics, including requirements relating to payment methods accepted by the clinic, direct dispensing of monitored prescription drugs, and having a medical director.

Justice

Act 22 (SB-35) eliminates the 48-hour waiting period for handgun purchases so that a firearms dealer may transfer a handgun immediately after receiving notice from the Department of Justice that the background check indicates that the purchaser is not prohibited from possessing a firearm under state or federal law.

Local law

Act 60 (SB-209) does all of the following:

1. Authorizes a local exposition district to assist in the development and construction of sports and entertainment arena facilities in this state.

2. Requires a local exposition district to enter into a development agreement with a professional basketball team or its affiliate to construct the sports and entertainment arena facilities, as well as a lease agreement. The district, the state, and sponsoring municipalities—in this case, the city of Milwaukee and Milwaukee County—must commit $250 million in financial assistance for the construction of the sports and entertainment arena facilities, and the team or its affiliates must also agree to provide $250 million in funding.

3. Requires the state to pay to the district for 20 years a $4 million annual payment, as well as reduces the shared revenue payment to Milwaukee County by $4 million per year for 20 years.

Act 176 (AB-568) does the following:

1. Prohibits the enactment or enforcement of local ordinances that require that rental units be inspected other than under certain circumstances.

2. Prohibits the enactment or enforcement of local ordinances that require rental units to be certified, registered, or licensed.

3. Restricts local inspection fees and occupancy or transfer of tenancy fees on rental units.

4. Prohibits the enactment or enforcement of local ordinances that require a landlord to register or obtain a license or certification in order to own or manage a residential rental property.

5. Requires a political subdivision to hold a public hearing before designating a property as a historic landmark or including a property in a historic district.

6. Allows an owner of property that is affected by a decision of a local landmarks commission to appeal the decision to the governing body of the political subdivision.

Act 391 (AB-582) prohibits a county from enacting a development moratorium, changes the notice requirements that a political subdivision must provide relating to potential zoning actions that could affect the use of a person's land, requires a court to resolve ambiguity in a zoning ordinance in favor of the free use of private property, and requires a supermajority vote for a political subdivision to enact a down zoning ordinance.

Natural resources

Act 55 (SB-21) makes changes to the laws relating to shoreland zoning. Current law requires all counties to enact shoreland zoning ordinances for their unincorporated areas and requires certain shorelands in cities and villages to be subject to shoreland zoning ordinances. The act specifies that shoreland zoning standards and ordinances apply to accessory structures in addition to principal structures located in a shoreland area and provides that if a city or village is required to enact an ordinance for shorelands in the city or village, the ordinance must be consistent with the requirements and limitations applicable to county shoreland zoning ordinances.

Occupational regulation

Act 16 (AB-143) establishes a statewide licensure program for transportation network companies, such as Uber and Lyft, which is administered by the

Department of Safety and Professional Services and includes specific requirements for transportation network companies and their drivers, including driver background checks, minimum automobile insurance levels, zero tolerance for a driver's use of drugs and alcohol during relevant times, passenger privacy protections, and nondiscrimination and accessibility requirements.

Real estate

Act 176 (AB-568) authorizes a landlord to terminate the tenancy of a tenant based on criminal activity committed by the tenant or a member of the tenant's household; makes remaining on property without consent criminal trespass and provides for the disposition of personal property left in rental property by a trespasser; creates a right-to-cure for certain tenants for certain breaches; and prohibits a local government from making the purchase or transfer of real property or the occupancy of residential real property contingent on whether a purchaser or other transferee takes certain actions with respect to the property.

Act 219 (SB-314) prohibits a person from obtaining title to or an interest in real property belonging to a state or political subdivision by adverse possession or prescriptive use and prohibits a state or political subdivision from obtaining title to or an interest in real property belonging to a person by adverse possession or prescriptive use.

State government

Act 55 (SB-21) authorizes an additional $101,193,900 in general obligation bonding authority during the 2015–17 fiscal biennium for new or revised state building projects.

Act 150 (AB-373) makes changes to the state civil service, including eliminating mandatory examinations and requiring applicants to file a resume with the Department of Administration; extending probationary periods; defining "just cause"; requiring layoffs to be based primarily on job performance; creating a grievance process for adverse employment decisions; and creating a new merit-based compensation program.

Taxation

Act 55 (SB-21) changes laws related to taxation as follows:

1. Modifies the state alternative minimum tax so that it is consistent with federal law changes to the federal alternative minimum tax.

2. Increases the individual income tax standard deduction for married tax filers.

Act 114 (SB-233) requires the Department of Revenue to distribute excess sales tax revenue collected from the local professional football stadium district to Brown County and the municipalities within Brown County.

Transportation

Act 55 (SB-21) authorizes $350 million in highway bonding if certain conditions are satisfied and the Joint Committee on Finance approves.

Trusts and estates; probate

Act 300 (AB-695) creates the Wisconsin Digital Property Act, which is based on the Revised Uniform Fiduciary Access to Digital Assets Act. The Wisconsin Digital Property Act governs the disclosure of digital property to a personal representative, agent under a power of attorney, trustee, or conservator or guardian of a protected person. ⬛

Significant decisions of the Wisconsin Supreme Court and Court of Appeals

June 2015 to December 2016

Wisconsin Supreme Court

MIRANDA WAIVER SUFFICIENT TO WAIVE RIGHT TO COUNSEL

In *State v. Delebreau*, 2015 WI 55, 362 Wis. 2d 542, 864 N.W.2d 852, the supreme court held that a defendant's *Miranda* waiver was sufficient to waive the defendant's constitutional right to have counsel present during a custodial interrogation. The court also held that such a waiver will not be presumed invalid simply because the defendant was represented by counsel.

Jesse Delebreau was arrested for delivering heroin. Approximately two weeks later, he was formally charged and made his initial appearance in court where he was represented by a public defender. While he was still in custody, investigators questioned Delebreau twice at the jail. At each interview, Delebreau waived his *Miranda* rights and did not ask for counsel. Before trial, Delebreau moved to suppress incriminating statements he made during the interviews, claiming that police had violated his constitutional right to have counsel present during the questioning. The circuit court denied the motion, the statements were introduced at trial, and a jury found him guilty. The court of appeals affirmed in a published opinion.

The supreme court affirmed in an opinion written by Justice Prosser. The court noted that the Sixth Amendment to the U.S. Constitution provides that, in all criminal prosecutions, the accused shall enjoy the right to have the assistance of counsel for his or her defense. Under prior Wisconsin Supreme Court precedent, if a defendant was formally charged with a crime and represented by counsel, the defendant was not required to affirmatively invoke his or her right to counsel. The court explained that the right to counsel arises when a defendant is charged with a crime and the defendant automatically invokes the right to counsel either by retaining counsel or by having counsel appointed. The court noted, however, that the legal landscape had changed.

In *Montejo v. Louisiana*, 556 U.S. 778 (2009), the U.S. Supreme Court declared that a defendant's waiver of his or her *Miranda* rights was sufficient to waive the defendant's Sixth Amendment right to counsel and that the waiver was not presumed invalid simply because the defendant was already represented by counsel. The Wisconsin Supreme Court concluded that *Montejo* effectively overruled prior Wisconsin precedent. Applying this new standard, the court found that Delebreau had given a valid *Miranda* waiver that also waived his right to have counsel present during the interrogation. Thus, Delebreau was not entitled to suppress his incriminating statements on Sixth Amendment grounds.

The court also interpreted the state analogue to the Sixth Amendment to determine whether it offered greater protections. The court found that, although the state constitution *may* provide a criminal defendant with rights beyond those afforded by the U.S. Constitution, in this case, the language of article I, section 7, of the Wisconsin Constitution did not differ so substantially from the federal Constitution so as to create a different right. Therefore, Delebreau also could not suppress his statements based on the Wisconsin Constitution.

Chief Justice Roggensack concurred and wrote separately because the majority opinion "overstated" the holding in *Montejo*. According to the concurrence, *Montejo* merely directs that a defendant must take affirmative action to invoke his or her Sixth Amendment right to have counsel present during police interrogation and that the right can be waived.

Justice Abrahamson dissented in an opinion joined by Justice A. W. Bradley. The dissent concluded that article I, section 7, of the Wisconsin Constitution stands apart from, and has meaning independent of, the Sixth Amendment to the U.S. Constitution. Although *Montejo* controls the interpretation of the Sixth Amendment, it does not control the interpretation of the Wisconsin Constitution. Thus, under prior Wisconsin Supreme Court precedent interpreting the Wisconsin Constitution, Delebreau's statements should have been suppressed.

WITHDRAWAL OF PLEA AGREEMENT BASED ON FAILURE TO WARN OF ADVERSE IMMIGRATION CONSEQUENCES

In three separate cases, the supreme court considered under what circumstances a noncitizen criminal defendant can withdraw a guilty plea because the defendant was not adequately warned about the immigration consequences of a conviction based on that plea. In the first two cases, the court considered what immigration information the *defendant's attorney* must provide to the defendant, and in the third case, the court considered what immigration information the *court* must provide to the defendant.

In *State v. Ortiz-Mondragon*, 2015 WI 73, 364 Wis. 2d 1, 866 N.W.2d 717, the supreme court considered whether defense counsel provided ineffective assistance when counsel failed to advise Fernando Ortiz-Mondragon that pleading no contest to the crime of substantial battery was certain to result in his deportation.

Ortiz-Mondragon pled no contest to substantial battery committed as an act of domestic abuse and other charges. In connection with the plea, Ortiz-Mondragon's attorney advised him that his plea could result in deportation, the exclusion of admission into this country, or the denial of naturalization under federal law. After serving his four-month jail sentence, Ortiz-Mondragon was deported from the United States.

Ortiz-Mondragon filed a motion for post-conviction relief to withdraw his no-contest plea. He argued that, based on U.S. Supreme Court precedent, his defense counsel provided deficient representation by failing to inform him that his no-contest plea was certain to result in his deportation and permanent exclusion from the United States. He relied on *Padilla v. Kentucky*, 559 U.S. 356 (2010), in which the U.S. Supreme Court held that, when immigration consequences are clear, a criminal defense attorney must give correct advice regarding those consequences to a noncitizen defendant. If the law is not succinct and straightforward, the attorney only needs to advise that a criminal conviction may carry a risk of adverse immigration consequences.

Ortiz-Mondragon claimed that he was certain to be deported because substantial battery is a "crime involving moral turpitude" under federal immigration law. Therefore, under *Padilla*, his counsel was deficient for failing to advise him that, if he pled no contest to the charge, deportation was certain. The circuit court denied the motion, and the court of appeals affirmed in a published opinion.

In an opinion written by Justice Ziegler, the Wisconsin Supreme Court affirmed. The court held that federal immigration law is not "succinct, clear, and explicit" on the question of whether Ortiz-Mondragon's substantial battery is a crime involving moral turpitude. The methodology for determining whether a crime qualifies as a crime involving moral turpitude varies by jurisdiction and is in a state of flux. Therefore, Ortiz-Mondragon's defense counsel only needed to advise him that the pending criminal charges may carry a risk of adverse immigration consequences. Because the attorney gave that advice, the attorney was not deficient, and Ortiz-Mondragon could not withdraw his plea.

Justice A. W. Bradley dissented in an opinion joined by Justice Abrahamson. The dissent argued that the majority's analysis of what constitutes a "crime involving moral turpitude" was unnecessary because a separate provision under federal immigration law clearly provides that a conviction of domestic violence renders a noncitizen deportable. Because the immigration consequences were clear, defense counsel's duty to give correct advice was likewise clear. The dissent concluded that the case should be remanded to the circuit court for a hearing to determine the nature and extent of the advice Ortiz-Mondragon's defense counsel gave him regarding the immigration consequences of his plea.

In *State v. Shata*, 2015 WI 74, 364 Wis. 2d 63, 868 N.W.2d 93, the supreme court considered whether defense counsel provided ineffective assistance when counsel failed to advise Shata that pleading guilty to a controlled substance offense would absolutely result in deportation.

Hatem Shata pled guilty to possession of marijuana with intent to deliver. In connection with the plea, Shata's attorney advised him that he faced a "strong chance" of deportation if convicted based on his plea. About four months after he was sentenced, Shata filed a post-conviction motion to withdraw his guilty plea. He argued that, under *Padilla*, his defense counsel provided deficient representation by failing to inform him that a conviction based on his guilty plea would absolutely result in deportation. He claimed that any noncitizen convicted of a controlled substance offense is automatically deportable, and therefore defense counsel should have advised him that deportation was absolutely certain. The circuit court denied the motion. The court of appeals reversed in an unpublished opinion.

In an opinion written by Justice Ziegler, the supreme court reversed the court of appeals. All parties agreed that Shata's controlled substance conviction made him "deportable." Nevertheless, the court found that deportation was not absolutely certain because the federal government has discretion in enforcing the nation's immigration laws, and executive action, including action by the U.S. Department of Homeland Security, could block deportation of a deportable noncitizen. In short, the advice given by Shata's attorney was correct—Shata's guilty plea carried a strong chance of deportation, but deportation was not absolutely certain.

Justice A. W. Bradley dissented in an opinion joined by Justice Abrahamson. The dissent argued that the case involved the same type of crime and the same immigration statute as in *Padilla*, and, therefore, the result should be the same. Defense counsel should have advised Shata that his conviction would make him "subject to automatic deportation." The dissent found that advising that "deportation is very likely" is not the same as advising that "deportation is presumptively mandatory," and, therefore, defense counsel's performance was deficient.

Finally, in *State v. Valadez*, 2016 WI 4, 366 Wis. 2d 332, 874 N.W.2d 514, the supreme court considered under what circumstances a criminal defendant can withdraw a guilty plea based on the circuit court's failure to provide statutory warnings regarding the immigration consequences of the plea.

Melisa Valadez became a lawful permanent resident (LPR) in 2001. In 2004 and 2005, she pled guilty to three separate charges related to possession of controlled substances. At her plea hearings, the circuit courts failed to warn Valadez, as required by statute, that her pleas may have immigration consequences. Valadez served jail time and completed all conditions of her probation. In 2013, Valadez filed a motion to withdraw her guilty pleas because, as a result of her convictions, she was unable to renew her LPR card and, if she left the country, she would likely be excluded from admission. The circuit court denied the motion, and the court of appeals certified the case to the supreme court.

In an opinion written by Justice Abrahamson, the supreme court reversed the circuit court's denial of the motion. The supreme court held that the relevant statute provides that, if the circuit court failed to properly advise a defendant regarding the immigration risks of a guilty plea, the court must allow the defendant to withdraw the plea if the defendant shows that the plea is likely to result in deportation, exclusion from admission, or denial of naturalization. In this case, there was no dispute that the circuit court did not provide the required warning. Therefore, the case centered on whether Valadez had shown that her plea was "likely" to result in adverse immigration consequences.

The court concluded that Valadez's convictions made her "inadmissible" under the immigration statutes. Thus, she had shown that she was "likely" to be excluded from admission, and it was not necessary for her to first leave the country and attempt to return so that the federal government actually took steps to exclude her. Therefore, the circuit court incorrectly denied Valadez's motion to withdraw her guilty pleas. The court declined to rule on whether the motion was timely because the parties agreed that it was.

Justice Ziegler concurred in part and dissented in part in an opinion joined by Justice Gableman. The opinion agreed that Valadez had proved that she was likely to be excluded from admission but dissented because there could be other impediments to withdrawal of her guilty pleas that the circuit court could address on remand, for example, arguments regarding any time limits applicable to the motion.

Justice Prosser dissented in an opinion joined by Chief Justice Roggensack. The dissent argued that the relevant statute does not grant an absolute right to plea withdrawal. Rather, supreme court precedent establishes that the state may prove that, despite the defect in the plea colloquy, the plea was knowing, intelligent, and voluntary. The dissent also argued that a reasonable time limit should apply to these types of motions.

Justice R. G. Bradley did not participate.

REASONABLE MISTAKE OF LAW AND REASONABLE SUSPICION IN A TRAFFIC STOP

In *State v. Houghton*, 2015 WI 79, 364 Wis. 2d 234, 868 N.W.2d 143, the supreme court held that a police officer's reasonable suspicion that a motorist has been or is violating a traffic law is sufficient for the officer to initiate a traffic stop, and held that an officer's objectively reasonable mistake of law may form the basis for the officer's reasonable suspicion.

In this case, an East Troy police officer pulled Richard Houghton over after observing Houghton's vehicle traveling without a front license plate and with an air freshener and GPS unit visible in the front windshield. Upon approaching the vehicle, the officer detected the odor of marijuana, which led him to conduct a search of the vehicle that resulted in the discovery of marijuana and associated paraphernalia. Houghton was charged with possession with intent to deliver and filed a motion to suppress evidence obtained during the search, arguing that the lack of a front license plate on his car and the items in his windshield were not violations of Wisconsin law, and consequently that the officer lacked a justification for the stop. The circuit court denied the motion, and Houghton was convicted. The court of appeals reversed.

The supreme court first addressed the general standard required for police to conduct stops related to traffic violations. The court noted that federal and Wisconsin cases have held that reasonable suspicion of a traffic violation provides the basis for a stop under certain circumstances. Furthermore, the court noted that reasonable suspicion is a lower standard for police to conduct a stop than is probable cause, requiring only specific and articulable facts that, when taken together with reasonable inferences from those facts, warrant intrusion. Houghton argued that, in a case in which the officer claims to have observed a traffic violation rather than to have merely suspected one, the stop must be based on probable cause. The court rejected this argument, concluding instead that police officers may initiate traffic stops whenever they have reasonable suspicion that a traffic law has been or will be violated.

The court next held that an objectively reasonable mistake of law by a police officer can form the basis for reasonable suspicion to conduct a traffic stop. Past Wisconsin cases had rejected this proposition. However, a recent

U.S. Supreme Court case, *Heien v. North Carolina*, 574 U.S. ___, 135 S. Ct. 530 (2014), held that an investigatory stop under these circumstances did not violate an individual's right to be free from unreasonable seizure under the Fourth Amendment to the U.S. Constitution. Noting that it had traditionally understood the Wisconsin Constitution's provision on search and seizure to have the same meaning as the Fourth Amendment, the court concluded that it would adopt the U.S. Supreme Court's reasoning.

Turning to the facts of the case, the court first determined that the presence of the air freshener and GPS unit attached to the front windshield of Houghton's vehicle did not violate any traffic laws. The court observed that the plain language of section 346.88 (3) (a) and (b) of the Wisconsin Statutes appeared to prohibit a driver from having almost any item attached to the front windshield of his or her vehicle. Nevertheless, the court interpreted these provisions to have a more narrow meaning. The court held that section 346.88 (3) (a), Wisconsin Statutes, prohibits only the attachment of signs, posters, and other items of a similar nature to the front windshield. The court held that section 346.88 (3) (b), Wisconsin Statutes, prohibits only objects that materially obstruct the driver's clear view through the windshield.

The court next concluded that the officer's interpretation that section 346.88, Wisconsin Statutes, prohibits the placement of any object on the front windshield was an objectively reasonable mistake of law. The court reasoned that the statute had never been interpreted before and that a reasonable judge could disagree with the court's construction of the statute. On the other hand, the court held that the officer's belief that Houghton violated the law by not having a front license plate displayed was an objectively unreasonable mistake of law or fact. Regardless, the court held that the officer had reasonable suspicion based on the officer's mistaken understanding of the statute. Consequently, the court determined that the traffic stop did not violate Houghton's rights under the Wisconsin Constitution.

Justice Abrahamson dissented, joined by Justice A. W. Bradley. Justice Abrahamson noted that past Wisconsin cases had rejected the idea that an officer's mistake of law can justify reasonable suspicion for a traffic stop. She disagreed with the majority's contention that the Wisconsin Constitution's provision on search and seizure has the same meaning as the U.S. Constitution's Fourth Amendment, asserting instead that the Wisconsin provision sets forth distinct rights. Moreover, Justice Abrahamson expressed concern that allowing a police officer's mistake of law to support a traffic stop would remove the incentive for officers to make certain that they properly understand the law.

Accordingly, she concluded that the stop in question was unlawful and that Houghton's conviction should be reversed.

JOHN DOE INVESTIGATIONS

After a John Doe proceeding was initiated in Milwaukee County, the investigation subsequently expanded to Columbia, Dane, Dodge, and Iowa counties. Although not consolidated, the proceedings were handled by a single special prosecutor and a single John Doe judge. In *State ex rel. Two Unnamed Petitioners v. Peterson*, 2015 WI 85, 363 Wis. 2d 1, 866 N.W.2d 165, the supreme court consolidated and addressed three cases arising from that investigation. In a subsequent decision, *State ex rel. Three Unnamed Petitioners v. Peterson*, 2015 WI 103, 365 Wis. 2d 351, 875 N.W.2d 49, the supreme court denied a motion for reconsideration of its decision in *Two Unnamed Petitioners*, while also denying a motion for stay and clarifying the court's mandate. The John Doe special prosecutor's investigation centered on allegedly illegal coordination between an unnamed candidate's campaign committee and issue advocacy organizations during the 2012 Wisconsin recall elections. Appeals on various issues ensued after the John Doe judge granted motions to quash the subpoenas and search warrants related to the investigation.

In the first of the three cases addressed in *Two Unnamed Petitioners*, the court considered an original action by certain targets of the John Doe investigation (the Unnamed Movants) seeking a declaration that the special prosecutor's theory of the case was invalid under Wisconsin law. The special prosecutor alleged two theories of illegal coordination as the bases for the litigation. First, the special prosecutor alleged that the issue advocacy organizations and the candidate's campaign committee worked "hand in glove," such that the organizations became mere subcommittees of the candidate's campaign committee. Section 11.10 (4), 2011–12 Wisconsin Statutes, provides that a committee that acts with the cooperation of a candidate is deemed a subcommittee of the candidate's personal campaign committee. Second, the special prosecutor alleged that the coordinated issue advocacy in question amounted to in-kind contributions because the issue advocacy was done for the benefit of the candidate. Under the special prosecutor's theory of the case, both of these provisions triggered campaign finance reporting requirements that were not met.

In an opinion written by Justice Gableman, the court granted the Unnamed Movants' request for a declaration finding the special prosecutor's theory of the case invalid and unsupported in law. The majority concluded that the definition of "political purposes" found in section 11.01 (16), 2011–12 Wisconsin Statutes, is unconstitutionally overbroad and vague under the U.S. and Wisconsin Constitutions because the language "is so sweeping that its sanctions may be applied to constitutionally protected conduct which the state is not permitted to regulate." The court held that a limiting construction should be applied, specifically, that "political purposes" must be limited to express advocacy and its functional equivalent. The court noted that express advocacy is speech that is clearly election related, whereas issue advocacy refers to "ordinary political speech about issues, policy, and public officials."

Because the court determined that the special prosecutor alleged only coordinated issue advocacy between the organizations and the candidate's campaign committee, the majority found that the alleged conduct was beyond the scope of Wisconsin campaign finance regulation. Accordingly, the majority held that the special prosecutor's theory of the case was invalid and ordered the John Doe investigation closed.

In the second case before the court in *Two Unnamed Petitioners*, the court held that the special prosecutor failed to prove that the reserve judge overseeing the John Doe investigation violated a plain legal duty when he exercised his discretion to quash the subpoenas and search warrants and ordered the return of all property seized by the special prosecutor. The court held that the reserve judge exercised his discretion under the John Doe statute, section 968.26, 2011–12 Wisconsin Statutes, to determine the extent of a John Doe investigation and further, that it is within the discretion of a trial court to quash subpoenas. The court found that supervisory writs (the relief requested) are not "appropriate vehicles" to review a judge's discretionary acts, and as such, the special prosecutor failed to show that the reserve judge violated a plain legal duty. Accordingly, the court denied the supervisory writ and affirmed the reserve judge's order.

In the third consolidated case before the court in *Two Unnamed Petitioners*, the court affirmed a court of appeals decision denying the Unnamed Movants' request for a supervisory writ. The court held that the Unnamed Movants failed to prove that either reserve judge involved violated a plain legal duty by 1) accepting an appointment as a reserve judge; 2) convening a multi-county John Doe proceeding; or 3) appointing a special prosecutor. Specifically, the court found that a judge's obligation to correctly find facts and apply the law is not the type of duty to be addressed through a supervisory writ procedure "as it would extend supervisory jurisdiction to a virtually unlimited range of decisions involving the finding of facts and application of law." The court found the judges did not violate any plain duty in accepting their appointments or their subsequent assignment to handle the John Doe proceeding. The court further found that the Wisconsin Statutes are silent regarding whether one judge can convene a multi-county John Doe proceeding and that, therefore, there is no prohibition nor violation of any plain legal duty. Finally, the court found that although the appointment of the special prosecutor may have been improper, the Unnamed Movants failed to prove a violation of any plain legal duty. Given the procedural posture of the case, the court did not need to reach the issue of the effect of an unlawful appointment; rather, it simply held that the requirements for issuance of a supervisory writ were not met.

Justice Prosser concurred, finding the subpoenas and search warrants were invalid because the subpoenas and search warrants were unconstitutionally overbroad and, further, that the special prosecutor's appointment was invalid. Justice Prosser's concurrence was joined in part by Justice Roggensack, and Justices Roggensack, Gableman, and Ziegler joined Justice Prosser in finding that the order appointing the special prosecutor lacked validity as a judge only has authority to appoint a special prosecutor if at least one of the nine conditions set forth in section 978.045 (1r), 2011–12 Wisconsin Statutes, is satisfied. The four concurring justices found that none of the conditions were satisfied.

Justice Ziegler also wrote a separate concurrence, writing to emphasize that, even if the search warrants issued by the John Doe judge were lawfully issued, their execution could be subject to a reasonableness analysis under the Fourth Amendment to the U.S. Constitution and the Wisconsin Constitution's counterpart.

Justice Abrahamson also wrote separately concurring in part and dissenting in part, finding that the majority "adopts an unprecedented and faulty interpretation of Wisconsin's campaign finance law and of the First Amendment." Among other things, Justice Abrahamson found that chapter 11, Wisconsin Statutes, does not regulate disbursements for issue advocacy made by independent political organizations, but that chapter 11 does require a candidate's campaign committee to report coordinated disbursements for issue advocacy as contributions received by the candidate or the candidate's campaign committee. Justice Crooks also wrote separately, concurring in part and dissenting in part. He disagreed with the majority opinion that section 11.06, 2011–12 Wisconsin Statutes, was unconstitutionally broad and vague in requiring reporting of in-kind contributions, including coordinated spending on issue advocacy.

He further noted that the special prosecutor had, in fact, alleged express advocacy as a secondary theory of criminal activity. Both Justice Abrahamson and Justice Crooks found the reporting requirement consistent with the U.S. and Wisconsin Constitutions and that the John Doe investigation should not have been terminated.

In the follow up *per curiam* opinion, *Three Unnamed Petitioners*, issued in December 2015, the court denied a motion for reconsideration, denied a motion for stay, but modified and clarified the order from *Two Unnamed Petitioners*. The court held that a majority of the court had ruled in *Two Unnamed Petitioners* that the special prosecutor's appointment was invalid. However, because neither the majority opinion nor the concurrence included a mandate regarding the effect of the determination that the appointment was invalid, there was no legal ruling on the issue of the special prosecutor's authority as of the issuance of *Two Unnamed Petitioners*. Because a majority of the court found the appointment invalid, the court ruled that the special prosecutor's authority to litigate the case terminated as of the date of the court's *per curiam* ruling in *Three Unnamed Petitioners*, except for the limited actions ordered by the court. The court noted that because the special prosecutor could no longer represent the prosecution, the court would be open to prompt review of motions to intervene by one or more of the district attorneys from the counties involved. The court denied reconsideration on whether the John Doe investigation should have been allowed to continue regarding coordination related to express advocacy, finding that the special prosecutor failed to raise the issue before the John Doe judge and therefore could not meet the standard for a supervisory writ to reverse the John Doe judge's order. Finally, the court modified its instructions regarding return of property seized in the investigation and the destruction of copies of documents and other materials relating to the investigation, delaying action until after the completion of proceedings in the U.S. Supreme Court or after the deadline for filing the petition for certiorari review, if no petition was filed.

Justice Abrahamson wrote separately in *Three Unnamed Petitioners*, concurring in part and dissenting in part, noting that the majority opinion in *Two Unnamed Petitioners* was flawed and that she therefore agreed it should be modified. However, she disagreed with the denial of the motion for reconsideration.

Justice A. W. Bradley did not participate in *Two Unnamed Petitioners*. Justice A. W. Bradley and Justice R. G. Bradley did not participate in *Three Unnamed Petitioners*, and Justice Crooks passed away while *Three Unnamed Petitioners* was pending and before final resolution by the court.

TRAFFIC STOPS BASED ON NON-CRIMINAL, NON-TRAFFIC OFFENSES

In *State v. Iverson*, 2015 WI 101, 365 Wis. 2d 302, 871 N.W.2d 661, the supreme court held that a law enforcement officer may conduct a warrantless traffic stop based on the officer's reasonable suspicion that an occupant of a vehicle has committed a non-traffic civil forfeiture offense.

In this case, a state patrol trooper observed a car drift within its lane and then stop at two different intersections with flashing yellow lights even though there was no traffic. The trooper then observed a lit cigarette being thrown from the vehicle and landing on the road, scattering its ashes. The trooper initiated a traffic stop based on the littering statute, section 287.81 (2) (a) and (b), Wisconsin Statutes, which establishes a $500 forfeiture for anyone who deposits or discharges solid waste on a highway or permits solid waste to be thrown from a vehicle operated by the person. A passenger in the car admitted discarding the cigarette, but the trooper ultimately cited the driver, Daniel Iverson, for drunk driving. After pleading not guilty, Iverson filed a motion to suppress evidence obtained following the traffic stop. The circuit court granted the motion and dismissed the case. The court of appeals affirmed, concluding that a non-traffic civil forfeiture does not provide a sufficient basis for a warrantless traffic stop.

In its reversal of the court of appeals decision, the supreme court addressed four issues: 1) whether throwing a cigarette butt onto a highway constitutes a violation of the littering statute; 2) whether the trooper had statutory authority to conduct a warrantless traffic stop in order to enforce the littering statute; 3) whether a state traffic patrol officer may conduct a warrantless traffic stop based on probable cause or reasonable suspicion that a violation of a non-traffic civil forfeiture law has occurred; and 4) whether, in this case, the trooper possessed probable cause or reasonable suspicion that a littering violation had occurred.

Addressing the first issue, the court held that a cigarette butt falls under the definition of "solid waste" in the littering statute because the definition includes the broad language "other discarded . . . materials." Addressing the second issue, the court held that a number of statutes provide a state trooper explicit authority to conduct traffic stops in order to investigate violations of the littering statute and to arrest violators under certain conditions.

The supreme court then addressed the issue of whether it is reasonable under the Fourth Amendment to the U.S. Constitution to conduct a traffic stop based on a non-traffic civil forfeiture offense. In a previous case, the supreme court stated that "[e]ven if no probable cause exist[s], a police officer may still conduct a traffic stop when, under the totality of the circumstances, he or she has grounds to reasonably suspect that a crime or traffic violation has been or will be committed." *State v. Popke*, 2009 WI 37, ¶ 23, 317 Wis. 2d 118, 765 N.W.2d 569. Relying on this, the court of appeals had concluded that an officer may only conduct a traffic stop if granted explicit authority under section 345.22 or 968.24, Wisconsin Statutes, which authorizes temporary questioning to investigate suspected criminal activity and warrantless arrest for traffic violations, respectively. The supreme court noted that this conclusion ignored other statutes (sections 23.58 and 110.07, Wisconsin Statutes) that explicitly authorize officers to investigate suspected violations of certain statutes, including the littering statute. The court also noted that *Popke* addressed a factual situation based only on criminal and traffic violations and, therefore, that its holding was limited to those issues.

The court also rejected the argument that the statutory categorization of civil forfeitures into traffic-related and non-traffic-related limits the authority of troopers to enforce non-traffic laws. The court held that, regardless of how it is categorized, the littering statute's language is broad enough to apply to highways, and the state traffic patrol has statutory authority to enforce it. Addressing the final question, the court held that, because the trooper testified that he saw a cigarette being ejected from the car and land on the highway, he had probable cause to believe someone in the car had violated the littering statute.

Justice Abrahamson, joined by Justice A. W. Bradley, concurred but objected to the majority's decision not to use a totality-of-the-circumstances test when analyzing the reasonableness of the traffic stop under the Fourth Amendment, and its use, instead, of a more abstract test looking at whether it is ever reasonable to conduct a traffic stop for littering.

Justice R. G. Bradley did not participate.

EMPLOYEES MUST BE PAID FOR TIME SPENT DONNING AND DOFFING

In *United Food & Commercial Workers Union, Local 1473 v. Hormel Foods Corp.*, 2016 WI 13, 367 Wis. 2d 131, 876 N.W.2d 99, the supreme court considered whether Hormel violated Wisconsin wage and hour laws by failing to pay its employees for the time they spent putting on (donning) and taking off (doffing) required clothing and equipment before and after their work shifts and unpaid lunch breaks.

Hormel operated a canning facility in Beloit, where employees prepared, cooked, and canned various food products. Federal regulations required Hormel to meet certain standards of cleanliness, quality, and safety including, for example, requiring employees to protect against food contamination by washing their hands and wearing clean clothing. Hormel's own rules required employees to wear hard hats, hearing protection, eye protection, hair nets, sanitary footwear, and clean clothing. The clothing and equipment was provided by Hormel and could not be worn outside the facility.

The circuit court found that the donning and doffing of the required clothing and equipment at the beginning and end of every work shift and during lunch breaks was integral and indispensable to the performance of the Hormel employees' principal activity of producing canned food products and awarded damages. Hormel appealed, and the court of appeals certified the appeal to the supreme court.

In an opinion written by Justice Abrahamson and joined by Justice A. W. Bradley, the court first agreed with the circuit court that the required donning and doffing was integral and indispensable.

The Wisconsin Administrative Code requires an employee to be paid for all time spent in activities that are integral and indispensable to the performance of the employee's principal work activity. The supreme court looked to section DWD 272.12 (2) (e) 1. c., Wisconsin Administrative Code, which provides an example of an integral part of a principal activity that justifies compensation: if an employee at a chemical plant cannot perform his or her principal activities without putting on certain clothes, then donning and doffing those clothes at the beginning and end of a workday would be an integral part of the employee's principal activity; however, if changing clothes is simply a convenience to the employee, it would not be an integral part of the employee's principal activity.

The supreme court also looked to *Weissman v. Tyson Prepared Goods, Inc.,* 2013 WI App 109, 350 Wis. 2d 380, 838 N.W.2d 502 (*Tyson Foods*), in which the court of appeals relied on the chemical plant example in section DWD 272.12 (2) (e), Wisconsin Administrative Code, to determine that the need to avoid food contamination at a meat processing plant made the donning and doffing of the clothing and equipment indispensable to the Tyson employees' principal work activities of manufacturing food and that the time spent donning and doffing was therefore compensable work time.

The supreme court noted that both in the chemical plant example in section DWD 272.12 (2) (e), Wisconsin Administrative Code, and in *Tyson Foods,* safety laws, rules of the employer, and the nature of the employees' work all required the employees to change clothes in order to do their jobs and that cleanliness and food safety were intrinsic elements of preparing and canning food at the Hormel facility.

The court disagreed with the argument that *Integrity Staffing Solutions, Inc. v. Busk*, 574 U.S. ___, 135 S. Ct. 513 (2014), overturned *Tyson Foods*. In *Integrity Staffing*, the U.S. Supreme Court held that employees' time spent waiting in line to undergo and undergoing security screenings to check for stolen merchandise was not integral and indispensable to the employees' principal work activity of retrieving and packaging products, because the screenings could have been eliminated without affecting the employees' ability to retrieve and package products. The Wisconsin Supreme Court held that *Integrity Staffing* was consistent with *Tyson Foods* even though the two cases reached different conclusions.

The court also disagreed that the compensation for the time spent donning and doffing the required clothing and equipment was not too minimal to merit compensation (*de minimis*). The *de minimis* rule allows employers to disregard otherwise compensable work when it concerns only a few seconds or minutes of work beyond scheduled work hours. The court found that the unpaid compensation of more than $500 for each employee, based on 24 hours per year of unpaid work time, was a substantial sum both for the employees and for Hormel.

Finally, Justices Abrahamson and A. W. Bradley declined to rule on whether employees' time spent donning and doffing required clothing and equipment during their lunch hours was compensable work time due to a lack of argument on appeal and instead simply accepted the circuit court's award of damages on this issue.

Chief Justice Roggensack concurred with the majority that the donning and doffing at the beginning and end of a workday was compensable work time and that the *de minimis* rule did not prevent compensation for that time but dissented on the issue of whether donning and doffing during lunch hours was compensable work time. The chief justice argued that leaving during a lunch break served no interest of Hormel and was not an integral part of the employees' principal work activities and that this time was therefore not compensable work time.

Justice Gableman, joined by Justice Ziegler, dissented, arguing that the donning and doffing of the required clothing and equipment was not integral and indispensable to the Hormel employees' principal activity of canning food.

GRANDPARENT VISITATION RIGHTS

In *S.A.M. v. Meister*, 2016 WI 22, 367 Wis. 2d 447, 876 N.W.2d 746, the supreme court considered grandparent visitation rights, specifically, the proper interpretation of section 767.43 (1), Wisconsin Statutes, and whether that statute unconstitutionally infringes on parents' due process rights. The court held that the statute does not require a grandparent, greatgrandparent, or stepparent who files a motion for visitation rights under that subsection to prove that he or she has maintained a relationship similar to a parent-child relationship with the child. The court further held that the statute does not unconstitutionally infringe on parents' constitutional rights.

Under section 767.43 (1), Wisconsin Statutes, a "grandparent, greatgrandparent, stepparent or person who has maintained a relationship similar to a parent-child relationship with the child" may file a petition for visitation rights, which a court may grant "if the parents have notice of the hearing and if the court determines that visitation is in the best interest of the child."

This statutory construction case arose from a petition by a paternal grandparent, Carol Meister, for visitation rights to her grandchildren following her son's divorce from the children's mother. A family court commissioner found that section 767.43 (1), Wisconsin Statutes, requires a grandparent to have a relationship similar to a parent-child relationship and, finding that such a relationship existed between Meister and her grandchildren, granted Meister visitation. The children's mother sought review of the commissioner's order. The circuit court also found that the statute requires a grandparent to have a relationship similar to a parent-child relationship but issued an order reversing the decision of the commissioner on the grounds that Meister did not have such a relationship with her grandchildren.

The children, represented by a guardian ad litem, appealed the circuit court's ruling. The court of appeals, relying on its own precedent, *Rogers v. Rogers*, 2007 WI App 50, 300 Wis. 2d 532, 731 N.W.2d 347, for interpreting the language now in section 767.43 (1), Wisconsin Statutes, affirmed the circuit court's ruling, holding that the statute requires that "'grandparents must have a parent-like relationship with the child' in order to qualify for visitation rights" and that Meister had not demonstrated that she maintained such a relationship with her grandchildren. The children then appealed, filing a petition for review with the supreme court, which was granted.

The supreme court, in a majority opinion by Justice Prosser, reversed the court of appeals. After examining the statute's history and the statutory language on its own and in the context of related statutory language in section 767.43 (3), Wisconsin Statutes, the court found that a "grandparent, greatgrandparent, or stepparent need not prove a parent-child relationship to succeed on a petition for visitation" and that the "parent-child relationship element applies only to a 'person' seeking visitation who is not a grandparent, greatgrandparent, or stepparent." The court also noted that, while its decision "eliminates one unintended impediment for grandparents," it does not guarantee grandparents will prevail on petitions for visitation, as a court must still consider the constitutional rights of the parents and determine, in its discretion, whether the facts and circumstances "warrant granting, modifying, or denying a visitation petition in the best interest of the child."

The court also held that its finding that the phrase "who has maintained a relationship similar to a parent-child relationship with the child" is inapplicable to grandparents, greatgrandparents, or stepparents does not conflict with parental constitutional rights because any court considering a petition under section 767.43 (1), Wisconsin Statutes, must, as part of making the necessary "best interest of the child" determination, "give special weight to a fit parent's opinions regarding the child's best interest."

Justice Abrahamson concurred, agreeing with the court's interpretation of section 767.43 (1), Wisconsin Statutes, but concluding that the court should not have ruled in the case, because review was sought by the children (through their guardian ad litem), and the statutory language limits the right to petition to grandparents, greatgrandparents, stepparents, and others who have maintained a relationship similar to a parent-child relationship with the child. As such, Justice Abrahamson concluded that the court did not have a statutory or other basis for considering the petition for review. Justice Abrahamson further stated that the majority's opinion could put the constitutionality of section 767.43 (3), Wisconsin Statutes, in doubt, due to the higher burden imposed upon grandparents of children born to unmarried parents than grandparents of those born to married parents.

Justice Ziegler, joined by Justice Gableman, also concurred, agreeing with the interpretation of section 767.43 (1), Wisconsin Statutes, and the outcome but finding that the statute is unambiguous and therefore disagreeing with the majority opinion to the extent that it acknowledges the statutory language is not "wholly unambiguous."

Justice R. G. Bradley did not participate.

SUPREMACY OF RULEMAKING POWERS FOR STATE SUPERINTENDENT OF PUBLIC INSTRUCTION

In *Coyne v. Walker*, 2016 WI 38, 368 Wis. 2d 444, 879 N.W.2d 520, the supreme court addressed whether provisions enacted by 2011 Wisconsin Act 21 that gave the governor and the state secretary of administration certain authority over agency rulemaking were unconstitutional as applied to rules promulgated by the state superintendent of public instruction (SPI), a constitutional office established by article X, section 1, of the Wisconsin Constitution. Article X, section 1, establishes the SPI and provides that the "supervision of public instruction" shall be vested in the SPI and "such other officers as the legislature shall direct." One of the primary issues in the case was whether rulemaking is a "supervisory" power under article X, section 1, and, if so, whether the Act 21 provisions violate the constitutional provision by giving the governor and secretary of administration a superior power over rulemaking conducted by the SPI.

In May 2011, Governor Scott Walker signed 2011 Wisconsin Act 21 into law. Act 21 made numerous changes to provisions in chapter 227 of the Wisconsin Statutes that delineate the process for state agencies to promulgate administrative rules. Among the changes in Act 21 were requirements that the governor approve agencies' initial "statements of scope" for proposed rulemaking and that the governor approve agencies' final drafts of proposed administrative rules. Another provision in Act 21 required certain rules to have the approval of the secretary of administration in order to proceed. Later in 2011, a number of parties (Coyne) filed suit, arguing that the provisions gave the governor and the secretary of administration equal or superior authority over the SPI and were therefore unconstitutional. The SPI sided with Coyne throughout the litigation.

The circuit court granted summary judgment to Coyne. Reasoning that the provisions could place the governor and the secretary of administration in a superior position over the SPI, the circuit court concluded that the provisions were unconstitutional as applied to the SPI. The court of appeals affirmed, citing language in the seminal case *Thompson v. Craney*, 199 Wis. 2d 674, 546 N.W.2d 123 (1996), for the proposition that rulemaking is a "supervisory power." Because the Act 21 provisions could allow the governor to withhold approval of a rule as a means of affecting the rule content, the court of appeals found that the Act 21 provisions were unconstitutional as applied to the SPI. The governor appealed the court of appeals ruling, and the supreme court granted review.

Five separate opinions were issued by members of the supreme court, with sharp disagreement among the justices about whether the case was ripe for adjudication as well as about the underlying merits. Justice Gableman, writing alone, authored the lead opinion. He concluded that the case was properly before the court as a declaratory action despite the Act 21 provisions not having yet been enforced against the SPI. As to the merits, Justice Gableman concluded that, although rulemaking is a power delegated to the SPI by the legislature, because rulemaking is the only means that is prescribed for the SPI and the Department of Public Instruction (DPI) to carry out their powers of supervision, it is therefore a "supervisory power" under article X, section 1. He then undertook a review of the history and text of the constitutional provision and the *Thompson* case, concluding that, under article X, section 1, other officers in whom the legislature may vest the supervision of public instruction must be other officers devoted to the supervision of public instruction who are supervised by the SPI. The governor and the secretary of administration, he concluded, would not qualify to serve as such other officers. Finally, Justice Gableman concluded that the Act 21 provisions gave the governor and secretary of administration unchecked power to stop a rule of the SPI. Based upon these conclusions, Justice Gableman concluded that the Act 21 provisions unconstitutionally vested the supervision of public instruction in the governor and the secretary of administration.

Justice Abrahamson, joined by Justice A. W. Bradley, wrote separately in concurrence. While she agreed that the provisions in Act 21 were unconstitutional as applied to the SPI, she took issue with the lead opinion's discussion of *Thompson* and the extent to which the legislature could reduce the role and duties of the SPI. Justice Prosser also wrote a concurring opinion. He agreed that the provisions were unconstitutional as giving the governor an absolute veto power over the SPI that would obstruct the SPI's ability to perform its constitutional duties but wrote separately to express his view that the holding in *Thompson* was unwarranted as it limited the legislature's ability to vest other officers with authority over education.

Chief Justice Roggensack dissented, joined by Justices R. G. Bradley and Ziegler. She concluded that rulemaking power exercised by the SPI and DPI was delegated by the legislature under article IV, section 1, of the Wisconsin Constitution and did not come from article X, section 1, and that the Act 21 provisions were therefore valid limitations on that legislatively delegated power. She also found there to be a lack of proof that the provisions had been unconstitutionally enforced against the SPI. Justice Ziegler also wrote separately, joined by Justice R. G. Bradley, to further detail her disagreement with the reasoning of the lead opinion. In her view, the legislature had broad authority to determine what it means to supervise public instruction and that this left the SPI "subject to the changing whims of the legislature."

WITHDRAWAL OF PLEA AGREEMENT BASED ON FAILURE TO WARN OF RISK OF CHAPTER 980 CIVIL COMMITMENT

In *State v. LeMere*, 2016 WI 41, 368 Wis. 2d 624, 879 N.W.2d 580, the supreme court concluded that the Sixth Amendment to the U.S. Constitution does not require defense counsel to inform a criminal defendant about the possibility of civil commitment under chapter 980, Wisconsin Statutes, when the defendant enters a plea to a sexually violent offense.

Stephen LeMere pled guilty to first-degree sexual assault of a child under the age of 13, and he was sentenced to 30 years of initial confinement followed by 15 years of extended supervision. After sentencing, LeMere filed a motion to withdraw his guilty plea, arguing that defense counsel was constitutionally deficient for failing to advise LeMere that he could be subject to lifetime commitment as a sexually violent person under chapter 980, Wisconsin Statutes. LeMere claimed that he would not have pled guilty if he had known of that risk. The circuit court denied the motion, and the court of appeals affirmed in an unpublished opinion.

The supreme court affirmed in an opinion written by Justice Prosser. The supreme court concluded that the Sixth Amendment does not require defense counsel to inform a criminal defendant about the possibility of future civil commitment under chapter 980, Wisconsin Statutes, when the defendant enters a plea to a sexually violent offense.

The Sixth Amendment guarantees a criminal defendant the right to have effective assistance of counsel for his or her defense, including during the plea bargaining process. Generally, defense counsel must advise the defendant of direct consequences of conviction, but not of collateral consequences. However, in *Padilla v. Kentucky*, 559 U.S. 356 (2010), the U.S. Supreme Court found that deportation is uniquely difficult to classify as either a direct or collateral consequence. Thus, the court established an exception to the general rule by declaring that defense counsel must advise defendants regarding potential immigration consequences of conviction.

The Wisconsin Supreme Court declined to create a similar exception for the risk of a civil commitment under chapter 980, Wisconsin Statutes. In reaching that decision, the court examined the differences between deportation and civil commitment and concluded that the "unique confluence of factors" that led the *Padilla* court to make an exception for deportation do not apply to civil commitment. Specifically, the court found that 1) deportation's unique nature weighs against creating an exception for civil commitment; 2) the consequences of a civil commitment are not as severe as deportation; 3) civil commitment is not penal in nature; 4) civil commitment is not an automatic result of the underlying conviction; 5) civil commitment is not enmeshed in the criminal process; and 6) no special vulnerability or class status warrants particularized consideration for persons convicted of sexually violent offenses.

Nevertheless, the court concluded that, although defense counsel is not required to advise a criminal defendant of the possibility of civil commitment, best practice is for defense counsel to discuss with the defendant any consequences of a plea that will have a meaningful impact on the defendant's decision to accept or reject a plea agreement.

Justice A. W. Bradley dissented in an opinion joined by Justice Abrahamson. The dissent concluded that, like deportation, a chapter 980 commitment is "a particularly severe and automatic penalty of a guilty plea that is closely connected to the criminal process." Thus, the dissent found that the Sixth Amendment requires defense counsel to advise a criminal defendant regarding the consequence of a chapter 980 commitment.

Justice R. G. Bradley did not participate.

HOME RULE

In *Black v. City of Milwaukee*, 2016 WI 47, 369 Wis. 2d 272, 882 N.W.2d 333, the Wisconsin Supreme Court held that the City of Milwaukee cannot require its employees to live within city limits.

Since 1938, Milwaukee's city charter required city employees to reside within city limits or face termination. In 2013, the Wisconsin legislature created section 66.0502 of the Wisconsin Statutes, which prohibited any city, village, town, county, or school district from requiring an employee to live within any jurisdictional limit. The Milwaukee Police Association sued the City of Milwaukee, arguing that the city was violating the statute by continuing to enforce its residency requirement, and sought money damages. The city argued that its residency requirement trumped the state statute based on the city's home rule authority under the Wisconsin Constitution.

Article XI, section 3 (1), of the Wisconsin Constitution, known as the home rule amendment, gives cities and villages the ability to determine their local affairs and government, subject only to other provisions in the state constitution and to "such enactments of the legislature of statewide concern as with uniformity shall affect every city or every village."

The court of appeals held that section 66.0502, Wisconsin Statutes, did not involve a matter of statewide concern and did not affect all municipalities uniformly, and that it therefore did not trump Milwaukee's residency requirement. According to the court, the facts in the record showed that only Milwaukee would be heavily affected by the statute and that the goal of enacting the statute was to target Milwaukee. The court of appeals also denied the police association's request for damages.

The supreme court, in an opinion by Justice Gableman, first looked to the court's prior home rule decisions to determine that a state statute can trump a municipal ordinance either when the statute addresses a matter of statewide concern or when the statute with uniformity affects every city or every village. The court went on to note that section 66.0502, Wisconsin Statutes, was a "mixed bag" of statewide and local interests: on the one hand, the legislature had an interest in allowing public employees the right to choose where they live; on the other hand, Milwaukee had an interest in maintaining its tax base, in efficiently delivering city services, and in having its employees share in a common community investment as city residents. However, the court stated that it would assume, without deciding, that the statute was a matter of local concern.

As to uniformity, the court held that a "statute satisfies the home rule amendment's uniformity requirement if it is, on its face, uniformly applicable to every city or village." The court found that, because the plain language of section 66.0502, Wisconsin Statutes, applies to all cities, villages, towns, counties, and school districts, the statute uniformly banned residency requirements. The court held that the statute satisfied the home rule amendment's uniformity requirement and, therefore, trumped Milwaukee's residency requirement. However, the court agreed with the court of appeals that the police association was not entitled to damages.

Justice R. G. Bradley wrote a separate concurrence, disagreeing with the majority's holding that a state statute can trump a municipal ordinance *either* when the statute addresses a matter of statewide concern or when the statute with uniformity affects every city or every village. Justice R. G. Bradley looked to the plain language of the amendment as well as the historical context, statements of the drafters, newspaper articles, and other documents surrounding the amendment's adoption to determine that, under the home rule amendment, a state statute can trump a municipal ordinance only when the statute *both* addresses a matter of statewide concern *and* with uniformity affects every city or village. However, Justice R. G. Bradley found that section 66.0502, Wisconsin Statutes, was a matter of statewide concern and was, on its face, uniformly applicable to every city or village, and therefore agreed with the majority that the statute barred Milwaukee from enforcing its residency requirement.

Justice A. W. Bradley, joined by Justice Abrahamson, concurred and dissented. The justices agreed that the police association was not entitled to damages, but found that Milwaukee should be able to enforce its residency requirement under the home rule amendment. The justices, like Justice R. G.

Bradley, disagreed with the majority's reading of the home rule amendment and determined that, to trump a municipal ordinance, a state statute must *both* address a matter of statewide concern *and* uniformly affect every city or village. The justices also disagreed with the majority's conclusion that a state statute may satisfy the uniformity requirement by being uniform on its face, and agreed with the court of appeals' findings that section 66.0502, Wisconsin Statutes, would have an outsize effect on Milwaukee, including a projected $649 million loss from the city's tax base.

BAR ON LICENSING FOR CHILD CARE PROVIDERS WITH HISTORY OF PUBLIC ASSISTANCE FRAUD

In *Blake v. Jossart*, 2016 WI 57, 370 Wis. 2d 1, 884 N.W.2d 484, Sonja Blake challenged a provision that permanently bars an individual who has been convicted of public assistance fraud from obtaining a child care license as unconstitutional. The supreme court upheld the law, finding that Blake failed to establish that the law violated equal protection or substantive due process or created an unconstitutional irrebuttable presumption.

Under Wisconsin law, any person providing child care to four or more children under the age of seven must obtain a child care center license and child care provider certification from the state. In addition, the Wisconsin Shares program provides child care subsidies to families meeting certain financial eligibility requirements who receive child care services from a child care provider certified by the Department of Children and Families. In 2009, following extensive reporting on widespread fraud within the Wisconsin Shares program, the legislature passed 2009 Wisconsin Act 76, which substantially changed the requirements for child care licensing and certification. Relevant to *Blake*, the new law created section 48.685 (5) (br) 5., Wisconsin Statutes, to impose a permanent bar prohibiting the state from licensing a child care center or certifying a child care provider if that individual had ever been convicted of an offense involving fraudulent activity as a participant of Wisconsin Shares or a number of other state and federal public assistance programs, including welfare.

Blake was a certified child care provider in Racine County from 2001 to 2006 and in 2008 received a new certification valid to June 2010. After Act 76 was passed, Racine County revoked Blake's child care certification because her criminal background check revealed a 1986 conviction of misdemeanor welfare fraud. Blake challenged the revocation, arguing that the permanent bar on her certification unconstitutionally violated her right to equal protection and due process, and created an impermissible irrebuttable presumption. Both the circuit court and the court of appeals upheld the statute as constitutional.

The supreme court also upheld the statute as constitutional, holding that the prohibition on licensing and certification for an individual with a conviction of public assistance fraud does not violate equal protection or substantive due process because Blake is not part of a suspect class, child care licensing and certification is not a fundamental right, and the legislation rationally advanced the state's interest in preventing fraud under Wisconsin Shares.

The court also considered the question of whether the statute violates the irrebuttable presumption doctrine. Under the irrebuttable presumption doctrine, if a statute creates a presumption that denies a person a fair opportunity to rebut, it violates the due process clause of the Fourteenth Amendment. Following precedent establishing an alternative standard for government benefits classification from the U.S. Supreme Court, the court held that the statute's requirements did not constitute an irrebuttable presumption but in this case rather were merely an application of an objective fact to Blake's eligibility.

Justices Abrahamson and A. W. Bradley dissented, opining that the sweeping nature of the permanent bar to child care licensing and certification based on welfare fraud was not rationally related to the purposes of preventing fraud against Wisconsin Shares or protecting children, families, and private employers in childcare, as stated by the majority. The dissent further argued that the consequence for Blake's 30-year old misdemeanor charge and $294 restitution was so disproportionate and overly harsh as to "shock the conscience" and therefore the statute violated substantive due process. The dissent also raised a concern that the retroactive and permanent effect of the statute violated the ex post facto clause of the constitution, which prohibits laws imposing an overly punitive after the fact penalty for a crime that has already been committed.

Wisconsin Court of Appeals

UNCONSTITUTIONALLY OVERBROAD STATUTE INVALIDATED

In *State v. Oatman*, 2015 WI App 76, 365 Wis. 2d 242, 871 N.W.2d 513, the court of appeals invalidated a statute, in its entirety, that prohibited a sex offender from photographing or otherwise recording an image of a child without the written consent of the child's parent or guardian.

Christopher Oatman was charged with 16 counts of violating section 948.14, Wisconsin Statutes, which prohibits a person who has a prior conviction for committing certain sex offenses from "intentionally [capturing] a representation of any minor without the written consent of the minor's parent, legal custodian, or guardian." The statute requires that the written consent state that the person seeking the consent is required to register as a sex offender. None of the images Oatman was charged with taking involved obscenity, child pornography, or nudity.

Oatman and the state entered into a stipulated agreement, wherein Oatman stipulated to the evidence of his guilt on eight charges, and the state agreed not to argue that Oatman had forfeited his right to challenge the constitutionality of section 948.14, Wisconsin Statutes. After being sentenced on the eight counts, Oatman appealed, arguing that the statute was overbroad and as such violated his First Amendment rights, as applied to him, and on its face.

The court of appeals noted that the constitutionality of a statute presents a question of law and is reviewed de novo. The court stated that, while statutes generally benefit from a presumption of constitutionality, when "the statute implicates the exercise of First Amendment rights, the burden shifts to the government to prove beyond a reasonable doubt that the statute passes constitutional muster."

Although Oatman challenged section 948.14, Wisconsin Statutes, on its face and as applied to the facts of his case, the court did not need to determine whether the statute was constitutional as applied to Oatman because it found that the statute was unconstitutional on its face.

The court quoted the state's brief as acknowledging that, if "the taking of photographs and video recordings for purely personal use were protected by the First Amendment, the State would concede that Wis. Stat. § 948.14 is overly broad." The court rejected the state's argument that First Amendment protections apply only to photographs that are created with an expressive or communicative intent and held that, even if the photographs were taken for purely personal use, the First Amendment analysis applies. The state also acknowledged, and the court found, that because the statute only regulates images of children, it is not content neutral, but is content-based. Content-based regulations are presumptively invalid and, in order to pass constitutional muster, must be the least restrictive means of achieving a compelling state interest.

The court found that, while the state "undeniably has a compelling interest in protecting children[,] Wis. Stat. § 948.14 does little, if anything, to further that interest." In addition to subjecting a child to inquiries by sex offenders as to whether the child has a parent or guardian available to consent to the capture of the child's image, the statute prohibits acts that are not harmful to children.

The court cited federal cases that determined that children are not harmed by nonobscene, nonpornographic photographs taken in public places and found that "[a]ccordingly, while we may dislike the fact that someone might have objectionable thoughts when viewing ordinary images of children, the State is constitutionally prohibited from precluding citizens from creating such images." Thus, the court concluded that section 948.14, Wisconsin Statutes, does little to further any compelling state interest, and, in banning the capture of any and all images of children, regardless of content, the statute was not narrowly tailored. The court stated that "it is difficult to imagine a content-based regulation that would be more *broadly* tailored."

Having determined that section 948.14, Wisconsin Statutes, was unconstitutionally broad on its face, the court considered the alternate remedies at hand. Generally, courts have three options: apply a limiting construction to rehabilitate the statute; sever the unconstitutional portions of a statute while leaving constitutional provisions intact; or invalidate the entire statute.

In this case, the state acknowledged, and the court held, that section 948.14, Wisconsin Statutes, was not amenable to a limiting construction or severance. The court thus invalidated the statute in its entirety and instructed the circuit court to dismiss the charges against Oatman.

CRIMINAL LAW PROCEDURE VIOLATIONS; EXCLUSION OF WITNESS AS REMEDY

In *State v. Prieto*, 2016 WI App 15, 366 Wis. 2d 794, 876 N.W.2d 154, the court of appeals upheld the circuit court's decision to exclude almost all of the state's witnesses after the prosecuting district attorney's persistent failure to respond to the defendant's requests for the names of the witnesses.

In May 2012, Caroline Prieto was charged with causing great bodily harm to a child. She made a prompt discovery demand for the district attorney to disclose all witnesses that the district attorney intended to call at trial. The district attorney ignored the discovery demand. More than a year and a half after Prieto was charged, the circuit court ordered the district attorney to provide its witness list within 60 days and scheduled the matter for trial in June 2014. The district attorney ignored the court order and did not provide its list of witnesses.

The trial was postponed and, at a hearing in August 2014, the court again ordered the district attorney to provide a list of witnesses. The district attorney did not do so.

In January 2015, with fewer than 20 days left before the scheduled trial date, Prieto moved the court to exclude any witness not already named by the state. The court granted the motion, excluding all witnesses but one expert witness the district attorney had identified. Fourteen days before trial, the district attorney submitted a list of witnesses and a motion for reconsideration of the court's exclusion order. The court denied the motion, and the state appealed.

The court of appeals noted that the state did not have, and did not offer, any good cause for its failure to submit a witness list. The state argued, however, that even absent good cause for its failure, the circuit court erred in imposing the strict remedy of excluding all but one of the named witnesses.

The court of appeals looked to statutory discovery provisions for its de novo determination of whether the district attorney violated the discovery statute, and, if it had, whether the circuit court erred in its imposition of a remedy. The court of appeals cited section 971.23 (1) (d), Wisconsin Statutes, which requires the district attorney, upon demand and "within a reasonable time before trial," to disclose a list of all witnesses and their addresses the district attorney intends to call at trial.

The court of appeals next cited section 971.23 (7m) (a), Wisconsin Statutes, which states in relevant part that "[t]he court shall exclude any witness not listed or evidence not presented for inspection or copying required by this section, unless good cause is shown for failure to comply." The court did note that, under section 971.23 (7m) (a) and (b), Wisconsin Statutes, the court could, in appropriate cases, grant a recess or a continuance or advise the jury of the state's failure to identify the witnesses.

The court of appeals acknowledged the state's contention that the remedy of exclusion is discretionary, not mandatory, but determined that it need not decide whether the statute requires exclusion because, even if the statute does allow for other remedies, the circuit court exercised proper discretion in excluding all unnamed witnesses.

The state argued, first, that it did not violate the discovery statute at all, because it listed its witnesses "within a reasonable time before trial." The court of appeals flatly rejected this argument, noting that the state had, over the course of years, ignored several circuit court orders and only offered up a witness list after the circuit court had entered its exclusion order. The court of appeals found that that was a violation of the discovery statute.

Turning next to the proper remedy, the state argued that exclusion should not be permitted in this case because Prieto could not prove that she was prejudiced by the district attorney's failure to identify the witnesses sooner. The court rejected this as well, noting that under the clear statutory language, the "burden was on the district attorney's office to show that it has good cause for this violation, not on Prieto to show that she was prejudiced."

The court acknowledged that exclusion was a severe sanction and stated that it "[shares] the circuit court's regret that the actions of the district attorney may prevent the merits of this case from being fully tried." However, the court reminded the district attorney that, ultimately, the extent of any sanctions brought to bear for discovery violations are within its own control and that it ignored repeated court orders and the statutory discovery mandates "at its peril."

In a concurring opinion, Judge Hagedorn agreed that the circuit court appropriately excluded the witnesses but stated that he would have affirmed that decision as a proper exercise of the judge's discretion to sanction the district attorney's violation of two court orders.

APPLICATION OF THE FEDERAL DRIVER'S PRIVACY PROTECTION ACT (DPPA) TO STATE PUBLIC RECORDS LAW

In *New Richmond News v. City of New Richmond*, 2016 WI App 43, 370 Wis. 2d 75, 881 N.W.2d 339, the court of appeals addressed the interaction between provisions in the federal Driver's Privacy Protection Act (DPPA) and provisions under Wisconsin law that provide for access to governmental records. The Wisconsin public records law generally provides for access to records of state and local governments and includes a policy statement containing a strong presumption in favor of access, though it allows records to be withheld pursuant to exceptions in state or federal law. Another state statute outside of the public records law specifically provides for access to traffic accident reports. The DPPA was enacted in 1994 to restrict the release of an individual's personal information contained in state motor vehicle records without his or her consent, applying a two-tier system prohibiting disclosure of certain types of personal identifying information. The provisions in the DPPA, however, contain a number of exceptions where disclosures are permitted. One such exception allows for disclosure for use by a governmental agency "in carrying out its functions," while another exception allows for disclosure for a use specifically authorized by a state law if the use is "related to the operation of a motor vehicle or public safety." The case addressed the interaction between the disclosure restrictions under the DPPA and the two state laws that require disclosure of public records.

The case originated with a request made by the New Richmond News newspaper to the City of New Richmond Police Department for copies of certain accident and incident reports. The police department responded to the request by noting that the DPPA requires redaction of information in the requested reports because the reports were prepared using information from state motor vehicle records. It cited a 2012 opinion of the U.S. Court of Appeals for the Seventh Circuit that employed a careful reading of the exceptions in the DPPA. The newspaper asked the police department to reconsider its decision, citing an informal Wisconsin attorney general opinion from 2008 that had concluded that the DPPA did not require such redactions. However, the police department stood by its decision and refused to provide unredacted versions of the reports, prompting a lawsuit by the newspaper. The circuit court granted summary judgment to the newspaper, concluding that the disclosures fell under the two exceptions in the DPPA or did not reveal personal information covered by the DPPA in the first place. The supreme court agreed to hear the case on a motion to bypass the court of appeals, but the case was remanded to the court of appeals after the death of Justice Crooks left the supreme court equally divided on whether to affirm or reverse the circuit court.

The court of appeals first addressed the Wisconsin statute specifically mandating that law enforcement agencies provide access to uniform traffic accident reports. Finding this use to be related to the operation of a motor vehicle or public safety, the court upheld the lower court's determination that disclosure of the unredacted accident reports was not prohibited by the DPPA.

The court of appeals then addressed whether disclosure in response to a public records request of information in the incident reports, which were not covered by the statute governing accident reports, was permitted under the DPPA's "agency functions" exception. The newspaper, noting that the state public records law declared responding to a public records request an "essential function" of government, argued that the duty under the public records law to provide access to public records upon request was an "agency function" that fell within the exception in the DPPA. The court of appeals rejected this argument, calling it an unreasonable reading of the DPPA that would lead to "untenable results" and defeat the purpose of the DPPA. The court also rejected the notion that police departments had any heightened need to comply with the public records law.

The court remanded the case back to the circuit court for consideration of whether disclosure served any other function other than compliance with the public records law. The court also remanded the case for a determination as to whether the information in question had actually been derived from state motor vehicle records, and not merely verified using such information. ⬛

4

STATISTICS AND REFERENCE

THE WISCONSIN CONSTITUTION

Last amended at the April 2015 election

Article V—Executive

Section

Article VI—Administrative

Section

Article VII—Judiciary

Section

1. Impeachment; trial
2. Court system
3. Supreme court: jurisdiction
4. Supreme court: election, chief justice, court system administration
5. Court of appeals
6. Circuit court: boundaries
7. Circuit court: election
8. Circuit court: jurisdiction
9. Judicial elections, vacancies
10. Judges: eligibility to office
11. Disciplinary proceedings
12. Clerks of circuit and supreme courts
13. Justices and judges: removal by address
14. Municipal court
15. Repealed
16. Repealed
17. Repealed
18. Repealed
19. Repealed
20. Repealed
21. Repealed
22. Repealed
23. Repealed
24. Justices and judges: eligibility for office; retirement

Article VIII—Finance

Section

1. Rule of taxation uniform; income, privilege and occupation taxes
2. Appropriations; limitation
3. Credit of state
4. Contracting state debts
5. Annual tax levy to equal expenses
6. Public debt for extraordinary expense; taxation
7. Public debt for public defense; bonding for public purposes
8. Vote on fiscal bills; quorum
9. Evidences of public debt
10. Internal improvements
11. Transportation fund

Article IX—Eminent domain and property of the state

Section

1. Jurisdiction on rivers and lakes; navigable waters
2. Territorial property
3. Ultimate property in lands; escheats

Article X—Education

Section

1. Superintendent of public instruction
2. School fund created; income applied
3. District schools; tuition; sectarian instruction; released time
4. Annual school tax
5. Income of school fund
6. State university; support
7. Commissioners of public lands
8. Sale of public lands

Preamble

We, the people of Wisconsin, grateful to Almighty God for our freedom, in order to secure its blessings, form a more perfect government, insure domestic tranquility and promote the general welfare, do establish this constitution.

Article I—Declaration of rights

Equality; inherent rights. Section 1. All people are born equally free and independent, and have certain inherent rights; among these are life, liberty and the pursuit of happiness; to secure these rights, governments are instituted, deriving their just powers from the consent of the governed.

Slavery prohibited. Section 2. There shall be neither slavery, nor involuntary servitude in this state, otherwise than for the punishment of crime, whereof the party shall have been duly convicted.

Free speech; libel. Section 3. Every person may freely speak, write and publish his sentiments on all subjects, being responsible for the abuse of that right, and no laws shall be passed to restrain or abridge the liberty of speech or of the press. In all criminal prosecutions or indictments for libel, the truth may be given in evidence, and if it shall appear to the jury that the matter charged as libelous be true, and was published with good motives and for justifiable ends, the party shall be acquitted; and the jury shall have the right to determine the law and the fact.

Right to assemble and petition. Section 4. The right of the people peaceably to assemble, to consult for the common good, and to petition the government, or any department thereof, shall never be abridged.

Trial by jury; verdict in civil cases. Section 5. The right of trial by jury shall remain inviolate, and shall extend to all cases at law without regard to the amount in controversy; but a jury trial may be waived by the parties in all cases in the manner prescribed by law. Provided, however, that the legislature may, from time to time, by statute provide that a valid verdict, in civil cases, may be based on the votes of a specified number of the jury, not less than five-sixths thereof.

Excessive bail; cruel punishments. Section 6. Excessive bail shall not be required, nor shall excessive fines be imposed, nor cruel and unusual punishments inflicted.

Rights of accused. Section 7. In all criminal prosecutions the accused shall enjoy the right to be heard by himself and counsel; to demand the nature and cause of the accusation against him; to meet the witnesses face to face; to have compulsory process to compel the attendance of witnesses in his behalf; and in prosecutions by indictment, or information, to a speedy public trial by an impartial jury of the county or district wherein the offense shall have been committed; which county or district shall have been previously ascertained by law.

Prosecutions; double jeopardy; self-incrimination; bail; habeas corpus. Section 8. (1) No person may be held to answer for a criminal offense without due process of law, and no person for the same offense may be put twice in jeopardy of punishment, nor may be compelled in any criminal case to be a witness against himself or herself.

(2) All persons, before conviction, shall be eligible for release under reasonable conditions designed to assure their appearance in court, protect members of the community from serious bodily harm or prevent the intimidation of witnesses. Monetary conditions of release may be imposed at or after the initial appearance only upon a finding that there is a reasonable basis to believe that the conditions are necessary to assure appearance in court. The legislature may authorize, by law, courts to revoke a person's release for a violation of a condition of release.

(3) The legislature may by law authorize, but may not require, circuit courts to deny release for a period not to exceed 10 days prior to the hearing required under this subsection to a person who is accused of committing a murder punishable by life imprisonment or a sexual assault punishable by a maximum imprisonment of 20 years, or who is accused of committing or attempting to commit a felony involving serious bodily harm to another or the threat of serious bodily harm to another and who has a previous conviction for committing or attempting to commit a felony involving serious bodily harm to another or the threat of serious bodily harm to another. The legislature may authorize by law, but may not require, circuit courts to continue to deny release to those accused persons for an additional period not to exceed 60 days following the hearing required under this subsection, if there is a requirement that there be a finding by the court based on clear and convincing evidence presented at a hearing that the accused committed the felony and a requirement that there be a finding by the court that available conditions of release will not adequately protect members of the community from serious bodily harm or prevent intimidation of witnesses. Any law enacted under

this subsection shall be specific, limited and reasonable. In determining the 10-day and 60-day periods, the court shall omit any period of time found by the court to result from a delay caused by the defendant or a continuance granted which was initiated by the defendant.

(4) The privilege of the writ of habeas corpus shall not be suspended unless, in cases of rebellion or invasion, the public safety requires it.

Remedy for wrongs. Section 9. Every person is entitled to a certain remedy in the laws for all injuries, or wrongs which he may receive in his person, property, or character; he ought to obtain justice freely, and without being obliged to purchase it, completely and without denial, promptly and without delay, conformably to the laws.

Victims of crime. Section 9m. This state shall treat crime victims, as defined by law, with fairness, dignity and respect for their privacy. This state shall ensure that crime victims have all of the following privileges and protections as provided by law: timely disposition of the case; the opportunity to attend court proceedings unless the trial court finds sequestration is necessary to a fair trial for the defendant; reasonable protection from the accused throughout the criminal justice process; notification of court proceedings; the opportunity to confer with the prosecution; the opportunity to make a statement to the court at disposition; restitution; compensation; and information about the outcome of the case and the release of the accused. The legislature shall provide remedies for the violation of this section. Nothing in this section, or in any statute enacted pursuant to this section, shall limit any right of the accused which may be provided by law.

Treason. Section 10. Treason against the state shall consist only in levying war against the same, or in adhering to its enemies, giving them aid and comfort. No person shall be convicted of treason unless on the testimony of two witnesses to the same overt act, or on confession in open court.

Searches and seizures. Section 11. The right of the people to be secure in their persons, houses, papers, and effects against unreasonable searches and seizures shall not be violated; and no warrant shall issue but upon probable cause, supported by oath or affirmation, and particularly describing the place to be searched and the persons or things to be seized.

Attainder; ex post facto; contracts. Section 12. No bill of attainder, ex post facto law, nor any law impairing the obligation of contracts, shall ever be passed, and no conviction shall work corruption of blood or forfeiture of estate.

Private property for public use. Section 13. The property of no person shall be taken for public use without just compensation therefor.

Feudal tenures; leases; alienation. Section 14. All lands within the state are declared to be allodial, and feudal tenures are prohibited. Leases and grants of agricultural land for a longer term than fifteen years in which rent or service of any kind shall be reserved, and all fines and like restraints upon alienation reserved in any grant of land, hereafter made, are declared to be void.

Equal property rights for aliens and citizens. Section 15. No distinction shall ever be made by law between resident aliens and citizens, in reference to the possession, enjoyment or descent of property.

Imprisonment for debt. Section 16. No person shall be imprisoned for debt arising out of or founded on a contract, expressed or implied.

Exemption of property of debtors. Section 17. The privilege of the debtor to enjoy the necessary comforts of life shall be recognized by wholesome laws, exempting a reasonable amount of property from seizure or sale for the payment of any debt or liability hereafter contracted.

Freedom of worship; liberty of conscience; state religion; public funds. Section 18. The right of every person to worship Almighty God according to the dictates of conscience shall never be infringed; nor shall any person be compelled to attend, erect or support any place of worship, or to maintain any ministry, without consent; nor shall any control of, or interference with, the rights of conscience be permitted, or any preference be given by law to any religious establishments or modes of worship; nor shall any money be drawn from the treasury for the benefit of religious societies, or religious or theological seminaries.

Religious tests prohibited. Section 19. No religious tests shall ever be required as a qualification for any office of public trust under the state, and no person shall be rendered incompetent to give evidence in any court of law or equity in consequence of his opinions on the subject of religion.

Military subordinate to civil power. Section 20. The military shall be in strict subordination to the civil power.

Rights of suitors. Section 21. (1) Writs of error shall never be prohibited, and shall be issued by such courts as the legislature designates by law.

(2) In any court of this state, any suitor may prosecute or defend his suit either in his own proper person or by an attorney of the suitor's choice.

Maintenance of free government. Section 22. The blessings of a free government can only be maintained by a firm adherence to justice, moderation, temperance, frugality and virtue, and by frequent recurrence to fundamental principles.

Transportation of school children. Section 23. Nothing in this constitution shall prohibit the legislature from providing for the safety and welfare of children by providing for the transportation of children to and from any parochial or private school or institution of learning.

Use of school buildings. Section 24. Nothing in this constitution shall prohibit the legislature from authorizing, by law, the use of public school buildings by civic, religious or charitable organizations during nonschool hours upon payment by the organization to the school district of reasonable compensation for such use.

Right to keep and bear arms. Section 25. The people have the right to keep and bear arms for security, defense, hunting, recreation or any other lawful purpose.

Right to fish, hunt, trap, and take game. Section 26. The people have the right to fish, hunt, trap, and take game subject only to reasonable restrictions as prescribed by law.

Article II—Boundaries

State boundary. Section 1. It is hereby ordained and declared that the state of Wisconsin doth consent and accept of the boundaries prescribed in the act of congress entitled "An act to enable the people of Wisconsin territory to form a constitution and state government, and for the admission of such state into the Union," approved August sixth, one thousand eight hundred and forty-six, to wit: Beginning at the northeast corner of the state of Illinois—that is to say, at a point in the center of Lake Michigan where the line of forty-two degrees and thirty minutes of north latitude crosses the same; thence running with the boundary line of the state of Michigan, through Lake Michigan, Green Bay, to the mouth of the Menominee river; thence up the channel of the said river to the Brule river; thence up said last-mentioned river to Lake Brule; thence along the southern shore of Lake Brule in a direct line to the center of the channel between Middle and South Islands, in the Lake of the Desert; thence in a direct line to the head waters of the Montreal river, as marked upon the survey made by Captain Cramm; thence down the main channel of the Montreal river to the middle of Lake Superior; thence through the center of Lake Superior to the mouth of the St. Louis river; thence up the main channel of said river to the first rapids in the same, above the Indian village, according to Nicollet's map; thence due south to the main branch of the river St. Croix; thence down the main channel of said river to the Mississippi; thence down the center of the main channel of that river to the northwest corner of the state of Illinois; thence due east with the northern boundary of the state of Illinois to the place of beginning, as established by "An act to enable the people of the Illinois territory to form a constitution and state government, and for the admission of such state into the Union on an equal footing with the original states," approved April 18th, 1818.

Enabling act accepted. Section 2. The propositions contained in the act of congress are hereby accepted, ratified and confirmed, and shall remain irrevocable without the consent of the United States; and it is hereby ordained that this state shall never interfere with the primary disposal of the soil within the same by the United States, nor with any regulations congress may find necessary for securing the title in such soil to bona fide purchasers thereof; and in no case shall nonresident proprietors be taxed higher than residents. Provided, that nothing in this constitution, or in the act of congress aforesaid, shall in any manner prejudice or affect the right of the state of Wisconsin to 500,000 acres of land granted to said state, and to be hereafter selected and located by and under the act of congress entitled "An act to appropriate the proceeds of the sales of the public lands, and grant pre-emption rights," approved September fourth, one thousand eight hundred and forty-one.

Article III—Suffrage

Electors. Section 1. Every United States citizen age 18 or older who is a resident of an election district in this state is a qualified elector of that district.

Implementation. Section 2. Laws may be enacted:

(1) Defining residency.

(2) Providing for registration of electors.

(3) Providing for absentee voting.

(4) Excluding from the right of suffrage persons:

(a) Convicted of a felony, unless restored to civil rights.

(b) Adjudged by a court to be incompetent or partially incompetent, unless the judgment specifies that the person is capable of understanding the objective of the elective process or the judgment is set aside.

(5) Subject to ratification by the people at a general election, extending the right of suffrage to additional classes.

Secret ballot. Section 3. All votes shall be by secret ballot.

Article IV—Legislative

Legislative power. Section 1. The legislative power shall be vested in a senate and assembly.

Legislature, how constituted. Section 2. The number of the members of the assembly shall never be less than fifty-four nor more than one hundred. The senate shall consist of a number not more than one-third nor less than one-fourth of the number of the members of the assembly.

Apportionment. Section 3. At its first session after each enumeration made by the authority of the United States, the legislature shall apportion and district anew the members of the senate and assembly, according to the number of inhabitants.

Representatives to the assembly, how chosen. Section 4. The members of the assembly shall be chosen biennially, by single districts, on the Tuesday succeeding the first Monday of November in even-numbered years, by the qualified electors of the several districts, such districts to be bounded by county, precinct, town or ward lines, to consist of contiguous territory and be in as compact form as practicable.

Senators, how chosen. Section 5. The senators shall be elected by single districts of convenient contiguous territory, at the same time and in the same manner as members of the assembly are required to be chosen; and no assembly district shall be divided in the formation of a senate district. The senate districts shall be numbered in the regular series, and the senators shall be chosen alternately from the odd and even-numbered districts for the term of 4 years.

Qualifications of legislators. Section 6. No person shall be eligible to the legislature who shall not have resided one year within the state, and be a qualified elector in the district which he may be chosen to represent.

Organization of legislature; quorum; compulsory attendance. Section 7. Each house shall be the judge of the elections, returns and qualifications of its own members; and a majority of each shall constitute a quorum to do business, but a smaller number may adjourn from day to day, and may compel the attendance of absent members in such manner and under such penalties as each house may provide.

Rules; contempts; expulsion. Section 8. Each house may determine the rules of its own proceedings, punish for contempt and disorderly behavior, and with the concurrence of two-thirds of all the members elected, expel a member; but no member shall be expelled a second time for the same cause.

Officers. Section 9. (1) Each house shall choose its presiding officers from its own members.

(2) The legislature shall provide by law for the establishment of a department of transportation and a transportation fund.

Journals; open doors; adjournments. Section 10. Each house shall keep a journal of its proceedings and publish the same, except such parts as require secrecy. The doors of each house shall be kept open except when the public welfare shall require secrecy. Neither house shall, without consent of the other, adjourn for more than three days.

Meeting of legislature. Section 11. The legislature shall meet at the seat of government at such time as shall be provided by law, unless convened by the governor in special session, and when so convened no business shall be transacted except as shall be necessary to accomplish the special purposes for which it was convened.

Ineligibility of legislators to office. Section 12. No member of the legislature shall, during the term for which he was elected, be appointed or elected to any civil office in the state, which shall have been created, or the emoluments of which shall have been increased, during the term for which he was elected.

Ineligibility of federal officers. Section 13. No person being a member of congress, or holding any military or civil office under the United States, shall be eligible to a seat in the legislature; and if any person shall, after his election as a member of the legislature, be elected to congress, or be appointed to any office, civil or military, under the government of the United States, his acceptance thereof shall vacate his seat. This restriction shall not prohibit a legislator from accepting short periods of active duty as a member of the reserve or from serving in the armed forces during any emergency declared by the executive.

Filling vacancies. Section 14. The governor shall issue writs of election to fill such vacancies as may occur in either house of the legislature.

Exemption from arrest and civil process. Section 15. Members of the legislature shall in all cases, except treason, felony and breach of the peace, be privileged from arrest; nor shall they be subject to any civil process, during the session of the legislature, nor for fifteen days next before the commencement and after the termination of each session.

Privilege in debate. Section 16. No member of the legislature shall be liable in any civil action, or criminal prosecution whatever, for words spoken in debate.

Enactment of laws. Section 17. (1) The style of all laws of the state shall be "The people of the state of Wisconsin, represented in senate and assembly, do enact as follows:".

(2) No law shall be enacted except by bill. No law shall be in force until published.

(3) The legislature shall provide by law for the speedy publication of all laws.

Title of private bills. Section 18. No private or local bill which may be passed by the legislature shall embrace more than one subject, and that shall be expressed in the title.

Origin of bills. Section 19. Any bill may originate in either house of the legislature, and a bill passed by one house may be amended by the other.

Yeas and nays. Section 20. The yeas and nays of the members of either house on any question shall, at the request of one-sixth of those present, be entered on the journal.

Powers of county boards. Section 22. The legislature may confer upon the boards of supervisors of the several counties of the state such powers of a local, legislative and administrative character as they shall from time to time prescribe.

Town and county government. Section 23. The legislature shall establish but one system of town government, which shall be as nearly uniform as practicable; but the legislature may provide for the election at large once in every 4 years of a chief executive officer in any county with such powers of an administrative character as they may from time to time prescribe in accordance with this section and shall establish one or more systems of county government.

Chief executive officer to approve or veto resolutions or ordinances; proceedings on veto. Section 23a. Every resolution or ordinance passed by the county board in any county shall, before it becomes effective, be presented to the chief executive officer. If he approves, he shall sign it; if not, he shall return it with his objections, which objections shall be entered at large upon the journal and the board shall proceed to reconsider the matter. Appropriations may be approved in whole or in part by the chief executive officer and the part approved shall become law, and the part objected to shall be returned in the same manner as provided for in other resolutions or ordinances. If, after such reconsideration, two-thirds of the members-elect of the county board agree to pass the resolution or ordinance or the part of the resolution or ordinance objected to, it shall become effective on the date prescribed but not earlier than the date of passage following reconsideration. In all such cases, the votes of the members of the county board shall be determined by ayes and noes and the names of the members voting for or against the resolution or ordinance or the part thereof objected to shall be entered on the journal. If any resolution or ordinance is not returned by the chief executive officer to the county board at its first meeting occurring not less than 6 days, Sundays excepted, after it has been presented to him, it shall become effective unless the county board has recessed or adjourned for a period in excess of 60 days, in which case it shall not be effective without his approval.

Gambling. Section 24. (1) Except as provided in this section, the legislature may not authorize gambling in any form.

(2) Except as otherwise provided by law, the following activities do not constitute consideration as an element of gambling:

(a) To listen to or watch a television or radio program.

(b) To fill out a coupon or entry blank, whether or not proof of purchase is required.

(c) To visit a mercantile establishment or other place without being required to make a purchase or pay an admittance fee.

(3) The legislature may authorize the following bingo games licensed by the state, but all profits shall accrue to the licensed organization and no salaries, fees or profits may be paid to any other organization or person: bingo games operated by religious, charitable, service, fraternal or veterans' organizations or those to which contributions are deductible for federal or state income tax purposes. All moneys received by the state that are attributable to bingo games shall be used for property tax relief for residents of this state

as provided by law. The distribution of moneys that are attributable to bingo games may not vary based on the income or age of the person provided the property tax relief. The distribution of moneys that are attributable to bingo games shall not be subject to the uniformity requirement of section 1 of article VIII. In this subsection, the distribution of all moneys attributable to bingo games shall include any earnings on the moneys received by the state that are attributable to bingo games, but shall not include any moneys used for the regulation of, and enforcement of law relating to, bingo games.

(4) The legislature may authorize the following raffle games licensed by the state, but all profits shall accrue to the licensed local organization and no salaries, fees or profits may be paid to any other organization or person: raffle games operated by local religious, charitable, service, fraternal or veterans' organizations or those to which contributions are deductible for federal or state income tax purposes. The legislature shall limit the number of raffles conducted by any such organization.

(5) This section shall not prohibit pari-mutuel on-track betting as provided by law. The state may not own or operate any facility or enterprise for pari-mutuel betting, or lease any state-owned land to any other owner or operator for such purposes. All moneys received by the state that are attributable to pari-mutuel on-track betting shall be used for property tax relief for residents of this state as provided by law. The distribution of moneys that are attributable to pari-mutuel on-track betting may not vary based on the income or age of the person provided the property tax relief. The distribution of moneys that are attributable to pari-mutuel on-track betting shall not be subject to the uniformity requirement of section 1 of article VIII. In this subsection, the distribution of all moneys attributable to pari-mutuel on-track betting shall include any earnings on the moneys received by the state that are attributable to pari-mutuel on-track betting, but shall not include any moneys used for the regulation of, and enforcement of law relating to, pari-mutuel on-track betting.

(6) (a) The legislature may authorize the creation of a lottery to be operated by the state as provided by law. The expenditure of public funds or of revenues derived from lottery operations to engage in promotional advertising of the Wisconsin state lottery is prohibited. Any advertising of the state lottery shall indicate the odds of a specific lottery ticket to be selected as the winning ticket for each prize amount offered. The net proceeds of the state lottery shall be deposited in the treasury of the state, to be used for property tax relief for residents of this state as provided by law. The distribution of the

net proceeds of the state lottery may not vary based on the income or age of the person provided the property tax relief. The distribution of the net proceeds of the state lottery shall not be subject to the uniformity requirement of section 1 of article VIII. In this paragraph, the distribution of the net proceeds of the state lottery shall include any earnings on the net proceeds of the state lottery.

(b) The lottery authorized under par. (a) shall be an enterprise that entitles the player, by purchasing a ticket, to participate in a game of chance if: 1) the winning tickets are randomly predetermined and the player reveals preprinted numbers or symbols from which it can be immediately determined whether the ticket is a winning ticket entitling the player to win a prize as prescribed in the features and procedures for the game, including an opportunity to win a prize in a secondary or subsequent chance drawing or game; or 2) the ticket is evidence of the numbers or symbols selected by the player or, at the player's option, selected by a computer, and the player becomes entitled to a prize as prescribed in the features and procedures for the game, including an opportunity to win a prize in a secondary or subsequent chance drawing or game if some or all of the player's symbols or numbers are selected in a chance drawing or game, if the player's ticket is randomly selected by the computer at the time of purchase or if the ticket is selected in a chance drawing.

(c) Notwithstanding the authorization of a state lottery under par. (a), the following games, or games simulating any of the following games, may not be conducted by the state as a lottery: 1) any game in which winners are selected based on the results of a race or sporting event; 2) any banking card game, including blackjack, baccarat or chemin de fer; 3) poker; 4) roulette; 5) craps or any other game that involves rolling dice; 6) keno; 7) bingo 21, bingo jack, bingolet or bingo craps; 8) any game of chance that is placed on a slot machine or any mechanical, electromechanical or electronic device that is generally available to be played at a gambling casino; 9) any game or device that is commonly known as a video game of chance or a video gaming machine or that is commonly considered to be a video gambling machine, unless such machine is a video device operated by the state in a game authorized under par. (a) to permit the sale of tickets through retail outlets under contract with the state and the device does not determine or indicate whether the player has won a prize, other than by verifying that the player's ticket or some or all of the player's symbols or numbers on the player's ticket have been selected in a chance drawing, or by verifying that the player's ticket has been randomly selected by a central system computer at the time of purchase; 10) any game that is similar to a game listed in this paragraph; or 11) any other game that is commonly considered to be a form of gambling and is not, or is not substantially similar to, a game conducted by the state under par. (a). No game conducted by the state under par. (a) may permit a player of the game to purchase a ticket, or to otherwise participate in the game, from a residence by using a computer, telephone or other form of electronic, telecommunication, video or technological aid.

Stationery and printing. Section 25. The legislature shall provide by law that all stationery required for the use of the state, and all printing authorized and required by them to be done for their use, or for the state, shall be let by contract to the lowest bidder, but the legislature may establish a maximum price; no member of the legislature or other state officer shall be interested, either directly or indirectly, in any such contract.

Extra compensation; salary change. Section 26. (1) The legislature may not grant any extra compensation to a public officer, agent, servant or contractor after the services have been rendered or the contract has been entered into.

(2) Except as provided in this subsection, the compensation of a public officer may not be increased or diminished during the term of office:

(a) When any increase or decrease in the compensation of justices of the supreme court or judges of any court of record becomes effective as to any such justice or judge, it shall be effective from such date as to every such justice or judge.

(b) Any increase in the compensation of members of the legislature shall take effect, for all senators and representatives to the assembly, after the next general election beginning with the new assembly term.

(3) Subsection (1) shall not apply to increased benefits for persons who have been or shall be granted benefits of any kind under a retirement system when such increased benefits are provided by a legislative act passed on a call of ayes and noes by a three-fourths vote of all the members elected to both houses of the legislature and such act provides for sufficient state funds to cover the costs of the increased benefits.

Suits against state. Section 27. The legislature shall direct by law in what manner and in what courts suits may be brought against the state.

Oath of office. Section 28. Members of the legislature, and all officers, executive and judicial, except such inferior officers as may be by law exempted, shall before they enter upon the duties of their respective offices, take and subscribe an oath or affirmation to support the constitution of the United States and the constitution of the state of Wisconsin, and faithfully to discharge the duties of their respective offices to the best of their ability.

Militia. Section 29. The legislature shall determine what persons shall constitute the militia of the state, and may provide for organizing and disciplining the same in such manner as shall be prescribed by law.

Elections by legislature. Section 30. All elections made by the legislature shall be by roll call vote entered in the journals.

Special and private laws prohibited. Section 31. The legislature is prohibited from enacting any special or private laws in the following cases:

(1) For changing the names of persons, constituting one person the heir at law of another or granting any divorce.

(2) For laying out, opening or altering highways, except in cases of state roads extending into more than one county, and military roads to aid in the construction of which lands may be granted by congress.

(3) For authorizing persons to keep ferries across streams at points wholly within this state.

(4) For authorizing the sale or mortgage of real or personal property of minors or others under disability.

(5) For locating or changing any county seat.

(6) For assessment or collection of taxes or for extending the time for the collection thereof.

(7) For granting corporate powers or privileges, except to cities.

(8) For authorizing the apportionment of any part of the school fund.

(9) For incorporating any city, town or village, or to amend the charter thereof.

General laws on enumerated subjects. Section 32. The legislature may provide by general law for the treatment of any subject for which lawmaking is prohibited by section 31 of this article. Subject to reasonable classifications, such laws shall be uniform in their operation throughout the state.

Auditing of state accounts. Section 33. The legislature shall provide for the auditing of state accounts and may establish such offices and prescribe such duties for the same as it shall deem necessary.

Continuity of civil government. Section 34. The legislature, in order to ensure continuity of state and local governmental operations in periods of emergency resulting from enemy action in the form of an attack, shall (1) forthwith provide for prompt and temporary succession to the powers and duties of public offices, of whatever nature and whether filled by election or appointment, the incumbents of which may become unavailable for carrying on the powers and duties of such offices, and (2) adopt such other measures as may be necessary and proper for attaining the objectives of this section.

Article V—Executive

Governor; lieutenant governor; term. Section 1. The executive power shall be vested in a governor who shall hold office for 4 years; a lieutenant governor shall be elected at the same time and for the same term.

Eligibility. Section 2. No person except a citizen of the United States and a qualified elector of the state shall be eligible to the office of governor or lieutenant governor.

Election. Section 3. The governor and lieutenant governor shall be elected by the qualified electors of the state at the times and places of choosing members of the legislature. They shall be chosen jointly, by the casting by each voter of a single vote applicable to both offices beginning with the general election in 1970. The persons respectively having the highest number of votes cast jointly for them for governor and lieutenant governor shall be elected; but in case two or more slates shall have an equal and the highest number of votes for governor and lieutenant governor, the two houses of the legislature, at its next annual session shall forthwith, by joint ballot, choose one of the slates so having an equal and the highest number of votes for governor and lieutenant governor. The returns of election for governor and lieutenant governor shall be made in such manner as shall be provided by law.

Powers and duties. Section 4. The governor shall be commander in chief of the military and naval forces of the state. He shall have power to convene the legislature on extraordinary occasions, and in case of invasion, or danger from the prevalence of contagious disease at the seat of government, he may convene them at any other suitable place within the state. He shall communicate to the legislature, at every session, the condition of the state, and recommend such matters to them for their consideration as he may deem expedient. He shall transact all necessary business with the officers of the government, civil and military. He shall expedite all such measures as may be resolved upon by the legislature, and shall take care that the laws be faithfully executed.

Pardoning power. Section 6. The governor shall have power to grant reprieves, commutations and pardons, after conviction, for all offenses, except treason and cases of impeachment, upon such conditions and with such restrictions and limitations as he may think proper, subject to such regulations as may be provided by law relative to the manner of applying for pardons. Upon conviction for treason he shall have the power to suspend the execution of the sentence until the case shall be reported to the legislature at its next meeting, when the legislature shall either pardon, or commute the sentence, direct the execution of the sentence, or grant a further reprieve. He shall annually communicate to the legislature each case of reprieve, commutation or pardon granted, stating the name of the convict, the crime of which he was convicted, the sentence and its date, and the date of the commutation, pardon or reprieve, with his reasons for granting the same.

Lieutenant governor, when governor. Section 7. (1) Upon the governor's death, resignation or removal from office, the lieutenant governor shall become governor for the balance of the unexpired term.

(2) If the governor is absent from this state, impeached, or from mental or physical disease, becomes incapable of performing the duties of the office, the lieutenant governor shall serve as acting governor for the balance of the unexpired term or until the governor returns, the disability ceases or the impeachment is vacated. But when the governor, with the consent of the legislature, shall be out of this state in time of war at the head of the state's military force, the governor shall continue as commander in chief of the military force.

Secretary of state, when governor. Section 8. (1) If there is a vacancy in the office of lieutenant governor and the governor dies, resigns or is removed from office, the secretary of state shall become governor for the balance of the unexpired term.

(2) If there is a vacancy in the office of lieutenant governor and the governor is absent from this state, impeached, or from mental or physical disease becomes incapable of performing the duties of the office, the secretary of state shall serve as acting governor for the balance of the unexpired term or until the governor returns, the disability ceases or the impeachment is vacated.

Governor to approve or veto bills; proceedings on veto. Section 10. (1) (a) Every bill which shall have passed the legislature shall, before it becomes a law, be presented to the governor.

(b) If the governor approves and signs the bill, the bill shall become law. Appropriation bills may be approved in whole or in part by the governor, and the part approved shall become law.

(c) In approving an appropriation bill in part, the governor may not create a new word by rejecting individual letters in the words of the enrolled bill, and may not create a new sentence by combining parts of 2 or more sentences of the enrolled bill.

(2) (a) If the governor rejects the bill, the governor shall return the bill, together with the objections in writing, to the house in which the bill originated. The house of origin shall enter the objections at large upon the journal and proceed to reconsider the bill. If, after such reconsideration, two-thirds of the members present agree to pass the bill notwithstanding the objections of the governor, it shall be sent, together with the objections, to the other house, by which it shall likewise be reconsidered, and if approved by two-thirds of the members present it shall become law.

(b) The rejected part of an appropriation bill, together with the governor's objections in writing, shall be returned to the house in which the bill originated. The house of origin shall enter the objections at large upon the journal and proceed to reconsider the rejected part of the appropriation bill. If, after such reconsideration, two-thirds of the members present agree to approve the rejected part notwithstanding the objections of the governor, it shall be sent, together with the objections, to the other house, by which it shall likewise be reconsidered, and if approved by two-thirds of the members present the rejected part shall become law.

(c) In all such cases the votes of both houses shall be determined by ayes and noes, and the names of the members voting for or against passage of the bill or the rejected part of the bill notwithstanding the objections of the governor shall be entered on the journal of each house respectively.

(3) Any bill not returned by the governor within 6 days (Sundays excepted) after it shall have been presented to the governor shall be law unless the legislature, by final adjournment, prevents the bill's return, in which case it shall not be law.

Article VI—Administrative

Election of secretary of state, treasurer and attorney general; term. Section 1. The qualified electors of this state, at the times and places of choosing the members of the legislature, shall in 1970 and every 4 years thereafter elect a secretary of state, treasurer and attorney general who shall hold their offices for 4 years.

Secretary of state; duties, compensation. Section 2. The secretary of state shall keep a fair record of the official acts of the legislature and executive department of the state, and shall, when required, lay the same and all matters relative thereto before either branch of the legislature. He shall perform such other duties as shall be assigned him by law. He shall receive as a compensation for his services yearly such sum as shall be provided by law, and shall keep his office at the seat of government.

Treasurer and attorney general; duties, compensation. Section 3. The powers, duties and compensation of the treasurer and attorney general shall be prescribed by law.

County officers; election, terms, removal; vacancies. Section 4. (1) (a) Except as provided in pars. (b) and (c) and sub. (2), coroners, registers of deeds, district attorneys, and all other elected county officers, except judicial officers, sheriffs, and chief executive officers, shall be chosen by the electors of the respective counties once in every 2 years.

(b) Beginning with the first general election at which the governor is elected which occurs after the ratification of this paragraph, sheriffs shall be chosen by the electors of the respective counties, or by the electors of all of the respective counties comprising each combination of counties combined by the legislature for that purpose, for the term of 4 years and coroners in counties in which there is a coroner shall be chosen by the electors of the respective counties, or by the electors of all of the respective counties comprising each combination of counties combined by the legislature for that purpose, for the term of 4 years.

(c) Beginning with the first general election at which the president is elected which occurs after the ratification of this paragraph, district attorneys, registers of deeds, county clerks, and treasurers shall be chosen by the electors of the respective counties, or by the electors of all of the respective counties comprising each combination of counties combined by the legislature for that purpose, for the term of 4 years and surveyors in counties in which the office of surveyor is filled by election shall be chosen by the electors of the respective counties, or by the electors of all of the respective counties comprising each combination of counties combined by the legislature for that purpose, for the term of 4 years.

(2) The offices of coroner and surveyor in counties having a population of 500,000 or more are abolished. Counties not having a population of 500,000 shall have the option of retaining the elective office of coroner or instituting a medical examiner system. Two or more counties may institute a joint medical examiner system.

(3) (a) Sheriffs may not hold any other partisan office.

(b) Sheriffs may be required by law to renew their security from time to time, and in default of giving such new security their office shall be deemed vacant.

(4) The governor may remove any elected county officer mentioned in this section except a county clerk, treasurer, or surveyor, giving to the officer a copy of the charges and an opportunity of being heard.

(5) All vacancies in the offices of coroner, register of deeds or district attorney shall be filled by appointment. The person appointed to fill a vacancy shall hold office only for the unexpired portion of the term to which appointed and until a successor shall be elected and qualified.

(6) When a vacancy occurs in the office of sheriff, the vacancy shall be filled by appointment of the governor, and the person appointed shall serve until his or her successor is elected and qualified.

Article VII—Judiciary

Impeachment; trial. Section 1. The court for the trial of impeachments shall be composed of the senate. The assembly shall have the power of impeaching all civil officers of this state for corrupt conduct in office, or for crimes and misdemeanors; but a majority of all the members elected shall concur in an impeachment. On the trial of an impeachment against the governor, the lieutenant governor shall not act as a member of the court. No judicial officer shall exercise his office, after he shall have been impeached, until his acquittal. Before the trial of an impeachment the members of the court shall take an oath or affirmation truly and impartially to try the impeachment according to evidence; and no person shall be convicted without the concurrence of two-thirds of the members present. Judgment in cases of impeachment shall not extend further than to removal from office, or removal from office and disqualification to hold any office of honor, profit or trust under the state; but the party impeached shall be liable to indictment, trial and punishment according to law.

Court system. Section 2. The judicial power of this state shall be vested in a unified court system consisting of one supreme court, a court of appeals, a circuit court, such trial courts of general uniform statewide jurisdiction as the legislature may create by law, and a municipal court if authorized by the legislature under section 14.

Supreme court: jurisdiction. Section 3. (1) The supreme court shall have superintending and administrative authority over all courts.

(2) The supreme court has appellate jurisdiction over all courts and may hear original actions and proceedings. The supreme court may issue all writs necessary in aid of its jurisdiction.

(3) The supreme court may review judgments and orders of the court of appeals, may remove cases from the court of appeals and may accept cases on certification by the court of appeals.

Supreme court: election, chief justice, court system administration. Section 4. (1) The supreme court shall have 7 members who shall be known as justices of the supreme court. Justices shall be elected for 10-year terms of office commencing with the August 1 next succeeding the election. Only one justice may be elected in any year. Any 4 justices shall constitute a quorum for the conduct of the court's business.

(2) The chief justice of the supreme court shall be elected for a term of 2 years by a majority of the justices then serving on the court. The justice so designated as chief justice may, irrevocably, decline to serve as chief justice or resign as chief justice but continue to serve as a justice of the supreme court.

(3) The chief justice of the supreme court shall be the administrative head of the judicial system and shall exercise this administrative authority pursuant to procedures adopted by the supreme court. The chief justice may assign any judge of a court of record to aid in the proper disposition of judicial business in any court of record except the supreme court.

Court of appeals. Section 5. (1) The legislature shall by law combine the judicial circuits of the state into one or more districts for the court of appeals and shall designate in each district the locations where the appeals court shall sit for the convenience of litigants.

(2) For each district of the appeals court there shall be chosen by the qualified electors of the district one or more appeals judges as prescribed by law, who shall sit as prescribed by law. Appeals judges shall be elected for 6-year terms and shall reside in the district from which elected. No alteration of district or circuit boundaries shall have the effect of removing an appeals

judge from office during the judge's term. In case of an increase in the number of appeals judges, the first judge or judges shall be elected for full terms unless the legislature prescribes a shorter initial term for staggering of terms.

(3) The appeals court shall have such appellate jurisdiction in the district, including jurisdiction to review administrative proceedings, as the legislature may provide by law, but shall have no original jurisdiction other than by prerogative writ. The appeals court may issue all writs necessary in aid of its jurisdiction and shall have supervisory authority over all actions and proceedings in the courts in the district.

Circuit court: boundaries. Section 6. The legislature shall prescribe by law the number of judicial circuits, making them as compact and convenient as practicable, and bounding them by county lines. No alteration of circuit boundaries shall have the effect of removing a circuit judge from office during the judge's term. In case of an increase of circuits, the first judge or judges shall be elected.

Circuit court: election. Section 7. For each circuit there shall be chosen by the qualified electors thereof one or more circuit judges as prescribed by law. Circuit judges shall be elected for 6-year terms and shall reside in the circuit from which elected.

Circuit court: jurisdiction. Section 8. Except as otherwise provided by law, the circuit court shall have original jurisdiction in all matters civil and criminal within this state and such appellate jurisdiction in the circuit as the legislature may prescribe by law. The circuit court may issue all writs necessary in aid of its jurisdiction.

Judicial elections, vacancies. Section 9. When a vacancy occurs in the office of justice of the supreme court or judge of any court of record, the vacancy shall be filled by appointment by the governor, which shall continue until a successor is elected and qualified. There shall be no election for a justice or judge at the partisan general election for state or county officers, nor within 30 days either before or after such election.

Judges: eligibility to office. Section 10. (1) No justice of the supreme court or judge of any court of record shall hold any other office of public trust, except a judicial office, during the term for which elected. No person shall be eligible to the office of judge who shall not, at the time of election or appointment, be a qualified elector within the jurisdiction for which chosen.

(2) Justices of the supreme court and judges of the courts of record shall

receive such compensation as the legislature may authorize by law, but may not receive fees of office.

Disciplinary proceedings. Section 11. Each justice or judge shall be subject to reprimand, censure, suspension, removal for cause or for disability, by the supreme court pursuant to procedures established by the legislature by law. No justice or judge removed for cause shall be eligible for reappointment or temporary service. This section is alternative to, and cumulative with, the methods of removal provided in sections 1 and 13 of this article and section 12 of article XIII.

Clerks of circuit and supreme courts. Section 12. (1) There shall be a clerk of circuit court chosen in each county organized for judicial purposes by the qualified electors thereof, who, except as provided in sub. (2), shall hold office for two years, subject to removal as provided by law.

(2) Beginning with the first general election at which the governor is elected which occurs after the ratification of this subsection, a clerk of circuit court shall be chosen by the electors of each county, for the term of 4 years, subject to removal as provided by law.

(3) In case of a vacancy, the judge of the circuit court may appoint a clerk until the vacancy is filled by an election.

(4) The clerk of circuit court shall give such security as the legislature requires by law.

(5) The supreme court shall appoint its own clerk, and may appoint a clerk of circuit court to be the clerk of the supreme court.

Justices and judges: removal by address. Section 13. Any justice or judge may be removed from office by address of both houses of the legislature, if two-thirds of all the members elected to each house concur therein, but no removal shall be made by virtue of this section unless the justice or judge complained of is served with a copy of the charges, as the ground of address, and has had an opportunity of being heard. On the question of removal, the ayes and noes shall be entered on the journals.

Municipal court. Section 14. The legislature by law may authorize each city, village and town to establish a municipal court. All municipal courts shall have uniform jurisdiction limited to actions and proceedings arising under ordinances of the municipality in which established. Judges of municipal courts may receive such compensation as provided by the municipality in which established, but may not receive fees of office.

Justices and judges: eligibility for office; retirement. Section 24. (1) To be eligible for the office of supreme court justice or judge of any court of record, a person must be an attorney licensed to practice law in this state and have been so licensed for 5 years immediately prior to election or appointment.

(2) Unless assigned temporary service under subsection (3), no person may serve as a supreme court justice or judge of a court of record beyond the July 31 following the date on which such person attains that age, of not less than 70 years, which the legislature shall prescribe by law.

(3) A person who has served as a supreme court justice or judge of a court of record may, as provided by law, serve as a judge of any court of record except the supreme court on a temporary basis if assigned by the chief justice of the supreme court.

Article VIII—Finance

Rule of taxation uniform; income, privilege and occupation taxes. Section 1. The rule of taxation shall be uniform but the legislature may empower cities, villages or towns to collect and return taxes on real estate located therein by optional methods. Taxes shall be levied upon such property with such classifications as to forests and minerals including or separate or severed from the land, as the legislature shall prescribe. Taxation of agricultural land and undeveloped land, both as defined by law, need not be uniform with the taxation of each other nor with the taxation of other real property. Taxation of merchants' stock-in-trade, manufacturers' materials and finished products, and livestock need not be uniform with the taxation of real property and other personal property, but the taxation of all such merchants' stock-in-trade, manufacturers' materials and finished products and livestock shall be uniform, except that the legislature may provide that the value thereof shall be determined on an average basis. Taxes may also be imposed on incomes, privileges and occupations, which taxes may be graduated and progressive, and reasonable exemptions may be provided.

Appropriations; limitation. Section 2. No money shall be paid out of the treasury except in pursuance of an appropriation by law. No appropriation shall be made for the payment of any claim against the state except claims of the United States and judgments, unless filed within six years after the claim accrued

Credit of state. Section 3. Except as provided in s. 7 (2) (a), the credit of the state shall never be given, or loaned, in aid of any individual, association or corporation.

Contracting state debts. Section 4. The state shall never contract any public debt except in the cases and manner herein provided.

Annual tax levy to equal expenses. Section 5. The legislature shall provide for an annual tax sufficient to defray the estimated expenses of the state for each year; and whenever the expenses of any year shall exceed the income, the legislature shall provide for levying a tax for the ensuing year, sufficient, with other sources of income, to pay the deficiency as well as the estimated expenses of such ensuing year.

Public debt for extraordinary expense; taxation. Section 6. For the purpose of defraying extraordinary expenditures the state may contract public debts (but such debts shall never in the aggregate exceed one hundred thousand dollars). Every such debt shall be authorized by law, for some purpose or purposes to be distinctly specified therein; and the vote of a majority of all the members elected to each house, to be taken by yeas and nays, shall be necessary to the passage of such law; and every such law shall provide for levying an annual tax sufficient to pay the annual interest of such debt and the principal within five years from the passage of such law, and shall specially appropriate the proceeds of such taxes to the payment of such principal and interest; and such appropriation shall not be repealed, nor the taxes be postponed or diminished, until the principal and interest of such debt shall have been wholly paid.

Public debt for public defense; bonding for public purposes. Section 7. (1) The legislature may also borrow money to repel invasion, suppress insurrection, or defend the state in time of war; but the money thus raised shall be applied exclusively to the object for which the loan was authorized, or to the repayment of the debt thereby created.

(2) Any other provision of this constitution to the contrary notwithstanding:

(a) The state may contract public debt and pledges to the payment thereof its full faith, credit and taxing power:

1. To acquire, construct, develop, extend, enlarge or improve land, waters, property, highways, railways, buildings, equipment or facilities for public purposes.

2. To make funds available for veterans' housing loans.

(b) The aggregate public debt contracted by the state in any calendar year pursuant to paragraph (a) shall not exceed an amount equal to the lesser of:

1. Three-fourths of one per centum of the aggregate value of all taxable property in the state; or

2. Five per centum of the aggregate value of all taxable property in the state less the sum of: a. the aggregate public debt of the state contracted pursuant to this section outstanding as of January 1 of such calendar year after subtracting therefrom the amount of sinking funds on hand on January 1 of such calendar year which are applicable exclusively to repayment of such outstanding public debt and, b. the outstanding indebtedness as of January 1 of such calendar year of any entity of the type described in paragraph (d) to the extent that such indebtedness is supported by or payable from payments out of the treasury of the state.

(c) The state may contract public debt, without limit, to fund or refund the whole or any part of any public debt contracted pursuant to paragraph (a), including any premium payable with respect thereto and any interest to accrue thereon, or to fund or refund the whole or any part of any indebtedness incurred prior to January 1, 1972, by any entity of the type described in paragraph (d), including any premium payable with respect thereto and any interest to accrue thereon.

(d) No money shall be paid out of the treasury, with respect to any lease, sublease or other agreement entered into after January 1, 1971, to the Wisconsin State Agencies Building Corporation, Wisconsin State Colleges Building Corporation, Wisconsin State Public Building Corporation, Wisconsin University Building Corporation or any similar entity existing or operating for similar purposes pursuant to which such nonprofit corporation or such other entity undertakes to finance or provide a facility for use or occupancy by the state or an agency, department or instrumentality thereof.

(e) The legislature shall prescribe all matters relating to the contracting of public debt pursuant to paragraph (a), including: the public purposes for which public debt may be contracted; by vote of a majority of the members elected to each of the 2 houses of the legislature, the amount of public debt which may be contracted for any class of such purposes; the public debt or other indebtedness which may be funded or refunded; the kinds of notes, bonds or other evidence of public debt which may be issued by the state; and the manner in which the aggregate value of all taxable property in the state shall be determined.

(f) The full faith, credit and taxing power of the state are pledged to the payment of all public debt created on behalf of the state pursuant to this section and the legislature shall provide by appropriation for the payment of the interest upon and instalments of principal of all such public debt as the same falls due, but, in any event, suit may be brought against the state to compel such payment.

(g) At any time after January 1, 1972, by vote of a majority of the members elected to each of the 2 houses of the legislature, the legislature may declare that an emergency exists and submit to the people a proposal to authorize the state to contract a specific amount of public debt for a purpose specified in such proposal, without regard to the limit provided in paragraph (b). Any such authorization shall be effective if approved by a majority of the electors voting thereon. Public debt contracted pursuant to such authorization shall thereafter be deemed to have been contracted pursuant to paragraph (a), but neither such public debt nor any public debt contracted to fund or refund such public debt shall be considered in computing the debt limit provided in paragraph (b). Not more than one such authorization shall be thus made in any 2-year period.

Vote on fiscal bills; quorum. Section 8. On the passage in either house of the legislature of any law which imposes, continues or renews a tax, or creates a debt or charge, or makes, continues or renews an appropriation of public or trust money, or releases, discharges or commutes a claim or demand of the state, the question shall be taken by yeas and nays, which shall be duly entered on the journal; and three-fifths of all the members elected to such house shall in all such cases be required to constitute a quorum therein.

Evidences of public debt. Section 9. No scrip, certificate, or other evidence of state debt, whatsoever, shall be issued, except for such debts as are authorized by the sixth and seventh sections of this article.

Internal improvements. Section 10. Except as further provided in this section, the state may never contract any debt for works of internal improvement, or be a party in carrying on such works.

(1) Whenever grants of land or other property shall have been made to the state, especially dedicated by the grant to particular works of internal improvement, the state may carry on such particular works and shall devote thereto the avails of such grants, and may pledge or appropriate the revenues derived from such works in aid of their completion.

(2) The state may appropriate money in the treasury or to be thereafter raised by taxation for:

(a) The construction or improvement of public highways.

(b) The development, improvement and construction of airports or other aeronautical projects.

(c) The acquisition, improvement or construction of veterans' housing.

(d) The improvement of port facilities.

(e) The acquisition, development, improvement or construction of railways and other railroad facilities.

(3) The state may appropriate moneys for the purpose of acquiring, preserving and developing the forests of the state. Of the moneys appropriated under the authority of this subsection in any one year an amount not to exceed two-tenths of one mill of the taxable property of the state as determined by the last preceding state assessment may be raised by a tax on property.

Transportation Fund. Section 11. All funds collected by the state from any taxes or fees levied or imposed for the licensing of motor vehicle operators, for the titling, licensing, or registration of motor vehicles, for motor vehicle fuel, or for the use of roadways, highways, or bridges, and from taxes and fees levied or imposed for aircraft, airline property, or aviation fuel or for railroads or railroad property shall be deposited only into the transportation fund or with a trustee for the benefit of the department of transportation or the holders of transportation-related revenue bonds, except for collections from taxes or fees in existence on December 31, 2010, that were not being deposited in the transportation fund on that date. None of the funds collected or received by the state from any source and deposited into the transportation fund shall be lapsed, further transferred, or appropriated to any program that is not directly administered by the department of transportation in furtherance of the department's responsibility for the planning, promotion, and protection of all transportation systems in the state except for programs for which there was an appropriation from the transportation fund on December 31, 2010. In this section, the term "motor vehicle" does not include any all-terrain vehicles, snowmobiles, or watercraft.

Article IX—Eminent domain and property of the state

Jurisdiction on rivers and lakes; navigable waters. Section 1. The state shall have concurrent jurisdiction on all rivers and lakes bordering on this state so far as such rivers or lakes shall form a common boundary to the state and any other state or territory now or hereafter to be formed, and bounded by the same; and the river Mississippi and the navigable waters leading into the Mississippi and St. Lawrence, and the carrying places between the same, shall be common highways and forever free, as well to the inhabitants of the state as to the citizens of the United States, without any tax, impost or duty therefor.

Territorial property. Section 2. The title to all lands and other property which have accrued to the territory of Wisconsin by grant, gift, purchase, forfeiture, escheat or otherwise shall vest in the state of Wisconsin.

Ultimate property in lands; escheats. Section 3. The people of the state, in their right of sovereignty, are declared to possess the ultimate property in and to all lands within the jurisdiction of the state; and all lands the title to which shall fail from a defect of heirs shall revert or escheat to the people.

Article X—Education

Superintendent of public instruction. Section 1. The supervision of public instruction shall be vested in a state superintendent and such other officers as the legislature shall direct; and their qualifications, powers, duties and compensation shall be prescribed by law. The state superintendent shall be chosen by the qualified electors of the state at the same time and in the same manner as members of the supreme court, and shall hold office for 4 years from the succeeding first Monday in July. The term of office, time and manner of electing or appointing all other officers of supervision of public instruction shall be fixed by law.

School fund created; income applied. Section 2. The proceeds of all lands that have been or hereafter may be granted by the United States to this state for educational purposes (except the lands heretofore granted for the purposes of a university) and all moneys and the clear proceeds of all property that may accrue to the state by forfeiture or escheat; and the clear proceeds of all fines collected in the several counties for any breach of the penal laws, and all moneys arising from any grant to the state where the purposes of such grant are not specified, and the 500,000 acres of land to which the state is entitled by the provisions of an act of congress, entitled "An act to appropriate the proceeds of the sales of the public lands and to grant pre-emption rights," approved September 4, 1841; and also the 5 percent of the net proceeds of the public lands to which the state shall become entitled on admission into the union (if congress shall consent to such appropriation of the 2 grants last mentioned) shall be set apart as a separate fund to be called "the school fund," the interest of which and all other revenues derived from the school lands shall be exclusively applied to the following objects, to wit:

(1) To the support and maintenance of common schools, in each school district, and the purchase of suitable libraries and apparatus therefor.

(2) The residue shall be appropriated to the support and maintenance of academies and normal schools, and suitable libraries and apparatus therefor.

District schools; tuition; sectarian instruction; released time. Section 3. The legislature shall provide by law for the establishment of district schools, which shall be as nearly uniform as practicable; and such schools shall be free and without charge for tuition to all children between the ages of 4 and 20 years; and no sectarian instruction shall be allowed therein; but the legislature by law may, for the purpose of religious instruction outside the district schools, authorize the release of students during regular school hours.

Annual school tax. Section 4. Each town and city shall be required to raise by tax, annually, for the support of common schools therein, a sum not less than one-half the amount received by such town or city respectively for school purposes from the income of the school fund.

Income of school fund. Section 5. Provision shall be made by law for the distribution of the income of the school fund among the several towns and cities of the state for the support of common schools therein, in some just proportion to the number of children and youth resident therein between the ages of four and twenty years, and no appropriation shall be made from the school fund to any city or town for the year in which said city or town shall fail to raise such tax; nor to any school district for the year in which a school shall not be maintained at least three months.

State university; support. Section 6. Provision shall be made by law for the establishment of a state university at or near the seat of state government, and for connecting with the same, from time to time, such colleges in different parts of the state as the interests of education may require. The proceeds of all lands that have been or may hereafter be granted by the United States to the state for the support of a university shall be and remain a perpetual fund to be called "the university fund," the interest of which shall be appropriated to the support of the state university, and no sectarian instruction shall be allowed in such university.

Commissioners of public lands. Section 7. The secretary of state, treasurer and attorney general, shall constitute a board of commissioners for the sale of the school and university lands and for the investment of the funds arising therefrom. Any two of said commissioners shall be a quorum for the transaction of all business pertaining to the duties of their office.

Sale of public lands. Section 8. Provision shall be made by law for the sale of all school and university lands after they shall have been appraised; and when any portion of such lands shall be sold and the purchase money shall not be paid at the time of the sale, the commissioners shall take security by mortgage upon the lands sold for the sum remaining unpaid, with seven per cent interest thereon, payable annually at the office of the treasurer. The commissioners shall be authorized to execute a good and sufficient conveyance to all purchasers of such lands, and to discharge any mortgages taken as security, when the sum due thereon shall have been paid. The commissioners shall have power to withhold from sale any portion of such lands when they shall deem it expedient, and shall invest all moneys arising from the sale of such lands, as well as all other university and school funds, in such manner as the legislature shall provide, and shall give such security for the faithful performance of their duties as may be required by law.

Article XI—Corporations

Corporations; how formed. Section 1. Corporations without banking powers or privileges may be formed under general laws, but shall not be created by special act, except for municipal purposes. All general laws or special acts enacted under the provisions of this section may be altered or repealed by the legislature at any time after their passage.

Property taken by municipality. Section 2. No municipal corporation shall take private property for public use, against the consent of the owner, without the necessity thereof being first established in the manner prescribed by the legislature.

Municipal home rule; debt limit; tax to pay debt. Section 3. (1) Cities and villages organized pursuant to state law may determine their local affairs and government, subject only to this constitution and to such enactments of the legislature of statewide concern as with uniformity shall affect every city or every village. The method of such determination shall be prescribed by the legislature.

(2) No county, city, town, village, school district, sewerage district or other municipal corporation may become indebted in an amount that exceeds an allowable percentage of the taxable property located therein equalized for state purposes as provided by the legislature. In all cases the allowable percentage shall be 5 percent except as specified in pars. (a) and (b):

(a) For any city authorized to issue bonds for school purposes, an additional 10 percent shall be permitted for school purposes only, and in such cases the territory attached to the city for school purposes shall be included in the total taxable property supporting the bonds issued for school purposes.

(b) For any school district which offers no less than grades one to 12 and which at the time of incurring such debt is eligible for the highest level of school aids, 10 percent shall be permitted.

(3) Any county, city, town, village, school district, sewerage district or other municipal corporation incurring any indebtedness under sub. (2) shall, before or at the time of doing so, provide for the collection of a direct annual tax sufficient to pay the interest on such debt as it falls due, and also to pay and discharge the principal thereof within 20 years from the time of contracting the same.

(4) When indebtedness under sub. (2) is incurred in the acquisition of lands by cities, or by counties or sewerage districts having a population of 150,000 or over, for public, municipal purposes, or for the permanent improvement thereof, or to purchase, acquire, construct, extend, add to or improve a sewage collection or treatment system which services all or a part of such city or county, the city, county or sewerage district incurring the indebtedness shall, before or at the time of so doing, provide for the collection of a direct annual tax sufficient to pay the interest on such debt as it falls due, and also to pay and discharge the principal thereof within a period not exceeding 50 years from the time of contracting the same.

(5) An indebtedness created for the purpose of purchasing, acquiring, leasing, constructing, extending, adding to, improving, conducting, controlling, operating or managing a public utility of a town, village, city or special district, and secured solely by the property or income of such public utility, and whereby no municipal liability is created, shall not be considered an indebtedness of such town, village, city or special district, and shall not be included in arriving at the debt limitation under sub. (2).

Acquisition of lands by state and subdivisions; sale of excess. Section 3a. The state or any of its counties, cities, towns or villages may acquire by gift, dedication, purchase, or condemnation lands for establishing, laying out, widening, enlarging, extending, and maintaining memorial grounds, streets, highways, squares, parkways, boulevards, parks, playgrounds, sites for public buildings, and reservations in and about and along and leading to any or all of the same; and after the establishment, layout, and completion of such improvements, may convey any such real estate thus acquired and not necessary for such improvements, with reservations concerning the future use and occupation of such real estate, so as to protect such public works and improvements, and their environs, and to preserve the view, appearance, light, air, and usefulness of such public works. If the governing body of a county, city, town or village elects to accept a gift or dedication of land made on condition that the land be devoted to a special purpose and the condition subsequently becomes impossible or impracticable, such governing body may by resolution or ordinance enacted by a two-thirds vote of its members elect either to grant the land back to the donor or dedicator or his heirs or accept from the donor or dedicator or his heirs a grant relieving the county, city, town or village of the condition; however, if the donor or dedicator or his heirs are unknown or cannot be found, such resolution or ordinance may provide for the commencement of proceedings in the manner and in the courts as the legislature shall designate for the purpose of relieving the county, city, town or village from the condition of the gift or dedication.

General banking law. Section 4. The legislature may enact a general banking law for the creation of banks, and for the regulation and supervision of the banking business.

Article XII—Amendments

Constitutional amendments. Section 1. Any amendment or amendments to this constitution may be proposed in either house of the legislature, and if the same shall be agreed to by a majority of the members elected to each of the two houses, such proposed amendment or amendments shall be entered on their journals, with the yeas and nays taken thereon, and referred to the legislature to be chosen at the next general election, and shall be published for three months previous to the time of holding such election; and if, in the legislature so next chosen, such proposed amendment or amendments shall be agreed to by a majority of all the members elected to each house, then it shall be the duty of the legislature to submit such proposed amendment or amendments to the people in such manner and at such time as the legislature shall prescribe; and if the people shall approve and ratify such amendment or amendments by a majority of the electors voting thereon, such amendment or amendments shall become part of the constitution; provided, that if more than one amendment be submitted, they shall be submitted in such manner that the people may vote for or against such amendments separately.

Constitutional conventions. Section 2. If at any time a majority of the senate and assembly shall deem it necessary to call a convention to revise or change this constitution, they shall recommend to the electors to vote for or against a convention at the next election for members of the legislature. And if it shall appear that a majority of the electors voting thereon have voted for a convention, the legislature shall, at its next session, provide for calling such convention.

Article XIII—Miscellaneous provisions

Political year; elections. Section 1. The political year for this state shall commence on the first Monday of January in each year, and the general election shall be held on the Tuesday next succeeding the first Monday of November in even-numbered years.

Eligibility to office. Section 3. (1) No member of congress and no person holding any office of profit or trust under the United States except postmaster, or under any foreign power, shall be eligible to any office of trust, profit or honor in this state.

(2) No person convicted of a felony, in any court within the United States, no person convicted in federal court of a crime designated, at the time of commission, under federal law as a misdemeanor involving a violation of public trust and no person convicted, in a court of a state, of a crime designated, at the time of commission, under the law of the state as a misdemeanor involving a violation of public trust shall be eligible to any office of trust, profit or honor in this state unless pardoned of the conviction.

(3) No person may seek to have placed on any ballot for a state or local elective office in this state the name of a person convicted of a felony, in any court within the United States, the name of a person convicted in federal court of a crime designated, at the time of commission, under federal law as a misdemeanor involving a violation of public trust or the name of a person convicted, in a court of a state, of a crime designated, at the time of commission, under the law of the state as a misdemeanor involving a violation of public trust, unless the person named for the ballot has been pardoned of the conviction.

Great seal. Section 4. It shall be the duty of the legislature to provide a great seal for the state, which shall be kept by the secretary of state, and all official acts of the governor, his approbation of the laws excepted, shall be thereby authenticated.

Legislative officers. Section 6. The elective officers of the legislature, other than the presiding officers, shall be a chief clerk and a sergeant at arms, to be elected by each house.

Division of counties. Section 7. No county with an area of nine hundred square miles or less shall be divided or have any part stricken therefrom, without submitting the question to a vote of the people of the county, nor unless a majority of all the legal voters of the county voting on the question shall vote for the same.

Removal of county seats. Section 8. No county seat shall be removed until the point to which it is proposed to be removed shall be fixed by law, and a majority of the voters of the county voting on the question shall have voted in favor of its removal to such point.

Election or appointment of statutory officers. Section 9. All county officers whose election or appointment is not provided for by this constitution shall be elected by the electors of the respective counties, or appointed by the boards of supervisors, or other county authorities, as the legislature shall direct. All city, town and village officers whose election or appointment is not provided for by this constitution shall be elected by the electors of such cities, towns and villages, or of some division thereof, or appointed by such authorities thereof as the legislature shall designate for that purpose. All other officers whose election or appointment is not provided for by this constitution, and all officers whose offices may hereafter be created by law, shall be elected by the people or appointed, as the legislature may direct.

Vacancies in office. Section 10. (1) The legislature may declare the cases in which any office shall be deemed vacant, and also the manner of filling the vacancy, where no provision is made for that purpose in this constitution.

(2) Whenever there is a vacancy in the office of lieutenant governor, the governor shall nominate a successor to serve for the balance of the unexpired term, who shall take office after confirmation by the senate and by the assembly.

Passes, franks and privileges. Section 11. No person, association, copartnership, or corporation, shall promise, offer or give, for any purpose, to any political committee, or any member or employe thereof, to any candidate for, or incumbent of any office or position under the constitution or laws, or under any ordinance of any town or municipality, of this state, or to any person at the request or for the advantage of all or any of them, any free pass or frank, or any privilege withheld from any person, for the traveling accommodation or transportation of any person or property, or the transmission of any message or communication.

No political committee, and no member or employee thereof, no candidate for and no incumbent of any office or position under the constitution or laws, or under any ordinance of any town or municipality of this state, shall ask for, or accept, from any person, association, copartnership, or corporation, or use, in any manner, or for any purpose, any free pass or frank, or any privilege withheld from any person, for the traveling accommodation or transportation of any person or property, or the transmission of any message or communication.

Any violation of any of the above provisions shall be bribery and punished as provided by law, and if any officer or any member of the legislature be guilty thereof, his office shall become vacant.

No person within the purview of this act shall be privileged from testifying in relation to anything therein prohibited; and no person having so testified shall be liable to any prosecution or punishment for any offense concerning which he was required to give his testimony or produce any documentary evidence.

Notaries public and regular employees of a railroad or other public utilities who are candidates for or hold public offices for which the annual compensation is not more than three hundred dollars to whom no passes or privileges are extended beyond those which are extended to other regular employees of such corporations are excepted from the provisions of this section.

Recall of elective officers. Section 12. The qualified electors of the state, of any congressional, judicial or legislative district or of any county may petition for the recall of any incumbent elective officer after the first year of the term for which the incumbent was elected, by filing a petition with the filing officer with whom the nomination petition to the office in the primary is filed, demanding the recall of the incumbent.

(1) The recall petition shall be signed by electors equalling at least twenty-five percent of the vote cast for the office of governor at the last preceding election, in the state, county or district which the incumbent represents.

(2) The filing officer with whom the recall petition is filed shall call a recall election for the Tuesday of the 6th week after the date of filing the petition or, if that Tuesday is a legal holiday, on the first day after that Tuesday which is not a legal holiday.

(3) The incumbent shall continue to perform the duties of the office until the recall election results are officially declared.

(4) Unless the incumbent declines within 10 days after the filing of the petition, the incumbent shall without filing be deemed to have filed for the recall election. Other candidates may file for the office in the manner provided by law for special elections. For the purpose of conducting elections under this section:

(a) When more than 2 persons compete for a nonpartisan office, a recall primary shall be held. The 2 persons receiving the highest number of votes in the recall primary shall be the 2 candidates in the recall election, except that if any candidate receives a majority of the total number of votes cast in the recall primary, that candidate shall assume the office for the remainder of the term and a recall election shall not be held.

(b) For any partisan office, a recall primary shall be held for each political party which is by law entitled to a separate ballot and from which more than one candidate competes for the party's nomination in the recall election. The person receiving the highest number of votes in the recall primary for each political party shall be that party's candidate in the recall election. Independent candidates and candidates representing political parties not entitled by law to a separate ballot shall be shown on the ballot for the recall election only.

(c) When a recall primary is required, the date specified under sub. (2) shall be the date of the recall primary and the recall election shall be held on the Tuesday of the 4th week after the recall primary or, if that Tuesday is a legal holiday, on the first day after that Tuesday which is not a legal holiday.

(5) The person who receives the highest number of votes in the recall election shall be elected for the remainder of the term.

(6) After one such petition and recall election, no further recall petition shall be filed against the same officer during the term for which he was elected.

(7) This section shall be self-executing and mandatory. Laws may be enacted to facilitate its operation but no law shall be enacted to hamper, restrict or impair the right of recall.

Marriage. Section 13. Only a marriage between one man and one woman shall be valid or recognized as a marriage in this state. A legal status identical or substantially similar to that of marriage for unmarried individuals shall not be valid or recognized in this state.

Article XIV—Schedule

Effect of change from territory to state. Section 1. That no inconvenience may arise by reason of a change from a territorial to a permanent state government, it is declared that all rights, actions, prosecutions, judgments, claims and contracts, as well of individuals as of bodies corporate, shall continue as if no such change had taken place; and all process which may be issued under the authority of the territory of Wisconsin previous to its admission into the union of the United States shall be as valid as if issued in the name of the state.

Territorial laws continued. Section 2. All laws now in force in the territory of Wisconsin which are not repugnant to this constitution shall remain in force until they expire by their own limitation or be altered or repealed by the legislature.

Common law continued in force. Section 13. Such parts of the common law as are now in force in the territory of Wisconsin, not inconsistent with this constitution, shall be and continue part of the law of this state until altered or suspended by the legislature.

Implementing revised structure of judicial branch. Section 16.

(4) The terms of office of justices of the supreme court serving on August 1, 1978, shall expire on the July 31 next preceding the first Monday in January on which such terms would otherwise have expired, but such advancement of the date of term expiration shall not impair any retirement rights vested in any such justice if the term had expired on the first Monday in January.

Under the Flag of France

Although American Indians lived in the area of present-day Wisconsin for several thousand years before the arrival of the French—numbering about 20,000 when the French arrived—the written history of the state began with the accounts of French explorers. The French explored the area, named places, and established trading posts, but left relatively little mark on it. They were interested in the fur trade, rather than agricultural settlement, and were never present in large numbers.

1634 Jean Nicolet: First known European to reach Wisconsin. Sought Northwest Passage.

1654–59 Pierre Esprit Radisson and Medart Chouart des Groseilliers: First of the fur traders in Wisconsin.

1661 Father Rene Menard: First missionary to Wisconsin Indians.

1665 Father Claude Allouez founded mission at La Pointe.

1666 Nicholas Perrot opened fur trade with Wisconsin Indians.

1672 Father Allouez and Father Louis Andre built St. Francois Xavier mission at De Pere.

Jean Nicolet, a French explorer, is the first known European to arrive in Wisconsin, making landfall in 1634 at Green Bay. He is depicted in this commissioned painting from 1907 meeting a group of Menominee Indians, wearing a Chinese robe and brandishing two pistols.

WHI IMAGE ID 1870

1673 Louis Jolliet and Father Jacques Marquette discovered Mississippi River.

1678 Daniel Greysolon Sieur du Lhut (Duluth) explored western end of Lake Superior.

(top) Father Jacques Marquette and Louis Jolliet traveled the Mississippi River in 1673. *(above left)* Lead mining by Indians in the southwest part of the state was first noticed by the French in 1690, and became a driving force for white settlement in the area during the 1800s. *(above right)* Important locations related to the Fox Indian Wars from 1701 to 1738 are shown in a historical map.

1685 Perrot made Commandant of the West.

1690 Perrot discovered lead mines in Wisconsin and Iowa.

1701–38 Fox Indian Wars.

1755 Wisconsin Indians, under Charles Langlade, helped defeat British General Braddock.

1763 Treaty of Paris. Wisconsin became part of British colonial territory.

Under the Flag of England

Wisconsin experienced few changes under British control. It remained the western edge of European penetration into the American continent, important only because of the fur trade. French traders plied their trade and British and colonial traders began to appear, but Europeans continued to be visitors rather than settlers.

1761 Fort at Green Bay accepted by English.

1763 Conspiracy of Pontiac. Two Englishmen killed by Indians at Muscoda.

1764 Charles Langlade settled at Green Bay. First permanent settlement.

1766 Jonathan Carver visited Wisconsin seeking Northwest Passage.

1774 Quebec Act made Wisconsin a part of Province of Quebec.

1781 Traditional date of settlement at Prairie du Chien.

1783 Second Treaty of Paris. Wisconsin became United States territory.

Achieving Territorial Status

In spite of the Treaty of Paris, Wisconsin remained British in all but title until after the War of 1812. In 1815, the American army established control. Gradually, Indian title to the southeastern half of the state was extinguished. Lead mining brought the first heavy influx of settlers and ended the dominance of the fur trade in the economy of the area. The lead mining period ran from about 1824 to 1861. Almost half of the 11,683 people who lived in the territory in 1836 were residents of the lead mining district in the southwestern corner of the state.

1787 Under the Northwest Ordinance of 1787, Wisconsin was made part of the Northwest Territory. The governing units for the Wisconsin area prior to statehood were:

1787–1800 Northwest Territory.

WHI IMAGE ID 27761

ω. H. Harrison

Future U.S. President William Henry Harrison was appointed governor of the Indiana Territory in 1800. The area included present-day Wisconsin until 1809.

1800–1809 Indiana Territory.

1809–1818 Illinois Territory.

1818–1836 Michigan Territory.

1836–1848 Wisconsin Territory.

1795 Jacques Vieau established trading posts at Kewaunee, Manitowoc, and Sheboygan. Made headquarters at Milwaukee.

1804 William Henry Harrison's treaty with Indians at St. Louis. United States extinguished Indian title to lead region (a cause of Black Hawk War).

1814 Fort Shelby built at Prairie du Chien. Captured by English and name changed to Fort McKay.

1815 War with England concluded. Fort McKay abandoned by British.

1816 Fort Shelby rebuilt at Prairie du Chien (renamed Fort Crawford). Astor's American Fur Company began operations in Wisconsin.

1818 Solomon Juneau bought trading post of Jacques Vieau at Milwaukee.

1820 Rev. Jedediah Morse preached first Protestant sermon in Wisconsin at Fort Howard (Green Bay) July 9. Henry Schoolcraft, James Doty, Lewis Cass made exploration trip through Wisconsin.

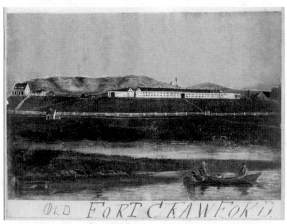

WHI IMAGE ID 5385

The military fort at Prairie du Chien was rebuilt in 1816 after the war with England and renamed Fort Crawford, the name it retains to this day.

1822 New York Indians (Oneida, Stockbridge, Munsee, and Brothertown) moved to Wisconsin. First mining leases in southwest Wisconsin.

1825 Indian Treaty established tribal boundaries.

WHI IMAGE ID 3773

Fort Howard on the Fox River at Green Bay, like Fort Crawford, was built to protect travel routes from invasion during the War of 1812. This lithograph from the 1840s shows the second fort built on higher ground.

1826–27 Winnebago Indian War. Surrender of Chief Red Bird.

1828 Fort Winnebago begun at Portage.

1832 Black Hawk War.

WHI IMAGE ID 31637

The building housing the Main Street offices of the *Green Bay Intelligencer*, the state's first newspaper, established in 1833.

1833 Land treaty with Indians cleared southern Wisconsin land titles. First newspaper, *Green Bay Intelligencer*, established.

1834 Land offices established at Green Bay and Mineral Point. First public road laid out.

1835 First steamboat arrived at Milwaukee. First bank in Wisconsin opened at Green Bay.

1836 Act creating Territory of Wisconsin signed April 20 by President Andrew Jackson. (Provisions of Ordinance of 1787 made part of the act.)

Wisconsin Territory

Wisconsin's population reached 305,000 by 1850. About half of the new immigrants were from New York and New England. The rest were principally from England, Scotland, Ireland, Germany, and Scandinavia. New York's Erie Canal gave Wisconsin a water outlet to the Atlantic Ocean and a route for new settlers. Wheat was the primary cash crop for most of the newcomers. State politics revolved around factions headed by James Doty and Henry Dodge. As political parties developed, the Democrats proved dominant throughout the period.

1836 Capital located at Belmont—Henry Dodge appointed governor, July 4, by President Andrew Jackson. First session of legislature. Madison chosen as permanent capital.

1837 Madison surveyed and platted. First Capitol begun. Panic of 1837—all territorial banks failed. Winnebago Indians ceded all claims to land in Wisconsin. Imprisonment for debt abolished.

WHI IMAGE ID 2613

WHI IMAGE ID 11337

WHI IMAGE ID 10476

Henry Dodge *(top left)* and James Doty *(top right)* both served as appointed governors of the Wisconsin Territory. *(above)* The first session of the territorial legislature was held in 1836 at this building in Belmont.

1838 Territorial legislature met in Madison. Milwaukee and Rock River Canal Company chartered.

1840 First school taxes authorized and levied.

WHI IMAGE ID 2963

Nathaniel Tallmadge was appointed governor of the Wisconsin Territory in 1844. The above portrait was painted when he served as a U.S. Senator for New York State.

1841 James Doty appointed governor by President John Tyler.

1842 C.C. Arndt shot and killed in legislature by James R. Vineyard.

1844 Nathaniel P. Tallmadge appointed governor. Wisconsin Phalanx (a utopian colony) established at Ceresco (Ripon).

1845 Dodge reappointed governor. Mormon settlement at Voree (Burlington). Swiss colony came to New Glarus.

1846 Congress passed enabling act for admission of Wisconsin as state. First Constitutional Convention met in Madison.

1847 Census population 210,546. First Constitution rejected by people. Second Constitutional Convention.

1848 Second Constitution adopted. President James K. Polk signed bill on May 29 making Wisconsin a state.

Say cheese: Wisconsin's newest symbol

State dairy product. Fourth-graders from Mineral Point Elementary School researched state symbols and were surprised to discover that there was no official state dairy product. The students proposed designating cheese as the new symbol to their legislators—Representative Todd Novak and Senator Howard Marklein *(bottom, left and right)*—who agreed to bring the idea to the legislature. Ella Kroll, Isabelle Coogan, Matthew Goninen *(below, left to right)*, and teacher Livia Doyle *(bottom, seated behind Senator Marklein)* testified for the proposal at a committee hearing held in March 2017 at the state capitol. The legislation later passed unanimously, and the governor signed the new symbol into law at the students' school on June 1, 2017, the first day of Dairy Month.

(ALL PHOTOS) JAY SALVO, LEGISLATIVE PHOTOGRAPHER

Coat of arms. The large shield at the center of the coat of arms is divided into quarters on which appear symbols for agriculture (plow), mining (pick and shovel), manufacturing (arm and hammer), and navigation (anchor). At the center of the large shield, a small shield and the band that encircles it represent the United States coat of arms and symbolize Wisconsin's membership in and loyalty to the United States. Supporting the large shield from the sides are a sailor holding a coil of rope and a yeoman resting on a pick. These figures represent labor on water and land. At the base of the large shield, a horn of plenty represents prosperity and abundance, and a pyramid of 13 lead ingots represents mineral wealth and the 13 original states of the United States. Above the large shield appears a badger, the state animal, and above the badger appears the state motto, "Forward."

Great seal. The great seal consists of the state coat of arms; the words "Great Seal of the State of Wisconsin" in a curve above; and a line of 13 stars, representing the 13 original states of the United States, in a curve below, all enclosed within an ornamental border. The great seal is used to authenticate the official acts of the governor other than the governor's approval of laws.

Flag. The state flag consists of the state coat of arms; the word "Wisconsin" in white letters above; and the statehood date "1848" in white numbers below, all centered on a royal blue field.

The Capitol abounds in the imagery of the badger, an animal associated with Wisconsin since the early 1800s. It was officially designated the state animal in 1957.

State flower. Wood violet (*Viola papilionacea*)

State tree. Sugar maple (*Acer saccharum*)

State animal. Badger (*Taxidea taxus*)

State bird. Robin (*Turdus migratorius*)

State fish. Muskellunge (*Esox masquinongy masquinongy* Mitchell)

State dog. American water spaniel

State insect. Honey bee (*Apis mellifera*)

State domestic animal. Dairy cow (*Bos taurus*)

State wildlife animal. White-tailed deer (*Odocoileus virginianus*)

State symbol of peace. Mourning dove (*Zenaidura macroura carolinensis* Linnaeus)

State fossil. Trilobite (*Calymene celebra*)

State mineral. Galena (lead sulfide)

State rock. Red granite

State soil. Antigo silt loam (*Typic glossoboralf*)

State beverage. Milk

State fruit. Cranberry (*Vaccinium macrocarpon*)

State grain. Corn (*Zea mays*)

State pastry. Kringle

State dance. Polka

State song. "On, Wisconsin," music by W. T. Purdy

On, Wisconsin! On, Wisconsin! Grand old badger state! We, thy loyal sons and daughters, Hail thee, good and great. ▪ On, Wisconsin! On, Wisconsin! Champion of the right, "Forward", our motto—God will give thee might!

State ballad. "Oh Wisconsin, Land of My Dreams," words by Erma Barrett, music by Shari A. Sarazin

Oh Wisconsin, land of beauty, with your hillsides and your plains, with your jackpine and your birch tree, and your oak of mighty frame. ▪ Land of rivers, lakes and valleys, land of warmth and winter snows, land of birds and beasts and humanity, oh Wisconsin, I love you so. ▪ Oh Wisconsin, land of my dreams. Oh Wisconsin, you're all I'll ever need. A little heaven here on earth could you be? Oh Wisconsin, land of my dreams. ▪ In the summer, golden grain fields; in the winter, drift of white snow; in the springtime, robins singing; in the autumn, flaming colors show. ▪ Oh I wonder who could wander, or who could want to drift for long, away from all your beauty, all your sunshine, all your sweet song? ▪ Oh Wisconsin, land of my dreams. Oh Wisconsin, you're all I'll ever need. A little heaven here on earth could you be? Oh Wisconsin, land of my dreams. ▪ And when it's time, let my spirit run free in Wisconsin, land of my dreams.

State waltz. "The Wisconsin Waltz," words and music by Eddie Hansen

Music from heaven throughout the years; the beautiful Wisconsin Waltz. Favorite song of the pioneers; the beautiful Wisconsin Waltz. ▪ Song of my heart on that last final day, when it is time to lay me away. One thing I ask is to let them play the beautiful Wisconsin Waltz. ▪ My sweetheart, my complete heart, it's for you when we dance together; the beautiful Wisconsin Waltz. I remember that September, before love turned into an ember, we danced to the Wisconsin Waltz. ▪ Summer ended, we intended that our lives then would both be blended, but somehow our planning got lost. ▪ Memory now sings a dream song, a faded love theme song; the beautiful Wisconsin Waltz.

State tartan. The thread count of the state tartan is 44 threads muted blue; 6 threads scarlet; 4 threads muted blue; 6 threads gray; 28 threads black; 40 threads dark green; 4 threads dark yellow; 40 threads dark green; 28 threads black; 22 threads muted blue; and 12 threads dark brown (half sett with full count at the pivots).

County vote for superintendent of public instruction, February 21, 2017 spring primary

	Tony Evers*	Lowell E. Holtz	John Humphries	Total
Adams	585	264	95	948
Ashland	893	101	49	1,047
Barron	1,190	374	172	1,740
Bayfield	1,457	178	96	1,732
Brown	8,941	2,920	1,134	13,011
Buffalo	597	178	66	843
Burnett	393	165	66	625
Calumet	1,605	594	251	2,452
Chippewa	1,922	572	242	2,736
Clark	891	387	166	1,447
Columbia	2,688	680	299	3,670
Crawford	719	130	86	939
Dane	60,046	4,793	2,677	67,720
Dodge	2,407	1,606	306	4,325
Door	1,602	350	133	2,093
Douglas	2,089	766	809	3,701
Dunn	1,561	342	147	2,054
Eau Claire	5,437	912	412	6,783
Florence	97	52	18	167
Fond du Lac	3,151	1,726	495	5,388
Forest	241	92	41	375
Grant	2,056	329	240	2,634
Green	1,888	379	160	2,439
Green Lake	462	251	95	809
Iowa	1,989	311	189	2,498
Iron	344	106	43	494
Jackson	675	187	91	955
Jefferson	3,149	1,544	305	5,016
Juneau	794	287	110	1,195
Kenosha	4,443	1,757	526	6,780
Kewaunee	619	218	85	923
La Crosse	5,992	848	632	7,486
Lafayette	814	172	105	1,094
Langlade	515	201	103	820
Lincoln	843	280	117	1,245
Manitowoc	2,656	1,405	543	4,616
Marathon	4,573	1,657	701	6,955
Marinette	980	511	212	1,706
Marquette	465	286	97	852
Menominee	51	13	8	72
Milwaukee	42,132	12,621	3,452	58,408
Monroe	1,285	415	121	1,828
Oconto	1,111	468	170	1,749
Oneida	1,332	382	150	1,880
Outagamie	6,838	2,081	751	9,684
Ozaukee	3,338	3,185	416	6,957
Pepin	305	66	22	393
Pierce	1,015	303	133	1,455
Polk	1,798	691	512	3,002
Portage	3,560	622	329	4,527
Price	552	197	65	814
Racine	6,707	4,344	1,146	12,239
Richland	1,002	149	90	1,242
Rock	5,889	1,283	530	7,723

County vote for superintendent of public instruction, February 21, 2017 spring primary, continued

	Tony Evers*	Lowell E. Holtz	John Humphries	Total
Rusk.	516	225	67	809
St. Croix.	1,763	592	257	2,627
Sauk.	3,656	779	306	4,742
Sawyer	593	154	99	851
Shawano	1,000	503	167	1,676
Sheboygan.	4,793	2,856	832	8,510
Taylor	442	213	100	758
Trempealeau	1,910	607	402	2,926
Vernon	1,527	319	150	2,000
Vilas	830	345	165	1,343
Walworth.	2,846	1,735	441	5,051
Washburn	577	172	67	820
Washington	3,553	4,272	690	8,537
Waukesha	12,050	12,992	1,791	26,881
Waupaca	1,658	742	221	2,624
Waushara.	611	296	97	1,004
Winnebago	6,000	1,904	798	8,728
Wood	2,543	961	407	3,923
Total.	**255,552**	**84,398**	**27,066**	**368,096**

Note: County totals include scattered votes. Write-in candidate Rick Melcher received a total of 377 votes.

*Incumbent.

Source: Official records of the Wisconsin Elections Commission.

County vote for superintendent of public instruction, April 4, 2017 spring election

	Tony Evers*	Lowell E. Holtz	Total		Tony Evers*	Lowell E. Holtz	Total
Adams	1,845	791	2,638	Iron	912	354	1,267
Ashland.	2,162	547	2,715	Jackson.	1,926	721	2,647
Barron.	3,489	1,663	5,164	Jefferson	5,687	3,428	9,125
Bayfield.	2,722	705	3,432	Juneau	1,912	866	2,786
Brown.	22,154	9,720	31,939	Kenosha	9,915	4,405	14,347
Buffalo	1,353	546	1,904	Kewaunee	1,406	699	2,105
Burnett	1,552	1,121	2,673	La Crosse	11,684	3,193	14,877
Calumet	3,087	1,612	4,699	Lafayette	1,969	608	2,580
Chippewa	4,557	1,867	6,424	Langlade	2,039	922	2,961
Clark.	2,560	1,349	3,916	Lincoln	2,261	895	3,160
Columbia.	5,027	1,865	6,903	Manitowoc.	9,287	4,998	14,335
Crawford	1,424	394	1,820	Marathon.	10,905	5,076	16,000
Dane	84,155	12,789	97,060	Marinette.	2,985	1,522	4,507
Dodge	8,007	4,679	12,708	Marquette	1,633	1,013	2,656
Door.	5,174	1,696	6,883	Menominee	132	43	175
Douglas.	4,108	1,832	5,981	Milwaukee	67,940	26,743	94,877
Dunn	3,070	1,136	4,206	Monroe.	2,658	940	3,604
Eau Claire.	8,611	2,114	10,734	Oconto	3,525	1,939	5,464
Florence	490	244	735	Oneida	3,608	1,537	5,228
Fond du Lac	7,405	4,376	11,795	Outagamie	13,072	5,479	18,553
Forest	989	399	1,390	Ozaukee	6,908	6,033	12,975
Grant	5,488	1,658	7,150	Pepin	690	231	921
Green	3,868	1,225	5,096	Pierce	2,210	928	3,138
Green Lake.	1,150	760	1,912	Polk	5,098	2,494	7,595
Iowa.	3,319	752	4,079	Portage	6,638	1,729	8,374

County vote for superintendent of public instruction, April 4, 2017 spring election, continued

	Tony Evers*	Lowell E. Holtz	Total		Tony Evers*	Lowell E. Holtz	Total
Price.	1,643	777	2,420	Vernon	4,288	1,332	5,620
Racine.	12,793	8,165	20,963	Vilas	2,847	1,483	4,334
Richland	2,083	558	2,641	Walworth.	6,153	4,188	10,362
Rock.	12,718	3,983	16,730	Washburn	1,525	670	2,199
Rusk	1,354	650	2,005	Washington	6,685	7,710	14,404
St. Croix.	4,340	2,108	6,462	Waukesha	23,906	25,152	49,118
Sauk.	5,921	1,847	7,768	Waupaca	4,863	2,440	7,303
Sawyer	2,209	921	3,136	Waushara	1,578	824	2,402
Shawano	3,804	2,280	6,085	Winnebago	11,997	5,239	17,260
Sheboygan.	8,459	5,265	13,735	Wood	5,687	2,414	8,101
Taylor	1,424	748	2,173	**Total**.	**495,010**	**212,709**	**708,711**
Trempealeau	3,947	1,319	5,277				

Note: County totals include scattered votes. Write-in candidate Rick Melcher received a total of 62 votes.
*Incumbent.
Source: Official records of the Wisconsin Elections Commission.

County vote for supreme court justice, February 16, 2016 spring primary

	Rebecca G. Bradley*	JoAnne F. Kloppenburg	Joe Donald	Total
Adams	738	800	88	1,628
Ashland.	351	785	73	1,209
Barron.	1,280	1,080	233	2,600
Bayfield.	649	1,450	123	2,229
Brown.	9,923	8,037	2,881	20,865
Buffalo	521	595	70	1,187
Burnett	444	311	76	834
Calumet	2,016	1,286	438	3,740
Chippewa	1,903	2,203	326	4,432
Clark.	1,163	906	123	2,192
Columbia.	2,224	3,163	388	5,778
Crawford	452	886	109	1,447
Dane	14,019	53,109	5,521	72,751
Dodge	4,329	2,409	646	7,384
Door.	1,302	1,547	471	3,323
Douglas.	849	1,061	214	2,129
Dunn	1,174	1,344	189	2,707
Eau Claire.	2,809	5,186	607	8,619
Florence	163	91	32	286
Fond du Lac	4,682	2,585	815	8,082
Forest	409	266	42	717
Grant	1,173	1,610	248	3,035
Green	1,267	2,127	233	3,630
Green Lake.	960	451	152	1,563
Iowa.	1,310	2,148	328	3,796
Iron	394	378	75	847
Jackson	611	930	103	1,644
Jefferson	5,109	3,876	923	9,926
Juneau	863	812	73	1,750
Kenosha	4,765	4,509	1,101	10,389
Kewaunee	1,695	1,150	568	3,413
La Crosse	3,712	6,115	895	10,722
Lafayette	492	695	98	1,285

County vote for supreme court justice, February 16, 2016 spring primary, continued

	Rebecca G. Bradley*	JoAnne F. Kloppenburg	Joe Donald	Total
Langlade	798	648	109	1,555
Lincoln	1,355	1,427	160	2,944
Manitowoc.	3,781	2,570	848	7,202
Marathon.	5,864	5,372	768	12,029
Marinette.	1,508	1,150	407	3,065
Marquette	786	570	83	1,439
Menominee	40	60	15	115
Milwaukee.	42,144	40,305	27,432	110,118
Monroe.	1,500	1,541	254	3,297
Oconto	1,852	1,277	493	3,622
Oneida	3,276	3,507	560	7,361
Outagamie.	6,243	5,134	1,703	13,080
Ozaukee	7,608	2,570	1,181	11,359
Pepin	184	278	29	491
Pierce	1,407	1,191	381	2,987
Polk	826	696	161	1,683
Portage.	2,901	4,858	441	8,210
Price.	642	679	90	1,411
Racine.	8,922	5,743	1,890	16,555
Richland	628	770	109	1,507
Rock.	3,885	6,464	859	11,208
Rusk	665	660	105	1,430
St. Croix.	1,917	1,517	490	3,933
Sauk.	2,165	3,505	385	6,055
Sawyer	1,243	1,005	245	2,497
Shawano	1,914	1,247	531	3,692
Sheboygan.	7,038	3,507	1,002	11,557
Taylor	731	516	77	1,326
Trempealeau	897	1,270	172	2,339
Vernon	1,021	1,578	138	2,737
Vilas	1,920	1,560	252	3,747
Walworth.	5,315	2,887	1,057	9,278
Washburn	885	839	210	1,937
Washington	12,087	3,424	1,365	16,876
Waukesha	32,533	9,316	3,550	45,418
Waupaca	2,200	1,573	571	4,346
Waushara.	1,113	729	244	2,086
Winnebago	6,022	5,438	1,644	13,122
Wood	3,365	3,447	473	7,285
Total.	**252,932**	**244,729**	**68,746**	**567,038**

Note: County totals include scattered votes.

*Incumbent.

Source: Official records of the Wisconsin Elections Commission.

County vote for supreme court justice, April 5, 2016 spring election

	Rebecca G. Bradley*	JoAnne F. Kloppenburg	Total
Adams	3,524	2,948	6,481
Ashland.	1,965	3,305	5,273
Barron.	7,412	6,347	13,773
Bayfield.	2,447	4,044	6,498
Brown.	47,989	34,854	83,053

County vote for supreme court justice, April 5, 2016 spring election, continued

	Rebecca G. Bradley*	JoAnne F. Kloppenburg	Total
Buffalo	2,557	2,045	4,611
Burnett	2,504	2,087	4,595
Calumet	11,083	6,363	17,446
Chippewa	11,106	9,398	20,504
Clark	5,635	3,639	9,274
Columbia	9,784	10,633	20,459
Crawford	2,455	2,782	5,238
Dane	60,264	156,986	217,809
Dodge	17,932	10,894	28,826
Door	6,824	6,181	13,028
Douglas	5,732	6,940	12,727
Dunn	6,546	6,468	13,014
Eau Claire	16,082	19,957	36,143
Florence	903	604	1,507
Fond du Lac	21,077	12,544	33,621
Forest	1,885	1,227	3,114
Grant	7,557	7,422	15,012
Green	5,730	7,505	13,256
Green Lake	4,272	2,202	6,481
Iowa	3,846	5,204	9,057
Iron	1,241	1,087	2,330
Jackson	3,130	3,271	6,401
Jefferson	16,213	12,121	28,407
Juneau	4,191	3,387	7,597
Kenosha	24,019	21,652	45,886
Kewaunee	5,051	3,016	8,067
La Crosse	17,957	22,062	40,019
Lafayette	2,581	2,731	5,315
Langlade	4,700	2,663	7,367
Lincoln	5,560	4,282	9,865
Manitowoc	17,268	10,236	27,546
Marathon	27,863	19,343	47,279
Marinette	8,531	5,463	13,994
Marquette	3,265	2,496	5,773
Menominee	318	402	720
Milwaukee	124,175	153,963	279,083
Monroe	7,152	5,849	13,021
Oconto	8,798	5,285	14,083
Oneida	7,775	6,616	14,416
Outagamie	35,613	25,469	61,082
Ozaukee	25,257	13,662	38,919
Pepin	1,154	1,085	2,239
Pierce	5,603	5,458	11,061
Polk	6,168	5,048	11,216
Portage	11,819	13,190	25,074
Price	2,950	2,346	5,296
Racine	33,887	25,400	59,287
Richland	2,854	3,137	5,999
Rock	21,780	26,578	48,509
Rusk	2,819	2,143	4,962
St. Croix	12,475	10,319	22,890
Sauk	10,011	11,458	21,469
Sawyer	3,114	2,786	5,908
Shawano	8,978	4,871	13,863
Sheboygan	25,640	15,083	40,801
Taylor	4,146	2,319	6,472
Trempealeau	4,552	4,403	8,963

County vote for supreme court justice, April 5, 2016 spring election, continued

	Rebecca G. Bradley*	JoAnne F. Kloppenburg	Total
Vernon	4,798	5,407	10,210
Vilas	5,489	3,670	9,177
Walworth	19,867	12,539	32,520
Washburn	3,043	2,773	5,827
Washington	37,351	14,488	51,839
Waukesha	111,235	51,185	162,757
Waupaca	10,386	6,517	16,920
Waushara	5,071	3,064	8,135
Winnebago	32,619	25,416	58,209
Wood	14,514	11,059	25,574
Total	1,020,092	928,377	1,953,147

Note: County totals include scattered votes. On May 5, 2016, the official canvas was recertified to correct an error Brown County found in the supreme court race. Data reflects correction.

*Incumbent.

Source: Official records of the Wisconsin Elections Commission.

County vote for supreme court justice, April 4, 2017 spring election

	Annette Ziegler*	Total		Annette Ziegler*	Total
Adams	1,980	1,980	La Crosse	10,527	10,527
Ashland	1,867	1,926	Lafayette	2,017	2,035
Barron	4,405	4,439	Langlade	2,362	2,363
Bayfield	2,414	2,566	Lincoln	2,324	2,356
Brown	23,574	24,027	Manitowoc	11,378	11,448
Buffalo	1,607	1,618	Marathon	12,270	12,492
Burnett	2,205	2,205	Marinette	3,721	3,721
Calumet	3,517	3,517	Marquette	2,194	2,220
Chippewa	4,904	4,904	Menominee	117	117
Clark	3,169	3,182	Milwaukee	54,826	57,631
Columbia	4,852	5,024	Monroe	3,038	3,070
Crawford	1,355	1,391	Oconto	4,598	4,598
Dane	53,726	60,214	Oneida	3,861	3,902
Dodge	9,729	9,729	Outagamie	13,446	13,446
Door	5,078	5,131	Ozaukee	9,391	9,629
Douglas	4,710	4,784	Pepin	711	711
Dunn	3,285	3,285	Pierce	2,582	2,582
Eau Claire	7,479	7,828	Polk	6,571	6,571
Florence	654	654	Portage	5,645	5,777
Fond du Lac	8,873	8,961	Price	1,749	1,749
Forest	1,140	1,143	Racine	14,989	14,989
Grant	5,707	5,781	Richland	1,991	2,020
Green	3,616	3,753	Rock	11,581	11,863
Green Lake	1,529	1,557	Rusk	1,642	1,647
Iowa	2,979	3,169	St. Croix	5,117	5,247
Iron	987	991	Sauk	5,213	5,213
Jackson	2,119	2,119	Sawyer	2,661	2,678
Jefferson	6,088	6,258	Shawano	5,155	5,155
Juneau	2,275	2,303	Sheboygan	10,452	10,572
Kenosha	10,026	10,189	Taylor	1,713	1,720
Kewaunee	1,730	1,730	Trempealeau	4,375	4,416

County vote for supreme court justice, April 4, 2017 spring election, continued

	Annette Ziegler*	Total		Annette Ziegler*	Total
Vernon	4,257	4,264	Waupaca	5,918	5,918
Vilas	3,290	3,330	Waushara	1,925	1,925
Walworth	7,653	7,769	Winnebago	11,469	11,722
Washburn	1,739	1,763	Wood	5,898	5,899
Washington	11,000	11,120	**Total**	**492,352**	**506,517**
Waukesha	33,407	33,984			

Note: County totals include scattered votes.

*Incumbent.

Source: Official records of the Wisconsin Elections Commission.

District vote for court of appeals judges, April 5, 2016 spring election

District I

County	Joan F. Kessler*	Total
Milwaukee	175,733	177,922
Total	**175,733**	**177,922**

District II

County	Paul F. Reilly*	Total
Calumet	12,592	12,592
Fond du Lac	23,756	23,756
Green Lake	5,027	5,039
Kenosha	30,631	31,004
Manitowoc	19,323	19,411
Ozaukee	25,557	25,557
Racine	38,813	38,813
Sheboygan	30,138	30,319
Walworth	23,279	23,487
Washington	35,430	35,430
Waukesha	103,115	103,929
Winnebago	40,553	40,885
Total	**388,214**	**390,222**

District III

County	Thomas M. Hruz*	Total
Ashland	3,192	3,203
Barron	11,330	11,359
Bayfield	4,177	4,184
Brown	56,023	56,470
Buffalo	3,482	3,495
Burnett	3,756	3,762
Chippewa	14,369	14,369
Door	8,754	8,812
Douglas	9,148	9,245
Dunn	10,142	10,142
Eau Claire	24,784	24,989
Florence	1,127	1,127
Forest	2,121	2,124

District vote for court of appeals judges, April 5, 2016 spring election, continued

District III, continued

County	Thomas M. Hruz*	Total
Iron	1,605	1,608
Kewaunee	6,221	6,221
Langlade	5,109	5,114
Lincoln	6,807	6,838
Marathon	34,900	35,077
Marinette	10,448	10,448
Menominee	312	320
Oconto	11,267	11,267
Oneida	9,952	10,003
Outagamie	42,409	42,409
Pepin	1,729	1,729
Pierce	9,291	9,291
Polk	9,354	9,354
Price	3,388	3,388
Rusk	3,529	3,529
St. Croix	18,172	18,288
Sawyer	4,484	4,505
Shawano	10,498	10,528
Taylor	4,441	4,449
Trempealeau	7,033	7,056
Vilas	6,284	6,321
Washburn	4,394	4,401
Total	**364,032**	**365,425**

District IV

County	Brian W. Blanchard*	Total
Adams	4,240	4,253
Clark	6,657	6,657
Columbia	14,082	14,169
Crawford	4,009	4,012
Dane	139,261	140,644
Dodge	20,464	20,464
Grant	11,775	11,856
Green	9,351	9,408
Iowa	6,823	6,836
Jackson	4,916	4,916
Jefferson	18,843	19,013
Juneau	6,014	6,027
La Crosse	27,029	27,029
Lafayette	3,943	3,954
Marquette	4,410	4,429
Monroe	10,580	10,612
Portage	15,553	15,658
Richland	4,330	4,341
Rock	34,590	34,882
Sauk	15,506	15,506
Vernon	7,612	7,621
Waupaca	13,197	13,248
Waushara	6,208	6,208
Wood	17,887	17,888
Total	**407,280**	**409,631**

Note: County totals include scattered votes.

*Incumbent.

Source: Official records of the Wisconsin Elections Commission.

District vote for court of appeals judges, April 4, 2017 spring election

District I

County	Bill Brash*	Total
Milwaukee	51,818	52,589
Total.	51,818	52,589

District II

County	Brian K. Hagedorn*	Total
Calumet	3,424	3,424
Fond du Lac	8,586	8,611
Green Lake.	1,481	1,483
Kenosha	9,590	9,677
Manitowoc.	10,963	11,010
Ozaukee	8,794	8,899
Racine.	14,295	14,295
Sheboygan.	10,059	10,099
Walworth.	7,384	7,443
Washington	9,732	9,784
Waukesha	30,811	31,063
Winnebago	11,031	11,135
Total.	126,150	126,923

District IV

County	Michael R. Fitzpatrick	Total
Adams	1,899	1,899
Clark	3,062	3,066
Columbia.	4,805	4,841
Crawford.	1,395	1,399
Dane	58,502	59,142
Dodge	9,463	9,463
Grant	5,697	5,730
Green.	3,598	3,621
Iowa	3,038	3,060
Jackson.	2,125	2,125
Jefferson	5,966	6,007
Juneau	2,270	2,282
La Crosse.	10,501	10,501
Lafayette.	2,020	2,023
Marquette.	2,137	2,145
Monroe	2,974	2,994
Portage.	5,604	5,632
Richland	1,962	1,968
Rock	11,927	12,035
Sauk.	5,177	5,177
Vernon	4,247	4,249
Waupaca	5,894	5,894
Waushara.	1,907	1,907
Wood.	5,706	5,706
Total.	161,876	162,866

Note: County totals include scattered votes.

*Incumbent.

Source: Official records of the Wisconsin Elections Commission.

Vote for circuit judges, February 16, 2016 spring primary

Counties in circuit	Branch	Candidates	Vote
Iowa	—	Tim Angel	586
		Margaret M. Koehler	1,197
		Timothy B. McKinley	1,086
		Larry Nelson	955
Kewaunee	—	Keith A. Mehn	1,564
		Andrew Naze	819
		Jeffrey Ronald Wisnicky	1,090
Portage	2	Trish Baker	2,702
		David R. Knaapen	2,222
		Jared Redfield	690
		Robert J. Shannon*	2,580
Walworth	2	Daniel S. Johnson	3,367
		Dan Necci	2,932
		Shannon Wynn	2,810

— Means the circuit has only one branch.   *Incumbent.

Source: Official records of the Wisconsin Elections Commission.

Vote for circuit judges, April 5, 2016 spring election

Counties in circuit	Branch	Candidates	Vote
Barron	1	James C. Babler*	12,364
Crawford	—	Lynn Marie Rider	4,327
Dane	3	Valerie L. Bailey-Rihn	132,270
	4	Everett Mitchell	132,939
	5	Nicholas J. McNamara*	131,068
	14	John D. Hyland	130,198
	15	Stephen Ehlke*	130,754
	17	Peter C. Anderson*	129,643
Eau Claire	1	John F. Manydeeds	18,850
		Brian H. Wright*	15,132
Fond du Lac	2	Peter L. Grimm*	25,290
	4	Gary R. Sharpe*	25,020
Iowa	—	Margaret M. Koehler	4,546
		Timothy B. McKinley	4,315
Juneau	1	John Pier Roemer*	6,384
Kewaunee	—	Keith A. Mehn	4,096
		Jeffrey Ronald Wisnicky	3,832
Lincoln	1	Jay R. Tlusty*	7,844
Marathon	2	Greg Huber*	37,240
Milwaukee	5	Mary M. Kuhnmuench*	171,093
	14	Christopher R. Foley*	175,825
	25	Stephanie Rothstein*	168,070
	31	Hannah C. Dugan	132,461
		Paul Rifelj*	70,098
	34	Glenn H. Yamahiro*	167,132
	44	Gwen Connolly	167,479
	45	Michelle Ackerman Havas*	99,225
		Jean Marie Kies	100,409
Monroe	2	Mark L. Goodman*	11,260
	3	J. David Rice*	11,100
Oconto	2	Jay Conley*	11,890
Pierce	—	Joseph D. Boles*	10,309
Portage	2	Trish Baker	10,515

Vote for circuit judges, April 5, 2016 spring election, continued

Counties in circuit	Branch	Candidates	Vote
		Robert J. Shannon*	12,551
Racine.	2	Eugene A. Gasiorkiewicz*.	40,407
	4	Mark Nielsen.	34,573
		Joseph W. Seifert	13,554
Rock.	2	Alan Bates*.	35,354
Rusk.	—	Steven P. Anderson*	2,542
		Richard J. Summerfield	2,319
St. Croix.	4	R. Michael Waterman*.	18,333
Sauk.	1	Michael Screnock*	15,773
	2	Kevin R. Calkins	9,403
		Wendy J. N. Klicko	10,757
Vilas	—	Neal A. Nielsen III*	7,354
Walworth.	2	Daniel S. Johnson.	16,420
		Dan Necci	13,385
	4	David M. Reddy*	24,024
Winnebago	3	Barbara Hart Key*	41,909
	5	John A. Jorgensen*	40,795

— Means the circuit has only one branch. *Incumbent.
Source: Official records of the Wisconsin Elections Commission.

Vote for circuit judges, February 21, 2017 spring primary

Counties in circuit	Branch	Candidates	Vote
Manitowoc.	3	Donald J. Chewning	482
		Bob Dewane.	2,148
		Patricia Koppa.	1,760
Polk	1	David D. Danielson.	764
		Malia Malone	930
		Daniel J. Tolan.	1,604
Trempealeau	—	Charles V. Feltes*	910
		Rian W. Radtke	1,142
		Rick Schaumberg.	1,087

— Means the circuit has only one branch. *Incumbent.
Source: Official records of the Wisconsin Elections Commission.

Vote for circuit judges, April 4, 2017 spring election

Counties in circuit	Branch	Candidates	Vote
Burnett	—	Melissia R. Christianson Mogen	1,850
		David Grindell.	1,085
Columbia.	2	W. Andrew Voigt*.	5,024
Dane	9	Richard G. Niess*	58,785
	12	Jill J. Karofsky	50,585
		Marilyn Townsend	37,110
Dodge	2	Martin De Vries*	7,988
		Randall E. Doyle.	4,476
Door.	2	David L. Weber*.	5,426
Fond du Lac	5	Robert Wirtz*	9,140

Vote for circuit judges, April 4, 2017 spring election, continued

Counties in circuit	Branch	Candidates	Vote
Grant	1	Robert P. VanDeHey*	6,086
Green Lake.	—	Mark Slate*	1,643
Iron	—	Patrick J. Madden*	1,081
Jefferson	4	Bennett J. Brantmeier	6,087
Kenosha	4	Anthony Milisauskas*	10,390
	7	Jodi L. Meier*	12,386
		John Anthony Ward	2,145
Manitowoc.	3	Bob Dewane	7,646
		Patricia Koppa	6,217
Marathon.	4	Gregory J. Strasser*	12,528
	5	Michael K. Moran*	12,780
Milwaukee	1	Maxine A. White*	55,038
	4	Michael J. Hanrahan*	52,096
	9	Paul Van Grunsven*	51,192
	10	Michelle Ackerman Havas	52,032
	13	Mary E. Triggiano*	52,348
	18	Pedro Colon*	54,247
	19	Dennis R. Cimpl*	51,670
	21	Cynthia Davis*	52,464
	33	Carl Ashley*	52,473
	35	Frederick C. Rosa*	52,864
	36	Jeffrey Kremers*	52,611
	47	Scott A. Wales	36,705
		Kristy Yang	49,342
Oconto	1	Michael T. Judge*	4,846
Outagamie.	1	Mark J. McGinnis*	14,032
Polk	1	Malia Malone	3,218
		Daniel J. Tolan.	4,839
	2	Jeff Anderson*	6,959
Racine.	3	Emily S. Mueller*	15,242
Rock.	6	John M. Wood*	11,822
Sheboygan.	2	Kent Hoffmann*	10,159
	3	Angela W. Sutkiewicz*	10,722
	5	Daniel Borowski*	10,143
Trempealeau	—	Rian W. Radtke	2,856
		Rick Schaumberg.	2,594
Vernon	—	Timothy J. Gaskell	2,512
		Darcy Rood	3,253
Washington	1	James G. Pouros*	10,004
	3	Todd K. Martens*	8,903
		Robert T. Olson	3,210
Waukesha	3	Ralph M. Ramirez*	31,937
	4	Lloyd V. Carter*	30,757
	11	William Domina*	31,326
Waupaca	1	Eric D. Hendrickson	2,568
		Dennis Krueger (write-in).	5
		Troy L. Nielsen.	4,522
Waushara.	—	Guy Dutcher*	2,078
Winnebago	2	Scott C. Woldt*	11,811
	6	Daniel J. Bissett*	11,715

— Means the circuit has only one branch. *Incumbent.

Source: Official records of the Wisconsin Elections Commission.

District vote for state senators, partisan and special primaries

Senate district	Assembly districts	Party	Candidates	Vote
June 23, 2015 special primary				
33	. . . . .97, 98, 99	Democrat	Sherryll Shaddock	676
		Republican	Brian Dorow	4,929
		Republican	Chris Kapenga.	5,559
		Republican	M.D. Langner	168
August 9, 2016 partisan primary				
2	. . . . . .4, 5, 6	Democrat	John N. Powers	4,323
		Republican	Robert Cowles*	11,168
4	. . . . . .10, 11, 12	Democrat	Mandela Barnes.	7,433
		Democrat	Lena C. Taylor*	11,454
6	. . . . . .16, 17, 18	Democrat	Michael Bonds	3,022
		Democrat	Thomas Harris.	3,166
		Democrat	LaTonya Johnson	9,583
8	. . . . . .22, 23, 24	Republican	Alberta Darling*	8,565
10	. . . . .28, 29, 30	Democrat	Diane Odeen	5,332
		Republican	Sheila E. Harsdorf*	6,488
12	. . . . .34, 35, 36	Democrat	Bryan Van Stippen	5,842
		Republican	Tom Tiffany*	10,257
14	. . . . .40, 41, 42	Democrat	Brian Smith	5,669
		Republican	Luther S. Olsen*	8,891
16	. . . . .46, 47, 48	Democrat	Mark Miller*	18,592
18	. . . . .52, 53, 54	Democrat	Mark L. Harris	5,165
		Democrat	John Lemberger	1,758
		Republican	Mark Elliott.	4,108
		Republican	Dan Feyen	5,225
20	. . . . .58, 59, 60	Republican	Duey Stroebel*	10,220
22	. . . . .64, 65, 66	Democrat	Robert W. Wirch*	6,006
24	. . . . .70, 71, 72	Democrat	Julie M. Lassa*.	9,147
		Republican	Patrick Testin	4,622
26	. . . . .76, 77, 78	Democrat	Fred A. Risser*	24,762
28	. . . . .82, 83, 84	Republican	Dmitry Becker (write-in)	3
		Republican	Dave Craig	13,637
30	. . . . .88, 89,90	Democrat	Dave Hansen*	4,956
		Republican	Eric Wimberger	7,203
32	. . . . .94, 95, 96	Democrat	Jared William Landry.	1,024
		Democrat	Jennifer Shilling*	10,957
		Republican	Dan Kapanke	5,754
		Republican	John Sarnowski	601

*Incumbent.

Source: Official records of the Wisconsin Elections Commission.

District vote for state senators, general and special elections

Senate district	Assembly districts	Party	Candidates	Vote	% of total[1]
November 4, 2014 general election					
1	1, 2, 3	Democrat	Dean P. Debroux	29,555	38.37
		Republican	Frank Lasee*	47,438	61.59
3	7, 8, 9	Democrat	Tim Carpenter*	29,291	97.10
5	13, 14, 15	Independant	Wendy Friedrich	20,020	26.17
		Republican	Leah Vukmir*	55,869	73.03
7	19, 20, 21	Democrat	Chris J. Larson*	41,950	59.50
		Republican	Jason Red Arnold	28,387	40.26
9	25, 26, 27	Democrat	Martha Laning	28,770	39.94
		Republican	Devin LeMahieu	43,186	59.95
11	31, 32, 33	Democrat	Dan Kilkenny	25,377	36.63
		Republican	Steve Nass	43,842	63.29
13	37, 38, 39	Democrat	Michelle Zahn	28,700	37.28
		Republican	Scott L. Fitzgerald*	48,255	62.69
15	43, 44, 45	Democrat	Janis Ringhand	36,389	59.47
		Republican	Brian Fitzgerald	24,760	40.47
17	49, 50, 51	Democrat	Pat Bomhack	28,179	44.85
		Republican	Howard Marklein	34,601	55.07
19	55, 56, 57	Democrat	Penny Bernard Schaber	31,135	42.76
		Republican	Roger Roth	41,628	57.17
21	61, 62, 63	Democrat	Randy Bryce	28,106	38.39
		Independant	Bill Thompkins (write-in)	34	0.05
		Republican	Van Wanggaard	44,967	61.42
23	67, 68, 69	Democrat	Phil Swanhorst	25,135	38.84
		Republican	Terry Moulton*	39,577	61.15
25	73, 74, 75	Democrat	Janet Bewley	35,055	51.16
		Republican	Dane Deutsch	33,445	48.81
27	79, 80, 81	Democrat	Jon B. Erpenbach*	61,920	97.51
29	85, 86, 87	Democrat	Paul Demain	23,917	34.26
		Republican	Jerry Petrowski*	45,887	65.73
31	91, 92, 93	Democrat	Kathleen Vinehout*	35,508	52.32
		Republican	Mel Pittman	32,317	47.62
33	97, 98, 99	Democrat	Sherryll Shaddock	20,899	26.07
		Republican	Paul Farrow*	59,199	73.86
April 7, 2015 special election					
20	58, 59, 60	Democrat	Nicholas J. Stamates (write-in)	23	0.1
		Republican	Duey Stroebel	23,347	98.77
July 21, 2015 special election					
33	97, 98, 99	Democrat	Sherryll Shaddock	2,798	27.96
		Republican	Chris Kapenga	7,191	71.86
November 8, 2016 general election					
2	4, 5, 6	Democrat	John N. Powers	30,796	34.95
		Republican	Robert Cowles*	57,269	65.00
4	10, 11, 12	Democrat	Lena C. Taylor*	62,099	98.33
6	16, 17, 18	Democrat	LaTonya Johnson	60,129	98.89
8	22, 23, 24	Republican	Alberta Darling*	77,331	95.51
10	28, 29, 30	Democrat	Diane Odeen	32,863	36.76
		Republican	Sheila E. Harsdorf*	56,496	63.20
12	34, 35, 36	Democrat	Bryan Van Stippen	33,713	37.04
		Republican	Tom Tiffany*	57,273	62.92

District vote for state senators, general and special elections, continued

Senate district	Assembly districts	Party	Candidates	Vote	% of total[1]
14	40, 41, 42	Democrat	Brian Smith	35,555	42.89
		Republican	Luther S. Olsen*	47,294	57.05
16	46, 47, 48	Democrat	Mark Miller*	77,047	98.39
18	52, 53, 54	Democrat	Mark L. Harris	36,366	44.06
		Republican	Dan Feyen	46,076	55.83
20	58, 59, 60	Republican	Duey Stroebel*	79,743	98.21
22	64, 65, 66	Democrat	Robert W. Wirch*	50,841	98.16
24	70, 71, 72	Democrat	Julie M. Lassa*	41,091	47.63
		Republican	Patrick Testin	45,139	52.32
26	76, 77, 78	Democrat	Fred A. Risser*	95,246	98.57
28	82, 83, 84	Republican	Dave Craig	70,269	98.10
30	88, 89, 90	Democrat	Dave Hansen*	40,214	51.27
		Republican	Eric Wimberger	38,175	48.67
32[2]	94, 95, 96	Democrat	Jennifer Shilling*	43,585	48.86
		Independent	Chip DeNure	2,093	2.35
		Republican	Dan Kapanke	43,524	48.79

*Incumbent.

1. Percentages do not add up to 100, as scattered votes have been omitted.   2. Results reflect recount findings.

Source: Official records of the Wisconsin Elections Commission.

District vote for representatives to the assembly, partisan and special primaries

Assembly district	Party	Candidates	Vote
September 1, 2015 special primary			
99	Rep.	Cindi Duchow	1,341
	Rep.	Scott Owens	737
	Rep.	Dave Westlake	1,101
	Rep.	Spencer Zimmerman . . .	146
August 9, 2016 partisan primary			
1	Dem.	Lynn Utesch	2,033
	Rep.	Joel Kitchens*	5,168
2	Rep.	Andre Jacque*	2,987
3	Dem.	Sharon M. Wasileski	1,514
	Rep.	Christopher Schaefer . . .	739
	Rep.	Bradley B. Schinke	1,218
	Rep.	Ron Tusler	2,589
	Rep.	Josh Young	197
4	Dem.	Tony Lee	1,769
	Rep.	David Steffen*	3,961
5	Dem.	Sam Kelly	1,357
	Rep.	Jim Steineke*	3,272
6	Dem.	William James Switalla . .	1,139
	Rep.	Gary Tauchen*	3,757
7	Dem.	Daniel G. Riemer*	2,767

Assembly district	Party	Candidates	Vote
	Lib.	Matthew Bughman	19
	Rep.	Zachary Marshall	880
8	Dem.	Laura Manriquez	381
	Dem.	JoCasta Zamarripa*	683
9	Dem.	Marisabel Cabrera	1,073
	Dem.	Josh Zepnick*	1,222
10	Dem.	David Bowen*	5,545
11	Dem.	Jason M. Fields	2,933
	Dem.	Darrol D. Gibson	2,063
12	Dem.	Frederick P. Kessler*	3,793
13	Rep.	Rob Hutton*	2,437
14	Dem.	Chris Rockwood	2,887
	Rep.	Dale Kooyenga*	2,489
15	Rep.	Joe Sanfelippo*	2,190
16	Dem.	Brandy Bond	418
	Dem.	Stephen Jansen	214
	Dem.	Edgar Lin	1,641
	Dem.	Leon D. Young*	2,211
17	Dem.	Kim Burns	1,635
	Dem.	David Crowley	3,303
	Dem.	Marcus Hart	887

District vote for representatives to the assembly, partisan and special primaries, continued

Assembly district	Party	Candidates	Vote
18	Dem.	Evan Goyke*	3,712
19	Dem.	Jonathan Brostoff*	5,278
20	Dem.	Julie Meyer.	2,374
	Dem.	Christine Sinicki*	3,530
21	Dem.	Frank Disco Gratke	781
	Dem.	John F. Redmond	1,771
	Rep.	Jessie Rodriguez*	2,713
22	Rep.	Janel Brandtjen*	2,992
23	Rep.	Jim Ott*	2,588
24	Rep.	Dan Knodl*	2,575
25	Dem.	Ronald J. Kossik	1,485
	Rep.	Paul Tittl*	2,182
26	Dem.	Evan Braun.	650
	Dem.	Rebecca Clarke	2,372
	Rep.	Terry Katsma*	2,109
27	Dem.	Nanette Bulebosh	2,029
	Rep.	Tyler Vorpagel*	2,051
28	Dem.	Jeff Peterson.	1,655
	Rep.	Adam Jarchow*	1,977
29	Dem.	Scottie E. Ard	1,103
	Dem.	Randy Knaack	1,047
	Rep.	Rob Stafsholt	1,352
	Rep.	Vince Trudell.	485
30	Dem.	Scott J. Nelson	1,786
	Rep.	Paul W. Berning	1,138
	Rep.	Shannon Zimmerman . . .	1,565
31	Dem.	Clinton Anderson.	1,652
	Dem.	Don Prestia	1,009
	Rep.	Amy Loudenbeck*	5,123
32	Dem.	Christine Welcher.	1,269
	Rep.	Tyler August*	4,892
33	Dem.	Brandon White	1,574
	Rep.	Cody Horlacher*	3,784
34	Dem.	Lawrence Dale.	630
	Dem.	Matthew N. Michalsen. .	2,109
	Rep.	Rob Swearingen*	4,291
35	Dem.	Renea Frederick.	999
	Dem.	Erik Pfantz	481
	Dem.	Derek Woellner	622
	Rep.	Mary Czaja*	2,140
36	Rep.	Jeffrey L. Mursau*	4,042
37	Dem.	Jordan Turner	1,773
	Rep.	John Jagler*	1,813
38	Dem.	Chris R. Gutschenritter . .	696
	Dem.	Scott Martin Michalak . . .	1,672
	Rep.	Joel Kleefisch*	2,764
39	Dem.	Jim Zahn	1,262
	Rep.	Mark L. Born*	1,916
40	Dem.	Dmitri Martin	1,793

Assembly district	Party	Candidates	Vote
	Rep.	Kevin Petersen*	4,357
41	Rep.	Joan Ballweg*	2,670
42	Dem.	George E. Ferriter.	2,357
	Rep.	Keith Ripp*	2,182
43	Dem.	Don Vruwink.	3,038
	Dem.	Anissa M. Welch.	2,207
	Rep.	Allison Hetz	2,091
44	Dem.	Debra Kolste*	4,555
45	Dem.	Mark Spreitzer*	2,619
46	Dem.	Gary Hebl*	4,195
47	Dem.	Jimmy Anderson	3,517
	Dem.	Julia Arata-Fratta	3,021
	Dem.	H. Tony Hartmann	1,336
48	Dem.	Melissa Agard Sargent* . .	7,400
49	Dem.	Jesse Bennett	1,855
	Rep.	Travis Tranel*	1,281
50	Dem.	Tom Crofton	925
	Dem.	Art Shrader.	2,192
	Rep.	Ed Brooks*	2,983
51	Dem.	Jeff Wright	3,011
	Rep.	Todd Novak*	1,934
52	Dem.	Paul G. Czisny	1,747
	Rep.	Jeremy Thiesfeldt*	3,653
53	Rep.	Michael Schraa*	2,820
54	Dem.	Gordon Hintz*	2,765
	Lib.	Jordan Hansen	21
55	Dem.	Bob Baker	1,485
	Rep.	Mike Rohrkaste*	2,506
56	Dem.	Mariana Stout	1,531
	Rep.	Dave Murphy*	3,952
57	Dem.	Amanda Stuck*	2,109
58	Rep.	Bob Gannon*	3,144
59	Rep.	Jesse Kremer*	3,128
60	Rep.	Robert Brooks*	3,623
61	Dem.	Amee Janus	1,374
	Rep.	Samantha Kerkman*	4,398
62	Rep.	Thomas Weatherston* . . .	5,209
63	Dem.	Andy Mitchell	1,624
	Rep.	Robin Vos*	5,369
64	Dem.	Peter W. Barca*	2,153
65	Dem.	Tod Ohnstad*	2,065
66	Dem.	Cory Mason*	1,693
	Lib.	George Meyers	20
67	Dem.	Denny D. Doughty	780
	Dem.	Dennis Hunt	1,813
	Rep.	Travis C. Hakes	647

District vote for representatives to the assembly, partisan and special primaries, continued

Assembly district	Party	Candidates	Vote
	Rep.	Michael Hanke	849
	Rep.	Rob Summerfield	1,231
	Rep.	Tony Zammit	328
68	Dem.	Howard White	2,135
	Rep.	Kathy Bernier*	1,267
69	Rep.	Bob Kulp*	2,342
70	Dem.	Mark Holbrook	2,326
	Rep.	Nancy Lynn VanderMeer*	2,225
71	Dem.	Katrina Shankland*	3,494
72	Dem.	Russ Brown	1,380
	Dem.	David Gorski	1,781
	Rep.	Scott S. Krug*	1,977
73	Dem.	Nick Milroy*	5,442
74	Dem.	Beth Meyers*	4,652
75	Dem.	Joe Huftel	3,687
	Rep.	Romaine Robert Quinn*	2,244
76	Dem.	Chris Taylor*	7,738
	Rep.	Jon Rygiewicz	238
77	Dem.	Terese Berceau*	8,809
78	Dem.	Lisa Subeck*	6,882
	Dem.	Jacob Wischmeier	1,170
79	Dem.	Dianne H. Hesselbein*	5,875
	Rep.	Jordan Zadra	1,123
80	Dem.	Luke Joseph	978
	Dem.	Sondy Pope*	5,210
81	Dem.	Dave Considine*	3,319
	Rep.	David J. Moore	1,324
82	Rep.	Ken Skowronski*	3,917
83	Rep.	Jordan Karweik	576
	Rep.	Karen L. Schuh	915

Assembly district	Party	Candidates	Vote
	Rep.	Steven A. Whittow	2,817
	Rep.	Chuck Wichgers	4,077
84	Rep.	Mike Kuglitsch*	2,854
85	Dem.	Mandy Wright	2,778
	Rep.	Patrick Snyder	1,968
86	Dem.	John H. Small	408
	Dem.	Nancy Stencil	1,942
	Rep.	John Spiros*	2,202
87	Dem.	Elizabeth Riley	1,704
	Rep.	James W. Edming*	2,949
88	Dem.	Noah Reif	1,531
	Rep.	John Macco*	3,218
89	Dem.	Heidi Fencl	1,280
	Rep.	John Nygren*	2,991
90	Dem.	Eric Genrich*	1,529
91	Dem.	Dana Wachs*	3,533
	Rep.	Bill Ingram	749
92	Dem.	Chris Danou*	2,811
	Rep.	Debbie Bork	808
	Rep.	Treig E. Pronschinske	960
93	Rep.	Warren Petryk*	1,590
94	Dem.	Steve Doyle*	3,346
	Rep.	Julian Bradley	1,970
95	Dem.	Jill Billings*	4,165
96	Dem.	Alicia Leinberger	2,956
	Rep.	Lee Nerison*	2,166
97	Rep.	Scott Allen*	2,977
98	Rep.	Adam Neylon*	2,748
99	Rep.	Cindi Duchow*	4,290

*Incumbent. Dem.–Democrat; Lib.–Libertarian; Rep.–Republican.
Source: Official records of the Wisconsin Elections Commission.

District vote for representatives to the assembly, general and special elections

Assembly district	Party	Candidates	Vote	% of total[1]
September 29, 2015 special election				
99	Democrat	Thomas D. Hibbard [2]	62	3.91
	Republican	Cindi Duchow	1,441	90.86
	Independent	Jan Brakken [2]	15	0.95
November 8, 2016 general election				
1	Democrat	Lynn Utesch	13,289	39.85
	Republican	Joel Kitchens*	20,044	60.11

District vote for representatives to the assembly, general and special elections, continued

Assembly district	Party	Candidates	Vote	% of total[1]
2	Republican	Andre Jacque*	20,039	69.29
	Independent	Mark Grams	8,837	30.56
3	Democrat	Sharon M. Wasileski	11,969	39.46
	Republican	Ron Tusler	18,361	60.54
4	Democrat	Tony Lee	12,016	40.23
	Republican	David Steffen*	17,817	59.65
5	Democrat	Sam Kelly	10,933	35.40
	Republican	Jim Steineke*	19,941	64.58
6	Democrat	William James Switalla	7,944	29.82
	Republican	Gary Tauchen*	18,690	70.15
7	Democrat	Daniel G. Riemer*	13,514	56.14
	Libertarian	Matthew Bughman	1,303	5.41
	Republican	Zachary Marshall	9,212	38.27
8	Democrat	JoCasta Zamarripa*	8,528	98.45
9	Democrat	Josh Zepnick*	12,142	97.97
10	Democrat	David Bowen*	21,228	99.11
11	Democrat	Jason M. Fields	18,418	98.76
12	Democrat	Frederick P. Kessler*	18,642	98.42
13	Democrat	Gregory Francis Walz-Chojnacki [2]	0	0.00
	Republican	Rob Hutton*	23,904	96.99
14	Democrat	Chris Rockwood	14,934	42.70
	Republican	Dale Kooyenga*	20,001	57.19
15	Republican	Joe Sanfelippo*	21,525	97.54
16	Democrat	Leon D. Young*	18,019	98.43
17	Democrat	David Crowley	21,715	99.07
18	Democrat	Evan Goyke*	18,006	98.87
19	Democrat	Jonathan Brostoff*	26,732	97.54
20	Democrat	Christine Sinicki*	21,222	97.02
21	Democrat	Jack Redmond	11,338	40.53
	Republican	Jessie Rodriguez*	16,589	59.30
22	Republican	Janel Brandtjen*	26,131	97.82
23	Republican	Jim Ott*	25,670	95.57
24	Republican	Dan Knodl*	24,047	96.48
25	Democrat	Ronald J. Kossik	9,305	34.89
	Republican	Paul Tittl*	17,325	64.97
26	Democrat	Rebecca Clarke	11,283	40.39
	Republican	Terry Katsma*	16,583	59.36
27	Democrat	Nanette Bulebosh	11,501	38.04
	Republican	Tyler Vorpagel*	18,644	61.66
28	Democrat	Jeff Peterson	9,837	33.88
	Republican	Adam Jarchow*	17,612	60.66
	Independent	Vincent Zilka	1,580	5.44
29	Democrat	Scottie E. Ard	10,661	38.83
	Republican	Rob Stafsholt	16,774	61.10
30	Democrat	Scott J. Nelson	12,358	38.94
	Republican	Shannon Zimmerman	17,790	56.05
	Independent	Aaron S. Taylor	1,574	4.96

District vote for representatives to the assembly, general and special elections, continued

Assembly district	Party	Candidates	Vote	% of total[1]
31	Democrat	Clinton Anderson.	10,348	35.88
	Republican	Amy Loudenbeck*	18,465	64.02
32	Democrat	Christine Welcher.	10,090	37.38
	Republican	Tyler August*	16,862	62.47
33	Democrat	Brandon White	11,246	37.34
	Republican	Cody Horlacher*	18,851	62.59
34	Democrat	Matthew N. Michalsen.	12,715	36.93
	Republican	Rob Swearingen*.	21,686	62.99
35	Democrat	Renea Frederick.	9,564	33.91
	Republican	Mary Czaja*	18,622	66.02
36	Republican	Jeffrey L. Mursau*	22,899	99.92
37	Democrat	Jordan Turner	10,990	38.10
	Republican	John Jagler*	17,821	61.78
38	Democrat	Scott Martin Michalak.	12,288	37.20
	Republican	Joel Kleefisch*.	20,708	62.70
39	Democrat	Jim Zahn	9,192	32.57
	Republican	Mark L. Born*	19,028	67.42
40	Democrat	Dmitri Martin	9,801	35.41
	Republican	Kevin Petersen*.	17,866	64.55
41	Republican	Joan Ballweg*	17,711	70.55
	Independent	Bradley Pearson.	7,382	29.40
42	Democrat	George E. Ferriter.	11,867	41.31
	Republican	Keith Ripp*.	16,842	58.63
43	Democrat	Don Vruwink.	16,179	54.56
	Republican	Allison Hetz	13,427	45.28
44	Democrat	Debra Kolste*	19,948	98.51
45	Democrat	Mark Spreitzer*	17,867	98.00
46	Democrat	Gary Hebl*	24,678	98.19
47	Democrat	Jimmy Anderson	19,154	68.47
	Independent	Adam Dahl.	8,596	30.73
48	Democrat	Melissa Agard Sargent*	26,534	98.76
49	Democrat	Jesse Bennett	11,344	42.94
	Republican	Travis Tranel*	15,056	56.99
50	Democrat	Art Shrader.	10,762	42.13
	Republican	Ed Brooks*	14,774	57.83
51	Democrat	Jeff Wright	13,189	48.62
	Republican	Todd Novak*.	13,912	51.29
52	Democrat	Paul G. Czisny	9,829	36.24
	Republican	Jeremy Thiesfeldt*	17,293	63.76
53	Republican	Michael Schraa*.	21,641	98.92
54	Democrat	Gordon Hintz*.	17,923	69.46
	Libertarian	Jordan Hansen	7,682	29.77
55	Democrat	Bob Baker	11,523	38.46
	Republican	Mike Rohrkaste*	18,393	61.40
56	Democrat	Mariana Stout.	11,551	35.45
	Republican	Dave Murphy*.	21,022	64.52
57	Democrat	Amanda Stuck*	19,048	98.68
	Independent	Mitchell Hanke[2].	12	0.06

District vote for representatives to the assembly, general and special elections, continued

Assembly district	Party	Candidates	Vote	% of total[1]
58	Republican	Bob Gannon*	25,457	98.13
59	Republican	Jesse Kremer*	25,847	99.27
60	Republican	Robert Brooks*	23,806	74.87
	Independent	David Pelikan	7,895	24.83
61	Democrat	Amee Janus	9,792	33.23
	Republican	Samantha Kerkman*	19,622	66.59
62	Republican	Thomas Weatherston*	22,523	100.00
63	Democrat	Andy Mitchell	10,487	35.84
	Republican	Robin Vos*	18,771	64.16
64	Democrat	Peter W. Barca*	18,799	97.67
65	Democrat	Tod Ohnstad*	16,112	97.84
66	Democrat	Cory Mason*	13,526	81.32
	Libertarian	George Meyers	3,107	18.68
67	Democrat	Dennis Hunt	10,308	35.69
	Republican	Rob Summerfield	18,574	64.31
68	Democrat	Howard White	11,263	41.83
	Republican	Kathy Bernier*	15,628	58.05
69	Republican	Bob Kulp*	21,443	99.68
70	Democrat	Mark Holbrook	10,266	37.68
	Republican	Nancy Lynn VanderMeer*	16,963	62.26
71	Democrat	Katrina Shankland*	21,834	98.90
72	Democrat	David Gorski	12,279	43.45
	Republican	Scott S. Krug*	15,972	56.52
73	Democrat	Nick Milroy*	22,107	98.17
74	Democrat	Beth Meyers*	22,624	99.36
75	Democrat	Joe Huftel	10,894	37.97
	Republican	Romaine Robert Quinn*	17,786	62.00
76	Democrat	Chris Taylor*	33,628	82.77
	Republican	Jon Rygiewicz	6,877	16.93
77	Democrat	Terese Berceau*	29,069	98.90
78	Democrat	Lisa Subeck*	25,362	78.90
	Independent	Chris V. Fisher	6,661	20.72
79	Democrat	Dianne H. Hesselbein*	23,211	63.84
	Republican	Jordan Zadra	13,105	36.04
80	Democrat	Sondy Pope*	26,250	98.19
81	Democrat	Dave Considine*	17,270	60.49
	Republican	David J. Moore	11,265	39.46
82	Republican	Ken Skowronski*	21,080	97.83
83	Republican	Chuck Wichgers	26,596	98.79
84	Republican	Mike Kuglitsch*	21,987	97.91
85	Democrat	Mandy Wright	12,837	46.52
	Republican	Patrick Snyder	14,722	53.35
86	Democrat	Nancy Stencil	11,142	35.43
	Republican	John Spiros*	18,246	58.01
	Independent	Michael A. Tauschek	2,047	6.51
87	Democrat	Elizabeth Riley	8,554	31.98
	Republican	James W. Edming*	18,179	67.97

District vote for representatives to the assembly, general and special elections, continued

Assembly district	Party	Candidates	Vote	% of total[1]
88	Democrat	Noah Reif.	11,312	38.88
	Republican	John Macco*.	17,742	60.99
89	Democrat	Heidi Fencl.	9,055	31.78
	Republican	John Nygren*	19,429	68.20
90	Democrat	Eric Genrich*	14,387	97.92
91	Democrat	Dana Wachs*	17,780	60.87
	Republican	Bill Ingram	11,341	38.82
92	Democrat	Chris Danou*	12,540	47.92
	Republican	Treig E. Pronschinske	13,605	51.99
93	Republican	Warren Petryk*	24,298	98.49
94	Democrat	Steve Doyle*.	16,721	52.63
	Republican	Julian Bradley	15,049	47.37
95	Democrat	Jill Billings*.	23,020	100.00
96	Democrat	Alicia Leinberger	10,186	38.89
	Republican	Lee Nerison*.	16,000	61.09
97	Republican	Scott Allen*	21,611	97.63
98	Republican	Adam Neylon*	25,592	98.39
99	Republican	Cindi Duchow*	28,597	98.86

*Incumbent.

1. Percentages do not add up to 100, as scattered votes have been omitted.   2. Write-in candidate.

Source: Official records of the Wisconsin Elections Commission.

County vote for U.S. senator, August 9, 2016 partisan primary

	Russ Feingold (Dem.)	Scott Harbach (Dem.)	Ron Johnson* (Rep.)	Phillip N. Anderson (Lib.)
Adams	1,026	145	662	11
Ashland.	857	33	287	2
Barron.	3,010	712	1,712	17
Bayfield.	1,978	194	564	1
Brown.	7,901	579	14,630	64
Buffalo	616	59	682	3
Burnett	481	73	647	8
Calumet	1,236	107	4,008	14
Chippewa	2,625	231	2,590	21
Clark.	812	88	1,105	6
Columbia.	3,168	255	1,811	15
Crawford	978	62	497	5
Dane	63,804	3,984	8,322	212
Dodge	2,441	356	3,198	21
Door.	1,389	59	3,020	9
Douglas.	4,562	938	985	10
Dunn	2,059	155	1,234	19
Eau Claire.	6,021	541	1,766	40
Florence	88	19	268	0
Fond du Lac	3,222	298	5,705	22

County vote for U.S. senator, August 9, 2016 partisan primary, continued

	Russ Feingold (Dem.)	Scott Harbach (Dem.)	Ron Johnson* (Rep.)	Phillip N. Anderson (Lib.)
Forest	296	39	354	3
Grant	1,728	169	1,132	11
Green	2,098	148	1,201	16
Green Lake	514	41	1,539	1
Iowa	1,852	161	603	6
Iron	572	100	284	2
Jackson	1,050	118	503	8
Jefferson	3,120	361	2,924	2
Juneau	1,071	75	2,066	8
Kenosha	5,569	461	8,861	31
Kewaunee	565	64	1,440	1
La Crosse	7,753	723	3,686	32
Lafayette	855	71	810	4
Langlade	681	66	688	8
Lincoln	1,116	196	1,016	2
Manitowoc	2,479	568	2,552	17
Marathon	5,397	388	4,869	24
Marinette	1,068	107	2,365	29
Marquette	637	68	805	2
Menominee	67	14	51	0
Milwaukee	65,725	10,774	21,629	185
Monroe	1,799	147	2,135	15
Oconto	1,158	143	2,993	32
Oneida	2,028	148	2,188	10
Outagamie	5,682	346	10,518	44
Ozaukee	3,626	622	5,587	31
Pepin	360	33	190	0
Pierce	1,429	109	1,343	10
Polk	1,397	150	1,634	12
Portage	4,252	395	1,235	11
Price	1,002	162	629	7
Racine	6,945	482	15,284	75
Richland	1,116	120	471	7
Rock	11,833	1,512	7,773	49
Rusk	607	55	917	11
St. Croix	2,259	181	3,479	26
Sauk	3,854	284	1,630	19
Sawyer	662	53	1,289	4
Shawano	955	102	2,856	9
Sheboygan	4,113	640	4,395	28
Taylor	490	50	745	3
Trempealeau	1,328	144	738	6
Vernon	1,892	168	1,137	15
Vilas	1,037	62	1,856	5
Walworth	3,098	237	9,525	19
Washburn	828	65	658	12
Washington	3,155	530	7,863	33
Waukesha	11,785	1,210	30,839	139
Waupaca	1,623	158	4,312	22
Waushara	830	123	1,233	13
Winnebago	6,630	549	7,282	46
Wood	3,531	516	2,949	20
Total	**303,791**	**33,096**	**248,754**	**1,625**

*Incumbent. Dem.–Democrat; Lib.–Libertarian; Rep.–Republican.

Source: Official records of the Wisconsin Elections Commission.

County vote for U.S. senator, November 8, 2016 general election

	Ron Johnson* (Rep.)	Russ Feingold (Dem.)	Phillip N. Anderson (Lib.)	County total
Adams	5,446	4,093	486	10,032
Ashland.	3,214	4,452	232	7,907
Barron.	12,893	8,699	754	22,350
Bayfield.	4,020	5,162	263	9,445
Brown.	71,760	51,008	4,616	127,438
Buffalo	3,851	2,746	285	6,883
Burnett	5,198	3,143	258	8,599
Calumet	16,485	9,197	937	26,619
Chippewa	17,339	12,661	1,324	31,324
Clark.	8,084	4,779	652	13,515
Columbia.	13,557	15,057	838	29,467
Crawford	3,671	3,708	270	7,651
Dane	80,670	220,344	5,775	306,960
Dodge	27,078	14,760	1,328	43,166
Door.	9,295	7,671	582	17,558
Douglas.	9,364	11,893	767	22,052
Dunn	11,425	9,491	896	21,812
Eau Claire.	24,650	27,527	1,940	54,160
Florence	1,770	759	85	2,614
Fond du Lac	32,464	17,131	1,734	51,329
Forest	2,589	1,651	199	4,443
Grant	12,197	10,926	801	23,932
Green	8,106	10,207	528	18,852
Green Lake.	6,215	2,774	329	9,319
Iowa.	4,679	7,226	294	12,206
Iron	1,949	1,361	90	3,402
Jackson	4,615	4,096	442	9,155
Jefferson	23,902	17,149	1,258	42,334
Juneau	6,441	4,697	408	11,549
Kenosha	37,540	35,670	2,621	75,900
Kewaunee	6,678	3,697	388	10,763
La Crosse	27,694	32,903	2,100	62,697
Lafayette	3,659	3,757	178	7,594
Langlade	6,007	3,465	415	9,889
Lincoln	8,031	5,785	743	14,564
Manitowoc.	23,769	14,299	1,785	39,881
Marathon.	38,570	27,812	2,518	68,937
Marinette.	12,597	6,502	773	19,872
Marquette	4,357	3,190	253	7,804
Menominee	303	844	84	1,231
Milwaukee	147,922	276,556	9,879	434,714
Monroe.	10,797	7,673	944	19,426
Oconto	13,004	6,061	745	19,810
Oneida	12,047	8,293	926	21,273
Outagamie.	53,252	37,067	3,448	93,768
Ozaukee	35,456	18,159	1,031	54,677
Pepin	2,097	1,491	111	3,699
Pierce	11,418	8,646	806	20,879
Polk	13,535	8,094	747	22,379
Portage.	17,547	18,985	1,397	37,952
Price.	4,282	2,955	314	7,551
Racine.	49,682	41,606	2,485	93,773
Richland	3,837	3,905	236	7,981
Rock.	30,487	42,437	2,388	75,353
Rusk	4,229	2,443	320	6,993
St. Croix.	27,406	17,713	1,563	46,700
Sauk.	14,127	16,323	937	31,387

County vote for U.S. senator, November 8, 2016 general election, continued

	Ron Johnson* (Rep.)	Russ Feingold (Dem.)	Phillip N. Anderson (Lib.)	County total
Sawyer	5,154	3,507	264	8,930
Shawano	12,794	6,114	758	19,666
Sheboygan	35,146	22,441	1,884	59,521
Taylor	6,177	2,828	384	9,390
Trempealeau	7,081	5,963	500	13,550
Vernon	6,712	6,887	522	14,121
Vilas	8,247	4,820	420	13,492
Walworth	30,786	18,358	1,672	50,855
Washburn	5,250	3,508	263	9,024
Washington	55,961	19,831	1,619	77,461
Waukesha	161,351	71,779	4,423	237,651
Waupaca	16,208	8,514	995	25,727
Waushara	7,579	3,834	491	11,904
Winnebago	46,843	36,077	3,288	86,286
Wood	20,925	15,175	1,542	37,643
Total	**1,479,471**	**1,380,335**	**87,531**	**2,948,741**
% of total vote	**50.17**	**46.81**	**2.97**	

Note: County totals include scattered votes. Republican write-in candidate John Schiess received a total of eight votes.

*Incumbent. Dem.–Democrat; Lib.–Libertarian; Rep.–Republican.

Source: Official records of the Wisconsin Elections Commission.

District vote for U.S. representatives, August 9, 2016 partisan primary

First congressional district

County	Ryan Solen (Dem.)	Tom Breu (Dem.)	Jason Lebeck (Lib.)	Paul Nehlen (Rep.)	Paul Ryan* (Rep.)
Kenosha	3,107	1,974	30	2,597	8,163
Milwaukee (part)	2,150	1,272	16	844	7,987
Racine	3,701	2,303	73	2,666	15,214
Rock (part)	2,999	2,973	21	1,364	5,319
Walworth (part)	1,419	921	17	1,967	8,474
Waukesha (part)	1,263	699	38	1,426	12,207
Total	**14,639**	**10,142**	**195**	**10,864**	**57,364**

Second congressional district

County	Mark Pocan* (Dem.)	Peter Theron (Rep.)
Dane	58,503	7,017
Green	1,903	1,058
Iowa	1,693	482
Lafayette	700	653
Richland (part)	137	80
Rock (part)	5,123	2,136
Sauk	3,402	1,440
Total	**71,461**	**12,866**

District vote for U.S. representatives, August 9, 2016 partisan primary, continued

Third congressional district

County	Ron Kind* (Dem.)	Myron Buchholz (Dem.)
Adams	865	224
Buffalo	567	101
Chippewa (part)	1,576	336
Crawford	852	169
Dunn	1,891	308
Eau Claire	4,972	1,595
Grant	1,561	315
Jackson (part)	893	177
Juneau (part)	756	112
La Crosse	6,975	1,523
Monroe (part)	1,537	257
Pepin	327	70
Pierce	1,341	192
Portage	3,701	780
Richland (part)	848	191
Trempealeau	1,211	254
Vernon	1,436	619
Wood (part)	2,011	466
Total	**33,320**	**7,689**

Fourth congressional district

County	Gwen S. Moore* (Dem.)	Gary R. George (Dem.)	Andy Craig (Lib.)
Milwaukee (part)	55,256	10,013	127
Waukesha (part)	0	0	0
Total	**55,256**	**10,013**	**127**

Fifth congressional district

County	Khary Penebaker (Dem.)	F. James Sensenbrenner, Jr.* (Rep.)	John Arndt (Lib.)
Dodge (part)	739	1,522	13
Jefferson	2,421	2,793	60
Milwaukee (part)	6,496	4,532	40
Walworth (part)	386	271	1
Washington	2,517	7,540	32
Waukesha (part)	6,794	17,545	97
Total	**19,353**	**34,203**	**243**

Sixth congressional district

County	Sarah Lloyd (Dem.)	W. Michael Slattery (Dem.)	Glenn Grothman* (Rep.)
Columbia	2,625	472	1,760
Dodge (part)	1,087	289	1,519
Fond du Lac	2,418	761	5,441
Green Lake	381	115	1,465
Manitowoc	1,437	1,329	2,383
Marquette	500	111	758
Milwaukee (part)	105	42	67
Ozaukee	2,675	727	5,237

District vote for U.S. representatives, August 9, 2016 partisan primary, continued

County	Sarah Lloyd (Dem.)	W. Michael Slattery (Dem.)	Glenn Grothman* (Rep.)
Sheboygan.	3,213	981	4,157
Waushara.	595	217	1,135
Winnebago (part).	4,616	1,415	5,873
Total.	19,652	6,459	29,795

Seventh congressional district

County	Mary Hoeft (Dem.)	Joel Lewis (Dem.)	Sean Duffy* (Rep.)	Donald Raihala (Rep.)
Ashland.	718	104	276	63
Barron.	3,052	614	1,630	133
Bayfield.	1,613	293	557	69
Burnett.	453	72	615	60
Chippewa (part)	678	149	1,448	144
Clark.	633	154	1,074	105
Douglas.	3,839	1,037	981	114
Florence	72	22	222	31
Forest.	239	51	346	33
Iron	458	126	267	27
Jackson (part).	63	16	116	10
Juneau (part)	171	51	418	74
Langlade.	559	103	661	47
Lincoln	853	442	1,036	105
Marathon.	4,075	1,356	4,885	393
Monroe (part).	106	26	256	35
Oneida	1,591	403	2,133	342
Polk	1,300	174	1,512	188
Price.	781	200	585	49
Rusk.	499	102	865	132
Sawyer	580	95	1,262	266
St. Croix.	1,938	405	3,303	372
Taylor.	414	76	732	73
Vilas.	839	133	2,113	351
Washburn	802	68	654	70
Wood (part)	963	259	1,554	170
Total.	27,289	6,531	29,501	3,456

Eighth congressional district

County	Tom Nelson (Dem.)	Mike Gallagher (Rep.)	Frank Lasee (Rep.)	Terry McNulty (Rep.)
Brown.	7,185	13,553	3,136	698
Calumet	1,192	3,049	1,318	220
Door.	1,280	2,355	773	595
Kewaunee	577	1,113	309	278
Marinette.	1,046	2,006	514	102
Menominee	91	52	19	5
Oconto	1,130	2,541	622	131
Outagamie.	5,603	8,862	2,414	635
Shawano	932	2,519	531	150
Waupaca.	1,582	3,582	901	257
Winnebago (part).	296	690	168	38
Total.	20,914	40,322	10,705	3,109

*Incumbent. Dem.–Democrat; Lib.–Libertarian; Rep.–Republican.

Source: Official records of the Wisconsin Elections Commission.

District vote for U.S. representatives, November 8, 2016 general election

First congressional district

County	Paul Ryan* (Rep.)	Ryan Solen (Dem.)	Spencer Zimmerman (Ind.)	Jason Lebeck (Lib.)
Kenosha	43,929	27,346	1,824	1,886
Milwaukee (part)	33,903	13,827	1,112	843
Racine.	57,538	30,995	2,040	1,880
Rock (part).	21,879	14,546	1,170	1,009
Walworth (part).	31,192	10,889	1,838	1,085
Waukesha (part)	41,631	9,400	1,445	783
Total.	**230,072**	**107,003**	**9,429**	**7,486**
% of total vote[1]	**64.95**	**30.21**	**2.66**	**2.11**

Second congressional district

County	Mark Pocan* (Dem.)	Peter Theron (Rep.)
Dane	215,374	79,395
Green	9,920	8,141
Iowa	7,176	4,496
Lafayette	3,616	3,474
Richland (part)	776	692
Rock (part)	20,758	14,316
Sauk	15,917	13,530
Total.	**273,537**	**124,044**
% of total vote[1]	**68.72**	**31.16**

Third congressional district

County	Ron Kind* (Dem.)	Ryan Peterson (Rep. write-in)
Adams	5,918	0
Buffalo	5,087	1
Chippewa (part)	12,980	43
Crawford	5,635	5
Dunn	16,022	10
Eau Claire.	39,113	22
Grant	17,672	2
Jackson (part)	6,147	3
Juneau (part)	5,942	9
La Crosse	46,541	22
Monroe (part)	12,180	32
Pepin	2,686	2
Pierce	15,428	2
Portage	26,024	3
Richland (part)	4,265	1
Trempealeau	10,253	4
Vernon	10,398	5
Wood (part)	15,110	3
Total.	**257,401**	**169**
% of total vote[1]	**98.86**	**0.06**

District vote for U.S. representatives, November 8, 2016 general election, continued

Fourth congressional district

County	Gwen S. Moore* (Dem.)	Robert R. Raymond (Ind.)	Andy Craig (Lib.)
Milwaukee (part)	220,181	33,494	32,183
Waukesha (part)	0	0	0
Total.	220,181	33,494	32,183
% of total vote[1]	76.74	11.67	11.22

Fifth congressional district

County	F. James Sensenbrenner, Jr.* (Rep.)	Khary Penebaker (Dem.)	John Arndt (Lib.)
Dodge (part).	13,810	4,360	809
Jefferson	25,438	13,758	1,982
Milwaukee (part)	38,212	31,238	3,385
Walworth (part).	2,412	2,495	300
Washington	56,888	15,567	2,697
Waukesha (part)	123,946	47,059	6,151
Total.	260,706	114,477	15,324
% of total vote[1]	66.70	29.29	3.92

Sixth congressional district

County	Glenn Grothman* (Rep.)	Sarah Lloyd (Dem.)	Jeff Dahlke (Ind.)
Columbia.	13,081	13,779	1,594
Dodge (part).	13,076	8,521	1,259
Fond du Lac	30,802	16,741	2,573
Green Lake.	5,960	2,599	490
Manitowoc.	22,223	13,210	2,993
Marquette	4,096	2,790	580
Milwaukee (part)	629	501	31
Ozaukee	34,127	16,793	2,111
Sheboygan.	33,767	21,918	2,447
Waushara.	7,114	3,624	714
Winnebago (part).	39,272	32,596	4,924
Total.	204,147	133,072	19,716
% of total vote[1]	57.15	37.26	5.52

Seventh congressional district

County	Sean Duffy* (Rep.)	Mary Hoeft (Dem.)
Ashland.	3,115	4,757
Barron.	12,818	9,121
Bayfield.	3,948	5,473
Burnett	5,312	3,094
Chippewa (part)	8,291	4,241
Clark.	9,018	4,258
Douglas.	9,542	12,349
Florence	1,787	707
Forest	2,819	1,440
Iron	2,012	1,320

District vote for U.S. representatives, November 8, 2016 general election, continued

County	Sean Duffy* (Rep.)	Mary Hoeft (Dem.)
Jackson (part)	666	288
Juneau (part)	1,811	923
Langlade	6,844	3,022
Lincoln	9,040	5,406
Marathon	43,492	24,284
Monroe (part)	1,530	706
Oneida	13,039	7,875
Polk	14,003	7,889
Price	4,555	2,849
Rusk	4,362	2,451
Sawyer	28,998	16,709
St. Croix	5,299	3,582
Taylor	6,830	2,442
Vilas	8,849	4,451
Washburn	5,342	3,558
Wood (part)	10,096	5,448
Total	**223,418**	**138,643**
% of total vote[1]	**61.67**	**38.27**

Eighth congressional district

County	Mike Gallagher (Rep.)	Tom Nelson (Dem.)
Brown	76,473	48,739
Calumet	17,307	8,985
Door	9,981	7,430
Kewaunee	7,232	3,418
Marinette	13,210	6,199
Menominee	346	830
Oconto	13,712	5,769
Outagamie	54,720	38,024
Shawano	13,286	6,012
Waupaca	16,945	8,335
Winnebago (part)	4,680	1,941
Total	**227,892**	**135,682**
% of total vote[1]	**62.65**	**37.30**

Note: Democratic write-in candidate Jerry Kobishop received a total of two votes. Wisconsin Green write-in candidate Wendy Gribben received a total of 16 votes.

*Incumbent. Dem.–Democrat; Ind.–Independent; Lib.–Libertarian; Rep.–Republican.

1. Percentages do not add up to 100, as scattered votes have been omitted.

Source: Official records of the Wisconsin Elections Commission.

Republican presidential primary vote, by county, April 5, 2016

	Ted Cruz	Donald J. Trump	John R. Kasich	Marco Rubio	Ben Carson	Jeb Bush	Rand Paul	Un-instructed delegation	Mike Huckabee	Chris Christie	Carly Fiorina	Rick Santorum	Jim Gilmore	Total
Adams	1,360	2,279	374	30	21	6	10	9	10	3	3	3	2	4,116
Ashland	795	1,269	312	24	28	10	4	2	5	2	1	1	3	2,458
Barron	3,559	4,216	922	105	86	28	20	15	12	20	6	8	1	9,013
Bayfield	926	1,600	448	40	22	8	7	7	6	8	2	3	0	3,079
Brown	25,684	18,761	5,080	470	191	121	95	65	52	35	33	23	9	50,696
Buffalo	999	1,397	323	21	16	13	5	7	2	5	1	3	1	2,795
Burnett	1,172	1,629	356	45	36	2	9	7	6	4	0	2	2	3,270
Calumet	6,134	4,054	1,200	95	63	26	26	8	19	9	8	5	2	11,649
Chippewa	5,567	5,839	1,108	82	68	37	28	21	17	14	13	5	2	12,802
Clark	2,739	2,865	392	52	29	20	18	85	11	4	3	4	2	6,224
Columbia	4,516	4,416	1,920	111	73	36	36	32	16	15	13	6	3	11,211
Crawford	1,009	1,216	352	25	27	8	13	5	6	7	3	3	1	2,681
Dane	26,395	20,922	20,134	601	306	175	227	170	89	67	58	29	12	69,404
Dodge	10,445	6,505	2,544	199	108	52	41	37	13	18	12	8	6	19,988
Door	3,193	2,953	1,105	95	40	29	13	22	18	5	5	7	1	7,499
Douglas	2,070	3,678	761	84	66	18	13	10	8	9	4	3	1	6,733
Dunn	3,473	3,076	763	50	51	22	17	12	16	10	4	5	1	7,500
Eau Claire	8,497	6,856	2,364	125	88	41	58	39	31	16	10	9	3	18,170
Florence	428	653	105	14	7	5	1	0	3	1	1	1	0	1,219
Fond du Lac	12,758	7,656	2,277	209	138	72	45	35	19	23	7	7	20	23,266
Forest	660	1,110	157	32	10	5	6	0	4	2	1	6	0	1,996
Grant	3,247	3,501	1,558	96	64	29	36	19	24	17	8	9	5	8,616
Green	2,467	2,828	1,455	48	52	25	21	49	16	5	5	6	2	6,993
Green Lake	2,148	1,985	436	46	28	15	6	9	8	11	4	6	3	4,706
Iowa	1,519	1,612	838	49	39	21	15	15	6	7	5	3	3	4,141
Iron	391	940	187	23	5	1	4	4	1	3	1	3	0	1,566
Jackson	1,228	1,808	288	30	25	12	9	6	13	6	4	3	2	3,434
Jefferson	9,343	5,769	2,571	175	84	58	50	32	19	23	14	8	5	18,195
Juneau	1,627	2,439	591	38	36	10	14	4	9	5	4	3	1	4,784
Kenosha	10,888	11,164	3,748	250	137	63	61	43	33	20	19	11	10	26,498
Kewaunee	2,480	2,087	380	61	32	13	7	8	10	4	3	3	0	5,090

Republican presidential primary vote, by county, April 5, 2016, continued

	Ted Cruz	Donald J. Trump	John R. Kasich	Marco Rubio	Ben Carson	Jeb Bush	Rand Paul	Un-instructed delegation	Mike Huckabee	Chris Christie	Carly Fiorina	Rick Santorum	Jim Gilmore	Total
La Crosse	7,447	8,279	3,634	203	138	50	80	37	36	24	18	8	3	19,957
Lafayette	1,069	1,229	564	37	31	13	9	21	14	4	3	3	0	2,998
Langlade	2,002	2,407	396	46	38	20	14	5	11	6	6	3	2	4,957
Lincoln	2,520	3,030	523	38	35	18	15	5	12	9	3	1	1	6,214
Manitowoc	9,329	6,445	1,420	157	88	37	24	32	17	16	10	7	5	17,618
Marathon	13,435	13,309	2,565	201	144	74	64	42	28	23	25	11	7	29,966
Marinette	3,725	4,635	644	103	51	23	7	18	14	14	3	4	2	9,244
Marquette	1,330	1,765	405	36	26	12	7	10	6	9	3	2	0	3,616
Menominee	76	78	22	3	0	0	0	1	0	0	0	0	0	180
Milwaukee	61,505	29,527	19,216	1,188	502	371	290	256	93	163	84	48	23	113,496
Monroe	3,032	3,595	994	74	80	32	34	23	20	9	6	10	3	7,925
Oconto	4,064	4,475	584	72	45	13	13	11	9	7	6	3	2	9,304
Oneida	3,242	4,337	1,168	81	44	33	32	18	12	9	9	2	0	8,997
Outagamie	18,603	13,942	4,074	340	158	86	103	42	46	30	33	12	6	37,478
Ozaukee	16,947	5,774	4,838	276	85	67	33	74	20	22	20	4	2	28,162
Pepin	546	607	154	9	9	3	2	0	3	1	1	0	1	1,337
Pierce	2,828	2,825	994	140	69	29	40	25	14	13	7	2	1	6,989
Polk	3,002	3,544	819	127	71	22	25	18	19	15	9	2	1	7,677
Portage	5,891	5,117	1,365	120	84	39	34	19	21	9	17	9	2	12,745
Price	1,165	1,699	253	27	32	8	8	4	6	5	1	3	2	3,213
Racine	18,738	11,763	5,281	351	158	117	79	72	40	36	26	13	9	36,683
Richland	1,160	1,438	519	40	28	14	12	9	8	5	0	3	2	3,243
Rock	9,049	10,283	4,760	186	143	86	52	65	39	35	15	17	6	24,795
Rusk	1,338	1,619	220	30	22	7	9	7	9	3	2	0	0	3,267
St. Croix	6,900	6,705	2,665	357	150	66	74	48	28	24	22	15	1	17,091
Sauk	3,906	4,699	2,196	124	73	43	25	20	25	29	5	7	2	11,154
Sawyer	1,150	2,038	475	33	26	11	6	7	8	3	4	2	2	3,773
Shawano	4,221	4,271	632	71	44	20	14	8	14	10	8	4	1	9,321
Sheboygan	15,659	6,815	3,267	234	108	69	55	48	36	31	18	15	9	26,396
Taylor	1,914	2,100	316	43	31	15	8	67	8	8	1	5	1	4,522
Trempealeau	1,779	2,414	541	44	17	18	10	0	10	6	2	1	1	4,852

	Ted Cruz	Donald J. Trump	John R. Kasich	Marco Rubio	Ben Carson	Jeb Bush	Rand Paul	Un-instructed delegation	Mike Huckabee	Chris Christie	Carly Fiorina	Rick Santorum	Jim Gilmore	Total
Vernon	1,880	2,439	637	53	47	18	17	9	12	6	4	6	0	5,135
Vilas	2,032	3,246	835	44	35	15	6	16	9	12	2	4	1	6,267
Walworth	10,738	7,546	3,348	189	104	57	28	58	31	21	10	10	8	22,187
Washburn	1,364	1,927	443	51	34	16	13	7	6	11	4	3	1	3,888
Washington	25,532	9,585	4,831	360	156	100	74	71	27	38	18	13	0	40,805
Waukesha	75,244	27,218	18,583	1,184	348	238	152	186	93	78	71	30	15	123,657
Waupaca	5,195	4,736	818	103	68	21	23	18	19	18	7	5	6	11,045
Waushara	2,485	2,480	407	48	44	20	6	3	8	10	3	6	3	5,523
Winnebago	16,085	13,324	3,966	310	191	127	84	97	59	29	20	18	7	34,390
Wood	7,235	6,947	1,481	133	127	45	23	27	32	12	11	7	5	16,085
Total	**533,079**	**387,295**	**155,902**	**10,591**	**5,660**	**3,054**	**2,519**	**2,281**	**1,424**	**1,191**	**772**	**511**	**245**	**1,105,944**

Note: County totals include scattered votes. Write-in candidate Victor Williams received a total of 39 votes.

Source: Official records of the Wisconsin Elections Commission.

Democratic presidential primary vote, by county, April 5, 2016

	Bernie Sanders	Hillary Clinton	Martin O'Malley	Un-instructed delegation	Total
Adams	1,515	1,375	10	11	2,912
Ashland	2,204	1,248	10	5	3,467
Barron	2,965	2,572	24	14	5,578
Bayfield	2,619	1,488	8	8	4,123
Brown	22,559	16,701	62	47	39,389
Buffalo	1,149	825	6	9	1,990
Burnett	936	918	8	10	1,872
Calumet	4,017	3,028	13	7	7,065
Chippewa	5,127	4,022	22	18	9,189
Clark	1,969	1,473	7	3	3,452
Columbia	6,460	4,187	10	19	10,679
Crawford	1,592	1,146	8	8	2,754
Dane	102,986	61,405	143	143	164,743
Dodge	6,249	4,505	23	13	10,790
Door	3,426	2,943	9	10	6,390
Douglas	4,512	3,577	31	32	8,163
Dunn	4,279	2,421	20	14	6,734
Eau Claire	13,674	7,689	22	31	21,429
Florence	293	175	4	2	474
Fond du Lac	7,385	5,519	23	13	12,940
Forest	667	610	4	8	1,291
Grant	4,491	3,068	27	12	7,599
Green	4,368	2,766	6	24	7,167
Green Lake	1,148	871	6	4	2,031
Iowa	3,202	2,164	11	11	5,391
Iron	563	437	7	9	1,018
Jackson	1,872	1,294	10	8	3,184
Jefferson	7,555	4,775	17	18	12,371
Juneau	1,839	1,355	12	4	3,210
Kenosha	14,653	10,897	40	31	25,647
Kewaunee	1,667	1,497	12	5	3,181
La Crosse	15,156	8,908	27	29	24,120
Lafayette	1,331	1,170	3	16	2,523
Langlade	1,447	1,192	10	10	2,659
Lincoln	2,442	1,732	8	8	4,191
Manitowoc	6,458	4,999	46	15	11,526
Marathon	11,673	8,061	53	33	19,827
Marinette	2,698	2,580	18	14	5,310
Marquette	1,321	994	7	6	2,332
Menominee	355	204	0	2	561
Milwaukee	93,668	100,798	261	214	195,057
Monroe	3,539	2,269	20	8	5,839
Oconto	2,590	2,422	19	15	5,047
Oneida	3,813	2,500	12	17	6,345
Outagamie	17,021	11,228	42	46	28,337
Ozaukee	6,897	6,587	13	16	13,513
Pepin	561	435	3	0	999
Pierce	3,208	2,343	25	26	5,602
Polk	2,476	2,165	29	15	4,685
Portage	9,351	5,088	36	24	14,506
Price	1,418	862	13	2	2,295
Racine	14,681	14,111	55	43	28,890
Richland	1,786	1,276	4	2	3,071
Rock	17,360	11,262	42	52	28,730
Rusk	1,092	816	7	4	1,919
St. Croix	5,679	4,895	46	33	10,664
Sauk	7,203	4,527	15	19	11,765

Democratic presidential primary vote, by county, April 5, 2016, continued

	Bernie Sanders	Hillary Clinton	Martin O'Malley	Un-instructed delegation	Total
Sawyer	1,654	976	7	8	2,648
Shawano	3,003	2,117	7	8	5,139
Sheboygan	8,952	7,145	36	47	16,189
Taylor	1,279	852	11	5	2,147
Trempealeau	2,430	1,989	13	0	4,444
Vernon	3,481	1,936	8	10	5,438
Vilas	2,147	1,414	4	6	3,573
Walworth	8,426	5,188	25	21	13,668
Washburn	1,419	1,058	12	7	2,500
Washington	7,690	6,388	22	20	14,120
Waukesha	26,442	24,835	67	63	51,441
Waupaca	3,894	2,585	17	14	6,515
Waushara	1,600	1,241	10	5	2,856
Winnebago	17,854	11,212	40	40	29,164
Wood	6,756	4,428	24	14	11,222
Total	570,192	433,739	1,732	1,488	1,007,600

Note: County totals include scattered votes. Write-in candidate Roque "Rocky" De La Fuente received a total of 18 votes.

Source: Official records of the Wisconsin Elections Commission.

Republican National Convention delegates, July 18–21, 2016, Cleveland, Ohio

Ted Cruz delegates and residence

At-large

Dave Anderson (alternate)	Wausau
Candee Arndt	Brookfield
Tyler August (alternate)	Delavan
Crystal Berg	Hartford
Kim Bliss	Darien
Mary Buestrin	Mequon
Rachel Campos-Duffy (alternate)	Wausau
Ardis Cerny (alternate)	Pewaukee
Brad Courtney	Whitefish Bay
Alberta Darling (alternate)	River Hills
Scott Fitzgerald	Juneau
Jennie Frederick (alternate)	Jackson
Keith Gilkes (alternate)	Madison
Bill Johnson	Hayward
Steve King	Janesville
Dean Knudson	Hudson
Mary Lazich (alternate)	New Berlin
Ginny Marschman (alternate)	Waukesha
Katie McCallum (alternate)	Middleton
Van Mobley (alternate)	Thiensville
John Nygren (alternate)	Marinette
Gerard Randall (alternate)	Milwaukee
Charlotte Rasmussen	Stanley
Sandra Ruggles (alternate)	Milwaukee
Brad Schimel	Waukesha
Tom Schreibel	Hartland
Duey Stroebel	Saukville
Don Taylor	Waukesha
Tommy Thompson	Madison
Jim Villa (alternate)	West Allis
Robin Vos	Burlington
Tonette Walker	Maple Bluff
Scott Walker	Maple Bluff

First congressional district

Rose-Ann Dieck	Greendale
Bill Folk (alternate)	Racine
Bill Jaeck	Franksville
Gene Hainault (alternate)	Kenosha
Bryan Steil	Janesville
Jonathan Steitz (alternate)	Pleasant Prairie

Second congressional district

David Blaska (alternate)	Madison
Nora Gard (alternate)	Beloit
Scott Grabins	Verona
Howard Marklein	Spring Green
Phil Prange (alternate)	Madison
Roger Stauter	Monona

Fourth congressional district

Andrew Davis (alternate)	Milwaukee
Greg Reiman (alternate)	Whitefish Bay
Patty Reiman	Whitefish Bay
John Savage (alternate)	Milwaukee

Republican National Convention delegates, July 18–21, 2016, Cleveland, Ohio, continued

Robert Spindell . . . . Milwaukee
Laurie Wolf . . . . Bayside

Fifth congressional district
Keith Best (alternate) . . . . Waukesha
Grace Degner (alternate) . . . . . Hustisford
James Geldreich . . . . West Bend
Kathy Kiernan . . . . Richfield
John Macy . . . . Oconomowoc
Jim Schildbach (alternate) . . . . Watertown

Sixth congressional district
Rohn Bishop (alternate). . . . . . Waupun
Jane Kautzer. . . . . Sheboygan

Lillian Nolan (alternate) . . . . . . Fond du Lac
Paul Tittl . . . . Manitowoc
Sridhar Vasudevan (alternate) . . Belgium
Don Zimmer. . . . . Manitowoc

Eighth congressional district
Barb Finger . . . . Oconto
Jerome Murphy. . . . . Appleton
Kelly Ruh . . . . Green Bay
Patti Schick (alternate) . . . . . . Hobart
Jeff Schoenfeldt (alternate) . . . Fitchburg
Tom Schumacher (alternate). . . De Pere

Donald Trump delegates and residence

Third congressional district
Scott Colburn . . . . Friendship
Tamara Deutsch (alternate) . . . Menomonie
Kathryn Heitman . . . . Lyndon Station
Sue Lynch (alternate) . . . . La Crosse
Larry Vangen (alternate) . . . . . La Crosse
Brian Westrate . . . . Fall Creek

Seventh congressional district
Jesse Garza . . . . Hudson
Adam Jarchow . . . . Balsam Lake
Lonnie Kennell (alternate) . . . . Hayward
Jim Miller. . . . . Hayward
Pam Travis (alternate) . . . . Neillsville
Paul Wharton (alternate) . . . . . Hayward

Source: Republican Party of Wisconsin.

Democratic National Convention delegates, July 25–28, 2016, Philadelphia, Pennsylvania

Hillary Clinton delegates and residence

Party leaders and elected officials
Peter Barca . . . . Kenosha
Tom Barrett . . . . Milwaukee
Thelma Sias . . . . Milwaukee
JoCasta Zamarripa . . . . Milwaukee

At-large
Sachin Chheda (alternate) . . . . Milwaukee
Heather Colburn . . . . Madison
Patrick Guarasci . . . . Milwaukee
Gretchen Hoover. . . . . Rhinelander
Ann Jacobs . . . . Milwaukee
David Jordan . . . . Oneida
Alexander Lasry . . . . Milwaukee
Gretchen Lowe . . . . Madison
Dian Palmer . . . . Brookfield

First congressional district
Margaret Andrietsch . . . . Mount Pleasant
Cory Mason . . . . Racine
Bradley Schwanda . . . . Oak Creek

Second congressional district
Luke Fuszard . . . . Middleton
Frank Long . . . . Madison
Sondra Milkie . . . . Madison
Crystal Miller . . . . Madison

Third congressional district
Veronica Burke . . . . Onalaska
Ryan Greendeer . . . . Black River Falls
Gary Hawley. . . . . Stevens Point

Fourth congressional district
Carmen Cabrera . . . . Milwaukee
Nancy Kaplan . . . . Glendale
Craig Mastantuono . . . . Milwaukee
LaKeshia Myers . . . . Milwaukee
Candice Owley (alternate) . . . . Milwaukee
Marla Stephens . . . . Whitefish Bay
Andrew Warner . . . . Whitefish Bay

Democratic National Convention delegates, July 25–28, 2016, Philadelphia, Pennsylvania, continued

Fifth congressional district
Ryan Champeau . . . . Waukesha
Tanya Lohr. . . . . West Bend

Sixth congressional district
Joan Kaeding . . . . Oshkosh
Deb Klock . . . . Plymouth
Joseph Messinger . . . . Cedarburg

Seventh congressional district
David Mettille. . . . . Ashland
Thomas Mettille . . . . Ashland
Melissa Schroeder . . . . Merrill

Eighth congressional district
Mary Ginnebaugh . . . . Green Bay
Mark Waltman . . . . Appleton

Bernie Sanders delegates and residence

Party leaders and elected officials
Jonathan Brostoff . . . . Milwaukee
Eric Genrich . . . . Green Bay
Bryan Kennedy . . . . Glendale
Dorothy Krause . . . . Fitchburg
Marcelia Nicholson . . . . Milwaukee
Paul Soglin. . . . . Madison

At-large
Omar Barberena . . . . Milwaukee
Kimberly Butler . . . . Balsam Lake
Anna Dvorak . . . . Milwaukee
Jarrett English. . . . . Milwaukee
Jens Jorgensen (alternate) . . . . Janesville
Solana Patterson-Ramos . . . . . Milwaukee
Martha Pincus . . . . Fox Point
Peter Rickman . . . . Milwaukee
Clinton Rodgers . . . . Brookfield
Jacqueline Spaight. . . . . Madison
Hailey Storsved . . . . Menomonee Falls
Brandon Yellowbird-Stevens . . Green Bay

First congressional district
Angela Aker . . . . Kenosha
Catherine Brandstetter . . . . . . Kenosha
David Palmer . . . . Mount Pleasant
Joshua Skolnick (alternate). . . . Williams Bay

Second congressional district
John Hendrick . . . . Madison
Maureen May-Grimm . . . . Mineral Point
Mahlon Mitchell (alternate) . . . Fitchburg
Christine McDonough. . . . . . . Sun Prairie
Tod Pulvermacher . . . . Arena
John Stanley. . . . . DeForest
Karla Stoebig . . . . Madison
Heidi Wegleitner . . . . Madison

Third congressional district
Obbie King . . . . La Crosse
Matthew LaRonge . . . . Plover
Alicia Leinberger . . . . Viroqua
Xong Xiong . . . . La Crosse

Fourth congressional district
Jaime Alvarado . . . . Milwaukee
Supreme Moore Omokunde . . . Milwaukee
Luz Sosa . . . . Milwaukee
Tomika Vukovic. . . . . Glendale
Walter Wilson . . . . Glendale

Fifth congressional district
Robert Hansen . . . . Greenfield
Joe Kanzleiter (alternate) . . . . . Menomonee Falls
Tracey Sperko. . . . . Wauwatosa
Michelle Zahn . . . . Juneau

Sixth congressional district
Paul Czisny . . . . Fond du Lac
Ryan Hamann . . . . Oshkosh
Patti VandeHei . . . . Plymouth

Seventh congressional district
Rebecca Bonesteel (alternate) . . Hudson
Maria Hutchinson . . . . Hudson
Lori Miller . . . . Weston
Joshua Renner . . . . Wausau

Eighth congressional district
Desiree May . . . . Green Bay
Eric Reimer . . . . Green Bay
Andrew Walsh . . . . Appleton

Unpledged delegates and residence

Tammy Baldwin. . . . . Madison
David Bowen . . . . Milwaukee
Christine Bremer Muggli . . . . . Wausau
Michael Childers . . . . La Pointe
Ron Kind . . . . La Crosse

Martha Laning . . . . Sheboygan
Martha Love . . . . Milwaukee
Gwen Moore . . . . Milwaukee
Mark Pocan . . . . Black Earth
Jason Rae . . . . Milwaukee

Source: Democratic Party of Wisconsin.

Presidential vote by county and municipality, November 8, 2016 general election

	Donald J. Trump/ Michael R. Pence (Rep.)	Hillary Clinton/ Tim Kaine (Dem.)		Donald J. Trump/ Michael R. Pence (Rep.)	Hillary Clinton/ Tim Kaine (Dem.)
Adams	**5,966**	**3,745**	Dallas, village	113	60
Adams, city	377	325	Dovre, town	231	138
Adams, town	377	207	Doyle, town	210	67
Big Flats, town.	300	169	Haugen, village	85	65
Colburn, town.	85	42	Lakeland, town	341	201
Dell Prairie, town	474	301	Maple Grove, town. . . .	342	110
Easton, town.	336	169	Maple Plain, town	257	207
Friendship, village	154	117	New Auburn, village (part)	7	2
Jackson, town	314	225	Oak Grove, town	298	177
Leola, town	116	18	Prairie Farm, town	169	92
Lincoln, town	98	76	Prairie Farm, village . . .	122	60
Monroe, town.	129	102	Prairie Lake, town.	555	261
New Chester, town. . . .	247	138	Rice Lake, city	2,116	1,554
New Haven, town.	176	145	Rice Lake, town	947	580
Preston, town	397	270	Sioux Creek, town	184	94
Quincy, town	357	269	Stanfold, town	243	122
Richfield, town	56	27	Stanley, town	834	407
Rome, town	1,169	715	Sumner, town	249	128
Springville, town	414	211	Turtle Lake, town	195	89
Strongs Prairie, town. . .	376	213	Turtle Lake, village (part)	220	129
Wisconsin Dells, city (part)	14	6	Vance Creek, town	210	113
Ashland	**3,303**	**4,226**	**Bayfield**	**4,124**	**4,953**
Agenda, town.	151	68	Ashland, city (part). . . .	0	0
Ashland, city (part). . . .	1,388	2,348	Barksdale, town.	220	233
Ashland, town.	147	144	Barnes, town.	293	254
Butternut, village.	84	86	Bayfield, city.	73	253
Chippewa, town	128	72	Bayfield, town.	146	327
Gingles, town	198	211	Bayview, town.	141	181
Gordon, town	94	49	Bell, town.	83	136
Jacobs, town.	204	120	Cable, town	299	193
La Pointe, town	53	159	Clover, town	76	86
Marengo, town	101	92	Delta, town	113	84
Mellen, city	152	140	Drummond, town	169	153
Morse, town	138	150	Eileen, town	220	178
Peeksville, town.	52	33	Grand View, town.	147	131
Sanborn, town	72	398	Hughes, town	163	130
Shanagolden, town . . .	32	28	Iron River, town.	384	322
White River, town.	309	128	Kelly, town	146	97
			Keystone, town	104	83
Barron	**13,614**	**7,889**	Lincoln, town	103	65
Almena, town.	306	148	Mason, town.	88	74
Almena, village	209	74	Mason, village.	18	20
Arland, town.	180	107	Namakagon, town	133	100
Barron, city.	759	511	Orienta, town	46	39
Barron, town.	255	97	Oulu, town	166	147
Bear Lake, town.	226	133	Pilsen, town	59	74
Cameron, village	504	245	Port Wing, town.	109	146
Cedar Lake, town.	471	210	Russell, town	89	405
Chetek, city	582	381	Tripp, town.	78	54
Chetek, town	651	375	Washburn, city	328	792
Clinton, town	220	112	Washburn, town	130	196
Crystal Lake, town	266	137	**Brown**	**67,210**	**53,382**
Cumberland, city	597	459	Allouez, village	3,764	3,651
Cumberland, town	269	166	Ashwaubenon, village. .	4,873	3,802
Dallas, town	191	78			

Presidential vote by county and municipality, November 8, 2016 general election, continued

	Donald J. Trump/ Michael R. Pence (Rep.)	Hillary Clinton/ Tim Kaine (Dem.)		Donald J. Trump/ Michael R. Pence (Rep.)	Hillary Clinton/ Tim Kaine (Dem.)
Bellevue, village	4,222	3,318	La Follette, town	166	129
De Pere, city	6,491	5,821	Lincoln, town	123	45
Denmark, village	646	361	Meenon, town.	370	165
Eaton, town	591	291	Oakland, town	312	243
Glenmore, town.	391	167	Roosevelt, town.	73	32
Green Bay, city	19,826	21,303	Rusk, town	163	76
Green Bay, town	800	363	Sand Lake, town	157	118
Hobart, village	2,623	1,701	Scott, town.	221	171
Holland, town	570	273	Siren, town.	349	156
Howard, village (part) . .	5,917	3,850	Siren, village.	218	127
Humboldt, town	488	222	Swiss, town	215	189
Lawrence, town.	1,906	990	Trade Lake, town	331	152
Ledgeview, town	2,469	1,580	Union, town	126	75
Morrison, town	653	173	Webb Lake, town	172	99
New Denmark, town. . .	598	294	Webster, village.	192	122
Pittsfield, town	1,079	480	West Marshland, town. .	143	42
Pulaski, village (part). . .	912	523	Wood River, town.	360	126
Rockland, town	692	338			
Scott, town.	1,294	868	**Calumet**	**15,367**	**9,642**
Suamico, village	4,749	2,200	Appleton, city (part) . . .	2,601	2,587
Wrightstown, town. . . .	820	365	Brillion, city	985	501
Wrightstown, village (part)	836	448	Brillion, town	568	195
			Brothertown, town. . . .	526	186
Buffalo	**4,048**	**2,525**	Charlestown, town	315	123
Alma, city.	225	173	Chilton, city	1,055	637
Alma, town.	95	78	Chilton, town	449	150
Belvidere, town	149	94	Harrison, town	153	118
Buffalo, town	224	150	Harrison, village (part). .	3,385	2,162
Buffalo City, city.	323	251	Hilbert, village	380	118
Canton, town	80	53	Kaukauna, city (part). . .	0	0
Cochrane, village	105	82	Kiel, city (part).	80	53
Cross, town	132	58	Menasha, city (part) . . .	763	662
Dover, town	128	84	New Holstein, city	912	614
Fountain City, city	192	190	New Holstein, town . . .	517	234
Gilmanton, town	128	62	Potter, village	109	24
Glencoe, town.	165	64	Rantoul, town	312	87
Lincoln, town	78	40	Sherwood, village	1,034	683
Maxville, town.	129	37	Stockbridge, town	629	260
Milton, town.	173	139	Stockbridge, village . . .	237	137
Modena, town.	90	66	Woodville, town	357	111
Mondovi, city	653	443			
Mondovi, town	157	82	**Chippewa**	**17,916**	**11,887**
Montana, town	95	39	Anson, town.	758	441
Naples, town	241	102	Arthur, town.	257	92
Nelson, town	210	88	Auburn, town	220	115
Nelson, village	88	63	Birch Creek, town.	191	116
Waumandee, town. . . .	188	87	Bloomer, city	1,092	577
			Bloomer, town	384	145
Burnett.	**5,410**	**2,949**	Boyd, village.	162	109
Anderson, town.	172	64	Cadott, village.	346	234
Blaine, town	66	31	Chippewa Falls, city . . .	2,982	2,934
Daniels, town	251	102	Cleveland, town.	318	117
Dewey, town.	166	94	Colburn, town.	295	108
Grantsburg, town.	365	163	Cooks Valley, town	267	107
Grantsburg, village. . . .	378	196	Cornell, city	415	207
Jackson, town	321	232	Delmar, town	299	120

Presidential vote by county and municipality, November 8, 2016 general election, continued

	Donald J. Trump/ Michael R. Pence (Rep.)	Hillary Clinton/ Tim Kaine (Dem.)		Donald J. Trump/ Michael R. Pence (Rep.)	Hillary Clinton/ Tim Kaine (Dem.)
Eagle Point, town	1,136	691	Thorp, city	453	250
Eau Claire, city (part). . .	449	463	Thorp, town	193	101
Edson, town	264	146	Unity, town	216	72
Estella, town	162	59	Unity, village (part). . . .	61	9
Goetz, town	258	150	Warner, town	167	62
Hallie, town	43	48	Washburn, town	108	32
Howard, town	245	134	Weston, town	196	100
Lafayette, town	1,880	1,379	Withee, town	191	78
Lake Hallie, village	1,836	1,391	Withee, village	156	71
Lake Holcombe, town . .	397	171	Worden, town	165	55
New Auburn, village (part)	152	46	York, town	222	100
Ruby, town.	158	57	**Columbia**	**14,163**	**13,528**
Sampson, town	344	133	Arlington, town	238	203
Sigel, town.	308	179	Arlington, village	227	215
Stanley, city (part)	540	327	Caledonia, town	369	454
Tilden, town	521	303	Cambria, village.	175	161
Wheaton, town	874	615	Columbus, city (part) . .	1,089	1,381
Woodmohr, town.	363	173	Columbus, town	206	134
Clark	**8,652**	**4,221**	Courtland, town	173	66
Abbotsford, city (part). .	373	232	Dekorra, town.	700	616
Beaver, town.	177	66	Doylestown, village . . .	61	63
Butler, town	36	14	Fall River, village	396	346
Colby, city (part)	339	169	Fort Winnebago, town. .	303	185
Colby, town	177	76	Fountain Prairie, town. .	245	228
Curtiss, village.	32	12	Friesland, village	114	37
Dewhurst, town.	127	66	Hampden, town	193	147
Dorchester, village (part)	197	79	Leeds, town	239	195
Eaton, town	168	60	Lewiston, town	343	305
Foster, town	53	20	Lodi, city	641	998
Fremont, town	348	121	Lodi, town	961	905
Grant, town	266	103	Lowville, town.	321	268
Granton, village.	112	55	Marcellon, town	291	202
Green Grove, town	147	62	Newport, town	216	149
Greenwood, city	285	203	Otsego, town	209	159
Hendren, town	116	63	Pacific, town	848	685
Hewett, town	109	54	Pardeeville, village	523	437
Hixon, town	133	69	Portage, city	1,710	2,033
Hoard, town	164	71	Poynette, village	530	621
Levis, town.	156	61	Randolph, town.	323	78
Longwood, town	141	68	Randolph, village (part) .	154	64
Loyal, city	358	177	Rio, village	246	250
Loyal, town.	189	48	Scott, town.	188	118
Lynn, town.	162	75	Springvale, town	180	120
Mayville, town.	235	100	West Point, town	556	645
Mead, town	89	45	Wisconsin Dells, city (part)	536	509
Mentor, town	147	78	Wyocena, town	487	422
Neillsville, city	595	409	Wyocena, village	172	129
Owen, city	220	174	**Crawford**	**3,836**	**3,419**
Pine Valley, town	400	205	Bell Center, village	19	16
Reseburg, town	109	72	Bridgeport, town	295	220
Seif, town.	62	34	Clayton, town	199	231
Sherman, town	229	81	De Soto, village (part) . .	18	29
Sherwood, town	72	68	Eastman, town	238	141
Stanley, city (part)	1	1	Eastman, village	111	55

Presidential vote by county and municipality, November 8, 2016 general election, continued

	Donald J. Trump/ Michael R. Pence (Rep.)	Hillary Clinton/ Tim Kaine (Dem.)		Donald J. Trump/ Michael R. Pence (Rep.)	Hillary Clinton/ Tim Kaine (Dem.)
Ferryville, village	52	70	Montrose, town	246	429
Freeman, town	208	183	Mount Horeb, village . .	1,205	2,591
Gays Mills, village.	95	119	Oregon, town	713	1,276
Haney, town	72	83	Oregon, village	1,753	3,818
Lynxville, village	43	28	Perry, town	163	306
Marietta, town	156	87	Pleasant Springs, town .	869	1,119
Mount Sterling, village .	33	47	Primrose, town	143	273
Prairie du Chien, city. . .	1,118	1,140	Rockdale, village	30	64
Prairie du Chien, town. .	268	178	Roxbury, town.	453	557
Scott, town.	113	114	Rutland, town	461	738
Seneca, town	238	191	Shorewood Hills, village	121	1,285
Soldiers Grove, village. .	114	117	Springdale, town	455	684
Steuben, village.	34	16	Springfield, town	703	833
Utica, town.	135	173	Stoughton, city	2,107	4,593
Wauzeka, town	119	72	Sun Prairie, city	5,153	10,281
Wauzeka, village	158	109	Sun Prairie, town	594	719
			Vermont, town	174	342
Dane	**71,275**	**217,697**	Verona, city	1,983	4,872
Albion, town.	463	592	Verona, town	462	757
Belleville, village (part) .	303	687	Vienna, town	444	422
Berry, town.	285	415	Waunakee, village	2,840	4,351
Black Earth, town	137	176	Westport, town	1,031	1,607
Black Earth, village	237	498	Windsor, village.	1,679	2,320
Blooming Grove, town .	294	665	York, town	191	194
Blue Mounds, town . . .	239	315			
Blue Mounds, village. . .	152	329	**Dodge**	**26,635**	**13,968**
Bristol, town.	1,100	1,132	Ashippun, town.	1,149	371
Brooklyn, village (part) .	157	331	Beaver Dam, city	3,322	3,398
Burke, town	762	1,076	Beaver Dam, town	1,143	866
Cambridge, village (part)	312	513	Brownsville, village. . . .	216	90
Christiana, town	323	363	Burnett, town	348	135
Cottage Grove, town. . .	921	1,374	Calamus, town	301	181
Cottage Grove, village. .	1,197	2,246	Chester, town	255	96
Cross Plains, town	394	498	Clyman, town	315	87
Cross Plains, village . . .	695	1,344	Clyman, village	110	66
Dane, town	276	222	Columbus, city (part) . .	0	0
Dane, village.	238	268	Elba, town	323	236
Deerfield, town	385	459	Emmet, town	556	178
Deerfield, village	478	735	Fox Lake, city	401	264
DeForest, village	1,720	2,897	Fox Lake, town	485	195
Dunkirk, town	463	683	Hartford, city (part). . . .	0	0
Dunn, town	1,148	1,911	Herman, town	571	98
Edgerton, city (part) . . .	26	28	Horicon, city	1,030	623
Fitchburg, city.	2,923	10,121	Hubbard, town	699	298
Madison, city	23,052	120,178	Hustisford, town	624	177
Madison, town	253	1,999	Hustisford, village	405	141
Maple Bluff, village. . . .	294	690	Iron Ridge, village	332	120
Marshall, village.	694	937	Juneau, city	563	353
Mazomanie, town	262	347	Kekoskee, village	54	25
Mazomanie, village . . .	304	551	Lebanon, town	661	225
McFarland, village	1,465	3,123	Leroy, town	387	112
Medina, town	342	378	Lomira, town	493	118
Middleton, city	2,488	8,727	Lomira, village.	812	317
Middleton, town	1,470	2,313	Lowell, town.	403	152
Monona, city	1,050	4,145	Lowell, village	112	41

Presidential vote by county and municipality, November 8, 2016 general election, continued

	Donald J. Trump/ Michael R. Pence (Rep.)	Hillary Clinton/ Tim Kaine (Dem.)		Donald J. Trump/ Michael R. Pence (Rep.)	Hillary Clinton/ Tim Kaine (Dem.)
Mayville, city.	1,605	836	Superior, city	4,642	6,828
Neosho, village	242	74	Superior, town	645	593
Oak Grove, town	363	184	Superior, village.	175	203
Portland, town	344	212	Wascott, town.	273	195
Randolph, village (part) .	364	208			
Reeseville, village.	190	102	**Dunn**	**11,486**	**9,034**
Rubicon, town.	1,063	225	Boyceville, village.	256	157
Shields, town.	228	99	Colfax, town	365	209
Theresa, town	464	123	Colfax, village	278	226
Theresa, village	477	183	Downing, village	89	28
Trenton, town	513	179	Dunn, town	396	337
Watertown, city (part) . .	2,563	1,474	Eau Galle, town	295	124
Waupun, city (part). . . .	1,355	755	Elk Mound, town	563	278
Westford, town	446	250	Elk Mound, village	182	150
Williamstown, town . . .	348	101	Grant, town	146	90
			Hay River, town	177	102
Door.	**8,580**	**8,014**	Knapp, village	162	56
Baileys Harbor, town. . .	327	441	Lucas, town	252	133
Brussels, town.	374	200	Menomonie, city	2,940	3,862
Clay Banks, town	129	104	Menomonie, town	911	730
Egg Harbor, town.	472	400	New Haven, town.	216	95
Egg Harbor, village.	80	113	Otter Creek, town	155	90
Ephraim, village.	89	140	Peru, town	78	38
Forestville, town	335	206	Red Cedar, town	703	449
Forestville, village	144	86	Ridgeland, village	61	48
Gardner, town.	424	245	Rock Creek, town.	315	198
Gibraltar, town	325	428	Sand Creek, town.	176	114
Jacksonport, town	275	232	Sheridan, town	169	63
Liberty Grove, town . . .	582	733	Sherman, town	318	163
Nasewaupee, town. . . .	703	461	Spring Brook, town. . . .	552	290
Sevastopol, town	974	780	Stanton, town	297	117
Sister Bay, village	267	358	Tainter, town.	795	556
Sturgeon Bay, city	2,120	2,447	Tiffany, town.	242	82
Sturgeon Bay, town . . .	271	224	Weston, town	187	97
Union, town	388	190	Wheeler, village.	57	49
Washington, town	301	226	Wilson, town.	153	103
Douglas	**9,661**	**11,357**	**Eau Claire**	**23,331**	**27,340**
Amnicon, town	303	307	Altoona, city.	1,717	1,816
Bennett, town.	209	140	Augusta, city.	361	232
Brule, town.	145	207	Bridge Creek, town. . . .	362	219
Cloverland, town	75	46	Brunswick, town	541	453
Dairyland, town.	82	24	Clear Creek, town.	252	149
Gordon, town	247	186	Drammen, town	239	164
Hawthorne, town.	328	246	Eau Claire, city (part). . .	13,077	19,185
Highland, town	103	97	Fairchild, town	100	37
Lake Nebagamon, village	381	288	Fairchild, village.	119	72
Lakeside, town	191	164	Fall Creek, village.	371	303
Maple, town	167	194	Lincoln, town	340	214
Oakland, town	305	336	Ludington, town	332	205
Oliver, village	97	143	Otter Creek, town	149	84
Parkland, town	306	336	Pleasant Valley, town . .	1,239	818
Poplar, village	210	123	Seymour, town	1,019	838
Solon Springs, town . . .	336	229	Union, town	755	610
Solon Springs, village . .	186	160	Washington, town	2,210	1,888
Summit, town	255	312	Wilson, town.	148	53

Presidential vote by county and municipality, November 8, 2016 general election, continued

	Donald J. Trump/ Michael R. Pence (Rep.)	Hillary Clinton/ Tim Kaine (Dem.)		Donald J. Trump/ Michael R. Pence (Rep.)	Hillary Clinton/ Tim Kaine (Dem.)
Florence	**1,898**	**665**	Laona, town	359	213
Aurora, town.	407	127	Lincoln, town	292	206
Commonwealth, town. .	161	60	Nashville, town	314	244
Fence, town	104	26	Popple River, town	10	12
Fern, town	94	23	Ross, town	57	11
Florence, town	782	335	Wabeno, town.	260	169
Homestead, town	185	52	**Grant**	**12,350**	**10,051**
Long Lake, town	76	29	Bagley, village.	92	84
Tipler, town	89	13	Beetown, town	216	79
			Bloomington, town . . .	142	53
Fond du Lac	**31,022**	**17,387**	Bloomington, village . .	203	134
Alto, town	506	68	Blue River, village.	91	84
Ashford, town	745	204	Boscobel, city	599	528
Auburn, town	1,084	265	Boscobel, town	90	82
Brandon, village	293	113	Cassville, town	123	59
Byron, town	697	212	Cassville, village	202	176
Calumet, town	564	229	Castle Rock, town.	87	47
Campbellsport, village .	643	242	Clifton, town	63	59
Eden, town.	473	121	Cuba City, city (part) . . .	384	400
Eden, village.	278	101	Dickeyville, village	274	223
Eldorado, town	608	197	Ellenboro, town.	178	95
Empire, town	1,095	546	Fennimore, city	550	452
Fairwater, village	111	43	Fennimore, town	152	73
Fond du Lac, city	9,988	7,900	Glen Haven, town	127	50
Fond du Lac, town	1,203	654	Harrison, town	157	87
Forest, town	485	141	Hazel Green, town	286	315
Friendship, town	931	425	Hazel Green, village (part)	261	271
Kewaskum, village (part)	0	0	Hickory Grove, town . . .	105	59
Lamartine, town	722	243	Jamestown, town.	644	349
Marshfield, town	444	168	Lancaster, city	902	710
Metomen, town	282	87	Liberty, town	145	72
Mount Calvary, village. .	203	71	Lima, town.	185	138
North Fond du Lac, village	1,229	978	Little Grant, town.	90	46
Oakfield, town.	259	97	Livingston, village (part)	124	134
Oakfield, village.	383	180	Marion, town	141	76
Osceola, town	801	251	Millville, town	47	41
Ripon, city	1,817	1,567	Montfort, village (part) .	122	124
Ripon, town	479	251	Mount Hope, town	68	32
Rosendale, town	284	99	Mount Hope, village . . .	40	30
Rosendale, village	397	159	Mount Ida, town	172	82
Springvale, town	282	91	Muscoda, town	190	98
St. Cloud, village	213	87	Muscoda, village (part) .	249	202
Taycheedah, town	1,818	856	North Lancaster, town. .	183	77
Waupun, city (part). . . .	1,157	540	Paris, town	237	125
Waupun, town	548	201	Patch Grove, town	92	63
			Patch Grove, village . . .	45	37
Forest	**2,787**	**1,579**	Platteville, city.	2,410	2,859
Alvin, town.	69	28	Platteville, town.	396	352
Argonne, town	187	71	Potosi, town	246	157
Armstrong Creek, town .	154	64	Potosi, village	198	143
Blackwell, town	37	17	Smelser, town	245	180
Caswell, town	35	12	South Lancaster, town. .	184	118
Crandon, city	504	253	Tennyson, village	99	68
Crandon, town	205	116	Waterloo, town	157	88
Freedom, town	143	74	Watterstown, town. . . .	91	65
Hiles, town	161	89			

Presidential vote by county and municipality, November 8, 2016 general election, continued

	Donald J. Trump/ Michael R. Pence (Rep.)	Hillary Clinton/ Tim Kaine (Dem.)		Donald J. Trump/ Michael R. Pence (Rep.)	Hillary Clinton/ Tim Kaine (Dem.)
Wingville, town	80	60	Brigham, town	229	372
Woodman, town	55	24	Clyde, town	68	111
Woodman, village	24	14	Cobb, village.	96	126
Wyalusing, town	107	77	Dodgeville, city	842	1,340
			Dodgeville, town	391	515
Green	**8,693**	**9,122**	Eden, town.	99	93
Adams, town	146	137	Highland, town	183	176
Albany, town	339	275	Highland, village	175	195
Albany, village.	198	245	Hollandale, village	31	104
Belleville, village (part) .	97	169	Linden, town	207	157
Brodhead, city (part). . .	688	563	Linden, village.	92	120
Brooklyn, town	294	352	Livingston, village (part)	2	0
Brooklyn, village (part) .	87	143	Mifflin, town	145	108
Browntown, village . . .	67	43	Mineral Point, city	463	839
Cadiz, town	274	161	Mineral Point, town . . .	243	215
Clarno, town.	376	232	Montfort, village (part) .	22	31
Decatur, town	499	389	Moscow, town.	136	185
Exeter, town	406	682	Muscoda, village (part) .	7	6
Jefferson, town	395	193	Pulaski, town	96	79
Jordan, town	174	129	Rewey, village.	38	55
Monroe, city	2,167	2,486	Ridgeway, town.	126	212
Monroe, town.	371	301	Ridgeway, village.	135	155
Monticello, village	239	353	Waldwick, town.	97	140
Mount Pleasant, town . .	158	151	Wyoming, town.	61	144
New Glarus, town.	338	441			
New Glarus, village. . . .	362	773	**Iron**	**2,081**	**1,275**
Spring Grove, town . . .	275	162	Anderson, town.	23	22
Sylvester, town	312	225	Carey, town	62	28
Washington, town	212	223	Gurney, town	41	41
York, town	219	294	Hurley, city.	396	281
			Kimball, town	171	112
Green Lake	**6,216**	**2,693**	Knight, town.	57	38
Berlin, city (part)	1,348	774	Mercer, town	634	309
Berlin, town	491	145	Montreal, city	232	175
Brooklyn, town	732	325	Oma, town.	155	84
Green Lake, city.	330	205	Pence, town	50	47
Green Lake, town.	503	169	Saxon, town	130	74
Kingston, town	203	60	Sherman, town	130	64
Kingston, village	114	43			
Mackford, town	237	42	**Jackson**.	**4,906**	**3,818**
Manchester, town	256	87	Adams, town	427	301
Markesan, city.	477	174	Albion, town.	345	248
Marquette, town	194	73	Alma, town.	281	152
Marquette, village	52	31	Alma Center, village . . .	102	96
Princeton, city.	384	182	Bear Bluff, town.	69	6
Princeton, town.	584	251	Black River Falls, city . . .	691	750
St. Marie, town	159	65	Brockway, town.	331	432
Seneca, town	152	67	City Point, town.	63	33
			Cleveland, town.	154	80
Iowa.	**4,809**	**6,669**	Curran, town.	85	69
Arena, town	325	436	Franklin, town.	100	91
Arena, village	150	222	Garden Valley, town . . .	142	74
Avoca, village	108	105	Garfield, town.	214	97
Barneveld, village.	215	375	Hixton, town.	203	99
Blanchardville, village			Hixton, village.	110	95
(part).	27	53	Irving, town	191	145

Presidential vote by county and municipality, November 8, 2016 general election, continued

	Donald J. Trump/ Michael R. Pence (Rep.)	Hillary Clinton/ Tim Kaine (Dem.)		Donald J. Trump/ Michael R. Pence (Rep.)	Hillary Clinton/ Tim Kaine (Dem.)
Knapp, town	141	47	Lyndon, town	328	267
Komensky, town	28	114	Lyndon Station, village .	97	90
Manchester, town	250	118	Marion, town	177	64
Melrose, town	135	81	Mauston, city	840	679
Melrose, village	119	129	Necedah, town	837	297
Merrillan, village	107	116	Necedah, village	219	138
Millston, town	59	30	New Lisbon, city	389	177
North Bend, town	136	120	Orange, town	172	89
Northfield, town	212	130	Plymouth, town	187	106
Springfield, town	114	94	Seven Mile Creek, town .	97	65
Taylor, village	97	71	Summit, town	202	112
			Union Center, village . .	60	33
Jefferson	**23,417**	**16,569**	Wisconsin Dells, city (part)	0	0
Aztalan, town	446	304	Wonewoc, town.	207	105
Cambridge, village (part)	11	30	Wonewoc, village.	178	133
Cold Spring, town	278	167			
Concord, town	799	337	**Kenosha**	**36,037**	**35,799**
Farmington, town	583	246	Brighton, town	589	259
Fort Atkinson, city	2,537	2,905	Bristol, village	1,819	854
Hebron, town	397	170	Genoa City, village (part)	0	0
Ixonia, town	1,875	666	Kenosha, city	15,835	22,873
Jefferson, city	1,705	1,547	Paddock Lake, village . .	834	495
Jefferson, town	749	383	Paris, town	568	293
Johnson Creek, village. .	844	554	Pleasant Prairie, village .	5,814	4,644
Koshkonong, town. . . .	1,211	769	Randall, town	1,105	518
Lac La Belle, village (part)	0	0	Salem, town	3,589	1,832
Lake Mills, city.	1,394	1,669	Silver Lake, village	751	383
Lake Mills, town.	561	575	Somers, town	296	232
Milford, town	362	222	Somers, village	2,123	1,900
Oakland, town	829	894	Twin Lakes, village	1,595	959
Palmyra, town.	487	234	Wheatland, town	1,119	557
Palmyra, village	581	264			
Sullivan, town	882	360	**Kewaunee**	**6,618**	**3,627**
Sullivan, village	222	104	Ahnapee, town	258	191
Sumner, town	291	203	Algoma, city	696	694
Waterloo, city	782	712	Carlton, town	368	181
Waterloo, town	282	191	Casco, town	425	179
Watertown, city (part) . .	3,981	2,120	Casco, village	184	83
Watertown, town.	771	286	Franklin, town.	356	184
Whitewater, city (part). .	557	657	Kewaunee, city	795	534
			Lincoln, town	316	142
Juneau	**7,130**	**4,073**	Luxemburg, town.	609	195
Armenia, town	231	115	Luxemburg, village. . . .	809	393
Camp Douglas, village. .	183	81	Montpelier, town.	530	223
Clearfield, town.	245	128	Pierce, town	229	193
Cutler, town	135	60	Red River, town	522	250
Elroy, city.	289	220	West Kewaunee, town. .	521	185
Finley, town	52	13			
Fountain, town	200	86	**La Crosse**	**26,378**	**32,406**
Germantown, town . . .	550	252	Bangor, town	172	104
Hustler, village	57	45	Bangor, village	353	340
Kildare, town	189	101	Barre, town.	459	228
Kingston, town	18	2	Burns, town	306	188
Lemonweir, town.	473	285	Campbell, town.	1,104	1,192
Lindina, town	214	164	Farmington, town	585	445
Lisbon, town	304	166	Greenfield, town	571	545

Presidential vote by county and municipality, November 8, 2016 general election, continued

	Donald J. Trump/ Michael R. Pence (Rep.)	Hillary Clinton/ Tim Kaine (Dem.)		Donald J. Trump/ Michael R. Pence (Rep.)	Hillary Clinton/ Tim Kaine (Dem.)
Hamilton, town	828	533	Price, town	86	42
Holland, town	1,274	934	Rolling, town	537	221
Holmen, village	2,188	2,234	Summit, town	69	22
La Crosse, city	9,050	15,948	Upham, town	325	160
Medary, town	440	462	Vilas, town	95	27
Onalaska, city	4,423	4,850	White Lake, village	86	56
Onalaska, town	1,718	1,380	Wolf River, town	303	135
Rockland, village (part) .	157	124			
Shelby, town	1,298	1,527	**Lincoln**	**8,401**	**5,371**
Washington, town	155	145	Birch, town	163	72
West Salem, village. . . .	1,297	1,227	Bradley, town	837	543
			Corning, town	293	144
Lafayette	**3,977**	**3,288**	Harding, town	146	87
Argyle, town	116	108	Harrison, town	327	194
Argyle, village	137	193	King, town	342	234
Belmont, town	184	118	Merrill, city	2,030	1,707
Belmont, village	214	199	Merrill, town	988	549
Benton, town	156	77	Pine River, town.	679	347
Benton, village	190	222	Rock Falls, town.	232	115
Blanchard, town	66	91	Russell, town	191	103
Blanchardville, village			Schley, town	322	131
(part)	105	178	Scott, town.	497	247
Cuba City, city (part) . . .	57	59	Skanawan, town	139	82
Darlington, city	454	504	Somo, town	47	14
Darlington, town	295	179	Tomahawk, city	853	651
Elk Grove, town	131	66	Tomahawk, town	184	88
Fayette, town	104	66	Wilson, town.	131	63
Gratiot, town	182	91			
Gratiot, village	48	51	**Manitowoc**	**23,244**	**14,538**
Hazel Green, village (part)	7	3	Cato, town	585	255
Kendall, town	112	57	Centerville, town	241	128
Lamont, town	84	66	Cleveland, village.	438	288
Monticello, town	46	14	Cooperstown, town . . .	468	228
New Diggings, town . . .	137	89	Eaton, town	310	139
Seymour, town	95	61	Francis Creek, village . .	222	114
Shullsburg, city	217	263	Franklin, town.	431	190
Shullsburg, town	87	70	Gibson, town	475	231
South Wayne, village. . .	116	72	Kellnersville, village . . .	100	57
Wayne, town.	155	63	Kiel, city (part).	1,093	633
White Oak Springs, town	44	18	Kossuth, town	730	355
Willow Springs, town . .	213	130	Liberty, town	512	180
Wiota, town	225	180	Manitowoc, city	7,806	6,341
			Manitowoc, town.	372	178
Langlade	**6,478**	**3,250**	Manitowoc Rapids, town	907	430
Ackley, town.	185	84	Maple Grove, town. . . .	352	80
Ainsworth, town	186	81	Maribel, village	106	57
Antigo, city.	1,953	1,288	Meeme, town	540	245
Antigo, town.	536	224	Mishicot, town	466	190
Elcho, town	495	246	Mishicot, village	455	253
Evergreen, town	195	72	Newton, town.	890	352
Langlade, town	180	90	Reedsville, village	364	165
Neva, town.	318	152	Rockland, town	392	119
Norwood, town	370	136	St. Nazianz, village	229	96
Parrish, town	41	14	Schleswig, town	721	363
Peck, town	139	43	Two Creeks, town.	145	69
Polar, town	379	157	Two Rivers, city	2,727	2,175

Presidential vote by county and municipality, November 8, 2016 general election, continued

	Donald J. Trump/ Michael R. Pence (Rep.)	Hillary Clinton/ Tim Kaine (Dem.)		Donald J. Trump/ Michael R. Pence (Rep.)	Hillary Clinton/ Tim Kaine (Dem.)
Two Rivers, town	593	347	Schofield, city	569	478
Valders, village	339	152	Spencer, town	531	233
Whitelaw, village	235	128	Spencer, village	543	298
			Stettin, town	932	479
Marathon	**39,014**	**26,481**	Stratford, village	537	217
Abbotsford, city (part). .	85	58	Texas, town	631	321
Athens, village	356	165	Unity, village (part). . . .	80	22
Bergen, town	254	165	Wausau, city	7,905	8,646
Berlin, town	380	132	Wausau, town	809	422
Bern, town	149	68	Weston, town	217	95
Bevent, town	347	247	Weston, village	4,059	2,964
Birnamwood, village (part)	4	7	Wien, town.	275	125
Brighton, town	204	41			
Brokaw, village	55	75	**Marinette**	**13,122**	**6,409**
Cassel, town	353	161	Amberg, town.	315	125
Cleveland, town.	513	222	Athelstane, town	215	93
Colby, city (part)	131	85	Beaver, town.	447	139
Day, town	413	165	Beecher, town.	285	104
Dorchester, village (part)	1	0	Coleman, village	227	102
Easton, town.	486	193	Crivitz, village	300	136
Eau Pleine, town	275	92	Dunbar, town	188	79
Edgar, village	442	267	Goodman, town	214	119
Elderon, town	235	97	Grover, town.	682	205
Elderon, village	59	28	Lake, town	466	175
Emmet, town	316	177	Marinette, city.	2,479	1,745
Fenwood, village	49	25	Middle Inlet, town	303	131
Frankfort, town	213	73	Niagara, city	444	233
Franzen, town.	209	80	Niagara, town	354	131
Green Valley, town	202	100	Pembine, town	280	134
Guenther, town	142	64	Peshtigo, city	895	516
Halsey, town.	187	61	Peshtigo, town	1,443	732
Hamburg, town	280	136	Porterfield, town	690	316
Harrison, town	121	49	Pound, town.	517	135
Hatley, village	192	82	Pound, village	110	30
Hewitt, town.	232	102	Silver Cliff, town.	216	95
Holton, town	300	84	Stephenson, town	1,240	569
Hull, town	226	68	Wagner, town	266	110
Johnson, town	239	107	Wausaukee, town.	415	189
Knowlton, town	685	409	Wausaukee, village. . . .	131	66
Kronenwetter, village . .	2,374	1,480			
Maine, village	904	486	**Marquette**	**4,709**	**2,808**
Marathon, town.	422	154	Buffalo, town	336	221
Marathon City, village . .	540	261	Crystal Lake, town	183	107
Marshfield, city (part) . .	222	175	Douglas, town.	277	181
McMillan, town	700	430	Endeavor, village	111	63
Mosinee, city	1,344	805	Harris, town	293	167
Mosinee, town	789	410	Mecan, town.	217	142
Norrie, town	330	173	Montello, city	348	289
Plover, town	223	111	Montello, town	370	191
Reid, town	410	244	Moundville, town.	137	99
Rib Falls, town.	410	124	Neshkoro, town.	218	108
Rib Mountain, town . . .	2,480	1,667	Neshkoro, village	123	69
Rietbrock, town.	330	136	Newton, town	158	69
Ringle, town	633	357	Oxford, town	295	157
Rothschild, village	1,480	1,283	Oxford, village.	153	86

Presidential vote by county and municipality, November 8, 2016 general election, continued

	Donald J. Trump/ Michael R. Pence (Rep.)	Hillary Clinton/ Tim Kaine (Dem.)		Donald J. Trump/ Michael R. Pence (Rep.)	Hillary Clinton/ Tim Kaine (Dem.)
Packwaukee, town	426	258	Sheldon, town.	156	55
Shields, town	202	106	Sparta, city.	1,884	1,646
Springfield, town	289	158	Sparta, town.	904	567
Westfield, town	275	154	Tomah, city	2,079	1,494
Westfield, village	298	183	Tomah, town	468	230
			Warrens, village.	146	59
Menominee	**267**	**1,002**	Wellington, town	125	108
Menominee, town	267	1,002	Wells, town.	171	90
			Wilton, town.	156	64
Milwaukee.	**126,069**	**288,822**	Wilton, village.	106	102
Bayside, village (part) . .	866	1,849	Wyeville, village.	36	19
Brown Deer, village . . .	2,038	4,408			
Cudahy, city	3,939	4,514	**Oconto . . . .**	**13,345**	**5,940**
Fox Point, village	1,425	2,790	Abrams, town	714	281
Franklin, city.	10,569	8,048	Bagley, town.	133	42
Glendale, city	2,309	5,313	Brazeau, town.	560	222
Greendale, village	4,136	3,815	Breed, town	267	79
Greenfield, city	9,290	8,767	Chase, town	1,057	455
Hales Corners, village . .	2,389	1,722	Doty, town	129	64
Milwaukee, city (part) . .	45,422	188,700	Gillett, city	358	196
Oak Creek, city	9,039	7,639	Gillett, town	439	94
River Hills, village.	494	585	How, town	229	72
St. Francis, city	2,002	2,676	Lakewood, town	365	192
Shorewood, village. . . .	1,407	6,527	Lena, town	264	98
South Milwaukee, city. .	4,757	4,818	Lena, village	164	84
Wauwatosa, city	10,037	16,314	Little River, town	379	154
West Allis, city.	12,808	13,668	Little Suamico, town . . .	1,922	774
West Milwaukee, village.	478	1,025	Maple Valley, town	269	86
Whitefish Bay, village . .	2,664	5,644	Morgan, town	408	136
			Mountain, town.	288	160
Monroe.	**11,356**	**7,052**	Oconto, city	1,179	737
Adrian, town.	280	118	Oconto, town	496	222
Angelo, town.	388	202	Oconto Falls, city	786	375
Byron, town	373	184	Oconto Falls, town	446	184
Cashton, village.	236	185	Pensaukee, town	524	243
Clifton, town.	136	79	Pulaski, village (part). . .	0	0
Glendale, town	197	89	Riverview, town.	287	193
Grant, town	181	49	Spruce, town	322	131
Greenfield, town	251	122	Stiles, town	527	246
Jefferson, town	171	105	Suring, village.	153	50
Kendall, village	110	79	Townsend, town	396	252
La Grange, town	627	336	Underhill, town	284	118
Lafayette, town	113	51			
Leon, town.	384	176	**Oneida . . . .**	**12,132**	**8,109**
Lincoln, town	319	94	Cassian, town	393	250
Little Falls, town	436	214	Crescent, town	712	525
Melvina, village	22	16	Enterprise, town	147	72
New Lyme, town	65	28	Hazelhurst, town	484	332
Norwalk, village.	108	92	Lake Tomahawk, town. .	399	224
Oakdale, town.	259	101	Little Rice, town.	159	58
Oakdale, village	69	37	Lynne, town	56	20
Ontario, village (part)	0	0	Minocqua, town	1,922	1,026
Portland, town	226	157	Monico, town	110	40
Ridgeville, town.	137	99	Newbold, town	965	670
Rockland, village (part) .	0	0	Nokomis, town	473	340
Scott, town.	37	5	Pelican, town	807	603

Presidential vote by county and municipality, November 8, 2016 general election, continued

	Donald J. Trump/ Michael R. Pence (Rep.)	Hillary Clinton/ Tim Kaine (Dem.)		Donald J. Trump/ Michael R. Pence (Rep.)	Hillary Clinton/ Tim Kaine (Dem.)
Piehl, town	32	17	Grafton, village	3,981	2,581
Pine Lake, town	852	658	Mequon, city	8,165	6,385
Rhinelander, city	1,504	1,540	Newburg, village (part) .	30	8
Schoepke, town	136	90	Port Washington, city . .	3,355	2,692
Stella, town	200	156	Port Washington, town .	606	282
Sugar Camp, town	717	361	Saukville, town	869	258
Three Lakes, town	1,026	448	Saukville, village	1,371	749
Woodboro, town	292	196	Thiensville, village	1,023	870
Woodruff, town	746	483			
			Pepin	**2,206**	**1,344**
Outagamie	**49,879**	**38,068**	Albany, town	191	111
Appleton, city (part) . . .	13,146	15,065	Durand, city	526	308
Bear Creek, village	85	52	Durand, town	252	98
Black Creek, town	460	194	Frankfort, town	98	67
Black Creek, village. . . .	428	191	Lima, town	200	98
Bovina, town	427	184	Pepin, town	226	160
Buchanan, town	2,110	1,497	Pepin, village	173	223
Center, town.	1,421	572	Stockholm, town	72	65
Cicero, town	312	175	Stockholm, village	22	27
Combined Locks, village	1,130	793	Waterville, town	290	114
Dale, town	1,100	413	Waubeek, town	156	73
Deer Creek, town	195	74			
Ellington, town	1,208	385	**Pierce**	**11,272**	**8,399**
Freedom, town	2,086	972	Bay City, village	129	67
Grand Chute, town	6,141	4,862	Clifton, town.	701	461
Greenville, town	4,226	1,963	Diamond Bluff, town. . .	183	73
Harrison, village (part). .	0	0	El Paso, town	226	128
Hortonia, town	427	177	Ellsworth, town	390	208
Hortonville, village	907	494	Ellsworth, village	779	518
Howard, village (part) . .	0	0	Elmwood, village	247	121
Kaukauna, city (part). . .	3,722	3,333	Gilman, town	309	229
Kaukauna, town	507	192	Hartland, town	346	120
Kimberly, village	1,749	1,562	Isabelle, town	91	57
Liberty, town	365	131	Maiden Rock, town. . . .	216	107
Little Chute, village . . .	2,933	2,123	Maiden Rock, village. . .	48	31
Maine, town	289	139	Martell, town	369	260
Maple Creek, town	223	80	Oak Grove, town	761	433
New London, city (part).	382	223	Plum City, village	163	109
Nichols, village	89	19	Prescott, city	1,125	845
Oneida, town	991	830	River Falls, city (part). . .	2,293	2,735
Osborn, town	476	196	River Falls, town.	640	654
Seymour, city	1,003	580	Rock Elm, town	122	94
Seymour, town	447	149	Salem, town	165	86
Shiocton, village	238	146	Spring Lake, town	202	107
Vandenbroek, town . . .	581	268	Spring Valley, village (part)	345	295
Wrightstown, village (part)	75	34	Trenton, town	579	315
			Trimbelle, town	611	274
Ozaukee	**30,464**	**20,170**	Union, town	232	72
Bayside, village (part) . .	28	46			
Belgium, town	560	273	**Polk**	**13,810**	**7,565**
Belgium, village.	826	349	Alden, town	994	463
Cedarburg, city	3,618	3,009	Amery, city.	692	562
Cedarburg, town	2,543	1,199	Apple River, town.	364	205
Fredonia, town	929	261	Balsam Lake, town	508	254
Fredonia, village	828	332	Balsam Lake, village . . .	267	144
Grafton, town	1,732	876	Beaver, town.	278	145

Presidential vote by county and municipality, November 8, 2016 general election, continued

	Donald J. Trump/ Michael R. Pence (Rep.)	Hillary Clinton/ Tim Kaine (Dem.)		Donald J. Trump/ Michael R. Pence (Rep.)	Hillary Clinton/ Tim Kaine (Dem.)
Black Brook, town	482	204	Rosholt, village	144	92
Bone Lake, town	235	142	Sharon, town	707	461
Centuria, village	188	103	Stevens Point, city	4,659	7,888
Clam Falls, town	178	89	Stockton, town	951	745
Clayton, town	280	183	Whiting, village	421	506
Clayton, village	125	58			
Clear Lake, town	309	104	**Price**.	**4,559**	**2,667**
Clear Lake, village	334	148	Catawba, town	82	41
Dresser, village	235	149	Catawba, village	30	24
Eureka, town.	605	258	Eisenstein, town	205	131
Farmington, town	705	275	Elk, town	368	221
Frederic, village	283	187	Emery, town	112	67
Garfield, town	558	270	Fifield, town	333	206
Georgetown, town	301	225	Flambeau, town.	185	86
Johnstown, town	132	116	Georgetown, town	66	19
Laketown, town.	347	189	Hackett, town	74	37
Lincoln, town	790	395	Harmony, town	88	39
Lorain, town	105	44	Hill, town	142	48
Luck, town	335	172	Kennan, town	104	57
Luck, village	294	232	Kennan, village	38	23
McKinley, town	121	56	Knox, town.	94	64
Milltown, town	416	225	Lake, town	376	263
Milltown, village	246	114	Ogema, town	292	105
Osceola, town	986	518	Park Falls, city	545	469
Osceola, village	644	447	Phillips, city	329	260
St. Croix Falls, city. . . .	571	455	Prentice, town.	163	60
St. Croix Falls, town. . . .	415	204	Prentice, village	177	82
Sterling, town	221	95	Spirit, town	122	43
Turtle Lake, village (part)	22	10	Worcester, town.	634	322
West Sweden, town . . .	244	125			
			Racine	**46,681**	**42,641**
Portage.	**17,305**	**18,529**	Burlington, city (part) . .	2,875	2,005
Alban, town	258	216	Burlington, town	2,195	1,059
Almond, town.	260	113	Caledonia, village.	8,076	5,768
Almond, village	116	69	Dover, town	1,332	524
Amherst, town	431	376	Elmwood Park, village. .	147	150
Amherst, village	260	262	Mount Pleasant, village .	7,291	6,784
Amherst Junction, village	118	76	North Bay, village.	63	78
Belmont, town	213	121	Norway, town	3,453	1,141
Buena Vista, town	411	228	Racine, city.	8,955	19,147
Carson, town	484	297	Raymond, town	1,628	671
Dewey, town.	298	251	Rochester, village.	1,527	588
Eau Pleine, town	343	217	Sturtevant, village	1,374	1,142
Grant, town	695	376	Union Grove, village . . .	1,475	714
Hull, town	1,558	1,511	Waterford, town	2,655	914
Junction City, village. . .	99	77	Waterford, village.	1,873	880
Lanark, town.	474	348	Wind Point, village	582	551
Linwood, town	373	271	Yorkville, town	1,180	525
Milladore, village (part) .	2	1			
Nelsonville, village	35	53	**Richland**	**4,013**	**3,569**
New Hope, town	182	273	Akan, town.	117	87
Park Ridge, village	136	186	Bloom, town.	116	95
Pine Grove, town	232	121	Boaz, village	23	33
Plover, town	514	318	Buena Vista, town	416	317
Plover, village	2,931	3,076	Cazenovia, village (part)	68	75
			Dayton, town	177	135

Presidential vote by county and municipality, November 8, 2016 general election, continued

	Donald J. Trump/ Michael R. Pence (Rep.)	Hillary Clinton/ Tim Kaine (Dem.)		Donald J. Trump/ Michael R. Pence (Rep.)	Hillary Clinton/ Tim Kaine (Dem.)
Eagle, town	138	81	Flambeau, town.	363	150
Forest, town	89	83	Glen Flora, village	23	11
Henrietta, town	110	121	Grant, town	236	114
Ithaca, town	158	136	Grow, town	169	33
Lone Rock, village	166	181	Hawkins, town	43	21
Marshall, town	174	104	Hawkins, village.	94	52
Orion, town	141	121	Hubbard, town	69	21
Richland, town	373	243	Ingram, village	20	10
Richland Center, city. . .	999	1,057	Ladysmith, city	792	507
Richwood, town	109	122	Lawrence, town.	90	26
Rockbridge, town	182	165	Marshall, town	148	47
Sylvan, town.	116	81	Murry, town	89	36
Viola, village (part)	71	95	Richland, town	64	39
Westford, town	133	118	Rusk, town	193	113
Willow, town.	122	103	Sheldon, village.	65	30
Yuba, village.	15	16	South Fork, town	47	18
			Strickland, town	92	64
Rock.	**31,493**	**39,339**	Stubbs, town	202	98
Avon, town.	204	116	Thornapple, town	316	90
Beloit, city	4,732	7,926	Tony, village	38	16
Beloit, town	2,063	1,783	True, town	99	46
Bradford, town	304	187	Washington, town	131	80
Brodhead, city (part). . .	13	14	Weyerhaeuser, village . .	56	43
Center, town.	293	299	Wilkinson, town.	21	7
Clinton, town	284	145	Willard, town	166	67
Clinton, village	527	361	Wilson, town.	49	12
Edgerton, city (part) . . .	918	1,635			
Evansville, city.	907	1,701	**St. Croix**	**26,222**	**17,482**
Footville, village	199	180	Baldwin, town.	346	151
Fulton, town.	926	908	Baldwin, village.	1,052	698
Harmony, town	753	717	Cady, town.	306	131
Janesville, city.	11,668	16,146	Cylon, town	236	108
Janesville, town.	1,041	1,036	Deer Park, village	82	21
Johnstown, town	251	192	Eau Galle, town	397	210
La Prairie, town	255	185	Emerald, town.	264	124
Lima, town.	325	252	Erin Prairie, town	240	129
Magnolia, town	184	188	Forest, town	220	72
Milton, city.	1,233	1,465	Glenwood, town	262	92
Milton, town.	843	721	Glenwood City, city . . .	338	186
Newark, town	524	317	Hammond, town	834	311
Orfordville, village	294	323	Hammond, village	481	341
Plymouth, town.	391	250	Hudson, city.	3,425	3,430
Porter, town	234	350	Hudson, town.	2,866	1,760
Rock, town.	663	641	Kinnickinnic, town	561	419
Spring Valley, town. . . .	224	163	New Richmond, city . . .	2,097	1,627
Turtle, town	814	526	North Hudson, village. .	1,108	930
Union, town	426	612	Pleasant Valley, town . .	146	110
			Richmond, town	1,150	575
Rusk.	**4,564**	**2,171**	River Falls, city (part). . .	816	928
Atlanta, town	221	82	Roberts, village	422	322
Big Bend, town	167	90	Rush River, town	162	101
Big Falls, town.	51	26	St. Joseph, town	1,375	908
Bruce, village	211	121	Somerset, town.	1,484	709
Cedar Rapids, town . . .	19	7	Somerset, village.	704	362
Conrath, village.	22	15	Spring Valley, village (part)	6	0
Dewey, town.	198	79			

Presidential vote by county and municipality, November 8, 2016 general election, continued

	Donald J. Trump/ Michael R. Pence (Rep.)	Hillary Clinton/ Tim Kaine (Dem.)		Donald J. Trump/ Michael R. Pence (Rep.)	Hillary Clinton/ Tim Kaine (Dem.)
Springfield, town	317	148	Exeland, village	51	32
Stanton, town	303	172	Hayward, city	558	393
Star Prairie, town	1,214	572	Hayward, town	975	674
Star Prairie, village	183	99	Hunter, town	197	186
Troy, town	1,779	1,219	Lenroot, town	492	299
Warren, town	633	294	Meadowbrook, town . .	65	12
Wilson, village.	57	30	Meteor, town	55	25
Woodville, village.	356	193	Ojibwa, town	113	51
			Radisson, town	152	64
Sauk.	**14,799**	**14,690**	Radisson, village	50	30
Baraboo, city.	2,361	2,900	Round Lake, town	403	243
Baraboo, town.	520	476	Sand Lake, town	304	205
Bear Creek, town	150	174	Spider Lake, town	174	108
Cazenovia, village (part)	3	3	Weirgor, town	144	45
Dellona, town	488	356	Winter, town.	393	188
Delton, town	597	492	Winter, village.	91	47
Excelsior, town	515	359			
Fairfield, town.	333	296	**Shawano**.	**12,769**	**6,068**
Franklin, town.	173	184	Almon, town.	194	81
Freedom, town	142	100	Angelica, town	686	221
Greenfield, town	279	265	Aniwa, town	170	74
Honey Creek, town. . . .	192	200	Aniwa, village	63	31
Ironton, town	165	85	Bartelme, town	72	221
Ironton, village	61	32	Belle Plaine, town	658	272
La Valle, town	460	291	Birnamwood, town. . . .	214	125
La Valle, village	102	60	Birnamwood, village (part)	182	117
Lake Delton, village . . .	568	537	Bonduel, village.	496	168
Lime Ridge, village	48	37	Bowler, village.	74	37
Loganville, village	88	46	Cecil, village	214	91
Merrimac, town.	323	313	Eland, village	47	58
Merrimac, village	147	118	Fairbanks, town.	243	56
North Freedom, village .	159	98	Germania, town.	110	70
Plain, village.	207	180	Grant, town	363	97
Prairie du Sac, town . . .	312	300	Green Valley, town	369	133
Prairie du Sac, village . .	820	1,324	Gresham, village	121	105
Reedsburg, city	2,071	1,757	Hartland, town	311	59
Reedsburg, town	388	236	Herman, town.	268	93
Rock Springs, village. . .	101	49	Hutchins, town	203	63
Sauk City, village	646	1,094	Lessor, town	490	141
Spring Green, town . . .	451	493	Maple Grove, town. . . .	320	147
Spring Green, village . .	271	573	Marion, city (part)	3	2
Sumpter, town	184	170	Mattoon, village	99	45
Troy, town	235	190	Morris, town.	131	79
Washington, town	212	139	Navarino, town	162	65
West Baraboo, village . .	325	312	Pella, town	378	98
Westfield, town	171	95	Pulaski, village (part). . .	42	18
Winfield, town.	282	183	Red Springs, town	190	219
Wisconsin Dells, city (part)	42	38	Richmond, town	740	257
Woodland, town	207	135	Seneca, town	176	88
			Shawano, city	2,083	1,399
Sawyer.	**5,185**	**3,503**	Tigerton, village	230	113
Bass Lake, town	560	659	Washington, town	669	282
Couderay, town	73	71	Waukechon, town	388	109
Couderay, village	22	26	Wescott, town.	1,107	532
Draper, town.	86	50	Wittenberg, town.	298	135
Edgewater, town	227	95	Wittenberg, village. . . .	205	167

Presidential vote by county and municipality, November 8, 2016 general election, continued

	Donald J. Trump/ Michael R. Pence (Rep.)	Hillary Clinton/ Tim Kaine (Dem.)		Donald J. Trump/ Michael R. Pence (Rep.)	Hillary Clinton/ Tim Kaine (Dem.)
Sheboygan	**32,514**	**23,000**	Stetsonville, village . . .	163	70
Adell, village.	208	51	Taft, town	103	36
Cascade, village.	245	105	Westboro, town.	286	70
Cedar Grove, village . . .	880	204			
Elkhart Lake, village . . .	338	308	**Trempealeau**	**7,366**	**5,636**
Glenbeulah, village . . .	145	96	Albion, town.	202	126
Greenbush, town	564	292	Arcadia, city	471	292
Herman, town.	679	320	Arcadia, town	573	318
Holland, town	1,084	306	Blair, city	241	241
Howards Grove, village .	1,139	679	Burnside, town	120	76
Kohler, village	726	562	Caledonia, town	287	187
Lima, town.	1,223	412	Chimney Rock, town. . .	84	63
Lyndon, town	621	234	Dodge, town.	130	95
Mitchell, town.	496	181	Eleva, village.	160	137
Mosel, town	290	153	Ettrick, town	333	313
Oostburg, village	1,465	240	Ettrick, village	136	116
Plymouth, city.	2,329	1,743	Gale, town	547	354
Plymouth, town.	1,180	590	Galesville, city.	395	333
Random Lake, village . .	593	237	Hale, town	328	226
Rhine, town	870	499	Independence, city. . . .	254	177
Russell, town	152	45	Lincoln, town	163	140
Scott, town.	818	208	Osseo, city	436	389
Sheboygan, city.	8,788	10,495	Pigeon, town	200	143
Sheboygan, town.	2,475	1,852	Pigeon Falls, village . . .	87	89
Sheboygan Falls, city . .	2,405	1,781	Preston, town	230	172
Sheboygan Falls, town .	682	278	Strum, village	229	251
Sherman, town	649	198	Sumner, town	240	177
Waldo, village	197	72	Trempealeau, town. . . .	548	421
Wilson, town.	1,273	859	Trempealeau, village. . .	482	362
			Unity, town	152	112
			Whitehall, city	338	326
Taylor	**6,579**	**2,393**			
Aurora, town.	135	39	**Vernon**	**7,004**	**6,371**
Browning, town.	325	73	Bergen, town	369	357
Chelsea, town	273	84	Chaseburg, village	82	64
Cleveland, town.	98	21	Christiana, town	282	200
Deer Creek, town	277	60	Clinton, town	127	104
Ford, town	93	37	Coon, town	208	200
Gilman, village	112	61	Coon Valley, village. . . .	192	189
Goodrich, town	205	60	De Soto, village (part) . .	68	50
Greenwood, town	239	73	Forest, town	140	98
Grover, town.	103	19	Franklin, town.	325	197
Hammel, town	294	94	Genoa, town.	189	212
Holway, town	189	62	Genoa, village.	54	70
Jump River, town	91	44	Greenwood, town	110	74
Little Black, town	382	142	Hamburg, town	258	233
Lublin, village	39	13	Harmony, town	173	138
Maplehurst, town.	133	31	Hillsboro, city	326	266
McKinley, town	142	24	Hillsboro, town	221	106
Medford, city	1,181	670	Jefferson, town	325	245
Medford, town	932	297	Kickapoo, town	132	121
Molitor, town	117	47	La Farge, village.	164	145
Pershing, town	44	30	Liberty, town	71	86
Rib Lake, town	273	86	Ontario, village (part) . .	111	69
Rib Lake, village.	232	103	Readstown, village	98	64
Roosevelt, town.	118	47	Stark, town.	100	92

Presidential vote by county and municipality, November 8, 2016 general election, continued

	Donald J. Trump/ Michael R. Pence (Rep.)	Hillary Clinton/ Tim Kaine (Dem.)		Donald J. Trump/ Michael R. Pence (Rep.)	Hillary Clinton/ Tim Kaine (Dem.)
Sterling, town	196	89	Walworth, town.	616	229
Stoddard, village	204	198	Walworth, village.	691	430
Union, town	120	92	Whitewater, city (part). .	2,119	2,990
Viola, village (part)	57	39	Whitewater, town.	464	335
Viroqua, city	888	1,187	Williams Bay, village . . .	810	568
Viroqua, town	493	418			
Webster, town.	133	172	**Washburn**	**5,436**	**3,282**
Westby, city	472	579	Barronett, town.	129	83
Wheatland, town	179	130	Bashaw, town	384	190
Whitestown, town	137	87	Bass Lake, town	214	80
			Beaver Brook, town . . .	251	146
Vilas	**8,166**	**4,770**	Birchwood, town	284	108
Arbor Vitae, town.	1,235	726	Birchwood, village	137	70
Boulder Junction, town .	417	245	Brooklyn, town	101	56
Cloverland, town	473	209	Casey, town	160	108
Conover, town.	544	275	Chicog, town	95	70
Eagle River, city	421	293	Crystal, town	106	47
Lac du Flambeau, town .	588	762	Evergreen, town	429	226
Land O'Lakes, town . . .	367	184	Frog Creek, town	51	23
Lincoln, town	1,026	484	Gull Lake, town	71	55
Manitowish Waters, town	349	130	Long Lake, town	226	155
Phelps, town.	524	220	Madge, town	189	156
Plum Lake, town	234	117	Minong, town	307	248
Presque Isle, town	303	218	Minong, village	133	78
St. Germain, town	850	420	Sarona, town	162	63
Washington, town	625	373	Shell Lake, city	363	320
Winchester, town.	210	114	Spooner, city	614	443
			Spooner, town	264	159
Walworth	**28,863**	**18,710**	Springbrook, town	160	82
Bloomfield, town	367	258	Stinnett, town.	80	32
Bloomfield, village	1,283	550	Stone Lake, town	185	88
Burlington, city (part) . .	0	1	Trego, town	341	196
Darien, town.	533	268			
Darien, village.	371	250	**Washington**	**51,740**	**20,852**
Delavan, city.	1,556	1,497	Addison, town.	1,548	400
Delavan, town.	1,568	971	Barton, town.	1,211	426
East Troy, town	1,677	629	Erin, town	1,795	584
East Troy, village	1,498	730	Farmington, town	1,655	465
Elkhorn, city	2,446	1,725	Germantown, town . . .	103	49
Fontana-on-Geneva Lake,			Germantown, village . .	7,473	3,879
village	538	382	Hartford, city (part). . . .	4,539	2,177
Geneva, town	1,586	938	Hartford, town	1,624	498
Genoa City, village (part)	758	400	Jackson, town	2,125	573
Lafayette, town	785	338	Jackson, village	2,635	1,028
La Grange, town	848	419	Kewaskum, town	526	145
Lake Geneva, city.	1,722	1,554	Kewaskum, village (part)	1,573	559
Linn, town	793	438	Milwaukee, city (part) . .	0	0
Lyons, town	1,198	574	Newburg, village (part) .	466	110
Mukwonago, village (part)	59	35	Polk, town	1,890	531
Richmond, town	592	359	Richfield, village	5,511	1,817
Sharon, town	320	151	Slinger, village.	1,986	758
Sharon, village	362	243	Trenton, town	2,127	679
Spring Prairie, town . . .	954	319	Wayne, town.	1,001	241
Sugar Creek, town	1,362	695	West Bend, city	9,847	5,175
Troy, town	987	434	West Bend, town	2,105	758

Presidential vote by county and municipality, November 8, 2016 general election, continued

	Donald J. Trump/ Michael R. Pence (Rep.)	Hillary Clinton/ Tim Kaine (Dem.)		Donald J. Trump/ Michael R. Pence (Rep.)	Hillary Clinton/ Tim Kaine (Dem.)
Waukesha	**142,543**	**79,224**	Larrabee, town	461	188
Big Bend, village	540	180	Lebanon, town	570	279
Brookfield, city	13,970	9,144	Lind, town	542	222
Brookfield, town	2,267	1,476	Little Wolf, town	551	153
Butler, village	560	323	Manawa, city	362	144
Chenequa, village	250	70	Marion, city (part)	372	144
Delafield, city	2,623	1,494	Matteson, town	365	133
Delafield, town	3,398	1,512	Mukwa, town	1,064	545
Dousman, village	852	371	New London, city (part) .	1,405	906
Eagle, town	1,496	564	Ogdensburg, village . . .	58	18
Eagle, village	812	240	Royalton, town	548	197
Elm Grove, village	2,285	1,706	St. Lawrence, town	257	110
Genesee, town	3,206	1,314	Scandinavia, town	345	254
Hartland, village	3,231	1,676	Scandinavia, village . . .	92	65
Lac La Belle, village (part)	133	57	Union, town	265	107
Lannon, village	452	225	Waupaca, city	1,339	1,172
Lisbon, town.	4,378	1,755	Waupaca, town	418	205
Menomonee Falls, village	12,614	8,227	Weyauwega, city	496	215
Merton, town	3,776	1,264	Weyauwega, town	221	75
Merton, village	1,407	429	Wyoming, town.	107	43
Milwaukee, city (part) . .	0	0			
Mukwonago, town	3,372	1,207	**Waushara**	**7,667**	**3,791**
Mukwonago, village (part)	2,667	1,255	Aurora, town.	378	155
Muskego, city	9,995	4,412	Berlin, city (part)	34	15
Nashotah, village.	583	238	Bloomfield, town	420	113
New Berlin, city	14,439	8,868	Coloma, town	234	123
North Prairie, village . . .	917	325	Coloma, village	146	70
Oconomowoc, city	5,835	3,222	Dakota, town	377	139
Oconomowoc, town . . .	3,887	1,483	Deerfield, town	240	144
Oconomowoc Lake, village	252	82	Hancock, town	198	89
Ottawa, town	1,647	689	Hancock, village	114	65
Pewaukee, city	5,925	2,874	Leon, town.	558	239
Pewaukee, village	2,708	1,583	Lohrville, village	122	73
Summit, village	1,908	891	Marion, town	753	365
Sussex, village.	3,838	1,990	Mount Morris, town . . .	442	230
Vernon, town	3,447	1,298	Oasis, town	157	76
Wales, village	1,090	547	Plainfield, town	182	58
Waukesha, city	18,246	14,577	Plainfield, village	215	148
Waukesha, town	3,537	1,656	Poy Sippi, town	331	131
			Redgranite, village	247	129
Waupaca	**16,209**	**8,451**	Richford, town	172	50
Bear Creek, town	275	93	Rose, town	204	147
Big Falls, village	28	10	Saxeville, town	392	179
Caledonia, town	655	259	Springwater, town	466	279
Clintonville, city.	1,145	631	Warren, town	203	115
Dayton, town	953	531	Wautoma, city.	431	286
Dupont, town	236	80	Wautoma, town.	467	241
Embarrass, village	110	41	Wild Rose, village.	184	132
Farmington, town	1,210	822			
Fremont, town	274	102	**Winnebago**	**43,445**	**37,047**
Fremont, village	297	105	Algoma, town	2,413	1,609
Harrison, town	169	87	Appleton, city (part) . . .	199	207
Helvetia, town.	276	102	Black Wolf, town	973	547
Iola, town.	366	164	Clayton, town	1,582	738
Iola, village.	377	249	Fox Crossing, village . . .	3,227	2,300
			Menasha, city (part) . . .	3,079	3,199

Presidential vote by county and municipality, November 8, 2016 general election, continued

	Donald J. Trump/ Michael R. Pence (Rep.)	Hillary Clinton/ Tim Kaine (Dem.)		Donald J. Trump/ Michael R. Pence (Rep.)	Hillary Clinton/ Tim Kaine (Dem.)
Menasha, town	1,674	1,669	Grand Rapids, town . . .	2,612	1,709
Neenah, city	6,221	6,103	Hansen, town	278	104
Neenah, town	1,197	842	Hewitt, village.	275	181
Nekimi, town	591	240	Hiles, town	74	20
Nepeuskun, town.	299	122	Lincoln, town	589	318
Omro, city	984	648	Marshfield, city (part) . .	4,605	3,761
Omro, town	849	433	Marshfield, town	290	136
Oshkosh, city	13,868	15,228	Milladore, town.	203	128
Oshkosh, town	975	556	Milladore, village (part) .	79	47
Poygan, town	493	216	Nekoosa, city	638	381
Rushford, town	599	263	Pittsville, city	270	126
Utica, town.	509	249	Port Edwards, town . . .	404	255
Vinland, town	716	428	Port Edwards, village . .	515	389
Winchester, town.	698	329	Remington, town.	93	42
Winneconne, town. . . .	941	498	Richfield, town	530	247
Winneconne, village . . .	842	434	Rock, town.	338	129
Wolf River, town	516	189	Rudolph, town	399	214
			Rudolph, village	140	101
Wood	**21,498**	**14,225**	Saratoga, town	1,738	913
Arpin, town	295	129	Seneca, town	363	255
Arpin, village	80	41	Sherry, town.	271	134
Auburndale, town	314	95	Sigel, town.	340	213
Aurburndale, village . . .	209	102	Vesper, village.	188	89
Biron, village.	232	178	Wisconsin Rapids, city. .	4,286	3,398
Cameron, town	202	79	Wood, town	306	140
Cary, town	163	70	**State totals**	**1,405,284**	**1,382,536**
Cranmoor, town	58	29			
Dexter, town.	121	72			

Note: Other president/vice president tickets received the following votes: Gary Johnson/Bill Weld (Libertarian)—106,674; Jill Stein/Ajamu Baraka (Wisconsin Green)—31,072; Darrell L. Castle/Scott N. Bradley (Constitution)—12,162; Evan McMullin/Nathan Johnson (write-in)—11,855; Monica Moorehead/Lamont Lilly (Workers World Party)—1,770; Rocky Roque De La Fuente/Michael Steinberg (American Delta Party)—1,502; Michael A. Maturen/Juan Munoz (write-in)—284; Tom Hoefling/Steve Schulin (write-in)—80; Chris Keniston/ Deacon Taylor (write-in)—67; Cherunda Fox/Roger Kushner (write-in)—47; Emidio Soltysik/Angela Nicole Walker (write-in)—33; Laurence Kotlikoff/Edward E. Leamer (write-in)—15; Joseph Maldonado (write-in)—4; Marshall Schoenke/James Creighton Mitchell Jr. (write-in)—1.

Source: Official records of the Wisconsin Elections Commission.

OFFICIALS IN GOVERNMENT AND POLITICS

State officers appointed by the governor, May 14, 2017

Accounting Examining Board [1] ($25/day [2])
Joseph Braunger . . . . expires 7/1/17
Gerald Denor 7/1/17
Glenn Michaelsen 7/1/17
Christine Anderson 7/1/18
Kathleen LaBrake 7/1/18
John Scheid .7/1/19
Todd Craft 7/1/20

Adjutant General (group 4 salary [2])
Major Gen. Donald P. Dunbar . . . . .expires 9/1/12

Administration, Department of, secretary [1] (group 8 salary [2])
Scott Neitzel . . . . . expires at governor's pleasure

Adult Offender Supervision Board, Interstate
Michael Bohren . . . . .expires 5/1/17
Robert Berry 5/1/19
Jay C. Laufenberg 5/1/19

Adult Offender Supervision, Interstate Compact Administrator
Tracy Hudrlik . . . . .expires 5/1/17

Aerospace Authority, Wisconsin [1]
Thomas Crabb . . . . .expires 6/30/10
Judith Schieble 6/30/10
Thomas Mullooly 6/30/11
Edward Wagner 6/30/11
Mark Hanna 6/30/12
Mark Lee 6/30/12

Affirmative Action, Council on
David Dunham . . . . .expires 7/1/11
Eileen Hocker 7/1/11
Sandra Ryan 7/1/11
Ronald Shaheed 7/1/11
Nancy Vue 7/1/11
Thressessa Childs 7/1/12
Janice Hughes 7/1/12
John Magerus 7/1/12
James Parker 7/1/12
Yolanda Santos Adams 7/1/12
Lakshmi Bharadwaj 7/1/13

Aging and Long-Term Care, Board on [1]
Eva Arnold . . . . .expires 5/1/17
Tanya Meyer 5/1/17
Michael Brooks 5/1/18
James Surprise 5/1/18
Dale B. Taylor [3] 5/1/20
Valerie A. Palarski [3] 5/1/21
Barbara Bechtel [3] 5/1/22

Agriculture, Trade and Consumer Protection, Board of [1] (not to exceed $35/day nor $1,000/year [2])
Andre Diercks . . . . .expires 5/1/17
Miranda Leis 5/1/17

Mark Schleitwiler 5/1/17
Dennis Badtke 5/1/19
Nicole Hansen 5/1/19
Dean Strauss 5/1/19
Kurt Hallstrand 5/1/21
Paul Palmby 5/1/21
Gregory Zwald 5/1/21

Agriculture, Trade and Consumer Protection, Department of, secretary [1] (group 6 salary [2])
Ben Brancel . . . . . . expires at governor's pleasure

Alcohol and Other Drug Abuse, State Council on
Craig Harper . . . . . expires at governor's pleasure
Mark C. Seidl . . . . governor's pleasure
Michael Waupoose . . . . governor's pleasure
Rebecca Wigg-Ninham . . . . . governor's pleasure
Joyce O'Donnell . . . . .expires 7/1/17
Mary Rasmussen 7/1/17
Scott A. Stokes 7/1/17
Norman Briggs 7/1/19
Sandy Hardie 7/1/19
Duncan M. Shrout 7/1/19

Architects, Landscape Architects, Professional Engineers, Designers and Professional Land Surveyors, Examining Board of [1] ($25/day [2])
Steven Nielsen . . . . .expires 7/1/09
Scott Berg 7/1/11
Ruth Johnson 7/1/11
Gary Kohlenberg 7/1/12
Daniel Fedderly 7/1/13
Thomas Gasperetti 7/1/13
Rosheen Styczinski 7/1/13
Bruce Bowden 7/1/14
Steven Hook 7/1/14
Matthew Fernholz 7/1/15
Andrew Gersich 7/1/15
Kristine Cotharn 7/1/17
Joseph Eberle 7/1/17
Joseph D. Frasch 7/1/17
Steven Wagner 7/1/17
Kenneth D. Arneson 7/1/18
Ralf Kelm 7/1/18
Mark Mayer 7/1/18
Matthew D. Wolfert 7/1/18
Andrew Albright 7/1/19
Michael J. Heberling 7/1/19
Christina C. Martin 7/1/19
Tim Garland 7/1/20
5 vacancies

Artistic Endowment Foundation [1] inactive

Arts Board
Barbara Munson . . . . .expires 5/1/11
John Hendricks 5/1/12
Sharon Stewart 5/1/13
LaMoine MacLaughlin 5/1/15

State officers appointed by the governor, May 14, 2017, continued

Heather McDonell 5/1/18
John H. Potter. 5/1/18
Robert Wagner 5/1/18
Karen A. Hoffman 5/1/19
Catherine L. Lange. 5/1/19
Kevin M. Miller 5/1/19
Matthew J. Wallock 5/1/19
Ann Brunner 5/1/20
Mary Gielow 5/1/20
Brian Kelsey 5/1/20
Frederick Schwertfeger 5/1/20

Athletic Trainers Affiliated Credentialing Board [1]
($25/day [2]**)**
Jack J. Johnsen . . . . .expires 7/1/17
Jay J. Davide. 7/1/18
Kurt Fielding [3] 7/1/19
Gregory Vergamini [3]. 7/1/20
2 vacancies

Auctioneer Board [1] **($25/day** [2]**)**
Timothy Sweeney . . . . .expires 5/1/12
Ronald Polacek 5/1/13
Leonard Yoap 5/1/14
James Wenzler 5/1/15
Heather Berlinski 5/1/16
Jerry Thiel .5/1/18
Randy J. Stockwell. 5/1/20

Banking Review Board [1] **($25/day, not to exceed**
$1,500/year [2]**)**
Douglas Farmer . . . . .expires 5/1/17
Robert C. Gorsuch 5/1/18
Debra R. Lins 5/1/19
Thomas J. Pamperin 5/1/20
Thomas E. Spitz. 5/1/22

Bradley Center Sports and Entertainment
Corporation, Board of Directors [1]
Rolen L. Womack . . . . .expires 7/1/13
Ted Kellner 7/1/16
Gary Sweeney 7/1/16
Ricardo Diaz 7/1/17
Patrick Lawton 7/1/18
Andrew Petzold 7/1/18
Lynn Sprangers. 7/1/18
Michael Grebe 7/1/20
Jeffrey A. Joerres 7/1/20
Sarah Zimmerman [3]. 7/1/20

Building Commission
Robert Brandherm . expires at governor's pleasure

Building Inspector Review Board
James Micech . . . . .expires 5/1/15
Benjamin E. Noffke 5/1/18

Burial Sites Preservation Board ($25/day [2])
Corina Williams . . . . .expires 7/1/10
Kathryn Eagan-Bruhy 7/1/13
David Grignon 7/1/14
Cynthia Stiles 7/1/14
Jennifer Haas 7/1/15

Cemetery Board [1] **($25/day** [2]**)**
Kathleen Cantu . . . . .expires 7/1/12
Clyde Rupnow 7/1/16
Patricia Grathen 7/1/18
Bernard Schroedl 7/1/18
Francis J. Groh [3] 7/1/20
John Reinemann 7/1/20

Child Abuse and Neglect Prevention Board
James Leonhart . . . . .expires 5/1/11
Jeffrey Lamont 5/1/17
Sandra J. McCormick 5/1/17
Notesong Thompson 5/1/17
Vicki M. Tylka 5/1/17
Jennifer L. Noyes 5/1/18
Kimberly Simac 5/1/18
Teri B. Zywicki 5/1/18
Kari A. Christenson 5/1/19
Molly J. Jasmer 5/1/19
Bernice C. Day 5/1/20
Monica Young . . . . expires at governor's pleasure

Children and Families, Department of, secretary [1]
(group 6 salary [2])
Eloise Anderson . . . expires at governor's pleasure

Chiropractic Examining Board [1] ($25/day [2])
John Church [3] . . . . .expires 7/1/17
Jeffrey Mackey 7/1/17
Juli McNeely. 7/1/17
Jeffrey A. King [3]. 7/1/19
Patricia Schumacher 7/1/19
Jacob J. Curtis [3] 7/1/20

Circus World Museum Foundation [1]
David Hoffman . . . expires at governor's pleasure

Claims Board
Katie Ignatowski . . . expires at governor's pleasure

College Savings Program Board [1]
John Wheeler . . . . .expires 5/1/15
Robert Kieckhefer 5/1/19
William L. Oemichen 5/1/19
Alberta Darling [3] 5/1/21
Rob Kreibich [3]. 5/1/21
Kimberly Shaul [3] 5/1/21

Commercial Building Code Council
Hunter Bohne . . . . .expires 7/1/15
Samuel Lawrence 7/1/16
Corey Rockweiler 7/1/16
Peter Scheuerman 7/1/16
Kevin Bierce 7/1/17
David Enigl 7/1/17
Steve Klessig 7/1/17
Irina Ragozin 7/1/17
Steven Howard 7/1/18
Brian J. Rinke 7/1/18

Controlled Substances Board
Subhadeep Barman . . . . .expires 5/1/19
Alan Bloom 5/1/20

State officers appointed by the governor, May 14, 2017, continued

Conveyance Safety Code Council
Jesse Kaysen . . . . .expires 7/1/09
Brian Hornung 7/1/15
Steven L. Ketelboeter 7/1/17
Ronald P. Mueller. 7/1/17
Jennie L. Macaluso. 7/1/18
William G. Grubbs, Jr. 7/1/19
Brian Rausch 7/1/19
Paul S. Rosenberg 7/1/19
Kenneth R. Smith 7/1/19

Corrections, Department of, secretary [1] **(group 6 salary** [2]**)**
Jon Litscher . . . . . . expires at governor's pleasure

Cosmetology Examining Board [1]
Kristin Allison . . . . .expires 7/1/16
Suresh Misra 7/1/18
Lori A. Paul .7/1/18
Gail Sengbusch 7/1/18
Denise Trokan [3] 7/1/19
Vicky McNally [3] 7/1/20
Kim S. Rank [3] 7/1/20
2 vacancies

Credit Union Review Board [1] **($25/day, not to exceed $1,500/year** [2]**)**
Colleen Woggon . . . . .expires 5/1/17
Lisa M. Greco 5/1/18
Danny Wollin 5/1/19
Christopher P. Butler 5/1/20
Sherri O. Stumpf 5/1/21

Credit Unions, Office of, director [1] **(group 3 salary** [2]**)**
Kim Santos . . . . . . expires at governor's pleasure

Crime Victims Rights Board
Rebecca St. John . . . . .expires 5/1/19

Criminal Penalties, Joint Review Committee on
Bradley Gehring . . . expires at governor's pleasure
Maury Straub . . . . governor's pleasure

Deaf and Hard of Hearing, Council for the
Michelle S. Cordova . . . . .expires 7/1/17
Nicole Everson 7/1/17
Karl Nollenberger 7/1/17
David H. Seligman. 7/1/17
Justin Vollmar 7/1/17
Thomas O'Connor 7/1/19
Steven Smart 7/1/19
Lisa D. Woods. 7/1/19

Deferred Compensation Board [1]
Jason A. Rothenberg . . . . .expires 7/1/17
Arthur Zimmerman 7/1/17
Gail Hanson .7/1/18
John M. Scherer 7/1/19
Edward D. Main 7/1/20

Dentistry Examining Board [1] **($25/day** [2]**)**
Leonardo Huck . . . . .expires 7/1/17
Timothy McConville 7/1/17

Wendy Pietz 7/1/17
Mark Braden 7/1/18
Eileen Donohoo 7/1/18
Lyndsay N. Knoell 7/1/18
Carrie Stempski 7/1/18
Beth Welter .7/1/18
Debra Beres [3] 7/1/20
2 vacancies

Developmental Disabilities, Board for People with ($50/day [2])
Elsa Diaz Bautista . . . . .expires 7/1/17
Pam Malin .7/1/17
Camille Nicklaus 7/1/17
Judith Quigley 7/1/17
Sheila Thornton 7/1/17
Jennifer A. Kuhr. 7/1/18
Ramsey A. Lee 7/1/18
Delores Sallis 7/1/18
Patrick Young 7/1/18
Wendy Ackley 7/1/19
Gail M. Bovy 7/1/19
Amy M. Burger 7/1/19
Lynn Carus .7/1/19
Michael D. Hineberg 7/1/19
Erica Larsen .7/1/19
Nathaniel Lentz 7/1/19
Carole Stuebe 7/1/19
Robert Kuhr .7/1/20
David Pinno .7/1/20
L. Lynn Stansberry-Brusnahan 7/1/20

Dietitians Affiliated Credentialing Board [1] ($25/ day [2])
David Joe . . . . .expires 7/1/18
Tara LaRowe 7/1/18
Jill D. Hoyt [3] 7/1/19
Scott Krueger [3] 7/1/19

Distance Learning Authorization Board
Barbara Lundberg . . expires at governor's pleasure

Domestic Abuse, Council on [1]
Mariana Rodriguez . . . . .expires 7/1/11
L. Kevin Hamberger 7/1/17
Jill Karofsky .7/1/17
Patricia Ninmann [3] 7/1/17
Renee J. Schulz-Stangl 7/1/17
Susan Sippel 7/1/17
Lena C. Taylor 7/1/18
Gerald A. Urbik 7/1/18
Shirley A. Armstrong [3] 7/1/19
Susan M. Perry [3] 7/1/19
Lisa Subeck .7/1/19
Mark M. Thomas [3] 7/1/19

Dry Cleaner Environmental Response Council
Kevin D. Braden . . . . .expires 7/1/17
Thomas McKay 7/1/17
David Cass .7/1/18
Jeanne Tarvin 7/1/18
Jim Fitzgerald 7/1/19
Richard W. Klinke 7/1/19

State officers appointed by the governor, May 14, 2017, continued

Economic Development Corporation, Wisconsin [1]
Daniel Ariens . . . . . expires at governor's pleasure
Raymond Dreger . . . . governor's pleasure
David J. Drury. . . . . governor's pleasure
Nancy Hernandez . . . . governor's pleasure
Lisa Mauer . . . . governor's pleasure
R.D. Nair . . . . governor's pleasure

Economic Development Corporation, Wisconsin, chief exececutive officer [1, 4]
Mark Hogan . . . . . expires at governor's pleasure

Education Commission of the States
Jessica Doyle . . . . . expires at governor's pleasure
Tracie Happel . . . . governor's pleasure
Bette Lang . . . . governor's pleasure
Demond Means . . . . governor's pleasure
John Reinemann . . . . governor's pleasure

Educational Approval Board ($25/day [2])
Crystal M. H. Cook . . expires at governor's pleasure
Robert Hein . . . . governor's pleasure
Mark S. Kapocius . . . . governor's pleasure
Donald Madelung . . . . governor's pleasure
Jo Oyama-Miller . . . . governor's pleasure
William Roden . . . . governor's pleasure
Katie Thiry . . . . governor's pleasure

Educational Communications Board [1]
Richard Lepping . . . . expires 5/1/17
Karen Schroeder 5/1/19
Rolf Wegenke 5/1/19
David Hutchison [3] 5/1/21
Eileen Littig . . . . . . expires at governor's pleasure

Elections Commission [1] (90% of the per diem of a temporary reserve judge assigned to the circuit court)
Beverly R. Gill . . . . expires 5/1/19
Julie M. Glancey 5/1/21

Electronic Recording Council
John Wilcox . . . . expires 7/1/13
Tyson Fettes 7/1/18
Jodi Helgeson 7/1/18
Michael McDonnell 7/1/18
Staci M. Hoffman 7/1/19
Michael Lenz 7/1/19
Sharon A. Martin 7/1/19

Emergency Management Division, administrator [1] (group 1 salary [2])
Brian Satula . . . . . . expires at governor's pleasure

Emergency Medical Services Board
Jerry R. Biggart . . . . expires 5/1/17
Craig Nelson 5/1/17
Michael Clark 5/1/18
Mario Colella 5/1/18
Donald F. Kimlicka 5/1/18
Carrie L. Meier 5/1/19
Gary L. Weiss 5/1/19
Steven W. Zils 5/1/19

Mark C. Fredrickson 5/1/20
Dustin E. Ridings 5/1/20
Gregory Neal West 5/1/20

Employee Trust Funds Board [1]
Victor Shier . . . . expires 5/1/17
Bob Ziegelbauer . . . expires at governor's pleasure

Employment Relations Commission [1] (group 5 salary [2])
Rodney Pasch . . . . expires 3/1/17
James Daley 3/1/19
James Scott 3/1/21

Ethics Commission [1] (90% of the per diem of a temporary reserve judge assigned to the circuit court)
Timothy M. Van Akkeren . . . . expires 5/1/19
James "Mac" Davis 5/1/21

Federal-State Relations Office, director (group 3 salary [2])
Jen Jinks . . . . expires at governor's pleasure

Financial Institutions, Department of, secretary [1] (group 6 salary [2])
Jay M. Risch . . . . . . expires at governor's pleasure

Forestry, Council on
R. Bruce Allison . . . expires at governor's pleasure
Janet Bewley . . . . governor's pleasure
Michael Bolton . . . . governor's pleasure
Dennis G. Brown . . . . governor's pleasure
Troy Brown . . . . governor's pleasure
Matt Dallman . . . . governor's pleasure
Paul J. DeLong . . . . governor's pleasure
Donald Friske . . . . governor's pleasure
James Heerey . . . . governor's pleasure
Jeanne Higgins . . . . governor's pleasure
Thomas Hittle . . . . governor's pleasure
James Hoppe . . . . governor's pleasure
William J. Horvath . . . . governor's pleasure
Mary Hubler . . . . governor's pleasure
James Kerkman . . . . governor's pleasure
Nick Milroy . . . . governor's pleasure
Kenneth Price . . . . governor's pleasure
Mark Rickenbach . . . . governor's pleasure
Robert Rogers . . . . governor's pleasure
Henry Schienebeck . . . . governor's pleasure
Jane Severt . . . . governor's pleasure
Jason Sjostrom . . . . governor's pleasure
Jeffrey C. Stier . . . . governor's pleasure
Paul Strong . . . . governor's pleasure
Tom Tiffany . . . . governor's pleasure
Richard Wedepohl . . . . governor's pleasure
Kenneth R. Zabel . . . . governor's pleasure

Fox River Navigational System Authority [1]
H. Bruce Enke . . . . expires 7/1/17
Jeffery Feldt 7/1/17
William Raaths 7/1/18
S. Timothy Rose 7/1/18
Kathryn A. Curren 7/1/19
John L. Vette 7/1/19

State officers appointed by the governor, May 14, 2017, continued

Funeral Directors Examining Board [1] ($25/day [2])
Eric Lengell . . . . .expires 7/1/16
Marla Michaelis 7/1/17
Dean Stensberg 7/1/17
Aziz K. Al-Sager. 7/1/18
Marc A. Eernisse 7/1/18
D. Bruce Carlson [3] 7/1/19

Geologists, Hydrologists and Soil Scientists, Examining Board of Professional [1] ($25/day [2])
Patricia Trochlell . . . . .expires 7/1/09
Ruth Johnson 7/1/10
John Hahn .7/1/11
Brenda Halminiak 7/1/12
Randall Hunt 7/1/12
Frederick Madison 7/1/12
Kenneth Bradbury 7/1/13
William Mode 7/1/13
Richard Beilfuss 7/1/14
James Robertson 7/1/14
Stephanie Williams 7/1/17

Great Lakes Commission
Lynn Dufrane . . . . .expires 7/1/17
Dean R. Haen 7/1/20
Ken Johnson . . . . . expires at governor's pleasure

Great Lakes Protection Fund [1]
Richard Meeusen . . . . .expires 1/9/15
Kevin L. Shafer 1/12/16

Groundwater Coordinating Council
Stephen Diercks . . . . .expires 7/1/17

Group Insurance Board ($25/day [2])
Terri Carlson . . . . .expires 5/1/17
Herschel Day 5/1/17
Michael Farrell 5/1/19
Charles Grapentine 5/1/19
Theodore Neitzke IV 5/1/19
Nancy L. Thompson 5/1/19
Bob Ziegelbauer . . . expires at governor's pleasure

Health and Educational Facilities Authority, Wisconsin [1]
Kevin Flaherty . . . . .expires 6/30/17
Tim Size 6/30/18
James Dietsche 6/30/19
Robert Van Meeteren [3] 6/30/20
Paul Mathews 6/30/21
Pamela Stanick [3] 6/30/22
James K. Oppermann [3] 7/1/23

Health Care Liability Insurance Plan/Injured Patients and Families Compensation Fund Board of Governors
Dennis Conta . . . . .expires 5/1/10
Gregory Banaszynski 5/1/17
Kim R. Hurtz 5/1/17
Carla Borda 5/1/18
Sridhar V. Vasudevan 5/1/19

Health Services, Department of, secretary [1] (group 9 salary [2])
Linda J. Seemeyer . . expires at governor's pleasure

Hearing and Speech Examining Board [1] ($25/day [2])
Melanie Blechl . . . . .expires 7/1/12
Mary Polenske 7/1/15
Thomas Sather 7/1/15
Samuel P. Gubbels 7/1/17
Barbara Johnson 7/1/17
Thomas Krier 7/1/17
Scott Larson 7/1/17
Patricia Willis 7/1/18
Steven Klapperich [3] 7/1/19
Robert R. Broeckert [3] 7/1/20

Higher Educational Aids Board
Nathaniel Helm-Quest . . . . .expires 5/1/16
Margaret A. Farrow 5/1/17
Jacob Lubenow 5/1/17
Robert T. Welch. 5/1/17
Benjamin Zellmer 5/1/17
Jeff Cichon. .5/1/18
Michelle Thompson 5/1/18
Stephen D. Willett 5/1/18
Steven D. Midthun 5/1/19
Kathleen A. Sahlhoff 5/1/19

Higher Educational Aids Board, executive secretary (group 3 salary [2])
John Reinemann . . . expires at governor's pleasure

Highway Safety, Council on
Gerald Powalisz . . . . .expires 7/1/16
Bria Dean 7/1/17
Robert Hinds 7/1/17
Donald Gutkowski. 7/1/18
J.D. Lind 7/1/18
Kurt Schultz 7/1/18
Richard G. Van Boxtel 7/1/18
Monica Young 7/1/18
John P. Mesich 7/1/19
Yash Wadhwa 7/1/19

Historic Preservation Review Board
Anne Biebel . . . . .expires 7/1/16
Bruce Block .7/1/16
Robert Gough 7/1/16
Daniel J. Joyce 7/1/17
Valentine Schute, Jr. 7/1/17
Carol J. McChesney Johnson 7/1/18
David V. Mollenhoff. 7/1/18
Neil Prendergast 7/1/18
Sissel Schroeder 7/1/18
Paul Wolter .7/1/18
Kubet Luchterhand 7/1/19
Melinda J. Young 7/1/19
Carlen I. Hatala 7/1/20
Daniel J. Stephans 7/1/20
Donna Zimmerman 7/1/20

State officers appointed by the governor, May 14, 2017, continued

Housing and Economic Development Authority, Wisconsin [1]
Perry Armstrong . . . . .expires 1/1/18
Bradley Guse .1/1/18
Ivan Gamboa .1/1/19
John Horning .1/1/19
Susan Shore 1/1/20
McArthur Weddle 1/1/20

Housing and Economic Development Authority, Wisconsin, executive director [1] (group 6 salary [2])
Wyman Winston . . . . .expires 1/3/17

Insurance, Commissioner of [1] (group 5 salary [2])
Ted Nickel . . . . expires at governor's pleasure

Interoperability Council
Melinda Allen . . . . .expires 5/1/09
Steven Hansen 5/1/13
Lynn Schubert 5/1/13
Jon Freund .5/1/15
Matthew Joski 5/1/15
William Stolte 5/1/15
Bradley Wentlandt 5/1/17
James D. Formea 5/1/19
Richard G. Van Boxtel 5/1/20

Interstate Juvenile Supervision, State Board for
Edward Brooks . . . . .expires 7/1/18
T. Christopher Dee 7/1/19

Invasive Species Council
Thomas Bressner . . . . .expires 7/1/17
James Kerkman 7/1/17
Gregory Long 7/1/17
Paul Schumacher 7/1/17
Kenneth F. Raffa 7/1/18
Hannah Spaul 7/1/19
Thomas Buechel 7/1/20

Investment and Local Impact Fund Board
Edward Brandis . . . . .expires 5/1/15
Kelly Klein .5/1/15
David Pajula 5/1/15
Robert Walesewicz 5/1/16
Leslie Kolesar 5/1/18
Emmer Schields, Jr. 5/1/18
Rick J. Hermus 5/1/20
Richard G. Chandler 5/1/20
Mark Hogan . . . . . . expires at governor's pleasure
2 vacancies

Investment Board, State of Wisconsin [1] ($50/day [2])
Mark Doll . . . . .expires 5/1/21
Barbara Nick 5/1/21
Paul Stewart 5/1/21
Norman Cummings [3] 5/1/23
Timothy R. Sheehy [3] 5/1/23
David Stein [3] 5/1/23

Judicial Commission [1] ($25/day [2])
Mark Barrette . . . . .expires 8/1/14
Eileen Burnett 8/1/14

William Cullinan 8/1/14
Steven C. Miller 8/1/17
Robert H. Papke 8/1/18

Judicial Council
Dennis Myers . . . . .expires 7/1/18
Benjamin J. Pliskie 7/1/19
Christian Gossett . . expires at governor's pleasure

Kickapoo Reserve Management Board ($25/day [2])
Tracy Littlejohn . . . . .expires 5/1/12
Adlai Mann .5/1/13
William L. Quackenbush 5/1/17
Richard T. Wallin 5/1/17
Paul Hayes .5/1/18
Reggie Nelson 5/1/18
Susan C. Cushing 5/1/19
Travis M. Downing 7/1/19
David M. Maxwell 5/1/19
Ronald M. Johnson 5/1/20
vacancy

Labor and Industry Review Commission [1] (group 5 salary [2])
Laurie McCallum . . . . .expires 3/1/17
Clarence Jordahl 3/1/19
David B. Falstad 3/1/21

Labor and Industry Review Commission, general counsel
Maria Gonzalez Knavel . . . .
. . . . expires at governor's pleasure

Laboratory of Hygiene Board
Michael Ricker . . . . .expires 5/1/13
Ruth Etzel .5/1/15
Jeffery Kindrai 5/1/17
James M. Morrison 5/1/18
Robert F. Corliss 5/1/19
Barry E. Irmen 5/1/19
Jim C. Wenzler 5/1/19

Lake Michigan Commercial Fishing Board
Charles W. Henriksen expires at governor's pleasure
Richard R. Johnson . . . . governor's pleasure
Michael Le Clair . . . . governor's pleasure
Mark Maricque . . . . governor's pleasure
Dan Pawlitzke . . . . governor's pleasure
Neil A. Schwarz . . . . governor's pleasure
Dean Swaer . . . . governor's pleasure

Lake States Wood Utilization Consortium inactive

Lake Superior Commercial Fishing Board
Jeff Bodin . . . . expires at governor's pleasure
Bill Damberg . . . . governor's pleasure
Maurine Halvorson . . . . governor's pleasure
Craig Hoopman . . . . governor's pleasure
vacancy

Land and Water Conservation Board [1] ($25/day [2])
Dennis Caneff . . . . .expires 5/1/14
Eric D. Birschbach 5/1/18
Lynn Harrison 5/1/19

State officers appointed by the governor, May 14, 2017, continued

Mark E. Cupp 5/1/20
vacancy

Law Enforcement Standards Board
Gary Cuskey . . . . .expires 5/1/14
James Arts 5/1/15
Jon Koch 5/1/15
John R. Gossage 5/1/18
Anna Ruzinski 5/1/18
Joseph Collins 5/1/19
Nathan Henriksen 5/1/19
Jean Galasinski 5/1/20
Laura Messner-Washer 5/1/20
Christopher Domagalski 5/1/21
Kim Gaffney 5/1/21
Jennifer Harper 5/1/21

Library and Network Development, Council on
Ewa Barczyk . . . . .expires 7/1/13
Bob Koechley 7/1/13
Kristi Williams 7/1/13
Cara Cavin .7/1/14
Patrick Wilkinson 7/1/14
Joshua Cowles 7/1/17
Thomas C. Kamenick 7/1/18
Douglas H. Lay 7/1/18
Bryan McCormick 7/1/18
Dennis Myers 7/1/18
Kathy Pletcher 7/1/18
Joan Robb .7/1/18
Lisa Sterrett 7/1/18
Mary Therese Boyle 7/1/19
Laurie J. Freund 7/1/19
Becki George 7/1/19
Jess M. Ripp 7/1/19
Terrence Berres 7/1/20
Miriam M. Erickson 7/1/20

Lower Fox River Remediation Authority [1]
Gregory B. Conway . . . . expires 6/30/11
Patrick Schillinger 6/30/11
Robert Cowles 6/30/13
Dave Hansen 6/30/13
David Stegeman 6/30/16
James Wall 6/30/16
vacancy

Lower Wisconsin State Riverway Board [1]
($25/day [2])
Frederick Madison . . . . .expires 5/1/13
Ritchie Brown 5/1/17
Gretchen F. G. La Budde 5/1/17
Robert J. Leys 5/1/17
Robert Cary 5/1/18
Richard McFarlane 5/1/18
Gerald Dorscheid [3]. 5/1/19
Steve A. Williamson 5/1/19
vacancy

Madison Cultural Arts District Board
Carol Toussaint . . . . .expires 7/1/14
Diane Kay Ballweg 7/1/16

Sheryl Theo .7/1/17
Susan Hamblin . . . . expires at governor's pleasure

**Marriage and Family Therapy, Professional
Counseling, and Social Work, Examining
Board of** [1] ($25/day [2])
Alice Hanson-Drew . . . . .expires 7/1/13
Jennifer Anderson-Meger 7/1/17
Kathleen M. Miller 7/1/17
Peter Fabian 7/1/18
Allison Gordon 7/1/18
Kristin Koger 7/1/18
Linda Pellmann [3]. 7/1/19
Monica S. Vick [3]. 7/1/19
Gregory Winkler [3] 7/1/19
Bridget Ellingboe 7/1/20
Elizabeth A. Krueger [3]. 7/1/20
Tammy H. Scheidegger [3] 7/1/20
vacancy

**Massage Therapy and Bodywork Therapy
Affiliated Credentialing Board** [1]
Carie Martin . . . . .expires 7/1/11
Amy Connell 7/1/12
Lillian Pounds 7/1/12
Xiping Zhou 7/1/12
June Motzer 7/1/13
Darlene Campo 7/1/18
Robert Coleman, Jr. [3] 7/1/18
Carla Hedtke [3] 7/1/18
Elizabeth Krizenesky 7/1/18
Carol Ostendorf 7/1/18
Sharon Pollock 7/1/18
Mark Richardson 7/1/18

**Medical College of Wisconsin, Incorporated, Board
of Trustees** [1]
Cory Nettles . . . . .expires 5/1/13
Elizabeth Brenner 5/1/15

Medical Education Review Committee inactive

Medical Examining Board [1] ($25/day [2])
Padmaja Doniparthi. . . . . .expires 7/1/17
David Roelke 7/1/17
Carolyn Ogland Vukich 7/1/17
Mary Jo Capodice 7/1/18
Kenneth Simons 7/1/18
Robert Zondag 7/1/18
Rodney Erickson [3] 7/1/19
Robert L. Zoeller [3] 7/1/19
Alaa A. Abd-Elsayed [3] 7/1/20
Michael Carton [3] 7/1/20
Bradley Kudick 7/1/20
Lee Ann R. Lau [3] 7/1/20
Timothy Westlake [3] 7/1/20

Mental Health, Council on
Mishelle O'Shasky . . . . .expires 7/1/13
David Stepien 7/1/15
Ann Catherine Veierstahler 7/1/16
Patrick Cork 7/1/17

State officers appointed by the governor, May 14, 2017, continued

Dori L. Richards	7/1/17
Edward F. Wall	7/1/17
Kathleen F. Enders	7/1/18
Tracey Hassinger	7/1/18
Monique M. Hicks	7/1/18
Richard Immler	7/1/18
Carol Keen	7/1/18
Sheli Metzger	7/1/18
Jacqueline J. Borthwick	7/1/19
Julie-Anne Braun	7/1/19
Barbara Buffington	7/1/19
Kathryn Bush	7/1/19
Beth A. Clay	7/1/19
Kimberlee M. Coronado	7/1/19
Inshirah Farhoud	7/1/19
Mark Lausch	7/1/19
Charlotte Matteson	7/1/19
Amy L. Polsin	7/1/19
Karen Iverson Riggers	7/1/19
Matthew Strittmater	7/1/19
Donna Wrenn	7/1/19

Midwest Interstate Low-Level Radioactive Waste Commission, Wisconsin commissioner [1]

Stanley York . . . . . expires at governor's pleasure

Midwest Interstate Passenger Rail Commission

Craig Anderson	expires 1/5/15
Dave Ross	expires at governor's pleasure

Midwestern Higher Education Commission

Margaret A. Farrow	expires 7/1/16
Rolf Wegenke	7/1/18
Don Madelung	expires at governor's pleasure

Migrant Labor, Council on

Enrique Figueroa	expires 7/1/12
Teresa Tellez-Giron	7/1/13
Steve Ziobro	7/1/13
Kevin Magee	7/1/14
Richard W. Okray	7/1/15
Guadalupe Rendon	7/1/16
John Bauknecht	7/1/17
Erica A. Kunze	7/1/17
Lupe G. Martinez	7/1/18
Jeanine M. McCain	7/1/18
Melissa K. Cuevas	7/1/19

Military and State Relations, Council on

Jamie Aulik	expires at governor's pleasure
Linda Fournier	governor's pleasure
Larry Olson	governor's pleasure
Daniel Zimmerman	governor's pleasure

Milwaukee Child Welfare Partnership Council

Marshall Murray	expires 7/1/13
Tony Shields	7/1/16
Mary Triggiano	7/1/16
Colleen M. Ellingson	7/1/17
Susan Gadacz	7/1/17
Mallory O'Brien	7/1/17
Sara Purtell Scullen	7/1/17

Delvyn L. Crawford	7/1/18
Willie Johnson, Jr.	7/1/18
Veneshia McKinney-Whitson	7/1/18
Mark M. Mertens	7/1/18
Anthony Staskunas	7/1/18
Steve F. Taylor	7/1/18
Christine P. Holmes	7/1/19
Monica Young	7/1/19

Mississippi River Parkway Commission

Frank Fiorenza	expires 2/1/12
Jill Billings	2/1/20
Dennis Donath	2/1/20
Jean Galasinski	2/1/20
Jaynne L. Lepke	2/1/20
Alan Lorenz	2/1/20
Howard Marklein	2/1/20
Robert Miller	2/1/20
Lee Nerison	2/1/20
Sherry Quamme	2/1/20
David Smith	2/1/20
Kathleen Vinehout	2/1/20
Thomas Vondrum	2/1/20

National and Community Service Board

Larry Kleinsteiber	expires 5/1/08
Maia Pearson	5/1/10
Martha Kerner	5/1/12
Thi Le	5/1/13
Scott Fromader	5/1/14
Sue Grady	5/1/14
Mark Mueller	5/1/14
Bob Guenther	5/1/15
Christine Beatty	5/1/17
Lisa Delmore	5/1/17
Robert Griffith	5/1/17
Kathleen Groat	5/1/17
James M. Langdon	5/1/17
Amy McDowell	5/1/17
Paula Horning	5/1/18
Angela Kringle	5/1/18
Margaret Jane Moore	5/1/18
Pamela Charles	5/1/19
Donald P. Dunbar	5/1/19
Anthony F. Hallman	5/1/19
Kate Jaeger	5/1/19
Susan Schwartz	5/1/19
Daniel Zimmerman	5/1/20
India McCanse	expires at governor's pleasure

Natural Resources, Department of, secretary [1]
(group 7 salary [2]**)**

Cathy Stepp . . . . . expires at governor's pleasure

Natural Resources Board [1]

Preston D. Cole	expires 5/1/19
Gary Zimmer	5/1/19
Julie Anderson	5/1/21
Frederick Prehn	5/1/21
William Bruins [3]	5/1/23
Terry N. Hilgenberg [3]	5/1/23
Gregory J. Kazmierski [3]	5/1/23

State officers appointed by the governor, May 14, 2017, continued

Nonmotorized Recreation and Transportation Trails Council
Rod Bartlow . . . . . expires at governor's pleasure
William Hauda . . . . governor's pleasure
Dana Johnson . . . . governor's pleasure
Anne Murphy . . . . governor's pleasure
Joel Patenaude . . . . governor's pleasure
Debbie Peterson . . . . governor's pleasure
David Phillips . . . . governor's pleasure
Ben Popp . . . . governor's pleasure
Geoffrey Snudden . . . . governor's pleasure
Blake Theisen . . . . governor's pleasure

Nursing, Board of [1] ($25/day [2])
Peter Kallio . . . . .expires 7/1/18
Sheryl Krause 7/1/18
Cheryl Streeter 7/1/18
Paul Abegglen 7/1/19
Lillian Nolan 7/1/19
Pamela K. White [3] 7/1/19
Beth Smith Houskamp [3] 7/1/20
Jennifer L. Eklof [3] 7/1/21
Luann Skarlupka [3] 7/1/21

Nursing Home Administrator Examining Board [1] ($25/day [2])
Susan Kinast-Porter . . . . .expires 7/1/09
Loreli Dickinson 7/1/11
Charles Hawkins 7/1/17
Kate Bertram 7/1/18
Brittany Cobb 7/1/18
Timothy Conroy 7/1/18
Stefanie Carton [3] 7/1/19
April Folgert [3] 7/1/19
Patrick Shaughnessy [3] 7/1/19

Occupational Therapists Affiliated Credentialing Board [1] ($25/day [2])
David Cooper . . . . .expires 7/1/11
Brian Holmquist 7/1/13
Corliss Rice .7/1/13
Gaye Meyer .7/1/18
Amy Summers 7/1/18
Mary C. Kassens [3] 7/1/19
Laura O'Brien [3] 7/1/19

Off-Highway Motorcycle Council
Mitch Winder . . . . .expires 3/1/18
Kira A. Benkert 3/1/19
Craig A. Johnson 3/1/19
Robert B. McConnell 3/1/20
Bryan T. Much 3/1/20

Off-Road Vehicle Council
Adam Harden . . . . expires 3/1/18
Rob McConnell 3/1/18
Robert A. Donahue 3/1/19
Bryan Much .3/1/19
Ernest G. Pulvermacher 3/1/19
David Traczyk 3/1/20
James Wisneski 3/1/20

Offender Reentry, Council on
Melinda Danforth . . . . .expires 7/1/11
Chuck Brendel 7/1/14
Michael Tobin 7/1/14
Angela M. Mancuso 7/1/17
Jonathon W. Nejedlo 7/1/17
Michael A. Oberbrunner 7/1/17
Antwayne M. Robertson 7/1/17
Michael R. Knetzger 7/1/18
Susan L. Opper 7/1/18
Karen J. Cumblad . . expires at governor's pleasure

Optometry Examining Board [1] ($25/day [2])
Ann Meier Carli . . . . .expires 7/1/14
Mark Jinkins 7/1/16
Richard L. Foss 7/1/17
Peter I. Sorce 7/1/18
Brian Hammes [3] 7/1/19
Robert C. Schulz [3] 7/1/20
John L. Sterling [3] 7/1/21

Parole Commission, chairperson [1] (group 2 salary [2])
Daniel J. Gabler [3] . . . . .expires 3/1/19

Perfusionists Examining Council ($25/day [2])
David Cobb . . . . .expires 7/1/10

Pharmacy Examining Board [1] ($25/day [2])
Philip Trapskin . . . . .expires 7/1/17
Cathy Winters 7/1/17
Grace D. Degner 7/1/18
Terry K. Maves 7/1/18
Thaddeus Schumacher 7/1/19
Franklin J. LaDien [3] 7/1/20
Kristi E. Sullivan [3] 7/1/20

Physical Disabilities, Council on
Jeffrey Fox . . . . .expires 7/1/11
Lewis Tyler .7/1/13
Joey Torkelson 7/1/15
Benjamin Barrett 7/1/16
Kurt Roskopf 7/1/16
Joanne Zimmerman 7/1/16
Michael Kindschi 7/1/17
Roberto Escamilla II 7/1/18
Ron J. Jansen 7/1/18
John Meissner 7/1/18
Noah Hershkowitz 7/1/19
Robert A. Nissen 7/1/19
Karen E. Secor 7/1/19
Monica Young . . . . expires at governor's pleasure

Physical Therapy Examining Board [1] ($25/day [2])
Lori Dominiczak . . . . .expires 7/1/17
Thomas Murphy 7/1/17
Sarah Olson 7/1/17
John Greany 7/1/19
Shari Berry [3] 7/1/20

Physician Assistants, Council on
Mary Pangman Schmitt . . . . .expires 7/1/08

State officers appointed by the governor, May 14, 2017, continued

Podiatry Affiliated Credentialing Board [1] ($25/day [2])
Thomas Komp . . . . .expires 7/1/17
William W. Weis [3] 7/1/19
Jeffery Giesking [3]. 7/1/20
vacancy

Prison Industries Board [1]
Lyle Balistreri . . . . .expires 5/1/08
Jose Carrillo .5/1/14
Bernie Spiegel 5/1/16
Tracey Isensee 5/1/18
James Jackson 5/1/19
James M. Langdon. 5/1/19
Bill Smith 5/1/19
Edward F. Wall [3]. 5/1/19

Psychology Examining Board [1] ($25/day [2])
Marcus P. Desmonde . . . . .expires 7/1/17
Rebecca Anderson 7/1/18
Christopher S. Gultch 7/1/18
David Thompson 7/1/18
Daniel Schroeder [3]. 7/1/19
Peter I. Sorce 7/1/20

Public Defender Board [1]
James Brennan . . . . .expires 5/1/13
Ellen Thorn 5/1/13
David Coon .5/1/18
Joseph T. Miotke 5/1/18
Mai N. Xiong 5/1/18
Regina Dunkin 5/1/19
Daniel M. Berkos [3] 5/1/20
Patrick Fiedler [3]. 5/1/20
John J. Hogan [3] 5/1/20

Public Health Council
A. Charles Post . . . . .expires 7/1/11
Mark Villalpando 7/1/11
Amy Bremel .7/1/13
Gretchen Sampson 7/1/13
James Sanders 7/1/13
Ann H. Hoffman 7/1/16
William Keeton 7/1/16
Sandra Mahkorn 7/1/16
Ruric Anderson 7/1/17
Terry Brandenburg 7/1/17
Mary Dorn .7/1/17
Gary D. Gilmore 7/1/17
Alan Schwartzstein 7/1/17
Jason Shrader 7/1/17
Michael Wallace 7/1/17
Bridget Clementi 7/1/18
Dale Hippensteel 7/1/18
Eric Krawczyk 7/1/18
Robert Leischow 7/1/18
Stephanie Schultz 7/1/18
Joan Theurer 7/1/18
Thai Vue 7/1/18
Darlene M. Weis 7/1/19

Public Records Board
Carl Buesing . . . . . expires at governor's pleasure
Carol Hemersbach . . . . governor's pleasure

Scott Kowalski . . . . governor's pleasure
Sandra Rudd . . . . governor's pleasure
Peter Sorce . . . . governor's pleasure

Public Service Commission [1] (group 5 salary [2])
Ellen Nowak. . . . . .expires 3/1/19
Michael Huebsch 3/1/21
Lon E. Roberts 3/1/23

Radiography Examining Board [1]
Donald Borst . . . . .expires 7/1/17
Michele Goodwiler 7/1/18
Thomas L. Frenn [3] 7/1/19
Tracy Marshall [3]. 7/1/20
Heidi Nichols 7/1/20
2 vacancies

Railroads, Commissioner of [1] (group 5 salary [2])
Yash Wadhwa . . . . .expires 3/1/23

Real Estate Appraisers Board [1] ($25/day [2])
Thomas Kneesel . . . . .expires 5/1/18
Lawrence Nicholson 5/1/18
Jennifer M. Espinoza-Coates 5/1/19
Steven Miner 5/1/19
Carl Clementi 5/1/20
Dennis Myers 5/1/21
vacancy

Real Estate Curriculum and Examinations, Council on
Lawrence Sager . . . . .expires 7/1/04
Paul G. Hoffman 7/1/06
Peter Sveum 7/1/06
Barbara McGill 7/1/10
Kathryne Kuhl 7/1/15
Robert Larson 7/1/15
Casey C. Clickner. 7/1/19
Robert G. Blakely 7/1/20
Kathy S. Zimmermann 7/1/20

Real Estate Examining Board [1] ($25/day [2])
Dennis Pierce . . . . .expires 7/1/13
Kitty Jedwabny 7/1/17
Richard J. Marino. 7/1/18
Brian McGrath 7/1/18
Michael J. Mulleady 7/1/18
Robert L. Webster 7/1/20
Jerry C. Lyons [3] 7/1/21

Recycling, Council on
James Birmingham . . . . .expires 1/5/15
Gary Harter 1/5/19
Carsten Jarrod Holter 1/5/19
David F. Keeling 1/5/19
Joseph Liebau 1/5/19
Heidi Woelfel 1/5/19
Jeff Zillich .1/5/19

Respiratory Care Practitioners Examining Council
vacancy

Retirement Board, Wisconsin ($25/day [2])
John David . . . . .expires 5/1/08

State officers appointed by the governor, May 14, 2017, continued

Wayne E. Koessl 5/1/09
Herbert Stinski .5/1/12
Mary Von Ruden 5/1/13
Steven Wilding .5/1/16
Julie Wathke 5/1/18
Scott Nordstrand. 5/1/20
vacancy

Retirement Systems, Joint Survey Committee on
Tim Pederson . . . . expires 2/14/15

Revenue, Deptartment of, secretary [1] (group 7 salary [2])
Rick Chandler . . . . expires at governor's pleasure

Rural Health Development Council
Erica Hoven . . . . .expires 7/1/09
Linda L. McFarlin 7/1/09
Byron Crouse .7/1/12
Tim Size 7/1/13
Charlie Walker 7/1/14
Jeremy Normington-Slay 7/1/15
Syed Ahmed .7/1/16
James O'Keefe 7/1/16
Blane Christman 7/1/17
Jacalyn Szehner 7/1/18
3 vacancies

Safety and Professional Services, Department of, secretary [1] (group 4 salary [2])
Laura E. Gutierrez . . expires at governor's pleasure

Savings Institutions Review Board [1] ($10/day [2])
Dennis P. Doyle. . . . . .expires 5/1/19
George Gary .5/1/19
Robert W. Holmes 5/1/19
Paul C. Adamski [3] 5/1/22
Charles Schmalz [3] 5/1/22

Sign Language Interpreter Council [1]
Debra Gorra Barash . . . . .expires 7/1/14
Carlos Jaramillo 7/1/14
Joel Mankowski 7/1/14
Faye Jordan Peters 7/1/14
Joseph Riggio 7/1/14
Steven Smart .7/1/14
Christopher Woodfill 7/1/14

Small Business Environmental Council
Sharon Klinger-Kingsley . . . . .expires 7/1/15
Amy J. Litscher 7/1/17
Jody A. Jansen 7/1/19

Small Business Regulatory Review Board
James Ring . . . . .expires 5/1/17
Connie Smith .5/1/17
Steven Davis .5/1/18
Erich Korth 5/1/18
Pravin Raikar .5/1/18
Melissa Remis 5/1/18
Guy Wood 5/1/18

Snowmobile Recreational Council [1]
Samuel J. Landes. . . . . .expires 7/1/17
Robert B. Lang 7/1/17
Andrew F. Malecki, Jr. 7/1/17
David Newman. 7/1/17
Michelle Voight 7/1/17
Thomas H. Chwala 7/1/18
Larry D. Erickson 7/1/18
Dale Mayo 7/1/18
Lee Van Zeeland 7/1/18
Arlyn H. Baumgarten 7/1/19
Beverly A. Dittmar 7/1/19
Gary Hilgendorf 7/1/19
Michael F. Holden 7/1/19
Steve W. Moran. 7/1/19
Nancy L. Olson 7/1/19

Southeast Wisconsin Professional Baseball Park District Board [1]
Kristine O'Meara . . . . .expires 7/1/15
Don Smiley 7/1/15
William L. McReynolds 7/1/17
John Wenum .7/1/17
Jim Ott 7/1/19
Thomas B. Schreibel [3] 7/1/19

Sporting Heritage Council
William Torhorst . . . . .expires 5/1/16

State Capitol and Executive Residence Board
Jay Fernholz . . . . .expires 5/1/15
Arlan Kay 5/1/15
Kathryn Neitzel 5/1/17
Marijo Reed .5/1/17
Lauren McManus Brown 5/1/19
Ronald L. Siggelkow 5/1/19

State Employees Suggestion Board
Danielle Johnson . . . . .expires 5/1/15
Paul Ruby 5/1/17
vacancy

State Fair Park Board [1] ($10/day, not to exceed $600/year [2])
Jim Sullivan ($0/day [2]) . . . . .expires 1/1/12
Leah Vukmir ($0/day [2]) 1/1/13
Keith Ripp ($0/day [2]) 1/1/13
Sue Rupnow .5/1/17
Susan Crane. .5/1/18
Dan Devine 5/1/19
James Villa 5/1/19
Aldo Madrigrano 5/1/20
John Yingling .5/1/20
Mary Maas [3] .5/1/21

State Historical Society of Wisconsin Board of Curators [1]
William Van Sant . . . . .expires 7/1/15
Keene Winters 7/1/17
George F. Jacobs, Jr. 7/1/19
Dave Anderson . . . expires at governor's pleasure

State officers appointed by the governor, May 14, 2017, continued

State Trails Council
Thomas Huber . . . . .expires 7/1/07
Jim Joque 7/1/11
Robbie Webber 7/1/13
Ken Carpenter 7/1/15
Phillip Johnsrud 7/1/15
Michael McFadzen 7/1/17
Kendal Neitzke 7/1/17
John Siegert .7/1/17
James White 7/1/17
Randy Harden 7/1/19
Doug Johnson 7/1/19
LuAna Schneider 7/1/19
Bryan T. Much 7/1/21

State Use Board
Michael Casey . . . . .expires 5/1/11
Nickolas George, Jr. 5/1/11
Bill Smith 5/1/11
Jean Zweifel .5/1/11
Tim Casper .5/1/13
Marie Danforth 5/1/13
David Dumke 5/1/13
Enid Glenn .5/1/17
James M. Langdon 5/1/17

Tax Appeals Commission [1] (group 4 salary [2])
David Wilmoth . . . . .expires 3/1/19
David Coon .3/1/21
Lorna Hemp Boll 3/1/23

Tax Exemptions, Joint Survey Committee on
Kimberly Shaul . . . . .expires 1/15/13

Teachers Retirement Board ($25/day [2])
Sandra Claflin-Chalton . . . . .expires 5/1/12
Gary Epping 5/1/18
David Schalow 5/1/19
Craig Hubbell ($0/day [2]) 5/1/18

Technical College System Board [1] ($100/year [2])
Philip Baranowski . . . . .expires 5/1/17
Hunter Kautz [3] 5/1/17
W. Kent Lorenz 5/1/19
Terrance McGowan 5/1/19
Stephen Mark Tyler 5/1/19
Becky Levzow 5/1/21
Kelly Tourdot 5/1/21
Mary Williams 5/1/21
John Schwantes [3] 5/1/23
Stephen D. Willett [3] 5/1/23

Tourism, Council on
Allyson Gommer . . . . .expires 7/1/16
Paul Cunningham 7/1/17
Apache B. Danforth 7/1/17
Stanton Peter Helland, Jr. 7/1/17
Deborah Archer 7/1/18
James Bolen 7/1/18
Kathy Kopp 7/1/18
Paul Upchurch 7/1/18
Stacey Watson 7/1/18
Cindy L. Burzinski 7/1/19

Brian Kelsey .7/1/19
Scott Krause 7/1/19
Lola Roeh 7/1/19
Joe Klimczak 7/1/20

Tourism, Department of, secretary [1] (group 6 salary [2])
Stephanie Klett . . . expires at governor's pleasure

Transportation, Department of, secretary [1] (group 7 salary [2])
Dave B. Ross [3] . . . . . expires at governor's pleasure

Transportation Projects Commission
Barbara Fleisner . . . expires at governor's pleasure
Jean M. Jacobson . . . . governor's pleasure
Michael Ryan . . . . governor's pleasure

Uniform Dwelling Code Council
Timothy Wiberg . . . . .expires 7/1/16
Peter Krabbe 7/1/17
Daniel Wald .7/1/17
Brian Wert .7/1/17
Abe J. Degnan 7/1/18
Steven J. Gryboski 7/1/18
W. Scott Satula 7/1/18
Mary L. Schroeder 7/1/18
Michael A. Coello 7/1/19
Jesse Jerabek 7/1/19
Mike Marthaler 7/1/19

Uniform State Laws, Commission on
John Macy . . . . .expires 5/1/17
Annette Kingsland Ziegler 5/1/19

University of Wisconsin Hospitals and Clinics Authority [1]
Carol L. Booth . . . . expires at governor's pleasure
Richard W. Choudoir . . . . governor's pleasure
Pablo Sanchez . . . . .expires 7/1/17
Andrew Hitt .7/1/19
David Ward .7/1/19
Lisa Reardon [3] 7/1/20
Gary Wolter [3] 7/1/20
John W. Litscher [3] 7/1/21

University of Wisconsin System, Board of Regents [1]
Lisa Erickson . . . . .expires 5/1/18
Tim Higgins .5/1/18
Gerald Whitburn 5/1/18
John Behling 5/1/19
Regina Millner 5/1/19
Ryan L. Ring [3] 5/1/19
Margaret Farrow 5/1/20
Janice Mueller 5/1/20
Jose Delgado 5/1/21
Eve M. Hall .5/1/21
Michael M. Grebe 5/1/22
Andrew Petersen 5/1/22
Tracey Klein .5/1/23
Bryan Steil .5/1/23
Robert B. Atwell [3] 5/1/24
Michael T. Jones [3] 5/1/24

State officers appointed by the governor, May 14, 2017, continued

Veterans Affairs, Board of[1]
Alan Richards . . . . .expires 5/1/13
John Townsend 5/1/13
Marvin Freedman 5/1/15
Peter Moran 5/1/15
Daniel Bohlin 5/1/17
Cathy Gorst .5/1/17
Leigh Neville-Neil 5/1/17
Kevin Nicholson 5/1/17
John Gaedke 5/1/19
Carl Krueger 5/1/19
Larry Kutschma 5/1/19

Veterans Affairs, Department of, secretary[1]
(group 6 salary[2])
Daniel J. Zimmerman . . . .
. . . . expires at governor's pleasure

Veterinary Diagnostic Laboratory Board
Casey Davis . . . . .expires 5/1/18
Alissa Grenawalt 5/1/18
James Meronek 5/1/19
Ray Pawlisch 5/1/19
Sandra C. Madland 5/1/20
Sheryl Shaw . . . . . expires at governor's pleasure

Veterinary Examining Board[1] ($25/day[2])
Robert Forbes . . . . .expires 7/1/17
Diane Dommer Martin 7/1/17
Lisa Weisensel Nesson 7/1/18
Dana Reimer 7/1/18
Sheldon Schall 7/1/18
Philip Johnson 7/1/19
Bruce Berth .7/1/20
Kevin S. Kreier 7/1/20

Waste Facility Siting Board[1] ($35/day[2])
James Schuerman . . . . .expires 5/1/13
Dale R. Shaver 5/1/17
Jeanette P. DeKeyser 5/1/18

Waterways Commission, Wisconsin[1]
Maureen Kinney . . . . .expires 3/1/14
Roger E. Walsh 3/1/18
James F. Rooney 3/1/19
Lee Van Zeeland 3/1/20
vacancy

Wisconsin Center District Board of Directors
James Kaminski . . . . .expires 5/1/17
James Kanter 5/1/17
Stephen H. Marcus 5/1/17

Wisconsin Compensation Rating Bureau
Daniel Burazin . . . . expires at governor's pleasure
Chris Reader . . . . governor's pleasure

Women's Council
Jane Clark . . . . .expires 7/1/11
Patricia M. Cadorin 7/1/17
Karen M. Katz 7/1/17
Katherine Mnuk 7/1/17
Mary Jo Baas 7/1/18
Brianna N. Buch 7/1/18
Jessie Nicholson 7/1/18
Michelle Mettner 7/1/19

Workforce Development, Department of, secretary[1] (group 6 salary[2])
Raymond Allen . . . expires at governor's pleasure

Note: List includes only appointments made by the governor to statutory bodies in state government. In many cases, additional members serve ex officio or are appointed by other means. The governor also appoints members of intrastate regional agencies and nonstatutory committees and makes temporary appointments under chapter 17, Wis. Stats., to elected state and county offices when vacancies occur.

1. Nominated by the governor and appointed with the advice and consent of the senate. Senate confirmation is required for secretaries of departments, members of commissions and commissioners, governing boards, examining boards, and other boards as designated by statute. 2. Members of boards and councils are reimbursed for actual and necessary expenses incurred in performing their duties. In addition, examining board members receive $25 per day for days worked, and members of certain other boards under section 15.07(5), Wis. Stats., receive a per diem as noted in the table. Section 20.923, Wis. Stats., places state officials in one of ten executive salary groups for which salary ranges have been established. Group salary ranges for the period June 28, 2015, to June 24, 2017, were: Group 1: $60,382–$99,632; Group 2: $65,208–$107,598; Group 3: $70,429–$116,210; Group 4: $76,066–$125,528; Group 5: $82,139–$135,533; Group 6: $88,712–$146,390; Group 7: $95,826–$158,122; Group 8: $103,480–$170,747; Group 9: $111,758–$184,413; Group 10: $120,702–$199,160. 3. Nominated by governor but not yet confirmed by senate. 4. Compensation set by Economic Development Corporation Board.

Source: Appointment lists maintained by governor's office and received by the Legislative Reference Bureau on or before May 14, 2017.

Circuit court judges, May 15, 2017

Counties in circuit	Branch	Court location	Judges	Term expires July 31
Adams	—	Friendship	Daniel Glen Wood	2021
Ashland.	—	Ashland	Robert E. Eaton	2018
Barron.	1	Barron	James C. Babler	2022
	2	Barron	J. Michael Bitney	2020
	3	Barron	Maureen D. Boyle.	2020
Bayfield.	—	Washburn	John P. Anderson	2021
Brown.	1	Green Bay	Donald R. Zuidmulder.	2021
	2	Green Bay	Tom Walsh	2018
	3	Green Bay	Tammy Jo Hock	2019
	4	Green Bay	Kendall M. Kelley	2021
	5	Green Bay	Marc A. Hammer	2021
	6	Green Bay	John P. Zakowski	2018
	7	Green Bay	Timothy A. Hinkfuss	2019
	8	Green Bay	William M. Atkinson	2021
Buffalo, Pepin	—	Alma	James J. Duvall	2018
Burnett	—	Siren	vacancy [1]	2017
Calumet	—	Chilton	Jeffrey S. Froehlich	2018
Chippewa	1	Chippewa Falls	Steven H. Gibbs [2]	2018
	2	Chippewa Falls	James Isaacson	2021
	3	Chippewa Falls	Steven R. Cray	2020
Clark.	—	Neillsville	Jon M. Counsell	2018
Columbia.	1	Portage	Todd J. Hepler	2021
	2	Portage	W. Andrew Voigt [3]	2017
	3	Portage	Alan White	2019
Crawford	—	Prairie du Chien	Lynn Marie Ryder.	2022
Dane	1	Madison	John Markson [4]	2020
	2	Madison	Josann M. Reynolds	2021
	3	Madison	Valerie L. Bailey-Rihn.	2022
	4	Madison	Everett Mitchell	2022
	5	Madison	Nicholas J. McNamara	2022
	6	Madison	Shelley J. Gaylord.	2021
	7	Madison	William E. Hanrahan	2020
	8	Madison	Frank D. Remington	2018
	9	Madison	Richard Niess [3]	2017
	10	Madison	Juan B. Colas	2021
	11	Madison	Ellen K. Berz	2018
	12	Madison	Clayton Kawski [2,5]	2017
	13	Madison	Julie Genovese	2021
	14	Madison	John D. Hyland	2022
	15	Madison	Stephen Ehlke.	2022
	16	Madison	Rhonda L. Lanford	2019
	17	Madison	Peter C. Anderson	2022
Dodge	1	Juneau	Brian A. Pfitzinger	2020
	2	Juneau	Martin J. De Vries [2,6]	2017
	3	Juneau	Joseph G. Sciascia	2019
	4	Juneau	Steven Bauer	2020
Door.	1	Sturgeon Bay	D. Todd Ehlers	2018
	2	Sturgeon Bay	David L. Weber [2,6]	2017
Douglas.	1	Superior	Kelly J. Thimm	2021
	2	Superior	George L. Glonek	2021
Dunn	1	Menomonie	James M. Peterson	2020
	2	Menomonie	Rod W. Smeltzer.	2021
Eau Claire.	1	Eau Claire	John F. Manydeeds.	2022
	2	Eau Claire	Michael Schumacher	2020
	3	Eau Claire	William M. Gabler.	2018
	4	Eau Claire	Jon M. Theisen	2018
	5	Eau Claire	Paul J. Lenz.	2018
Florence, Forest. . . .	—	Crandon	Leon D. Stenz	2020

Circuit court judges, May 15, 2017, continued

Counties in circuit	Branch	Court location	Judges	Term expires July 31
Fond du Lac	1	Fond du Lac	Dale L. English.	2020
	2	Fond du Lac	Peter L. Grimm	2022
	3	Fond du Lac	Richard J. Nuss	2021
	4	Fond du Lac	Gary R. Sharpe	2022
	5	Fond du Lac	Robert J. Wirtz [3]	2017
Grant	1	Lancaster	Robert P. VanDeHey [3]	2017
	2	Lancaster	Craig R. Day	2021
Green	1	Monroe	Jim Beer	2021
	2	Monroe	Thomas J. Vale.	2021
Green Lake	—	Green Lake	Mark Slate [3]	2017
Iowa	—	Dodgeville	Margaret M. Koehler.	2022
Iron	—	Hurley	Patrick John Madden [3]	2017
Jackson	—	Black River Falls	Anna L. Becker	2021
Jefferson	1	Jefferson	Jennifer L. Weston	2021
	2	Jefferson	William F. Hue	2019
	3	Jefferson	Robert F. Dehring [2]	2018
	4	Jefferson	Randy R. Koschnick [7]	2017
Juneau	1	Mauston	John Pier Roemer.	2022
	2	Mauston	Paul S. Curran	2020
Kenosha	1	Kenosha	David Mark Bastianelli.	2021
	2	Kenosha	Jason A. Rossell.	2018
	3	Kenosha	Bruce E. Schroeder.	2020
	4	Kenosha	Anthony Milisauskas [3]	2017
	5	Kenosha	David P. Wilk.	2021
	6	Kenosha	Mary K. Wagner.	2021
	7	Kenosha	Jodi L. Meier [2, 6]	2017
	8	Kenosha	Chad G. Kerkman.	2021
Kewaunee	—	Kewaunee	Keith A. Mehn.	2022
La Crosse	1	La Crosse	Ramona A. Gonzalez.	2019
	2	La Crosse	Elliott Levine.	2019
	3	La Crosse	Todd Bjerke	2019
	4	La Crosse	Scott L. Horne.	2019
	5	La Crosse	Gloria Doyle.	2021
Lafayette	—	Darlington	Duane M. Jorgenson.	2021
Langlade	—	Antigo	John Rhode	2021
Lincoln	1	Merrill	Jay R. Tlusty.	2022
	2	Merrill	Robert Russell.	2019
Manitowoc	1	Manitowoc	Mark R. Rohrer	2019
	2	Manitowoc	Gary Bendix	2018
	3	Manitowoc	Jerome L. Fox [8]	2017
Marathon	1	Wausau	Jill N. Falstad.	2021
	2	Wausau	Gregory Huber	2022
	3	Wausau	Lamont K. Jacobson	2020
	4	Wausau	Gregory J. Strasser [2, 6]	2017
	5	Wausau	Mike Moran [3]	2017
Marinette	1	Marinette	David G. Miron	2020
	2	Marinette	James A. Morrison	2019
Marquette	—	Montello	Bernard Ben Bult	2019
Menominee, Shawano	1	Shawano	James R. Habeck	2020
	2	Shawano	William F. Kussel, Jr.	2018
Milwaukee	1	Milwaukee	Maxine Aldridge White [3]	2017
	2	Wauwatosa	Joe Donald.	2021
	3	Milwaukee	Clare L. Fiorenza	2021
	4	Milwaukee	Michael J. Hanrahan [2, 6]	2017
	5	Milwaukee	Mary Kuhnmuench.	2022
	6	Milwaukee	Ellen Brostrom	2021
	7	Milwaukee	Thomas J. McAdams.	2020
	8	Milwaukee	William Sosnay	2018

Circuit court judges, May 15, 2017, continued

Counties in circuit	Branch	Court location	Judges	Term expires July 31
	9	Milwaukee	Paul R. Van Grunsven [3]	2017
	10	Milwaukee	Timothy G. Dugan [9]	2017
	11	Milwaukee	Dave Swanson	2019
	12	Milwaukee	David L. Borowski	2021
	13	Milwaukee	Mary Triggiano [3]	2017
	14	Milwaukee	Christopher R. Foley	2022
	15	Milwaukee	J.D. Watts	2021
	16	Wauwatosa	Michael J. Dwyer	2021
	17	Milwaukee	Carolina Maria Stark	2018
	18	Wauwatosa	Pedro Colón [3]	2017
	19	Wauwatosa	Dennis R. Cimpl [3]	2017
	20	Milwaukee	Dennis P. Moroney [10]	2018
	21	Milwaukee	Cynthia M. Davis [2, 6]	2017
	22	Milwaukee	Timothy M. Witkowiak	2021
	23	Milwaukee	Lindsey Grady	2018
	24	Milwaukee	Janet Protasiewicz	2020
	25	Milwaukee	Stephanie Rothstein	2022
	26	Milwaukee	William Pocan	2019
	27	Milwaukee	Kevin E. Martens	2020
	28	Wauwatosa	Mark A. Sanders	2018
	29	Milwaukee	Richard J. Sankovitz	2021
	30	Milwaukee	Jeffrey A. Conen	2021
	31	Milwaukee	Hannah C. Dugan	2022
	32	Milwaukee	Laura Gramling Perez	2020
	33	Milwaukee	Carl Ashley [3]	2017
	34	Milwaukee	Glenn H. Yamahiro	2022
	35	Milwaukee	Frederick C. Rosa [3]	2017
	36	Milwaukee	Jeffrey A. Kremers [3]	2017
	37	Wauwatosa	T. Christopher Dee	2021
	38	Milwaukee	Jeffrey A. Wagner	2018
	39	Milwaukee	Jane Carroll	2018
	40	Milwaukee	Rebecca Dallett	2020
	41	Wauwatosa	John J. DiMotto	2020
	42	Milwaukee	David A. Hansher	2021
	43	Milwaukee	Marshall B. Murray	2018
	44	Milwaukee	Gwen Connolly	2022
	45	Wauwatosa	Jean Marie Kies	2022
	46	Milwaukee	David Feiss	2021
	47	Milwaukee	John Siefert [11]	2017
Monroe	1	Sparta	Todd L. Ziegler	2019
	2	Sparta	Mark L. Goodman	2022
	3	Sparta	J. David Rice	2022
Oconto	1	Oconto	Michael T. Judge [3]	2017
	2	Oconto	Jay N. Conley	2022
Oneida	1	Rhinelander	Patrick F. O'Melia	2020
	2	Rhinelander	Michael H. Bloom	2018
Outagamie	1	Appleton	Mark McGinnis [3]	2017
	2	Appleton	Nancy J. Krueger	2020
	3	Appleton	Mitchell J. Metropulos	2020
	4	Appleton	Greg Gill, Jr.	2018
	5	Appleton	Michael W. Gage	2021
	6	Appleton	Vincent Biskupic	2021
	7	Appleton	John A. Des Jardins	2018
Ozaukee	1	Port Washington	Paul V. Malloy	2021
	2	Port Washington	Joe Voiland	2019
	3	Port Washington	Sandy A. Williams	2021
Pierce	—	Ellsworth	Joe Boles	2022
Polk	1	Balsam Lake	Daniel J. Tolan [2, 6]	2017
	2	Balsam Lake	Jeff Anderson [3]	2017

Circuit court judges, May 15, 2017, continued

Counties in circuit	Branch	Court location	Judges	Term expires July 31
Portage	1	Stevens Point	Thomas B. Eagon	2018
	2	Stevens Point	Robert J. Shannon	2022
	3	Stevens Point	Thomas T. Flugaur	2018
Price	—	Phillips	Douglas T. Fox	2020
Racine	1	Racine	Wynne Laufenberg [2]	2018
	2	Racine	Eugene Gasiorkiewicz	2022
	3	Racine	Emily S. Mueller [3]	2017
	4	Racine	Mark Nielsen	2022
	5	Racine	Mike Piontek	2018
	6	Racine	David W. Paulson	2021
	7	Racine	Charles H. Constantine	2020
	8	Racine	Faye M. Flancher	2021
	9	Racine	Robert S. Repischak [2]	2018
	10	Racine	Timothy D. Boyle	2018
Richland	—	Richland Center	Andrew Sharp	2018
Rock	1	Janesville	James P. Daley	2020
	2	Janesville	Alan Bates	2022
	3	Janesville	Michael Fitzpatrick	2021
	4	Janesville	Daniel T. Dillon	2019
	5	Janesville	Mike Haakenson	2021
	6	Janesville	John M. Wood [2,6]	2017
	7	Janesville	Barbara W. McCrory	2018
Rusk	—	Ladysmith	Steven P. Anderson	2022
St. Croix	1	Hudson	Eric J. Lundell	2020
	2	Hudson	Edward F. Vlack III	2019
	3	Hudson	Scott R. Needham	2018
	4	Hudson	R. Michael Waterman	2022
Sauk	1	Baraboo	Michael P. Screnock	2022
	2	Baraboo	Wendy J. N. Klicko	2022
	3	Baraboo	Guy D. Reynolds	2018
Sawyer	—	Hayward	John Yackel	2021
Sheboygan	1	Sheboygan	L. Edward Stengel	2021
	2	Sheboygan	Kent Hoffman [2,6]	2017
	3	Sheboygan	Angela Sutkiewicz [3]	2017
	4	Sheboygan	Rebecca Persick	2021
	5	Sheboygan	Daniel J. Borowski [2,6]	2017
Taylor	—	Medford	Ann Knox-Bauer	2021
Trempealeau	—	Whitehall	Charles V. Feltes [2,12]	2017
Vernon	—	Viroqua	Michael J. Rosborough [13]	2017
Vilas	—	Eagle River	Neal A. Nielsen	2022
Walworth	1	Elkhorn	Phillip A. Koss	2018
	2	Elkhorn	Daniel S. Johnson	2022
	3	Elkhorn	Kristine E. Drettwan	2021
	4	Elkhorn	David M. Reddy	2022
Washburn	—	Shell Lake	Eugene D. Harrington	2021
Washington	1	West Bend	James Pouros [3]	2017
	2	West Bend	James K. Muehlbauer	2020
	3	West Bend	Todd Martens [3]	2017
	4	West Bend	Andrew T. Gonring	2018
Waukesha	1	Waukesha	Michael O. Bohren	2019
	2	Waukesha	Jennifer Dorow	2018
	3	Waukesha	Ralph M. Ramirez [3]	2017
	4	Waukesha	Lloyd V. Carter [3]	2017
	5	Waukesha	Lee Sherman Dreyfus, Jr.	2020
	6	Waukesha	Patrick C. Haughney	2020
	7	Waukesha	Maria S. Lazar	2021
	8	Waukesha	Michael P. Maxwell	2021
	9	Waukesha	Michael Aprahamian	2021
	10	Waukesha	Paul Bugenhagen, Jr.	2021

Circuit court judges, May 15, 2017, continued

Counties in circuit	Branch	Court location	Judges	Term expires July 31
	11	Waukesha	William Domina[3]	2017
	12	Waukesha	Kathryn W. Foster.	2018
Waupaca	1	Waupaca	Philip M. Kirk[14]	2017
	2	Waupaca	Vicki Taggatz Clussman	2020
	3	Waupaca	Raymond S. Huber	2018
Waushara.	—	Wautoma	Guy Dutcher[3]	2017
Winnebago	1	Oshkosh	Thomas J. Gritton	2018
	2	Oshkosh	Scott C. Woldt[3]	2017
	3	Oshkosh	Barbara Hart Key	2022
	4	Oshkosh	Karen L. Seifert	2018
	5	Oshkosh	John Jorgensen.	2022
	6	Oshkosh	Daniel J. Bissett[3]	2017
Wood	1	Wisconsin Rapids	Gregory J. Potter	2020
	2	Wisconsin Rapids	Nicholas J. Brazeau, Jr.	2018
	3	Wisconsin Rapids	Todd P. Wolf	2021

— Means the circuit has only one branch.

1. Melissia R. Christianson Mogen was newly elected on April 4, 2017, for a six-year term to commence on August 1, 2017. 2. Appointed by the governor. 3. Reelected on April 4, 2017, for a six-year term to commence on August 1, 2017. 4. Retiring June 2, 2017; appointee will serve to 2018. 5. Jill J. Karofsky was newly elected on April 4, 2017, for a six-year term to commence on August 1, 2017. 6. Newly elected on April 4, 2017, for a six-year term to commence on August 1, 2017. 7. Bennett J. Brantmeier was newly elected on April 4, 2017, for a six-year term to commence on August 1, 2017. 8. Bob Dewane was newly elected on April 4, 2017, for a six-year term to commence on August 1, 2017. 9. Michelle Ackerman Havas was newly elected on April 4, 2017, for a six-year term to commence on August 1, 2017. 10. Retiring June 22, 2017; appointee will serve to 2018. 11. Kristy Yang was newly elected on April 4, 2017, for a six-year term to commence on August 1, 2017. 12. Rian W. Radtke was newly elected on April 4, 2017, for a six-year term to commence on August 1, 2017. 13. Darcy Rood was newly elected on April 4, 2017, for a six-year term to commence on August 1, 2017. 14. Troy L. Nielsen was newly elected on April 4, 2017, for a six-year term to commence on August 1, 2017.

Sources: 2015–2016 Wisconsin Statutes; Wisconsin Elections Commission, department data, April 2017; governor's appointment notices; The Third Branch newsletter, Winter/Spring 2017 and previous issues.

Wisconsin county officers: county clerks, June 2017

	Clerk	Website
Adams	Cindy Phillippi (D)	www.co.adams.wi.gov
Ashland.	Heather W. Schutte (D)	www.co.ashland.wi.us
Barron.	DeeAnn Cook (R)	www.barroncountywi.gov
Bayfield.	Scott S. Fibert (D)	www.bayfieldcounty.org
Brown.	Sandy Juno (R)	www.co.brown.wi.us
Buffalo	Roxann M. Halverson (D)	www.buffalocounty.com
Burnett	Wanda Hinrichs (D)	www.burnettcounty.com
Calumet	Beth A. Hauser (R)	www.co.calumet.wi.us
Chippewa	Sandi Frion (D)	www.co.chippewa.wi.us
Clark.	Christina M. Jensen (R)	www.co.clark.wi.us
Columbia.	Susan M. Moll (R)	www.co.columbia.wi.us
Crawford	Janet Geisler (R)	www.crawfordcountywi.org
Dane	Scott McDonell (D)	www.countyofdane.com
Dodge	Karen J. Gibson (R)	www.co.dodge.wi.gov
Door.	Jill M. Lau (R)	www.co.door.wi.gov
Douglas.	Susan T. Sandvick (D)	www.douglascountywi.org
Dunn	Julie A. Wathke (D)	www.co.dunn.wi.us
Eau Claire.	Janet K. Loomis (D)	www.co.eau-claire.wi.us

Wisconsin county officers: county clerks, June 2017, continued

	Clerk	Website
Florence	Donna Trudell (R)	www.florencecountywi.com
Fond du Lac	Lisa Freiberg (R)	www.fdlco.wi.gov
Forest	Nora Matuszewski (R)	www.co.forest.wi.gov
Grant	Linda K. Gebhard (R)	www.co.grant.wi.gov
Green	Michael J. Doyle (I)	www.co.green.wi.gov
Green Lake	Elizabeth Otto (R)	www.co.green-lake.wi.us
Iowa	Gregory T. Klusendorf (D)	www.iowacounty.org
Iron	Michael Saari (D)	www.co.iron.wi.gov
Jackson	Kyle Deno (D)	www.co.jackson.wi.us
Jefferson	Barbara A. Frank (R)	www.jeffersoncountywi.gov
Juneau	Terri L. Wafle-Treptow (R)	www.co.juneau.wi.gov
Kenosha	Mary T. Schuch-Krebs (D)	www.co.kenosha.wi.us
Kewaunee	Jamie Annoye (D)	www.kewauneeco.org
La Crosse	Ginny Dankmeyer (D)	www.lacrossecounty.org
Lafayette	Carla M. Jacobson (R)	www.co.lafayette.wi.gov
Langlade	Judy Nagel (D)	www.co.langlade.wi.us
Lincoln	Christopher Marlowe (R)	www.co.lincoln.wi.us
Manitowoc	Lois Kiel (R)	www.co.manitowoc.wi.us
Marathon	Nan Kottke (D)	www.co.marathon.wi.us
Marinette	Kathy Brandt (R)	www.marinettecounty.com
Marquette	Gary L. Sorensen (R)	www.co.marquette.wi.us
Menominee	Sarah Lyons (D)	www.co.menominee.wi.us
Milwaukee	George L. Christenson (D)	www.milwaukeecounty.org
Monroe	Shelley Bohl (R)	www.co.monroe.wi.us
Oconto	Kim Pytleski (R)	www.co.oconto.wi.us
Oneida	Tracy Hartman (R)	www.co.oneida.wi.gov
Outagamie	Lori J. O'Bright (R)	www.outagamie.org
Ozaukee	Julianne B. Winkelhorst (R)	www.co.ozaukee.wi.us
Pepin	Audrey Bauer (R)	www.co.pepin.wi.us
Pierce	Jamie R. Feuerhelm (D)	www.co.pierce.wi.us
Polk	Sharon Jorgenson (R)	www.co.polk.wi.us
Portage	Shirley M. Simonis (D)	www.co.portage.wi.us
Price	Jean Gottwald (D)	www.co.price.wi.us
Racine	Wendy M. Christensen (R)	http://racinecounty.com
Richland	Victor V. Vlasak (R)	www.co.richland.wi.us
Rock	Lisa Tollefson (D)	www.co.rock.wi.us
Rusk	Loren Beebe (D)	www.ruskcounty.org
St. Croix	Cindy Campbell (D)	www.co.saint-croix.wi.us
Sauk	Rebecca C. Evert (R)	www.co.sauk.wi.us
Sawyer	Carol Williamson (R)	www.sawyercountygov.org
Shawano	Pamela Schmidt (R)	www.co.shawano.wi.us
Sheboygan	Jon Dolson (R)	www.sheboygancounty.com
Taylor	Bruce P. Strama (D)	www.co.taylor.wi.us
Trempealeau	Paul L. Syverson (D)	www.tremplocounty.com
Vernon	Ronald Hoff (R)	www.vernoncounty.org
Vilas	David R. Alleman (R)	www.co.vilas.wi.us
Walworth	Kimberly S. Bushey (R)	www.co.walworth.wi.us
Washburn	Lolita Olson (R)	www.co.washburn.wi.us
Washington	Ashley Reichert (R)	www.co.washington.wi.us
Waukesha	Kathleen O. Novack (R)	www.waukeshacounty.gov
Waupaca	Jill Lodewegen (R)	www.co.waupaca.wi.us
Waushara	Melanie Rendon Stake (R)	www.co.waushara.wi.us
Winnebago	Susan T. Ertmer (R)	www.co.winnebago.wi.us
Wood	Cynthia Cepress (D)	www.co.wood.wi.us

Note: County clerks are elected at the general election for four-year terms.

D–Democrat; I–Independent; R–Republican.

Source: Data collected from county clerks by Wisconsin Legislative Reference Bureau, March 2017.

Wisconsin county officers: county board chair; executive (or alternative); treasurer, June 2017

	County board chair (# of supervisors)	Executive, administrator, administrative coordinator	Treasurer
Adams	John West (20)	Barb Petkovsek (interim AC)	Jani Zander (D)
Ashland	Pete Russo (21)	Jeff Beirl (CA)	Tracey Hoglund (D)
Barron	James Miller (29)	Jeff French (CA)	Yvonne Ritchie (R)
Bayfield	Dennis M. Pocernich (13)	Mark Abeles–Allison (CA)	Daniel R. Anderson (D)
Brown	Patrick Moynihan, Jr. (26)	Troy Streckenbach (CE)	Paul Zeller (R)
Buffalo	Douglas Kane (14)	Sonya Hansen (AC)	Tina Anibas (R)
Burnett	Donald Taylor (21)	Nathan Ehalt (CA)	Judith Dykstra (R)
Calumet	Alice M. Connors (21)	Todd M. Romenesko (CA)	Michael V. Schlaak (R)
Chippewa	Anson Albarado (15)	Frank Pascarella (CA)	Patricia Schimmel (D)
Clark	Wayne Hendrickson (29)	Clinton Langreck (AC)	Mary J. Domanico (R)
Columbia	Vern E. Gove (28)	Susan Moll (AC)	Deborah A. Raimer (R)
Crawford	Tom Cornford (17)	Dan McWilliams (AC)	Deanne Lutz (D)
Dane	Sharon Corrigan (37)	Joseph Parisi (CE)	Adam Gallagher (D)
Dodge	Russell Kottke (33)	Jim Mielke (CA)	Patti Hilker (R)
Door	David Lienau (21)	Ken Pabich (CA)	Jay Zahn (R)
Douglas	Mark Liebaert (21)	Andrew G. Lisak (CA)	Carol Jones (D)
Dunn	Steven Rasmussen (29)	Paul R. Miller (CA)	Megan Mittlestadt (R)
Eau Claire	Gregg Moore (29)	Kathryn Schauf (CA)	Glenda J. Lyons (D)
Florence	Jeanette Bomberg (12)	Donna Trudell (AC)	Donna Liebergen (R)
Fond du Lac	Martin F. Farrell (25)	Allen J. Buechel (CE)	Brenda A. Schneider (R)
Forest	Paul Millan (21)	Nora Matuszewski (AC)	Christy Conley (D)
Grant	Robert C. Keeney (17)	Linda K. Gebhard (AC)	Louise Ketterer (R)
Green	Arthur F. Carter (31)	Michael J. Doyle (AC)	Sherri Hawkins (R)
Green Lake	Harley Reabe (19)	Catherine Schmit (CA)	Amanda R. Toney (R)
Iowa	John M. Meyers (21)	Larry Bierke (CA)	Connie Johnson (D)
Iron	Joe Pinardi (15)	Michael Saari (AC)	Clara J. Maki (D)
Jackson	Ray Ransom (19)	Kyle Deno (AC)	JoAnne Forsting Leonard (D)
Jefferson	James Schroeder (30)	Ben Wehmeier (CA)	John E. Jensen (R)
Juneau	Alan K. Peterson (21)	Alan K. Peterson (AC)	Denise Giebel (R)
Kenosha	Kimberly Breunig (23)	Jim Kreuser (CE)	Teri Jacobson (D)
Kewaunee	Robert A. Weidner (20)	Scott Feldt (CA)	Michelle Dax (R)
La Crosse	Tara Johnson (29)	Steve O'Malley (CA)	Shawn Handland (D)
Lafayette	Jack Sauer (16)	Jack Sauer (AC)	Becky Taylor (R)
Langlade	David Solin (21)	Robin J. Stowe (CC)	Tammy Wilhelm (D)
Lincoln	Robert Lee (22)	Randy Scholz (AC)	Diana Petruzates (R)
Manitowoc	Jim Brey (25)	Bob Ziegelbauer (CE)	Nancy Saueressig (R)
Marathon	Kurt Gibbs (38)	Brad Karger (CA)	Audrey Jensen (R)
Marinette	Mark Anderson (30)	John Lefebvre (CA)	Bev A. Noffke (R)
Marquette	Robert C. Miller (17)	Gary Sorensen (AC)	Diana Campbell (R)
Menominee	Elizabeth Moses (7)	Jeremy Weso (AC)	Louise Madosh (D)
Milwaukee	Theodore Lipscomb, Sr. (18)	Chris Abele (CE)	David Cullen (D)
Monroe	Cedric Schnitzler (16)	Jim Bialecki (CA)	Annette Erickson (R)
Oconto	Lee Rymer (31)	Kevin Hamann (AC)	Tanya Peterson (R)
Oneida	David Hintz (21)	Lisa Charbarneau (AC)	Kristina Ostermann (D)
Outagamie	Jeff Nooyen (36)	Thomas Nelson (CE)	Jack C. Voight (R)
Ozaukee	Lee Schlenvogt (26)	Jason Dzwinel (interim CA)	Joshua Morrison (R)
Pepin	Dwight Jelle (12)	Pamela DeWitt (AC)	Nancy Richardson (R)
Pierce	Jeff Holst (17)	Jo Ann Miller (AC)	Kathy Fuchs (R)
Polk	Dean K. Johansen (15)	Dana Frey (CA)	Amanda Nissen (D)
Portage	O. Philip Idsvoog (25)	Patty Dreier (CE)	Thomas Mallison (D)
Price	Bruce Jilka (13)	Nicholas Trimner (CA)	Lynn Neeck (D)
Racine	Russell A. Clark (21)	Jonathan Delagrave (CE)	Jane F. Nikolai (R)
Richland	Jeanetta Kirkpatrick (21)	Victor V. Vlasak (AC)	Julie Keller (R)
Rock	J. Russell Podzilni (29)	Joshua M. Smith (CA)	Michelle Roettger (D)
Rusk	Peter Boss (19)	Ted East (AC)	Verna Nielsen (R)
St. Croix	Roger Larson (19)	Patrick Thompson (CA)	Denise Anderson (R)
Sauk	Marty Krueger (31)	Alene Kleczek Bolin (AC)	Elizabeth Geoghegan (R)

Wisconsin county officers: county board chair; executive (or alternative); treasurer, June 2017, continued

County board chair (# of supervisors)	Executive, administrator, administrative coordinator	Treasurer
Sawyer . . . . Ron Kinsley (15)	Thomas Hoff (CA)	Dianne Ince (R)
Shawano . . . . . . Jerry Erdmann (27)	Brent Miller (AC)	Debra Wallace (R)
Sheboygan. . . . . Thomas G. Wegner (25)	Adam Payne (CA)	Laura Henning-Lorenz (D)
Taylor . . . . Jim Metz (17)	Marie Koerner (AC)	Sarah Holtz (R)
Trempealeau . . . Dick Miller (17)	Paul L. Syverson (AC)	Laurie Halama (D)
Vernon . . . . Dennis Brault (29)	Ronald Hoff (AC)	Rachel Hanson (R)
Vilas . . . . Ronald De Bruyne (21)	David R. Alleman (AC)	Jerri Radtke (R)
Walworth. . . . . . Nancy Russell (11)	David A. Bretl (CA)	Valerie Etzel (R)
Washburn . . . . . Thomas Mackie (21)	Lolita Olson (AC)	Nicole Tims (R)
Washington . . . . Rick Gundrum (26)	Joshua Schoemann (CA)	Jane Merten (R)
Waukesha . . . . . Paul L. Decker (25)	Paul Farrow (CE)	Pamela F. Reeves (R)
Waupaca . . . . . . Dick Koeppen (27)	Amanda Welch (AC)	Mark Sether (R)
Waushara. . . . . . Donna R. Kalata (11)	Robert J. Sivick (CA)	Elaine Wedell (R)
Winnebago . . . . David W. Albrecht (36)	Mark L. Harris (CE)	Mary E. Krueger (R)
Wood . . . . Lance Pliml (19)	Lance Pliml (AC)	Heather L. Gehrt (D)

Note: The county board is composed of supervisors who are elected at the nonpartisan spring election for two-year terms (but Milwaukee supervisors elected before 2016 were elected for four-year terms). The county board elects one of its members to be its chair. County executives are elected at the nonpartisan spring election for four-year terms. In lieu of electing a county executive, a county can choose to appoint a county administrator or to designate a county official to serve as the county's administrative coordinator. Treasurers are elected at the general election for four-year terms.

A–appointed to fill a vacancy; AC–administrative coordinator; CA–county administrator; CC–corporation counsel; CE–county executive; D–Democrat; R–Republican.

Source: Data collected from county clerks by Wisconsin Legislative Reference Bureau, March 2017.

Wisconsin county officers: clerk of circuit court; register of deeds; surveyor, June 2017

Clerk of circuit court	Register of deeds	Surveyor[1]
Adams . . . . Kathleen R. Dye (D)	Jodi Helgeson (R)	Gregory Rhinehart
Ashland. . . . . Kerrie Ferrando (D)	Karen Miller (D)	Dave Carlson
Barron. . . . . Sharon Millermon (R)	Margo Katterhagen (R)	Mark Netterlund
Bayfield. . . . . Kay L. Cederberg (D)	Denise Tarasewicz (D)	Robert Mick
Brown. . . . . John A. Vander Leest (R)	Cheryl Berken (R)	Terry VanHout
Buffalo . . . . Roselle Schlosser (R)	Carol Burmeister (D)	Joe Nelsen
Burnett . . . . Trudy Schmidt (D)	Jeanine Chell (D)	Jason Towne
Calumet . . . . Connie Daun (R)	Tamara Alten (R)	Bradley Buechel
Chippewa . . . . Karen Hepfler (D)	Marge L. Geissler (D)	Samuel I. Wenz
Clark. . . . . Heather Bravener (D)	Peggy L. Walter (R)	Wade Pettit
Columbia. . . . . Susan Raimer (R)	Karen A. Manske (R)	Jim Grothman
Crawford . . . . Donna Steiner (D)	Melissa Nagel (D)	Richard Marks
Dane . . . . Carlo Esqueda (D)	Kristi Chlebowski (D)	Dan Frick
Dodge . . . . Lynn Hron (R)	Christine Planasch (R)	Mike Canniff
Door. . . . . Connie DeFere (R)	Carey Petersilka (R)	None
Douglas. . . . . Michele L. Wick (D)	Tracy Middleton (D)	Matt Johnson
Dunn . . . . Katie Schalley (A)	Heather Kuhn (D)	Thomas Carlson
Eau Claire. . . . . Susan Schaffer (D)	Kathryn A. Christenson (D)	Dean Roth
Florence . . . . Tanya Neuens (R)	Pattie Gehlhoff (R)	None
Fond du Lac . . . . . . Ramona Geib (R)	James M. Krebs (R)	Peter Kuen
Forest . . . . Penny Carter (D)	Cortney M. Britten (D)	None
Grant . . . . Tina McDonald (R)	Marilyn Pierce (R)	Jay P. Adams

Wisconsin county officers: clerk of circuit court; register of deeds; surveyor, June 2017, continued

	Clerk of circuit court	Register of deeds	Surveyor[1]
Green	Barbara Miller (R)	Cynthia Meudt (R)	None
Green Lake	Amy Thoma (R)	Sarah Guenther (R)	None
Iowa	Lia N. Gust (R)	Dixie L. Edge (D)	None
Iron	Karen Ransanici (D)	Daniel Soine (D)	Todd Maki
Jackson	Jan Moennig (D)	Shari Marg (D)	Ethan Remus
Jefferson	Carla J. Robinson (R)	Staci M. Hoffman (R)	Jim Morrow
Juneau	Patty Schluter (R)	Stacy Havill (R)	Gary Dechant
Kenosha	Rebecca Matoska-Mentink (D)	JoEllyn M. Storz (D)	Robert W. Merry
Kewaunee	Rebecca Deterville (D)	Germaine Bertrand (D)	Kip Inman
La Crosse	Pamela Radtke (R)	Cheryl McBride (R)	Bryan Meyer
Lafayette	Catherine McGowan (R)	Joseph G. Boll (R)	Aaron Austin
Langlade	Marilyn Baraniak (D)	Chet Haatvedt (D)	David Tlusty
Lincoln	Marie Peterson (A)	Sarah Koss (R)	Anthony Dallman
Manitowoc	Lynn Zigmunt (D)	Kristi L. Tuesburg (R)	None
Marathon	Shirley Lang (R)	Dean Stratz (R)	Christopher Fieri
Marinette	Sheila M. Dudka (R)	Renee Miller (R)	None
Marquette	Shari Rudolph (R)	Bette Krueger (R)	Vacant
Menominee	Pamela Frechette (D)	Louise Madosh (D)	None
Milwaukee	John Barrett (D)	John La Fave (D)	Kurt W. Bauer
Monroe	Shirley Chapiewsky (R)	Deb Brandt (R)	Gary Dechant
Oconto	Michael C. Hodkiewicz (R)	Annette Behringer (R)	Brian Gross
Oneida	Brenda Behrle (R)	Kyle Franson (R)	None
Outagamie	Barb Bocik (R)	Sarah R. Van Camp (R)	James A. Hebert
Ozaukee	Mary Lou Mueller (R)	Ronald A. Voigt (R)	None
Pepin	Audrey Lieffring (R)	Monica J. Bauer (R)	Cedar Corporation
Pierce	Peg M. Feuerhelm (D)	Julie Hines (D)	James Filkins
Polk	Jobie Bainbridge (R)	Sally Spanel (D)	Steve Geiger
Portage	Lisa M. Roth (A)	Cynthia Wisinski (D)	Thomas J. Trzinski (I)
Price	Chris Cress (D)	Judith Chizek (D)	Alfred Schneider
Racine	Samuel A. Christensen (R)	Tyson Fettes (R)	None
Richland	Stacy Kleist (R)	Susan Triggs (R)	Todd T. Rummler
Rock	Jackie Gackstatter (D)	Sandy Disrud (D)	Brad Heuer
Rusk	Lori Gorsegner (A)	Carol Johnson (D)	None
St. Croix	Kristi Severson (D)	Beth Pabst (D)	Brian V. Halling
Sauk	Carrie Wastlick (A)	Brent Bailey (R)	Patrick Dederich (R)
Sawyer	Sarah Jungbluth (R)	Paula Chisser (R)	Dan Ploeger
Shawano	Susan M. Krueger (R)	Amy Dillenburg (R)	David Yurk
Sheboygan	Melody Lorge (I)	Ellen Schleicher (D)	Edgar Harvey, Jr.
Taylor	Rose M. Thums (R)	Sara Nuernberger (D)	Robert Meyer
Trempealeau	Michelle Weisenberger (D)	Rose Ottum (D)	Joe Nelson
Vernon	Sheila Olson (R)	Konna Spaeth (R)	None
Vilas	Courtney Szuta (A)	Christine Walker (R)	Thomas Boettcher (R)
Walworth	Sheila T. Reiff (R)	Donna Pruess (R)	None
Washburn	Shannon Anderson (A)	Renee M. Bell (R)	Steven Waak
Washington	Theresa Russell (R)	Sharon Martin (R)	Scott M. Schmidt
Waukesha	Kathleen A. Madden (R)	James Behrend (R)	Robert W. Merry
Waupaca	Terrie Tews-Liebe (R)	Michael Mazemke (R)	Joseph S. Glodowski
Waushara	Melissa M. Zamzow (R)	Heather Schwersenska (R)	Jerry Smart
Winnebago	Melissa Pingel (R)	Natalie Strohmeyer (R)	None
Wood	Cindy Joosten (R)	Susan Ginter (R)	Kevin Boyer

Note: Clerks of circuit court, registers of deeds, and surveyors are elected at the general election for four-year terms. In lieu of electing a surveyor, a county can choose to appoint one.

A–Appointed to fill a vacancy; D–Democrat; I–Independent; R–Republican.

1. Surveyors are appointed unless party designation is shown.

Source: Data collected from county clerks by Wisconsin Legislative Reference Bureau, March 2017.

Wisconsin county officers: district attorney; sheriff; coroner (or alternative), June 2017

	District attorney	Sheriff	Coroner/medical examiner
Adams	Tania M. Bonnett (I)	Sam Wollin (D)	Marilyn Rogers (ME)
Ashland.	Kelly McNight (D)	Michael Brennan, Sr. (D)	Barbara Beeksma (R)
Barron.	Angela L. Beranek (D)	Chris Fitzgerald (D)	Mary A. Ricci (ME)
Bayfield	Kimberly Lawton (D)	Paul Susienka (D)	Gary Victorson (D)
Brown.	David L. Lasee (R)	John R. Gossage (R)	Vincent Tranchida (ME)
Buffalo	Thomas Clark (D)	Mike Schmidtknecht (R)	Peter Samb (R)
Burnett	William L. Norine (R)	Ronald L. Wilhelm, Jr. (R)	Michael Maloney (ME)
Calumet	Nathan F. Haberman (R)	Mark R. Ott (R)	Michael Klaeser (ME)
Chippewa	Steven H. Gibbs (R)	James Kowalczyk (D)	Ronald Patten (D)
Clark.	Kerra Stumbris (D)	Greg Herrick (R)	Richard J. Schleifer (R)
Columbia.	Jane E. Kohlwey (R)	Dennis Richards (R)	Angela Hinze (ME)
Crawford	Timothy Baxter (D)	Dale McCullick (D)	Joe Morovits (D)
Dane	Ismael R. Ozanne (D)	David J. Mahoney (D)	Vincent Tranchida (ME)
Dodge	Kurt Klomberg (R)	Dale Schmidt (R)	Patrick Schoebel (ME)
Door.	Colleen Nordin (R)	Steve Delarwelle (R)	Contracts with Brown County
Douglas.	Mark Fruehauf (D)	Thomas Dalbec (D)	Darrell Witt (ME)
Dunn	Andrea Nodolf (R)	Dennis P. Smith (D)	Christopher H. Kruse (ME)
Eau Claire.	Gary King (D)	Ron D. Cramer (R)	Christopher H. Kruse (ME)
Florence	Doug Drexler (D)	Jeff Rickaby (R)	Mary Johnson (R)
Fond du Lac	Eric Toney (R)	Mylan C. Fink, Jr. (R)	P. Douglas Kelley (ME)
Forest	Charles Simono (D)	John Dennee (D)	Larry Mathein (ME)
Grant	Lisa Riniker (R)	Nate Dreckman (R)	Ronald Sturmer (R)
Green	Craig Nolen (R)	Mark A. Rohloff (R)	None[2]
Green Lake.	Andrew Christenson (R)	Mark Podoll (R)	Amanda Thoma (R)
Iowa.	Larry Nelson (D)	Steven R. Michek (R)	Wendell F. Hamlin (R)
Iron	Matthew Tingstad (D)	Tony Furyk (D)	Diane Simonich (D)
Jackson.	Gerald Fox (D)	Duane Waldera (D)	Karla Wood (D)
Jefferson	Susan V. Happ (D)	Paul Milbrath (R)	Nichol Tesch (ME)
Juneau	Kenneth Hamm (R)	Brent Oleson (R)	Linda Mitchel-May (A)
Kenosha	Michael Graveley (D)	David Beth (R)	Patrice Hall (ME)
Kewaunee	Andrew Naze (D)	Matthew Joski (R)	Rory Groessl (D)
La Crosse	Tim Gruenke (D)	Steve Helgeson (R)	Tim Candahl (ME)
Lafayette	Jenna Gill (R)	Reginald Gill (R)	Linda Gebhardt (D)
Langlade	Elizabeth Constable (R)	Mark Westen (A)	Larry Shadick (R)
Lincoln	Galen Bayne-Allison (D)	Jeff Jaeger (R)	Paul Proulx (R)
Manitowoc.	Jacalyn LaBre (R)	Robert Hermann (D)	Curtis Green (D)
Marathon.	Theresa Wetzsteon (D)	Scott Parks (R)	Jessica Blahnik (ME)
Marinette.	Allen R. Brey (D)	Jerry Sauve (R)	George F. Smith (R)
Marquette	Chad Hendee (R)	Kim Gaffney (R)	Thomas Wastart II (R)
Menominee[1].	Gregory Parker (R)	Robert Summers (D)	Patrick Roberts (ME)
Milwaukee	John T. Chisholm (D)	David A. Clarke, Jr. (D)	Brian L. Peterson (ME)
Monroe.	Kevin Croninger (R)	Scott Perkins (R)	Bob Smith (ME)
Oconto	Ed Burke (R)	Michael Jansen (R)	Barry Irmen (ME)
Oneida	Michael Schiek (R)	Grady Hartman (R)	Larry Mathein (ME)
Outagamie.	Carrie Schneider (R)	Bradley G. Gehring (R)	Ruth A. Wulgaert (R)
Ozaukee	Adam Y. Gerol (R)	James G. Johnson (R)	Timothy J. Deppisch (R)
Pepin	Jon D. Seifert (D)	Joel D. Wener (R)	Christy Rundquist (I)
Pierce	Sean Froelich (D)	Nancy Hove (D)	John Worsing (ME)
Polk	Jeffrey L. Kemp (R)	Pete Johnson (R)	Jonn Dinnies (ME)
Portage.	Louis J. Molepske, Jr. (D)	Michael Lukas (D)	Scott W. Rifleman (R)
Price.	Mark Fuhr (D)	Brian Schmidt (R)	James Dalbesio, III (D)
Racine.	Patricia J. Hanson (R)	Christopher Schmaling (R)	Michael Payne (ME)
Richland	Jennifer M. Harper (R)	Jim Bindl (R)	James Rossing (I)
Rock.	David J. O'Leary (D)	Robert D. Spoden (D)	Vincent Tranchida (ME)
Rusk.	Annette Barna (D)	Jeffery Wallace (R)	Jim Rassbach (ME)
St. Croix.	Michael Nieskes (R)	John A. Shilts (R)	Patty Schachtner (ME)
Sauk.	Kevin R. Calkins (I)	Chip Meister (R)	Greg L. Hahn (R)
Sawyer	Bruce Poquette (R)	Mark Kelsey (R)	Dave Dokkestul (R)

Wisconsin county officers: district attorney; sheriff; coroner (or alternative), June 2017, continued

District attorney	Sheriff	Coroner/medical examiner
Shawano[1] . . . . Gregory Parker (R)	Adam Bieber (R)	Brian Westfahl (A)
Sheboygan. . . . . . . Joel Urmanski (R)	Todd Priebe (R)	David Leffin (ME)
Taylor . . . . Kristi Tlusty (D)	Bruce A. Daniels (D)	Scott Perrin (ME)
Trempealeau . . . . . Taavi McMahon (D)	Richard Anderson (D)	Bonnie Kindschy (D)
Vernon . . . . Timothy Gaskell (R)	John B. Spears (R)	Janet Reed (R)
Vilas . . . . Martha Milanowski (R)	Joseph A. Fath (R)	Paul Tirpe (R)
Walworth. . . . . Zeke Wiedenfeld (R)	Kurt Picknell (R)	Lynda Biedrzycki (ME)
Washburn . . . . Angeline E. Winton (D)	Terry C. Dryden (R)	Angela Pank (A)
Washington . . . . . . Mark Bensen (R)	Dale Schmidt (R)	Lynda Biedrzycki (ME)
Waukesha . . . . Susan L. Opper (R)	Eric J. Severson (R)	Lynda Biedrzycki (ME)
Waupaca . . . . Veronica Isherwood (R)	Bradly Hardel (R)	Barry Tomaras (R)
Waushara. . . . . Scott Blader (R)	Jeffrey L. Nett (R)	Roland B. Handel (R)
Winnebago . . . . . . Christian Gossett (R)	John Matz (R)	Barry Busby (R)
Wood . . . . Craig Lambert (R)	Thomas Reichert (D)	Dara Borre Hamm (D)

Note: District attorneys, sheriffs, and coroners are elected at the general election for four-year terms. In lieu of electing a coroner, a county can choose to appoint a medical examiner.

A–Appointed to fill a vacancy; D–Democrat; I–Independent; ME–medical examiner; R–Republican.

1. Menominee and Shawano counties comprise a single prosecutorial unit, served by a single district attorney.   2. Duties are fulfilled by Green County Chief Deputy Coroner, Jody Makos.

Source: Data collected from county clerks by Wisconsin Legislative Reference Bureau, March 2017.

Tribal chairpersons and contact information, February 2017

Tribe and chairperson	Contact information
Bad River Band of Lake Superior Chippewa. . . . . Robert Blanchard	P.O. Box 39, Odanah 54861-0039 715-682-7111; www.badriver-nsn.gov
Forest County Potawatomi Community . . . . Harold "Gus" Frank	P.O. Box 340, Crandon 54520-0346 715-478-7200; www.fcpotawatomi.com
Ho-Chunk Nation . . . . Wilfrid Cleveland (president)	P.O. Box 667, Black River Falls 54615-0667 715-284-9343; www.ho-chunknation.com
Lac Courte Oreilles Band of Lake Superior Chippewa . . Michael "Mic" Isham	13394 W. Trepania Road, Hayward 54843-2186 715-634-8934; www.lco-nsn.gov
Lac du Flambeau Band of Lake Superior Chippewa. . . . Joseph Wildcat, Sr. (president)	P.O. Box 67, Lac du Flambeau 54538-0067 715-588-3303; www.ldftribe.com
Menominee Nation . . . . Gary Besaw	P.O. Box 910, Keshena 54135-0910 715-799-5114; www.menominee-nsn.gov
Oneida Nation of Wisconsin. . . . . Cristina Danforth	P.O. Box 365, Oneida 54155-0365 920-869-4380; www.oneida-nsn.gov
Red Cliff Band of Lake Superior Chippewa . . . . Bryan Bainbridge	88385 Pike Road, Hwy. 13, Bayfield 54814-0529 715-779-3700; www.redcliff-nsn.gov
St. Croix Chippewa Community . . . . Lewis Taylor	24663 Angeline Avenue, Webster 54893-9246 715-349-2195; www.stcciw.com
Sokaogon Chippewa Community . . . . Chris McGeshick	3051 Sand Lake Road, Crandon 54520-8815 715-478-7500; www.sokaogonchippewa.com
Stockbridge-Munsee Band of Mohican Indians . . . . . . Shannon Holsey (president)	P.O. Box 70, Bowler 54416-9801 715-793-4111; www.mohican-nsn.gov

Sources: Wisconsin State Tribal Relations Initiative, http://witribes.wi.gov [February 2017] and individual tribal websites.

Political parties qualifying for ballot status as of June 2017

in the order they will be listed on the ballot

Republican Party of Wisconsin

---

148 East Johnson Street, Madison, WI 53703; 608-257-4765; www.wisgop.org

Executive director . . . . Mark Morgan
Political director . . . . .Phil Curry
Deputy political director . . . . .Josh Zdroik
Research director. . . . . Charles Nichols
Research assistant . . . . Edward Meyers
Press secretary . . . . .Alec Zimmerman
Office manager. . . . . Benjamin Stelter
Controller/operations director . . . . Ben Heath
Finance director . . . . .Richelle Flackey
Data director . . . . David Bredemus
Grassroots director. . . . . Carlton Huffman
Telemarketing manager. . . . . .Richard Dickie

Executive Committee

Party officers . . . . .Brad Courtney, Whitefish Bay, *chair*; Tom Schreibel, Hartland, *1st vice chair*;
Crystal Berg, Hartford, *2nd vice chair*; Laurie Forcier, Eau Claire, *3rd vice chair*;
Andrew Davis, Milwaukee, *4th vice chair*; Mike Jones, Milwaukee, *finance chair*;
Katie McCallum, Middleton, *secretary*; Andrew Hitt, Appleton, *treasurer*;
Steve King Sr., Janesville, *national committeeman*;
Mary Buestrin, River Hills, *national committeewoman*
Immediate past chair . . . . Reince Priebus, Kenosha
At-large member . . . . Maripat Krueger, Menomonie
Wisconsin African American Council chair .Gerard Randall, Milwaukee
Wisconsin Republican Labor Council chair . . . . Van Wanggaard, Racine
Wisconsin Hispanic Heritage Council chair . . . . Ivan Gamboa, Greendale
CD 1 representative . . . . Kim Travis, Williams Bay, *chair*; Carol Brunner, Franklin, *1st vice chair*
CD 2 representative . . . . Kim Babler, Madison, *chair*; Tim McCumber, Merrimac, *1st vice chair*
CD 3 representative . . . . Brian Westrate, Fall Creek, *chair*; Julian Bradley, La Crosse, *1st vice chair*
CD 4 representative . . . . Bob Spindell, Milwaukee, *chair*; Doug Haag, Milwaukee, *1st vice chair*
CD 5 representative . . . . Kathy Kiernan, Richfield, *chair*; Keith Best, Waukesha, *1st vice chair*
CD 6 representative . . . . Darryl Carlson, Sheboygan, *chair*; Janet Reabe, Green Lake, *1st vice chair*
CD 7 representative . . . . Jim Miller, Hayward, *chair*; Jesse Garza, Hudson, *1st vice chair*
CD 8 representative . . . . Kelly Ruh, Green Bay, *chair*; Bill Berglund, Sturgeon Bay, *1st vice chair*

Democratic Party of Wisconsin

---

15 N Pinckney Street, Suite 200, Madison, WI 53703; 608-255-5172; www.wisdems.org

Executive director . . . . Jason Sidener
Communications director . . . . .Brandon Weathersby
Party affairs director. . . . . Cassi Fenili
Deputy party affairs director. . . . . .McKinley Kant
Organizing director . . . . .Staci O'Brien
Political and research director. . . . . .George Gillis
Candidate services director . . . . Sam Voorhees
Deputy candidate services director . . . . .Brian Evans
Finance director . . . . .Kesha Bozeman
Voter file manager . . . . .Will Hoffman
Compliance director. . . . . Breianna Hasenzahl-Reeder
Office manager. . . . . Tom McCann

State Administrative Committee

Party officers . . . . Martha Laning, Sheboygan, *chair*; David Bowen, Milwaukee, *1st vice chair*;
Mandela Barnes, Milwaukee, *2nd vice chair*; Meg Andrietsch, Racine, *secretary*;
Randy Udell, Madison, *treasurer*

Political parties qualifying for ballot status as of June 2017, continued

---

Democratic Party of Wisconsin, continued

National committee members. . . . . Janet Bewley, Mason; Martha Love, Milwaukee; Khary Penebaker, Hartland; Andrew Werthmann, Eau Claire; Jason Rae, Milwaukee

College Democrats representative . . . . Shea Senger, Milwaukee

Young Democrats representative. . . . . .Sarah Smith, Milwaukee

Milwaukee County chair . . . . .Rob Hansen, Greenfield

At-large members . . . . Penny Bernard Schaber, Appleton; Michael Childers, La Pointe; Paul DeMain; Hayward; David Duran, Lodi; Luke Fuszard, Middleton; Ryan Greendeer, Black River Falls; Gail Hohenstein, Green Bay; Melissa Lemke, Racine; Sarah Lloyd, Wisconsin Dells; Gretchen Lowe, Madison; Dian Palmer, Brookfield; Mary Lang Sollinger, Madison; Yee L. Xiong, Weston

County Chairs Association chair. . . . . Peter Hellios, Granton

Assembly representative . . . . JoCasta Zamarripa, Milwaukee

Senate representative. . . . . Janis Ringhand, Evansville

CD 1 representative . . . . Mary Jonker, Kenosha, *chair*; Matt Lowe, Muskego

CD 2 representative . . . . .Christine Welcher, Stoughton, *chair*; Mike Martez Johnson, Madison

CD 3 representative . . . . Lisa Herrmann, Eau Claire, *chair*; George Wilbur, La Farge

CD 4 representative . . . . .Terrell Martin, Milwaukee, *chair*; Michelle Bryant, Milwaukee

CD 5 representative . . . . .Justin Koestler, Waukesha, *chair*; Karen Kirsch, Greenfield

CD 6 representative . . . . .Ben Stepanek, Oshkosh, *chair*; Debra Dassow, Cedarburg

CD 7 representative . . . . .Melissa Schroeder, Merrill, *chair*; Paul Knuth, Rhinelander

CD 8 representative . . . . .Mary Ginnebaugh, Green Bay, *chair*; Mark Waltman, Appleton

---

Libertarian Party of Wisconsin

PO Box 20815, Greenfield, WI 53220; 800-236-9236; info@lpwi.org; www.lpwi.org

Executive Committee

Party officers . . . .*chair*, vacant; Phillip Anderson, Madison, *vice chair*; Andy Craig, Milwaukee, *secretary*; Patrick Baird, Madison, *treasurer*

At-large members . . . . .Stephen Nass, Middleton; George Meyers, Racine

CD 1 representative . . . . Jim Sewell, Racine; Donna Harmon, Oak Creek, *alternate*

CD 2 representative . . . . .Terry Gray, Madison; Peter Augelli, Verona, *alternate*

CD 3 representative . . . . .vacant

CD 4 representative . . . . Kenneth Morgan, Milwaukee; Diane Mielke, Milwaukee, *alternate*

CD 5 representative . . . . vacant

CD 6 representative . . . . Brian Defferding, Neenah; Adam Markert, Menasha, *alternate*

CD 7 representative . . . . Robert Burke, Hudson; Nathan Gall, Hayward, *alternate*

CD 8 representative . . . . Tyler Danke, Fremont

Wisconsin Green Party

PO Box 1701, Madison, WI 53701-1701; info@wisconsingreenparty.org; www.wisconsingreenparty.org

Coordinating Council

Party officers . . . . Michael White, *cochair*; Dace Zeps, *cochair*; Molly Katzfey, *recording secretary*; David Schwab, *corresponding secretary*; Bobby Gifford, *operations treasurer*; Pete Karas, *elections treasurer*

CD 1 representative . . . . .Sondra Plunkett

CD 2 representative . . . . Read Eldred

CD 3 representative . . . . .Joseph Behn

CD 4 representative . . . . .Tiffany Anderson, Josh Anderson

CD 5 representative . . . . .Alan Schultz, Eugene Barufkin

CD 6 representative . . . . Thomas Ward, Jeff Reese

CD 7 representative . . . . Melissa Thomas

CD 8 representative . . . . .2 seats vacant

Political parties qualifying for ballot status as of June 2017,
continued

Constitution Party of Wisconsin

PO Box 070344, Milwaukee, WI 53207-1918; 608-561-7996; constitutionpartyofwisconsin@gmail.com;
www.constitutionpartyofwisconsin.com

State Committee

Party officers . . . . Andrew Zuelke, Ripon, *chair;* Jerry Broitzman, Milwaukee, *vice chair;*
Terry Larson, Mayville, *communications director;* Nigel Brown, Janesville, *secretary;*
Ralph Denson, Milwaukee, *treasurer;*
CD 1 representative . . . . Michael Skott, Union Grove; Glen E. L. Petroski, Kenosha
CD 2 representative . . . . vacant
CD 3 representative . . . . Lorraine Decker, La Crosse
CD 4 representative . . . . Colin Hudson, Milwaukee
CD 5 representative . . . . .vacant
CD 6 representative . . . . .Dino Bohlman, Eden
CD 7 representative . . . . Larry Oftedahl, Barron
CD 8 representative . . . . Mark Gabriel, Appleton

CD–congressional district

Sources: Republican Party of Wisconsin, Democratic Party of Wisconsin, Libertarian Party of Wisconsin, Wisconsin Green Party, Constitution Party of Wisconsin.

POPULATION AND POLITICAL SUBDIVISIONS

Wisconsin population since 1840

Year	Population	% increase	Rural	Urban (%)[1]	Density[2]
1840.	30,945	—	30,945	0	0.6
1850.	305,391	886.9	276,768	28,623 (9.4)	5.6
1860.	775,881	154.1	664,007	111,874 (14.4)	14.1
1870.	1,054,670	35.9	847,471	207,099 (19.6)	19.2
1880.	1,315,497	24.7	998,293	317,204 (24.1)	24.0
1890.	1,693,330	28.7	1,131,044	562,286 (33.2)	30.9
1900.	2,069,042	22.2	1,278,829	790,213 (38.2)	37.4
1910.	2,333,860	12.8	1,329,540	1,004,320 (43.0)	42.6
1920.	2,632,067	12.8	1,387,209	1,244,858 (47.3)	47.6
1930.	2,939,006	11.7	1,385,163	1,553,843 (52.9)	53.0
1940.	3,137,587	6.7	1,458,443	1,679,144 (53.5)	57.3
1950.	3,434,575	9.5	1,446,687	1,987,888 (57.9)	62.7
1960.	3,951,777	15.1	1,429,598	2,522,179 (63.8)	72.2
1970.	4,417,821	11.8	1,507,313	2,910,418 (65.9)	81.3
1980.	4,705,642	6.5	1,685,035	3,020,732 (64.2)	86.6
1990.	4,891,769	4.0	1,679,813	3,211,956 (65.7)	90.1
2000.	5,363,715	9.6	1,700,032	3,663,643 (68.3)	98.8
2010.	5,686,986	6.0	1,697,348	3,989,638 (70.2)	105.0

1. The "urban" definition was revised beginning with the 1950 census.   2. Population per square mile of land area.

Sources: U.S. Department of Commerce, U.S. Census Bureau; Wisconsin Department of Administration, Demographic Services Center, *Time Series of The Final Official Population Estimates and Census Counts for Wisconsin Counties*, October 10, 2016.

Wisconsin 2010 census by sex, race, and Hispanic origin

	Total population	Male	Female	White	Black or African American	American Indian/ Alaska Native	Asian or Pacific Islander	Some other race	Two or more races	Hispanic origin (any race)
Adams . . .	20,875	11,221	9,654	19,409	633	205	86	266	276	783
Ashland. . .	16,157	8,082	8,075	13,662	48	1,791	63	56	537	302
Barron. . . .	45,870	22,814	23,056	44,076	407	406	226	236	519	862
Bayfield. . .	15,014	7,716	7,298	13,024	46	1,435	49	29	431	158
Brown. . . .	248,007	122,658	125,349	214,415	5,491	6,715	6,828	9,155	5,403	17,985
Buffalo . . .	13,587	6,859	6,728	13,253	37	38	28	122	109	237
Burnett . . .	15,457	7,806	7,651	14,163	81	718	55	67	373	194
Calumet . .	48,971	24,543	24,428	46,187	246	203	1,047	705	583	1,690
Chippewa .	62,415	32,404	30,011	59,504	982	310	788	182	649	800
Clark.	34,690	17,577	17,113	33,338	80	174	135	773	190	1,292
Columbia. .	56,833	28,935	27,898	54,468	717	277	330	441	600	1,444
Crawford . .	16,644	8,575	8,069	16,080	296	39	66	36	127	150
Dane	488,073	241,411	246,662	413,631	25,347	1,730	23,201	12,064	12,100	28,925
Dodge . . .	88,759	46,679	42,080	83,294	2,381	385	513	1,309	877	3,522
Door.	27,785	13,679	14,106	26,839	144	162	116	249	275	671
Douglas. . .	44,159	22,087	22,072	41,166	486	868	384	82	1,173	494
Dunn	43,857	22,133	21,724	41,545	220	168	1,158	228	538	626
Eau Claire. .	98,736	48,351	50,385	91,946	874	471	3,328	519	1,598	1,804
Florence . .	4,423	2,262	2,161	4,306	10	31	14	14	48	37
Fond du Lac	101,633	49,926	51,707	95,674	1,305	471	1,169	1,700	1,314	4,368
Forest	9,304	4,724	4,580	7,690	76	1,256	24	32	226	138

Wisconsin 2010 census by sex, race, and Hispanic origin,
continued

	Total popu-lation	Male	Female	White	Black or African Amer-ican	American Indian/ Alaska Native	Asian or Pacific Islander	Some other race	Two or more races	Hispanic origin (any race)
Grant	51,208	26,636	24,572	49,655	588	103	317	221	324	649
Green	36,842	18,241	18,601	35,593	140	65	209	490	345	1,033
Green Lake	19,051	9,509	9,542	18,428	88	52	91	268	124	743
Iowa.	23,687	11,878	11,809	23,127	87	36	134	102	201	336
Iron	5,916	2,959	2,957	5,790	3	36	18	13	56	35
Jackson. . .	20,449	10,874	9,575	18,258	400	1,271	73	144	303	519
Jefferson . .	83,686	41,638	42,048	78,632	681	257	578	2,479	1,059	5,555
Juneau . . .	26,664	14,029	12,635	25,077	557	398	122	188	322	687
Kenosha . .	166,426	82,444	83,982	139,416	11,052	814	2,482	7,880	4,782	19,592
Kewaunee .	20,574	10,460	10,114	19,955	69	77	65	219	189	463
La Crosse . .	114,638	55,961	58,677	105,540	1,610	493	4,770	371	1,854	1,741
Lafayette . .	16,836	8,582	8,254	16,292	39	48	58	303	96	522
Langlade . .	19,977	10,032	9,945	19,267	72	191	63	100	284	324
Lincoln . . .	28,743	14,412	14,331	27,929	157	100	134	131	292	340
Manitowoc	81,442	40,489	40,953	76,402	442	450	2,060	1,069	1,019	2,565
Marathon. .	134,063	67,308	66,755	122,446	841	634	7,178	1,223	1,741	2,992
Marinette. .	41,749	20,758	20,991	40,559	108	238	227	176	441	522
Marquette .	15,404	7,808	7,596	14,920	77	86	68	126	127	391
Menominee	4,232	2,098	2,134	451	19	3,701	1	6	54	178
Milwaukee .	947,735	457,717	490,018	574,656	253,764	6,808	32,785	51,429	28,293	126,039
Monroe. . .	44,673	22,648	22,025	41,940	512	510	329	764	618	1,661
Oconto . . .	37,660	19,194	18,466	36,418	73	467	116	198	388	519
Oneida . . .	35,998	17,993	18,005	34,787	152	323	193	82	461	385
Outagamie	176,695	88,130	88,565	161,238	1,736	2,982	5,294	2,728	2,717	6,359
Ozaukee . .	86,395	42,340	44,055	82,010	1,177	208	1,529	483	988	1,956
Pepin	7,469	3,780	3,689	7,337	21	19	14	35	43	72
Pierce	41,019	20,420	20,599	39,614	232	151	308	201	513	623
Polk	44,205	22,177	22,028	42,807	96	454	166	226	456	656
Portage. . .	70,019	34,984	35,035	65,981	383	265	1,983	546	861	1,853
Price	14,159	7,180	6,979	13,750	39	54	126	42	148	153
Racine. . . .	195,408	96,771	98,637	155,731	21,767	781	2,174	10,046	4,909	22,546
Richland . .	18,021	9,042	8,979	17,540	82	46	99	119	135	360
Rock.	160,331	78,815	81,516	140,513	7,978	516	1,669	5,948	3,707	12,124
Rusk.	14,755	7,371	7,384	14,398	61	74	42	37	143	173
St. Croix. . .	84,345	42,218	42,127	80,914	552	313	923	483	1,160	1,692
Sauk.	61,976	30,848	31,128	58,588	357	769	350	1,156	756	2,675
Sawyer . . .	16,557	8,393	8,164	13,123	77	2,757	49	42	509	268
Shawano . .	41,949	20,921	21,028	37,254	143	3,172	193	366	821	905
Sheboygan	115,507	58,010	57,497	103,861	1,684	444	5,345	2,297	1,876	6,329
Taylor	20,689	10,559	10,130	20,248	58	43	64	128	148	316
Trempealeau	28,816	14,638	14,178	27,230	62	63	127	1,086	248	1,667
Vernon . . .	29,773	14,854	14,919	29,085	109	61	99	145	274	394
Vilas.	21,430	10,861	10,569	18,658	35	2,370	62	45	260	268
Walworth. .	102,228	51,237	50,991	93,935	980	308	888	4,604	1,513	10,578
Washburn .	15,911	7,924	7,987	15,343	36	186	65	49	232	208
Washington	131,887	65,393	66,494	126,317	1,155	401	1,445	1,052	1,517	3,385
Waukesha .	389,891	191,355	198,536	363,963	4,914	1,066	10,852	4,041	5,055	16,123
Waupaca . .	52,410	26,447	25,963	50,916	154	258	200	425	457	1,307
Waushara. .	24,496	12,893	11,603	23,012	454	131	108	509	282	1,329
Winnebago	166,994	83,952	83,042	154,445	2,975	1,036	3,880	2,188	2,470	5,784
Wood	74,749	36,777	37,972	71,048	393	587	1,328	593	800	1,680
Total.	**5,686,986**	**2,822,400**	**2,864,586**	**4,902,067**	**359,148**	**54,526**	**131,061**	**135,867**	**104,317**	**336,056**

Sources: U.S. Department of Commerce, U.S. Census Bureau, P.L. 94-171 Redistricting File, processed by Wisconsin Demographic Services Center and the Applied Population Laboratory of UW-Madison, May 2011.

Basic data on Wisconsin counties

County (year created)[1]	County seat	Full value 2015 assessment (1,000)[2]	Population 2016 estimate	Population % change[3]	Population 2016 rank	Land area in sq. miles[4]	2016 density/ sq. mile[5]
Adams (1848)	Friendship	$2,410,884	20,730	-0.69	52	645.7	32.1
Ashland (1860)	Ashland.	1,193,763	15,975	-1.13	60	1,045.0	15.3
Barron (1859)	Barron.	3,851,193	46,372	1.09	30	862.7	53.8
Bayfield (1845)	Washburn	2,556,255	15,206	1.28	64	1,477.9	10.3
Brown (1818)	Green Bay	19,332,587	257,897	3.99	4	529.7	486.9
Buffalo (1853)	Alma.	1,088,267	13,704	0.86	67	671.6	20.4
Burnett (1856).	Meenon.	2,468,753	15,544	0.56	62	821.9	18.9
Calumet (1836)	Chilton	3,669,398	51,669	5.51	29	318.2	162.4
Chippewa (1845) . . .	Chippewa Falls . .	4,971,654	64,135	2.76	24	1,008.4	63.6
Clark (1853)	Neillsville	1,911,308	34,888	0.57	41	1,209.8	28.8
Columbia (1846) . . .	Portage.	4,988,178	57,066	0.41	26	765.5	74.5
Crawford (1818). . . .	Prairie du Chien. .	1,127,441	16,744	0.60	59	570.7	29.3
Dane (1836)	Madison	53,916,407	518,538	6.24	2	1,197.2	433.1
Dodge (1836)	Juneau	5,991,793	89,962	1.36	17	875.6	102.7
Door (1851)	Sturgeon Bay . . .	6,920,415	28,127	1.23	45	482.0	58.4
Douglas (1854)	Superior	3,336,979	44,415	0.58	33	1,304.1	34.1
Dunn (1854).	Menomonie	2,802,597	44,575	1.64	32	850.1	52.4
Eau Claire (1856) . . .	Eau Claire.	7,499,942	101,731	3.03	16	638.0	159.5
Florence (1881)	Florence	623,906	4,473	1.13	71	488.2	9.2
Fond du Lac (1836). .	Fond du Lac	7,066,200	103,290	1.63	14	719.6	143.5
Forest (1885).	Crandon	1,105,407	9,279	-0.27	68	1,014.1	9.1
Grant (1836)	Lancaster.	3,003,073	53,107	3.71	27	1,146.9	46.3
Green (1836).	Monroe	2,721,777	36,907	0.18	39	584.0	63.2
Green Lake (1858) . .	Green Lake.	2,240,329	19,143	0.48	55	349.4	54.8
Iowa (1829)	Dodgeville	1,887,078	23,829	0.60	48	762.6	31.2
Iron (1893)	Hurley.	965,479	5,901	-0.25	70	758.2	7.8
Jackson (1853)	Black River Falls . .	1,567,145	20,743	1.44	50	987.7	21.0
Jefferson (1836). . . .	Jefferson	6,488,642	84,262	0.69	20	556.5	151.4
Juneau (1856).	Mauston	1,919,250	27,022	1.34	46	766.9	35.2
Kenosha (1850)	Kenosha	13,180,389	167,658	0.74	8	272.0	616.4
Kewaunee (1852). . .	Kewaunee	1,951,894	20,723	0.72	53	342.5	60.5
La Crosse (1851) . . .	La Crosse	8,717,923	118,038	2.97	12	451.7	261.3
Lafayette (1846). . . .	Darlington	1,077,361	16,961	0.74	57	633.6	26.8
Langlade (1879). . . .	Antigo	1,677,319	19,995	0.09	54	870.6	23.0
Lincoln (1874).	Merrill.	2,314,396	28,787	0.15	44	879.0	32.7
Manitowoc (1836) . .	Manitowoc.	5,202,783	81,404	-0.05	21	589.1	138.2
Marathon (1850) . . .	Wausau	9,852,983	135,483	1.06	10	1,545.0	87.7
Marinette (1879) . . .	Marinette.	3,604,171	41,413	-0.80	36	1,399.4	29.6
Marquette (1836). . .	Montello	1,514,044	15,425	0.14	63	455.6	33.9
Menominee (1961). .	Keshena	288,738	4,256	0.57	72	357.6	11.9
Milwaukee (1834) . .	Milwaukee	58,553,179	948,930	0.13	1	241.4	3,930.9
Monroe (1854)	Sparta.	3,042,763	45,865	2.67	31	900.8	50.9
Oconto (1851).	Oconto	3,616,763	38,195	1.42	38	998.0	38.3
Oneida (1885).	Rhinelander	6,742,092	36,208	0.58	40	1,113.0	32.5
Outagamie (1851) . .	Appleton	13,650,745	182,365	3.21	6	637.5	286.1
Ozaukee (1853)	Port Washington . .	10,970,707	87,879	1.72	18	233.1	377.0
Pepin (1858).	Durand	565,217	7,414	-0.74	69	232.0	32.0
Pierce (1853).	Ellsworth	2,996,431	41,320	0.73	37	573.8	72.0
Polk (1853).	Balsam Lake	4,229,719	44,236	0.07	34	914.0	48.4
Portage (1836)	Stevens Point . . .	5,344,210	70,883	1.23	23	800.7	88.5
Price (1879)	Phillips	1,391,246	14,086	-0.52	66	1,254.4	11.2
Racine (1836)	Racine.	13,896,029	195,294	-0.06	5	332.5	587.4
Richland (1842)	Richland Center. .	1,072,880	17,954	-0.37	56	586.2	30.6
Rock (1836)	Janesville.	9,926,025	159,886	-0.28	9	718.1	222.7
Rusk (1901)	Ladysmith	1,226,516	14,783	0.19	65	913.6	16.2
St. Croix (1840)	Hudson	8,062,751	86,858	2.98	19	722.3	120.3

Basic data on Wisconsin counties, continued

County (year created)[1]	County seat	Full value 2015 assess- ment (1,000)[2]	Population 2016 estimate	Population % change[3]	2016 rank	Land area in sq. miles[4]	2016 density/ sq. mile[5]
Sauk (1840)	Baraboo	6,829,472	62,187	0.34	25	830.9	74.8
Sawyer (1883)	Hayward	3,434,332	16,754	1.19	58	1,257.3	13.3
Shawano (1853). . . .	Shawano	2,978,852	41,755	-0.46	35	893.1	46.8
Sheboygan (1836) . .	Sheboygan.	8,645,086	115,050	-0.40	13	511.3	225.0
Taylor (1875).	Medford	1,395,486	20,741	0.25	51	974.9	21.3
Trempealeau (1854) .	Whitehall.	1,992,373	29,395	2.01	43	733.0	40.1
Vernon (1851)	Viroqua	1,841,679	30,114	1.15	42	791.6	38.0
Vilas (1893).	Eagle River.	6,749,757	21,662	1.08	49	856.6	25.3
Walworth (1836) . . .	Elkhorn	13,374,833	102,593	0.36	15	555.1	184.8
Washburn (1883) . . .	Shell Lake	2,352,892	15,929	0.11	61	797.1	20.0
Washington (1836). .	West Bend	13,367,424	134,137	1.71	11	430.7	311.4
Waukesha (1846) . . .	Waukesha	50,187,625	396,449	1.68	3	549.6	721.3
Waupaca (1851). . . .	Waupaca	3,849,849	52,320	-0.17	28	747.7	70.0
Waushara (1851) . . .	Wautoma.	2,403,249	24,471	-0.10	47	626.2	39.1
Winnebago (1840) . .	Oshkosh	12,071,659	169,032	1.22	7	434.5	389.0
Wood (1856).	Wisconsin Rapids	4,832,608	74,998	0.33	22	793.1	94.6
Total.		490,602,544	5,775,120	1.55		54,157.8	106.6

1. Counties are created by legislative act. Depending on the date, Wisconsin counties were created by the Michigan Territorial Legislature (1818–1836), the Wisconsin Territorial Legislature (1836–1848), or the Wisconsin State Legislature (after 1848). 2. Reflects actual market value of all taxable general property, including personal property and real estate, as determined by the Wisconsin Department of Revenue. 3. Change from 2010 U.S. census. 4. Determined by 2010 census. 5. 2016 density calculated by Wisconsin Legislative Reference Bureau.

Sources: Wisconsin Department of Revenue, Division of State and Local Finance, *Town, Village, and City Taxes 2013: Taxes Levied 2013—Collected 2014*, 2014; U.S. Census Bureau, Census 2010 Summary File 1, March 2015.

Wisconsin population by county and municipality

	2010 census	2016 esti- mate	% change		2010 census	2016 esti- mate	% change
Adams	**20,875**	**20,730**	**-0.69**	**Ashland**	**16,157**	**15,975**	**-1.13**
Adams, city	1,967	1,942	-1.27	Agenda, town	422	424	0.47
Adams, town	1,345	1,364	1.41	Ashland, city (part)	8,216	8,039	-2.15
Big Flats, town.	1,018	1,034	1.57	Ashland, town.	594	591	-0.51
Colburn, town.	223	230	3.14	Butternut, village	375	371	-1.07
Dell Prairie, town	1,590	1,626	2.26	Chippewa, town	374	372	-0.53
Easton, town.	1,130	1,117	-1.15	Gingles, town	778	788	1.29
Friendship, village	725	723	-0.28	Gordon, town	283	285	0.71
Jackson, town	1,003	1,006	0.30	Jacobs, town.	722	708	-1.94
Leola, town	308	306	-0.65	La Pointe, town	261	265	1.53
Lincoln, town	296	297	0.34	Marengo, town	390	392	0.51
Monroe, town	398	404	1.51	Mellen, city	731	717	-1.92
New Chester, town	2,254	2,009	-10.87	Morse, town	493	499	1.22
New Haven, town.	655	659	0.61	Peeksville, town.	141	141	0.00
Preston, town	1,393	1,398	0.36	Sanborn, town	1,331	1,315	-1.20
Quincy, town	1,163	1,173	0.86	Shanagolden, town . . .	125	125	0.00
Richfield, town	158	158	0.00	White River, town.	921	943	2.39
Rome, town	2,720	2,748	1.03				
Springville, town	1,318	1,317	-0.08	**Barron**	**45,870**	**46,372**	**1.09**
Strongs Prairie, town. . .	1,150	1,159	0.78	Almena, town	858	858	0.00
Wisconsin Dells, city (part)	61	60	-1.64	Almena, village	677	650	-3.99

Wisconsin population by county and municipality, continued

	2010 census	2016 esti-mate	% change		2010 census	2016 esti-mate	% change
Arland, town.	789	827	4.82	Orienta, town	122	122	0.00
Barron, city.	3,423	3,388	-1.02	Oulu, town.	527	534	1.33
Barron, town.	873	872	-0.11	Pilsen, town	210	215	2.38
Bear Lake, town.	659	660	0.15	Port Wing, town.	368	372	1.09
Cameron, village	1,783	1,834	2.86	Russell, town	1,279	1,366	6.80
Cedar Lake, town. . . .	948	966	1.90	Tripp, town.	231	238	3.03
Chetek, city	2,221	2,212	-0.41	Washburn, city	2,117	2,104	-0.61
Chetek, town	1,644	1,664	1.22	Washburn, town	530	544	2.64
Clinton, town	879	897	2.05				
Crystal Lake, town	757	762	0.66	**Brown.**	**248,007**	**257,897**	**3.99**
Cumberland, city	2,170	2,182	0.55	Allouez, village	13,975	13,711	-1.89
Cumberland, town	876	876	0.00	Ashwaubenon, village. .	16,963	17,029	0.39
Dallas, town	565	574	1.59	Bellevue, village	14,570	15,337	5.26
Dallas, village	409	390	-4.65	De Pere, city	23,800	24,592	3.33
Dovre, town	849	873	2.83	Denmark, village	2,123	2,181	2.73
Doyle, town	453	464	2.43	Eaton, town	1,508	1,601	6.17
Haugen, village	287	285	-0.70	Glenmore, town.	1,135	1,132	-0.26
Lakeland, town	975	980	0.51	Green Bay, city	104,057	105,079	0.98
Maple Grove, town. . . .	979	988	0.92	Green Bay, town	2,035	2,083	2.36
Maple Plain, town	803	815	1.49	Hobart, village	6,182	8,543	38.19
New Auburn, village (part)	20	28	40.00	Holland, town	1,519	1,558	2.57
Oak Grove, town	948	966	1.90	Howard, village (part) . .	17,399	19,295	10.90
Prairie Farm, town	573	593	3.49	Humboldt, town	1,311	1,336	1.91
Prairie Farm, village . . .	473	462	-2.33	Lawrence, town.	4,284	4,973	16.08
Prairie Lake, town.	1,532	1,558	1.70	Ledgeview, town	6,555	7,558	15.30
Rice Lake, city	8,419	8,599	2.14	Morrison, town	1,599	1,620	1.31
Rice Lake, town	3,060	3,101	1.34	New Denmark, town. . .	1,541	1,580	2.53
Sioux Creek, town	655	670	2.29	Pittsfield, town	2,608	2,708	3.83
Stanfold, town	719	727	1.11	Pulaski, village (part). . .	3,321	3,300	-0.63
Stanley, town	2,546	2,577	1.22	Rockland, town	1,734	1,815	4.67
Sumner, town	798	817	2.38	Scott, town.	3,545	3,624	2.23
Turtle Lake, town	624	633	1.44	Suamico, village	11,346	12,281	8.24
Turtle Lake, village (part)	957	959	0.21	Wrightstown, town. . . .	2,221	2,275	2.43
Vance Creek, town	669	665	-0.60	Wrightstown, village (part)	2,676	2,686	0.37
Bayfield	**15,014**	**15,206**	**1.28**	**Buffalo**	**13,587**	**13,704**	**0.86**
Ashland, city (part). . . .	0	0	0.00	Alma, city.	781	769	-1.54
Barksdale, town.	723	731	1.11	Alma, town.	297	303	2.02
Barnes, town.	769	772	0.39	Belvidere, town	396	403	1.77
Bayfield, city.	487	485	-0.41	Buffalo, town	705	705	0.00
Bayfield, town.	680	693	1.91	Buffalo City, city.	1,023	1,018	-0.49
Bayview, town.	487	492	1.03	Canton, town	305	313	2.62
Bell, town.	263	270	2.66	Cochrane, village	450	447	-0.67
Cable, town	825	828	0.36	Cross, town	377	390	3.45
Clover, town	223	221	-0.90	Dover, town	486	501	3.09
Delta, town	273	275	0.73	Fountain City, city	859	854	-0.58
Drummond, town	463	432	-6.70	Gilmanton, town	426	437	2.58
Eileen, town	681	696	2.20	Glencoe, town.	485	493	1.65
Grand View, town.	468	473	1.07	Lincoln, town	162	167	3.09
Hughes, town	383	387	1.04	Maxville, town.	309	311	0.65
Iron River, town.	1,123	1,157	3.03	Milton, town.	534	547	2.43
Kelly, town	463	473	2.16	Modena, town.	354	360	1.69
Keystone, town	378	374	-1.06	Mondovi, city	2,777	2,771	-0.22
Lincoln, town	287	291	1.39	Mondovi, town	469	474	1.07
Mason, town.	315	319	1.27	Montana, town	284	282	-0.70
Mason, village.	93	93	0.00	Naples, town	691	704	1.88
Namakagon, town	246	249	1.22	Nelson, town	571	612	7.18
				Nelson, village	374	373	-0.27

Wisconsin population by county and municipality, continued

	2010 census	2016 esti- mate	% change		2010 census	2016 esti- mate	% change
Waumandee, town. . . .	472	470	-0.42	Boyd, village.	552	554	0.36
Burnett.	**15,457**	**15,544**	**0.56**	Cadott, village.	1,437	1,458	1.46
Anderson, town.	398	400	0.50	Chippewa Falls, city . . .	13,661	13,965	2.23
Blaine, town	197	197	0.00	Cleveland, town.	864	878	1.62
Daniels, town	649	654	0.77	Colburn, town.	856	892	4.21
Dewey, town.	516	515	-0.19	Cooks Valley, town	805	830	3.11
Grantsburg, town.	1,136	1,145	0.79	Cornell, city	1,467	1,462	-0.34
Grantsburg, village. . . .	1,341	1,332	-0.67	Delmar, town	936	970	3.63
Jackson, town.	773	792	2.46	Eagle Point, town.	3,053	3,173	3.93
La Follette, town	536	537	0.19	Eau Claire, city (part). . .	1,981	2,049	3.43
Lincoln, town	309	312	0.97	Edson, town	1,089	1,084	-0.46
Meenon, town.	1,163	1,158	-0.43	Estella, town	433	432	-0.23
Oakland, town	827	847	2.42	Goetz, town	762	792	3.94
Roosevelt, town.	199	203	2.01	Hallie, town	161	175	8.70
Rusk, town	409	420	2.69	Howard, town.	798	804	0.75
Sand Lake, town	531	535	0.75	Lafayette, town	5,765	5,988	3.87
Scott, town.	494	503	1.82	Lake Hallie, village	6,448	6,916	7.26
Siren, town.	936	944	0.85	Lake Holcombe, town . .	1,031	1,042	1.07
Siren, village.	806	796	-1.24	New Auburn, village (part)	528	521	-1.33
Swiss, town	790	791	0.13	Ruby, town.	494	496	0.40
Trade Lake, town	823	829	0.73	Sampson, town	892	921	3.25
Union, town	340	343	0.88	Sigel, town.	1,044	1,041	-0.29
Webb Lake, town	311	312	0.32	Stanley, city (part)	3,602	3,618	0.44
Webster, village.	653	653	0.00	Tilden, town	1,485	1,511	1.75
West Marshland, town. .	367	368	0.27	Wheaton, town	2,701	2,777	2.81
Wood River, town.	953	958	0.52	Woodmohr, town.	932	958	2.79
Calumet	**48,971**	**51,669**	**5.51**	**Clark**	**34,690**	**34,888**	**0.57**
Appleton, city (part) . . .	11,088	11,731	5.80	Abbotsford, city (part). .	1,616	1,599	-1.05
Brillion, city	3,148	3,262	3.62	Beaver, town.	885	891	0.68
Brillion, town	1,486	1,521	2.36	Butler, town	96	96	0.00
Brothertown, town. . . .	1,329	1,332	0.23	Colby, city (part)	1,354	1,332	-1.62
Charlestown, town. . . .	775	781	0.77	Colby, town	874	897	2.63
Chilton, city	3,933	3,939	0.15	Curtiss, village.	216	212	-1.85
Chilton, town	1,143	1,154	0.96	Dewhurst, town.	323	330	2.17
Harrison, town	10,839	1,188	-89.04	Dorchester, village (part)	871	869	-0.23
Harrison, village (part)[1] .	NA	10,749	NA	Eaton, town	712	716	0.56
Hilbert, village	1,132	1,186	4.77	Foster, town	95	97	2.11
Kaukauna, city (part). . .	0	0	0.00	Fremont, town	1,265	1,272	0.55
Kiel, city (part).	309	317	2.59	Grant, town	916	938	2.40
Menasha, city (part) . . .	2,209	2,637	19.38	Granton, village.	355	355	0.00
New Holstein, city	3,236	3,204	-0.99	Green Grove, town	756	757	0.13
New Holstein, town . . .	1,508	1,519	0.73	Greenwood, city	1,026	1,023	-0.29
Potter, village	253	251	-0.79	Hendren, town	499	504	1.00
Rantoul, town	798	810	1.50	Hewett, town	293	296	1.02
Sherwood, village	2,713	2,959	9.07	Hixon, town	808	818	1.24
Stockbridge, town	1,456	1,498	2.88	Hoard, town	841	847	0.71
Stockbridge, village . . .	636	651	2.36	Levis, town.	492	498	1.22
Woodville, town	980	980	0.00	Longwood, town	858	863	0.58
Chippewa	**62,415**	**64,135**	**2.76**	Loyal, city.	1,261	1,255	-0.48
Anson, town	2,076	2,170	4.53	Loyal, town.	826	835	1.09
Arthur, town	759	772	1.71	Lynn, town.	861	883	2.56
Auburn, town	697	711	2.01	Mayville, town.	961	952	-0.94
Birch Creek, town.	517	528	2.13	Mead, town	321	331	3.12
Bloomer, city	3,539	3,559	0.57	Mentor, town	584	584	0.00
Bloomer, town	1,050	1,088	3.62	Neillsville, city.	2,463	2,431	-1.30
				Owen, city	940	936	-0.43

Wisconsin population by county and municipality, continued

	2010 census	2016 esti-mate	% change		2010 census	2016 esti-mate	% change
Pine Valley, town	1,157	1,172	1.30	Clayton, town	958	945	-1.36
Reseburg, town	776	791	1.93	De Soto, village (part) . .	108	106	-1.85
Seif, town.	172	172	0.00	Eastman, town	739	753	1.89
Sherman, town	882	915	3.74	Eastman, village	428	430	0.47
Sherwood, town	220	226	2.73	Ferryville, village	176	183	3.98
Stanley, city (part)	6	6	0.00	Freeman, town	686	706	2.92
Thorp, city	1,621	1,629	0.49	Gays Mills, village.	491	505	2.85
Thorp, town	808	826	2.23	Haney, town	309	316	2.27
Unity, town	878	906	3.19	Lynxville, village	132	134	1.52
Unity, village (part). . . .	139	138	-0.72	Marietta, town	470	489	4.04
Warner, town	669	676	1.05	Mount Sterling, village .	211	210	-0.47
Washburn, town	290	288	-0.69	Prairie du Chien, city. . .	5,911	5,874	-0.63
Weston, town	699	699	0.00	Prairie du Chien, town. .	1,073	1,074	0.09
Withee, town	966	983	1.76	Scott, town.	462	475	2.81
Withee, village	487	482	-1.03	Seneca, town	866	901	4.04
Worden, town	666	683	2.55	Soldiers Grove, village. .	592	576	-2.70
York, town	886	879	-0.79	Steuben, village.	131	123	-6.11
				Utica, town.	661	682	3.18
Columbia	**56,833**	**57,066**	**0.41**	Wauzeka, town	422	419	-0.71
Arlington, town	806	809	0.37	Wauzeka, village	711	697	-1.97
Arlington, village	819	824	0.61	**Dane**	**488,073**	**518,538**	**6.24**
Caledonia, town	1,378	1,403	1.81	Albion, town.	1,951	1,975	1.23
Cambria, village.	767	763	-0.52	Belleville, village (part) .	1,848	1,854	0.32
Columbus, city (part) . .	4,991	5,066	1.50	Berry, town.	1,127	1,140	1.15
Columbus, town	646	654	1.24	Black Earth, town	483	484	0.21
Courtland, town	525	530	0.95	Black Earth, village	1,338	1,388	3.74
Dekorra, town	2,311	2,338	1.17	Blooming Grove, town .	1,815	1,799	-0.88
Doylestown, village . . .	297	293	-1.35	Blue Mounds, town . . .	968	997	3.00
Fall River, village	1,712	1,732	1.17	Blue Mounds, village. . .	855	938	9.71
Fort Winnebago, town. .	825	826	0.12	Bristol, town	3,765	4,169	10.73
Fountain Prairie, town. .	887	892	0.56	Brooklyn, village (part) .	936	953	1.82
Friesland, village	356	354	-0.56	Burke, town	3,284	3,341	1.74
Hampden, town	574	581	1.22	Cambridge, village (part)	1,348	1,362	1.04
Leeds, town	774	773	-0.13	Christiana, town	1,235	1,259	1.94
Lewiston, town	1,225	1,232	0.57	Cottage Grove, town. . .	3,875	3,824	-1.32
Lodi, city	3,050	3,087	1.21	Cottage Grove, village. .	6,192	6,635	7.15
Lodi, town	3,273	3,312	1.19	Cross Plains, town	1,507	1,551	2.92
Lowville, town.	1,008	1,019	1.09	Cross Plains, village . . .	3,538	3,842	8.59
Marcellon, town	1,102	1,105	0.27	Dane, town	990	1,004	1.41
Newport, town	586	589	0.51	Dane, village.	995	1,090	9.55
Otsego, town	693	696	0.43	DeForest, village	8,936	9,388	5.06
Pacific, town	2,707	2,714	0.26	Deerfield, town	1,585	1,611	1.64
Pardeeville, village	2,115	2,105	-0.47	Deerfield, village	2,319	2,451	5.69
Portage, city	10,324	10,251	-0.71	Dunkirk, town	1,945	1,942	-0.15
Poynette, village	2,528	2,525	-0.12	Dunn, town	4,931	4,940	0.18
Randolph, town.	769	773	0.52	Edgerton, city (part) . . .	97	131	35.05
Randolph, village (part) .	472	469	-0.64	Fitchburg, city.	25,260	27,635	9.40
Rio, village	1,059	1,059	0.00	Madison, city	233,209	247,207	6.00
Scott, town.	905	914	0.99	Madison, town	6,279	6,341	0.99
Springvale, town	520	533	2.50	Maple Bluff, village. . . .	1,313	1,304	-0.69
West Point, town	1,955	1,991	1.84	Marshall, village.	3,862	3,859	-0.08
Wisconsin Dells, city (part)	2,440	2,416	-0.98	Mazomanie, town	1,090	1,100	0.92
Wyocena, town	1,666	1,691	1.50	Mazomanie, village . . .	1,652	1,668	0.97
Wyocena, village	768	747	-2.73	McFarland, village	7,808	8,044	3.02
				Medina, town	1,376	1,386	0.73
Crawford.	**16,644**	**16,744**	**0.60**	Middleton, city	17,442	19,317	10.75
Bell Center, village	117	116	-0.85	Middleton, town	5,877	6,399	8.88
Bridgeport, town	990	1,030	4.04				

Wisconsin population by county and municipality, continued

	2010 census	2016 estimate	% change		2010 census	2016 estimate	% change
Monona, city	7,533	7,864	4.39	Neosho, village	574	572	-0.35
Montrose, town.	1,081	1,096	1.39	Oak Grove, town	1,080	1,075	-0.46
Mount Horeb, village . .	7,009	7,142	1.90	Portland, town	1,079	1,091	1.11
Oregon, town	3,184	3,242	1.82	Randolph, village (part) .	1,339	1,318	-1.57
Oregon, village	9,231	9,797	6.13	Reeseville, village.	708	707	-0.14
Perry, town.	729	742	1.78	Rubicon, town.	2,207	2,249	1.90
Pleasant Springs, town .	3,154	3,234	2.54	Shields, town	554	566	2.17
Primrose, town	731	736	0.68	Theresa, town	1,075	1,085	0.93
Rockdale, village	214	213	-0.47	Theresa, village	1,262	1,258	-0.32
Roxbury, town.	1,794	1,870	4.24	Trenton, town	1,293	1,312	1.47
Rutland, town	1,966	2,003	1.88	Watertown, city (part) . .	8,459	8,586	1.50
Shorewood Hills, village	1,565	2,077	32.72	Waupun, city (part). . . .	7,864	8,067	2.58
Springdale, town	1,904	1,954	2.63	Westford, town	1,228	1,233	0.41
Springfield, town	2,734	2,869	4.94	Williamstown, town . . .	755	764	1.19
Stoughton, city	12,611	12,819	1.65				
Sun Prairie, city	29,364	32,613	11.06	**Door**.	**27,785**	**28,127**	**1.23**
Sun Prairie, town	2,326	2,381	2.36	Baileys Harbor, town. . .	1,022	1,044	2.15
Vermont, town	819	824	0.61	Brussels, town.	1,136	1,139	0.26
Verona, city	10,619	12,100	13.95	Clay Banks, town	382	391	2.36
Verona, town	1,948	1,975	1.39	Egg Harbor, town.	1,342	1,359	1.27
Vienna, town	1,482	1,532	3.37	Egg Harbor, village. . . .	201	203	1.00
Waunakee, village	12,097	13,322	10.13	Ephraim, village.	288	289	0.35
Westport, town	3,950	4,012	1.57	Forestville, town	1,096	1,107	1.00
Windsor, village[2]	6,345	7,145	12.61	Forestville, village	430	428	-0.47
York, town	652	648	-0.61	Gardner, town.	1,194	1,209	1.26
				Gibraltar, town	1,021	1,034	1.27
				Jacksonport, town	705	711	0.85
Dodge	**88,759**	**89,962**	**1.36**	Liberty Grove, town . . .	1,734	1,752	1.04
Ashippun, town.	2,559	2,596	1.45	Nasewaupee, town. . . .	2,061	2,098	1.80
Beaver Dam, city	16,214	16,799	3.61	Sevastopol, town	2,628	2,685	2.17
Beaver Dam, town	3,962	4,029	1.69	Sister Bay, village	876	905	3.31
Brownsville, village. . . .	581	593	2.07	Sturgeon Bay, city	9,144	9,237	1.02
Burnett, town	904	907	0.33	Sturgeon Bay, town . . .	818	822	0.49
Calamus, town	1,048	1,047	-0.10	Union, town	999	1,001	0.20
Chester, town	687	701	2.04	Washington, town	708	713	0.71
Clyman, town	774	784	1.29				
Clyman, village	422	415	-1.66	**Douglas**	**44,159**	**44,415**	**0.58**
Columbus, city (part) . .	0	0	0.00	Amnicon, town	1,155	1,198	3.72
Elba, town	996	1,005	0.90	Bennett, town	597	615	3.02
Emmet, town	1,302	1,313	0.84	Brule, town.	656	671	2.29
Fox Lake, city	1,519	1,509	-0.66	Cloverland, town	210	203	-3.33
Fox Lake, town	2,465	2,460	-0.20	Dairyland, town	184	183	-0.54
Hartford, city (part). . . .	0	0	0.00	Gordon, town	636	637	0.16
Herman, town.	1,108	1,133	2.26	Hawthorne, town.	1,136	1,117	-1.67
Horicon, city	3,655	3,752	2.65	Highland, town	311	300	-3.54
Hubbard, town	1,774	1,792	1.01	Lake Nebagamon, village	1,069	1,081	1.12
Hustisford, town	1,373	1,398	1.82	Lakeside, town	693	706	1.88
Hustisford, village	1,123	1,119	-0.36	Maple, town	744	765	2.82
Iron Ridge, village	929	938	0.97	Oakland, town	1,136	1,172	3.17
Juneau, city	2,814	2,748	-2.35	Oliver, village	399	431	8.02
Kekoskee, village	161	160	-0.62	Parkland, town	1,220	1,242	1.80
Lebanon, town	1,659	1,664	0.30	Poplar, village	603	612	1.49
Leroy, town	1,002	996	-0.60	Solon Springs, town . . .	910	926	1.76
Lomira, town	1,137	1,156	1.67	Solon Springs, village . .	600	600	0.00
Lomira, village.	2,430	2,432	0.08	Summit, town	1,063	1,073	0.94
Lowell, town.	1,190	1,205	1.26	Superior, city	27,244	27,237	-0.03
Lowell, village	340	336	-1.18	Superior, town	2,166	2,212	2.12
Mayville, city	5,154	5,092	-1.20	Superior, village.	664	674	1.51

Wisconsin population by county and municipality, continued

	2010 census	2016 esti-mate	% change		2010 census	2016 esti-mate	% change
Wascott, town.	763	760	-0.39	Fern, town	159	160	0.63
				Florence, town	2,002	2,007	0.25
Dunn	**43,857**	**44,575**	**1.64**	Homestead, town	336	343	2.08
Boyceville, village.	1,086	1,089	0.28	Long Lake, town	157	159	1.27
Colfax, town	1,186	1,256	5.90	Tipler, town	142	146	2.82
Colfax, village	1,158	1,123	-3.02				
Downing, village	265	263	-0.75	**Fond du Lac**.	**101,633**	**103,290**	**1.63**
Dunn, town	1,524	1,537	0.85	Alto, town	1,045	1,062	1.63
Eau Galle, town	757	772	1.98	Ashford, town	1,747	1,771	1.37
Elk Mound, town	1,792	1,904	6.25	Auburn, town	2,352	2,388	1.53
Elk Mound, village	878	872	-0.68	Brandon, village	879	875	-0.46
Grant, town	385	392	1.82	Byron, town	1,634	1,656	1.35
Hay River, town	558	566	1.43	Calumet, town	1,470	1,496	1.77
Knapp, village	463	462	-0.22	Campbellsport, village .	2,016	2,008	-0.40
Lucas, town	764	769	0.65	Eden, town.	1,028	1,039	1.07
Menomonie, city	16,264	16,338	0.45	Eden, village.	875	892	1.94
Menomonie, town	3,366	3,470	3.09	Eldorado, town	1,462	1,482	1.37
New Haven, town.	677	686	1.33	Empire, town	2,797	2,818	0.75
Otter Creek, town	501	505	0.80	Fairwater, village	371	367	-1.08
Peru, town	242	244	0.83	Fond du Lac, city	43,021	43,381	0.84
Red Cedar, town	2,086	2,151	3.12	Fond du Lac, town	3,015	3,553	17.84
Ridgeland, village	273	273	0.00	Forest, town	1,080	1,078	-0.19
Rock Creek, town.	1,000	1,036	3.60	Friendship, town	2,675	2,710	1.31
Sand Creek, town.	570	578	1.40	Kewaskum, village (part)	0	0	0.00
Sheridan, town	454	468	3.08	Lamartine, town	1,737	1,775	2.19
Sherman, town	849	877	3.30	Marshfield, town	1,138	1,144	0.53
Spring Brook, town. . . .	1,558	1,639	5.20	Metomen, town.	741	735	-0.81
Stanton, town	791	792	0.13	Mount Calvary, village. .	762	569	-25.33
Tainter, town.	2,319	2,410	3.92	North Fond du Lac, village	5,014	5,237	4.45
Tiffany, town.	618	623	0.81	Oakfield, town.	703	709	0.85
Weston, town	594	601	1.18	Oakfield, village.	1,075	1,097	2.05
Wheeler, village.	348	346	-0.57	Osceola, town	1,865	1,865	0.00
Wilson, town.	531	533	0.38	Ripon, city	7,733	7,833	1.29
				Ripon, town	1,400	1,422	1.57
Eau Claire	**98,736**	**101,731**	**3.03**	Rosendale, town	695	705	1.44
Altoona, city.	6,706	7,345	9.53	Rosendale, village	1,063	1,046	-1.60
Augusta, city.	1,550	1,537	-0.84	Springvale, town	707	718	1.56
Bridge Creek, town. . . .	1,900	1,909	0.47	St. Cloud, village	477	474	-0.63
Brunswick, town	1,624	1,839	13.24	Taycheedah, town	4,205	4,485	6.66
Clear Creek, town.	821	847	3.17	Waupun, city (part). . . .	3,476	3,505	0.83
Drammen, town	783	812	3.70	Waupun, town	1,375	1,395	1.45
Eau Claire, city (part). . .	63,950	65,332	2.16				
Fairchild, town	343	355	3.50	**Forest**.	**9,304**	**9,279**	**-0.27**
Fairchild, village.	550	547	-0.55	Alvin, town.	157	155	-1.27
Fall Creek, village.	1,315	1,302	-0.99	Argonne, town	512	508	-0.78
Lincoln, town	1,096	1,142	4.20	Armstrong Creek, town .	409	411	0.49
Ludington, town	1,063	1,081	1.69	Blackwell, town	332	323	-2.71
Otter Creek, town	500	499	-0.20	Caswell, town	91	89	-2.20
Pleasant Valley, town . .	3,044	3,237	6.34	Crandon, city	1,920	1,875	-2.34
Seymour, town	3,209	3,328	3.71	Crandon, town	650	655	0.77
Union, town	2,663	2,806	5.37	Freedom, town	345	346	0.29
Washington, town	7,134	7,314	2.52	Hiles, town.	311	316	1.61
Wilson, town.	485	499	2.89	Laona, town	1,212	1,205	-0.58
				Lincoln, town	955	968	1.36
Florence	**4,423**	**4,473**	**1.13**	Nashville, town	1,064	1,079	1.41
Aurora, town.	1,036	1,061	2.41	Popple River, town	44	42	-4.55
Commonwealth, town. .	399	404	1.25	Ross, town	136	134	-1.47
Fence, town	192	193	0.52	Wabeno, town	1,166	1,173	0.60

Wisconsin population by county and municipality, continued

	2010 census	2016 esti- mate	% change		2010 census	2016 esti- mate	% change
				Albany, town	1,106	1,125	1.72
Grant	**51,208**	**53,107**	**3.71**	Albany, village.	1,018	1,010	-0.79
Bagley, village.	379	375	-1.06	Belleville, village (part) .	537	533	-0.74
Beetown, town	777	789	1.54	Brodhead, city (part). . .	3,203	3,187	-0.50
Bloomington, town . . .	350	356	1.71	Brooklyn, town	1,083	1,112	2.68
Bloomington, village . .	735	739	0.54	Brooklyn, village (part) .	465	463	-0.43
Blue River, village.	434	434	0.00	Browntown, village . . .	280	280	0.00
Boscobel, city	3,231	3,198	-1.02	Cadiz, town	815	811	-0.49
Boscobel, town	376	373	-0.80	Clarno, town.	1,166	1,163	-0.26
Cassville, town	416	413	-0.72	Decatur, town	1,767	1,780	0.74
Cassville, village	947	943	-0.42	Exeter, town	2,023	2,060	1.83
Castle Rock, town.	248	258	4.03	Jefferson, town	1,217	1,231	1.15
Clifton, town.	385	397	3.12	Jordan, town	641	635	-0.94
Cuba City, city (part) . . .	1,877	1,881	0.21	Monroe, city	10,827	10,717	-1.02
Dickeyville, village	1,061	1,059	-0.19	Monroe, town	1,245	1,243	-0.16
Ellenboro, town.	525	543	3.43	Monticello, village	1,217	1,220	0.25
Fennimore, city	2,497	2,508	0.44	Mount Pleasant, town . .	598	604	1.00
Fennimore, town	612	614	0.33	New Glarus, town.	1,335	1,365	2.25
Glen Haven, town	417	419	0.48	New Glarus, village. . . .	2,172	2,164	-0.37
Harrison, town	495	503	1.62	Spring Grove, town . . .	874	891	1.95
Hazel Green, town	1,132	1,141	0.80	Sylvester, town	1,004	1,010	0.60
Hazel Green, village (part)	1,243	1,254	0.88	Washington, town	809	820	1.36
Hickory Grove, town . . .	455	495	8.79	York, town	910	945	3.85
Jamestown, town.	2,076	2,169	4.48				
Lancaster, city	3,868	3,811	-1.47	**Green Lake**	**19,051**	**19,143**	**0.48**
Liberty, town	553	557	0.72	Berlin, city (part)	5,435	5,429	-0.11
Lima, town	805	801	-0.50	Berlin, town	1,140	1,144	0.35
Little Grant, town.	283	282	-0.35	Brooklyn, town	1,826	1,859	1.81
Livingston, village (part)	657	654	-0.46	Green Lake, city.	960	983	2.40
Marion, town	572	589	2.97	Green Lake, town.	1,154	1,159	0.43
Millville, town	166	168	1.20	Kingston, town	1,064	1,085	1.97
Montfort, village (part) .	622	625	0.48	Kingston, village	326	326	0.00
Mount Hope, town	300	299	-0.33	Mackford, town	560	561	0.18
Mount Hope, village . . .	225	227	0.89	Manchester, town	1,022	1,047	2.45
Mount Ida, town	561	565	0.71	Markesan, city.	1,476	1,444	-2.17
Muscoda, town	769	772	0.39	Marquette, town	531	542	2.07
Muscoda, village (part) .	1,249	1,218	-2.48	Marquette, village	150	152	1.33
North Lancaster, town. .	509	528	3.73	Princeton, city.	1,214	1,197	-1.40
Paris, town	702	719	2.42	Princeton, town.	1,434	1,445	0.77
Patch Grove, town	339	340	0.29	St. Marie, town	351	359	2.28
Patch Grove, village . . .	198	199	0.51	Seneca, town	408	411	0.74
Platteville, city.	11,224	12,824	14.26				
Platteville, town.	1,509	1,551	2.78	**Iowa**.	**23,687**	**23,829**	**0.60**
Potosi, town	849	854	0.59	Arena, town	1,456	1,488	2.20
Potosi, village	688	682	-0.87	Arena, village	834	825	-1.08
Smelser, town	794	798	0.50	Avoca, village	637	629	-1.26
South Lancaster, town. .	843	867	2.85	Barneveld, village.	1,231	1,238	0.57
Tennyson, village	355	366	3.10	Blanchardville, village			
Waterloo, town	550	573	4.18	(part)	177	180	1.69
Watterstown, town. . . .	330	337	2.12	Brigham, town	1,034	1,065	3.00
Wingville, town	357	363	1.68	Clyde, town	306	311	1.63
Woodman, town	185	195	5.41	Cobb, village.	458	465	1.53
Woodman, village	132	131	-0.76	Dodgeville, city	4,693	4,676	-0.36
Wyalusing, town	346	351	1.45	Dodgeville, town	1,708	1,758	2.93
				Eden, town	355	366	3.10
				Highland, town	750	765	2.00
Green	**36,842**	**36,907**	**0.18**	Highland, village	842	841	-0.12
Adams, town	530	538	1.51	Hollandale, village	288	286	-0.69

Wisconsin population by county and municipality, continued

	2010 census	2016 estimate	% change		2010 census	2016 estimate	% change
Linden, town	847	842	-0.59	**Jefferson**	**83,686**	**84,262**	**0.69**
Linden, village.	549	543	-1.09	Aztalan, town	1,457	1,460	0.21
Livingston, village (part)	7	7	0.00	Cambridge, village (part)	109	108	-0.92
Mifflin, town	585	595	1.71	Cold Spring, town	727	774	6.46
Mineral Point, city	2,487	2,491	0.16	Concord, town	2,072	2,085	0.63
Mineral Point, town . . .	1,033	1,052	1.84	Farmington, town	1,380	1,388	0.58
Montfort, village (part) .	96	99	3.13	Fort Atkinson, city	12,368	12,441	0.59
Moscow, town.	576	600	4.17	Hebron, town	1,094	1,100	0.55
Muscoda, village (part) .	50	36	-28.00	Ixonia, town	4,385	4,711	7.43
Pulaski, town	400	405	1.25	Jefferson, city	7,973	7,985	0.15
Rewey, village.	292	285	-2.40	Jefferson, town	2,178	2,182	0.18
Ridgeway, town.	568	562	-1.06	Johnson Creek, village. .	2,738	2,933	7.12
Ridgeway, village.	653	642	-1.68	Koshkonong, town. . . .	3,692	3,694	0.05
Waldwick, town.	473	478	1.06	Lac La Belle, village (part)	1	1	0.00
Wyoming, town.	302	299	-0.99	Lake Mills, city.	5,708	5,883	3.07
				Lake Mills, town.	2,070	2,087	0.82
Iron	**5,916**	**5,901**	**-0.25**	Milford, town	1,099	1,113	1.27
Anderson, town.	58	59	1.72	Oakland, town	3,100	3,087	-0.42
Carey, town	163	159	-2.45	Palmyra, town.	1,186	1,175	-0.93
Gurney, town	159	164	3.14	Palmyra, village	1,781	1,773	-0.45
Hurley, city.	1,547	1,504	-2.78	Sullivan, town	2,208	2,217	0.41
Kimball, town	498	491	-1.41	Sullivan, village	669	672	0.45
Knight, town.	211	206	-2.37	Sumner, town	832	796	-4.33
Mercer, town	1,407	1,439	2.27	Waterloo, city	3,333	3,371	1.14
Montreal, city	807	805	-0.25	Waterloo, town	909	907	-0.22
Oma, town.	289	300	3.81	Watertown, city (part) . .	15,402	15,409	0.05
Pence, town	163	161	-1.23	Watertown, town.	1,975	1,968	-0.35
Saxon, town	324	321	-0.93	Whitewater, city (part). .	3,240	2,942	-9.20
Sherman, town	290	292	0.69				
				Juneau	**26,664**	**27,022**	**1.34**
Jackson.	**20,449**	**20,743**	**1.44**	Armenia, town	699	742	6.15
Adams, town	1,342	1,377	2.61	Camp Douglas, village. .	601	615	2.33
Albion, town.	1,210	1,242	2.64	Clearfield, town.	728	735	0.96
Alma, town.	1,044	1,099	5.27	Cutler, town	326	331	1.53
Alma Center, village . . .	503	509	1.19	Elroy, city.	1,442	1,379	-4.37
Bear Bluff, town.	138	135	-2.17	Finley, town	97	95	-2.06
Black River Falls, city . . .	3,622	3,623	0.03	Fountain, town	555	573	3.24
Brockway, town.	2,828	2,857	1.03	Germantown, town . . .	1,471	1,627	10.61
City Point, town.	182	179	-1.65	Hustler, village	194	195	0.52
Cleveland, town.	481	496	3.12	Kildare, town	681	706	3.67
Curran, town.	343	321	-6.41	Kingston, town	91	88	-3.30
Franklin, town.	448	460	2.68	Lemonweir, town.	1,743	1,761	1.03
Garden Valley, town . . .	422	434	2.84	Lindina, town	718	713	-0.70
Garfield, town	638	682	6.90	Lisbon, town.	912	914	0.22
Hixton, town.	652	669	2.61	Lyndon, town	1,384	1,405	1.52
Hixton, village.	433	427	-1.39	Lyndon Station, village .	500	490	-2.00
Irving, town	751	768	2.26	Marion, town	426	429	0.70
Knapp, town.	299	312	4.35	Mauston, city	4,423	4,489	1.49
Komensky, town	509	512	0.59	Necedah, town	2,327	2,380	2.28
Manchester, town	704	711	0.99	Necedah, village	916	917	0.11
Melrose, town	470	499	6.17	New Lisbon, city	2,554	2,567	0.51
Melrose, village	503	496	-1.39	Orange, town	570	573	0.53
Merrillan, village	542	530	-2.21	Plymouth, town.	597	598	0.17
Millston, town.	159	164	3.14	Seven Mile Creek, town .	358	352	-1.68
North Bend, town	488	501	2.66	Summit, town	646	656	1.55
Northfield, town	639	652	2.03	Union Center, village . .	200	197	-1.50
Springfield, town	623	607	-2.57	Wisconsin Dells, city (part)	2	0	-100.00
Taylor, village	476	481	1.05				

Wisconsin population by county and municipality, continued

	2010 census	2016 estimate	% change		2010 census	2016 estimate	% change
Wonewoc, town.	687	688	0.15	Belmont, village	986	993	0.71
Wonewoc, village.	816	807	-1.10	Benton, town	504	512	1.59
				Benton, village	973	964	-0.92
Kenosha	**166,426**	**167,658**	**0.74**	Blanchard, town	264	275	4.17
Brighton, town	1,456	1,458	0.14	Blanchardville, village			
Bristol, village	4,914	5,003	1.81	(part)	648	640	-1.23
Genoa City, village (part).	6	6	0.00	Cuba City, city (part) . . .	209	216	3.35
Kenosha, city	99,218	99,489	0.27	Darlington, city	2,451	2,421	-1.22
Paddock Lake, village . .	2,992	2,983	-0.30	Darlington, town	875	888	1.49
Paris, town	1,504	1,505	0.07	Elk Grove, town	551	576	4.54
Pleasant Prairie, village .	19,719	20,438	3.65	Fayette, town	376	416	10.64
Randall, town	3,180	3,183	0.09	Gratiot, town	550	554	0.73
Salem, town[3]	12,067	12,096	0.24	Gratiot, village	236	231	-2.12
Silver Lake, village[3]. . . .	2,411	2,400	-0.46	Hazel Green, village (part)	13	13	0.00
Somers, town	9,597	1,234	-87.14	Kendall, town	454	466	2.64
Somers, village[4].	NA	8,462	NA	Lamont, town	314	318	1.27
Twin Lakes, village	5,989	6,049	1.00	Monticello, town	133	135	1.50
Wheatland, town	3,373	3,352	-0.62	New Diggings, town . . .	502	514	2.39
				Seymour, town	446	451	1.12
Kewaunee	**20,574**	**20,723**	**0.72**	Shullsburg, city	1,226	1,215	-0.90
Ahnapee, town	940	932	-0.85	Shullsburg, town	354	352	-0.56
Algoma, city	3,167	3,151	-0.51	South Wayne, village. . .	489	488	-0.20
Carlton, town	1,014	1,026	1.18	Wayne, town.	490	495	1.02
Casco, town	1,165	1,181	1.37	White Oak Springs, town	118	120	1.69
Casco, village	583	594	1.89	Willow Springs, town . .	758	757	-0.13
Franklin, town	993	1,002	0.91	Wiota, town	856	854	-0.23
Kewaunee, city	2,952	2,915	-1.25				
Lincoln, town	948	944	-0.42	**Langlade**.	**19,977**	**19,995**	**0.09**
Luxemburg, town.	1,469	1,492	1.57	Ackley, town.	524	529	0.95
Luxemburg, village. . . .	2,515	2,583	2.70	Ainsworth, town	469	462	-1.49
Montpelier, town	1,306	1,328	1.68	Antigo, city.	8,234	8,197	-0.45
Pierce, town	833	831	-0.24	Antigo, town.	1,412	1,407	-0.35
Red River, town	1,393	1,414	1.51	Elcho, town	1,233	1,249	1.30
West Kewaunee, town. .	1,296	1,330	2.62	Evergreen, town	495	506	2.22
				Langlade, town	473	480	1.48
La Crosse.	**114,638**	**118,038**	**2.97**	Neva, town.	902	899	-0.33
Bangor, town	615	618	0.49	Norwood, town	913	900	-1.42
Bangor, village	1,459	1,520	4.18	Parrish, town	91	88	-3.30
Barre, town.	1,234	1,260	2.11	Peck, town	349	361	3.44
Burns, town	947	955	0.84	Polar, town.	984	996	1.22
Campbell, town.	4,314	4,330	0.37	Price, town	228	221	-3.07
Farmington, town	2,061	2,083	1.07	Rolling, town	1,504	1,518	0.93
Greenfield, town	2,060	2,116	2.72	Summit, town	163	160	-1.84
Hamilton, town	2,436	2,467	1.27	Upham, town	676	684	1.18
Holland, town	3,701	3,967	7.19	Vilas, town	233	223	-4.29
Holmen, village	9,005	9,623	6.86	White Lake, village	363	359	-1.10
La Crosse, city	51,320	52,377	2.06	Wolf River, town	731	756	3.42
Medary, town	1,461	1,498	2.53				
Onalaska, city	17,736	18,646	5.13	**Lincoln**	**28,743**	**28,787**	**0.15**
Onalaska, town	5,623	5,743	2.13	Birch, town.	594	673	13.30
Rockland, village (part) .	594	628	5.72	Bradley, town	2,408	2,455	1.95
Shelby, town.	4,715	4,707	-0.17	Corning, town	883	884	0.11
Washington, town	558	544	-2.51	Harding, town.	372	380	2.15
West Salem, village. . . .	4,799	4,956	3.27	Harrison, town	833	842	1.08
				King, town	855	879	2.81
Lafayette.	**16,836**	**16,961**	**0.74**	Merrill, city	9,661	9,522	-1.44
Argyle, town	436	446	2.29	Merrill, town.	2,980	3,002	0.74
Argyle, village	857	851	-0.70	Pine River, town.	1,869	1,886	0.91
Belmont, town	767	800	4.30				

Wisconsin population by county and municipality, continued

	2010 census	2016 esti-mate	% change		2010 census	2016 esti-mate	% change
Rock Falls, town	618	639	3.40	Eau Pleine, town	773	762	-1.42
Russell, town	677	678	0.15	Edgar, village	1,479	1,468	-0.74
Schley, town.	934	925	-0.96	Elderon, town	606	618	1.98
Scott, town.	1,432	1,436	0.28	Elderon, village	179	176	-1.68
Skanawan, town	391	397	1.53	Emmet, town	931	941	1.07
Somo, town	114	118	3.51	Fenwood, village	152	147	-3.29
Tomahawk, city	3,397	3,332	-1.91	Frankfort, town	670	659	-1.64
Tomahawk, town	416	427	2.64	Franzen, town	578	585	1.21
Wilson, town.	309	312	0.97	Green Valley, town	541	547	1.11
				Guenther, town	341	345	1.17
Manitowoc	**81,442**	**81,404**	**-0.05**	Halsey, town.	651	659	1.23
Cato, town	1,566	1,577	0.70	Hamburg, town	918	920	0.22
Centerville, town	645	642	-0.47	Harrison, town	374	369	-1.34
Cleveland, village.	1,485	1,515	2.02	Hatley, village	574	605	5.40
Cooperstown, town . . .	1,292	1,299	0.54	Hewitt, town.	606	622	2.64
Eaton, town	833	832	-0.12	Holton, town	873	885	1.37
Francis Creek, village . .	669	663	-0.90	Hull, town	750	745	-0.67
Franklin, town.	1,264	1,259	-0.40	Johnson, town	985	984	-0.10
Gibson, town	1,344	1,338	-0.45	Knowlton, town.	1,910	1,934	1.26
Kellnersville, village . . .	332	329	-0.90	Kronenwetter, village . .	7,210	7,536	4.52
Kiel, city (part).	3,429	3,451	0.64	Maine, village[2]	2,337	2,341	0.17
Kossuth, town	2,090	2,086	-0.19	Marathon, town.	1,048	1,048	0.00
Liberty, town	1,281	1,288	0.55	Marathon City, village . .	1,524	1,568	2.89
Manitowoc, city.	33,736	33,783	0.14	Marshfield, city (part) . .	900	969	7.67
Manitowoc, town.	1,083	1,098	1.39	McMillan, town	1,968	2,014	2.34
Manitowoc Rapids, town	2,150	2,146	-0.19	Mosinee, city	3,988	4,013	0.63
Maple Grove, town. . . .	835	833	-0.24	Mosinee, town	2,174	2,196	1.01
Maribel, village	351	343	-2.28	Norrie, town	976	988	1.23
Meeme, town	1,446	1,458	0.83	Plover, town	689	685	-0.58
Mishicot, town	1,289	1,291	0.16	Reid, town	1,215	1,245	2.47
Mishicot, village	1,442	1,442	0.00	Rib Falls, town.	993	1,005	1.21
Newton, town	2,264	2,293	1.28	Rib Mountain, town . . .	6,825	6,917	1.35
Reedsville, village	1,206	1,197	-0.75	Rietbrock, town.	981	983	0.20
Rockland, town	1,001	1,002	0.10	Ringle, town	1,711	1,728	0.99
St. Nazianz, village	783	776	-0.89	Rothschild, village	5,269	5,325	1.06
Schleswig, town	1,963	1,988	1.27	Schofield, city	2,169	2,207	1.75
Two Creeks, town.	437	425	-2.75	Spencer, town	1,581	1,625	2.78
Two Rivers, city	11,712	11,566	-1.25	Spencer, village.	1,925	1,936	0.57
Two Rivers, town	1,795	1,779	-0.89	Stettin, town.	2,554	2,564	0.39
Valders, village	962	957	-0.52	Stratford, village	1,578	1,600	1.39
Whitelaw, village	757	748	-1.19	Texas, town	1,615	1,607	-0.50
				Unity, village (part)	204	201	-1.47
Marathon	**134,063**	**135,483**	**1.06**	Wausau, city	39,106	38,909	-0.50
Abbotsford, city (part). .	694	680	-2.02	Wausau, town	2,229	2,339	4.93
Athens, village	1,105	1,102	-0.27	Weston, town	639	661	3.44
Bergen, town	641	637	-0.62	Weston, village	14,868	15,338	3.16
Berlin, town	945	941	-0.42	Wien, town.	825	849	2.91
Bern, town	591	605	2.37				
Bevent, town	1,118	1,121	0.27	**Marinette**	**41,749**	**41,413**	**-0.80**
Birnamwood, village (part)	16	20	25.00	Amberg, town.	726	735	1.24
Brighton, town	612	609	-0.49	Athelstane, town	504	508	0.79
Brokaw, village	251	241	-3.98	Beaver, town.	1,146	1,169	2.01
Cassel, town	911	921	1.10	Beecher, town	724	735	1.52
Cleveland, town.	1,488	1,512	1.61	Coleman, village	724	726	0.28
Colby, city (part)	498	499	0.20	Crivitz, village	984	959	-2.54
Day, town	1,085	1,092	0.65	Dunbar, town	1,094	632	-42.23
Dorchester, village (part)	5	4	-20.00	Goodman, town	619	620	0.16
Easton, town.	1,111	1,131	1.80				

Wisconsin population by county and municipality, continued

	2010 census	2016 esti- mate	% change		2010 census	2016 esti- mate	% change
Grover, town.	1,768	1,806	2.15	Wauwatosa, city	46,396	47,160	1.65
Lake, town	1,135	1,158	2.03	West Allis, city.	60,411	60,164	-0.41
Marinette, city.	10,968	10,878	-0.82	West Milwaukee, village.	4,206	4,181	-0.59
Middle Inlet, town	840	834	-0.71	Whitefish Bay, village . .	14,110	14,216	0.75
Niagara, city	1,624	1,602	-1.35				
Niagara, town	853	871	2.11	**Monroe. . . . .**	**44,673**	**45,865**	**2.67**
Pembine, town	889	886	-0.34	Adrian, town.	762	794	4.20
Peshtigo, city	3,502	3,449	-1.51	Angelo, town	1,296	1,316	1.54
Peshtigo, town	4,057	4,105	1.18	Byron, town	1,342	1,360	1.34
Porterfield, town	1,971	2,003	1.62	Cashton, village.	1,102	1,107	0.45
Pound, town.	1,425	1,422	-0.21	Clifton, town.	690	697	1.01
Pound, village.	377	377	0.00	Glendale, town	667	690	3.45
Silver Cliff, town.	491	505	2.85	Grant, town	495	500	1.01
Stephenson, town	3,006	3,064	1.93	Greenfield, town	707	719	1.70
Wagner, town	681	694	1.91	Jefferson, town	819	858	4.76
Wausaukee, town.	1,066	1,107	3.85	Kendall, village	472	469	-0.64
Wausaukee, village. . . .	575	568	-1.22	La Grange, town	2,007	2,009	0.10
				Lafayette, town	396	551	39.14
Marquette	**15,404**	**15,425**	**0.14**	Leon, town	1,086	1,129	3.96
Buffalo, town	1,221	1,240	1.56	Lincoln, town	835	847	1.44
Crystal Lake, town	484	492	1.65	Little Falls, town	1,523	1,581	3.81
Douglas, town.	725	735	1.38	Melvina, village	104	104	0.00
Endeavor, village	468	460	-1.71	New Lyme, town	168	174	3.57
Harris, town	790	794	0.51	Norwalk, village.	638	638	0.00
Mecan, town.	686	688	0.29	Oakdale, town.	772	791	2.46
Montello, city	1,495	1,461	-2.27	Oakdale, village	297	293	-1.35
Montello, town	1,033	1,040	0.68	Ontario, village (part) . .	0	0	0.00
Moundville, town.	552	567	2.72	Portland, town	808	832	2.97
Neshkoro, town.	561	552	-1.60	Ridgeville, town.	501	519	3.59
Neshkoro, village.	434	424	-2.30	Rockland, village (part) .	0	0	0.00
Newton, town.	547	549	0.37	Scott, town.	135	134	-0.74
Oxford, town	885	891	0.68	Sheldon, town.	727	750	3.16
Oxford, village.	607	597	-1.65	Sparta, city.	9,522	9,804	2.96
Packwaukee, town	1,416	1,416	0.00	Sparta, town.	3,128	3,181	1.69
Shields, town	550	547	-0.55	Tomah, city	9,093	9,345	2.77
Springfield, town	830	836	0.72	Tomah, town	1,400	1,435	2.50
Westfield, town	866	878	1.39	Warrens, village.	363	356	-1.93
Westfield, village	1,254	1,258	0.32	Wellington, town	621	648	4.35
				Wells, town.	519	537	3.47
Menominee	**4,232**	**4,256**	**0.57**	Wilton, town.	1,027	1,056	2.82
Menominee, town	4,232	4,256	0.57	Wilton, village.	504	501	-0.60
				Wyeville, village.	147	140	-4.76
Milwaukee.	**947,735**	**948,930**	**0.13**				
Bayside, village (part) . .	4,300	4,275	-0.58	**Oconto . . . .**	**37,660**	**38,195**	**1.42**
Brown Deer, village . . .	11,999	12,305	2.55	Abrams, town	1,856	1,895	2.10
Cudahy, city	18,267	18,192	-0.41	Bagley, town.	291	289	-0.69
Fox Point, village	6,701	6,678	-0.34	Brazeau, town	1,284	1,301	1.32
Franklin, city.	35,451	35,741	0.82	Breed, town	712	730	2.53
Glendale, city	12,872	12,724	-1.15	Chase, town	3,005	3,088	2.76
Greendale, village	14,046	14,123	0.55	Doty, town	260	264	1.54
Greenfield, city	36,720	36,404	-0.86	Gillett, city	1,386	1,370	-1.15
Hales Corners, village . .	7,692	7,652	-0.52	Gillett, town	1,043	1,024	-1.82
Milwaukee, city (part) . .	594,833	594,667	-0.03	How, town	516	533	3.29
Oak Creek, city	34,451	35,206	2.19	Lakewood, town	816	832	1.96
River Hills, village.	1,597	1,577	-1.25	Lena, town	727	718	-1.24
St. Francis, city	9,365	9,458	0.99	Lena, village	564	562	-0.35
Shorewood, village. . . .	13,162	13,134	-0.21	Little River, town	1,094	1,115	1.92
South Milwaukee, city. .	21,156	21,073	-0.39	Little Suamico, town . . .	4,799	5,058	5.40

Wisconsin population by county and municipality, continued

	2010 census	2016 esti- mate	% change		2010 census	2016 esti- mate	% change
Maple Valley, town	662	667	0.76	Howard, village (part) . .	0	0	0.00
Morgan, town	984	997	1.32	Kaukauna, city (part). . .	15,462	15,894	2.79
Mountain, town.	822	824	0.24	Kaukauna, town	1,238	1,285	3.80
Oconto, city	4,513	4,521	0.18	Kimberly, village	6,468	6,679	3.26
Oconto, town	1,335	1,350	1.12	Liberty, town	867	873	0.69
Oconto Falls, city	2,891	2,867	-0.83	Little Chute, village . . .	10,449	10,976	5.04
Oconto Falls, town	1,265	1,270	0.40	Maine, town	866	883	1.96
Pensaukee, town	1,381	1,391	0.72	Maple Creek, town	619	606	-2.10
Pulaski, village (part). . .	0	0	0.00	New London, city (part).	1,610	1,627	1.06
Riverview, town.	725	731	0.83	Nichols, village	273	269	-1.47
Spruce, town	835	844	1.08	Oneida, town	4,678	4,702	0.51
Stiles, town	1,489	1,519	2.01	Osborn, town	1,170	1,205	2.99
Suring, village	544	536	-1.47	Seymour, city	3,451	3,441	-0.29
Townsend, town	979	992	1.33	Seymour, town	1,193	1,191	-0.17
Underhill, town	882	907	2.83	Shiocton, village	921	926	0.54
Oneida	**35,998**	**36,208**	**0.58**	Vandenbroek, town	1,474	1,535	4.14
Cassian, town	985	992	0.71	Wrightstown, village (part)	151	169	11.92
Crescent, town	2,033	2,062	1.43	**Ozaukee**	**86,395**	**87,879**	**1.72**
Enterprise, town	315	316	0.32	Bayside, village (part) . .	89	90	1.12
Hazelhurst, town	1,273	1,286	1.02	Belgium, town.	1,415	1,427	0.85
Lake Tomahawk, town. .	1,043	1,041	-0.19	Belgium, village.	2,245	2,292	2.09
Little Rice, town.	306	313	2.29	Cedarburg, city	11,412	11,530	1.03
Lynne, town	141	142	0.71	Cedarburg, town	5,760	5,887	2.20
Minocqua, town	4,453	4,510	1.28	Fredonia, town	2,172	2,165	-0.32
Monico, town	309	303	-1.94	Fredonia, village	2,160	2,191	1.44
Newbold, town	2,719	2,739	0.74	Grafton, town	4,053	4,137	2.07
Nokomis, town	1,371	1,439	4.96	Grafton, village	11,459	11,549	0.79
Pelican, town	2,764	2,815	1.85	Mequon, city	23,132	23,870	3.19
Piehl, town.	86	86	0.00	Newburg, village (part) . .	97	96	-1.03
Pine Lake, town.	2,740	2,757	0.62	Port Washington, city . .	11,250	11,495	2.18
Rhinelander, city	7,798	7,665	-1.71	Port Washington, town .	1,643	1,659	0.97
Schoepke, town.	387	391	1.03	Saukville, town	1,822	1,828	0.33
Stella, town	650	642	-1.23	Saukville, village	4,451	4,450	-0.02
Sugar Camp, town	1,694	1,711	1.00	Thiensville, village	3,235	3,213	-0.68
Three Lakes, town	2,131	2,162	1.45				
Woodboro, town	813	836	2.83	**Pepin**	**7,469**	**7,414**	**-0.74**
Woodruff, town	1,987	2,000	0.65	Albany, town	676	675	-0.15
				Durand, city	1,931	1,872	-3.06
Outagamie	**176,695**	**182,365**	**3.21**	Durand, town	742	747	0.67
Appleton, city (part) . . .	60,045	61,071	1.71	Frankfort, town	343	352	2.62
Bear Creek, village	448	447	-0.22	Lima, town.	702	683	-2.71
Black Creek, town	1,259	1,246	-1.03	Pepin, town	721	735	1.94
Black Creek, village. . . .	1,316	1,318	0.15	Pepin, village	837	821	-1.91
Bovina, town	1,145	1,163	1.57	Stockholm, town	197	203	3.05
Buchanan, town	6,755	6,916	2.38	Stockholm, village	66	66	0.00
Center, town.	3,402	3,497	2.79	Waterville, town	831	829	-0.24
Cicero, town	1,103	1,107	0.36	Waubeek, town	423	431	1.89
Combined Locks, village	3,328	3,515	5.62				
Dale, town	2,731	2,803	2.64	**Pierce**	**41,019**	**41,320**	**0.73**
Deer Creek, town.	637	646	1.41	Bay City, village	500	496	-0.80
Ellington, town	2,758	2,931	6.27	Clifton, town.	2,012	2,050	1.89
Freedom, town	5,842	6,005	2.79	Diamond Bluff, town. . .	469	461	-1.71
Grand Chute, town. . . .	20,919	22,083	5.56	El Paso, town	681	704	3.38
Greenville, town	10,309	11,545	11.99	Ellsworth, town	1,146	1,164	1.57
Harrison, village (part)[5]	NA	0	NA	Ellsworth, village	3,284	3,293	0.27
Hortonia, town	1,097	1,091	-0.55	Elmwood, village	817	813	-0.49
Hortonville, village. . . .	2,711	2,720	0.33	Gilman, town	959	981	2.29

Wisconsin population by county and municipality, continued

	2010 census	2016 esti-mate	% change		2010 census	2016 esti-mate	% change
Hartland, town	827	850	2.78	Almond, town	680	670	-1.47
Isabelle, town	281	283	0.71	Almond, village	448	439	-2.01
Maiden Rock, town. . . .	589	599	1.70	Amherst, town	1,325	1,335	0.75
Maiden Rock, village. . .	119	120	0.84	Amherst, village	1,035	1,058	2.22
Martell, town	1,185	1,193	0.68	Amherst Junction, village	377	375	-0.53
Oak Grove, town	2,150	2,179	1.35	Belmont, town	616	620	0.65
Plum City, village	599	597	-0.33	Buena Vista, town	1,198	1,200	0.17
Prescott, city.	4,258	4,255	-0.07	Carson, town	1,305	1,308	0.23
River Falls, city (part). . .	11,851	11,920	0.58	Dewey, town.	932	940	0.86
River Falls, town.	2,271	2,303	1.41	Eau Pleine, town	908	958	5.51
Rock Elm, town	485	491	1.24	Grant, town	1,906	1,915	0.47
Salem, town	510	520	1.96	Hull, town	5,346	5,380	0.64
Spring Lake, town	563	573	1.78	Junction City, village. . .	439	439	0.00
Spring Valley, village (part)	1,346	1,362	1.19	Lanark, town	1,527	1,544	1.11
Trenton, town	1,829	1,840	0.60	Linwood, town	1,121	1,122	0.09
Trimbelle, town	1,679	1,682	0.18	Milladore, village (part) .	0	0	0.00
Union, town	609	591	-2.96	Nelsonville, village	155	157	1.29
				New Hope, town	718	710	-1.11
Polk	**44,205**	**44,236**	**0.07**	Park Ridge, village	491	495	0.81
Alden, town	2,786	2,790	0.14	Pine Grove, town	937	932	-0.53
Amery, city.	2,902	2,918	0.55	Plover, town	1,701	1,731	1.76
Apple River, town.	1,146	1,160	1.22	Plover, village	12,123	12,603	3.96
Balsam Lake, town	1,411	1,396	-1.06	Rosholt, village	506	491	-2.96
Balsam Lake, village . . .	1,009	1,010	0.10	Sharon, town	1,982	2,018	1.82
Beaver, town.	835	838	0.36	Stevens Point, city	26,717	26,895	0.67
Black Brook, town	1,325	1,340	1.13	Stockton, town	2,917	2,983	2.26
Bone Lake, town	717	722	0.70	Whiting, village	1,724	1,685	-2.26
Centuria, village	948	943	-0.53				
Clam Falls, town	596	612	2.68	**Price**.	**14,159**	**14,086**	**-0.52**
Clayton, town	975	986	1.13	Catawba, town	269	270	0.37
Clayton, village	571	567	-0.70	Catawba, village	110	101	-8.18
Clear Lake, town	899	898	-0.11	Eisenstein, town	630	619	-1.75
Clear Lake, village	1,070	1,061	-0.84	Elk, town	988	1,001	1.32
Dresser, village	895	899	0.45	Emery, town	297	290	-2.36
Eureka, town.	1,649	1,668	1.15	Fifield, town	901	902	0.11
Farmington, town	1,836	1,843	0.38	Flambeau, town.	489	478	-2.25
Frederic, village	1,137	1,133	-0.35	Georgetown, town	171	170	-0.58
Garfield, town	1,692	1,694	0.12	Hackett, town	169	167	-1.18
Georgetown, town	977	989	1.23	Harmony, town	222	222	0.00
Johnstown, town	534	528	-1.12	Hill, town	333	333	0.00
Laketown, town.	961	972	1.14	Kennan, town	356	348	-2.25
Lincoln, town	2,208	2,206	-0.09	Kennan, village	135	126	-6.67
Lorain, town	284	279	-1.76	Knox, town.	341	342	0.29
Luck, town	930	909	-2.26	Lake, town	1,128	1,123	-0.44
Luck, village	1,119	1,096	-2.06	Ogema, town	713	717	0.56
McKinley, town	347	352	1.44	Park Falls, city	2,462	2,476	0.57
Milltown, town	1,226	1,230	0.33	Phillips, city	1,478	1,433	-3.04
Milltown, village	917	912	-0.55	Prentice, town.	475	474	-0.21
Osceola, town	2,855	2,869	0.49	Prentice, village.	660	653	-1.06
Osceola, village	2,568	2,598	1.17	Spirit, town	277	278	0.36
St. Croix Falls, city.	2,133	2,097	-1.69	Worcester, town.	1,555	1,563	0.51
St. Croix Falls, town. . . .	1,165	1,162	-0.26				
Sterling, town	790	775	-1.90	**Racine**	**195,408**	**195,294**	**-0.06**
Turtle Lake, village (part)	93	92	-1.08	Burlington, city (part) . .	10,464	10,591	1.21
West Sweden, town . . .	699	692	-1.00	Burlington, town	6,502	6,454	-0.74
				Caledonia, village.	24,705	24,917	0.86
Portage.	**70,019**	**70,883**	**1.23**	Dover, town.	4,051	4,036	-0.37
Alban, town	885	880	-0.56	Elmwood Park, village . .	497	497	0.00

Wisconsin population by county and municipality, continued

	2010 census	2016 esti- mate	% change		2010 census	2016 esti- mate	% change
Mount Pleasant, village .	26,197	26,369	0.66	Milton, town.	2,923	2,939	0.55
North Bay, village.	241	232	-3.73	Newark, town	1,541	1,523	-1.17
Norway, town	7,948	7,973	0.31	Orfordville, village	1,442	1,450	0.55
Racine, city.	78,860	78,165	-0.88	Plymouth, town.	1,235	1,168	-5.43
Raymond, town.	3,870	3,950	2.07	Porter, town	945	955	1.06
Rochester, village.	3,682	3,736	1.47	Rock, town.	3,196	3,178	-0.56
Sturtevant, village	6,970	6,961	-0.13	Spring Valley, town. . . .	746	739	-0.94
Union Grove, village . . .	4,915	4,900	-0.31	Turtle, town	2,388	2,366	-0.92
Waterford, town	6,344	6,349	0.08	Union, town	2,099	2,109	0.48
Waterford, village.	5,368	5,378	0.19	**Rusk. . . . .**	**14,755**	**14,783**	**0.19**
Wind Point, village	1,723	1,694	-1.68	Atlanta, town	592	575	-2.87
Yorkville, town	3,071	3,092	0.68	Big Bend, town	358	370	3.35
Richland	**18,021**	**17,954**	**-0.37**	Big Falls, town	140	139	-0.71
Akan, town.	403	393	-2.48	Bruce, village	779	771	-1.03
Bloom, town.	512	511	-0.20	Cedar Rapids, town . . .	41	38	-7.32
Boaz, village	156	155	-0.64	Conrath, village.	95	94	-1.05
Buena Vista, town	1,869	1,894	1.34	Dewey, town.	545	558	2.39
Cazenovia, village (part)	314	306	-2.55	Flambeau, town.	1,059	1,069	0.94
Dayton, town	693	686	-1.01	Glen Flora, village	92	88	-4.35
Eagle, town	531	523	-1.51	Grant, town	813	814	0.12
Forest, town	352	352	0.00	Grow, town	427	420	-1.64
Henrietta, town.	493	487	-1.22	Hawkins, town	153	160	4.58
Ithaca, town.	619	630	1.78	Hawkins, village.	305	304	-0.33
Lone Rock, village	888	877	-1.24	Hubbard, town	204	201	-1.47
Marshall, town	567	571	0.71	Ingram, village	78	82	5.13
Orion, town	579	582	0.52	Ladysmith, city	3,414	3,367	-1.38
Richland, town	1,379	1,357	-1.60	Lawrence, town.	311	307	-1.29
Richland Center, city. . .	5,184	5,178	-0.12	Marshall, town	688	697	1.31
Richwood, town	533	524	-1.69	Murry, town	277	282	1.81
Rockbridge, town	734	716	-2.45	Richland, town	232	235	1.29
Sylvan, town.	555	557	0.36	Rusk, town	525	548	4.38
Viola, village (part)	477	478	0.21	Sheldon, village.	237	232	-2.11
Westford, town	530	529	-0.19	South Fork, town	120	116	-3.33
Willow, town.	579	582	0.52	Strickland, town	280	291	3.93
Yuba, village	74	66	-10.81	Stubbs, town	579	583	0.69
Rock.	**160,331**	**159,886**	**-0.28**	Thornapple, town	774	796	2.84
Avon, town.	608	595	-2.14	Tony, village	113	110	-2.65
Beloit, city	36,966	36,657	-0.84	True, town	296	296	0.00
Beloit, town	7,662	7,616	-0.60	Washington, town	339	350	3.24
Bradford, town	1,121	1,084	-3.30	Weyerhaeuser, village . .	238	228	-4.20
Brodhead, city (part). . .	90	94	4.44	Wilkinson, town.	40	40	0.00
Center, town.	1,066	1,054	-1.13	Willard, town	505	515	1.98
Clinton, town	930	936	0.65	Wilson, town.	106	107	0.94
Clinton, village	2,154	2,108	-2.14	**St. Croix . . . .**	**84,345**	**86,858**	**2.98**
Edgerton, city (part) . . .	5,364	5,414	0.93	Baldwin, town.	928	932	0.43
Evansville, city.	5,012	5,190	3.55	Baldwin, village.	3,957	3,956	-0.03
Footville, village	808	801	-0.87	Cady, town.	821	840	2.31
Fulton, town.	3,252	3,277	0.77	Cylon, town	683	688	0.73
Harmony, town	2,569	2,574	0.19	Deer Park, village.	216	210	-2.78
Janesville, city.	63,575	63,470	-0.17	Eau Galle, town	1,139	1,204	5.71
Janesville, town.	3,434	3,464	0.87	Emerald, town.	853	847	-0.70
Johnstown, town.	778	765	-1.67	Erin Prairie, town	688	676	-1.74
La Prairie, town	834	821	-1.56	Forest, town	629	628	-0.16
Lima, town.	1,280	1,266	-1.09	Glenwood, town	785	784	-0.13
Magnolia, town.	767	754	-1.69	Glenwood City, city . . .	1,242	1,221	-1.69
Milton, city.	5,546	5,519	-0.49	Hammond, town	2,102	2,143	1.95

Wisconsin population by county and municipality, continued

	2010 census	2016 esti-mate	% change		2010 census	2016 esti-mate	% change
Hammond, village	1,922	1,891	-1.61	Troy, town	794	804	1.26
Hudson, city	12,719	13,584	6.80	Washington, town	1,007	1,015	0.79
Hudson, town	8,461	8,582	1.43	West Baraboo, village . .	1,414	1,470	3.96
Kinnickinnic, town	1,722	1,759	2.15	Westfield, town	571	554	-2.98
New Richmond, city . . .	8,375	8,807	5.16	Winfield, town	856	859	0.35
North Hudson, village . .	3,768	3,757	-0.29	Wisconsin Dells, city (part)	175	175	0.00
Pleasant Valley, town . .	515	527	2.33	Woodland, town	790	802	1.52
Richmond, town	3,272	3,437	5.04	**Sawyer**	**16,557**	**16,754**	**1.19**
River Falls, city (part) . . .	3,149	3,309	5.08	Bass Lake, town	2,377	2,414	1.56
Roberts, village	1,651	1,621	-1.82	Couderay, town	401	398	-0.75
Rush River, town	508	501	-1.38	Couderay, village	88	87	-1.14
St. Joseph, town	3,842	3,904	1.61	Draper, town	204	211	3.43
Somerset, town	4,036	4,163	3.15	Edgewater, town	519	525	1.16
Somerset, village	2,635	2,670	1.33	Exeland, village	196	195	-0.51
Spring Valley, village (part)	6	10	66.67	Hayward, city	2,318	2,373	2.37
Springfield, town	932	949	1.82	Hayward, town	3,567	3,571	0.11
Stanton, town	900	893	-0.78	Hunter, town	678	683	0.74
Star Prairie, town	3,504	3,551	1.34	Lenroot, town	1,279	1,321	3.28
Star Prairie, village	561	553	-1.43	Meadowbrook, town . .	131	139	6.11
Troy, town	4,705	5,107	8.54	Meteor, town	158	152	-3.80
Warren, town	1,591	1,636	2.83	Ojibwa, town	249	251	0.80
Wilson, village	184	182	-1.09	Radisson, town	405	398	-1.73
Woodville, village.	1,344	1,336	-0.60	Radisson, village	241	239	-0.83
				Round Lake, town	977	998	2.15
Sauk	**61,976**	**62,187**	**0.34**	Sand Lake, town	813	820	0.86
Baraboo, city	12,048	12,013	-0.29	Spider Lake, town	351	357	1.71
Baraboo, town	1,672	1,685	0.78	Weirgor, town	332	329	-0.90
Bear Creek, town	595	608	2.18	Winter, town	960	975	1.56
Cazenovia, village (part)	4	13	225.00	Winter, village	313	318	1.60
Dellona, town	1,552	1,569	1.10				
Delton, town	2,391	2,412	0.88	**Shawano**	**41,949**	**41,755**	**-0.46**
Excelsior, town	1,575	1,569	-0.38	Almon, town	584	576	-1.37
Fairfield, town	1,077	1,075	-0.19	Angelica, town	1,793	1,814	1.17
Franklin, town	652	654	0.31	Aniwa, town	541	533	-1.48
Freedom, town	447	453	1.34	Aniwa, village	260	250	-3.85
Greenfield, town	932	937	0.54	Bartelme, town	819	804	-1.83
Honey Creek, town. . . .	733	726	-0.95	Belle Plaine, town	1,855	1,852	-0.16
Ironton, town	660	656	-0.61	Birnamwood, town. . . .	763	780	2.23
Ironton, village	253	254	0.40	Birnamwood, village (part)	802	787	-1.87
La Valle, town	1,302	1,330	2.15	Bonduel, village.	1,478	1,484	0.41
La Valle, village	367	353	-3.81	Bowler, village.	302	289	-4.30
Lake Delton, village . . .	2,914	2,922	0.27	Cecil, village	570	558	-2.11
Lime Ridge, village	162	157	-3.09	Eland, village	202	197	-2.48
Loganville, village	300	293	-2.33	Fairbanks, town	616	604	-1.95
Merrimac, town	942	969	2.87	Germania, town.	332	323	-2.71
Merrimac, village	420	421	0.24	Grant, town	991	981	-1.01
North Freedom, village .	701	678	-3.28	Green Valley, town	1,089	1,088	-0.09
Plain, village	773	761	-1.55	Gresham, village	586	582	-0.68
Prairie du Sac, town . . .	1,144	1,126	-1.57	Hartland, town	904	897	-0.77
Prairie du Sac, village . .	3,972	4,053	2.04	Herman, town	776	766	-1.29
Reedsburg, city	9,200	9,303	1.12	Hutchins, town	600	593	-1.17
Reedsburg, town	1,293	1,280	-1.01	Lessor, town	1,263	1,281	1.43
Rock Springs, village. . .	362	306	-15.47	Maple Grove, town	972	952	-2.06
Sauk City, village	3,410	3,422	0.35	Marion, city (part)	25	26	4.00
Spring Green, town . . .	1,697	1,699	0.12	Mattoon, village	438	428	-2.28
Spring Green, village . .	1,628	1,625	-0.18	Morris, town	453	449	-0.88
Sumpter, town	1,191	1,186	-0.42	Navarino, town	446	444	-0.45

Wisconsin population by county and municipality, continued

	2010 census	2016 esti- mate	% change		2010 census	2016 esti- mate	% change
Pella, town	865	867	0.23	Lublin, village	118	117	-0.85
Pulaski, village (part)	218	216	-0.92	Maplehurst, town	335	334	-0.30
Red Springs, town	925	939	1.51	McKinley, town	458	452	-1.31
Richmond, town	1,864	1,868	0.21	Medford, city	4,326	4,372	1.06
Seneca, town	558	556	-0.36	Medford, town	2,606	2,650	1.69
Shawano, city	9,305	9,219	-0.92	Molitor, town	324	330	1.85
Tigerton, village	741	728	-1.75	Pershing, town	180	177	-1.67
Washington, town	1,895	1,914	1.00	Rib Lake, town	852	864	1.41
Waukechon, town	1,021	1,048	2.64	Rib Lake, village	910	897	-1.43
Wescott, town	3,183	3,205	0.69	Roosevelt, town	473	466	-1.48
Wittenberg, town	833	824	-1.08	Stetsonville, village	541	529	-2.22
Wittenberg, village	1,081	1,033	-4.44	Taft, town	430	422	-1.86
				Westboro, town	684	692	1.17
Sheboygan	**115,507**	**115,050**	**-0.40**				
Adell, village	516	514	-0.39	**Trempealeau**	**28,816**	**29,395**	**2.01**
Cascade, village	709	695	-1.97	Albion, town	653	662	1.38
Cedar Grove, village	2,113	2,099	-0.66	Arcadia, city	2,925	3,055	4.44
Elkhart Lake, village	967	958	-0.93	Arcadia, town	1,779	1,815	2.02
Glenbeulah, village	463	456	-1.51	Blair, city	1,366	1,380	1.02
Greenbush, town	2,565	2,549	-0.62	Burnside, town	511	511	0.00
Herman, town	2,151	2,091	-2.79	Caledonia, town	920	934	1.52
Holland, town	2,239	2,249	0.45	Chimney Rock, town	241	231	-4.15
Howards Grove, village	3,188	3,221	1.04	Dodge, town	389	386	-0.77
Kohler, village	2,120	2,108	-0.57	Eleva, village	670	677	1.04
Lima, town	2,982	2,976	-0.20	Ettrick, town	1,237	1,250	1.05
Lyndon, town	1,542	1,547	0.32	Ettrick, village	524	522	-0.38
Mitchell, town	1,304	1,308	0.31	Gale, town	1,695	1,745	2.95
Mosel, town	790	781	-1.14	Galesville, city	1,481	1,498	1.15
Oostburg, village	2,887	2,941	1.87	Hale, town	1,037	1,056	1.83
Plymouth, city	8,445	8,467	0.26	Independence, city	1,336	1,366	2.25
Plymouth, town	3,195	3,188	-0.22	Lincoln, town	823	840	2.07
Random Lake, village	1,594	1,576	-1.13	Osseo, city	1,701	1,703	0.12
Rhine, town	2,134	2,135	0.05	Pigeon, town	891	905	1.57
Russell, town	377	367	-2.65	Pigeon Falls, village	411	408	-0.73
Scott, town	1,836	1,817	-1.03	Preston, town	953	976	2.41
Sheboygan, city	49,288	48,653	-1.29	Strum, village	1,114	1,122	0.72
Sheboygan, town	7,271	7,435	2.26	Sumner, town	810	833	2.84
Sheboygan Falls, city	7,775	7,853	1.00	Trempealeau, town	1,756	1,817	3.47
Sheboygan Falls, town	1,718	1,721	0.17	Trempealeau, village	1,529	1,637	7.06
Sherman, town	1,505	1,497	-0.53	Unity, town	506	507	0.20
Waldo, village	503	493	-1.99	Whitehall, city	1,558	1,559	0.06
Wilson, town	3,330	3,355	0.75				
				Vernon	**29,773**	**30,114**	**1.15**
Taylor	**20,689**	**20,741**	**0.25**	Bergen, town	1,364	1,370	0.44
Aurora, town	422	426	0.95	Chaseburg, village	284	290	2.11
Browning, town	905	928	2.54	Christiana, town	931	945	1.50
Chelsea, town	806	811	0.62	Clinton, town	1,358	1,393	2.58
Cleveland, town	268	262	-2.24	Coon, town	728	744	2.20
Deer Creek, town	768	768	0.00	Coon Valley, village	765	754	-1.44
Ford, town	268	267	-0.37	De Soto, village (part)	179	183	2.23
Gilman, village	410	372	-9.27	Forest, town	634	648	2.21
Goodrich, town	510	511	0.20	Franklin, town	1,140	1,177	3.25
Greenwood, town	638	642	0.63	Genoa, town	789	805	2.03
Grover, town	256	255	-0.39	Genoa, village	253	244	-3.56
Hammel, town	713	724	1.54	Greenwood, town	847	840	-0.83
Holway, town	973	959	-1.44	Hamburg, town	973	983	1.03
Jump River, town	375	370	-1.33	Harmony, town	755	794	5.17
Little Black, town	1,140	1,144	0.35	Hillsboro, city	1,417	1,405	-0.85

Wisconsin population by county and municipality, continued

	2010 census	2016 esti- mate	% change		2010 census	2016 esti- mate	% change
Hillsboro, town	807	815	0.99	Sharon, town	907	895	-1.32
Jefferson, town	1,143	1,156	1.14	Sharon, village	1,605	1,586	-1.18
Kickapoo, town	626	656	4.79	Spring Prairie, town . . .	2,181	2,172	-0.41
La Farge, village.	746	701	-6.03	Sugar Creek, town	3,943	3,935	-0.20
Liberty, town	252	267	5.95	Troy, town	2,353	2,355	0.08
Ontario, village (part) . .	554	553	-0.18	Walworth, town.	1,702	1,692	-0.59
Readstown, village	415	420	1.20	Walworth, village.	2,816	2,836	0.71
Stark, town.	363	382	5.23	Whitewater, city (part). .	11,150	11,455	2.74
Sterling, town	633	617	-2.53	Whitewater, town.	1,471	1,487	1.09
Stoddard, village	774	796	2.84	Williams Bay, village . . .	2,564	2,580	0.62
Union, town	700	721	3.00	**Washburn**	**15,911**	**15,929**	**0.11**
Viola, village (part)	222	222	0.00	Barronett, town	442	443	0.23
Viroqua, city	4,362	4,362	0.00	Bashaw, town	946	959	1.37
Viroqua, town	1,718	1,747	1.69	Bass Lake, town	505	521	3.17
Webster, town.	778	811	4.24	Beaver Brook, town . . .	713	720	0.98
Westby, city	2,200	2,224	1.09	Birchwood, town	478	487	1.88
Wheatland, town	561	581	3.57	Birchwood, village	442	434	-1.81
Whitestown, town	502	508	1.20	Brooklyn, town	254	254	0.00
Vilas.	**21,430**	**21,662**	**1.08**	Casey, town	353	360	1.98
Arbor Vitae, town.	3,316	3,340	0.72	Chicog, town	234	226	-3.42
Boulder Junction, town .	933	944	1.18	Crystal, town	267	264	-1.12
Cloverland, town	1,029	1,038	0.87	Evergreen, town	1,135	1,134	-0.09
Conover, town.	1,235	1,242	0.57	Frog Creek, town	130	128	-1.54
Eagle River, city	1,398	1,416	1.29	Gull Lake, town	186	188	1.08
Lac du Flambeau, town .	3,441	3,468	0.78	Long Lake, town	624	630	0.96
Land O'Lakes, town . . .	861	874	1.51	Madge, town	508	518	1.97
Lincoln, town	2,423	2,454	1.28	Minong, town	917	935	1.96
Manitowish Waters, town	566	585	3.36	Minong, village	527	519	-1.52
Phelps, town.	1,200	1,248	4.00	Sarona, town	384	383	-0.26
Plum Lake, town	491	497	1.22	Shell Lake, city	1,347	1,367	1.48
Presque Isle, town	618	632	2.27	Spooner, city	2,682	2,623	-2.20
St. Germain, town	2,085	2,066	-0.91	Spooner, town	706	719	1.84
Washington, town	1,451	1,470	1.31	Springbrook, town	445	431	-3.15
Winchester, town.	383	388	1.31	Stinnett, town.	246	235	-4.47
				Stone Lake, town	508	506	-0.39
Walworth	**102,228**	**102,593**	**0.36**	Trego, town	932	945	1.39
Bloomfield, town	6,278	1,581	-74.26				
Bloomfield, village[4] . . .	NA	4,643	NA	**Washington**	**131,887**	**134,137**	**1.71**
Burlington, city (part) . .	0	0	0.00	Addison, town.	3,495	3,456	-1.12
Darien, town.	1,693	1,696	0.18	Barton, town.	2,637	2,646	0.34
Darien, village.	1,580	1,589	0.57	Erin, town	3,747	3,763	0.43
Delavan, city.	8,463	8,414	-0.58	Farmington, town	4,014	4,040	0.65
Delavan, town.	5,285	5,254	-0.59	Germantown, town . . .	254	245	-3.54
East Troy, town	4,021	4,045	0.60	Germantown, village . .	19,749	20,008	1.31
East Troy, village	4,281	4,343	1.45	Hartford, city (part). . . .	14,223	14,627	2.84
Elkhorn, city	10,084	9,897	-1.85	Hartford, town	3,609	3,582	-0.75
Fontana-on-Geneva Lake, village.	1,672	1,677	0.30	Jackson, town	4,134	4,371	5.73
				Jackson, village	6,753	6,911	2.34
Geneva, town	4,993	5,033	0.80	Kewaskum, town	1,053	1,056	0.28
Genoa City, village (part)	3,036	3,038	0.07	Kewaskum, village (part)	4,004	4,015	0.27
Lafayette, town	1,979	1,973	-0.30	Milwaukee, city (part) . .	0	0	0.00
La Grange, town	2,454	2,468	0.57	Newburg, village (part) .	1,157	1,165	0.69
Lake Geneva, city.	7,651	7,771	1.57	Polk, town	3,937	3,991	1.37
Linn, town	2,383	2,424	1.72	Richfield, village	11,300	11,537	2.10
Lyons, town	3,698	3,699	0.03	Slinger, village.	5,068	5,338	5.33
Mukwonago, village (part)	101	166	64.36	Trenton, town	4,732	4,757	0.53
Richmond, town	1,884	1,889	0.27	Wayne, town	2,169	2,195	1.20

Wisconsin population by county and municipality, continued

	2010 census	2016 estimate	% change		2010 census	2016 estimate	% change
West Bend, city	31,078	31,676	1.92	Lebanon, town	1,665	1,674	0.54
West Bend, town	4,774	4,758	-0.34	Lind, town	1,579	1,594	0.95
Waukesha	**389,891**	**396,449**	**1.68**	Little Wolf, town	1,424	1,431	0.49
Big Bend, village	1,290	1,314	1.86	Manawa, city	1,371	1,328	-3.14
Brookfield, city	37,920	37,806	-0.30	Marion, city (part)	1,235	1,223	-0.97
Brookfield, town	6,116	6,058	-0.95	Matteson, town	936	924	-1.28
Butler, village	1,841	1,828	-0.71	Mukwa, town	2,930	2,965	1.19
Chenequa, village	590	589	-0.17	New London, city (part)	5,685	5,655	-0.53
Delafield, city	7,085	7,165	1.13	Ogdensburg, village	185	179	-3.24
Delafield, town	8,400	8,281	-1.42	Royalton, town	1,434	1,444	0.70
Dousman, village	2,302	2,334	1.39	St. Lawrence, town	710	699	-1.55
Eagle, town	3,507	3,503	-0.11	Scandinavia, town	1,066	1,066	0.00
Eagle, village	1,950	1,973	1.18	Scandinavia, village	363	361	-0.55
Elm Grove, village	5,934	5,943	0.15	Union, town	806	804	-0.25
Genesee, town	7,340	7,384	0.60	Waupaca, city	6,069	6,052	-0.28
Hartland, village	9,110	9,179	0.76	Waupaca, town	1,173	1,184	0.94
Lac La Belle, village (part)	289	288	-0.35	Weyauwega, city	1,900	1,905	0.26
Lannon, village	1,107	1,167	5.42	Weyauwega, town	583	565	-3.09
Lisbon, town	10,157	10,291	1.32	Wyoming, town	329	303	-7.90
Menomonee Falls, village	35,626	36,907	3.60	**Waushara**	**24,496**	**24,471**	**-0.10**
Merton, town	8,338	8,402	0.77	Aurora, town	985	997	1.22
Merton, village	3,346	3,504	4.72	Berlin, city (part)	89	88	-1.12
Milwaukee, city (part)	0	0	0.00	Bloomfield, town	1,052	1,069	1.62
Mukwonago, town	7,959	8,014	0.69	Coloma, town	753	743	-1.33
Mukwonago, village (part)	7,254	7,606	4.85	Coloma, village	450	455	1.11
Muskego, city	24,135	24,534	1.65	Dakota, town	1,227	1,231	0.33
Nashotah, village	1,395	1,361	-2.44	Deerfield, town	737	758	2.85
New Berlin, city	39,584	40,227	1.62	Hancock, town	528	534	1.14
North Prairie, village	2,141	2,175	1.59	Hancock, village	417	406	-2.64
Oconomowoc, city	15,759	16,656	5.69	Leon, town	1,439	1,432	-0.49
Oconomowoc, town	8,408	8,611	2.41	Lohrville, village	402	394	-1.99
Oconomowoc Lake, village	595	589	-1.01	Marion, town	2,038	2,037	-0.05
Ottawa, town	3,859	3,897	0.98	Mount Morris, town	1,097	1,114	1.55
Pewaukee, city	13,195	14,148	7.22	Oasis, town	389	400	2.83
Pewaukee, village	8,166	8,106	-0.73	Plainfield, town	550	543	-1.27
Summit, village[2]	4,674	4,751	1.65	Plainfield, village	862	852	-1.16
Sussex, village	10,518	10,797	2.65	Poy Sippi, town	931	917	-1.50
Vernon, town	7,601	7,647	0.61	Redgranite, village	2,149	2,139	-0.47
Wales, village	2,549	2,540	-0.35	Richford, town	612	639	4.41
Waukesha, city	70,718	71,699	1.39	Rose, town	640	647	1.09
Waukesha, town	9,133	9,175	0.46	Saxeville, town	986	993	0.71
Waupaca	**52,410**	**52,320**	**-0.17**	Springwater, town	1,274	1,280	0.47
Bear Creek, town	823	816	-0.85	Warren, town	668	657	-1.65
Big Falls, village	61	57	-6.56	Wautoma, city	2,218	2,154	-2.89
Caledonia, town	1,627	1,666	2.40	Wautoma, town	1,278	1,281	0.23
Clintonville, city	4,559	4,521	-0.83	Wild Rose, village	725	711	-1.93
Dayton, town	2,748	2,763	0.55	**Winnebago**	**166,994**	**169,032**	**1.22**
Dupont, town	738	735	-0.41	Algoma, town	6,822	6,974	2.23
Embarrass, village	404	389	-3.71	Appleton, city (part)	1,490	1,484	-0.40
Farmington, town	3,974	4,000	0.65	Black Wolf, town	2,410	2,442	1.33
Fremont, town	597	592	-0.84	Clayton, town	3,951	4,061	2.78
Fremont, village	679	676	-0.44	Menasha, city (part)	15,144	14,936	-1.37
Harrison, town	468	472	0.85	Menasha, town[6]	18,498	18,741	1.31
Helvetia, town	636	630	-0.94	Neenah, city	25,501	26,050	2.15
Iola, town	971	984	1.34	Neenah, town	3,237	3,539	9.33
Iola, village	1,301	1,288	-1.00	Nekimi, town	1,429	1,427	-0.14
Larrabee, town	1,381	1,375	-0.43	Nepeuskun, town	710	734	3.38

Wisconsin population by county and municipality, continued

	2010 census	2016 esti-mate	% change		2010 census	2016 esti-mate	% change
Omro, city	3,517	3,558	1.17	Hewitt, village.	828	832	0.48
Omro, town	2,116	2,174	2.74	Hiles, town.	167	162	-2.99
Oshkosh, city	66,083	66,717	0.96	Lincoln, town	1,564	1,572	0.51
Oshkosh, town	2,475	2,473	-0.08	Marshfield, city (part) . .	18,218	18,232	0.08
Poygan, town	1,301	1,309	0.61	Marshfield, town	764	776	1.57
Rushford, town	1,561	1,581	1.28	Milladore, town	690	685	-0.72
Utica, town.	1,299	1,316	1.31	Milladore, village (part) .	276	276	0.00
Vinland, town	1,765	1,742	-1.30	Nekoosa, city	2,580	2,563	-0.66
Winchester, town.	1,763	1,784	1.19	Pittsville, city	874	875	0.11
Winneconne, town. . . .	2,350	2,389	1.66	Port Edwards, town . . .	1,427	1,417	-0.70
Winneconne, village . . .	2,383	2,407	1.01	Port Edwards, village . .	1,818	1,780	-2.09
Wolf River, town	1,189	1,194	0.42	Remington, town.	268	256	-4.48
				Richfield, town	1,628	1,632	0.25
Wood	**74,749**	**74,998**	**0.33**	Rock, town.	855	862	0.82
Arpin, town	929	962	3.55	Rudolph, town	1,028	1,034	0.58
Arpin, village	333	326	-2.10	Rudolph, village	439	430	-2.05
Auburndale, town	860	843	-1.98	Saratoga, town	5,142	5,184	0.82
Aurburndale, village . . .	703	707	0.57	Seneca, town	1,120	1,113	-0.63
Biron, village.	839	824	-1.79	Sherry, town.	803	807	0.50
Cameron, town	511	469	-8.22	Sigel, town	1,051	1,053	0.19
Cary, town	424	424	0.00	Vesper, village.	584	582	-0.34
Cranmoor, town	168	162	-3.57	Wisconsin Rapids, city. .	18,367	18,630	1.43
Dexter, town.	359	355	-1.11	Wood, town	796	789	-0.88
Grand Rapids, town . . .	7,646	7,701	0.72				
Hansen, town	690	683	-1.01				

1. This part of this village was created from part of the town of the same name after April 1, 2010. 2. This village was created from the entire town of the same name after April 1, 2010; the 2010 figure reflects the data for the previously existing town. 3. The town of Salem and the village of Silver Lake merged to become the village of Salem Lakes on February 14, 2017. 4. This village was created from part of the town of the same name after April 1, 2010. 5. This part of this village was created from part of the town of Buchanan after April 1, 2010. 6. Part of this town became the village of Fox Crossing on April 20, 2016. The initial population of Fox Crossing was 10,649, according to the certificate of incorporation issued for the village by the secretary of administration.

Sources: Wisconsin Department of Administration, Demographic Services Center, *January 1, 2016 Final Population Estimates*, October 2016; Wisconsin Department of Administration, Municipal Data System, *Certificate of Incorporation: Village of Fox Crossing*, April 20, 2016.

Wisconsin cities, May 1, 2017

City	Year incor-porated	County	2010 census	2016 estimate	% change
One first class city (150,000 or more)[1]					
Milwaukee	1846	Milwaukee, Washington, Waukesha	594,833	594,667	-0.03
15 second class cities (39,000–149,999)[1]					
Appleton.	1857	Calumet, Outagamie, Winnebago.	72,623	74,286	2.29
Eau Claire[2]	1872	Chippewa, Eau Claire	65,931	67,381	2.20
Fond du Lac[2] . . .	1852	Fond du Lac	43,021	43,381	0.84
Green Bay	1854	Brown.	104,057	105,079	0.98
Janesville[2]	1853	Rock.	63,575	63,470	-0.17
Kenosha	1850	Kenosha	99,218	99,489	0.27
La Crosse	1856	La Crosse	51,320	52,377	2.06
Madison	1856	Dane	233,209	247,207	6.00
Oshkosh[2]	1853	Winnebago	66,083	66,717	0.96

Wisconsin cities, May 1, 2017, continued

City	Year incorporated	County	2010 census	2016 estimate	% change
Racine.	1848	Racine.	78,860	78,165	-0.88
Sheboygan.	1853	Sheboygan.	49,288	48,653	-1.29
Waukesha	1895	Waukesha	70,718	71,699	1.39
Wausau	1872	Marathon	39,106	38,909	-0.50
Wauwatosa	1897	Milwaukee	46,396	47,160	1.65
West Allis.	1906	Milwaukee	60,411	60,164	-0.41

33 third class cities (10,000–38,999) [1]

City	Year incorporated	County	2010 census	2016 estimate	% change
Baraboo	1882	Sauk.	12,048	12,013	-0.29
Beaver Dam	1856	Dodge	16,214	16,799	3.61
Beloit[2].	1857	Rock.	36,966	36,657	-0.84
Brookfield	1954	Waukesha	37,920	37,806	-0.30
Burlington	1900	Racine, Walworth	10,464	10,591	1.21
Chippewa Falls . .	1869	Chippewa	13,661	13,965	2.23
Cudahy	1906	Milwaukee	18,267	18,192	-0.41
De Pere	1883	Brown.	23,800	24,592	3.33
Fort Atkinson[2]. . .	1878	Jefferson	12,368	12,441	0.59
Franklin.	1956	Milwaukee	35,451	35,741	0.82
Glendale	1950	Milwaukee	12,872	12,724	-1.15
Greenfield	1957	Milwaukee	36,720	36,404	-0.86
Hartford	1883	Dodge, Washington	14,223	14,627	2.84
Kaukauna	1885	Calumet, Outagamie.	15,462	15,894	2.79
Manitowoc.	1870	Manitowoc.	33,736	33,783	0.14
Marinette.	1887	Marinette.	10,968	10,878	-0.82
Marshfield	1883	Marathon, Wood	19,118	19,201	0.43
Menasha	1874	Calumet, Winnebago	17,353	17,573	1.27
Middleton	1963	Dane	17,442	19,317	10.75
Muskego	1964	Waukesha	24,135	24,534	1.65
Neenah	1873	Winnebago	25,501	26,050	2.15
New Berlin	1959	Waukesha	39,584	40,227	1.62
Oak Creek	1955	Milwaukee	34,451	35,206	2.19
Oconomowoc. . .	1875	Waukesha	15,759	16,656	5.69
Pewaukee	1999	Waukesha	13,195	14,148	7.22
River Falls.	1875	Pierce, St. Croix	15,000	15,229	1.53
Stevens Point . . .	1858	Portage.	26,717	26,895	0.67
Sun Prairie	1958	Dane	29,364	32,613	11.06
Superior	1858	Douglas.	27,244	27,237	-0.03
Two Rivers[2]	1878	Manitowoc.	11,712	11,566	-1.25
Watertown.	1853	Dodge, Jefferson	23,861	23,995	0.56
West Bend	1885	Washington	31,078	31,676	1.92
Wisconsin Rapids	1869	Wood	18,367	18,630	1.43

141 fourth class cities (Under 10,000) [1]

City	Year incorporated	County	2010 census	2016 estimate	% change
Abbotsford.	1965	Clark, Marathon.	2,310	2,279	-1.34
Adams	1926	Adams	1,967	1,942	-1.27
Algoma	1879	Kewaunee	3,167	3,151	-0.51
Alma.	1885	Buffalo	781	769	-1.54
Altoona.	1887	Eau Claire.	6,706	7,345	9.53
Amery.	1919	Polk	2,902	2,918	0.55
Antigo	1885	Langlade	8,234	8,197	-0.45
Arcadia	1925	Trempealeau	2,925	3,055	4.44
Ashland.	1887	Ashland, Bayfield	8,216	8,039	-2.15
Augusta.	1885	Eau Claire.	1,550	1,537	-0.84
Barron.	1887	Barron.	3,423	3,388	-1.02
Bayfield.	1913	Bayfield.	487	485	-0.41
Berlin	1857	Green Lake, Waushara	5,524	5,517	-0.13
Black River Falls . .	1883	Jackson.	3,622	3,623	0.03
Blair	1949	Trempealeau	1,366	1,380	1.02
Bloomer	1920	Chippewa	3,539	3,559	0.57

Wisconsin cities, May 1, 2017, continued

City	Year incorporated	County	2010 census	2016 estimate	% change
Boscobel	1873	Grant	3,231	3,198	-1.02
Brillion	1944	Calumet	3,148	3,262	3.62
Brodhead.	1891	Green, Rock	3,293	3,281	-0.36
Buffalo City	1859	Buffalo	1,023	1,018	-0.49
Cedarburg	1885	Ozaukee	11,412	11,530	1.03
Chetek	1891	Barron.	2,221	2,212	-0.41
Chilton	1877	Calumet	3,933	3,939	0.15
Clintonville.	1887	Waupaca	4,559	4,521	-0.83
Colby	1891	Clark, Marathon.	1,852	1,831	-1.13
Columbus	1874	Columbia, Dodge.	4,991	5,066	1.50
Cornell	1956	Chippewa	1,467	1,462	-0.34
Crandon	1898	Forest	1,920	1,875	-2.34
Cuba City.	1925	Grant, Lafayette.	2,086	2,097	0.53
Cumberland	1885	Barron.	2,170	2,182	0.55
Darlington	1877	Lafayette	2,451	2,421	-1.22
Delafield	1959	Waukesha	7,085	7,165	1.13
Delavan.	1897	Walworth.	8,463	8,414	-0.58
Dodgeville	1889	Iowa.	4,693	4,676	-0.36
Durand	1887	Pepin	1,931	1,872	-3.06
Eagle River.	1937	Vilas	1,398	1,416	1.29
Edgerton	1883	Dane, Rock.	5,461	5,545	1.54
Elkhorn	1897	Walworth.	10,084	9,897	-1.85
Elroy	1885	Juneau	1,442	1,379	-4.37
Evansville.	1896	Rock	5,012	5,190	3.55
Fennimore	1919	Grant	2,497	2,508	0.44
Fitchburg.	1983	Dane	25,260	27,635	9.40
Fountain City . . .	1889	Buffalo	859	854	-0.58
Fox Lake	1938	Dodge	1,519	1,509	-0.66
Galesville.	1942	Trempealeau	1,481	1,498	1.15
Gillett	1944	Oconto	1,386	1,370	-1.15
Glenwood City . .	1895	St. Croix.	1,242	1,221	-1.69
Green Lake.	1962	Green Lake.	960	983	2.40
Greenwood	1891	Clark.	1,026	1,023	-0.29
Hayward	1915	Sawyer	2,318	2,373	2.37
Hillsboro	1885	Vernon	1,417	1,405	-0.85
Horicon.	1897	Dodge	3,655	3,752	2.65
Hudson	1857	St. Croix.	12,719	13,584	6.80
Hurley.	1918	Iron	1,547	1,504	-2.78
Independence. . .	1942	Trempealeau	1,336	1,366	2.25
Jefferson	1878	Jefferson	7,973	7,985	0.15
Juneau	1887	Dodge	2,814	2,748	-2.35
Kewaunee	1883	Kewaunee	2,952	2,915	-1.25
Kiel	1920	Calumet, Manitowoc.	3,738	3,768	0.80
Ladysmith	1905	Rusk.	3,414	3,367	-1.38
Lake Geneva. . . .	1883	Walworth.	7,651	7,771	1.57
Lake Mills[2]	1905	Jefferson	5,708	5,883	3.07
Lancaster.	1878	Grant	3,868	3,811	-1.47
Lodi	1941	Columbia.	3,050	3,087	1.21
Loyal	1948	Clark.	1,261	1,255	-0.48
Manawa	1954	Waupaca	1,371	1,328	-3.14
Marion	1898	Shawano, Waupaca	1,260	1,249	-0.87
Markesan.	1959	Green Lake.	1,476	1,444	-2.17
Mauston	1883	Juneau	4,423	4,489	1.49

Wisconsin cities, May 1, 2017, continued

City	Year incorporated	County	2010 census	2016 estimate	% change
Mayville.	1885	Dodge	5,154	5,092	-1.20
Medford	1889	Taylor	4,326	4,372	1.06
Mellen	1907	Ashland.	731	717	-1.92
Menomonie	1882	Dunn	16,264	16,338	0.45
Mequon	1957	Ozaukee	23,132	23,870	3.19
Merrill.	1883	Lincoln	9,661	9,522	-1.44
Milton.	1969	Rock.	5,546	5,519	-0.49
Mineral Point . . .	1857	Iowa.	2,487	2,491	0.16
Mondovi	1889	Buffalo	2,777	2,771	-0.22
Monona	1969	Dane	7,533	7,864	4.39
Monroe.	1882	Green	10,827	10,717	-1.02
Montello	1938	Marquette	1,495	1,461	-2.27
Montreal	1924	Iron	807	805	-0.25
Mosinee	1931	Marathon.	3,988	4,013	0.63
Neillsville.	1882	Clark.	2,463	2,431	-1.30
Nekoosa	1926	Wood	2,580	2,563	-0.66
New Holstein . . .	1926	Calumet	3,236	3,204	-0.99
New Lisbon	1889	Juneau	2,554	2,567	0.51
New London. . . .	1877	Outagamie, Waupaca	7,295	7,282	-0.18
New Richmond . .	1885	St. Croix.	8,375	8,807	5.16
Niagara	1992	Marinette.	1,624	1,602	-1.35
Oconto	1869	Oconto	4,513	4,521	0.18
Oconto Falls	1919	Oconto	2,891	2,867	-0.83
Omro	1944	Winnebago	3,517	3,558	1.17
Onalaska	1887	La Crosse	17,736	18,646	5.13
Osseo	1941	Trempealeau	1,701	1,703	0.12
Owen	1925	Clark.	940	936	-0.43
Park Falls	1912	Price.	2,462	2,476	0.57
Peshtigo	1903	Marinette.	3,502	3,449	-1.51
Phillips	1891	Price.	1,478	1,433	-3.04
Pittsville	1887	Wood	874	875	0.11
Platteville[2]	1876	Grant	11,224	12,824	14.26
Plymouth.	1877	Sheboygan.	8,445	8,467	0.26
Port Washington .	1882	Ozaukee	11,250	11,495	2.18
Portage.	1854	Columbia.	10,324	10,251	-0.71
Prairie du Chien. .	1872	Crawford	5,911	5,874	-0.63
Prescott.	1857	Pierce	4,258	4,255	-0.07
Princeton.	1920	Green Lake.	1,214	1,197	-1.40
Reedsburg	1887	Sauk	9,200	9,303	1.12
Rhinelander	1894	Oneida	7,798	7,665	-1.71
Rice Lake	1887	Barron.	8,419	8,599	2.14
Richland Center. .	1887	Richland	5,184	5,178	-0.12
Ripon	1858	Fond du Lac	7,733	7,833	1.29
St. Croix Falls . . .	1958	Polk	2,133	2,097	-1.69
St. Francis	1951	Milwaukee	9,365	9,458	0.99
Schofield	1951	Marathon.	2,169	2,207	1.75
Seymour	1879	Outagamie	3,451	3,441	-0.29
Shawano	1874	Shawano	9,305	9,219	-0.92
Sheboygan Falls .	1913	Sheboygan.	7,775	7,853	1.00
Shell Lake	1961	Washburn	1,347	1,367	1.48
Shullsburg	1889	Lafayette	1,226	1,215	-0.90
South Milwaukee	1897	Milwaukee	21,156	21,073	-0.39
Sparta.	1883	Monroe.	9,522	9,804	2.96
Spooner	1909	Washburn	2,682	2,623	-2.20
Stanley	1898	Chippewa, Clark	3,608	3,624	0.44
Stoughton	1882	Dane	12,611	12,819	1.65

Wisconsin cities, May 1, 2017, continued

City	Year incorporated	County	2010 census	2016 estimate	% change
Sturgeon Bay . . .	1883	Door.	9,144	9,237	1.02
Thorp	1948	Clark.	1,621	1,629	0.49
Tomah	1883	Monroe	9,093	9,345	2.77
Tomahawk	1891	Lincoln	3,397	3,332	-1.91
Verona	1977	Dane	10,619	12,100	13.95
Viroqua	1885	Vernon	4,362	4,362	0.00
Washburn	1904	Bayfield.	2,117	2,104	-0.61
Waterloo	1962	Jefferson	3,333	3,371	1.14
Waupaca	1875	Waupaca	6,069	6,052	-0.28
Waupun	1878	Dodge, Fond du Lac	11,340	11,572	2.05
Wautoma.	1901	Waushara.	2,218	2,154	-2.89
Westby	1920	Vernon	2,200	2,224	1.09
Weyauwega	1939	Waupaca	1,900	1,905	0.26
Whitehall.	1941	Trempealeau	1,558	1,559	0.06
Whitewater[2]. . . .	1885	Jefferson, Walworth	14,390	14,397	0.05
Wisconsin Dells . .	1925	Adams, Columbia, Juneau, Sauk.	2,678	2,651	-1.01

1. A city is initially classified according to its population when it incorporates. If its population changes, a city can take action to change its classification, but if it does not take such action, its classification remains unchanged.   2. One of ten cities with a city manager.

Sources: Wisconsin Department of Administration, Demographic Services Center, *Official Final Estimates, 1/1/2016, Wisconsin Municipalities, with Comparison to Census 2010*, October 2016; League of Wisconsin Municipalities, *2016–2017 Directory of Wisconsin City and Village Officials*, July 2016; and data compiled by Wisconsin Legislative Reference Bureau.

Wisconsin villages, May 1, 2017

Village	Year incorporated	County	2010 census	2016 estimate	% change
Adell	1918	Sheboygan.	516	514	-0.39
Albany	1918	Green	1,018	1,010	-0.79
Allouez	1986	Brown.	13,975	13,711	-1.89
Alma Center	1902	Jackson	503	509	1.19
Almena.	1945	Barron.	677	650	-3.99
Almond	1905	Portage.	448	439	-2.01
Amherst	1899	Portage.	1,035	1,058	2.22
Amherst Junction	1912	Portage.	377	375	-0.53
Aniwa	1899	Shawano	260	250	-3.85
Arena	1923	Iowa	834	825	-1.08
Argyle	1903	Lafayette	857	851	-0.70
Arlington	1945	Columbia.	819	824	0.61
Arpin	1978	Wood	333	326	-2.10
Ashwaubenon[1].	1977	Brown.	16,963	17,029	0.39
Athens	1901	Marathon.	1,105	1,102	-0.27
Auburndale	1881	Wood	703	707	0.57
Avoca	1870	Iowa	637	629	-1.26
Bagley	1919	Grant	379	375	-1.06
Baldwin	1875	St. Croix.	3,957	3,956	-0.03
Balsam Lake	1905	Polk	1,009	1,010	0.10
Bangor	1899	La Crosse.	1,459	1,520	4.18

Wisconsin villages, May 1, 2017, continued

Village	Year incorporated	County	2010 census	2016 estimate	% change
Barneveld	1906	Iowa	1,231	1,238	0.57
Bay City	1909	Pierce	500	496	-0.80
Bayside [1]	1953	Milwaukee, Ozaukee	4,389	4,365	-0.55
Bear Creek	1902	Outagamie	448	447	-0.22
Belgium	1922	Ozaukee	2,245	2,292	2.09
Bell Center	1901	Crawford	117	116	-0.85
Belleville	1892	Dane, Green	2,385	2,387	0.08
Bellevue	2003	Brown	14,570	15,337	5.26
Belmont	1894	Lafayette	986	993	0.71
Benton	1892	Lafayette	973	964	-0.92
Big Bend	1928	Waukesha	1,290	1,314	1.86
Big Falls	1925	Waupaca	61	57	-6.56
Birchwood	1921	Washburn	442	434	-1.81
Birnamwood	1895	Marathon, Shawano	818	807	-1.34
Biron	1910	Wood	839	824	-1.79
Black Creek	1904	Outagamie	1,316	1,318	0.15
Black Earth	1901	Dane	1,338	1,388	3.74
Blanchardville	1890	Iowa, Lafayette	825	820	-0.61
Bloomfield	2011	Walworth	NA	4,643	NA
Bloomington	1880	Grant	735	739	0.54
Blue Mounds	1912	Dane	855	938	9.71
Blue River	1916	Grant	434	434	0.00
Boaz	1939	Richland	156	155	-0.64
Bonduel	1916	Shawano	1,478	1,484	0.41
Bowler	1923	Shawano	302	289	-4.30
Boyceville	1922	Dunn	1,086	1,089	0.28
Boyd	1891	Chippewa	552	554	0.36
Brandon	1881	Fond du Lac	879	875	-0.46
Bristol	2009	Kenosha	4,914	5,003	1.81
Brokaw	1903	Marathon	251	241	-3.98
Brooklyn	1905	Dane, Green	1,401	1,416	1.07
Brown Deer [1]	1955	Milwaukee	11,999	12,305	2.55
Brownsville	1952	Dodge	581	593	2.07
Browntown	1890	Green	280	280	0.00
Bruce	1901	Rusk	779	771	-1.03
Butler	1913	Waukesha	1,841	1,828	-0.71
Butternut	1903	Ashland	375	371	-1.07
Cadott	1895	Chippewa	1,437	1,458	1.46
Caledonia	2005	Racine	24,705	24,917	0.86
Cambria	1866	Columbia	767	763	-0.52
Cambridge	1891	Dane, Jefferson	1,457	1,470	0.89
Cameron	1894	Barron	1,783	1,834	2.86
Campbellsport	1902	Fond du Lac	2,016	2,008	-0.40
Camp Douglas	1893	Juneau	601	615	2.33
Cascade	1914	Sheboygan	709	695	-1.97
Casco	1920	Kewaunee	583	594	1.89
Cashton	1901	Monroe	1,102	1,107	0.45
Cassville	1882	Grant	947	943	-0.42
Catawba	1922	Price	110	101	-8.18
Cazenovia	1902	Richland, Sauk	318	319	0.31
Cecil	1905	Shawano	570	558	-2.11
Cedar Grove	1899	Sheboygan	2,113	2,099	-0.66
Centuria	1904	Polk	948	943	-0.53
Chaseburg	1922	Vernon	284	290	2.11
Chenequa	1928	Waukesha	590	589	-0.17
Clayton	1909	Polk	571	567	-0.70
Clear Lake	1894	Polk	1,070	1,061	-0.84
Cleveland	1958	Manitowoc	1,485	1,515	2.02

Wisconsin villages, May 1, 2017, continued

Village	Year incorporated	County	2010 census	2016 estimate	% change
Clinton	1882	Rock.	2,154	2,108	-2.14
Clyman	1924	Dodge	422	415	-1.66
Cobb	1902	Iowa.	458	465	1.53
Cochrane	1910	Buffalo	450	447	-0.67
Coleman	1903	Marinette.	724	726	0.28
Colfax.	1904	Dunn	1,158	1,123	-3.02
Coloma	1939	Waushara.	450	455	1.11
Combined Locks	1920	Outagamie.	3,328	3,515	5.62
Conrath	1915	Rusk.	95	94	-1.05
Coon Valley	1907	Vernon	765	754	-1.44
Cottage Grove	1924	Dane	6,192	6,635	7.15
Couderay	1922	Sawyer	88	87	-1.14
Crivitz	1974	Marinette.	984	959	-2.54
Cross Plains	1920	Dane	3,538	3,842	8.59
Curtiss	1917	Clark.	216	212	-1.85
Dallas	1903	Barron.	409	390	-4.65
Dane	1899	Dane	995	1,090	9.55
Darien	1951	Walworth.	1,580	1,589	0.57
Deerfield	1891	Dane	2,319	2,451	5.69
Deer Park	1913	St. Croix.	216	210	-2.78
DeForest	1891	Dane	8,936	9,388	5.06
Denmark	1915	Brown.	2,123	2,181	2.73
De Soto	1886	Crawford, Vernon.	287	289	0.70
Dickeyville	1947	Grant	1,061	1,059	-0.19
Dorchester	1901	Clark, Marathon.	876	873	-0.34
Dousman	1917	Waukesha	2,302	2,334	1.39
Downing	1909	Dunn	265	263	-0.75
Doylestown	1907	Columbia.	297	293	-1.35
Dresser	1919	Polk	895	899	0.45
Eagle	1899	Waukesha	1,950	1,973	1.18
Eastman	1909	Crawford	428	430	0.47
East Troy	1900	Walworth.	4,281	4,343	1.45
Eden	1912	Fond du Lac	875	892	1.94
Edgar	1898	Marathon.	1,479	1,468	-0.74
Egg Harbor	1964	Door.	201	203	1.00
Eland	1905	Shawano	202	197	-2.48
Elderon	1917	Marathon.	179	176	-1.68
Eleva	1902	Trempealeau	670	677	1.04
Elkhart Lake	1894	Sheboygan.	967	958	-0.93
Elk Mound	1909	Dunn	878	872	-0.68
Ellsworth.	1887	Pierce	3,284	3,293	0.27
Elm Grove [1]	1955	Waukesha	5,934	5,943	0.15
Elmwood	1905	Pierce	817	813	-0.49
Elmwood Park	1960	Racine.	497	497	0.00
Embarrass	1895	Waupaca	404	389	-3.71
Endeavor	1946	Marquette	468	460	-1.71
Ephraim	1919	Door.	288	289	0.35
Ettrick	1948	Trempealeau	524	522	-0.38
Exeland	1920	Sawyer	196	195	-0.51
Fairchild	1880	Eau Claire.	550	547	-0.55
Fairwater	1921	Fond du Lac	371	367	-1.08
Fall Creek	1906	Eau Claire.	1,315	1,302	-0.99
Fall River	1903	Columbia.	1,712	1,732	1.17
Fenwood	1904	Marathon.	152	147	-3.29
Ferryville	1912	Crawford	176	183	3.98
Fontana-on-Geneva Lake	1924	Walworth.	1,672	1,677	0.30
Footville	1918	Rock.	808	801	-0.87

Wisconsin villages, May 1, 2017, continued

Village	Year incorporated	County	2010 census	2016 estimate	% change
Forestville	1960	Door	430	428	-0.47
Fox Crossing [1,2,3]	2016	Winnebago	NA	10,649	NA
Fox Point [1]	1926	Milwaukee	6,701	6,678	-0.34
Francis Creek	1960	Manitowoc	669	663	-0.90
Frederic	1903	Polk	1,137	1,133	-0.35
Fredonia	1922	Ozaukee	2,160	2,191	1.44
Fremont	1882	Waupaca	679	676	-0.44
Friendship	1907	Adams	725	723	-0.28
Friesland	1946	Columbia	356	354	-0.56
Gays Mills	1900	Crawford	491	505	2.85
Genoa	1935	Vernon	253	244	-3.56
Genoa City	1901	Kenosha, Walworth	3,042	3,044	0.07
Germantown	1927	Washington	19,749	20,008	1.31
Gilman	1914	Taylor	410	372	-9.27
Glenbeulah	1913	Sheboygan	463	456	-1.51
Glen Flora	1915	Rusk	92	88	-4.35
Grafton	1896	Ozaukee	11,459	11,549	0.79
Granton	1916	Clark	355	355	0.00
Grantsburg	1887	Burnett	1,341	1,332	-0.67
Gratiot	1891	Lafayette	236	231	-2.12
Greendale [1]	1939	Milwaukee	14,046	14,123	0.55
Gresham	1908	Shawano	586	582	-0.68
Hales Corners	1952	Milwaukee	7,692	7,652	-0.52
Hammond	1880	St. Croix	1,922	1,891	-1.61
Hancock	1902	Waushara	417	406	-2.64
Harrison [4]	2013	Calumet, Outagamie	NA	10,749	NA
Hartland	1891	Waukesha	9,110	9,179	0.76
Hatley	1912	Marathon	574	605	5.40
Haugen	1918	Barron	287	285	-0.70
Hawkins	1922	Rusk	305	304	-0.33
Hazel Green	1867	Grant, Lafayette	1,256	1,267	0.88
Hewitt	1973	Wood	828	832	0.48
Highland	1873	Iowa	842	841	-0.12
Hilbert	1898	Calumet	1,132	1,186	4.77
Hixton	1920	Jackson	433	427	-1.39
Hobart	2003	Brown	6,182	8,543	38.19
Hollandale	1910	Iowa	288	286	-0.69
Holmen	1946	La Crosse	9,005	9,623	6.86
Hortonville	1894	Outagamie	2,711	2,720	0.33
Howard	1959	Brown, Outagamie	17,399	19,295	10.90
Howards Grove	1967	Sheboygan	3,188	3,221	1.04
Hustisford	1870	Dodge	1,123	1,119	-0.36
Hustler	1914	Juneau	194	195	0.52
Ingram	1907	Rusk	78	82	5.13
Iola	1892	Waupaca	1,301	1,288	-1.00
Iron Ridge	1913	Dodge	929	938	0.97
Ironton	1914	Sauk	253	254	0.40
Jackson	1912	Washington	6,753	6,911	2.34
Johnson Creek	1903	Jefferson	2,738	2,933	7.12
Junction City	1911	Portage	439	439	0.00
Kekoskee	1958	Dodge	161	160	-0.62
Kellnersville	1971	Manitowoc	332	329	-0.90
Kendall	1894	Monroe	472	469	-0.64
Kennan	1903	Price	135	126	-6.67
Kewaskum	1895	Fond du Lac, Washington	4,004	4,015	0.27
Kimberly	1910	Outagamie	6,468	6,679	3.26

Wisconsin villages, May 1, 2017, continued

Village	Year incorporated	County	2010 census	2016 estimate	% change
Kingston	1923	Green Lake.	326	326	0.00
Knapp	1905	Dunn	463	462	-0.22
Kohler	1912	Sheboygan.	2,120	2,108	-0.57
Kronenwetter	2002	Marathon.	7,210	7,536	4.52
La Farge	1899	Vernon	746	701	-6.03
La Valle	1883	Sauk	367	353	-3.81
Lac La Belle	1931	Jefferson, Waukesha	290	289	-0.34
Lake Delton	1954	Sauk	2,914	2,922	0.27
Lake Hallie	2003	Chippewa	6,448	6,916	7.26
Lake Nebagamon	1907	Douglas.	1,069	1,081	1.12
Lannon	1930	Waukesha	1,107	1,167	5.42
Lena	1921	Oconto	564	562	-0.35
Lime Ridge	1910	Sauk	162	157	-3.09
Linden	1900	Iowa	549	543	-1.09
Little Chute	1899	Outagamie.	10,449	10,976	5.04
Livingston	1914	Grant, Iowa.	664	661	-0.45
Loganville	1917	Sauk	300	293	-2.33
Lohrville	1910	Waushara	402	394	-1.99
Lomira	1899	Dodge	2,430	2,432	0.08
Lone Rock	1886	Richland	888	877	-1.24
Lowell	1894	Dodge	340	336	-1.18
Lublin	1915	Taylor	118	117	-0.85
Luck	1905	Polk	1,119	1,096	-2.06
Luxemburg	1908	Kewaunee	2,515	2,583	2.70
Lyndon Station	1903	Juneau	500	490	-2.00
Lynxville	1899	Crawford	132	134	1.52
Maiden Rock	1887	Pierce	119	120	0.84
Maine [5]	2015	Marathon.	2,337	2,341	0.17
Maple Bluff	1930	Dane	1,313	1,304	-0.69
Marathon City	1884	Marathon.	1,524	1,568	2.89
Maribel	1963	Manitowoc.	351	343	-2.28
Marquette	1958	Green Lake.	150	152	1.33
Marshall	1905	Dane	3,862	3,859	-0.08
Mason	1925	Bayfield.	93	93	0.00
Mattoon	1901	Shawano	438	428	-2.28
Mazomanie	1885	Dane	1,652	1,668	0.97
McFarland	1920	Dane	7,808	8,044	3.02
Melrose	1914	Jackson.	503	496	-1.39
Melvina	1922	Monroe.	104	104	0.00
Menomonee Falls [1]. . . .	1892	Waukesha	35,626	36,907	3.60
Merrillan	1881	Jackson.	542	530	-2.21
Merrimac	1899	Sauk	420	421	0.24
Merton	1922	Waukesha	3,346	3,504	4.72
Milladore	1933	Portage, Wood	276	276	0.00
Milltown	1910	Polk	917	912	-0.55
Minong	1915	Washburn	527	519	-1.52
Mishicot	1950	Manitowoc.	1,442	1,442	0.00
Montfort	1893	Grant, Iowa.	718	724	0.84
Monticello	1891	Green	1,217	1,220	0.25
Mount Calvary	1962	Fond du Lac	762	569	-25.33
Mount Hope	1919	Grant	225	227	0.89
Mount Horeb	1899	Dane	7,009	7,142	1.90
Mount Pleasant	2003	Racine.	26,197	26,369	0.66
Mount Sterling	1936	Crawford	211	210	-0.47
Mukwonago	1905	Walworth, Waukesha	7,355	7,772	5.67
Muscoda	1894	Grant, Iowa.	1,299	1,254	-3.46
Nashotah	1957	Waukesha	1,395	1,361	-2.44

Wisconsin villages, May 1, 2017, continued

Village	Year incorporated	County	2010 census	2016 estimate	% change
Necedah	1870	Juneau	916	917	0.11
Nelson	1978	Buffalo	374	373	-0.27
Nelsonville	1913	Portage	155	157	1.29
Neosho	1902	Dodge	574	572	-0.35
Neshkoro	1906	Marquette	434	424	-2.30
New Auburn	1902	Barron, Chippewa	548	549	0.18
Newburg	1973	Ozaukee, Washington	1,254	1,261	0.56
New Glarus	1901	Green	2,172	2,164	-0.37
Nichols	1967	Outagamie	273	269	-1.47
North Bay	1951	Racine	241	232	-3.73
North Fond du Lac	1903	Fond du Lac	5,014	5,237	4.45
North Freedom	1893	Sauk	701	678	-3.28
North Hudson	1912	St. Croix	3,768	3,757	-0.29
North Prairie	1919	Waukesha	2,141	2,175	1.59
Norwalk	1894	Monroe	638	638	0.00
Oakdale	1988	Monroe	297	293	-1.35
Oakfield	1903	Fond du Lac	1,075	1,097	2.05
Oconomowoc Lake	1959	Waukesha	595	589	-1.01
Ogdensburg	1912	Waupaca	185	179	-3.24
Oliver	1917	Douglas	399	431	8.02
Ontario	1890	Vernon, Monroe	554	553	-0.18
Oostburg	1909	Sheboygan	2,887	2,941	1.87
Oregon	1883	Dane	9,231	9,797	6.13
Orfordville	1900	Rock	1,442	1,450	0.55
Osceola	1886	Polk	2,568	2,598	1.17
Oxford	1912	Marquette	607	597	-1.65
Paddock Lake	1960	Kenosha	2,992	2,983	-0.30
Palmyra	1866	Jefferson	1,781	1,773	-0.45
Pardeeville	1894	Columbia	2,115	2,105	-0.47
Park Ridge	1938	Portage	491	495	0.81
Patch Grove	1921	Grant	198	199	0.51
Pepin	1860	Pepin	837	821	-1.91
Pewaukee	1876	Waukesha	8,166	8,106	-0.73
Pigeon Falls	1956	Trempealeau	411	408	-0.73
Plain	1912	Sauk	773	761	-1.55
Plainfield	1882	Waushara	862	852	-1.16
Pleasant Prairie	1989	Kenosha	19,719	20,438	3.65
Plover	1971	Portage	12,123	12,603	3.96
Plum City	1909	Pierce	599	597	-0.33
Poplar	1917	Douglas	603	612	1.49
Port Edwards	1902	Wood	1,818	1,780	-2.09
Potosi	1887	Grant	688	682	-0.87
Potter	1980	Calumet	253	251	-0.79
Pound	1914	Marinette	377	377	0.00
Poynette	1892	Columbia	2,528	2,525	-0.12
Prairie du Sac	1885	Sauk	3,972	4,053	2.04
Prairie Farm	1901	Barron	473	462	-2.33
Prentice	1899	Price	660	653	-1.06
Pulaski	1910	Brown, Oconto, Shawano	3,539	3,516	-0.65
Radisson	1953	Sawyer	241	239	-0.83
Randolph	1870	Columbia, Dodge	1,811	1,787	-1.33
Random Lake	1907	Sheboygan	1,594	1,576	-1.13
Readstown	1898	Vernon	415	420	1.20
Redgranite	1904	Waushara	2,149	2,139	-0.47
Reedsville	1892	Manitowoc	1,206	1,197	-0.75
Reeseville	1899	Dodge	708	707	-0.14
Rewey	1902	Iowa	292	285	-2.40

Wisconsin villages, May 1, 2017, continued

Village	Year incorporated	County	2010 census	2016 estimate	% change
Rib Lake	1902	Taylor	910	897	-1.43
Richfield	2008	Washington	11,300	11,537	2.10
Ridgeland	1921	Dunn	273	273	0.00
Ridgeway	1902	Iowa	653	642	-1.68
Rio	1887	Columbia	1,059	1,059	0.00
River Hills	1930	Milwaukee	1,597	1,577	-1.25
Roberts	1945	St. Croix	1,651	1,621	-1.82
Rochester	1912	Racine	3,682	3,736	1.47
Rockdale	1914	Dane	214	213	-0.47
Rockland	1919	La Crosse, Monroe	594	628	5.72
Rock Springs	1894	Sauk	362	306	-15.47
Rosendale	1915	Fond du Lac	1,063	1,046	-1.60
Rosholt	1907	Portage	506	491	-2.96
Rothschild	1917	Marathon	5,269	5,325	1.06
Rudolph	1960	Wood	439	430	-2.05
St. Cloud	1909	Fond du Lac	477	474	-0.63
St. Nazianz	1956	Manitowoc	783	776	-0.89
Salem Lakes [6]	2017	Kenosha	14,478	14,496	0.12
Sauk City	1854	Sauk	3,410	3,422	0.35
Saukville	1915	Ozaukee	4,451	4,450	-0.02
Scandinavia	1894	Waupaca	363	361	-0.55
Sharon	1892	Walworth	1,605	1,586	-1.18
Sheldon	1917	Rusk	237	232	-2.11
Sherwood	1968	Calumet	2,713	2,959	9.07
Shiocton	1903	Outagamie	921	926	0.54
Shorewood [1]	1900	Milwaukee	13,162	13,134	-0.21
Shorewood Hills	1927	Dane	1,565	2,077	32.72
Siren	1948	Burnett	806	796	-1.24
Sister Bay	1912	Door	876	905	3.31
Slinger	1869	Washington	5,068	5,338	5.33
Soldiers Grove	1888	Crawford	592	576	-2.70
Solon Springs	1920	Douglas	600	600	0.00
Somers [2]	2015	Kenosha	NA	8,462	NA
Somerset	1915	St. Croix	2,635	2,670	1.33
South Wayne	1911	Lafayette	489	488	-0.20
Spencer	1902	Marathon	1,925	1,936	0.57
Spring Green	1869	Sauk	1,628	1,625	-0.18
Spring Valley	1895	Pierce, St. Croix	1,352	1,372	1.48
Star Prairie	1900	St. Croix	561	553	-1.43
Stetsonville	1949	Taylor	541	529	-2.22
Steuben	1900	Crawford	131	123	-6.11
Stockbridge	1908	Calumet	636	651	2.36
Stockholm	1903	Pepin	66	66	0.00
Stoddard	1911	Vernon	774	796	2.84
Stratford	1910	Marathon	1,578	1,600	1.39
Strum	1948	Trempealeau	1,114	1,122	0.72
Sturtevant	1907	Racine	6,970	6,961	-0.13
Suamico	2003	Brown	11,346	12,281	8.24
Sullivan	1915	Jefferson	669	672	0.45
Summit	2010	Waukesha	4,674	4,751	1.65
Superior	1949	Douglas	664	674	1.51
Suring	1914	Oconto	544	536	-1.47
Sussex	1924	Waukesha	10,518	10,797	2.65
Taylor	1919	Jackson	476	481	1.05
Tennyson	1940	Grant	355	366	3.10
Theresa	1898	Dodge	1,262	1,258	-0.32
Thiensville	1910	Ozaukee	3,235	3,213	-0.68

Wisconsin villages, May 1, 2017, continued

Village	Year incorporated	County	2010 census	2016 estimate	% change
Tigerton	1896	Shawano	741	728	-1.75
Tony	1911	Rusk	113	110	-2.65
Trempealeau	1867	Trempealeau	1,529	1,637	7.06
Turtle Lake	1898	Barron, Polk	1,050	1,051	0.10
Twin Lakes	1937	Kenosha	5,989	6,049	1.00
Union Center	1913	Juneau	200	197	-1.50
Union Grove	1893	Racine	4,915	4,900	-0.31
Unity	1903	Clark, Marathon	343	339	-1.17
Valders	1919	Manitowoc	962	957	-0.52
Vesper	1948	Wood	584	582	-0.34
Viola	1899	Richland, Vernon	699	700	0.14
Waldo	1922	Sheboygan	503	493	-1.99
Wales	1922	Waukesha	2,549	2,540	-0.35
Walworth	1901	Walworth	2,816	2,836	0.71
Warrens	1973	Monroe	363	356	-1.93
Waterford	1906	Racine	5,368	5,378	0.19
Waunakee	1893	Dane	12,097	13,322	10.13
Wausaukee	1924	Marinette	575	568	-1.22
Wauzeka	1890	Crawford	711	697	-1.97
Webster	1916	Burnett	653	653	0.00
West Baraboo	1956	Sauk	1,414	1,470	3.96
Westfield	1902	Marquette	1,254	1,258	0.32
West Milwaukee	1906	Milwaukee	4,206	4,181	-0.59
Weston	1996	Marathon	14,868	15,338	3.16
West Salem	1893	La Crosse	4,799	4,956	3.27
Weyerhaeuser	1906	Rusk	238	228	-4.20
Wheeler	1922	Dunn	348	346	-0.57
Whitefish Bay [1]	1892	Milwaukee	14,110	14,216	0.75
White Lake	1926	Langlade	363	359	-1.10
Whitelaw	1958	Manitowoc	757	748	-1.19
Whiting	1947	Portage	1,724	1,685	-2.26
Wild Rose	1904	Waushara	725	711	-1.93
Williams Bay	1919	Walworth	2,564	2,580	0.62
Wilson	1911	St. Croix	184	182	-1.09
Wilton	1890	Monroe	504	501	-0.60
Wind Point	1954	Racine	1,723	1,694	-1.68
Windsor [5]	2015	Dane	6,345	7,145	12.61
Winneconne	1887	Winnebago	2,383	2,407	1.01
Winter	1973	Sawyer	313	318	1.60
Withee	1901	Clark	487	482	-1.03
Wittenberg	1893	Shawano	1,081	1,033	-4.44
Wonewoc	1878	Juneau	816	807	-1.10
Woodman	1917	Grant	132	131	-0.76
Woodville	1911	St. Croix	1,344	1,336	-0.60
Wrightstown	1901	Brown, Outagamie	2,827	2,855	0.99
Wyeville	1923	Monroe	147	140	-4.76
Wyocena	1909	Columbia	768	747	-2.73
Yuba	1935	Richland	74	66	-10.81

Note: There are 411 villages in Wisconsin as of May 1, 2017.

NA–Not Applicable

1. One of ten villages with an appointed village manager.   2. This village was created from part of a town after the date reflected by the 2010 data.   3. The 2016 population estimate for Fox Crossing comes from the village's certificate of incorporation, dated April 20, 2016.   4. This village was created from parts of two towns after the date reflected by the 2010 data.   5. This village was created from a whole town after the date reflected by the 2010 data. The 2010 figure reflects the data for the previously existing town.   6. This village

was created on February 14, 2017, by the merger of a whole village and a whole town. The 2010 and 2016 figures reflect the combined data for the previously existing village and town.

Sources: Wisconsin Department of Administration, Demographic Services Center, *Official Final Estimates, 1/1/2016, Wisconsin Municipalities, with Comparison to Census 2010*, October 2016; Wisconsin Department of Administration, Municipal Data System, *Certificate of Incorporation: Village of Fox Crossing*, April 20, 2016; League of Wisconsin Municipalities, *2016–2017 Directory of Wisconsin City and Village Officials*, July 2016; and data compiled by Wisconsin Legislative Reference Bureau.

Wisconsin cities and villages over 10,000 population, January 1, 2016

City or village (county)	2016 estimate[1]	2010 census	% change	2016 rank	2010 non-white[2]	2010 Hispanic or Latino origin[3]
Cities						
Milwaukee (Milwaukee, Washington, Waukesha)	594,667	594,833	-0.03	1	271,607	103,007
Madison (Dane).	247,207	233,209	6.00	2	40,798	15,948
Green Bay (Brown)	105,079	104,057	0.98	3	13,912	13,896
Kenosha (Kenosha).	99,489	99,218	0.27	4	14,121	16,130
Racine (Racine)	78,165	78,860	-0.88	5	20,362	16,309
Appleton (Calumet, Outagamie, Winnebago) . .	74,286	72,623	2.29	6	7,124	3,643
Waukesha (Waukesha)	71,699	70,718	1.39	7	5,321	8,529
Eau Claire (Chippewa, Eau Claire)	67,381	65,931	2.20	8	5,116	1,268
Oshkosh (Winnebago).	66,717	66,083	0.96	9	5,539	1,770
Janesville (Rock)	63,470	63,575	-0.17	10	3,689	3,421
West Allis (Milwaukee).	60,164	60,411	-0.41	11	5,094	5,770
La Crosse (La Crosse).	52,377	51,320	2.06	12	4,885	1,012
Sheboygan (Sheboygan)	48,653	49,288	-1.29	13	6,314	4,866
Wauwatosa (Milwaukee)	47,160	46,396	1.65	14	4,361	1,450
Fond du Lac (Fond du Lac)	43,381	43,021	0.84	15	2,695	2,742
New Berlin (Waukesha)	40,227	39,584	1.62	16	2,256	1,036
Wausau (Marathon)	38,909	39,106	-0.50	17	5,891	1,149
Brookfield (Waukesha)	37,806	37,920	-0.30	18	3,545	853
Beloit (Rock).	36,657	36,966	-0.84	20	7,149	6,332
Greenfield (Milwaukee)	36,404	36,720	-0.86	21	3,043	3,087
Franklin (Milwaukee)	35,741	35,451	0.82	22	4,168	1,592
Oak Creek (Milwaukee)	35,206	34,451	2.19	23	3,282	2,582
Manitowoc (Manitowoc)	33,783	33,736	0.14	24	2,486	1,695
Sun Prairie (Dane)	32,613	29,364	11.06	25	3,749	1,253
West Bend (Washington)	31,676	31,078	1.92	26	1,049	1,213
Fitchburg (Dane)	27,635	25,260	9.40	27	4,464	4,341
Superior (Douglas)	27,237	27,244	-0.03	28	2,166	382
Stevens Point (Portage)	26,895	26,717	0.67	29	1,946	696
Neenah (Winnebago)	26,050	25,501	2.15	31	1,163	967
De Pere (Brown).	24,592	23,800	3.33	33	1,207	511
Muskego (Waukesha)	24,534	24,135	1.65	34	529	545
Watertown (Dodge, Jefferson).	23,995	23,861	0.56	35	706	1,731
Mequon (Ozaukee).	23,870	23,132	3.19	36	1,760	467
South Milwaukee (Milwaukee).	21,073	21,156	-0.39	37	1,100	1,699
Middleton (Dane).	19,317	17,442	10.75	40	1,764	984
Marshfield (Marathon, Wood)	19,201	19,118	0.43	42	796	452
Onalaska (La Crosse).	18,646	17,736	5.13	43	1,539	276
Wisconsin Rapids (Wood).	18,630	18,367	1.43	44	1,186	535
Cudahy (Milwaukee).	18,192	18,267	-0.41	45	1,142	1,769
Menasha (Calumet, Winnebago)	17,573	17,353	1.27	46	954	1,204
Beaver Dam (Dodge).	16,799	16,214	3.61	48	502	1,210
Oconomowoc (Waukesha)	16,656	15,759	5.69	49	422	559
Menomonie (Dunn)	16,338	16,264	0.45	50	1,176	276

Wisconsin cities and villages over 10,000 population, January 1, 2016, continued

City or village (county)	2016 estimate[1]	2010 census	% change	2016 rank	2010 non- white[2]	2010 Hispanic or Latino origin[3]
Kaukauna (Calumet, Outagamie)	15,894	15,462	2.79	51	654	407
River Falls (Pierce, St. Croix).	15,229	15,000	1.53	54	673	270
Hartford (Dodge, Washington)	14,627	14,223	2.84	55	425	686
Whitewater (Jefferson, Walworth)	14,397	14,390	0.05	56	1,009	1,372
Pewaukee (Waukesha)	14,148	13,195	7.22	58	667	281
Chippewa Falls (Chippewa).	13,965	13,661	2.23	60	605	221
Hudson (St. Croix)	13,584	12,719	6.80	62	539	347
Platteville (Grant).	12,824	11,224	14.26	65	535	179
Stoughton (Dane)	12,819	12,611	1.65	66	554	230
Glendale (Milwaukee)	12,724	12,872	-1.15	67	2,499	465
Fort Atkinson (Jefferson)	12,441	12,368	0.59	69	315	1,128
Verona (Dane).	12,100	10,619	13.95	72	617	258
Baraboo (Sauk)	12,013	12,048	-0.29	73	487	446
Waupun (Dodge, Fond du Lac)	11,572	11,340	2.05	74	1,651	217
Two Rivers (Manitowoc).	11,566	11,712	-1.25	75	536	224
Cedarburg (Ozaukee)	11,530	11,412	1.03	78	367	197
Port Washington (Ozaukee)	11,495	11,250	2.18	79	457	347
Marinette (Marinette)	10,878	10,968	-0.82	81	271	149
Monroe (Green)	10,717	10,827	-1.02	84	252	526
Burlington (Racine, Walworth).	10,591	10,464	1.21	85	327	898
Portage (Columbia)	10,251	10,324	-0.71	86	811	414
Villages						
Menomonee Falls (Waukesha).	36,907	35,626	3.60	19	2,789	697
Mount Pleasant (Racine)	26,369	26,197	0.66	30	2,714	2,181
Caledonia (Racine).	24,917	24,705	0.86	32	1,563	1,303
Pleasant Prairie (Kenosha)	20,438	19,719	3.65	38	1,141	1,332
Germantown (Washington)	20,008	19,749	1.31	39	1,334	400
Howard (Brown, Outagamie).	19,295	17,399	10.90	41	919	410
Ashwaubenon (Brown)	17,029	16,963	0.39	47	1,375	471
Weston (Marathon)	15,338	14,868	3.16	52	1,670	301
Bellevue (Brown)	15,337	14,570	5.26	53	970	1,359
Whitefish Bay (Milwaukee)	14,216	14,110	0.75	57	1,060	399
Greendale (Milwaukee)	14,123	14,046	0.55	59	805	667
Allouez (Brown).	13,711	13,975	-1.89	61	1,252	383
Waunakee (Dane).	13,322	12,097	10.13	63	416	269
Shorewood (Milwaukee)	13,134	13,162	-0.21	64	1,416	447
Plover (Portage).	12,603	12,123	3.96	68	684	393
Brown Deer (Milwaukee)	12,305	11,999	2.55	70	4,358	471
Suamico (Brown)	12,281	11,346	8.24	71	242	112
Grafton (Ozaukee)	11,549	11,459	0.79	76	421	266
Richfield (Washington)	11,537	11,300	2.10	77	304	162
Little Chute (Outagamie)	10,976	10,449	5.04	80	337	327
Sussex (Waukesha).	10,797	10,518	2.65	82	431	249
Harrison (Calumet, Outagamie)[4]	10,749	NA	NA	83	NA	NA

1. Population estimates are based on the corrected 2010 census totals. Race and ethnicity data have not been adjusted since the 2010 census.   2. In the 2010 census, respondents were allowed to choose more than one race. The column "nonwhite" includes all who chose at least one race other than white.   3. "Hispanic or Latino Origin" represents ethnicity and includes people of Cuban, Mexican, Puerto Rican, South or Central American, or other Spanish culture or origin, regardless of race.   4. This village was created from parts of two towns after the date reflected by the 2010 data.

Sources: Wisconsin Department of Administration, Demographic Services Center, *Official Final Estimates, 1/1/2016, Wisconsin Municipalities, with Comparison to Census 2010,* October 2016, and *Population and Hispanic & Non-Hispanic Data, Wisconsin Municipalities, Census 2000 and 2010 Comparisons; Based on Census 2010 Geography,* March 2011.

Wisconsin towns over 2,500 population, January 1, 2016

Town (county)	2016 estimate	2010 census	% change	Town (county)	2016 estimate	2010 census	% change
Addison (Washington) . .	3,456	3,495	-1.12	Ledgeview (Brown)	7,558	6,555	15.30
Alden (Polk)	2,790	2,786	0.14	Lima (Sheboygan)	2,976	2,982	-0.20
Algoma (Winnebago) . . .	6,974	6,822	2.23	Lisbon (Waukesha).	10,291	10,157	1.32
Arbor Vitae (Vilas)	3,340	3,316	0.72	Little Suamico (Oconto). .	5,058	4,799	5.40
Ashippun (Dodge)	2,596	2,559	1.45	Lodi (Columbia).	3,312	3,273	1.19
Barton (Washington) . . .	2,646	2,637	0.34	Lyons (Walworth).	3,699	3,698	0.03
Beaver Dam (Dodge). . . .	4,029	3,962	1.69	Madison (Dane).	6,341	6,279	0.99
Beloit (Rock)	7,616	7,662	-0.60	Medford (Taylor)	2,650	2,606	1.69
Bristol (Dane)	4,169	3,765	10.73	Menasha (Winnebago) . .	18,741	18,498	1.31
Brockway (Jackson)	2,857	2,828	1.03	Menominee (Menominee)	4,256	4,232	0.57
Brookfield (Waukesha) . .	6,058	6,116	-0.95	Menomonie (Dunn)	3,470	3,366	3.09
Buchanan (Outagamie) . .	6,916	6,755	2.38	Merrill (Lincoln).	3,002	2,980	0.74
Burke (Dane).	3,341	3,284	1.74	Merton (Waukesha)	8,402	8,338	0.77
Burlington (Racine)	6,454	6,502	-0.74	Middleton (Dane).	6,399	5,877	8.88
Campbell (La Crosse) . . .	4,330	4,314	0.37	Milton (Rock)	2,939	2,923	0.55
Cedarburg (Ozaukee) . . .	5,887	5,760	2.20	Minocqua (Oneida).	4,510	4,453	1.28
Center (Outagamie)	3,497	3,402	2.79	Mukwa (Waupaca)	2,965	2,930	1.19
Chase (Oconto)	3,088	3,005	2.76	Mukwonago (Waukesha) .	8,014	7,959	0.69
Clayton (Winnebago) . . .	4,061	3,951	2.78	Neenah (Winnebago) . . .	3,539	3,237	9.33
Cottage Grove (Dane) . . .	3,824	3,875	-1.32	Newbold (Oneida)	2,739	2,719	0.74
Dale (Outagamie).	2,803	2,731	2.64	Norway (Racine)	7,973	7,948	0.31
Dayton (Waupaca)	2,763	2,748	0.55	Oakland (Jefferson)	3,087	3,100	-0.42
Delafield (Waukesha) . . .	8,281	8,400	-1.42	Oconomowoc (Waukesha)	8,611	8,408	2.41
Delavan (Walworth)	5,254	5,285	-0.59	Onalaska (La Crosse) . . .	5,743	5,623	2.13
Dover (Racine)	4,036	4,051	-0.37	Oneida (Outagamie). . . .	4,702	4,678	0.51
Dunn (Dane).	4,940	4,931	0.18	Oregon (Dane)	3,242	3,184	1.82
Eagle (Waukesha)	3,503	3,507	-0.11	Osceola (Polk)	2,869	2,855	0.49
Eagle Point (Chippewa) . .	3,173	3,053	3.93	Ottawa (Waukesha)	3,897	3,859	0.98
East Troy (Walworth). . . .	4,045	4,021	0.60	Pacific (Columbia)	2,714	2,707	0.26
Ellington (Outagamie). . .	2,931	2,758	6.27	Pelican (Oneida)	2,815	2,764	1.85
Empire (Fond du Lac) . . .	2,818	2,797	0.75	Peshtigo (Marinette). . . .	4,105	4,057	1.18
Erin (Washington)	3,763	3,747	0.43	Pine Lake (Oneida)	2,757	2,740	0.62
Farmington (Washington)	4,040	4,014	0.65	Pittsfield (Brown)	2,708	2,608	3.83
Farmington (Waupaca) . .	4,000	3,974	0.65	Pleasant Springs (Dane). .	3,234	3,154	2.54
Fond du Lac (Fond du Lac)	3,553	3,015	17.84	Pleasant Valley (Eau Claire)	3,237	3,044	6.34
Freedom (Outagamie). . .	6,005	5,842	2.79	Plymouth (Sheboygan) . .	3,188	3,195	-0.22
Friendship (Fond du Lac) .	2,710	2,675	1.31	Polk (Washington)	3,991	3,937	1.37
Fulton (Rock)	3,277	3,252	0.77	Randall (Kenosha)	3,183	3,180	0.09
Genesee (Waukesha) . . .	7,384	7,340	0.60	Raymond (Racine)	3,950	3,870	2.07
Geneva (Walworth)	5,033	4,993	0.80	Rib Mountain (Marathon)	6,917	6,825	1.35
Grafton (Ozaukee)	4,137	4,053	2.07	Rice Lake (Barron)	3,101	3,060	1.34
Grand Chute (Outagamie)	22,083	20,919	5.56	Richmond (St. Croix)	3,437	3,272	5.04
Grand Rapids (Wood) . . .	7,701	7,646	0.72	Rock (Rock)	3,178	3,196	-0.56
Greenbush (Sheboygan) .	2,549	2,565	-0.62	Rome (Adams)	2,748	2,720	1.03
Greenville (Outagamie) . .	11,545	10,309	11.99	St. Joseph (St. Croix)	3,904	3,842	1.61
Harmony (Rock).	2,574	2,569	0.19	Salem (Kenosha)	12,096	12,067	0.24
Hartford (Washington) . .	3,582	3,609	-0.75	Saratoga (Wood)	5,184	5,142	0.82
Hayward (Sawyer)	3,571	3,567	0.11	Scott (Brown)	3,624	3,545	2.23
Holland (La Crosse).	3,967	3,701	7.19	Sevastopol (Door)	2,685	2,628	2.17
Hudson (St. Croix)	8,582	8,461	1.43	Seymour (Eau Claire). . . .	3,328	3,209	3.71
Hull (Portage)	5,380	5,346	0.64	Sheboygan (Sheboygan) .	7,435	7,271	2.26
Ixonia (Jefferson)	4,711	4,385	7.43	Shelby (La Crosse)	4,707	4,715	-0.17
Jackson (Washington). . .	4,371	4,134	5.73	Somerset (St. Croix)	4,163	4,036	3.15
Janesville (Rock)	3,464	3,434	0.87	Sparta (Monroe)	3,181	3,128	1.69
Koshkonong (Jefferson). .	3,694	3,692	0.05	Springfield (Dane)	2,869	2,734	4.94
Lac du Flambeau (Vilas). .	3,468	3,441	0.78	Stanley (Barron)	2,577	2,546	1.22
Lafayette (Chippewa) . . .	5,988	5,765	3.87	Star Prairie (St. Croix) . . .	3,551	3,504	1.34
Lawrence (Brown)	4,973	4,284	16.08	Stephenson (Marinette). .	3,064	3,006	1.93

Wisconsin towns over 2,500 population, January 1, 2016,
continued

Town (county)	2016 estimate	2010 census	% change	Town (county)	2016 estimate	2010 census	% change
Stettin (Marathon)	2,564	2,554	0.39	Waterford (Racine)	6,349	6,344	0.08
Stockton (Portage)	2,983	2,917	2.26	Waukesha (Waukesha) . .	9,175	9,133	0.46
Sugar Creek (Walworth). .	3,935	3,943	-0.20	Wescott (Shawano).	3,205	3,183	0.69
Taycheedah (Fond du Lac)	4,485	4,205	6.66	West Bend (Washington) .	4,758	4,774	-0.34
Trenton (Washington) . . .	4,757	4,732	0.53	Westport (Dane)	4,012	3,950	1.57
Troy (St. Croix).	5,107	4,705	8.54	Wheatland (Kenosha) . . .	3,352	3,373	-0.62
Union (Eau Claire)	2,806	2,663	5.37	Wheaton (Chippewa) . . .	2,777	2,701	2.81
Vernon (Waukesha)	7,647	7,601	0.61	Wilson (Sheboygan)	3,355	3,330	0.75
Washington (Eau Claire). .	7,314	7,134	2.52	Yorkville (Racine)	3,092	3,071	0.68

Sources: Wisconsin Department of Administration, Demographic Services Center, *Official Final Estimates, 1/1/2016, Wisconsin Municipalities, with Comparison to Census 2010*, October 2016.

Wisconsin governors since 1848

	Party	Service	Residence[1]
Nelson Dewey.	Democrat	6/7/1848–1/5/1852	Lancaster
Leonard James Farwell	Whig	1/5/1852–1/2/1854	Madison
William Augustus Barstow	Democrat	1/2/1854–3/21/1856	Waukesha
Arthur McArthur[2]	Democrat	3/21/1856–3/25/1856	Milwaukee
Coles Bashford	Republican	3/25/1856–1/4/1858	Oshkosh
Alexander William Randall	Republican	1/4/1858–1/6/1862	Waukesha
Louis Powell Harvey[3]	Republican	1/6/1862–4/19/1862	Shopiere
Edward Salomon	Republican	4/19/1862–1/4/1864	Milwaukee
James Taylor Lewis.	Republican	1/4/1864–1/1/1866	Columbus
Lucius Fairchild	Republican	1/1/1866–1/1/1872	Madison
Cadwallader Colden Washburn	Republican	1/1/1872–1/5/1874	La Crosse
William Robert Taylor	Democrat	1/5/1874–1/3/1876	Cottage Grove
Harrison Ludington	Republican	1/3/1876–1/7/1878	Milwaukee
William E. Smith.	Republican	1/7/1878–1/2/1882	Milwaukee
Jeremiah McLain Rusk.	Republican	1/2/1882–1/7/1889	Viroqua
William Dempster Hoard	Republican	1/7/1889–1/5/1891	Fort Atkinson
George Wilbur Peck	Democrat	1/5/1891–1/7/1895	Milwaukee
William Henry Upham.	Republican	1/7/1895–1/4/1897	Marshfield
Edward Scofield.	Republican	1/4/1897–1/7/1901	Oconto
Robert Marion La Follette, Sr.[4].	Republican	1/7/1901–1/1/1906	Madison
James O. Davidson.	Republican	1/1/1906–1/2/1911	Soldiers Grove
Francis Edward McGovern	Republican	1/2/1911–1/4/1915	Milwaukee
Emanuel Lorenz Philipp.	Republican	1/4/1915–1/3/1921	Milwaukee
John James Blaine	Republican	1/3/1921–1/3/1927	Boscobel
Fred R. Zimmerman	Republican	1/3/1927–1/7/1929	Milwaukee
Walter Jodok Kohler, Sr..	Republican	1/7/1929–1/5/1931	Kohler
Philip Fox La Follette.	Republican	1/5/1931–1/2/1933	Madison
Albert George Schmedeman.	Democrat	1/2/1933–1/7/1935	Madison
Philip Fox La Follette.	Progressive	1/7/1935–1/2/1939	Madison
Julius Peter Heil.	Republican	1/2/1939–1/4/1943	Milwaukee
Walter Samuel Goodland[3, 5]	Republican	1/4/1943–3/12/1947	Racine
Oscar Rennebohm	Republican	3/12/1947–1/1/1951	Madison
Walter Jodok Kohler, Jr..	Republican	1/1/1951–1/7/1957	Kohler
Vernon Wallace Thomson.	Republican	1/7/1957–1/5/1959	Richland Center
Gaylord Anton Nelson.	Democrat	1/5/1959–1/7/1963	Madison
John W. Reynolds.	Democrat	1/7/1963–1/4/1965	Green Bay
Warren Perley Knowles	Republican	1/4/1965–1/4/1971	New Richmond
Patrick Joseph Lucey[4].	Democrat	1/4/1971–7/6/1977	Madison
Martin James Schreiber.	Democrat	7/6/1977–1/1/1979	Milwaukee
Lee Sherman Dreyfus	Republican	1/1/1979–1/3/1983	Stevens Point
Anthony Scully Earl	Democrat	1/3/1983–1/5/1987	Madison
Tommy George Thompson[4]	Republican	1/5/1987–2/1/2001	Elroy
Scott McCallum.	Republican	2/1/2001–1/6/2003	Fond du Lac
James Edward Doyle, Jr..	Democrat	1/6/2003–1/3/2011	Madison
Scott Kevin Walker	Republican	1/3/2011–	Wauwatosa

Note: Prior to 1971, the term of office was two years rather than four. Prior to 1885, the term of office began in January of an even-numbered rather than an odd-numbered year.

1. Residence at the time of election. 2. Served as acting governor during dispute over outcome of gubernatorial election. 3. Died in office. 4. Resigned. 5. Served as acting governor for the 1943–44 term following the death of Governor-elect Orland Loomis.

Sources: "Wisconsin's Former Governors," 1960 *Wisconsin Blue Book*, pp. 69–206; *Blue Book* biographies.

Vote for governor in general elections since 1848

1848
Nelson Dewey[1]—D 19,875
John H. Tweedy[1]—W 14,621
Charles Durkee[1]—I 1,134
Total. 35,309

1849
Nelson Dewey—D 16,649
Alexander L. Collins—W . . 11,317
Warren Chase—I 3,761
Total. 31,759

1851
Leonard J. Farwell—W . . . 22,319
Don A. J. Upham—D 21,812
Total. 44,190

1853
William A. Barstow—D . . . 30,405
Edward D. Holton—R. . . . 21,886
Henry S. Baird—W 3,304
Total. 55,683

1855
William A. Barstow[2]—D . . 36,355
Coles Bashford—R 36,198
Total. 72,598

1857
Alexander W. Randall—R . 44,693
James B. Cross—D 44,239
Total. 90,058

1859
Alexander W. Randall—R . 59,999
Harrison C. Hobart—D . . . 52,539
Total. 112,755

1861
Louis P. Harvey—R 53,777
Benjamin Ferguson—D . . 45,456
Total. 99,258

1863
James T. Lewis—R. 72,717
Henry L. Palmer—D. 49,053
Total. 122,029

1865
Lucius Fairchild—R 58,332
Harrison C. Hobart—D . . . 48,330
Total. 106,674

1867
Lucius Fairchild—R 73,637
John J. Tallmadge—D . . . 68,873
Total. 142,522

1869
Lucius Fairchild—R 69,502
Charles D. Robinson—D . . 61,239
Total. 130,781

1871
Cadwallader C. Washburn—R
. 78,301
James R. Doolittle—D . . . 68,910
Total. 147,274

1873
William R. Taylor—D 81,599
Cadwallader C. Washburn—R
. 66,224
Total. 147,856

1875
Harrison Ludington—R . . 85,155
William R. Taylor—D . . . 84,314
Total. 170,070

1877
William E. Smith—R. 78,759
James A. Mallory—D 70,486
Edward P. Allis—G. 26,216
Collin M. Campbell—S 2,176
Total. 178,122

1879
William E. Smith—R. . . . 100,535
James G. Jenkins—D 75,030
Reuben May—G. 12,996
Total. 189,005

1881
Jeremiah M. Rusk—R. . . . 81,754
N.D. Fratt—D. 69,797
T.D. Kanouse—Pro 13,225
Edward P. Allis—G 7,002
Total. 171,856

1884
Jeremiah M. Rusk—R . . . 163,214
N.D. Fratt—D. 143,945
Samuel D. Hastings—Pro . .8,545
William L. Utley—G 4,274
Total. 319,997

1886
Jeremiah M. Rusk—R . . . 133,247
Gilbert M. Woodward—D 114,529
John Cochrane—PPop. . . 21,467
John Myers Olin—Pro . . . 17,089
Total. 286,368

1888
William D. Hoard—R . . . 175,696
James Morgan—D 155,423
E.G. Durant—Pro 14,373
D. Frank Powell—L 9,196
Total. 354,714

1890
George W. Peck—D. . . . 160,388
William D. Hoard—R . . . 132,068
Charles Alexander—Pro . . 11,246
Reuben May—UL 5,447
Total. 309,254

1892
George W. Peck—D. . . . 178,095
John C. Spooner—R . . . 170,497
Thomas C. Richmond—Pro 13,185
C.M. Butt—PPop. 9,638
Total. 371,559

1894
William H. Upham—R . . 196,150
George W. Peck—D. . . . 142,250
D. Frank Powell—PPop. . . 25,604
John F. Cleghorn—Pro . . . 11,240
Total. 375,449

1896
Edward Scofield—R. . . . 264,981
Willis C. Silverthorn—D . 169,257
Joshua H. Berkey—Pro . . .8,140
Christ Tuttrop—SL 1,306
Robert Henderson—Nat. . . . 407
Total. 444,110

1898
Edward Scofield—R. . . . 173,137
Hiram W. Sawyer—D . . . 135,353
Albinus A. Worsley—PPop. .8,518
Eugene W. Chafin—Pro . . .8,078
Howard Tuttle—SDA 2,544
Henry Riese—SL. 1,473
Total. 329,430

1900
Robert M. La Follette—R. 264,419
Louis G. Bomrich—D . . . 160,674
J. Burritt Smith—Pro 9,707
Howard Tuttle—SD 6,590
Frank R. Wilke—SL 509
Total. 441,900

1902
Robert M. La Follette—R. 193,417
David S. Rose—D 145,818
Emil Seidel—SD 15,970
Edwin W. Drake—Pro. 9,647
Henry E.D. Puck—SL 791
Total. 365,676

Vote for governor in general elections since 1848, continued

1904
Robert M. La Follette—R. 227,253
George W. Peck—D. . . . 176,301
William A. Arnold—SD . . . 24,857
Edward Scofield—NR. . . . 12,136
William H. Clark—Pro. 8,764
Charles M. Minkley—SL 249
Total. 449,570

1906
James O. Davidson—R . . 183,558
John A. Aylward—D . . . 103,311
Winfield R. Gaylord—SD . . 24,437
Ephraim L. Eaton—Pro. . . .8,211
Ole T. Rosaas—SL 455
Total. 320,003

1908
James O. Davidson—R . . 242,935
John A. Aylward—D . . . 165,977
H.D. Brown—SD 28,583
Winfred D. Cox—Pro 11,760
Herman Bottema—SL 393
Total. 449,656

1910
Francis E. McGovern—R . 161,619
Adolph H. Schmitz—D . . . 110,442
William A. Jacobs—SD . . . 39,547
Byron E. Van Keuren—Pro. .7,450
Fred G. Kremer—SL. 430
Total. 319,522

1912
Francis E. McGovern—R . 179,360
John C. Karel—D 167,316
Carl D. Thompson—SD. . . 34,468
Charles L. Hill—Pro 9,433
William H. Curtis—SL. 3,253
Total. 393,849

1914
Emanuel L. Philipp—R . . 140,787
John C. Karel—D 119,509
John J. Blaine—I. 32,560
Oscar Ameringer—SD . . . 25,917
David W. Emerson—Pro . . .6,279
John Vierthaler—I. 352
Total. 325,430

1916
Emanuel L. Philipp—R . . 229,889
Burt Williams—D 164,555
Rae Weaver—Soc 30,649
George McKerrow—Pro . . .9,193
Total. 434,340

1918
Emanuel L. Philipp—R . . 155,799
Henry A. Moehlenpah—D 112,576
Emil Seidel—SD 57,523
William C. Dean—Pro. 5,296
Total. 331,582

1920
John J. Blaine—R 366,247
Robert McCoy—D. 247,746
William Coleman—S 71,126
Henry H. Tubbs—Pro 6,047
Total. 691,294

1922
John J. Blaine—R 367,929
Arthur A. Bentley—ID . . . 51,061
Louis A. Arnold—S 39,570
M.L. Welles—Pro. 21,438
Arthur A. Dietrich—ISL. . . .1,444
Total. 481,828

1924
John J. Blaine—R 412,255
Martin L. Lueck—D 317,550
William F. Quick—S 45,268
Adolph R. Bucknam—Pro . 11,516
Severi Alanne—IW 4,107
Farrand K. Shuttleworth—IPR 4,079
Jose Snover—SL. 1,452
Total. 796,432

1926
Fred R. Zimmerman—R . 350,927
Charles Perry—I 76,507
Virgil H. Cady—D 72,627
Herman O. Kent—S 40,293
David W. Emerson—Pro . . .7,333
Alex Gorden—SL 4,593
Total. 552,912

1928
Walter J. Kohler, Sr—R . . 547,738
Albert G. Schmedeman—D 394,368
Otto R. Hauser—S. 36,924
Adolph R. Bucknam—Pro . .6,477
Joseph Ehrhardt—IL 1,938
Alvar J. Hayes—IW 1,420
Total. 989,143

1930
Philip F. La Follette—R . . 392,958
Charles E. Hammersley—D 170,020
Frank B. Metcalfe—S 25,607
Alfred B. Taynton—Pro. . . 14,818
Fred B. Blair—IC 2,998
Total. 606,825

1932
Albert G. Schmedeman—D
. . . . 590,114
Walter J. Kohler, Sr—R . . 470,805
Frank B. Metcalfe—S 56,965
William C. Dean—Pro. 3,148
Fred B. Blair—Com 2,926
Joe Ehrhardt—SL 398
Total. 1,124,502

1934
Philip F. La Follette—P . . 373,093
Albert G. Schmedeman—D
. 359,467
Howard Greene—R 172,980
George A. Nelson—S 44,589
Morris Childs—IC 2,454
Thomas W. North—IPro 857
Joe Ehrhardt—ISL. 332
Total. 953,797

1936
Philip F. La Follette—P . . 573,724
Alexander Wiley—R. . . . 363,973
Arthur W. Lueck—D. . . . 268,530
Joseph F. Walsh—U 27,934
Joseph Ehrhardt—SL. 1,738
August F. Fehlandt—Pro. . .1,008
Total. 1,237,095

1938
Julius P. Heil—R 543,675
Philip F. La Follette—P . . . 353,381
Harry W. Bolens—D. 78,446
Frank W. Smith—U 4,564
John Schleier, Jr—ISL. 1,459
Total. 981,560

1940
Julius P. Heil—R 558,678
Orland S. Loomis—P . . . 546,436
Francis E. McGovern—D. 264,985
Fred B. Blair—Com 2,340
Louis Fisher—SL. 1,158
Total. 1,373,754

1942
Orland S. Loomis—P . . . 397,664
Julius P. Heil—R 291,945
William C. Sullivan—D . . . 98,153
Frank P. Zeidler—S 11,295
Fred Bassett Blair—IC 1,092
Georgia Cozzini—ISL. 490
Total. 800,985

Vote for governor in general elections since 1848, continued

1944
Walter S. Goodland—R. . 697,740
Daniel W. Hoan—D 536,357
Alexander O. Benz—P . . . 76,028
George A. Nelson—S 9,183
Georgia Cozzini—I (ISL) . . .1,122
Total. 1,320,483

1946
Walter S. Goodland—R. . 621,970
Daniel W. Hoan—D 406,499
Walter H. Uphoff—S 8,996
Sigmund G. Eisenscher—IC 1,857
Jerry R. Kenyon—ISL 959
Total. 1,040,444

1948
Oscar Rennebohm—R . . 684,839
Carl W. Thompson—D . . 558,497
Henry J. Berquist—PP . . . 12,928
Walter H. Uphoff—S 9,149
James E. Boulton—ISW 356
Georgia Cozzini—ISL 328
Total. 1,266,139

1950
Walter J. Kohler, Jr—R . . 605,649
Carl W. Thompson—D . . 525,319
M. Michael Essin—PP. 3,735
William O. Hart—S 3,384
Total. 1,138,148

1952
Walter J. Kohler, Jr—R . 1,009,171
William Proxmire—D . . . 601,844
M. Michael Essin—I 3,706
Total. 1,615,214

1954
Walter J. Kohler, Jr—R . . 596,158
William Proxmire—D . . . 560,747
Arthur Wepfer—I 1,722
Total. 1,158,666

1956
Vernon W. Thomson—R . 808,273
William Proxmire—D . . . 749,421
Total. 1,557,788

1958
Gaylord A. Nelson—D . . 644,296
Vernon W. Thomson—R . 556,391
Wayne Leverenz—I 1,485
Total. 1,202,219

1960
Gaylord A. Nelson—D . . 890,868
Philip G. Kuehn—R 837,123
Total. 1,728,009

1962
John W. Reynolds—D. . . 637,491
Philip G. Kuehn—R 625,536
Adolf Wiggert—I 2,477
Total. 1,265,900

1964
Warren P. Knowles—R . . 856,779
John W. Reynolds—D. . . 837,901
Total. 1,694,887

1966
Warren P. Knowles—R . . 626,041
Patrick J. Lucey—D 539,258
Adolf Wiggert—I 4,745
Total. 1,170,173

1968
Warren P. Knowles—R . . 893,463
Bronson C. La Follette—D 791,100
Adolf Wiggert—I 3,225
Robert Wilkinson—I 1,813
Total. 1,689,738

1970
Patrick J. Lucey—D 728,403
Jack B. Olson—R. 602,617
Leo J. McDonald—A 9,035
Georgia Cozzini—I (SL). . . .1,287
Samuel K. Hunt—I (SW) . . . 888
Myrtle Kastner—I (PLS) 628
Total. 1,343,160

1974
Patrick J. Lucey—D 628,639
William D. Dyke—R 497,189
William H. Upham—A . . . 33,528
Crazy Jim[3]—I. 12,107
William Hart—I (DS) 5,113
Fred Blair—I (C) 3,617
Georgia Cozzini—I (SL). . . .1,492
Total. 1,181,685

1978
Lee S. Dreyfus—R 816,056
Martin J. Schreiber—D. . . 673,813
Eugene R. Zimmerman—C . 6,355
John C. Doherty—I 2,183
Adrienne Kaplan—I (SW) . .1,548
Henry A. Ochsner—I (SL) . . . 849
Total. 1,500,996

1982
Anthony S. Earlv—D . . . 896,872
Terry J. Kohler—R 662,738
Larry Smiley—Lib 9,734
James P. Wickstrom—Con . .7,721
Peter Seidman—I (SW). . . .3,025
Total. 1,580,344

1986
Tommy G. Thompson—R
. . . . 805,090
Anthony S. Earl—D 705,578
Kathryn A. Christensen—LF 10,323
Darold E. Wall—I. 3,913
Sanford Knapp—I. 1,668
Total. 1,526,573

1990
Tommy G. Thompson—R
. . . . 802,321
Thomas A. Loftus—D. . . 576,280
Total. 1,379,727

1994
Tommy G. Thompson—R 1,051,326
Charles J.Chvala—D . . . 482,850
David S. Harmon—Lib . . . 11,639
Edward J. Frami—Tax. 9,188
Michael J. Mangan—I . . .8,150
Total. 1,563,835

1998
Tommy G. Thompson—R
. 1,047,716
Ed Garvey—D 679,553
Jim Mueller—Lib 11,071
Edward J. Frami—Tax. . . . 10,269
Mike Mangan—I. 4,985
A-Ja-mu Muhammad—I . . .1,604
Jeffrey L. Smith—WG. 14
Total. 1,756,014

2002
Jim Doyle—D 800,515
Scott McCallum—R. . . . 734,779
Ed Thompson—Lib 185,455
Jim Young—WG. 44,111
Alan D. Eisenberg—I 2,847
Ty A. Bollerud—I. 2,637
Mike Mangan—I. 1,710
Aneb Jah Rasta Sensas-Utcha
Nefer-I—I 929
Total. 1,775,349

2006
Jim Doyle—D 1,139,115
Mark Green—R 979,427
Nelson Eisman—WG 40,709
Total. 2,161,700

2010
Scott Walker—R 1,128,941
Tom Barrett—D 1,004,303
Jim Langer—I 10,608
James James—I 8,273
Total[4]. 2,160,832

Vote for governor in general elections since 1848, continued

June 5, 2012 recall election	
Scott Walker—R	1,335,585
Tom Barrett—D	1,164,480
Hari Trivedi—I	14,463
Total	**2,516,065**

2014	
Scott Walker—R	1,259,706
Mary Burke—D	1,122,913
Robert Burke—I (Lib)	18,720
Dennis Fehr—I (Peo)	7,530
Total	**2,410,314**

Note: A candidate whose party did not receive 1% of the vote for a statewide office in the previous election or who failed to meet the alternative requirement of section 5.62, Wis. Stats., is listed on the Wisconsin ballot as "independent." When a candidate's party affiliation is listed as "I," followed by a party designation in parentheses, "independent" was the official ballot listing, but a party designation was found by the Wisconsin Legislative Reference Bureau in newspaper reports.

Totals include scattered votes for other candidates.

A—American	ISL—Independent Socialist Labor	PPop—People's (Populist)
C—Conservative	ISW—Independent Socialist	Pro—Prohibition
Com—Communist	Worker	R—Republican
Con—Constitution	IW—Independent Worker	S—Socialist
D—Democrat	L—Labor	SD—Social Democrat
DS—Democratic Socialist	LF—Labor-Farm/Laborista-	SDA—Social Democrat of
G—Greenback	Agrario	America
I—Independent	Lib—Libertarian	SL—Socialist Labor
IC—Independent Communist	Nat—National	SW—Socialist Worker
ID—Independent Democrat	NR—National Republic	Tax—U.S. Taxpayers
IL—Independent Labor	P—Progressive	U—Union
IPR—Independent Prohibition	Peo—People's	UL—Union Labor
Republic	PLS—Progressive Labor Socialist	W—Whig
IPro—Independent Prohibition	PP—People's Progressive	WG—Wisconsin Green

1. Votes for Dewey and Tweedy are from 1874 *Blue Book*; Durkee vote is based on county returns, as filed in the Office of the Secretary of State, but returns from Manitowoc and Winnebago Counties were missing. Without these 2 counties, Dewey had 19,605 votes and Tweedy had 14,514 votes.   2. Barstow's plurality was set aside in *Atty. Gen. ex rel. Bashford v. Barstow*, 4 Wis. 567 (1855) because of irregularities in the election returns.   3. Legal name.   4. Total includes 6,780 votes for the Libertarian ticket, which had a candidate for lieutenant governor, but no candidate for governor.

Source: Canvass reports and Wisconsin Elections Commission records.

Wisconsin lieutenant governors since 1848

	Party	Service	Residence[1]
John E. Holmes	Democrat	1848–1850	Jefferson
Samuel W. Beall	Democrat	1850–1852	Taycheedah
Timothy Burns	Democrat	1852–1854	La Crosse
James T. Lewis	Republican	1854–1856	Columbus
Arthur McArthur[2]	Democrat	1856–1858	Milwaukee
Erasmus D. Campbell	Democrat	1858–1860	La Crosse
Butler G. Noble	Republican	1860–1862	Whitewater
Edward Salomon[3]	Republican	1862–1864	Milwaukee
Wyman Spooner	Republican	1864–1870	Elkhorn
Thaddeus C. Pound	Republican	1870–1872	Chippewa Falls
Milton H. Pettit[4]	Republican	1872–3/23/73	Kenosha
Charles D. Parker	Democrat	1874–1878	Pleasant Valley
James M. Bingham	Republican	1878–1882	Chippewa Falls
Sam S. Fifield	Republican	1882–1887	Ashland
George W. Ryland	Republican	1887–1891	Lancaster
Charles Jonas	Democrat	1891–1895	Racine
Emil Baensch	Republican	1895–1899	Manitowoc
Jesse Stone	Republican	1899–1903	Watertown
James O. Davidson[5]	Republican	1903–1907	Soldiers Grove

Wisconsin lieutenant governors since 1848, continued

	Party	Service	Residence[1]
William D. Connor	Republican	1907–1909	Marshfield
John Strange	Republican	1909–1911	Oshkosh
Thomas Morris	Republican	1911–1915	La Crosse
Edward F. Dithmar	Republican	1915–1921	Baraboo
George F. Comings	Republican	1921–1925	Eau Claire
Henry A. Huber	Republican	1925–1933	Stoughton
Thomas J. O'Malley	Democrat	1933–1937	Milwaukee
Henry A. Gunderson[6]	Progressive	1937–10/16/37	Portage
Herman L. Ekern[7]	Progressive	5/16/38–1939	Madison
Walter S. Goodland[8]	Republican	1939–1945	Racine
Oscar Rennebohm[9]	Republican	1945–1949	Madison
George M. Smith	Republican	1949–1955	Milwaukee
Warren P. Knowles	Republican	1955–1959	New Richmond
Philleo Nash	Democrat	1959–1961	Wisconsin Rapids
Warren P. Knowles	Republican	1961–1963	New Richmond
Jack Olson	Republican	1963–1965	Wisconsin Dells
Patrick J. Lucey	Democrat	1965–1967	Madison
Jack Olson	Republican	1967–1971	Wisconsin Dells
Martin J. Schreiber[10]	Democrat	1971–1979	Milwaukee
Russell A. Olson	Republican	1979–1983	Randall
James T. Flynn	Democrat	1983–1987	West Allis
Scott McCallum[11]	Republican	1987–2/1/01	Fond du Lac
Margaret A. Farrow[12]	Republican	5/9/01–2003	Pewaukee
Barbara Lawton	Democrat	2003–2011	Green Bay
Rebecca Kleefisch	Republican	2011–	Oconomowoc

Note: Prior to 1971, the term of office was two years rather than four. Prior to 1885, the term of office began in January of an even-numbered rather than an odd-numbered year. Prior to 1979, lieutenant governors did not cease to hold the office of lieutenant governor while acting in place of a governor who had died or resigned.

1. Residence at the time of election. 2. Served as acting governor 3/21/1856 to 3/25/1856 during dispute over outcome of gubernatorial election. 3. Became acting governor on the death of Governor Harvey, 4/19/1862. 4. Died in office. 5. Became acting governor when Governor La Follette resigned, 1/1/1906. 6. Resigned. 7. Appointed to serve the rest of Gunderson's term. 8. Became acting governor on the death of Governor-elect Orland Loomis, 1/1/1943. 9. Became acting governor on the death of Governor Goodland, 3/12/1947. 10. Became acting governor when Governor Lucey resigned, 7/6/1977. 11. Became governor when Governor Thompson resigned, 2/1/2001. 12. Appointed to serve the rest of McCallum's term.

Source: Wisconsin Legislative Reference Bureau, *Wisconsin Blue Book*, various editions, and bureau records.

Wisconsin attorneys general since 1848

	Party	Service	Residence[1]
James S. Brown	Democrat	1848–1850	Milwaukee
S. Park Coon	Democrat	1850–1852	Milwaukee
Experience Estabrook	Democrat	1852–1854	Geneva
George B. Smith	Democrat	1854–1856	Madison
William R. Smith	Democrat	1856–1858	Mineral Point
Gabriel Bouck	Democrat	1858–1860	Oshkosh
James H. Howe[2]	Republican	1860–1862	Green Bay
Winfield Smith[3]	Republican	1862–1866	Milwaukee
Charles R. Gill	Republican	1866–1870	Watertown
Stephen Steele Barlow	Republican	1870–1874	Dellona
Andrew Scott Sloan	Republican	1874–1878	Beaver Dam
Alexander Wilson	Republican	1878–1882	Mineral Point
Leander F. Frisby	Republican	1882–1887	West Bend
Charles E. Estabrook	Republican	1887–1891	Manitowoc

Wisconsin attorneys general since 1848, continued

	Party	Service	Residence[1]
James L. O'Connor	Democrat	1891–1895	Madison
William H. Mylrea	Republican	1895–1899	Wausau
Emmett R. Hicks	Republican	1899–1903	Oshkosh
Lafayette M. Sturdevant	Republican	1903–1907	Neillsville
Frank L. Gilbert	Republican	1907–1911	Madison
Levi H. Bancroft	Republican	1911–1913	Richland Center
Walter C. Owen[4]	Republican	1913–1918	Maiden Rock
Spencer Haven[5]	Republican	1918–1919	Hudson
John J. Blaine	Republican	1919–1921	Boscobel
William J. Morgan	Republican	1921–1923	Milwaukee
Herman L. Ekern	Republican	1923–1927	Madison
John W. Reynolds	Republican	1927–1933	Green Bay
James E. Finnegan	Democrat	1933–1937	Milwaukee
Orlando S. Loomis	Progressive	1937–1939	Mauston
John E. Martin[2]	Republican	1939–6/1/48	Madison
Grover L. Broadfoot[6]	Republican	6/5/48–11/12/48	Mondovi
Thomas E. Fairchild[7]	Democrat	11/12/48–1951	Verona
Vernon W. Thomson	Republican	1951–1957	Richland Center
Stewart G. Honeck	Republican	1957–1959	Madison
John W. Reynolds	Democrat	1959–1963	Green Bay
George Thompson	Republican	1963–1965	Madison
Bronson C. La Follette	Democrat	1965–1969	Madison
Robert W. Warren[2]	Republican	1969–10/8/74	Green Bay
Victor A. Miller[8]	Democrat	10/8/74–11/25/74	St. Nazianz
Bronson C. La Follette[9]	Democrat	11/25/74–1987	Madison
Donald J. Hanaway	Republican	1987–1991	Green Bay
James E. Doyle	Democrat	1991–2003	Madison
Peggy A. Lautenschlager	Democrat	2003–2007	Fond du Lac
J.B. Van Hollen	Republican	2007–2015	Waunakee
Brad D. Schimel	Republican	2015–	Waukesha

Note: Prior to 1971, the term of office was two years rather than four. Prior to 1885, the term of office began in January of an even-numbered rather than an odd-numbered year.

1. Residence at the time of election. 2. Resigned. 3. Appointed 10/7/1862 to serve the rest of Howe's term. 4. Resigned 1/7/1918. 5. Appointed to serve the rest of Owen's term. 6. Appointed to serve the rest of Martin's term. Resigned. 7. Attorney General-elect Fairchild appointed to serve the rest of Martin's term. 8. Appointed to serve the rest of Warren's term. Resigned. 9. Attorney General-elect La Follette appointed to serve the rest of Warren's term.

Source: Wisconsin Legislative Reference Bureau, *Wisconsin Blue Book*, various editions, and bureau records.

Wisconsin superintendents of public instruction since 1849

	Service	Residence[1]
Eleazer Root	1849–1852	Waukesha
Azel P. Ladd	1852–1854	Shullsburg
Hiram A. Wright	1854–1855	Prairie du Chien
A. Constantine Barry	1855–1858	Racine
Lyman C. Draper	1858–1860	Madison
Josiah L. Pickard	1860–1864	Platteville
John G. McMynn	1864–1868	Racine
Alexander J. Craig	1868–1870	Madison
Samuel Fallows	1870–1874	Milwaukee
Edward Searing	1874–1878	Milton
William Clarke Whitford	1878–1882	Milton
Robert Graham	1882–1887	Oshkosh

Wisconsin superintendents of public instruction since 1849, continued

	Service	Residence[1]
Jesse B. Thayer	1887–1891	River Falls
Oliver Elwin Wells	1891–1895	Appleton
John Q. Emery	1895–1899	Albion
Lorenzo D. Harvey	1899–1903	Milwaukee
Charles P. Cary	1903–1921	Delavan
John Callahan	1921–1949	Madison
George Earl Watson	1949–1961	Wauwatosa
Angus B. Rothwell[2]	1961–7/1/66	Manitowoc
William C. Kahl[3]	7/1/66–1973	Madison
Barbara Thompson	1973–1981	Madison
Herbert J. Grover[4]	1981–4/9/93	Cottage Grove
John T. Benson	1993–2001	Marshall
Elizabeth Burmaster	2001–2009	Madison
Tony Evers	2009–	Madison

Note: Prior to 1971, the term of office was two years rather than four. Prior to 1885, the term of office began in January of an even-numbered rather than an odd-numbered year. From 1905 onward, the term of office began in July rather than in January and the office was filled at the nonpartisan spring election rather than at the November general election.

1. Residence at the time of election. 2. Resigned. 3. Appointed to serve the rest of Rothwell's term.
4. Resigned. Lee Sherman Dreyfus was appointed to serve as "interim superintendent" for the rest of Grover's term but did not officially become superintendent.

Source: Wisconsin Legislative Reference Bureau, *Wisconsin Blue Book*, various editions, and bureau records.

Wisconsin secretaries of state since 1848

	Party	Service	Residence[1]
Thomas McHugh	Democrat	1848–1850	Delavan
William A. Barstow	Democrat	1850–1852	Waukesha
Charles D. Robinson	Democrat	1852–1854	Green Bay
Alexander T. Gray	Democrat	1854–1856	Janesville
David W. Jones	Democrat	1856–1860	Belmont
Lewis P. Harvey	Republican	1860–1862	Shopiere
James T. Lewis	Republican	1862–1864	Columbus
Lucius Fairchild	Republican	1864–1866	Madison
Thomas S. Allen	Republican	1866–1870	Mineral Point
Llywelyn Breese	Republican	1870–1874	Portage
Peter Doyle	Democrat	1874–1878	Prairie du Chien
Hans B. Warner	Republican	1878–1882	Ellsworth
Ernst G. Timme	Republican	1882–1891	Kenosha
Thomas J. Cunningham	Democrat	1891–1895	Chippewa Falls
Henry Casson	Republican	1895–1899	Viroqua
William H. Froehlich	Republican	1899–1903	Jackson
Walter L. Houser	Republican	1903–1907	Mondovi
James A. Frear	Republican	1907–1913	Hudson
John S. Donald	Republican	1913–1917	Mt. Horeb
Merlin Hull	Republican	1917–1921	Black River Falls
Elmer S. Hall	Republican	1921–1923	Green Bay
Fred R. Zimmerman	Republican	1923–1927	Milwaukee
Theodore Dammann	Republican	1927–1935	Milwaukee
Theodore Dammann	Progressive	1935–1939	Milwaukee
Fred R. Zimmerman[2]	Republican	1939–12/14/54	Milwaukee
Louis Allis[3]	Republican	12/16/54–1/3/55	Milwaukee
Mrs. Glenn M. Wise[4]	Republican	1/3/55–1957	Madison
Robert C. Zimmerman	Republican	1957–1975	Madison

Wisconsin secretaries of state since 1848, continued

	Party	Service	Residence[1]
Douglas J. La Follette	Democrat	1975–1979	Kenosha
Mrs. Vel R. Phillips	Democrat	1979–1983	Milwaukee
Douglas J. La Follette	Democrat	1983–	Madison

Note: Prior to 1971, the term of office was two years rather than four. Prior to 1885, the term of office began in January of an even-numbered rather than an odd-numbered year.

1. Residence at the time of election. 2. Died after being reelected for a new term but before the new term began. 3. Appointed to serve the rest of Zimmerman's unfinished term. 4. Appointed to serve Zimmerman's new term.

Source: Wisconsin Legislative Reference Bureau, *Wisconsin Blue Book*, various editions, and bureau records.

Wisconsin state treasurers since 1848

	Party	Service	Residence[1]
Jarius C. Fairchild	Democrat	1848–1852	Madison
Edward H. Janssen	Democrat	1852–1856	Cedarburg
Charles Kuehn	Democrat	1856–1858	Manitowoc
Samuel D. Hastings	Republican	1858–1866	Trempealeau
William E. Smith	Republican	1866–1870	Fox Lake
Henry Baetz	Republican	1870–1874	Manitowoc
Ferdinand Kuehn	Democrat	1874–1878	Milwaukee
Richard Guenther	Republican	1878–1882	Oshkosh
Edward C. McFetridge	Republican	1882–1887	Beaver Dam
Henry B. Harshaw	Republican	1887–1891	Oshkosh
John Hunner	Democrat	1891–1895	Eau Claire
Sewell A. Peterson	Republican	1895–1899	Rice Lake
James O. Davidson	Republican	1899–1903	Soldiers Grove
John J. Kempf[2]	Republican	1903–7/30/04	Milwaukee
Thomas M. Purtell[3]	Republican	7/30/04–1905	Cumberland
John J. Kempf	Republican	1905–1907	Milwaukee
Andrew H. Dahl	Republican	1907–1913	Westby
Henry Johnson	Republican	1913–1923	Suring
Solomon Levitan	Republican	1923–1933	Madison
Robert K. Henry	Democrat	1933–1937	Jefferson
Solomon Levitan	Progressive	1937–1939	Madison
John M. Smith[4]	Republican	1939–8/17/47	Shell Lake
John L. Sonderegger[5]	Republican	8/19/47–9/30/48	Madison
Clyde M. Johnston (appointed from staff)[5]		10/1/48–1949	Madison
Warren R. Smith[4]	Republican	1949–12/4/57	Milwaukee
Mrs. Dena A. Smith[5]	Republican	12/5/57–1959	Milwaukee
Eugene M. Lamb	Democrat	1959–1961	Milwaukee
Mrs. Dena A. Smith[4]	Republican	1961–2/20/68	Milwaukee
Harold W. Clemens[5]	Republican	2/21/68–1971	Oconomowoc
Charles P. Smith	Democrat	1971–1991	Madison
Cathy S. Zeuske	Republican	1991–1995	Shawano
Jack C. Voight	Republican	1995–2007	Appleton
Dawn Marie Sass	Democrat	2007–2011	Milwaukee
Kurt W. Schuller	Republican	2011–2015	Eden
Matt Adamczyk	Republican	2015–	Wauwatosa

Note: Prior to 1971, the term of office was two years rather than four. Prior to 1885, the term of office began in January of an even-numbered rather than an odd-numbered year.

1. Residence at the time of election. 2. Vacated office by failure to give the required bond. 3. Appointed to serve the rest of Kempf's term. 4. Died in office. 5. Appointed.

Source: Wisconsin Legislative Reference Bureau, *Wisconsin Blue Book*, various editions, and bureau records.

Justices of the Wisconsin Supreme Court since 1836

	Service	Residence[1]
Judges during the territorial period		
Charles Dunn (Chief Justice)[2]	1836–1848	
William C. Frazier	1836–1838	
David Irvin	1836–1838	
Andrew G. Miller	1836–1848	
Circuit judges who served as justices 1848–1853[3]		
Alexander W. Stow	1848–1851 (C.J.)	Fond du Lac
Levi Hubbell	1848–1853 (C.J. 1851)	Milwaukee
Edward V. Whiton	1848–1853 (C.J. 1852–53)	Janesville
Charles H. Larrabee	1848–1853	Horicon
Mortimer M. Jackson	1848–1853	Mineral Point
Wiram Knowlton	1850–1853	Prairie du Chien
Timothy O. Howe	1851–1853	Green Bay
Justices since 1853		
Edward V. Whiton	1853–1859 (C.J.)	Janesville
Samuel Crawford	1853–1855	New Diggings
Abram D. Smith	1853–1859	Milwaukee
Orsamus Cole	1855–1892 (C.J. 1880–92)	Potosi
Luther S. Dixon[4]	1859–1874 (C.J.)	Portage
Byron Paine[4]	1859–1864, 1867–71	Milwaukee
Jason Downer[4]	1864–1867	Milwaukee
William P. Lyon[4]	1871–1894 (C.J. 1892–94)	Racine
Edward G. Ryan[4]	1874–1880 (C.J.)	Racine
David Taylor	1878–1891	Sheboygan
Harlow S. Orton	1878–1895 (C.J. 1894–95)	Madison
John B. Cassoday[4]	1880–1907 (C.J. 1895–07)	Janesville
John B. Winslow[4]	1891–1920 (C.J. 1907–20)	Racine
Silas U. Pinney	1892–1898	Madison
Alfred W. Newman	1894–1898	Trempealeau
Roujet D. Marshall[4]	1895–1918	Chippewa Falls
Charles V. Bardeen[4]	1898–1903	Wausau
Joshua Eric Dodge[4]	1898–1910	Milwaukee
Robert G. Siebecker[5]	1903–1922 (C.J. 1920–22)	Madison
James C. Kerwin	1905–1921	Neenah
William H. Timlin	1907–1916	Milwaukee
Robert M. Bashford[4]	Jan.–June 1908	Madison
John Barnes	1908–1916	Rhinelander
Aad J. Vinje[4]	1910–1929 (C.J. 1922–29)	Superior
Marvin B. Rosenberry[4]	1916–1950 (C.J. 1929–50)	Wausau
Franz C. Eschweiler[4]	1916–1929	Milwaukee
Walter C. Owen	1918–1934	Maiden Rock
Burr W. Jones[4]	1920–1926	Madison
Christian Doerfler[4]	1921–1929	Milwaukee
Charles H. Crownhart[4]	1922–1930	Madison
E. Ray Stevens	1926–1930	Madison
Chester A. Fowler[4]	1929–1948	Fond du Lac
Oscar M. Fritz[4]	1929–1954 (C.J. 1950–54)	Milwaukee
Edward T. Fairchild[4]	1929–1957 (C.J. 1954–57)	Milwaukee
John D. Wickhem[4]	1930–1949	Madison
George B. Nelson[4]	1930–1942	Stevens Point
Theodore G. Lewis[4]	Nov. 15–Dec. 5, 1934	Madison
Joseph Martin[4]	1934–1946	Green Bay
Elmer E. Barlow[4]	1942–1948	Arcadia
James Ward Rector[4]	1946–1947	Madison
Henry P. Hughes	1948–1951	Oshkosh
John E. Martin[4]	1948–1962 (C.J. 1957–62)	Green Bay
Grover L. Broadfoot[4]	1948–1962 (C.J. Jan.–May 1962)	Mondovi
Timothy Brown[4]	1949–1964 (C.J. 1962–64)	Madison

Justices of the Wisconsin Supreme Court since 1836, continued

	Service	Residence[1]
Edward J. Gehl	1950–1956	Hartford
George R. Currie[4]	1951–1968 (C.J. 1964–68)	Sheboygan
Roland J. Steinle[4]	1954–1958	Milwaukee
Emmert L. Wingert[4]	1956–1959	Madison
Thomas E. Fairchild	1957–1966	Verona
E. Harold Hallows[4]	1958–1974 (C.J. 1968–74)	Milwaukee
William H. Dieterich	1959–1964	Milwaukee
Myron L. Gordon	1962–1967	Milwaukee
Horace W. Wilkie[4]	1962–1976 (C.J. 1974–76)	Madison
Bruce F. Beilfuss	1964–1983 (C.J. 1976–83)	Neillsville
Nathan S. Heffernan[4]	1964–1995 (C.J. 1983–95)	Sheboygan
Leo B. Hanley[4]	1966–1978	Milwaukee
Connor T. Hansen[4]	1967–1980	Eau Claire
Robert W. Hansen	1968–1978	Milwaukee
Roland B. Day[4]	1974–1996 (C.J. 1995–96)	Madison
Shirley S. Abrahamson[4]	1976– (C.J. 1996–2015)	Madison
William G. Callow	1978–1992	Waukesha
John L. Coffey	1978–1982	Milwaukee
Donald W. Steinmetz	1980–1999	Milwaukee
Louis J. Ceci[4]	1982–1993	Milwaukee
William A. Bablitch	1983–2003	Stevens Point
Jon P. Wilcox[4]	1992–2007	Wautoma
Janine P. Geske[4]	1993–1998	Milwaukee
Ann Walsh Bradley	1995–	Wausau
N. Patrick Crooks	1996–2015	Green Bay
David T. Prosser, Jr.[4]	1998–2016	Appleton
Diane S. Sykes[4]	1999–2004	Milwaukee
Patience D. Roggensack	2003– (C.J. 2015–)	Madison
Louis B. Butler, Jr.[4]	2004–2008	Milwaukee
Annette K. Ziegler	2007–	West Bend
Michael J. Gableman	2008–	Webster
Rebecca Grassl Bradley[4]	2015–	Milwaukee
Daniel Kelly[4]	2016–	North Prairie

Note: The structure of the Wisconsin Supreme Court has varied. There were three justices during the territorial period. From 1848 to 1853, circuit judges acted as supreme court judges—five from 1848 to 1850 and six from 1850 to 1853. From 1853 to 1877, there were three elected justices. The number was increased to five in 1877, and to seven in 1903.

C.J.—chief justice.

1. Residence at the time of election or appointment.   2. Before 1889, the chief justice was elected or appointed to the position. From 1889 to 2015, the most senior justice seved as chief justice. From 2015 onward, the justices have elected one of themselves to be chief justice for a two-year term.   3. Circuit judges acted as Supreme Court justices from1848 to 1853.   4. Initially appointed to the court.   5. Siebecker was elected April 7, 1903, but prior to inauguration for his elected term was appointed April 9, 1903, to fill the vacancy caused by the death of Justice Bardeen.

Sources: Wisconsin Legislative Reference Bureau, *Wisconsin Blue Book*, 1935, 1944, 1977; Wisconsin Elections Commission; Wisconsin Supreme Court, *Wisconsin Reports*, various volumes.

Senate presidents, or presidents pro tempore, and assembly speakers since 1848

Session	Senate presidents or presidents pro tempore[1]	Residence[2]	Assembly speakers	Residence[2]
1848.	—	—	Ninian E. Whiteside—D	Lafayette County
1849.	—	—	Harrison C. Hobart—D	Sheboygan
1850.	—	—	Moses M. Strong—D	Mineral Point
1851.	—	—	Frederick W. Horn—D	Cedarburg
1852.	E.B. Dean, Jr.—D	Madison	James M. Shafter—W	Sheboygan
1853.	Duncan C. Reed—D	Milwaukee	Henry L. Palmer—D	Milwaukee
1854.	Benjamin Allen—D	Hudson	Frederick W. Horn—D	Cedarburg
1855.	Eleazor Wakeley—D	Whitewater	Charles C. Sholes—R	Kenosha
1856.	Louis Powell Harvey—R	Shopiere	William Hull—D	Grant County
1857.	—	—	Wyman Spooner—R	Elkhorn
1858.	Hiram H. Giles—R	Stoughton	Frederick S. Lovell—R	Kenosha County
1859.	Dennison Worthington—R	Summit	William P. Lyon—R	Racine
1860.	Moses M. Davis—R	Portage	William P. Lyon—R	Racine
1861.	Alden I. Bennett—R	Beloit	Amasa Cobb—R	Mineral Point
1862.	Frederick O. Thorp—D	West Bend	James W. Beardsley—UD	Prescott
1863.	Wyman Spooner—R	Elkhorn	J. Allen Barber—R	Lancaster
1864.	Smith S. Wilkinson—R	Prairie du Sac	William W. Field—U	Fennimore
1865.	Willard H. Chandler—U	Windsor	William W. Field—U	Fennimore
1866.	Willard H. Chandler—U	Windsor	Henry D. Barron—U	St. Croix Falls
1867.	George F. Wheeler—U	Nanuapa	Angus Cameron—U	La Crosse
1868.	Newton M. Littlejohn—R	Whitewater	Alexander M. Thomson—R	Janesville
1869.	George C. Hazelton—R	Boscobel	Alexander M. Thomson—R	Janesville
1870.	David Taylor—R	Sheboygan	James M. Bingham—R	Palmyra
1871.	Charles G. Williams—R	Janesville	William E. Smith—R	Fox Lake
1872.	Charles G. Williams—R	Janesville	Daniel Hall—R	Watertown
1873.	Henry L. Eaton—R	Lone Rock	Henry D. Barron—R	St. Croix Falls
1874.	John C. Holloway—R	Lancaster	Gabriel Bouck—D	Oshkosh
1875.	Henry D. Barron—R	St. Croix Falls	Frederick W. Horn—R	Cedarburg
1876.	Robert L.D. Potter—R	Wautoma	Sam S. Fifield—R	Ashland
1877.	William H. Hiner—R	Fond du Lac	John B. Cassoday—R	Janesville
1878.	Levi W. Barden—R	Portage	Augustus R. Barrows—GB	Chippewa Falls
1879.	William T. Price—R	Black River Falls	David M. Kelly—R	Green Bay
1880.	Thomas B. Scott—R	Grand Rapids	Alexander A. Arnold—R	Galesville
1881.	Thomas B. Scott—R	Grand Rapids	Ira B. Bradford—R	Augusta
1882.	George B. Burrows—R	Madison	Franklin L. Gilson—R	Ellsworth
1883.	George W. Ryland—R	Lancaster	Earl P. Finch—D	Oshkosh
1885.	Edward S. Minor—R	Sturgeon Bay	Hiram O. Fairchild—R	Marinette
1887.	Charles K. Erwin—R	Tomah	Thomas B. Mills—R)	Millston
1889.	Thomas A. Dyson—R	La Crosse	Thomas B. Mills—R	Millston
1891.	Frederick W. Horn—D	Cedarburg	James J. Hogan—D	La Crosse
1893.	Robert J. MacBride—D	Neillsville	Edward Keogh—D	Milwaukee
1895.	Thompson D. Weeks—R	Whitewater	George B. Burrows—R	Madison
1897.	Lyman W. Thayer—R	Ripon	George A. Buckstaff—R	Oshkosh
1899.	Lyman W. Thayer—R	Ripon	George H. Ray—R	La Crosse
1901.	James J. McGillivray—R	Black River Falls	George H. Ray—R	La Crosse
1903–05 . .	James J. McGillivray—R	Black River Falls	Irvine L. Lenroot—R	West Superior
1907.	James H. Stout—R	Menomonie	Herman L. Ekern—R	Whitehall
1909.	James H. Stout—R	Menomonie	Levi H. Bancroft—R	Richland Center
1911.	Harry C. Martin—R	Darlington	C.A. Ingram—R	Durand
1913.	Harry C. Martin—R	Darlington	Merlin Hull—R	Black River Falls
1915.	Edward T. Fairchild—R	Milwaukee	Lawrence C. Whittet—R	Edgerton
1917.	Timothy Burke—R	Green Bay	Lawrence C. Whittet—R	Edgerton
1919.	Willard T. Stevens—R	Rhinelander	Riley S. Young—R	Darien
1921.	Timothy Burke—R	Green Bay	Riley S. Young—R	Darien
1923.	Henry A. Huber—R	Stoughton	John L. Dahl—R	Rice Lake
1925.	Howard Teasdale—R	Sparta	Herman Sachtjen[3]—R	Madison
			George A. Nelson[3]—R	Milltown

Senate presidents, or presidents pro tempore, and assembly speakers since 1848, continued

Session	Senate presidents or presidents pro tempore[1]	Residence[2]	Assembly speakers	Residence[2]
1927.	William L. Smith—R	Neillsville	John W. Eber—R	Milwaukee
1929.	Oscar H. Morris—R	Milwaukee	Charles B. Perry—R	Wauwatosa
1931.	Herman J. Severson—P	Iola	Charles B. Perry—R	Wauwatosa
1933.	Orland S. Loomis—R	Mauston	Cornelius T. Young—D	Milwaukee
1935.	Harry W. Bolens—D	Port Washington	Jorge W. Carow—P	Ladysmith
1937.	Walter J. Rush—P	Neillsville	Paul R. Alfonsi—P	Pence
1939.	Edward J. Roethe—R	Fennimore	Vernon W. Thomson—R	Richland Center
1941–43 . .	Conrad Shearer—R	Kenosha	Vernon W. Thomson—R	Richland Center
1945.	Conrad Shearer—R	Kenosha	Donald C. McDowell—R	Soldiers Grove
1947.	Frank E. Panzer—R	Brownsville	Donald C. McDowell—R	Soldiers Grove
1949.	Frank E. Panzer—R	Brownsville	Alex L. Nicol—R	Sparta
1951–53 . .	Frank E. Panzer—R	Brownsville	Ora R. Rice—R	Delavan
1955.	Frank E. Panzer—R	Brownsville	Mark Catlin, Jr.—R	Appleton
1957.	Frank E. Panzer—R	Brownsville	Robert G. Marotz—R	Shawano
1959.	Frank E. Panzer—R	Brownsville	George Molinaro—D	Kenosha
1961.	Frank E. Panzer—R	Brownsville	David J. Blanchard—R	Edgerton
1963.	Frank E. Panzer—R	Brownsville	Robert D. Haase—R	Marinette
1965.	Frank E. Panzer—R	Brownsville	Robert T. Huber—D	West Allis
1967–69 . .	Robert P. Knowles—R	New Richmond	Harold V. Froehlich—R	Appleton
1971.	Robert P. Knowles—R	New Richmond	Robert T. Huber[4]—D	West Allis
			Norman C. Anderson[4]—D	Madison
1973.	Robert P. Knowles—R	New Richmond	Norman C. Anderson—D	Madison
1975.	Fred A. Risser—D	Madison	Norman C. Anderson—D	Madison
1977–81 . .	Fred A. Risser—D	Madison	Edward G. Jackamonis—D	Waukesha
1983–89 . .	Fred A. Risser—D	Madison	Thomas A. Loftus—D	Sun Prairie
1991.	Fred A. Risser—D	Madison	Walter J. Kunicki—D	Milwaukee
1993.	Fred A. Risser[5]—D	Madison	Walter J. Kunicki—D	Milwaukee
	Brian D. Rude[5]—R	Coon Valley		
1995.	Brian D. Rude[6]—R	Coon Valley	David T. Prosser, Jr.—R	Appleton
	Fred A. Risser[6]—D	Madison		
1997.	Fred A. Risser[7]—D	Madison	Ben Brancel[8]—R	Endeavor
	Brian D. Rude[7]—R	Coon Valley	Scott R. Jensen[8]—R	Waukesha
1999.	Fred A. Risser—D	Madison	Scott R. Jensen—R	Waukesha
2001.	Fred A. Risser—D	Madison	Scott R. Jensen—R	Waukesha
2003–05 . .	Alan J. Lasee—R	De Pere	John Gard—R	Peshtigo
2007.	Fred A. Risser—D	Madison	Michael D. Huebsch—R	West Salem
2009.	Fred A. Risser—D	Madison	Michael J. Sheridan—D	Janesville
2011.	Michael G. Ellis[9]—R	Neenah	Jeff Fitzgerald—R	Horicon
	Fred A. Risser[9]—D	Madison		
2013.	Michael G. Ellis—R	Neenah	Robin J. Vos—R	Burlington
2015.	Mary A. Lazich—R	New Berlin	Robin J. Vos—R	Burlington
2017.	Roger Roth—R	Appleton	Robin J. Vos—R	Burlington

Note: Political party indicated is for session elected and is obtained from newspaper accounts for some early legislators.

D–Democrat; GB–Greenback; P–Progressive; R–Republican; U–Union; UD–Union Democrat; W–Whig.

1. Prior to May 1, 1979, the president pro tempore is listed because the lieutenant governor, rather than a legislator, was the president of the senate under the constitution until that time.   2. Residence at the time of election.   3. Nelson was elected to serve at special session, 4/15/26 to 4/16/26, as Sachtjen had resigned.
4. Anderson was elected speaker 1/18/72 after Huber resigned   5. A new president was elected on 4/20/93 after a change in party control following two special elections.   6. A new president was elected on 7/9/96 after a change in party control following a recall election.   7. A new president was elected on 4/21/98 after a change in party control following a special election.   8. Jensen was elected speaker 11/4/97 after Brancel resigned.   9. A new president was elected on 7/17/12 after a change in party control following a recall election.

Sources: Senate and Assembly Journals; Wisconsin Legislative Reference Bureau records.

Majority and minority leaders of the Wisconsin Legislature since 1937

Session	Senate majority	Senate minority	Assembly majority	Assembly minority
1937...	Maurice Coakley—R	NA	NA	NA
1939...	Maurice Coakley—R	Philip Nelson—P	NA	Paul Alfonsi—P
1941...	Maurice Coakley—R	Cornelius Young—D	Mark Catlin, Jr.—R	Andrew Biemiller—P
				Robert Tehan—D
1943...	Warren Knowles[1]—R	NA	Mark Catlin, Jr.—R	Elmer Genzmer—D
	John Byrnes[1]—R			Lyall Beggs—P
1945...	Warren Knowles—R	Anthony Gawronski—D	Vernon Thomson—R	Lyall Beggs—P
				Leland McParland—D
1947...	Warren Knowles—R	Robert Tehan—D	Vernon Thomson—R	Leland McParland—D
1949...	Warren Knowles—R	NA	Vernon Thomson—R	Leland McParland—D
1951...	Warren Knowles—R	Gaylord Nelson—D	Arthur Mockrud—R	George Molinaro—D
1953...	Warren Knowles—R	Henry Maier—D	Mark Catlin, Jr.—R	George Molinaro—D
1955...	Paul Rogan[2]—R	Henry Maier—D	Robert Marotz—R	Robert Huber—D
1957...	Robert Travis—R	Henry Maier—D	Warren Grady—R	Robert Huber—D
1959...	Robert Travis—R	Henry Maier—D	Keith Hardie—D	David Blanchard—R
1961...	Robert Travis—R	William Moser[3]—D	Robert Haase—R	Robert Huber—D
1963...	Robert Knowles—R	Richard Zaborski—D	Paul Alfonsi—R	Robert Huber—D
1965...	Robert Knowles—R	Richard Zaborski—D	Frank Nikolay—D	Robert Haase[4]—R
				Paul Alfonsi[4]—R
1967...	Jerris Leonard—R	Fred Risser—D	J. Curtis McKay—R	Robert Huber—D
1969...	Ernest Keppler—R	Fred Risser—D	Paul Alfonsi—R	Robert Huber—D
1971...	Ernest Keppler—R	Fred Risser—D	Norman Anderson[5]—D	Harold Froehlich—R
			Anthony Earl[5]—D	
1973...	Raymond Johnson—R	Fred Risser—D	Anthony Earl—D	John Shabaz—R
1975...	Wayne Whittow[6]—D	Clifford Krueger—R	Terry Willkom—D	John Shabaz—R
	William Bablitch[6]—D			
1977...	William Bablitch—D	Clifford Krueger—R	James Wahner—D	John Shabaz—R
1979...	William Bablitch—D	Clifford Krueger—R	James Wahner[7]—D	John Shabaz—R
			Gary Johnson[7]—D	
1981...	William Bablitch[9]—D	Walter Chilsen—R	Thomas Loftus—D	John Shabaz[8]—R
	Timothy Cullen[9]—D			Tommy Thompson[8]—R
1983...	Timothy Cullen—D	James Harsdorf—R	Gary Johnson—D	Tommy Thompson—R
1985...	Timothy Cullen—D	Susan Engeleiter—R	Dismas Becker—D	Tommy Thompson—R
1987...	Joseph Strohl—D	Susan Engeleiter—R	Thomas Hauke—D	Betty Jo Nelsen—R
1989...	Joseph Strohl—D	Michael Ellis—R	Thomas Hauke—D	David Prosser—R
1991...	David Helbach—D	Michael Ellis—R	David Travis—D	David Prosser—R
1993...	David Helbach[10]—D	Michael Ellis[10]—R	David Travis—D	David Prosser—R
	Michael Ellis[10]—R	David Helbach[10,11]—D		
		Robert Jauch[11]—D		
1995...	Michael Ellis[13]—R	Robert Jauch[12]—D	Scott Jensen—R	Walter Kunicki—D
		Charles Chvala[12,13]—D		
	Charles Chvala[13]—D	Michael Ellis[13]—R		
1997...	Charles Chvala[14]—D	Michael Ellis[14]—R	Steven Foti—R	Walter Kunicki[15]—D
	Michael Ellis[14]—R	Charles Chvala[14]—D		Shirley Krug[15]—D
1999...	Charles Chvala—D	Michael Ellis[16]—R	Steven Foti—R	Shirley Krug—D
		Mary Panzer[16]—R		
2001...	Charles Chvala—D	Mary Panzer—R	Steven Foti—R	Shirley Krug—D
	Russell Decker[17]—D			Spencer Black[18]—D
	Fred Risser[17]—D			
	Jon Erpenbach[17]—D			
2003...	Mary Panzer[19]—R	Jon Erpenbach—D	Steven Foti—R	James Kreuser—D
	Scott Fitzgerald[19]—R			
	Dale Schultz[20]—R	Judith Robson[20]—D		
2005...	Dale Schultz—R	Judith Robson—D	Michael Huebsch—R	James Kreuser—D
2007...	Judith Robson—D	Scott Fitzgerald—R	Jeff Fitzgerald—R	James Kreuser—D
	Russell Decker[21]—D			
2009...	Russell Decker[22]—D	Scott Fitzgerald—R	Thomas Nelson—D	Jeff Fitzgerald—R
	Dave Hansen[22]—D			

Majority and minority leaders of the Wisconsin Legislature since 1937, continued

Session	Senate majority	Senate minority	Assembly majority	Assembly minority
2011 . . .	Scott Fitzgerald—R	Mark Miller—D	Scott Suder—R	Peter Barca—D
	Mark Miller[23]—D	Scott Fitzgerald[23]—R		
2013 . . .	Scott Fitzgerald—R	Chris Larson—D	Scott Suder[24]—R	Peter Barca—D
			Bill Kramer[25]—R	
			Pat Strachota—R	
2015 . . .	Scott Fitzgerald—R	Jennifer Shilling—D	Jim Steineke—R	Peter Barca—D
2017 . . .	Scott Fitzgerald—R	Jennifer Shilling—D	Jim Steineke—R	Peter Barca—D

Note: Majority and minority leaders, who are chosen by the party caucuses in each house, were first recognized officially in the senate and assembly rules in 1963. Prior to the 1977 session, these positions were also referred to as "floor leader."

D–Democrat; P–Progressive; R–Republican. NA–Not available.

1. Knowles granted leave of absence to return to active duty in U.S. Navy; Byrnes chosen to succeed him on 4/30/1943.   2. Resigned after sine die adjournment.   3. Resigned 1/30/1962.   4. Haase resigned 9/15/1965; Alfonsi elected 10/4/1965.   5. Earl elected 1/18/1972 to succeed Anderson who became assembly speaker. 6. Whittow resigned 4/30/1976; Bablitch elected 5/17/1976.   7. Wahner resigned 1/28/1980; Johnson elected 1/28/1980.   8. Shabaz resigned 12/18/1981; Thompson elected 12/21/1981.   9. Bablitch resigned 5/26/1982; Cullen elected 5/26/1982.   10. Democrats controlled senate from 1/4/1993 to 4/20/1993 when Republicans assumed control after a special election.   11. Helbach resigned 5/12/1993; Jauch elected 5/12/1993. 12. Jauch resigned 10/17/1995; Chvala elected 10/24/1995.   13. Republicans controlled senate from 1/5/1995 to 6/13/1996 when Democrats assumed control after a recall election.   14. Democrats controlled the senate from 1/6/1997 to 4/21/1998 when Republicans assumed control after a special election. 15. Kunicki resigned 6/3/1998; Krug elected 6/3/1998.   16. Ellis resigned 1/25/2000; Panzer elected 1/25/2000.   17. Decker and Risser elected co-leaders 10/22/2002. Erpenbach elected leader 12/4/2002. 18. Black elected 5/1/2001.   19. Panzer resigned 9/17/2004; Fitzgerald elected 9/17/2004.   20. Schultz elected 11/9/2004; Robson elected 11/9/2004.   21. Decker elected 10/24/2007.   22. Hansen replaced Decker as leader, 12/15/2010.   23. After a resignation on 3/16/12 resulted in a 16–16 split, Fitzgerald and Miller served as co-leaders. A recall election gave Democrats control of the senate as of 7/17/12.   24. Suder resigned 9/3/13; Kramer elected 9/4/13.   25. Kramer removed 3/4/14; Strachota elected 3/4/14.

Sources: *Wisconsin Blue Book*, various editions; Senate and Assembly Journals; newspaper accounts.

Chief clerks and sergeants at arms of the legislature since 1848

	Senate		Assembly	
Session	Chief clerk	Sergeant at arms	Chief clerk	Sergeant at arms
1848	Henry G. Abbey	Lyman H. Seaver	Daniel N. Johnson	John Mullanphy
1849	William R. Smith	F. W. Shollner	Robert L. Ream	Felix McLinden
1850	William R. Smith	James Hanrahan	Alex T. Gray	E. R. Hugunin
1851	William Hull	E. D. Masters	Alex T. Gray	C. M. Kingsbury
1852	John K. Williams	Patrick Cosgrove	Alex T. Gray	Elisha Starr
1853	John K. Williams	Thomas Hood	Thomas McHugh	Richard F. Wilson
1854	Samuel G. Bugh	J. M. Sherwood	Thomas McHugh	William H. Gleason
1855	Samuel G. Bugh	William H. Gleason	David Atwood	William Blake
1856	Byron Paine	Joseph Baker	James Armstrong	Egbert Mosely
1857	William H. Brisbane	Alanson Filer	William C. Webb	William C. Rogers
1858	John L. V. Thomas	Nathaniel L. Stout	L. H. D. Crane	Francis Massing
1859	Hiram Bowen	Asa Kinney	L. H. D. Crane	Emmanual Munk
1860	J. H. Warren	Asa Kinney	L. H. D. Crane	Joseph Gates
1861	J. H. Warren	J. A. Hadley	L. H. D. Crane	Craig B. Peebe
1862	J. H. Warren	B. U. Caswell	John S. Dean	A. A. Huntington
1863	Frank M. Stewart	Luther Bashford	John S. Dean	A. M. Thompson
1864	Frank M. Stewart	Nelson Williams	John S. Dean	A. M. Thompson
1865	Frank M. Stewart	Nelson Williams	John S. Dean	Alonzo Wilcox
1866	Frank M. Stewart	Nelson Williams	E. W. Young	L. M. Hammond
1867	Leander B. Hills	Asa Kinney	E. W. Young	Daniel Webster

Chief clerks and sergeants at arms of the legislature since 1848,
continued

	Senate		Assembly	
Session	Chief clerk	Sergeant at arms	Chief clerk	Sergeant at arms
1868.	Leander B. Hills	W. H. Hamilton	E. W. Young	C. L. Harris
1869.	Leander B. Hills	W. H. Hamilton	E. W. Young	Rolin C. Kelly
1870.	Leander B. Hills	E. M. Rogers	E. W. Young	Ole C. Johnson
1871.	O. R. Smith	W. W. Baker	E. W. Young	Sam S. Fifield
1872.	J. H. Waggoner	W. D. Hoard	E. W. Young	Sam S. Fifield
1873.	J. H. Waggoner	Albert Emonson	E. W. Young	O. C. Bissel
1874.	J. H. Waggoner	O. U. Aiken	George W. Peck	Joseph Deuster
1875.	Fred A. Dennett	O. U. Aiken	R. M. Strong	J. W. Brackett
1876.	A. J. Turner	E. T. Gardner	R. M. Strong	Elisha Starr
1877.	A. J. Turner	C. E. Bullard	W. A. Nowell	Thomas B. Reid
1878.	A. J. Turner[1]	L. J. Brayton	Jabez R. Hunter	Anton Klaus
	Charles E. Bross[1]			
1879.	Charles E. Bross	Chalmers Ingersoll	John E. Eldred	Miletus Knight
1880.	Charles E. Bross	Chalmers Ingersoll	John E. Eldred	D. H. Pulcifer
1881.	Charles E. Bross	W. W. Baker	John E. Eldred	G. W. Church
1882.	Charles E. Bross	A. T. Glaze	E. D. Coe	D. E. Welch
1883.	Charles E. Bross	A. D. Thorp	I. T. Carr	Thomas Kennedy
1885.	Charles E. Bross	Hubert Wolcott	E. D. Coe	John M. Ewing
1887.	Charles E. Bross	T. J. George	E. D. Coe	William A. Adamson
1889.	Charles E. Bross	T J. George	E. D. Coe	F. E. Parsons
1891.	J. P. Hume	John A. Barney	George W. Porth	Patrick Whelan
1893.	Sam J. Shafer	John B. Becker	George W. Porth	Theodore Knapstein
1895.	Walter L. Houser	Charles Pettibone	W. A. Nowell	B. F. Millard
1897.	Walter L. Houser	Charles Pettibone	W. A. Nowell	C. M. Hambright
1899.	Walter L. Houser	Charles Pettibone	W. A. Nowell	James H. Agen
1901.	Walter L. Houser	Charles Pettibone	W. A. Nowell	A. M. Anderson
1903.	Theodore W. Goldin	Sanfield McDonald	C. O. Marsh	A. M. Anderson
1905.	L .K. Eaton	R. C. Falconer	C. O. Marsh	Nicholas Streveler
1907.	A. R. Emerson	R. C. Falconer	C. E. Shaffer	W. S. Irvine
1909.	F. E. Andrews	R. C. Falconer	C. E. Shaffer	W. S. Irvine
1911–13 . . .	F. M. Wylie	C. A. Leicht	C. E. Shaffer	W. S. Irvine
1915.	O. G. Munson	F. E. Andrews	C. E. Shaffer	W. S. Irvine
1917.	O. G. Munson	F. E. Andrews	C. E. Shaffer	T. G. Cretney
1919.	O. G. Munson	John Turner	C. E. Shaffer	T. G. Cretney
1921.	O. G. Munson	Vincent Kielpinski	C. E. Shaffer	T. G. Cretney
1923.	F. W. Schoenfeld	C. A. Leicht	C. E. Shaffer	T. W. Bartingale
1925.	F. W. Schoenfeld	C. A. Leicht	C. E. Shaffer	C. E. Hanson
1927–29 . . .	O. G. Munson	George W. Rickeman	C. E. Shaffer	C. F. Moulton
1931.	R. A. Cobban	Emil A. Hartman	C. E. Shaffer	Gustave Rheingans
1933.	R. A. Cobban	Emil A. Hartman	John J. Slocum	George C. Faust
1935–37 . . .	Lawrence R. Larsen	Emil A. Hartman	Lester R. Johnson	Gustave Rheingans
1939.	Lawrence R. Larsen	Emil A. Hartman	John J. Slocum	Robert A. Merrill
1941–43 . . .	Lawrence R. Larsen	Emil A. Hartman	Arthur L. May	Norris J. Kellman
1945.	Lawrence R. Larsen	Harold E. Damon	Arthur L. May	Norris J. Kellman
1947–53 . . .	Thomas M. Donahue	Harold E. Damon	Arthur L. May	Norris J. Kellman
1955–57 . . .	Lawrence R. Larsen	Harold E. Damon	Arthur L. May	Norris J. Kellman
1959.	Lawrence R. Larsen	Harold E. Damon	Norman C. Anderson	Thomas H. Browne
1961.	Lawrence R. Larsen	Harold E. Damon	Robert G. Marotz	Norris J. Kellman
1963.	Lawrence R. Larsen	Harold E. Damon	Kenneth E. Priebe	Norris J. Kellman
1965.	Lawrence R. Larsen[2]	Harold E. Damon	James P. Buckley	Thomas H. Browne
	William P. Nugent[2]			
1967.	William P. Nugent	Harry O. Levander	Arnold W. F. Langner[3]	Louis C. Romell
			Wilmer H. Struebing[3]	
1969.	William P. Nugent	Kenneth Nicholson	Wilmer H. Struebing	Louis C. Romell
1971.	William P. Nugent	Kenneth Nicholson	Thomas P. Fox	William F. Quick
1973.	William P. Nugent	Kenneth Nicholson	Thomas S. Hanson	William F. Quick
1975.	Glenn E. Bultman	Robert M. Thompson	Everett E. Bolle	Raymond J. Tobiasz

Chief clerks and sergeants at arms of the legislature since 1848,
continued

Session	Senate Chief clerk	Senate Sergeant at arms	Assembly Chief clerk	Assembly Sergeant at arms
1977.	Donald J. Schneider	Robert M. Thompson	Everett E. Bolle	Joseph E. Jones
1979.	Donald J. Schneider	Daniel B. Fields	Marcel Dandeneau	Joseph E. Jones
1981.	Donald J. Schneider	Daniel B. Fields	David R. Kedrowski	Lewis T. Mittness
1983.	Donald J. Schneider	Daniel B. Fields	Joanne M. Duren	Lewis T. Mittness
1985.	Donald J. Schneider	Daniel B. Fields	Joanne M. Duren	Patrick Essie
1987.	Donald J. Schneider	Daniel B. Fields	Thomas T. Melvin	Patrick Essie
1989–91 . . .	Donald J. Schneider	Daniel B. Fields	Thomas T. Melvin	Robert G. Johnston
1993.	Donald J. Schneider	Daniel B. Fields[4] Jon H. Hochkammer[4]	Thomas T. Melvin	Robert G. Johnston
1995.	Donald J. Schneider	Jon H. Hochkammer	Thomas T. Melvin [5] Charles R. Sanders [5]	John A. Scocos
1997.	Donald J. Schneider	Jon H. Hochkammer	Charles R. Sanders	John A. Scocos[6] Denise L. Solie[6]
1999.	Donald J. Schneider	Jon H. Hochkammer	Charles R. Sanders	Denise L. Solie
2001.	Donald J. Schneider	Jon H. Hochkammer[7]	John A. Scocos[7]	Denise L. Solie
2003.	Donald J. Schneider[8] Robert J. Marchant[8]	Edward A. Blazel	Patrick E. Fuller	Richard A. Skindrud
2005–07 . . .	Robert J. Marchant	Edward A. Blazel	Patrick E. Fuller	Richard A. Skindrud
2009.	Robert J. Marchant	Edward A. Blazel	Patrick E. Fuller	William M. Nagy
2011.	Robert J. Marchant[9]	Edward A. Blazel	Patrick E. Fuller	Anne Tonnon Byers
2013–17 . . .	Jeffrey Renk	Edward A. Blazel	Patrick E. Fuller	Anne Tonnon Byers

1. Bross elected 2/6/78; Turner resigned 2/7/78.   2. Larsen died 3/2/65; Nugent elected 3/31/65.   3. Langner resigned 5/2/67; Struebing elected 5/16/67.   4. Fields served until 8/2/93. Randall Radtke served as acting sergeant from 8/3/93 to 11/3/93. Hochkammer elected 1/25/94.   5. Melvin retired 1/31/95; Sanders elected 5/24/95.   6. Scocos resigned 9/25/97; Solie elected 1/15/98.   7. Scocos resigned 2/25/02. Hochkammer resigned 9/2/02. No replacement was elected for either.   8. Schneider resigned 7/4/03; Marchant elected 1/20/04.   9. Marchant resigned 1/2/12.

Sources: Wisconsin Legislative Reference Bureau, *Wisconsin Blue Book*, various editions; journals and organizing resolutions of each house.

Political composition of the Wisconsin Legislature since 1885

Session[1]	Senate[2] D	R	P	S	SD	Assembly[3] D	R	P	S	SD
1885.	13	20	—	—	—	39	61	—	—	—
1887.	6	25	—	—	—	30	57	—	—	—
1889.	6	24	—	—	—	29	71	—	—	—
1891.	19	14	—	—	—	66	33	—	—	—
1893.	26	7	—	—	—	56	44	—	—	—
1895.	13	20	—	—	—	19	81	—	—	—
1897.	4	29	—	—	—	8	91	—	—	—
1899.	2	31	—	—	—	19	81	—	—	—
1901.	2	31	—	—	—	18	82	—	—	—
1903.	3	30	—	—	—	25	75	—	—	—
1905.	4	28	—	—	1	11	85	—	—	4
1907.	5	27	—	—	1	19	76	—	—	5
1909.	4	28	—	—	1	17	80	—	—	3
1911.	4	27	—	—	2	29	59	—	—	12
1913.	9	23	—	—	1	37	57	—	—	6
1915.	11	21	—	—	1	29	63	—	—	8
1917.	6	24	—	3	—	14	79	—	7	—
1919.	2	27	—	4	—	5	79	—	16	—

Political composition of the Wisconsin Legislature since 1885,
continued

Session[1]	Senate[2]					Assembly[3]				
	D	R	P	S	SD	D	R	P	S	SD
1921.	2	27	—	4	—	2	92	—	6	—
1923.	—	30	—	3	—	1	89	—	10	—
1925.	—	30	—	3	—	1	92	—	7	—
1927.	—	31	—	2	—	3	89	—	8	—
1929.	—	31	—	2	—	6	90	—	3	—
1931.	1	30	—	2	—	2	89	—	9	—
1933.	9	23	—	1	—	59	13	24	3	—
1935.	13	6	14	—	—	35	17	45	3	—
1937.	9	8	16	—	—	31	21	46	2	—
1939.	6	16	11	—	—	15	53	32	—	—
1941.	3	24	6	—	—	15	60	25	—	—
1943.	4	23	6	—	—	14	73	13	—	—
1945.	6	22	5	—	—	19	75	6	—	—
1947.	5	27	1	—	—	11	88	—	—	—
1949.	3	27	—	—	—	26	74	—	—	—
1951.	7	26	—	—	—	24	75	—	—	—
1953.	7	26	—	—	—	25	75	—	—	—
1955.	8	24	—	—	—	36	64	—	—	—
1957.	10	23	—	—	—	33	67	—	—	—
1959.	12	20	—	—	—	55	45	—	—	—
1961.	13	20	—	—	—	45	55	—	—	—
1963.	11	22	—	—	—	46	53	—	—	—
1965.	12	20	—	—	—	52	48	—	—	—
1967.	12	21	—	—	—	47	53	—	—	—
1969.	10	23	—	—	—	48	52	—	—	—
1971.	12	20	—	—	—	67	33	—	—	—
1973.	15	18	—	—	—	62	37	—	—	—
1975.	18	13	—	—	—	63	36	—	—	—
1977.	23	10	—	—	—	66	33	—	—	—
1979.	21	10	—	—	—	60	39	—	—	—
1981.	19	14	—	—	—	59	39	—	—	—
1983.	17	14	—	—	—	59	40	—	—	—
1985.	19	14	—	—	—	52	47	—	—	—
1987.	19	11	—	—	—	54	45	—	—	—
1989.	20	13	—	—	—	56	43	—	—	—
1991.	19	14	—	—	—	58	41	—	—	—
1993[4]	15	15	—	—	—	52	47	—	—	—
1995[4]	16	17	—	—	—	48	51	—	—	—
1997[4]	17	16	—	—	—	47	52	—	—	—
1999.	17	16	—	—	—	44	55	—	—	—
2001.	18	15	—	—	—	43	56	—	—	—
2003.	15	18	—	—	—	41	58	—	—	—
2005.	14	19	—	—	—	39	60	—	—	—
2007.	18	15	—	—	—	47	52	—	—	—
2009.	18	15	—	—	—	52	46	—	—	—
2011[4]	14	19	—	—	—	38	60	—	—	—
2013.	15	18	—	—	—	39	59	—	—	—
2015.	14	18	—	—	—	36	63	—	—	—
2017.	13	20	—	—	—	35	64	—	—	—

Note: The number of assembly districts was reduced from 100 to 99 beginning in 1973. There have been 33 senate districts since 1862. Any deviation of a session's total from these numbers indicates vacant seats.

— Represents zero; D–Democrat; P–Progressive; R–Republican; S–Socialist; SD–Social Democrat.

1. Political composition at inauguration.   2. Miscellaneous affiliations for senate seats not shown in the table are: one Independent and one People's (1887); one Independent and 2 Union Labor (1889).
3. Miscellaneous affiliations for assembly seats not shown: 3 Independent, 4 Independent Democrat, and 6 People's (1887); one Union Labor (1891); one Fusion (1897); one Independent (1929, 2009, 2011);

one Independent Republican (1933). 4. In the 1993, 1995, and 1997 Legislatures, majority control of the senate shifted during the session. On 4/20/93, vacancies were filled resulting in a total of 16 Democrats and 17 Republicans; on 6/16/96, there were 17 Democrats and 16 Republicans; on 4/19/98, there were 16 Democrats and 17 Republicans. 5. A series of recall elections during the session resulted in a switch in majority control of the senate, with 17 Democrats and 16 Republicans as of 7/16/12.

Sources: Pre-1943 data compiled from the Secretary of State, *Officers of Wisconsin: U.S., State, Judicial, Congressional, Legislative and County Officers*, 1943 and earlier editions, and the *Wisconsin Blue Book*, various editions. Later data compiled from Wisconsin Legislative Reference Bureau sources.

Wisconsin legislative sessions since 1848

	Opening/final adjournment	Days	Measures introduced			Bills vetoed[1] (overridden)	Laws enacted
			Bills	Joint Res.	Res.		
1848.	6/5–8/21	78	217	0	0	0	155
1849.	1/10–4/2	83	428	0	0	2(1)	220
1850.	1/9–2/11	34	438	0	0	1	284
1851.	1/8–3/17	69	707	0	0	9	407
1852.	1/14–4/19	97	813	0	0	3(1)	504
1853.	1/12–7/13	183	1,145	0	0	6	521
1854.	1/11–4/3	83	880	0	0	2	437
1855.	1/10–4/2	83	955	0	0	6	500
1856.	1/9–10/14	288	1,242	0	0	1	688
1857.	1/14–3/9	55	895	0	0	0	517
1858.	1/13–5/17	125	1,364	157	342	28	436
1859.	1/12–3/21	69	986	113	143	9	680
1860.	1/11–4/2	83	1,024	69	246	2	489
1861.	1/9–4/17	99	857	100	235	2	387
1861 SS.	5/15–5/27	13	28	24	34	0	15
1862.	1/8–6/17	161	1,008	125	207	36²(8)	514
1862 SS.	9/10–9/26	17	43	25	37	0	17
1863.	1/14–4/2	79	895	101	157	10(1)	383
1864.	1/13–4/4	83	835	66	141	0	509
1865.	1/11–4/10	90	1,132	82	190	2	565
1866.	1/10–4/12	93	1,107	64	208	5	733
1867.	1/9–4/11	93	1,161	97	161	2	790
1868.	1/8–3/6	59	987	73	119	2(2)	692
1869.	1/13–3/11	58	887	52	81	14(1)	657
1870.	1/12–3/17	65	1,043	54	89	2	666
1871.	1/11–3/25	74	1,066	55	82	4	671
1872.	1/10–3/26	77	709	79	124	2	322
1873.	1/8–3/20	72	611	62	122	4	308
1874.	1/14–3/12	58	688	91	111	2	349
1875.	1/13–3/6	53	637	39	93	2	344
1876.	1/12–3/14	63	715	57	115	2	415
1877.	1/10–3/8	58	720	59	95	4	384
1878.	1/9–3/21	72	735	79	134	2	342
1878 SS.	6/4–6/7	4	6	14	10	0	5
1879.	1/8–3/5	57	610	49	105	0	256
1880.	1/14–3/17	64	669	58	93	3	323
1881.	1/12–4/4	83	780	104	100	6	334
1882.	1/11–3/31	80	728	57	90	6	330
1883.	1/10–4/4	85	705	75	100	2	360
1885.	1/14–4/13	90	963	97	108	8	471
1887.	1/12–4/15	94	1,293	114	60	10	553
1889.	1/9–4/19	101	1,355	136	82	6(1)	529
1891.	1/14–4/25	102	1,216	137	91	10(1)	483
1892 SS.	6/28–7/1	4	4	7	16	0	1
1892 SS.	10/17–10/27	11	8	6	14	0	2
1893.	1/11–4/21	101	1,124	135	86	6	312
1895.	1/9–4/20	102	1,154	139	88	0	387

Wisconsin legislative sessions since 1848, continued

	Opening/final adjournment	Days	Measures introduced			Bills vetoed[1] (overridden)	Laws enacted
			Bills	Joint Res.	Res.		
1896 SS	2/18–2/28	11	3	11	15	0	1
1897	1/13–8/20	220	1,077	155	39	19(1)	381
1899	1/11–5/4	114	910	113	40	3	357
1901	1/9–5/15	127	1,091	81	39	24	470
1903	1/14–5/23	130	1,115	65	81	23	451
1905	1/11–6/21	162	1,357	134	101	22	523
1905 SS	12/4–12/19	16	24	15	26	0	17
1907	1/9–7/16	189	1,685	205	84	28(1)	677
1909	1/13–6/18	157	1,567	213	49	22	550
1911	1/11–7/15	186	1,710	267	37	15	665
1912 SS	4/30–5/6	7	41	7	6	0	22
1913	1/8–8/9	214	1,847	175	79	24	778
1915	1/13–8/24	224	1,560	220	79	15	637
1916 SS	10/10–10/11	2	2	8	4	0	2
1917	1/10–7/16	188	1,439	229	115	18	679
1918 SS	2/19–3/9	19	27	22	28	2	16
1918 SS	9/24–9/25	2	2	6	9	0	2
1919	1/8–7/30	204	1,350	268	100	39	703
1919 SS	9/4–9/8	5	7	4	6	0	7
1920 SS	5/25–6/4	11	46	10	22	2	32
1921	1/12–7/14	184	1,199	207	93	41(1)	591
1922 SS	3/22–3/28	7	10	7	12	1	4
1923	1/10–7/14	186	1,247	215	93	52	449
1925	1/14–6/29	167	1,144	200	115	73	454
1926 SS	4/15–4/16	2	1	8	12	0	1
1927	1/12–8/13	214	1,341	235	167	90(2)	542
1928 SS	1/24–2/4	12	20	35	23	0	5
1928 SS	3/6–3/13	8	13	9	17	0	2
1929	1/9–9/20	255	1,366	278	185	44	530
1931	1/14–6/27	165	1,429	291	160	56	487
1931 SS	11/24/31–2/5/32	74	99	93	83	2	31
1933	1/11–7/25	196	1,411	324	157	15	496
1933 SS	12/11/33–2/3/34	55	45	160	53	0	20
1935	1/9–9/27	262	1,662	346	190	27	556
1937	1/13–7/2	171	1,404	228	127	10	432
1937 SS	9/15–10/16	32	28	18	23	0	15
1939	1/11–10/6	269	1,559	268	133	22	535
1941	1/8–6/6	150	1,368	160	109	17	333
1943	1/13/43–1/22/44	375	1,153	202	136	39(20)	577
1945	1/10–9/6	240	1,156	208	109	30(5)	590
1946 SS	7/29–7/30	2	2	6	14	0	2
1947	1/8–9/11	247	1,220	195	97	10(1)	615
1948 SS	7/19–7/20	2	0	5	11	0	0
1949	1/12–9/13	245	1,432	188	86	17(2)	643
1951	1/10–6/14	156	1,559	157	73	18	735
1953	1/14–11/6	297	1,593	175	70	31(3)	687
1955	1/12–10/21	283	1,503	256	74	38	696
1957	1/9–9/27	262	1,512	246	71	35(1)	706
1958 SS	6/11–6/13	3	3	7	13	0	3
1959	1/14/59–5/27/60	500	1,769	272	84	36(4)	696
1961	1/11/61–1/9/63	729	1,592	295	68	70(2)	689
1963	1/9/63–1/13/65	736	1,619	241	110	72(4)	580
1963 SS	12/10–12/12	3	8	10	10	0	3
1965[3]	1/13/65–1/2/67	720	1,818	293	86	24(1)	666
1967	1/11/67–1/6/69	727	1,700	215	61	18	355
1969	1/6/69–1/4/71	729	2,014	232	101	34(1)	501
1969 SS[4]	9/29/69–1/17/70	111	5	5	8	0	1
1970 SS	12/22	1	0	1	5	0	0

Wisconsin legislative sessions since 1848, continued

	Opening/final adjournment	Days	Measures introduced			Bills vetoed[1] (overridden)	Laws enacted
			Bills	Joint Res.	Res.		
1971.	1/4/71–1/1/73	729	2,568	291	121	32(3)	336
1972 SS	4/19–4/28	10	9	4	4	0	6
1973.	1/1/73–1/6/75	736	2,501	277	126	13	332
1973 SS	12/17–12/21	5	3	2	6	0	2
1974 SS	4/29–6/13	46	12	1	4	0	6
1974 SS[5]	11/19–11/20	2	2	0	0	0	1
1975.	1/6/75–1/3/77	729	2,325	169	88	36(6)	414
1975 SS	12/9–12/11	3	13	1	2	1	6
1976 SS	5/18	1	2	2	3	0	1
1976 SS[5]	6/15–6/17	3	13	4	3	0	9
1976 SS	9/8	1	4	1	4	0	2
1977.	1/3/77–1/3/79	730	2,053	182	48	21(4)	442
1977 SS	6/30	1	0	1	2	0	0
1977 SS	11/7–11/11	5	6	4	2	0	5
1978 SS[5]	6/13–6/15	3	2	5	2	0	2
1978 SS	12/20	1	2	4	2	0	2
1979.	1/3/79–1/5/81	734	1,920	203	40	19(3)	350
1979 SS	9/5	1	10	3	2	0	5
1980 SS[6]	1/22–1/25	4	8	3	2	0	0
1980 SS	6/3– 7/3	31	20	14	2	0	7
1981.	1/5/81–1/3/83	729	1,987	176	70	10(2)	381
1981 SS[7]	11/4–11/17	14	6	3	2	0	3
1982 SS[7]	4/6–5/20	45	4	2	2	1	1
1982 SS[7]	5/26–5/28	3	13	7	2	0	9
1983.	1/3/83–1/7/85	736	1,902	173	50	3	521
1983 SS	1/4–1/6	3	2	2	1	0	2
1983 SS	4/12–4/14	3	1	1	0	0	1
1983 SS	7/11–7/14	4	5	3	1	0	4
1983 SS	10/18–10/28	11	12	1	0	0	11
1984 SS	2/2–4/4	63	2	1	0	0	0
1984 SS	5/22–5/24	3	12	5	1	0	11
1985.	1/7/85–1/5/87	729	1,624	171	41	7	293
1985 SS	3/19–3/21	3	6	1	0	0	3
1985 SS	9/24–10/19	26	22	1	0	0	17
1985 SS	10/31	1	1	3	0	0	1
1985 SS	11/20	1	24	2	0	0	12
1986 SS	1/27–5/30	124	1	4	0	0	1
1986 SS	3/24–3/26	3	1	1	0	0	1
1986 SS	5/20–5/29	10	44	3	0	0	12
1986 SS	7/15	1	3	1	0	0	2
1987[8]	1/5/87–1/3/89	730	1,631	196	21	35	413
1987 SS	9/15–9/16	2	2	1	0	0	2
1987 SS	11/18/87–6/7/88	203	19	3	0	3	5
1988 SS	6/30	1	4	1	3	0	2
1989.	1/3/89–1/7/91	735	1,557	244	45	35	361
1989 SS	10/10/89–3/22/90	164	52	6	0	0	7
1990 SS	5/15/90	1	7	1	0	0	0
1991.	1/7/91–1/4/93	729	1,676	244	32	33	318
1991 SS	1/29/–7/4	157	16	1	0	0	2
1991 SS	10/15/91–5/21/92	220	9	2	0	0	1
1992 SS[6]	4/14–6/4	52	7	1	2	0	2
1992 SS	6/1	1	0	2	0	0	0
1992 SS	8/25–9/15	22	1	1	2	0	1
1993.	1/4/93–1/3/95	730	2,147	207	47	8	491
1994 SS	5/18–5/19	2	6	1	0	0	3
1994 SS[9]	6/7–6/23	17	3	4	0	0	3
1995.	1/3/95–1/6/97	735	1,780	163	38	4	467
1995 SS	1/4	1	1	1	0	0	1

Wisconsin legislative sessions since 1848, continued

	Opening/final adjournment	Days	Measures introduced			Bills vetoed[1] (overridden)	Laws enacted
			Bills	Joint Res.	Res.		
1995 SS	9/5–10/12	36	1	1	0	0	1
1997	1/6/97–1/4/99	729	1,508	183	30	3	333
1998 SS[10]	4/21–5/21	31	13	2	2	0	5
1999[11]	1/4/99–1/3/01	731	1,498	168	52	5	196
1999 SS[5]	10/27–11/11	16	3	1	0	0	1
2000 SS	5/4–5/9	8	2	2	1	0	1
2001	1/3/01–1/6/03	734	1,436	174	75	0	106
2001 SS[5]	5/1–5/3	3	1	0	0	0	1
2002 SS[5]	1/22–7/8	168	1	2	7	0	1
2002 SS[5]	5/13–5/15	3	2	0	0	0	1
2003[12]	1/6/03–1/3/05	729	1,567	164	78	54	326
2003 SS	1/30–2/20	22	1	0	0	0	1
2005[13]	1/3/05–1/3/07	731	1,967	196	76	47	489
2005 SS	1/12–1/20	9	2	0	0	0	1
2006 SS	2/14–3/7	22	2	0	0	0	1
2007	1/3/07–1/5/09	733	1,574	230	50	1	239
2007 SS	1/11–2/1	22	2	1	0	0	1
2007 SS	10/15–10/23	9	2	0	0	0	0
2007 SS	12/11/07–5/14/08	156	1	1	0	0	0
2008 SS	3/12–5/14	65	1	4	2	0	1
2008 SS	4/17–5/15	29	1	4	2	0	1
2009[14]	1/5/09–1/3/11	729	1,720	221	44	6	406
2009 SS	6/24–6/27	4	1	0	0	0	0
2009 SS	12/16–3/4/10	79	2	0	0	0	0
2011[15]	1/3/11–1/7/13	735	1,325	211	48	0	267
2011 SS	1/4–9/27	267	27	1	3	0	12
2011 SS	9/29–12/8	71	48	0	0	0	7
2013	1/7/13–1/5/15	730	1,627	214	37	1	373
2013 SS	10/10–11/12	34	8	0	0	0	4
2013 SS	12/2–12/19	18	2	0	0	0	1
2014 SS	1/23–3/20	57	4	0	0	0	2
2015[16]	1/5/15–1/3/17	730	1,830	236	45	2	392

Res.–resolution; SS–special session.

1. Partial vetoes not included. See executive vetoes table.   2. Does not include 18 bills that the lieutenant governor asserted had been vetoed by pocket veto when the governor, to whom they had been sent, died without signing them.   3. Although 1965 Legislature adjourned to 1/11/67, terms automatically expired on 1/2/67.   4. Senate adjourned the special session 11/15/69; assembly, 1/17/70.   5. Special session met concurrently with regular session.   6. Legislature met concurrently in extraordinary and special session.   7. Legislature met concurrently in special session and extended floorperiod.   8. Extraordinary sessions held in February, September, and November 1987 and April, May, and June 1988. May 1988 extraordinary session ran concurrently with May 1988 veto review period and with June 1988 extraordinary session.   9. Extraordinary session held in June 1994.   10. Extraordinary session held in April 1998.   11. Extraordinary session held in April and May 2000.   12. Extraordinary sessions held in February, July, and August 2003; December 2003–February 2004; March 2004; May 2004; and July 2004.   13. Extraordinary sessions held in July 2005 and April 2006.   14. Extraordinary sessions held in February, May, June, and December 2009 and December 2010.   15. Extraordinary sessions held in June and July 2011.   16. Extraordinary sessions held in February, July, and November 2015.

Sources: *Bulletin of the Proceedings of the Wisconsin Legislature*, various editions; and Senate and Assembly Journals.

Executive vetoes since 1931

Session	Bills vetoed (overridden)	Partial vetoes (overridden)	Budget bill partial vetoes[1] (overridden)
1931	58	2	12
1933	15	1	12
1935	27	4	0
1937	10	1	0
1939[2]	22	4	1
1941	17	1	1
1943	39 (20)	1 (1)	0
1945	30 (5)	2 (1)	1
1947	10 (1)	1	2
1949	17 (2)	2 (1)	0
1951	18	2	0
1953[3]	31 (3)	4	2
1955	38	0	0
1957	35 (1)	3	2
1959	36 (4)	1	0
1961	70 (2)	3	2
1963	72 (4)	1	0
1965	24 (1)	4	1
1967	18	5	0
1969	34 (1)	11	27
1971	32 (3)	8	12
1973	13	18 (3)	38 (2)
1975	37 (6)	22 (4)	42 (5)
1977	21 (4)	16 (3)	67 (21)
1979	19 (3)	9 (2)	45 (1)
1981[4]	11 (2)	11 (1)	121
1983	3	11 (1)	70 (6)
1985	7	7 (1)	78 (2)
1987	38	20	290
1989	35	28	203
1991	33	13	457
1993	8	24	78
1995	4	21	112
1997	3	8	152
1999	5	9	255
2001	0	3	315
2003	54	10	131
2005	47	2	139
2007	1	4	33
2009	6	5	81
2011	0	3	50
2013	1	4	57
2015	2	5	104

1. The number of individual veto statements in the governor's veto message. 2. Attorney general ruled veto of 1939 SB-43 was void and it became law (see Vol. 28, *Opinions of the Attorney General*, p. 423). 3. 1953 AB-141, partially vetoed in two separate sections by separate veto messages, is counted as one. 4. Attorney general ruled several vetoes "ineffective" because the governor failed to express his objections (see Vol. 70, *Opinions of the Attorney General*, p. 189).

Source: Compiled by Wisconsin Legislative Reference Bureau from the *Bulletin of the Proceedings of the Wisconsin Legislature* and the Assembly and Senate Journals.

History of proposed constitutional amendments since 1854

Article	Section	Subject	Election result	Vote totals	Date	Proposed amendment
IV	4	Assemblymen, 2-year terms	rejected	6,549–11,580	Nov. 1854	1854 Ch. 89
IV	5	Senators, 4-year terms	rejected	6,348–11,885	Nov. 1854	1854 Ch. 89
IV	11	Biennial legislative sessions	rejected	6,752–11,589	Nov. 1854	1854 Ch. 89
V	5	Governor's salary, changed from $1,250 to $2,500 a year	rejected	14,519–32,612	Nov. 1862	1862 JR 6
IV	21	Change legislators' pay to $350 a year	ratified	58,363–24,418	Nov. 1867	1866 JR 3
V	5	Change governor's salary from $1,250 to $5,000 a year	ratified	47,353–41,764	Nov. 1869	1869 JR 2
V	9	Change lieutenant governor's salary to $1,000 a year	ratified	47,353–41,764	Nov. 1869	1869 JR 2
I	8	Grand jury system modified	ratified	48,894–18,606	Nov. 1870	1870 JR 3
IV	31, 32	Private and local laws, prohibited on 9 subjects	ratified	54,087–3,675	Nov. 1871	1871 JR 1
VII	4	Supreme court, 1 chief and 4 associate justices	rejected	16,272–29,755	Nov. 1872	1872 JR 8
XI	3	Indebtedness of municipalities limited to 5%	ratified	66,061–1,509	Nov. 1874	1873 JR 4
VII	4	Supreme court, 1 chief and 4 associate justices	ratified	79,140–16,763	Nov. 1877	1877 JR 1
VIII	2	Claims against state, 6-year limit	ratified	33,046–3,371	Nov. 1877	1877 JR 4
IV	4, 5, 11	Biennial sessions; assemblymen 2-year, senators 4-year terms	ratified	53,532–13,936	Nov. 1881	1881 AJR 7[1]
IV	21	Change legislators' pay to $500 a year	ratified	53,532–13,936	Nov. 1881	1881 AJR 7[1]
III	1	Voting residence 30 days; in municipalities voter registration	ratified	36,223–5,347	Nov. 1882	1882 JR 5
VI	4	County officers except judicial, vacancies filled by appointment	ratified	60,091–8,089	Nov. 1882	1882 JR 3
VII	12	Clerk of court, full term election	ratified	60,091–8,089	Nov. 1882	1882 JR 3
XIII	1	Political year; biennial elections	ratified	60,091–8,089	Nov. 1882	1882 JR 3
X	1	State superintendent, qualifications and pay fixed by legislature	rejected	12,967–18,342	Nov. 1888	1887 JR 4
VII	4	Supreme court, composed of 5 justices of supreme court	ratified	125,759–14,712	Apr. 1889	1889 JR 3
IV	31	Cities incorporated by general law	ratified	15,718–9,015	Nov. 1892	1891 JR 4
X	1	State superintendent, pay fixed by law	rejected	38,752–56,506	Nov. 1896	1895 JR 2
VIII	7	Circuit judges, additional in populous counties	ratified	45,823–41,513	Apr. 1897	1897 JR 9
X	1	State superintendent, nonpartisan 4-year term, pay fixed by law	ratified	71,550–57,411	Nov. 1902	1901 JR 3
XI	4	General banking law authorized	ratified	64,836–44,620	Nov. 1902	1901 JR 2
XI	5	Banking law referenda requirement repealed	ratified	64,836–44,620	Nov. 1902	1901 JR 2
XIII	11	Free passes prohibited	ratified	67,781–40,697	Nov. 1902	1901 JR 9
VII	4	Supreme court, 7 justices, 10-year terms	ratified	51,377–39,857	Apr. 1903	1903 JR 7
III	1	Suffrage for full citizens only	ratified	85,838–36,733	Nov. 1908	1907 JR 25
V	10	Governor's approval of bills in 6 days	ratified	85,958–27,270	Nov. 1908	1907 JR 13
VIII	1	Income tax	ratified	85,696–37,729	Nov. 1908	1907 JR 29
VIII	10	Highways, appropriations for	ratified	116,421–46,739	Nov. 1908	1907 JR 18

Art.	Sec.	Proposal	Result	Vote	Election	Reference
IV	3	Apportionment after each federal census.	ratified	54,932–52,634	Nov. 1910	1909 JR 55
IV	21	Change legislators' pay to $1,000 a year.	rejected	44,153–76,278	Nov. 1910	1909 JR 7
VIII	10	Water power and forests, appropriations for [2]	rejected	62,468–45,924 [2]	Nov. 1910	1909 Ch. 514
VII	10	Judges' salaries, time of payment.	ratified	44,855–34,865	Nov. 1912	1911 JR 24
XI	3	City or county debt for lands, discharge within 50 years.	ratified	46,369–34,975	Nov. 1912	1911 JR 42
XI	3a	Public parks, playgrounds, etc.	ratified	48,424–33,931	Nov. 1912	1911 JR 48
IV	1	Initiative and referendum	rejected	84,934–148,536	Nov. 1914	1913 JR 22
IV	21	Change legislators' pay to $600 a year, 2 cents a mile for additional round trips	rejected	68,907–157,202	Nov. 1914	1913 JR 24
VII	6,7	Judicial circuits, decreased number, additional judges.	rejected	63,311–154,827	Nov. 1914	1913 JR 26
VIII	—	State annuity insurance.	rejected	59,909–170,338	Nov. 1914	1913 JR 35
VIII	—	State insurance.	rejected	58,490–165,966	Nov. 1914	1913 JR 12
XI	1	Home rule of cities and villages	rejected	86,020–141,472	Nov. 1914	1913 JR 21
XI	—	Municipal power of condemnation.	rejected	61,122–154,945	Nov. 1914	1913 JR 25
XII	1	Constitutional amendments, submission after 3/5 approval by one legislature	rejected	71,734–160,761	Nov. 1914	1913 JR 17
XII	—	Constitution amended upon petition	rejected	68,435–150,215	Nov. 1914	1913 JR 22
XIII	—	Recall of civil officers.	rejected	81,628–144,386	Nov. 1914	1913 JR 15
IV	21	Legislators' pay fixed by law.	rejected	126,243–132,258	Apr. 1920	1919 JR 37
VII	6,7	Judicial circuits, decreased number, additional judges.	rejected	113,786–116,436	Apr. 1920	1919 JR 92
I	5	Jury verdict, 5/6 in civil cases	ratified	171,433–156,820	Nov. 1922	1921 JR 36
VI	4	Sheriffs, no limit on successive terms	rejected	161,832–207,594	Nov. 1922	1921 JR 37
XI	—	Municipal indebtedness for public utilities.	rejected	105,234–219,639	Apr. 1924	1923 JR 18
IV	21	Change legislators' pay to $750 a year.	rejected	189,635–250,236	Nov. 1924	1923 JR 64
VII	7	Circuit judges, additional in populous counties	ratified	240,207–226,562	Nov. 1924	1923 JR 57
VIII	10	Forestry, appropriations for	ratified	336,360–173,563	Nov. 1924	1923 JR 34
XI	3	Home rule for cities and villages	ratified	299,792–190,165	Nov. 1926	1925 JR 52
V	5	Governor's salary fixed by law.	ratified	202,156–188,302	Nov. 1926	1925 JR 16
XIII	12	Recall of elective officials.	ratified	205,868–201,125	Apr. 1927	1927 JR 17
IV	21	Change legislators' pay to $1,000 for session.	rejected	151,786–199,260	Apr. 1927	1927 JR 13
VIII	1	Severance tax: forests, minerals.	ratified	179,217–141,888	Apr. 1929	1929 JR 6
IV	21	Legislators' salary repealed; to be fixed by law.	ratified	237,250–212,846	Apr. 1929	1929 JR 13
VI	4	Sheriffs succeeding themselves for 2 terms	ratified	259,881–210,964	Nov. 1930	1929 JR 43
V	10	Item veto on appropriation bills	ratified	252,655–153,703	Nov. 1932	1931 JR 52
V	5	Governor's salary provision repealed; fixed by law	ratified	452,605–275,175	Nov. 1932	1931 JR 53
V	9	Lieutenant governor's salary repealed; fixed by law	ratified	427,768–267,120	Nov. 1932	1931 JR 58
VII	1	Wording of section corrected	ratified	436,113–221,563	Nov. 1932	1931 JR 71
XI	3	Municipal indebtedness for public utilities.	ratified	401,194–279,631	Nov. 1932	
III	1	Women's suffrage	ratified	411,088–166,745	Nov. 1934	1933 JR 76
XIII	11	Free passes, permitted as specified.	ratified	365,971–361,799	Nov. 1936	1935 JR 98
VIII	1	Installment payment of real estate taxes	ratified	330,971–134,808	Apr. 1941	1941 JR 18

History of proposed constitutional amendments since 1854, continued

Article	Section	Subject	Election result	Vote totals	Date	Proposed amendment
VII	15	Justice of peace, abolish office in first class cities	ratified	160,965–113,408	Apr. 1945	1945 JR 2
VIII	10	Aeronautical program	ratified	187,111–101,169	Apr. 1945	1945 JR 3
VI	4	Sheriffs, no limit on successive terms	rejected	121,144–170,131	Apr. 1946	1945 JR 47
IV	33	Auditing of state accounts	ratified	480,938–308,072	Nov. 1946	1945 JR 73
VI	2	Auditing (part of same proposal)	ratified	480,938–308,072	Nov. 1946	1945 JR 73
X	3	Public transportation of school children to any school	rejected	437,817–545,475	Nov. 1946	1945 JR 78
XI	2	Repeal; relating to exercise of eminent domain by municipalities	rejected	210,086–807,318	Nov. 1948	1947 JR 48
II	2	Prohibition on taxing federal lands repealed	rejected	245,412–297,237	Apr. 1949	1949 JR 2
VIII	10	Allow internal improvement debt for veterans' housing	ratified	311,576–290,736	Apr. 1949	1949 JR 1
II	2	Prohibition on taxing federal lands repealed	ratified	305,612–186,284	Apr. 1951	1951 JR 7
XI	3	City debt limit 8% for combined city and school purposes	ratified	313,739–191,897	Apr. 1951	1951 JR 6
IV	3, 4, 5	Apportionment based on area and population[3]	rejected	433,043–406,133 [3]	Apr. 1953	1953 JR 9
VII	9	Judicial elections to full terms	ratified	386,972–345,094	Apr. 1953	1953 JR 12
VII	24	Judges: qualifications, retirement	ratified	380,214–177,929	Apr. 1955	1955 JR 14
XI	3	School debt limit, equalized value	ratified	320,376–228,641	Apr. 1955	1955 JR 12
IV	26	Teachers' retirement benefits	ratified	365,560–255,284	Apr. 1956	1955 JR 17
VI	4	Sheriffs, no limit on successive terms	rejected	269,722–328,603	Apr. 1956	1955 JR 53
XI	3a	Municipal acquisition of land for public purposes	ratified	376,692–193,544	Apr. 1956	1955 JR 36
XIII	11	Free passes, not for public use	rejected	188,715–380,207	Apr. 1956	1955 JR 54
VIII	10	Port development	ratified	472,177–451,045	Apr. 1960	1959 JR 15
XI	3	Debt limit in populous counties, 5% of equalized valuation	ratified	686,104–529,467	Nov. 1960	1959 JR 32
IV	26	Salary increases during term for various public officers	rejected	297,066–307,575	Apr. 1961	1961 JR 11
IV	34	Continuity of civil government	ratified	498,869–132,728	Apr. 1961	1961 JR 10
VI	4	Sheriffs, no limit on successive terms	rejected	283,495–388,238	Apr. 1961	1961 JR 9
VIII	1	Personal property classified for tax purposes	ratified	381,881–220,434	Apr. 1961	1961 JR 13
XI	2	Municipal eminent domain, abolished jury verdict of necessity	ratified	348,406–259,566	Apr. 1961	1961 JR 12
XI	3	Debt limit 10% of equalized valuation for integrated aid school district	ratified	409,963–224,783	Apr. 1961	1961 JR 8
IV	3	"Indians not taxed" exclusion removed from apportionment formula	ratified	631,296–259,577	Nov. 1962	1961 JR 32
VI	23	County executive: 4-year terms	ratified	527,075–331,393	Nov. 1962	1961 JR 64
VI	4	County executive: 2-year terms	ratified	527,075–331,393	Nov. 1962	1961 JR 64
XI	23a	County executive veto power	ratified	524,240–319,378	Nov. 1962	1961 JR 64
IV	3	Time for apportionment of seats in the state legislature	rejected	232,851–277,014	Apr. 1963	1963 JR 9
IV	26	Salary increases during term for justices and judges	rejected	216,205–335,774	Apr. 1963	1963 JR 7

Art.	Sec.	Subject	Result	Vote	Submitted	Joint resolution
XI	3	Equalized value debt limit	ratified	285,296–231,702	Apr. 1963	1963 JR 8
VIII	10	Maximum state appropriation for forestry increased	rejected	440,978–536,724	Apr. 1964	1963 JR 32
XI	3	Property valuation for debt limit adjusted	rejected	336,994–572,276	Apr. 1964	1963 JR 33
XII	1	Constitutional amendments, submission of related items in a single proposition	rejected	317,676–582,045	Apr. 1964	SS 1963 JR 1[4]
VI	4	Coroner and surveyor abolished in counties of 500,000.	ratified	380,059–215,169	Apr. 1965	1965 JR 5
IV	24	Lotteries, definition revised	ratified	454,390–194,327	Apr. 1965	1965 JR 2
IV	13	Legislators on active duty in armed forces	ratified	362,935–189,641	Apr. 1966	1965 JR 14
VII	2	Establishment of inferior courts.	ratified	321,434–216,341	Apr. 1966	1965 JR 50
VII	15	Justices of the peace abolished.	ratified	321,434–216,341	Apr. 1966	1965 JR 50
XI	3	Special district public utility debt limit	ratified	307,502–199,919	Apr. 1966	1965 JR 51
I	23	Transportation of children to private schools	ratified	494,236–377,107	Apr. 1967	1967 JR 13
IV	26	Judicial salary increased during term	ratified	489,989–328,292	Apr. 1967	1967 JR 17
V	1m, 1n	4-year term for governor and lieutenant governor	ratified	534,368–310,478	Apr. 1967	1967 JR 10
V	3	Joint election of governor and lieutenant governor	ratified	507,339–312,267	Apr. 1967	1967 JR 11
VI	1m	4-year term for secretary of state	ratified	520,326–311,974	Apr. 1967	1967 JR 10
VI	1n	4-year term for state treasurer.	ratified	514,280–314,873	Apr. 1967	1967 JR 10
VI	1p	4-year term for attorney general	ratified	515,962–311,603	Apr. 1967	1967 JR 10
VI	4	Sheriffs, no limit on successive terms	ratified	508,242–324,544	Apr. 1967	1967 JR 12
IV	11	Legislative sessions, more than one permitted in biennium	ratified	670,757–267,997	Apr. 1968	1967 JR 48
VII	24	Uniform retirement date for justices and circuit judges	ratified	734,046–215,455	Apr. 1968	1967 JR 56
VII	24	Temporary appointment of justices and circuit judges	ratified	678,249–245,807	Apr. 1968	1967 JR 25
VIII	10	Forestry appropriation from sources other than property tax	ratified	652,705–286,512	Apr. 1968	1967 JR 25
IV	23	Uniform county government modified	ratified	326,445–321,851	Apr. 1969	1969 JR 2
IV	23a	County executive to have veto power	ratified	326,445–321,851	Apr. 1969	1969 JR 2
VIII	7	State public debt for specified purposes allowed	ratified	411,062–258,366	Apr. 1969	1969 JR 3
I	24	Private use of school buildings	ratified	871,707–298,016	Apr. 1972	1971 JR 27
IV	23	County government systems authorized	ratified	571,285–515,255	Apr. 1972	1971 JR 13
VI	4	Coroner/medical examiner option	ratified	795,497–323,930	Apr. 1972	1971 JR 21
X	3	Released time for religious instruction	ratified	595,075–585,511	Apr. 1972	1971 JR 28
I	25	Equality of the sexes.	rejected	447,240–520,936	Apr. 1973	1973 JR 5
IV	24	Charitable bingo authorized.	ratified	645,544–391,499	Apr. 1973	1973 JR 3
IV	26	Increased benefits for retired public employees.	ratified	396,051–315,545	Apr. 1973	1973 JR 15
VII	13	Removal of judges by 2/3 vote of legislature for cause.	ratified	493,496–193,867	Apr. 1974	1973 JR 25
VIII	1	Taxation of agricultural lands	ratified	353,377–340,518	Apr. 1974	1973 JR 29
VIII	3, 7	Public debt for veterans' housing.	ratified	385,915–300,232	Apr. 1974	1973 JR 3
VIII	7, 10	Internal improvements for transportation facilities[5]	rejected	342,396–341,291[5]	Apr. 1975	1975 JR 2
XI	3	Exclusion of certain debt from municipal debt limit	rejected	310,434–337,925	Apr. 1975	1975 JR 3

History of proposed constitutional amendments since 1854, continued

Article	Section	Subject	Election result	Vote totals	Date	Proposed amendment
XIII	2	Dueling: repeal of disenfranchisement	ratified	395,616–282,726	Apr. 1975	1975 JR 4
XI	3	Municipal indebtedness increased up to 10% of equalized valuation	rejected	328,097–715,420	Apr. 1976	1975 JR 6
VIII	7(2)(a), 10	Internal improvements for transportation facilities[5]	rejected	722,658–935,152	Nov. 1976[5]	1975 JR 2
IV	24	Charitable raffle games authorized	ratified	483,518–300,473	Apr. 1977	1977 JR 6
VII	2	Unified court system [also affected I 21; IV 17, 26; VII 3–11, 14, 16–23; XIV 16(1)–(4)]	ratified	490,437–215,939	Apr. 1977	1977 JR 7
VII	5	Court of appeals created [also affected I 21(1); VII 2, 3(3); XIV 16(5)]	ratified	455,350–229,316	Apr. 1977	1977 JR 7
VII	11, 13	Court system disciplinary proceedings	ratified	565,087–151,418	Apr. 1977	1977 JR 7
VII	24	Retirement age for justices and judges set by law	ratified	506,207–244,170	Apr. 1977	1977 JR 7
IV	23	Town government uniformity	rejected	179,011–383,395	Apr. 1978	1977 JR 18
V	7,8	Gubernatorial succession	ratified	538,959–187,440	Apr. 1979	1979 JR 3
XIII	10	Lieutenant governor vacancy	ratified	540,186–181,497	Apr. 1979	1979 JR 3
IV	9	Senate presiding officer	ratified	372,734–327,008	Apr. 1979	1979 JR 3
V	1	4-year constitutional officer terms (improved wording) [also affected V 1m; VI 1, 1m, 1n, 1p]	ratified	533,620–164,768	Apr. 1979	1979 JR 3
I	8	Right to bail[6]	ratified	505,092–185,405[6]	Apr. 1981	1981 JR 8
XI	1,4	Obsolete corporation and banking provisions	ratified	418,997–186,898	Apr. 1981	1981 JR 9
XI	3	Indebtedness period for sewage collection or treatment systems	ratified	386,792–250,866	Apr. 1981	1981 JR 7
XIII	12	Primaries in recall elections	ratified	366,635–259,820	Apr. 1981	1981 JR 6
VI	4	Counties responsible for acts of sheriff	ratified	316,156–219,752	Apr. 1982	1981 JR 15
I	1, 18	Gender-neutral wording [also affected X 1, 2]	ratified	771,267–479,053	Nov. 1982	1981 JR 29
IV	3	Military personnel treatment in redistricting	ratified	834,188–321,331	Nov. 1982	1981 JR 29
IV	4,5	Obsolete 1881 amendment reference	ratified	919,349–238,884	Nov. 1982	1981 JR 29
IV	30	Elections by legislature	ratified	977,438–193,679	Nov. 1982	1981 JR 29
X	1	Obsolete reference to election and term of superintendent of public instruction	ratified	934,236–215,961	Nov. 1982	1981 JR 29
X	2	Obsolete reference to military draft exemption purchase; school fund	ratified	887,488–295,693	Nov. 1982	1981 JR 29
XIV	3	Obsolete transition from territory to statehood [also affected XIV 4–12; XIV 14, 15]	ratified	926,875–223,213	Nov. 1982	1981 JR 29
XIV	16(1)	Obsolete transitional provisions of 1977 court reorganization [also affected XIV 16(2), (3), (5)]	ratified	882,091–237,698	Nov. 1982	1981 JR 29
XIV	16(4)	Terms on supreme court effective date provision	ratified	960,540–190,366	Nov. 1982	1981 JR 29
I	1	Rewording to parallel Declaration of Independence	ratified	419,699–65,418	Apr. 1986	1985 JR 21
III	1–6	Revision of suffrage defined by general law	ratified	401,911–83,183	Apr. 1986	1985 JR 14
XIII	1	Modernizing constitutional text	ratified	404,273–82,512	Apr. 1986	1985 JR 14
XIII	5	Obsolete suffrage right on Indian land	ratified	381,339–102,090	Apr. 1986	1985 JR 14
IV	24(5)	Permitting pari-mutuel on-track betting	ratified	580,089–529,729	Apr. 1987	1987 JR 3
IV	24(6)	Authorizing the creation of a state lottery	ratified	739,181–391,942	Apr. 1987	1987 JR 4

Article	Section	Description		Date	Resolution	Vote
VIII	1	Authorizing income tax credits or refunds for property or sales taxes	rejected	Apr. 1989	1989 JR 2	405,765–406,863
V	10	Redefining the partial veto power of the governor	ratified	Apr. 1990	1989 JR 39	387,068–252,481
VIII	10	Providing housing for persons of low or moderate income	rejected	Apr. 1991	1991 JR 2	295,823–402,921
VIII	7(2)(a)1	Railways and other railroad facilities [also created VIII 10]	ratified	Apr. 1992	1991 JR 9	650,592–457,690
IV	26	Legislative and judiciary compensation, effective date	ratified	Apr. 1992	1991 JR 13	736,832–348,645
VIII	1	Residential property tax reduction	rejected	Nov. 1992	1991 JR 14	675,876–1,536,975
I	9m	Crime victims	ratified	Apr. 1993	1993 JR 2	861,405–163,087
IV	24	Gambling, limiting "lottery"; divorce under general law [also affected IV 31, 32].	ratified	Apr. 1993	1993 JR 3	623,987–435,180
I	3	Removal of unnecessary references to masculine gender [also affected I 3, 7, 9, 19, 21(2); IV 6, 12, 13, 23a; V 4, 6; VI 2; VII 1, 12; XI 3a; XIII 4, 11, 12(6)].	rejected	Apr. 1995	1995 JR 3	412,032–498,801
IV	24(6)(a)	Authorizing sports lottery dedicated to athletic facilities	rejected	Apr. 1995	1995 JR 2	348,818–618,377
VII	10(1)	Removal of restriction on judges holding nonjudicial public office after resignation during the judicial term.	rejected	Apr. 1995	1995 JR 4	390,744–503,239
XIII	3	Eligibility to seek or hold public office if convicted of a felony or a misdemeanor involving violation of a public trust	ratified	Nov. 1996	1995 JR 28	1,292,934–543,516
I	25	Guaranteeing the right to keep and bear arms	ratified	Nov. 1998	1997 JR 21	1,205,873–425,052
VI	4(1), (3), (5), (6)	4-year term for sheriff; sheriffs permitted to hold nonpartisan office; allowed legislature to provide for election to fill vacancy during term.	ratified	Nov. 1998	1997 JR 18	1,161,942–412,508
IV	24(3), (5), (6)	Distributing state lottery, bingo and pari-mutuel proceeds for property tax	ratified	Apr. 1999	1999 JR 2	648,903–105,976
I	26	Right to fish, hunt, trap, and take game	ratified	Apr. 2003	2003 JR 8	668,459–146,182
VI	4(1), (3), (4)	4-year term for county clerks, treasurers, clerks of circuit court, district attorneys, coroners, elected surveyors, and registers of deeds [also affected VII 12]	ratified	Apr. 2005	2005 JR 2	534,742–177,037
XIII	13	Marriage between one man and one woman	ratified	Nov. 2006	2005 JR 30	1,264,310–862,924
V	10(1)(c)	Gubernatorial partial veto power	ratified	Apr. 2008	2007 JR 26	575,582–239,613
IV	9(2)	Department of transportation and transportation fund [also created VIII 11].	ratified	Nov. 2014	2013 JR 1	1,733,101–434,806
VIII	1	Election of Chief Justice of the supreme court.	ratified	Apr. 2015	2015 JR 2	433,533–384,503

Note: To amend the Wisconsin Constitution, it is necessary for two consecutive legislatures to adopt an identical amendment (known as "first consideration" and "second consideration") and for a majority of the electorate to ratify the amendment at a subsequent election. See Art. XII, Sec. 1. JR 41 of 1925, which became Joint Rule 16 of the Wisconsin Legislature, established a new procedure to incorporate the "submission to the people" clause into the proposal at second approval.

Since the adoption of the Wisconsin Constitution in 1848, the electorate has voted 145 out of 196 times to amend a total of 128 sections of the constitution (excluding the same vote for more than one item but including a vote that was later resubmitted by the legislature and two votes that were declared invalid by the courts). The Wisconsin Legislature adopted 158 acts or joint resolutions to submit these changes to the electorate. Ch.–chapter; JR–joint resolution; SS–special session.

1. No other number was assigned to this joint resolution. 2. Ratified but declared invalid by Supreme Court in *State ex rel. Owen v. Donald*, 160 Wis. 21 (1915). 3. Ratified but declared invalid by Supreme Court in *State ex rel. Thomson v. Zimmerman*, 264 Wis. 644 (1953). 4. Special session December 1964. 5. Recount resulted in rejection (342,132 to 342,309). However, the Dane County Circuit Court ruled the recount invalid due to election irregularities and required that the referendum be resubmitted to the electorate. Resubmitted to the electorate November 1976 by the 1975 Wisconsin Legislature through Ch. 224, s.145r, Laws of 1975. 6. As a result of a Dane County Circuit Court injunction, vote totals were certified April 7, 1982, by the Board of State Canvassers.

Sources: Official records of the Wisconsin Elections Commission; *Laws of Wisconsin*, 2015 and previous volumes.

Statewide referenda other than constitutional amendments since 1849

Subject	Election result	Vote totals	Date	Submitting law
Extend suffrage to colored persons [1]	Approved	5,265–4,075	Nov. 1849	1849 Ch. 137
State banks; advisory	Approved	31,289–9,126	Nov. 1851	1851 Ch. 143
General banking law.	Approved	32,826–8,711	Nov. 1852	1852 Ch. 479
Liquor prohibition; advisory	Approved	27,519–24,109	Nov. 1853	1853 Ch. 101
Extend suffrage to colored persons	Rejected	28,235–41,345	Nov. 1857	1857 Ch. 44
Amend general banking law; redemption of bank notes	Approved	27,267–2,837	Nov. 1858	1858 Ch. 98
Amend general banking law; circulation of bank notes	Approved	57,646–2,515	Nov. 1861	1861 Ch. 242
Amend general banking law; interest rate 7% per year	Approved	46,269–7,794	Nov. 1862	1862 Ch. 203
Extend suffrage to colored persons [1]	Rejected	46,588–55,591	Nov. 1865	1865 Ch. 414
Amend general banking law; taxing shareholders	Approved	49,714–19,151	Nov. 1866	1866 Ch. 102
Amend general banking law; winding up circulation.	Approved	45,796–11,842	Nov. 1867	1866 Ch. 143; 1867 JR 12
Abolish office of bank comptroller	Approved	15,499–1,948	Nov. 1868	1868 Ch. 28
Incorporation of savings banks and savings societies	Approved	4,029–3,069	Nov. 1876	1876 Ch. 384
Women's suffrage upon school matters	Approved	43,581–38,998	Nov. 1886	1885 Ch. 211
Revise 1897 banking law; banking department under commission.	Rejected	86,872–92,607	Nov. 1898	1897 Ch. 303
Primary election law	Approved	130,366–80,102	Nov. 1904	1903 Ch. 451
Pocket ballots and coupon voting systems	Rejected	45,958–111,139	Apr. 1906	1905 Ch. 522
Women's suffrage	Rejected	135,545–227,024	Nov. 1912	1911 Ch. 227
Soldiers' bonus financed by 3-mill property tax and income tax.	Approved	165,762–57,324	Sept. 1919	1919 Ch. 667
Wisconsin prohibition enforcement act.	Approved	419,309–199,876	Nov. 1920	1919 Ch. 556
U.S. prohibition act (Volstead Act); memorializing Congress to amend	Approved	349,443–177,603	Nov. 1926	1925 JR 47
Repeal of Wisconsin prohibition enforcement act; advisory	Approved	350,337–196,402	Nov. 1926	1925 JR 47
Modification of Wisconsin prohibition enforcement act; advisory.	Approved	321,688–200,545	Apr. 1929	1929 JR 16
County distribution of auto licenses; advisory	Rejected	183,716–368,674	Apr. 1931	1931 JR 11
Sunday blue law repeal; advisory.	Approved	396,436–271,786	Apr. 1932	1931 JR 114
Old-age pensions; advisory	Approved	531,915–154,729	Apr. 1934	SS 1933 JR 64
Teacher tenure law repeal; advisory	Approved	403,782–372,524	Apr. 1940	1939 JR 100
Property tax levy for high school aid; 2 mills of assessed valuation	Rejected	131,004–410,315	Apr. 1944	1943 Ch. 525
Daylight saving time; advisory.	Rejected	313,091–379,740	Apr. 1947	1947 JR 4
3% retail sales tax for veterans bonus; advisory	Rejected	258,497–825,990	Nov. 1948	1947 JR 62
4-year term for constitutional officers; advisory.	Rejected	210,821–328,613	Apr. 1951	1951 JR 13
Apportionment of legislature by area and population; advisory.	Rejected	689,615–753,092	Nov. 1952	1951 Ch. 728

Subject	Election result	Vote totals	Date	Submitting law
New residents entitled to vote for president and vice president.	Approved	550,056–414,680	Nov. 1954	1953 Ch. 76
Statewide educational television tax-supported; advisory	Rejected	308,385–697,262	Nov. 1954	1953 JR 66
Daylight saving time.	Approved	578,661–480,656	Apr. 1957	1957 Ch. 6
Ex-residents entitled to vote for president and vice president	Approved	627,279–229,375	Nov. 1962	1961 Ch. 512
Gasoline tax increase for highway construction; advisory.	Rejected	150,769–889,364	Apr. 1964	SS 1963 JR 3
New residents entitled to vote after 6 months.	Approved	582,389–256,246	Nov. 1966	1965 Chs. 88,89
State control and funding of vocational education; advisory.	Rejected	292,560–409,789	Apr. 1969	1969 JR 4
Recreational lands bonding; advisory.	Approved	361,630–322,882	Apr. 1969	1969 JR 5
Water pollution abatement bonding; advisory	Approved	446,763–246,968	Apr. 1969	1969 JR 5
New residents entitled to vote after 10 days	Approved	1,017,887–660,875	Nov. 1976	1975 Ch. 85
Presidential voting revised.	Approved	782,181–424,386	Nov. 1978	1977 Ch. 394
Overseas voting revised.	Approved	658,289–524,029	Nov. 1978	1977 Ch. 394
Public inland lake protection and rehabilitation districts	Approved	1,210,452–355,024	Nov. 1980	1979 Ch. 299
Nuclear weapons moratorium and reduction; advisory	Approved	641,514–205,018	Sept. 1982	1981 JR 38
Nuclear waste site locating; advisory	Rejected	78,327–628,414	Apr. 1983	1983 JR 1
Gambling casinos on excursion vessels; advisory	Rejected	465,432–604,289	Apr. 1993	1991 WisAct 321
Gambling casino restrictions; advisory	Approved	646,827–416,722	Apr. 1993	1991 WisAct 321
Video poker and other forms of video gambling allowed; advisory.	Rejected	358,045–702,864	Apr. 1993	1991 WisAct 321
Pari-mutuel on-track betting continuation; advisory.	Approved	548,580–507,403	Apr. 1993	1991 WisAct 321
State-operated lottery continuation; advisory.	Approved	773,306–287,585	Apr. 1993	1991 WisAct 321
Extended suffrage in federal elections to adult children of U.S. citizens living abroad	Approved	1,293,458–792,975	Nov. 2000	1999 WisAct 182
Death penalty; advisory.	Approved	1,166,571–934,508	Nov. 2006	2005 JR 58

Note: Statewide referendum questions are submitted to the electorate by the Wisconsin Legislature: 1) to ratify a law extending the right of suffrage (as required by the state constitution); 2) to ratify a law that has been passed contingent on voter approval; or 3) to seek voter opinion through an advisory referendum. Since 1848, the Wisconsin Legislature has presented 53 referendum questions to the Wisconsin electorate through the passage of acts or joint resolutions; 39 were ratified. Prior to statehood, the territorial legislature sent four questions to the electorate, as follows: Formation of a state government, submitted by Territorial Laws 1846, page 5 (Jan.31), approved April 1846, 12,334 votes for, 2,487 against; Ratification of first constitution, submitted by Art. XIX, Sec. 9 of 1846 Constitution, rejected April 1847, 14,119 votes for, 20,231 against; Extend suffrage to colored persons, submitted by supplemental resolution to 1846 Constitution, rejected April 1847, 7,664 votes for, 14,615 against; Ratification of second constitution, submitted by Art. XIV, Sec. 9 of 1848 Constitution, approved March 1848, 16,799 votes for, 6,384 against.

Ch.–chapter; JR–joint resolution; SS–special session.

1. In *Gillespie v. Palmer*, 20 Wis. 544 (1866), the Wisconsin Supreme Court ruled that Chapter 137, Laws of 1849, extending suffrage to colored persons, was ratified November 6, 1849.

Sources: Official records of the Wisconsin Elections Commission; *Laws of Wisconsin*, 2015 and previous volumes.

Wisconsin vote in presidential elections since 1848

1848—4 electoral votes
Lewis Cass—D 15,001
Zachary Taylor—W 13,747
Martin Van Buren—FS . . . 10,418
Total. 39,166

1852—5 electoral votes
Franklin Pierce—D 33,658
Winfield Scott—W 22,210
John P. Hale—FS. 8,814
Total. 64,682

1856—5 electoral votes
John C. Fremont—R 66,090
James Buchanan—D 52,843
Millard Fillmore—A. 579
Total. 119,512

1860—5 electoral votes
Abraham Lincoln—R 86,113
Stephen A. Douglas—D . . 65,021
John C. Breckinridge—SoD . . 888
John Bell—CU 161
Total. 152,183

1864—8 electoral votes
Abraham Lincoln—R 83,458
George B. McClellan—D . . 65,884
Total. 149,342

1868—8 electoral votes
Ulysses S. Grant—R 108,857
Horatio Seymour—D 84,707
Total. 193,564

1872—10 electoral votes
Ulysses S. Grant—R 104,994
Horace Greeley—D & LR . . 86,477
Charles O'Conor—D 834
Total. 192,305

1876—10 electoral votes
Rutherford B. Hayes—R . 130,668
Samuel J. Tilden—D . . . 123,927
Peter Cooper—G 1,509
Green Clay Smith—Pro. 27
Total. 256,131

1880—10 electoral votes
James A. Garfield—R . . . 144,398
Winfield S. Hancock—D . 114,644
James B. Weaver—G 7,986
John W. Phelps—A 91
Neal Dow—Pro 68
Total. 267,187

1884—11 electoral votes
James G. Blaine—R 161,157
Grover Cleveland—D . . . 146,477
John P. St. John—Pro 7,656
Benjamin F. Butler—G 4,598
Total. 319,888

1888—11 electoral votes
Benjamin Harrison—R   176,553
Grover Cleveland—D . . . 155,232
Clinton B. Fisk—Pro. 14,277
Alson J. Streeter—UL. 8,552
Total. 354,614

1892—12 electoral votes
Grover Cleveland—D. . . . 177,325
Benjamin Harrison—R . . 171,101
John Bidwell—Pro 13,136
James B. Weaver—PPop . . 10,019
Total. 371,581

1896—12 electoral votes
William McKinley—R . . . 268,135
William J. Bryan—D. . . . 165,523
Joshua Levering—Pro 7,507
John M. Palmer—ND 4,584
Charles H. Matchett—SL. . .1,314
Charles E. Bentley—Nat . . . 346
Total. 447,409

1900—12 electoral votes
William McKinley—R . . . 265,760
William J. Bryan—D. . . . 159,163
John G. Wooley—Pro. . . . 10,027
Eugene V. Debs—SD 7,048
Joseph F. Malloney—SL 503
Total. 442,501

1904—13 electoral votes
Theodore Roosevelt—R . 280,164
Alton B. Parker—D 124,107
Eugene V. Debs—SD 28,220
Silas C. Swallow—Pro 9,770
Thomas E. Watson—PPop . . . 530
Charles H. Corregan—SL . . . 223
Total. 443,014

1908—13 electoral votes
William H. Taft—R 247,747
William J. Bryan—D. . . . 166,632
Eugene V. Debs—SD 28,164
Eugene W. Chafin—Pro . . 11,564
August Gillhaus—SL 314
Total. 454,421

1912—13 electoral votes
Woodrow Wilson—D . . . 164,230
William H. Taft—R. 130,596
Theodore Roosevelt—P . . 62,448
Eugene V. Debs—SD 33,476
Eugene W. Chafin—Pro . . .8,584
Arthur E. Reimer—SL. 632
Total. 399,966

1916—13 electoral votes
Charles E. Hughes—R . . 220,822
Woodrow Wilson—D . . . 191,363
Allan Benson—S. 27,631
J. Frank Hanly—Pro. 7,318
Total. 447,134

1920—13 electoral votes
Warren G. Harding—R . . 498,576
James M. Cox—D 113,422
Eugene V. Debs—S 80,635
Aaron S. Watkins—Pro 8,647
Total. 701,280

1924—13 electoral votes
Robert M. La Follette—P . 453,678
Calvin Coolidge—R 311,614
John W. Davis—D 68,096
William Z. Foster—Wrk 3,834
Herman P. Faris—Pro 2,918
Total. 840,140

1928—13 electoral votes
Herbert Hoover—R 544,205
Alfred E. Smith—D 450,259
Norman Thomas—S 18,213
William F. Varney—Pro 2,245
William Z. Foster—Wrk 1,528
Verne L. Reynolds—SL 381
Total. 1,016,831

1932—12 electoral votes
Franklin D. Roosevelt—D 707,410
Herbert Hoover—R 347,741
Norman Thomas—S 53,379
William Z. Foster—Com . . .3,112
William D. Upshaw—Pro. . .2,672
Verne L. Reynolds—SL 494
Total. 1,114,808

1936—12 electoral votes
Franklin D. Roosevelt—D 802,984
Alfred M. Landon—R . . . 380,828
William Lemke—U 60,297
Norman Thomas—S 10,626
Earl Browder—Com. 2,197
David L. Calvin—Pro 1,071
John W. Aiken—SL 557
Total. 1,258,560

Wisconsin vote in presidential elections, since 1848, continued

1940—12 electoral votes
Franklin D. Roosevelt—D   704,821
Wendell Willkie—R 679,206
Norman Thomas—S   15,071
Earl Browder—Com. 2,394
Roger Babson—Pro. 2,148
John W. Aiken—SL 1,882
Total. 1,405,522

1944—12 electoral votes
Thomas Dewey—R 674,532
Franklin D. Roosevelt—D 650,413
Norman Thomas—S 13,205
Edward Teichert—I 1,002
Total. 1,339,152

1948—12 electoral votes
Harry S Truman—D 647,310
Thomas Dewey—R 590,959
Henry Wallace—PP 25,282
Norman Thomas—S 12,547
Edward Teichert—I 399
Farrell Dobbs—ISW 303
Total. 1,276,800

1952—12 electoral votes
Dwight D. Eisenhower—R 979,744
Adlai E. Stevenson—D . . 622,175
Vincent Hallinan—IP 2,174
Farrell Dobbs—ISW 1,350
Darlington Hoopes—IS . . .1,157
Eric Hass—ISL 770
Total. 1,607,370

1956—12 electoral votes
Dwight D. Eisenhower—R 954,844
Adlai E. Stevenson—D . . 586,768
T. Coleman Andrews—I (Con)
. 6,918
Darlington Hoopes—I (S) . . . 754
Eric Hass—I (SL) 710
Farrell Dobbs—I (SW) 564
Total. 1,550,558

1960—12 electoral votes)
Richard M. Nixon—R . . . 895,175
John F. Kennedy—D . . . 830,805
Farrell Dobbs—I (SW) 1,792
Eric Hass—I (SL) 1,310
Total. 1,729,082

1964—12 electoral votes
Lyndon B. Johnson—D 1,050,424
Barry M. Goldwater—R. . . 638,495
Clifton DeBerry—I (SW) . . .1,692
Eric Hass—I (SL) 1,204
Total. 1,691,815

1968—12 electoral votes
Richard M. Nixon—R . . . 809,997
Hubert H. Humphrey—D 748,804
George C. Wallace—I (A) . 127,835
Henning A. Blomen—I (SL) .1,338
Frederick W. Halstead
—I (SW) 1,222
Total. 1,689,196

1972—11 electoral votes
Richard M. Nixon—R . . . 989,430
George S. McGovern—D. 810,174
John G. Schmitz—A. . . . 47,525
Benjamin M. Spock—I (Pop)
. 2,701
Louis Fisher—I (SL) 998
Gus Hall—I (Com) 663
Evelyn Reed—I (SW) 506
Total. 1,851,997

1976—11 electoral votes
Jimmy Carter—D 1,040,232
Gerald R. Ford—R 1,004,987
Eugene J. McCarthy—I. . . 34,943
Lester Maddox—A 8,552
Frank P. Zeidler—I (S) 4,298
Roger L. MacBride—I (Lib). .3,814
Peter Camejo—I (SW) 1,691
Margaret Wright—I (Pop) . . . 943
Gus Hall—I (Com) 749
Lyndon H. LaRouche, Jr—
I (USL). 738
Jules Levin—I (SL). 389
Total. 2,104,175

1980—11 electoral votes
Ronald Reagan—R . . . 1,088,845
Jimmy Carter—D 981,584
John Anderson—I. 160,657
Ed Clark—I (Lib) 29,135
Barry Commoner—I (Cit) . .7,767
John Rarick—I (Con) 1,519
David McReynolds—I (S) . . . 808
Gus Hall—I (Com) 772
Deirdre Griswold—I (WW) . . 414
Clifton DeBerry—I (SW) 383
Total. 2,273,221

1984—11 electoral votes
Ronald Reagan—R . . . 1,198,800
Walter F. Mondale—D . . 995,847
David Bergland—Lib 4,884
Bob Richards—Con. 3,864
Lyndon H. LaRouche, Jr—I . 3,791
Sonia Johnson—I (Cit) 1,456
Dennis L. Serrette—I (WIA) .1,007
Larry Holmes—I (WW) 619
Gus Hall—I (Com) 597
Melvin T. Mason—I (SW). . . . 445
Total. 2,212,018

1988—11 electoral votes
Michael S. Dukakis—D
. . . . 1,126,794
George Bush—R. 1,047,499
Ronald Paul—I (Lib). 5,157
David E. Duke—I (Pop). . . .3,056
James Warren—I (SW) . . .2,574
Lyndon H. LaRouche, Jr—I (NER)
. 2,302
Lenora B. Fulani—I (NA) . . .1,953
Total. 2,191,612

1992—11 electoral votes
Bill Clinton—D. 1,041,066
George Bush—R. 930,855
Ross Perot—I. 544,479
Andre Marrou—Lib. 2,877
James Gritz—I (AFC) 2,311
Ron Daniels—LF. 1,883
Howard Phillips—I (Tax) . . .1,772
J. Quinn Brisben—I (S) 1,211
John Hagelin—NL. 1,070
Lenora B. Fulani—I (NA) 654
Lyndon H. LaRouche, Jr—I (ER)
. . . . 633
Jack Herer—I (Gr) 547
Eugene A. Hem—3rd. 405
James Warren—I (SW) 390
Total. 2,531,114

1996—11 electoral votes
Bill Clinton—D. 1,071,971
Bob Dole—R 845,029
Ross Perot—Rfm 227,339
Ralph Nader—I (WG) . . . 28,723
Howard Phillips—Tax. 8,811
Harry Browne—Lib 7,929
John Hagelin—I (NL) 1,379
Monica Moorehead—I (WW)
. 1,333
Mary Cal Hollis—I (S) 848
James E. Harris—I (SW) 483
Total. 2,196,169

2000—11 electoral votes
Al Gore—D 1,242,987
George W. Bush—R. . . 1,237,279
Ralph Nader—WG 94,070
Pat Buchanan—I (Rfm). . . 11,446
Harry Browne—Lib 6,640
Howard Phillips—Con . . .2,042
Monica G. Moorehead—I (WW)
. 1,063
John Hagelin—I (Rfm) 878
James Harris—I (SW) 306
Total. 2,598,607

Wisconsin vote in presidential elections since 1848, continued

2004—10 electoral votes
John F. Kerry—D. 1,489,504
George W. Bush—R. . . 1,478,120
Ralph Nader—I (TBL) 16,390
Michael Badnarik—Lib. . . .6,464
David Cobb—WG 2,661
Walter F. Brown—I (SPW) . . .471
James Harris—I (SW) 411
Total. 2,997,007

2012—10 electoral votes
Barack Obama—D . . . 1,620,985
Mitt Romney—R. 1,407,966
Gary Johnson—I (Lib) . . . 20,439
Jill Stein—I (Grn) 7,665
Virgil Goode—Con 4,930
Jerry White—I (SE) 553
Gloria La Riva—I (S&L) 526
Total. 3,068,434

2008—10 electoral votes
Barack Obama—D . . . 1,677,211
John McCain—R. 1,262,393
Ralph Nader—I 17,605
Bob Barr—Lib 8,858
Chuck Baldwin—I (Con) . . .5,072
Cynthia McKinney—WG . . .4,216
Jeffrey J. Wamboldt—I (WtP) . 764
Brian Moore—I (SocUSA) . . .540
Gloria La Riva—I (S&L) 237
Total. 2,983,417

2016—10 electoral votes
Donald J. Trump—R . . 1,405,284
Hillary Clinton—D. . . . 1,382,536
Gary Johnson—Lib 106,674
Jill Stein—WG 31,072
Darrell L. Castle—Con . . . 12,162
Monica Moorehead—I (WW)
. 1,770
Rocky Roque De La Fuente—I (AD)
. 1,502
Total. 2,976,150

Note: The party designation listed for a candidate is taken from the Congressional Quarterly *Guide to U.S. Elections*. A candidate whose party did not receive 1% of the vote for a statewide office in the previous election or who failed to meet the alternative requirement of section 5.62, Wis. Stats., must be listed on the Wisconsin ballot as "independent." In this listing, candidates whose party affiliations appear as "I," followed by a party designation in parentheses, were identified on the ballot simply as "independent" although they also provided a party designation or statement of principle.

Under the Electoral College system, each state is entitled to electoral votes equal in number to its total congressional delegation of U.S. Senators and U.S. Representatives.

Some totals include scattered votes for other candidates.

A—American (Know Nothing)
AD—American Delta
AFC—America First Coalition
Cit—Citizens
Com—Communist
Con—Constitution
CU—Constitutional Union
D—Democrat
ER—Independents for Economic Recovery
FS—Free Soil
G—Greenback
Gr—Grassroots
Grn—Green
I—Independent
IP—Independent Progressive
IS—Independent Socialist
ISL—Independent Socialist Labor
ISW—Independent Socialist Worker

LF—Labor–Farm/Laborista-Agrario
Lib—Libertarian
LR—Liberal Republican
NA—New Alliance
Nat—National
ND—National Democrat
NER—National Economic Recovery
NL—Natural Law
P—Progressive
Pop—Populist
PP—People's Progressive
PPop—People's (Populist)
Pro—Prohibition
R—Republican
Rfm—Reform
S—Socialist
SD—Social Democrat
SE—Socialist Equality

SL—Socialist Labor
S&L—Party for Socialism and Liberation
SocUSA—Socialist Party USA
SoD—Southern Democrat
SPW—Socialist Party of Wis.
SW—Socialist Worker
Tax—U.S. Taxpayers
TBL—The Better Life
3rd—Third Party
U—Union
UL—Union Labor
USL—U.S. Labor
W—Whig
WG—Wisconsin Greens
WIA—Wis. Independent Alliance
Wrk—Workers
WtP—We, the People
WW—Worker's World

Sources: Official records of the Wisconsin Elections Commission and Congressional Quarterly, *Guide to U.S. Elections*, 1994.

Wisconsin members of the U.S. Senate since 1848

Class 1		Class 3	
	Term		Term
Henry Dodge—D	1848–1857	Isaac P. Walker—D.	1848–1855
James R. Doolittle—R	1857–1869	Charles Durkee—UR	1855–1861
Matthew H. Carpenter—R. . . .	1869–1875	Timothy O. Howe—UR	1861–1879
Angus Cameron[1]—R	1875–1881	Matthew H. Carpenter—R.	1879–1881
Philetus Sawyer—R.	1881–1893	Angus Cameron[1]—R	1881–1885
John Lendrum Mitchell—D . . .	1893–1899	John C. Spooner—R	1885–1891
Joseph Very Quarles—R	1899–1905	William F. Vilas—D	1891–1897
Robert M. La Follette, Sr.[2]—R . .	1906–1925	John C. Spooner—R	1897–1907
Robert M. La Follette, Jr.[3]—R. .	1925–1935	Isaac Stephenson[5]—R	1907–1915
Robert M. La Follette, Jr.—P. . .	1935–1947	Paul O. Husting—D	1915–1917
Joseph R. McCarthy—R	1947–1957	Irvine L. Lenroot[6]—R.	1918–1927
William Proxmire[4]—D	1957–1989	John J. Blaine—R	1927–1933
Herbert H. Kohl—D.	1989–2013	F. Ryan Duffy—D	1933–1939
Tammy Baldwin—D.	2013–	Alexander Wiley—R.	1939–1963
		Gaylord A. Nelson—D	1963–1981
		Robert W. Kasten, Jr.—R	1981–1993
		Russell D. Feingold—D.	1993–2011
		Ron Johnson—R.	2011–

Note: Each state has two U.S. Senators, and each serves a six–year term. They were elected by their respective state legislatures until passage of the 17th Amendment to the U.S. Constitution on April 8, 1913, which provided for popular election. Article I, Section 3, Clause 2, of the U.S. Constitution divides senators into three classes so that one–third of the senate is elected every two years. Wisconsin's seats were assigned to Class 1 and Class 3 at statehood.

D–Democrat; P–Progressive; R–Republican; UR–Union Republican.

1. Not a candidate for reelection to Class 1 seat, but elected 3/10/1881 to fill vacancy caused by death of Class 3 Senator Carpenter on 2/24/1881. 2. Elected 1/25/1905 but continued to serve as governor until 1/1/1906. 3. Elected 9/29/1925 to fill vacancy caused by death of Robert La Follette, Sr., on 6/18/1925. 4. Elected 8/27/1957 to fill vacancy caused by death of McCarthy on 5/2/1957. 5. Elected 5/17/1907 to fill vacancy caused by resignation of Spooner on 4/30/1907. 6. Elected 5/2/1918 to fill vacancy caused by death of Husting on 10/21/1917.

Source: Wisconsin Legislative Reference Bureau records.

Wisconsin members of the U.S. House of Representatives since 1848

	Party	District	Term	Residence
Adams, Henry C.	Rep.	2	1903–1906	Madison
Amlie, Thomas R	Rep., Prog.	1	1931–1933; 1935–1939	Elkhorn
Aspin, Les	Dem.	1	1971–1993	East Troy
Atwood, David	Rep.	2	1870–1871	Madison
Babbitt, Clinton.	Dem.	1	1891–1893	Beloit
Babcock, Joseph W.	Rep.	3	1893–1907	Necedah
Baldus, Alvin.	Dem.	3	1975–1981	Menomonie
Baldwin, Tammy	Dem.	2	1999–2013	Madison
Barber, J. Allen	Rep.	3	1871–1875	Lancaster
Barca, Peter W.	Dem.	1	1993–1995	Kenosha
Barnes, Lyman E	Dem.	8	1893–1895	Appleton
Barney, Samuel S	Rep.	5	1895–1903	West Bend
Barrett, Thomas M	Dem.	5	1993–2003	Milwaukee
Barwig, Charles	Dem.	2	1889–1895	Mayville
Beck, Joseph D	Rep.	7	1921–1929	Viroqua
Berger, Victor L	Soc.	5	1911–1913; 1919; 1923–1929	Milwaukee

Wisconsin members of the U.S. House of Representatives since 1848, continued

	Party	District	Term	Residence
Biemiller, Andrew J.	Dem.	5	1945–1947; 1949–1951	Milwaukee
Billinghurst, Charles	Rep.	3	1855–1859	Juneau
Blanchard, George W	Rep.	1	1933–1935	Edgerton
Boileau, Gerald J	Rep., Prog.	8, 7	1931–1939	Wausau
Bolles, Stephen	Rep.	1	1939–1941	Janesville
Bouck, Gabriel.	Dem.	6	1877–1881	Oshkosh
Bragg, Edward S	Dem.	5, 2	1877–1883; 1885–1887	Fond du Lac
Brickner, George H.	Dem.	5	1889–1895	Sheboygan Falls
Brophy, John C	Rep.	4	1947–1949	Milwaukee
Brown, James S	Dem.	1	1863–1865	Milwaukee
Brown, Webster E.	Rep.	9, 10	1901–1907	Rhinelander
Browne, Edward E	Rep.	8	1913–1931	Waupaca
Burchard, Samuel D	Dem.	5	1875–1877	Beaver Dam
Burke, Michael E	Dem.	6, 2	1911–1917	Beaver Dam
Bushnell, Allen R	Dem.	3	1891–1893	Madison
Byrnes, John W	Rep.	8	1945–1973	Green Bay
Cannon, Raymond J	Dem.	4	1933–1939	Milwaukee
Cary, William J.	Rep.	4	1907–1919	Milwaukee
Caswell, Lucien B	Rep.	2, 1	1875–1883; 1885–1891	Fort Atkinson
Cate, George W	Reform	8	1875–1877	Stevens Point
Clark, Charles B	Rep.	6	1887–1891	Neenah
Classon, David G	Rep.	9	1917–1923	Oconto
Cobb, Amasa	Rep.	3	1863–1871	Mineral Point
Coburn, Frank P.	Dem.	7	1891–1893	West Salem
Cole, Orasmus.	Whig	2	1849–1851	Potosi
Cook, Samuel A	Rep.	6	1895–1897	Neenah
Cooper, Henry Allen	Rep.	1	1893–1919; 1921–1931	Racine
Cornell, Robert J	Dem.	8	1975–1979	De Pere
Dahle, Herman B	Rep.	2	1899–1903	Mount Horeb
Darling, Mason C	Dem.	2	1848–1849	Fond du Lac
Davidson, James H.	Rep.	6, 8	1897–1913; 1917–1918	Oshkosh
Davis, Glenn R.	Rep.	2, 9	1947–1957; 1965–1975	Waukesha
Deuster, Peter V.	Dem.	4	1879–1885	Milwaukee
Dilweg, La Vern R.	Dem.	8	1943–1945	Green Bay
Doty, James D.	Dem.	3	1849–1853	Neenah
Duffy, Sean P.	Rep.	7	2011–	Ashland
Durkee, Charles.	Free Soil	1	1849–1853	Kenosha
Eastman, Ben C	Dem.	2	1851–1855	Platteville
Eldredge, Charles A	Dem.	4, 5	1863–1875	Fond du Lac
Esch, John Jacob	Rep.	7	1899–1921	La Crosse
Flynn, Gerald T	Dem.	1	1959–1961	Racine
Frear, James A.	Rep.	10, 9	1913–1935	Hudson
Froehlich, Harold V.	Rep.	8	1973–1975	Appleton
Gallagher, Mike	Rep.	8	2017–	Green Bay
Gehrmann, Bernard J	Prog.	10	1935–1943	Mellen
Green, Mark A.	Rep.	8	1999–2007	Green Bay
Griffin, Michael	Rep.	7	1894–1899	Eau Claire
Griswold, Harry W	Rep.	3	1939–1941	West Salem
Grothman, Glenn.	Rep.	6	2015–	Glenbeulah
Guenther, Richard W.	Rep.	6, 2	1881–1889	Oshkosh
Gunderson, Steven.	Rep.	3	1981–1997	Osseo
Hanchett, Luther	Rep.	2	1861–1862	Plover
Haugen, Nils P.	Rep.	8, 10	1887–1895	Black River Falls
Hawkes, Charles, Jr.	Rep.	2	1939–1941	Horicon
Hazelton, George C	Rep.	3	1877–1883	Boscobel
Hazelton, Gerry W	Rep.	2	1871–1875	Columbus
Henney, Charles W	Dem.	2	1933–1935	Portage
Henry, Robert K.	Rep.	2	1945–1947	Jefferson

Wisconsin members of the U.S. House of Representatives since 1848, continued

	Party	District	Term	Residence
Hopkins, Benjamin F.	Rep.	2	1867–1870	Madison
Hudd, Thomas R	Dem.	5	1886–1889	Green Bay
Hughes, James	Dem.	8	1933–1935	De Pere
Hull, Merlin	Prog.	7, 9	1929–1931; 1935–1953	Black River Falls
Humphrey, Herman L	Rep.	7	1877–1883	Hudson
Jenkins, John J	Rep.	10, 11	1895–1909	Chippewa Falls
Johns, Joshua L	Rep.	8	1939–1943	Appleton
Johnson, Jay	Dem.	8	1997–1999	New Franken
Johnson, Lester R.	Dem.	9	1953–1965	Black River Falls
Jones, Burr W	Dem.	3	1883–1885	Madison
Kading, Charles A.	Rep.	2	1927–1933	Watertown
Kagen, Steve.	Dem.	8	2007–2011	Appleton
Kasten, Robert W., Jr.	Rep.	9	1975–1979	Waukesha
Kastenmeier, Robert W	Dem.	2	1959–1991	Sun Prairie
Keefe, Frank B	Rep.	6	1939–1951	Oshkosh
Kersten, Charles J.	Rep.	5	1947–1949; 1951–1955	Whitefish Bay
Kimball, Alanson M.	Rep.	6	1875–1877	Waushara
Kind, Ron.	Dem.	3	1997–	La Crosse
Kleczka, Gerald D.	Dem.	4	1984–2005	Milwaukee
Kleczka, John C	Rep.	4	1919–1923	Milwaukee
Klug, Scott L	Rep.	2	1991–1999	Madison
Konop, Thomas F	Dem.	9	1911–1917	Kewaunee
Kopp, Arthur W	Rep.	3	1909–1913	Platteville
Kustermann, Gustav	Rep.	9	1907–1911	Green Bay
La Follette, Robert M., Sr	Rep.	3	1885–1891	Madison
Laird, Melvin R	Rep.	7	1953–1969	Marshfield
Lampert, Florian	Rep.	6	1918–1930	Oshkosh
Larrabee, Charles H	Dem.	3	1859–1861	Horicon
Lenroot, Irvine L	Rep.	11	1909–1918	Superior
Lynch, Thomas	Dem.	9	1891–1895	Antigo
Lynde, William Pitt	Dem.	1, 4	1848–1849; 1875–1879	Milwaukee
Macy, John B.	Dem.	3	1853–1855	Fond du Lac
Magoon, Henry S.	Rep.	3	1875–1877	Darlington
McCord, Myron H.	Rep.	9	1889–1891	Merrill
McDill, Alexander S	Rep.	8	1873–1875	Plover
McIndoe, Walter D	Rep.	6	1863–1867	Wausau
McMurray, Howard J.	Dem.	5	1943–1945	Milwaukee
Miller, Lucas M	Dem.	6	1891–1893	Oshkosh
Minor, Edward S	Rep.	8, 9	1895–1907	Sturgeon Bay
Mitchell, Alexander	Dem.	1, 4	1871–1875	Milwaukee
Mitchell, John L	Dem.	4	1891–1893	Milwaukee
Monahan, James G.	Rep.	3	1919–1921	Darlington
Moody, James P.	Dem.	5	1983–1993	Milwaukee
Moore, Gwen	Dem.	4	2005–	Milwaukee
Morse, Elmer A	Rep.	10	1907–1913	Antigo
Murphy, James W.	Dem.	3	1907–1909	Platteville
Murray, Reid F.	Rep.	7	1939–1953	Ogdensburg
Nelson, Adolphus P	Rep.	11	1918–1923	Grantsburg
Nelson, John Mandt	Rep.	2, 3	1906–1919; 1921–1933	Madison
Neumann, Mark W	Rep.	1	1995–1999	Janesville
Obey, David R	Dem.	7	1969–2011	Wausau
O'Konski, Alvin E	Rep.	10	1943–1973	Mercer
O'Malley, Thomas D. P.	Dem.	5	1933–1939	Milwaukee
Otjen, Theobald.	Rep.	4	1895–1907	Milwaukee
Paine, Halbert E.	Rep.	1	1865–1871	Milwaukee
Peavey, Hubert H.	Rep.	11, 10	1923–1935	Washburn
Petri, Thomas E	Rep.	6	1979–2015	Fond du Lac
Pocan, Mark	Dem.	2	2013–	Madison

Wisconsin members of the U.S. House of Representatives since 1848, continued

	Party	District	Term	Residence
Potter, John F	Rep.	1	1857–1863	East Troy
Pound, Thaddeus C.	Rep.	8	1877–1883	Chippewa Falls
Price, Hugh H	Rep.	8	1887	Black River Falls
Price, William T	Rep.	8	1883–1886	Black River Falls
Race, John A.	Dem.	6	1965–1967	Fond du Lac
Randall, Clifford E.	Rep.	1	1919–1921	Kenosha
Rankin, Joseph	Dem.	5	1883–1886	Manitowoc
Reilly, Michael K.	Dem.	6	1913–1917; 1930–1939	Fond du Lac
Reuss, Henry S.	Dem.	5	1955–1983	Milwaukee
Ribble, Reid J.	Rep.	8	2011–2017	Appleton
Roth, Toby	Rep.	8	1979–1997	Appleton
Rusk, Jeremiah M.	Rep.	6, 7	1871–1877	Viroqua
Ryan, Paul	Rep.	1	1999–	Janesville
Sauerhering, Edward	Rep.	2	1895–1899	Mayville
Sauthoff, Harry	Prog.	2	1935–1939; 1941–1945	Madison
Sawyer, Philetus	Rep.	5, 6	1865–1875	Oshkosh
Schadeberg, Henry C	Rep.	1	1961–1965; 1967–1971	Burlington
Schafer, John C	Rep.	4	1923–1933; 1939–1941	Milwaukee
Schneider, George J	Rep., Prog.	9, 8	1923–1933; 1935–1939	Appleton
Sensenbrenner, F. James, Jr.	Rep.	9, 5	1979–	Menomonee Falls
Shaw, George B	Rep.	7	1893–1894	Eau Claire
Sloan, A. Scott.	Rep.	3	1861–1863	Beaver Dam
Sloan, Ithamar C	Rep.	2	1863–1867	Janesville
Smith, Henry.	Union Labor	4	1887–1889	Milwaukee
Smith, Lawrence H	Rep.	1	1941–1959	Racine
Somers, Peter J	Dem.	4	1893–1895	Milwaukee
Stafford, William H	Rep.	5	1903–1911; 1913–1919; 1921–1923; 1929–1933	Milwaukee
Stalbaum, Lynn E	Dem.	1	1965–1967	Racine
Steiger, William A.	Rep.	6	1967–1978	Oshkosh
Stephenson, Isaac	Rep.	9	1883–1889	Marinette
Stevenson, William H	Rep.	3	1941–1949	La Crosse
Stewart, Alexander.	Rep.	9	1895–1901	Wausau
Sumner, Daniel H	Dem.	2	1883–1885	Waukesha
Tewes, Donald E	Rep.	2	1957–1959	Waukesha
Thill, Lewis D.	Rep.	5	1939–1943	Milwaukee
Thomas, Ormsby B	Rep.	7	1885–1891	Prairie du Chien
Thomson, Vernon W	Rep.	3	1961–1975	Richland Center
Van Pelt, William K	Rep.	6	1951–1963	Fond du Lac
Van Schaick, Isaac W	Rep.	4	1885–1887; 1889–1891	Milwaukee
Voigt, Edward	Rep.	2	1917–1927	Sheboygan
Washburn, Cadwallader C	Rep.	2 6	1855–1861; 1867–1871	Mineral Point, La Crosse
Wasielewski, Thaddeus F	Dem.	4	1941–1947	Milwaukee
Weisse, Charles H.	Dem.	6	1903–1911	Sheboygan Falls
Wells, Daniel, Jr	Dem.	1	1853–1857	Milwaukee
Wells, Owen A.	Dem.	6	1893–1895	Fond du Lac
Wheeler, Ezra	Dem.	5	1863–1865	Berlin
Williams, Charles G.	Rep.	1	1873–1883	Janesville
Winans, John	Dem.	1	1883–1885	Janesville
Withrow, Gardner R	Rep., Prog.	7, 3	1931–1939; 1949–1961	La Crosse
Woodward, Gilbert M	Dem.	7	1883–1885	La Crosse
Zablocki, Clement J	Dem.	4	1949–1983	Milwaukee

Dem.–Democrat; Prog.–Progressive; Rep.–Republican; Soc.–Socialist.

Sources: Wisconsin Legislative Reference Bureau, *Wisconsin Blue Book*, various editions; Congressional Quarterly, *Guide to U.S. Elections*, 1985; and official election records.

Wisconsin members of the U.S. House of Representatives since 1943, by district

District	Name	Party	Term	Residence
1	Lawrence H. Smith	Rep.	1941–1959	Racine
	Gerald T. Flynn	Dem.	1959–1961	Racine
	Henry C. Schadeberg	Rep.	1961–1965; 1967–1971	Burlington
	Lynn E. Stalbaum	Dem.	1965–1967	Racine
	Les Aspin[1]	Dem.	1971–1993	East Troy
	Peter W. Barca[1]	Dem.	1993–1995	Kenosha
	Mark W. Neumann	Rep.	1995–1999	Janesville
	Paul Ryan	Rep.	1999–	Janesville
2	Harry Sauthoff	Prog.	1941–1945	Madison
	Robert K. Henry	Rep.	1945–1947	Jefferson
	Glenn R. Davis	Rep.	1947–1957	Waukesha
	Donald E. Tewes	Rep.	1957–1959	Waukesha
	Robert W. Kastenmeier	Dem.	1959–1991	Sun Prairie
	Scott L. Klug	Rep.	1991–1999	Madison
	Tammy Baldwin	Dem.	1999–2013	Madison
	Mark Pocan	Dem.	2013–	Madison
3	William H. Stevenson	Rep.	1941–1949	La Crosse
	Gardner R. Withrow	Rep.	1949–1961	La Crosse
	Vernon W. Thomson	Rep.	1961–1975	Richland Center
	Alvin Baldus	Dem.	1975–1981	Menomonie
	Steven Gunderson	Rep.	1981–1997	Osseo
	Ron Kind	Dem.	1997–	La Crosse
4[3]	Thaddeus F. Wasielewski	Dem.	1941–1947	Milwaukee
	John C. Brophy	Rep.	1947–1949	Milwaukee
	Clement J. Zablocki[2]	Dem.	1949–1983	Milwaukee
	Gerald D. Kleczka[2]	Dem.	1984–2005	Milwaukee
	Gwen Moore	Dem.	2005–	Milwaukee
5[3]	Howard J. McMurray	Dem.	1943–1945	Milwaukee
	Andrew J. Biemiller	Dem.	1945–1947; 1949–1951	Milwaukee
	Charles J. Kersten	Rep.	1947–1949; 1951–1955	Whitefish Bay
	Henry S. Reuss	Dem.	1955–1983	Milwaukee
	James P. Moody	Dem.	1983–1993	Milwaukee
	Thomas M. Barrett	Dem.	1993–2003	Milwaukee
	F. James Sensenbrenner, Jr.	Rep.	2003–	Menomonee Falls
6	Frank B. Keefe	Rep.	1939–1951	Oshkosh
	William K. Van Pelt	Rep.	1951–1965	Fond du Lac
	John A. Race	Dem.	1965–1967	Fond du Lac
	William A. Steiger[4]	Rep.	1967–1978	Oshkosh
	Thomas E. Petri[4]	Rep.	1979–2015	Fond du Lac
	Glenn Grothman	Rep.	2015–	Glenbeulah
7	Reid F. Murray	Rep.	1939–1953	Ogdensburg
	Melvin R. Laird[5]	Rep.	1953–1969	Marshfield
	David R. Obey[5]	Dem.	1969–2011	Wausau
	Sean P. Duffy	Rep.	2011–	Ashland
8	La Vern R. Dilweg	Dem.	1943–1945	Green Bay
	John R. Byrnes	Rep.	1945–1973	Green Bay
	Harold V. Froehlich	Rep.	1973–1975	Appleton
	Robert J. Cornell	Dem.	1975–1979	De Pere
	Toby Roth	Rep.	1979–1997	Appleton
	Jay Johnson	Dem.	1997–1999	New Franken
	Mark A. Green	Rep.	1999–2007	Green Bay
	Steve Kagen	Dem.	2007–2011	Appleton
	Reid J. Ribble	Rep.	2011–2017	Appleton
	Mike Gallagher	Rep.	2017–	Green Bay

Wisconsin members of the U.S. House of Representatives since 1943, by district, continued

District	Name	Party	Term	Residence
9[3,6]	Merlin Hull	Prog.	1935–1953	Black River Falls
	Lester R. Johnson	Dem.	1953–1965	Black River Falls
	Glenn R. Davis	Rep.	1965–1975	Waukesha
	Robert W. Kasten	Rep.	1975–1979	Thiensville
	F. James Sensenbrenner, Jr.	Rep.	1979–2003	Menomonee Falls
10[7]	Alvin E. O'Konski	Rep.	1943–1973	Rhinelander

Dem.–Democrat; Prog.–Progressive; Rep.–Republican.

1. Aspin resigned 1/20/1993, to become U.S. Secretary of Defense. Barca was elected in a special election, 5/4/1993.   2. Zablocki died 12/3/1983. Kleczka was elected in a special election, 4/3/1984.   3. In the congressional reapportionment following the 2000 census, Wisconsin's delegation was reduced from nine to eight members. The previous 4th, 5th, and 9th districts were reconfigured into the new 4th and 5th districts.   4. Steiger died 12/4/1978, following his November 1978 election. Petri was elected in a special election, 4/3/1979.   5. Laird resigned 1/21/1969, to become U.S. Secretary of Defense. Obey was elected in a special election, 4/1/1969.   6. In the congressional redistricting following the 1960 census, the previous 9th District in western Wisconsin ceased to exist and a new 9th District was created in the Waukesha-Milwaukee metropolitan area.   7. In the congressional reapportionment following the 1970 census, Wisconsin's delegation was reduced from ten members to nine members.

Sources: 1944 *Wisconsin Blue Book* and Wisconsin Legislative Reference Bureau data.

INDEX